Hotels and Country Inns of Character and Charm in France

Fodor's RIVAGES

HOTELS AND COUNTRY INNS
of Character and Charm
IN FRANCE

Conceived by
Michelle Gastaut, Jean and Tatiana de Beaumont,
Anne Deren, with Livia Roubaud

Project editor
Michelle Gastaut

Fodor's Travel Publications, Inc.
New York • Toronto • London • Sydney • Auckland

While every care has been taken to ensure the accuracy of the information in this guide, time brings change, and consequently the publisher cannot accept responsibility for errors that may occur. Prudent travelers will therefore want to call ahead to verify prices and other "perishable" information.

Published in the United States by Fodor's Travel Publications, Inc.
Published in France by Payot/Rivages

Fodor's is a registered trademark of Fodor's Travel Publications, Inc.

ISBN 0-679-03159-6
Second Edition

**Hotels and Country Inns
of Character and Charm in France**

Translators: Marie Elise Palmier Chatelaine, Anne Norris, Edmund Swinglehurst, Christina Thistlethwayte
Layout: Marie Gastaut
Cover design: Fabrizio La Rocca
Front cover photograph: Le Chaufourg en Périgord (Aquitaine), photo by François Tissier;
back cover: Moulin d'Hauterive (Burgundy)

Special Sales

Printed in Italy by Litho Service
10 9 8 7 6 5 4 3 2 1

BIENVENUE

Welcome to the world of hotels with character and charm in France. This edition contains 550 hotels, including 60 small hotels in Paris, 50 properties appear in the guide for the first time. All have been selected for charm, quality of welcome, food and hotelkeeping. They range from the comparatively simple to the luxurious.

When choosing among them, remember that you cannot expect as much of a room costing 200F as you can of one costing 600F or more. Please also note that the prices given were quoted to us at the end of 1994 and may change.

When you make your reservation be sure to ask for the exact prices for half board *(demi-pension)* or full board *(pension)* as they can vary depending on the number in your party and the length of your stay. Half board is often obligatory. Note that rooms are generally held only until 6 or 7PM; if you are going to be late, let the hotel know.

STAR RATING

The government's hotel-rating organization assigns stars, from one to four, based on the comfort of a hotel, with special weight given to the number of bathrooms and toilets in relation to the number of rooms. This star rating has nothing at all to do with subjective criteria such as charm or the quality of the hospitality which are among our most important criteria. Some of the hotels in this guide have no stars–and that is because the hoteliers have never asked the government to rate them.

HOW TO USE THE GUIDE

Hotels are listed by regions, and within each region in alphabetical order by *département* and district. The number of the page on which a hotel is described corresponds to the number on the flag that pinpoints the property's location on the road map and to the numbers in the table of contents and index. The phrase "major credit cards" means that Diner's, Amex, Visa, Eurocard and MasterCard are all accepted.

PLEASE LET US KNOW...

If you are impressed by a small hotel or inn not featured here, one that you think ought to be included in the guide, let us know so that we can visit it.

Please also tell us if you are disappointed by one of our choices. Write us at Fodor's Travel Publications, 201 E. 50th Str., New York, NY 10022.

IMPORTANT NOTE:

Beginning October 18, 1996, you should add two figures to the existing telephone numbers in France, depending on the region: 01, 02, 03, 04, etc. These have been indicated in the Guide with an asterisk (*):

Example: Tel. (0)4* 91.54.83.53

From january 1 to October 15, 1996, dial:
91.54.83.53

Beginning October 18, 1996, dial:

From a foreign country:
33/4 91.54.83.53

In France:
04.91.54.83.53

CONTENTS LIST

Hotels listing by region
Map of France
Road maps

Hotels :

Paris 1
Alsace-Lorraine 32
Aquitaine 62
Auvergne-Limousin 107
Burgundy 129
Brittany 147
Centre – Loire Valley 191
Champagne-Picardie 219
Corsica 228
Franche-Comté 244
Ile–de–France 249
Languedoc-Roussillon 259
Midi-Pyrénées 290
Nord – Pas-de-Calais 332
Normandy 337
Pays-de-la-Loire 371
Poitou-Charentes 391
Provence – Riviera 400
Rhône-Alpes 496

Index 548
Week-ends around Paris 559

CONTENTS

P A R I S

RIVE GAUCHE

Notre-Dame - La Cité - Map 38:
- Hôtel de Notre-Dame 5ᵉ (690-790F) 1
- Les Rives de Notre-Dame 5ᵉ (950-1500F) 1B
- Hôtel du Parc Saint-Séverin 4ᵉ (600-1500F) 2

Ile Saint-Louis - Map 38:
- Hôtel des Deux Iles 4ᵉ (720-830F) 2B
- Hôtel du Jeu de Paume 4ᵉ (820-1395F) 3

Quartier Latin - Map 38:
- Hôtel Relais Christine 6ᵉ (1630-1800F) 3B
- Left Bank Saint-Germain Hôtel 6ᵉ (895-990F) 4
- Hôtel du Lys 6ᵉ (360-420F) 4B
- Hôtel Prince de Conti 6ᵉ (990F) 5
- Hôtel des Grands Hommes 5ᵉ (610-710F) 5B
- Hôtel des Trois Collèges 5ᵉ (450-600F) 6

Jardin des Plantes - Map 38:
- Résidence Les Gobelins 13ᵉ (400-455F) 6B

Parc Montsouris - Map 37:
- Hôtel du Parc Montsouris 14ᵉ (310-370F) 7

Montparnasse - Map 37:
- Hôtel Raspail-Montparnasse 14ᵉ (860-1210F) 7B
- Hôtel Danemark 6ᵉ (590-790F) 8
- L'Atelier Montparnasse 6ᵉ (700-950F) 8B
- Hôtel Ferrandi 6ᵉ (460-980F) 9
- Hôtel Sainte-Beuve 6ᵉ (700-1300F) 9B
- Hôtel Le Saint-Grégoire 6ᵉ (790-93F) 10

Luxembourg - Map 37:
- L'Abbaye Saint-Germain 6ᵉ (900-1600F) 10B
- Hôtel de Seine 6ᵉ (800-900F) 11
- Relais Saint-Germain 6ᵉ (1530-1950F) 11B
- Hôtel de l'Odéon 6ᵉ (740-920F) 12

   – Relais Médicis 6e (995-1495F) 12B
   – Le Clos Médicis 6e (886-986F) 13

Saint-Germain-des-Prés - Map 37:
   – Hôtel Le Régent 6e (750-950F) 13B
   – Hôtel de Fleurie 6e (650-1200F) 14
   – Hôtel les Marronniers 6e (700-850F) 14B
   – Hôtel d'Angleterre 6e (600-1100F) 15

Faubourg Saint-Germain - Map 37:
   – Hôtel des Saints-Pères 6e (456-1512F) 15B
   – Hôtel Lénox-Saint-Germain 7e (590-830F) 16
   – Hôtel de l'Université 7e (800-1300F) 16B
   – Hôtel de l'Académie 7e (690-890F) 17
   – Hôtel Montalembert 6e (1960-2080F) 17B
   – Hôtel Bersoly's 7e (580-680F) 18
   – Hôtel de Nevers 7e (410-440F) 18B
   – Hôtel de Suède 7e (650F) 19

Tour Eiffel - Map 37:
   – Hôtel de la Tulipe 7e (518-568F) 19B
   – Hôtel Saint-Dominique 7e (430-515F) 20
   – Hôtel de Tourville 7e (690-990F) 20B
   – Hôtel du Bailli de Suffren 15e (660-695F) 21

RIVE DROITE

Porte Maillot - La Défense - Map 37:
   – Hôtel Pergolèse 16e (960-1220F) 21B
   – Hôtel de Banville 17e (760F) 22
   – Le Jardin de Neuilly 17e (650-1050F) 22B

Etoile - Champs-Elysées - Map 37:
   – Hôtel Galileo 8e (800-950F) 23
   – Hôtel du Bois 16e (495-595F) 23B
   – Hôtel Raphaël-Paris 16e (1720-4020F) 24
   – Hôtel Franklin-Roosevelt 8e (790-890F) 24B

Madeleine-Opéra - Map 37:
   – Hôtel Queen Mary 8e (810-890F) 25
   – Hôtel Lido 8e (800-930F) 25B
   – Hôtel Beau Manoir 8e (995-1155F) 26
   – Hôtel Mansart 8e (656-960F) 26B

Tuileries - Louvre - Map 38
   – Hôtel de la Place du Louvre 1e (682-812F) 27
   – Le Relais du Louvre 1e (800-900F) 27B
   – Hôtel Brighton 1e (660-910F) 28
   – Hôtel de la Tamise 1e (750F) 28B
   – Hôtel Louvre Saint-Honoré 1e (762-862F) 29

Marais - Bastille - Map 38:
   – Hôtel de la Bretonnerie 4e (630-750F) 29B
   – Hôtel Saint-Paul-le Marais 4e (630F) 30
   – Hôtel Caron de Beaumarchais 4e (620-690F) 30B
   – Pavillon de la Reine 3e (1400-1600F) 31

Montmartre - Map 38:
   – TimHôtel Montmartre 18e (550F) 31B

A L S A C E – L O R R A I N E

BAS-RHIN

Itterswiller - Map 12:
 – Hôtel Arnold (270-595F)..32

Mittelbergheim - Map 12:
 – Hôtel Gilg (250-400F) 33

Obernai - Map 12:
 – La Cour d'alsace (695-800F)...34

Oberhaslach - Map 12:
 – Relais des Marches de l'est (190-210F)...35

Obersteinbach - Map 13:
 – Hôtel Anthon (260-290F) 36

La Petite-Pierre - Map 12:
 – Auberge d'Imsthal (280-600F)...37

Les Quelles - Map 12:
 – Hôtel Neuhauser (270-310F) 38

Strasbourg - Map 13:
 – Hôtel du Dragon (475-640F) 39

Wangenbourg - Map 12:
 – Parc Hôtel (304-412F) 40

La Wantzenau - Map 13:
 – Le Moulin de La Wantzenau (310-410F) 41

HAUT-RHIN

Buhl - Murbach - Map 20:
 – Hostellerie Saint-Barnabé (310-560F) 42

Colmar - Map 12:
 – Hostellerie Le Maréchal (550-1200F) 43

Illhaeusern - Map 12:
 – Hôtel La Clairière (560-950F) 44
 – Les Hirondelles (240-260F)..45

Lapoutroie - Map 12:
 – Auberge Les Alisiers (350F) 46

Ribeauvillé - Map 12:
 – Hôtel Le Clos Saint-Vincent (700-935F) 47
 – Hostellerie des Seigneurs de Ribeaupierre (470-540F) 48

La Rochette - Map 12:
 – Hôtel de la Rochette (250F)..49

Sainte-Croix-en-Plaine - Map 12:
 – Hôtel Au Moulin (230-400F) 50

Thannenkirsch - Map 12:
 – Auberge La Meunière (270-350F) 51

Thierenbach - Map 20:
 – Hôtel Les Violettes (540-740F)...52

MEURTHE-ET MOSELLE

Rehainviller - Map 12:
 – Château d'Adoménil (480-850F) 53

MOSELLE

Rugy - Map 12:
 – La Bergerie (300-380F) 54

Thionville - Map 12:
 – L'Horizon (680-780F)..55
Turquestein - Map 12:
 – Auberge du Kiboki (370-400F)...56

VOSGES
Gérardmer - Map 12:
 – Hostellerie des Bas-Rupts (380-780F)..57
Plombières-les-Bains - Map 20:
 – Hôtel de la Fontaine Stanislas (145-300F).....................................58
Les Rouges-Eaux - Map 12:
 – Auberge de la Cholotte (400F)...59
Le Thillot - Map 20:
 – Chalets des Ayes (340-420F)...60
Le Valtin - Map 12
 – Auberge du Val Joli (150-320F)..61

A Q U I T A I N E

DORDOGNE
Brantôme - Map 23:
 – Le Chatenet (490-580F)...62
 – Domaine de la Roseraie (360-680F)...63
Le Buisson-de-Cadoin - Map 23:
 – Hôtel du Manoir de Bellerive (750F)...64
Carsac-Aillac - Map 23:
 – Le Relais du Touron (390-485F.)...65
Coly - Map 23:
 – Manoir d'Hautegente (500-950F)...66
Les Eyzies-de-Tayac - Map 23:
 – Hôtel Cro-Magnon (350-550F)...67
 – Hôtel Les Glycines (360-410F)...68
 – Moulin de la Beune (280-300F)..69
Limeuil - Map 23:
 – Au Bon Accueil (130-160F)...70
Marnac - Map 23:
 – La Grande Marque (286F)...71
Mavaleix - Map 23:
 – Château de Mavaleix (260-410F)..72
Millac - Map 23:
 – La Métairie (450-600F)...73
Le Reclaud-de-Bouny-Bas - Map 23:
 – Auberge du Noyer (400-480F)..74
La Roque-Gageac - Map 23:
 – La Plume d'Oie (350-380F)...75
Saint-Cyprien-en-Périgord - Map 23:
 – Hôtel L' Abbaye (550-680F)..76
Saint-Saud-en-Périgord - Map 23:
 – Hostellerie Saint-Jacques (330-450F)...77

Sourzac- Map 23:
 – Le Chaufourg en Périgord (700-1150F) 78
Trémolat - Map 23:
 – Le Vieux Logis (740-1290F)...79
Vieux-Mareuil - Map 23:
 – Château de Vieux-Mareuil (500-1000F) 80

GIRONDE
Arcachon - Map 22:
 – Villa Teresa - Hôtel Semiramis (580-630F) 81
Bouliac - Map 22:
 – Hauterive Hôtel Saint-James (650-850F) 82
Castelnau-de-Médoc - Map 22:
 – Château du Foulon (450F)...83
Lugon - Map 22:
 – Hostellerie du Vieux Raquine (420-600F) 84
Ruch - Map 22:
 – Château Lardier (230-340F) 85
Saint-Ciers-de-Canesse - Map 22:
 – La Closerie des Vignes (360F)...86

LANDES
Eugénie-les-Bains - Map 29:
 – Le Couvent aux Herbes (1 000-1700F) 87
 – La Maison Rose (480-580F)...88
 – Auberge de la Ferme aux Grives (550-600F) 89
Grenade-sur-Adour - Map 29:
 – Pain, Adour et Fantaisie (380-700F) 90
Port-de-Lanne - Map 29:
 – La Vieille Auberge (230-450F) 91
Sabres - Map 29
 – Auberge des Pins (230-450F)...92

LOT-ET-GARONNE
Astaffort - Map 30:
 – Le Square (350F)...93
Poudenas - Map 30:
 – A la Belle Gasconne (530-670F)...94
Puymirol - Map 30:
 – Les Loges de l'Aubergade (750-1410F)...95

PYRENEES-ATLANTIQUES
Barcus - Map 29:
 – Chez Chilo (205-495F)...96
Arbonne-Biarritz - Map 28:
 – Hôtel Laminak (350-560F) 97
Biarritz - Map 28:
 – Le Château du Clair de Lune (430-680F) 98
 – Le Saint-Charles (250-420F)...99
Bidart-Biarritz - Map 28:
 – Villa L'Arche (450-750F)...100
Ciboure - Map 28:
 – Lehen Tokia (500-800F) 101

Esterençuby - Map 28:
– Artzaïn Etchea (220F) 102
Saint-Etienne-de-Baïgorry - Map 28:
– Hôtel Arcé (420-680F) 103
Saint-Jean-de-Luz - Map 28:
– La Devinière (500-650F)..104
Sare - Map 28:
– Hôtel Arraya (480-540F) 105
Ustaritz - Map 28:
– Hôtel La Patoula (350-470F)..106

A U V E R G N E - L I M O U S I N

ALLIER
Bourbon-L'Archambault- Map 18:
– Grand Hôtel Montespant-Talleyrand (280-330F) 107
Coulandon - Map 18:
– Le Chalet (360-460F)...108
Target - Map 25:
– Château de Boussac (600-800F) 109
Tronçais - Map 17:
– Le Tronçais (260-344F) 110

CANTAL
Boisset - Map 24:
– Auberge de Concasty (315-490F) 111
Champagnac - Map 24:
– Château de Lavendès (420-560F) 112
Champs-sur-Tarentaine - Map 24:
– Auberge du Vieux Chêne (320-420F) 113
Lanau - Chaudes-Aigues - Map 25:
– Auberge du Pont de Lanau (270-350F) 114
Le Theil - Map 24:
– Hostellerie de la Maronne (350-600F) 115
Pailherols - Map 24:
– Auberge des Montagnes (198-260F) 116
Vitrac - Map 24:
– Auberge de la Tomette (260-280F) 117

HAUTE-LOIRE
La Chaise-Dieu - Map 25:
– Hôtel de L'Echo et de l'Abbaye (300-350F)................................118
Moudeyres - Map 25:
– Le Pré Bossu (430-590F in half board)......................................119

CORREZE
Beaulieu-sur-Dordogne- Map 24:
– Hôtel le Turenne (250-280F)...120
Collonges-la-Rouge - Map 24:
– Relais de St-Jacques-de-Compostelle (170-300F) 121

Pont du Chambon - Map 24:
  – Au Rendez-Vous des Pêcheurs (235-265F)..122
Saint-Robert - Map 23:
  – La Maison Anglaise (220-350F) 123
Saint-Viance - Map 23:
  – Auberge des Prés de la Vézère (250-350F) 124
Turenne- Map 23 and 24:
  – La Maison des Chanoines (300-370F).. 125

CREUSE
Saint-Georges-la-Pouge - Map 24:
  – Domaine des Mouillères (200-370F) 126

HAUTE-VIENNE
La Roche l'Abeille - Map 23:
  – Moulin de la Gorce (700-900F)..127

PUY-DE-DOME
Saint-Gervais-d'Auvergne - Map 24:
  – Castel-Hôtel 1904 (260-280F) 128

B   U   R   G   U   N   D   Y

CÔTE-D'OR
Aloxe-Corton - Map 19:
  – Hôtel Clarion (600-800F) 129
Arnay-le-Duc - Map 19:
  – Chez Camille (395F) 130
Beaune - Map 19:
  – Hôtel Le Home (325-450F) 131
Levernois-Beaune- Map 19:
  – Hôtel Le Parc (200-460F)...132
Challanges-Beaune- Map 19:
  – Château de Challanges (480F).. 133
Curtil-Vergy - Map 19:
  – Le Manassès (400F) 134
Val-Suzon - Map 19:
  – Hostellerie du Val-Suzon (400-500F)..135

SAONE-ET-LOIRE
Bourbon-Lancy - Map 18:
  – Manoir de Sornat (350-650F)...136
Chagny - Map 19:
  – Hostellerie du Château de Bellecroix (580-1000F) 137
Cluny - Map 19:
  – Hôtel de Bourgogne (390-490F)...138
Louhans - Map 19:
  – Moulin de Bourgchâteau (240-300F)...139
Saint-Gervais-en-Vallière - Map 19:
  – Moulin d'Hauterive (530-600F) 140

Tournus - Map 19:
 – La Montagne de Brancion (450-750F)......................................141

YONNE
La Celle-Saint-Cyr - Map 18:
 – La Fontaine aux Muses (390F) 142
Charny - Prunoy - Map 18:
 – Château de Prunoy (500-700F) 143
Mailly-le-Château - Map 18:
 – Le Castel (230-340F)..144
Val-de-Mercy- Map 18:
 – Auberge du Château (350-490F)... 145
Villeneuve-sur-Yonne - Map 10 and 18:
 – La Lucarne aux Chouettes(490-650F)......................................146

B   R   I   T   T   A   N   Y

CÔTES-D'ARMOR
Brélidy - Map 5:
 – Château Hôtel de Brélidy (420-755F)......................................147
Dinan - Map 6:
 – Hôtel d'Avaugour (480-560F) 148
Louargat - Map 5:
 – Manoir du Cleuziou (380-420F) 149
Paimpol - Map 5:
 – Le Repaire de Kerroc'h (480F) 150
Perros-Guirec - Map 5:
 – Hôtel Le Sphinx (490-550F) 151
Planguenoual - Map 6:
 – Domaine du Val (450-900F)...152
Pléven - Map 6:
 – Manoir de Vaumadeuc (490-950F)...153
Plévenon - Fréhel - Map 6:
 – Le Fanal (240-320F)...154
Fréhel -   Map 6:
 – Relais de Fréhel (237-287F)...155
Plouers-sur-Rance - *Map 6* :
 – Manoir de Rigourdaine (290-390F)..156
Trébeurden - Map 5:
 – Ti-Al-Lannec (630-1050F)...157
Beg-Leguer - Lannion - Map 5:
 – Manoir de Crec'h-Goulifen (350-420F).....................................158
Tréguier - Map 5:
 – Kastell Dinec'h (420-490F)...159

FINISTERE
Bénodet - Map 5:
 – Le Minaret (260-420F) 160
 – Domaine Kéréven (280-375F) 161

Douarnenez - Map 5:
 – Hôtel Ty Mad (230-320F) 162
Plonévez-Porzay - Map 5:
 – Manoir de Moëllien (330-350F) 163
Pointe-du-Raz - Map 4:
 – Hôtel de L'Iroise (150-200F) 164
Pont-Aven - Map 5:
 – Moulin de Rosmadec (470F) 165
Pont-l'Abbé - Map 5:
 – Château de Kernuz (350-600F) 166
Portsall - *Map 4* :
 – La Demeure Océane (250-350F) 167
Roscoff - Map 5:
 – Le Brittany (460-630F) 168
Sainte-Anne-la-Palud- Map 5:
 – Hôtel de la Plage (750-1350F) 169
Trégunc - Map 5:
 – Les Grandes Roches (300-400F) 170
Saint-Antoine - Map 5:
 – Hôtel Ménez (250-290F) 171

ILLE-ET-VILAINE
Cancale - Map 6:
 – Hôtel Richeux (750-1550F) 172
 – Hôtel Les Rimains (750-850F) 173
Pleugueneuc - Map 6:
 – Château de la Motte Beaumanoir (900F) 174
Pleurtuit - Map 6:
 – Manoir de la Rance (450-800F) 175
Saint-Malo - Map 6:
 – La Korrigane (400-800F) 176
 – L'Ascott Hôtel (400-600F) 177

MORBIHAN
Belle-Ile-en-Mer - Map 5:
 – Hôtel Village La Désirade (390-560F) 178
 – Petit Hôtel Les Pougnots (530F) 179
Billiers-Musillac - Map 14:
 – Domaine de Rochevilaine (750-1150F) 180
Hennebont - Map 5:
 – Les Chaumières de Kernavien (380-680F) 181
Le Gréo - Map 14:
 – Logis Parc er Gréo (280-450F) 182
Ile de Groix - Map 5:
 – Hôtel de la Marine (217-440F) 183
Ilé aux Moines - Map 14:
 – Le San Francisco (315-525F) 184
Landévant - Map 5:
 – Au Vieux Chêne (150-230F) 185
Lesnevé - *Saint-Avé* - Map 14:
 – Moulin de Lesnuhé (230-250F) 186
Locmariaquer - Map :
 – Hôtel des Trois Fontaines (295-550F) 187

Plouhinec - Map 5:
– Hôtel de Kerlon (270-300F)...188
Plouharnel - Map 5:
– Hostellerie Les Ajoncs d'Or (280-380F) 189
La Roche-Bernard - Nivillac - Map 14:
– Domaine de Bodeuc (550F) 190

CENTRE - LOIRE VALLEY

CHER
Bannegon - Map 17:
– Auberge du Moulin de Chaméron (330-500F) 191
Brinon-sur-Sauldre - Map 17:
– La Solognote (310-420F) 192
Nançay - Map 17:
– Auberge des Meaulnes (450F) 193
Saint-Hilaire-de-Court - Map 17:
– Château de la Beuvrière (350-480F)...194

EURE-ET-LOIR
Cloyes-sur-le-Loir - Map 16:
– Hostellerie Saint-Jacques (320-480F)...195

INDRE
Argenton-sur-Creuse - Le Vivier - Map 16:
– Château du Vivier (300-580F) 196
– Manoir de Boisvillers (230-380F) 197
Le Blanc - Map 16:
– Domaine de l'Etape (220-440F) 198
Bouesse - Map 17:
– Château de Bouesse (480F) 199
Saint-Chartier - Map 17:
– Château de la Vallée Bleue (325-550F)..200

INDRE-ET-LOIRE
Chenonceaux - Map 16:
– Hôtel du Bon Laboureur et du Château (320-600F) 201
Civray-en-Touraine - Map 16:
– Hostellerie du Château de l'Isle (290-400F) 202
Chinon - Map 16:
– Hôtel Diderot (300-400F)..203
Loches - Map 16:
– Hôtel George Sand (260-650F)...204
Montbazon-en-Touraine - Map 16:
– Domaine de la Tortinière (455-890F)...205
Montlouis-sur-Loire - Map 16:
– Château de la Bourdaisière (550-1100F)..206
Vernou-sur-Brenne - Map 16:
– Hostellerie Les Perce-Neige (200-280F)...207

LOIR-ET-CHER

Chaumont-sur-Tharonne - Map 17:
  – La Croix Blanche (300-500F) 208
Chissay-en-Touraine - Map 16:
  – Château de Chissay (550-910F) 209
Nouan-le-Fuzelier - Map 17:
  – Hôtel Les Charmilles (340-380F) 210
Onzain - Map 16:
  – Hôtel Château des Tertres (390-500F) 211
Ouchamps - Map 16:
  – Relais des Landes (495-745F) 212
Troo - Map 16:
  – Château de la Voûte (370-550F)...213
La Ville-aux-Clercs - Map 16:
  – Manoir de la Forêt (290-340F)..214

LOIRET

Beaugency - Map 17:
  – Hôtel de l'Abbaye (510-560F)..215
  – Hôtel de la Sologne: (250-410F)...216
Combreux - Map 17
  – L'Auberge de Combreux (315-495F) 217
Sury-aux-Bois - Map 17:
  – Domaine de Chicamour (365F)...218

CHAMPAGNE - PICARDIE

AISNE

Longpont - Map 10:
  – Hôtel de l'Abbaye (175-320F) 219
Neuville-Saint-Amand - Map 2:
  – Hostellerie Le Château (330-390F)..220
Sainte-Preuve -Map 3:
  – Château de Barive (480-580F) 221

AUBE

La Vove - Map 10:
  – Auberge de la Scierie (390-490F)..222

MARNE

Etoges - Map 10:
  – Château d'Etoges (550-700F) 223

OISE

Ermenonville - Map 9:
  – Hôtel Le Prieuré (450-500F) 224
Saint-Jean-aux-Bois - Map 9:
  – A la Bonne Idée (385-430F)..225

MEUSE

Futeau - Map 11:
  – A l'Orée du Bois (340-360F)..226

SOMME

Routhiauville - Map 1:
 — Auberge Le Fiacre (350-380F) 227

C O R S I C A

CORSE-DU-SUD

Ajaccio - Map 36:
 — Hôtel Dolce Vita (435-970F) 228
Bonifacio - Map 36:
 — Hôtel Genovese (700-1500F) 229
 — Résidence du Centre Nautique (450-950F) 230
Cala Rossa - Porto-Vecchio - Map 36:
 — Grand Hôtel Cala Rossa (500-2000F) 231
Evisa - Map 36:
 — L' Aïtone (200-550F)..232
Piana - Map 36:
 — Les Roches Rouges (265-280F) 233
Porticcio - Map 36:
 — Le Maquis (1780-2480F in half board) 234
Serriera - Map 36:
 — Hôtel L' Aiglon (210-360F)...235

HAUTE-CORSE

Calvi - Map 36:
 — Hôtel Balanéa (300-1200F) 236
 — Auberge de la Signoria (450-1100F)...............................237
L'Argentella-Calvi - Map 36:
 — Marina d'Argentella (350-450F in half board)..............238
Feliceto - Map 36:
 — Hôtel Mare e Monti (283-297F) 239
Ile-Rousse - Map 36:
 — La Bergerie (250-450F) 240
Rogliano - Map 36:
 — U Sant'Agnellu (220-320F) 241
Erbalunga - Map 36:
 — Hôtel Castel Brando (380-530F) 242
San-Martino-di-Lota - Map 36:
 — Hôtel de la Corniche (300-450F) 243

F R A N C H E - C O M T É

DOUBS

Goumois - Map 20:
 — Auberge Le Moulin du Plain (204à 295F) 244
 — Hôtel Taillard (280-350F)..245

JURA

Champagnole - Map 20:
  – Hôtel de la Vouivre (320–410F) 246
Les Planches-près-Arbois - Map 19:
  – Le Moulin de la Mère Michelle (380–680F) 247
Les Rousses - Map 20:
  – Hôtel de France (285–515F) 248

I L E - D E - F R A N C E

ESSONNE

Fontaine-la-Rivière - Map 9:
  – Auberge de Courpain (350F) 249
Itteville - Map 9:
  – Auberge de l'Ile du Saussay (350F) 250

SEINE-ET-MARNE

Barbizon - Map 9:
  – Hostellerie de la Clé d'Or (420–480F) 251
  – Hostellerie Les Pléiades (420–550F) 252
La Ferté-sous-Jouarre- Map 10:
  – Château des Bondons (400–550F) 253
Flagy - Map 9
  – Au Moulin (310–500F) 254
Provins - Map 10:
  – Hostellerie Aux Vieux Remparts (395–650F) 255
Saint-Augustin - Map 10:
  – La Louveterie (500F) 256
Thomery - Map 9:
  – Hostellerie Le Vieux Logis (400F) 257
Germigny-l'Evêque - Map 9:
  – Hôtel Le Gonfalon (280–360F) 258

L A N G U E D O C - R O U S S I L L O N

AUDE

Carcassonne - Map 31:
  – Dame Carcas (400–600F) 259
Durban - Map 31:
  – Château Haut-Gléon (250–280F) 260
Gincla - Map 31:
  – Hostellerie du Grand Duc (250–320F) 261
Ornaisons - Map 31:
  – Relais du Val d'Orbieu (580–690F) 262

GARD

Aigaliers- Map 33:
  − La Buissonnière (250-280F) 263
Aigues-Mortes - Map 32:
  − Hôtel Les Arcades (460-550F) 264
  − Hôtel Les Templiers (400-700F) 265
Collias - Map 33:
  − Hostellerie Le Castellas (500-590F)...266
Les Coudoulières - Map 33:
  − La Bégude Saint-Pierre (440-700F)...267
Cornillon - Map 33:
  − La Vieille Fontaine (550-850F) 268
Marguerittes - Map 33:
  − L'Hacienda (400-550F) 269
Mus - Map 32:
  − Auberge de la Paillère (350F)..270
Nîmes - Map 32:
  − Hôtel Imperator (680-850F)..271
  − Royal Hôtel (250-480F)...272
Saint-Médiers - Map 33:
  − Le Mas d'Oléandre (240F) 273
Sommières - Map 32:
  − Auberge du Pont Romain (260-440F) 274
Tavel - Map 33:
  − Auberge du Seigneur (250-280F)..275
Tornac-Anduze - Map 32:
  − Demeures du Ranquet (580-800F)...276
Uzès - Arpaillargues - Map 33:
  − Hôtel Marie d'Agoult (400-1100F) 277
Uzès - Map 33:
  − Hôtel d'Entraigues (280-650F) 278
Villeneuve-lès-Avignon - Map 33:
  − Hôtel de l'Atelier (240-420F) 279

HÉRAULT

Madières - Map 32:
  − Château de Madières (560-960F) 280
Minerve - Map 31:
  − Relais Chantovent (220F)..281
Olargues - Map 31:
  − Domaine de Rieumégé (350-518F) 282

LOZERE

Meyrueis - Map 32:
  − Château d'Ayres (360-800F)...283
Le Pont-de-Montvert - Map 32:
  − Hôtel Chantoiseau (400-480F)...284

PYRÉNÉES-ORIENTALES

Céret - Map 31:
  − La Terrasse au Soleil (595-795F) 285
  − Le Mas des Trilles (420-950F) 286

Collioure - Map 31:
 − Hôtel Casa Païral (350-690F) 287
Llo - Map 31:
 − Auberge L' Atalaya (620F) 288
Mont-Louis - Map 31:
 − Lou Rouballou (150-300F) 289

M I D I - P Y R E N E E S

ARIEGE
Camon - Map 31:
 − Château de Camon (500-1 000F) 290
Mirepoix - Map 30:
 − La Maison des Consuls (300F) 291
Saint-Girons - Map 30:
 − Hôtel Eychenne (280-530F) 292
 − Château de Seignan (320-850F) 293

AVEYRON
Castelpers - Map 31:
 − Château de Castelpers (375-465F) 294
Najac - Map 31:
 − Hôtel Longcol (550-750F) 295
 − Oustal del Barry (300-450F) 296
Peyreleau - Le Rozier - Map 31 and 32:
 − Grand Hôtel de la Muse et du Rozier (410-650F) 297
Plaisance - Map 31:
 − Hostellerie Les Magnolias (225-300F) 298
Saint-Jean-du-Bruel - Map 32:
 − Hôtel du Midi-Papillon (95-191F) 299
Saint-Saturnin-de-Lenne- Map 31:
 − Château Saint Saturnin (450-980F) 300
Sauveterre-de-Rouergue - Map 31:
 − Le Sénéchal (450-550F) 301

GERS
Condom - Map 30:
 − Hôtel des Trois Lys (380-550F) 302
Lectoure - Map 30:
 − Hôtel de Bastard (220-320F) 303
Plaisance-du-Gers - Map 30:
 − Le Ripa Alta (300F) 304
Projan - Map 29:
 − Château de Projan (180-350F) 305
Saint-Martin-d'Armagnac - Map 29:
 − Auberge du Bergerayre (300F) 306
Ségos - Map 29:
 − Domaine de Bassibé (300F) 307

Solomiac - Map 30:
– Auberge d'Enrose (300F) 308

HAUTE-GARONNE
Cadours - Map 30:
– La Demeure d'en Jourdou (280-420F) 309
Saint-Félix-Lauragais - Map 31:
– Auberge du Poids Public (250-300F) 310
Sauveterre-de-Comminges - Map 30:
– Hostellerie des 7 Molles (600-760F) 311

LOT
Cardaillac - Map 24:
– Chez Marcel (135F) 312
Gluges - Map 24:
– Hôtel Les Falaises (210-320F) 313
Lacave - Map 23:
– Château de la Treyne (300F) 314
– Le Pont de l'Ouysse (500F) 315
Lascabanes - Map 30:
– La Petite Auberge (300F) 316
Le Vert - Mauroux - Map 30:
– Hostellerie Le Vert (270-340F) 317
Martel - Map 23 and 24:
– Relais Sainte-Anne (280-850F) 318
Lamagdelaine - Cahors - Map 30:
– Claude Marco (280-850F) 319
Rocamadour - Lafage - Map 24:
– Hôtel Les Vieilles Tours (210-450F) 320
Rocamadour - La Rhue - Map 24:
– Domaine de la Rhue (370-570F) 321
Saint-Céré - Map 24:
– Hôtel Ric (300-380F) 322
Saint-Cirq-Lapopie - Map 31:
– Hôtel de la Pelissaria (400-600F) 323
– Auberge du Sombral (400F) 324
Touzac - Map 30:
– La Source Bleue (250-450F) 325

TARN
Albi - Map 31:
– Hostellerie Saint-Antoine (450-750F) 326
Cuq-Toulza - Map 31:
– Cuq-en-Terrasse (350-450F) 327
Lacabarède - Map 31:
– Demeure de Flore (400F) 328
Pont-de-L'Arn - Map 31:
– Château de Montlédier (430-590F) 329
– La Métairie Neuve (290-550F) 330

TARN-ET-GARONNE
Saint-Beauzeuil - Map 30:
– Château de L'Hoste (210-260F) 331

N O R D - P A S - D E - C A L A I S

NORD

Sebourg - Map 3:
  – Le Jardin Fleuri (200-300F) 332
Valenciennes - Map 3:
  – Auberge du Bon Fermier (480-700F) 333

PAS-DE-CALAIS

Gosnay - Map 2:
  – Chartreuse du Val Saint-Esprit (400-900F) 334
Recques-sur-Hem - Map 1:
  – Château de Cocove (435-690F) 335
Hesdin-l'Abbé - Map 1:
  – Hôtel Cléry (450-590F) 336

N O R M A N D Y

CALVADOS

Bavent - Map 7:
  – Hostellerie du Moulin du Pré (220-340F) 337
Bayeux - Map 7:
  – Hôtel d'Argouges (190-420F) 338
Beuvron-en-Auge - Map 8:
  – Auberge de la Boule d'Or (230F) 339
Le Breuil-en-Bessin - Map 7:
  – Hostellerie du Château de Goville (425-695F) 340
Crépon - Map 7:
  – Ferme Hôtel La Rançonnière (295-420F) 341
Escures-Commes - Map 7:
  – La Chenevière (700-1100F) 342
Honfleur - Map 8:
  – Hôtel l'Ecrin (370-900F) 343
Pont-d'Ouilly - Map 7:
  – Auberge Saint-Christophe (270F) 344

EURE

Les Andelys - Map 8:
  – La Chaîne d'Or (395-740F) 345
Balisne - Map 8:
  – Relais Moulin de Balisne (350-450F) 346
Bazincourt-sur-Epte - Map 9:
  – Château de la Rapée (410-510F) 347
Le Bec-Hellouin - Map 8:
  – Auberge de l'Abbaye (380-420F) 348
Cocherel - Map 8:
  – La Ferme de Cocherel (350-400F) 349
Connelles- Map 8:
  – Le Moulin de Connelles (600-800F) 350
Douains - Map 8:
  – Château de Brécourt (670-1040F) 351

Pont-Audemer - Map 8:
– Auberge du Vieux Puits (270-420F) 352
Saint-Aubin-le-Vertueux - Map 8:
– Hostellerie du Moulin Fouret (235F) 353
La Saussaye - Map 8:
– Le Manoir des Saules (450-1150F) 354
Le Vaudreuil - Map 8:
– Hôtel du Golf (225-350F) 355

MANCHE
Agneaux - *Saint-Lô* - Map 7:
– Hôtel du Château d'Agneaux (370-700F) 356
Barfleur - Map 7:
– Hôtel Le Conquérant (200-360F) 357
Courtils - Map 7:
– Manoir de Roche Torin (450-800F) 358
Ducey - Map 7:
– Auberge de la Sélune (270-295F) 359
Granville - Map 6:
– Hôtel des Bains (250-650F) 360
Hébécrevone - Map 7:
– Château de la Roque (330-520F) 361
Saint-Vaast-la-Hougue - Map 7:
– Hôtel de France et des Fuchsias (290-400F) 362
Trelly - Map 7:
– Verte Campagne (220-380F) 363

ORNE
Condeau - Map 8:
– Moulin de Villeray (390-950F) 364
La Croix-Gauthier - *Bagnoles-de-L'Orne* - Map 7:
– Manoir du Lys (300-650F) 365

SEINE-MARITIME
Bézancourt - Map 1 and 9:
– Château du Landel (470-750F) 366
Croix-Mare - Map 1 and 8:
– Auberge du Val au Cesne (350F) 367
Martin-Eglise - Map 1:
– Auberge du Clos Normand (270-370F) 368
Sassetot-le-Mauconduit - Map 8:
– Château de Sassetot-le-Mauconduit (470-730F) 369
Varengeville - Map 1:
– Hôtel de la Terrasse (240-310F) 370

P A Y S   D E   L A   L O I R E

LOIRE-ATLANTIQUE
Pornichet - Map 14:
– Hôtel Sud-Bretagne (600-800F) 371
Saint-Lyphard - Map 14:
– Auberge de Kerhinet (270F) 372

Les Sorinières - Map 14:
— Abbaye de Villeneuve (390-935F)..373

MAINE-ET-LOIRE
Champigné - Map 15:
— Château des Briottières (550-750F)..374
Saumur - Map 15:
— Hôtel Anne d'Anjou (450F) 375

MAYENNE
Saulges - Map 15:
— Hôtel L' Ermitage (390-550F) 376

SARTHE
La Flèche - Map 15:
— Relais Cicéro (495-675F) 377
Luché-Pringé - Map 16:
— Auberge du Port-des-Roches (230-300F) 378
La Potardière - *Crosmières*- Map 15:
— Haras de la Potardière (550F) 379
Saint-Paterne - Map 8:
— Château de Saint-Paterne (450-650F) 380

VENDÉE
Bouin - Map 14:
— Hôtel du Martinet (265-340F) 381
Challans - Map 14:
— Château de la Vérie (350-880F) 382
— Hôtel de l'Antiquité (260-400F) 383
Ile d'Yeu - Map 14:
— Flux Hôtel (280F)...384
Noirmoutier-en-L'Ile - Map 14:
— Hôtel du Général d'Elbée (350-715F) 385
— Fleur de Sel (375-620F)..386
— Hôtel Les Prateaux (305-760F) 387
La Roche-sur-Yon - Map 14:
— Logis de La Couperie (295-480F)..388
Tiffauges - Map 15:
— Hôtel La Barbacane (280-355F) 389
Velluire - Map 15:
— Auberge de la Rivière (410F) 390

P O I T O U - C H A R E N T E S

CHARENTE
Cognac - Map 22:
— Les Pigeons Blancs (350-450F)..391
Nieul - Map 23:
— Château de Nieuil (700-1200F) 392

CHARENTE-MARITIME
Ile d'Oléron - Map 22:
　– Hôtel L'Ecailler (335-410F) 393
Ile de Ré - Map 22:
　– Hôtel Le Chat Botté (380-500F) 394
Pons - Map 22:
　– Hôtel de Bordeaux (260F) 395
La Rochelle - Map 22:
　– Hôtel France et d'Angleterre et Champlain (310-535F) 396
Vaux-sur-Mer - Map 22:
　– Résidence de Rohan (300-700F) 397

DEUX-SEVRES
Coulon - Map 15:
　– Au Marais (250-600F) 398
Saint-Maixent-l'Ecole - Map 15:
　– Le Logis Saint-Martin (360-460F) 399

P R O V E N C E - R I V I E R A

ALPES-DE-HAUTE-PROVENCE
Esparron-de-Verdon - Map 34:
　– Le Roumanin (320F) 400
Forcalquier - Map 34:
　– Auberge Charembeau (350F) 401
Pierrerue - *Forcalquier* - Map 34:
　– La Fare (800F) 402
Moustiers-Sainte-Marie - Map 34:
　– Bastide de Moustiers (800-1300F) 403
　– La Ferme Rose (350-380F) 404
Praloup-Les Molanès - Map 34:
　– Auberge du Clos Sorel (520-650F) 405
Reillanne- Map 33:
　– Auberge de Reillanne (360F) 406
Super-Sauze- Map 34:
　– Le Pyjama (330-430F) 407

HAUTES-ALPES
Serre-Chevalier - *Saint-Chaffrey* Map 27:
　– Le Clos de Chantemerle (200-450F) 408
　– La Boule de Neige (270-630F) 409

ALPES-MARITIMES
Antibes - Map 35:
　– Mas de la Pagane (550F) 410
Cannes - Map 34:
　– Hôtel de Paris (550-750F) 411

Coaraze - Map 35:
  − Auberge du Soleil (330-495F) 412
Miramar Théoule - Map 34:
  − La Tour de L'Esquillon (400-800F) 413
Mougins - Map 34:
  − Le Manoir de l'Etang (600-900F) 414
Nice - Map 35:
  − Hôtel La Pérouse (650-1300F) 415
  − Hôtel Windsor (400-670F) 416
Peillon - Map 35:
  − Auberge de la Madone (430-780F) 417
Roquebrune Village - Map 35:
  − Hôtel Les Deux Frères (495F) 418
Roquefort-les-Pins - Map 34:
  − Auberge du Colombier (350-550F) 419
Saint-Jean-Cap-Ferrat - Map 35:
  − Hôtel Brise Marine (640-695F) 420
Saint-Paul-de-Vence - Map 34:
  − Hôtel Le Hameau (440-600F) 421
Vence - Map 34:
  − Auberge des Seigneurs et du Lion d'Or (324-354F) 422
  − La Roseraie (410-550F) 423
Villefranche-sur-Mer - Map 35:
  − Hôtel Welcome (580-890F) 424

BOUCHES-DU-RHÔNE

Aix-en-Provence - Map 33:
  − Villa Gallici (880-2450F) 425
  − Hôtel des Quatre-Dauphins (320-380F) 426
Arles - Map 33:
  − Hôtel d'Arlatan (455-695F) 427
  − Grand Hôtel Nord-Pinus (700-900F) 428
Barbentane - Map 33:
  − Hôtel Castel-Mouisson (280-330F) 429
Les Baux-de-Provence - Map 33:
  − Hôtel La Benvengudo (520-670F) 430
  − Le Mas d'Aigret (450-1100F) 431
Cassis - Map 33:
  − Les Roches Blanches (900F) 432
  − Le Clos des Arômes (295-570F) 433
Eygalières - Map 33:
  − Auberge Provençale (285-500F) 434
  − Mas doù Pastré (320-550F) 435
Gémenos - Map 33:
  − Relais de la Magdelaine (545-750F) 436
Marseille - Map 33:
  − New Hôtel Bompard (370-400F) 437
Mausanne-les-Alpilles- Map 33:
  − L'Oustaloun (260-395F) 438
Saint-Andiol - Map 33:
  − Le Berger des Abeilles (300-350F) 439

Saintes-Maries-de-la-Mer - Map 33:
  – Hostellerie de Cacharel (530F)..440
  – Mas du Clarousset (750F)..441
  – Mas doù Juge (750F in half board)......................................442
Saint-Rémy-de-Provence - Map 33:
  – Château des Alpilles (900-1080F)..443
  – Château de Roussan (360-750F)...444
  – Mas des Carassins (380-500F)..445
Le Sambuc- Map 33:
  – Le Mas de Peint (980-1500F)..446

VAR
Les Adrets-de-L' Estérel - Map 34:
  – Hôtel Le Chrystalin (380-430F)..447
Les Arcs-sur-Argens - Map 34:
  – Logis du Guetteur (450F)...448
La Cadière-d'Azur - Map 34:
  – Hostellerie Bérard (425-740F)...449
Callas - Map 34:
  – Hostellerie Les Gorges de Pennafort (480-630F).........................450
Callian - Map 34:
  – Auberge du Puits Jaubert (225-250F).....................................451
Cotignac - Map 34:
  – Hostellerie Lou Calen (290-620F)..452
La Croix Valmer - Map 34:
  – Château de Valmer (735-1260F)...453
Fayence - Map 34:
  – Moulin de la Camandoule (460-655F)......................................454
Flassans-sur-Issole - Map 34:
  – La Grillade au feu de bois (400-550F)...................................455
Fox-Amphoux - Map 34:
  – Auberge du Vieux Fox (280-380F)...456
Grimaud - Map 34:
  – La Boulangerie (660-690F)..457
  – Le Verger (550-850F)...458
Ile de Port-Cros - Map 34:
  – Le Manoir (720-980F in half board)......................................459
Ile de Porquerolles - Map 34:
  – Les Glycines (550-650F)..460
Moissac-Bellevue - Map 34:
  – Hôtel Le Calalou (510-600F)...461
Roquebrune-sur-Argens - Map 34:
  – La Maurette (350-450F)...462
Saint-Aygulf - Map 34:
  – Hôtel Plein Soleil (650-850F)... 463
Saint-Tropez - Map 34:
  – Hôtel Le Pré de la Mer (490-680F).......................................464
  – La Ferme d'Augustin (580-1600F)...465
  – Hôtel Le Bouis (750-1150F)..466
  – La Ferme d'Hermès (600-850F)..467
  – La Figuière (500-900F)...468

Seillans - Map 34:
  – Hôtel des Deux Rocs (260-520F)...469
Toulon- Map 34:
  – Les Bastidières (450-800F) 470
Tourtour - Map 34:
  – Auberge Saint-Pierre (360-510F)..471
Trigance - Map 34:
  – Château de Trigance (550-700F)...472

VAUCLUSE

Avignon - Map 33:
  – Hôtel de la Mirande (1400-2100F)..473
  – Hôtel d'Europe (620-1650F)..474
  – L'Anastasy (300-350F)..475
Le Barroux - Map 33:
  – Les Géraniums (210-250F)..476
Bollène - Map 33:
  – Château de Rocher - La Belle Ecluse (220-370F) 477
Bonnieux - Map 33:
  – Hostellerie Prieuré (500-590F)..478
Crillon-le-Brave - Map 33:
  – Hostellerie de Crillon-le-Brave (750-1450F)......................................479
Entrechaux - Map 33:
  – Hostellerie La Manescale (400-560F) 480
Gigondas - Map 33:
  – Les Florets (350-410F) 481
Gordes - Map 33:
  – Ferme de la Huppe (600F)..482
  – Les Romarins (420-680F) 483
Isle sur la Sorgue - Map 33:
  – Mas de Cure Bourse (320-550F) 484
Lagnes - Map 33:
  – Mas des Grès (400-600F) 485
Oppède-le-Vieux - Map 33:
  – Mas des Capelans (400-800F) 486
Orange - Map 33:
  – Hôtel Arène (340-440F) 487
Piolenc - Map 33:
  – L'Orangerie (190-380F)..488
Le Pontet - Map 33:
  – Auberge de Cassagne (490-1380F)...489
Roussillon - Map 33:
  – Mas de Garrigon (780F) 490
Saignon - Map 33:
  – Auberge du Presbytère (200-400F)...491
Sérignan - Map 33:
  – Hostellerie du Vieux Château (300-800F) 492
Vaison-la-Romaine - Map 33:
  – Hostellerie Le Beffroi (435-630F)..493
Velleron- Map 33:
  – Hostellerie La Grangette (550-950F)..494
Venasque - Map 33:
  – Auberge de la Fontaine (700F the suite)...495

R H Ô N E - A L P E S

AIN

Ambérieux-en-Dombes - Map 26:
  – Auberge Les Bichonnières (240-320F) 496
Echenevex - Map 20:
  – Auberge des Chasseurs (400-600F) 497
Pérouges - Map 26:
  – Ostellerie du Vieux Pérouges (450-900F) 498

ARDECHE

Beaulieu - Map *32:*
  – Hôtel de la Santoline (290-370F) 499
Lamastre - Map 26:
  – Château d'Urbilhac (550-700F) 500
Saint-Agrève - Map 26:
  – Domaine de Rilhac (330-430F) 501
Saint-Cierge-la-Serre - Map 26:
  – Grangeon (290-490F) 502

DROME

La Chapelle-en-Vercors - Map 26:
  – Hôtel Bellier (300-440F) 503
Cliousclat - Map 26:
  – La Treille Muscate (280-500F) 504
Grignan - Map 33:
  – Manoir de la Roseraie (630-1050F) 505
Malataverne - Map 33:
  – Domaine du Colombier (de 450-860F) 506
Mirmande - Map 26:
  – La Capitelle (290-460F) 507
Solérieux - Map 33:
  – Ferme Saint-Michel (310-350F) 508
Vauvaneys-la Rochette - Map 26:
  – Auberge de la Rochette (400F) 509

ISERE

Chichilianne - Map 26:
  – Château de Passières (280-450F) 510
Chonas-l'Amballan - Map 26:
  – Domaine de Clairefontaine (180-380F) 511
Les Deux-Alpes - Map 27:
  – Chalet Mounier (335-780F) 512
Grenoble - Eybens - Map 26:
  – Château de la Commanderie (415-630F) 513
Saint-Lattier - Map 26:
  – Le Lièvre Amoureux (320-460F) 514
Villars-de-Lans - Map 26:
  – Hôtel Le Christiania (395-580F) 515

RHÔNE

Lyon - Map 26:
– Hôtel des Artistes (370-450F) 516

SAVOIE

Courchevel - Map 27:
– La Sivolière (850-1950F) 517
– Le Lodge Nogentil Hôtel 850-950F 518

Grésy-sur-Isère - Map 27:
– La Tour de Pacoret (280-450F) 519

Méribel-les-Allues Map 27:
– Hôtel Adray-Télébar (550-750F) 520
– Le Yéti (590-970F in half board) 521

Montpasey - *Tioulevé* Map 27:
– Le Relais du Lac Noir (195F)...................................522

La Rochette - Map 27:
– Les Châtaigniers (350-490F) 523

Les Saisies - Map 27:
– Hôtel Le Calgary (275-560F in half board) 524

Val d'Isère - Map 27:
– Le Blizzard (515-1210F) 525
– La Savoyarde (500-850F in half board) 526

Val Thorens - Map 27:
– Hôtel Fitz Roy 1000-1900F in half board).....................527

HAUTE-SAVOIE

Le Bettex - *Saint-Gervais* - Map 27:
– Chalet Rémy (220F)..528

Chamonix - Map 27:
– Hôtel La Savoyarde (400-580F) 529

Chamonix - *Le Lavancher* - Map 27:
– Hôtel du Jeu de Paume (790-990F)............................530
– Chalet Hôtel Beausoleil (350-565F)...........................531

Chamonix - *Les Praz* - Map 27:
– Hôtel Le Labrador (530-850F) 532

Combloux - Map 27:
– Au Cœur des Prés (330-500F) 533

Cordon - Map 27:
– Les Roches Fleuries (460-650F) 534

Doussard - Map 27:
– Marceau Hôtel (470F)..535

Les Gets - Map 27:
– Chalet-Hôtel Crychar (350-595F)..............................536

Les Houches - Map 27:
– Chalet-Hôtel Peter Pan (195-270F) 537

Manigod - Map 27:
– Hôtel de La Croix Fry (500-1500F) 538

Megève - Map 27:
– Le Mont Blanc (600-1030F) 539
– Les Fermes de Marie (770-1030F in half board)................540
– Le Coin du Feu (770-1030F) 541

– Le Fer-Cheval (565-860F per 1 pers.) 542
– Ferme Hôtel Duvillard (811-1054F) 543
– Le Mégevan (400-600F)..544
Morzine - Map 27:
– La Bergerie (350-500F) 545
Talloires - Map 27:
– Hôtel Beau Site (410-795F)..546

* Prices shown in brackets are prices for a double room, sometimes with half board. For precise details, go to the page mentioned.

We remind you that, from October 1996, the dialing codes will change. Please refer to the page before the table of contents.

KEY TO THE MAPS

Scale: 1:1,000,000
Maps 30 & 31: scale: 1:1,180,000

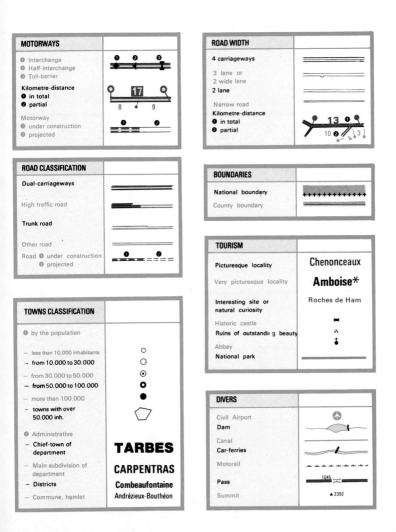

MOTORWAYS

- ❶ Interchange
- ❷ Half-interchange
- ❸ Toll-barrier

Kilometre-distance
- ❶ in total
- ❷ partial

Motorway
- ❶ under construction
- ❷ projected

ROAD WIDTH

4 carriageways

3 lane or
2 wide lane
2 lane
Narrow road
Kilometre-distance
- ❶ in total
- ❷ partial

ROAD CLASSIFICATION

Dual-carriageways

High traffic road

Trunk road

Other road

Road ❶ under construction
     ❷ projected

BOUNDARIES

National boundary
County boundary

TOURISM

Picturesque locality   Chenonceaux

Very picturesque locality   **Amboise**✳

Interesting site or   Roches de Ham
natural curiosity

Historic castle
Ruins of outstanding beauty

Abbey
National park

TOWNS CLASSIFICATION

- ❶ by the population

- — less than 10,000 inhabitants
- → from 10.000 to 30.000
- — from 30.000 to 50.000
- — from 50.000 to 100.000
- — more than 100.000
- — towns with over 50.000 inh.

- ❷ Administrative
- — Chief-town of department   **TARBES**
- — Main subdivision of department   **CARPENTRAS**
- — Districts   **Combeaufontaine**
- — Commune, hamlet   Andrézieux-Bouthéon

DIVERS

Civil Airport
Dam

Canal
Car-ferries

Motorail

Pass

Summit   ▲ 2392

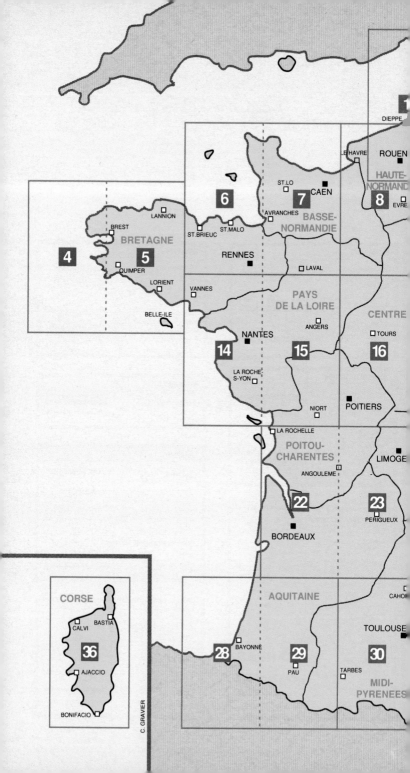

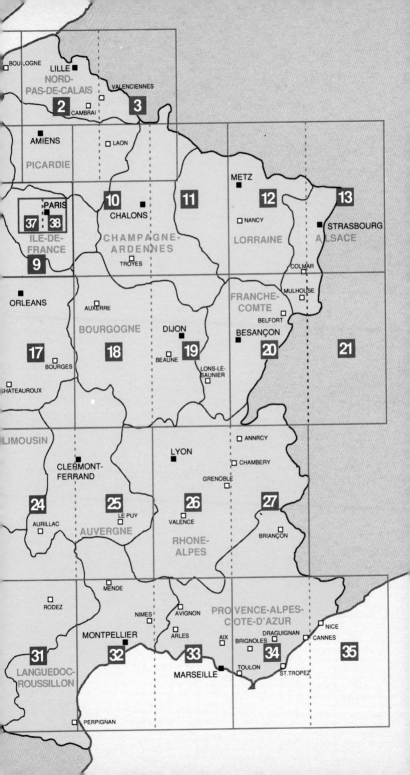

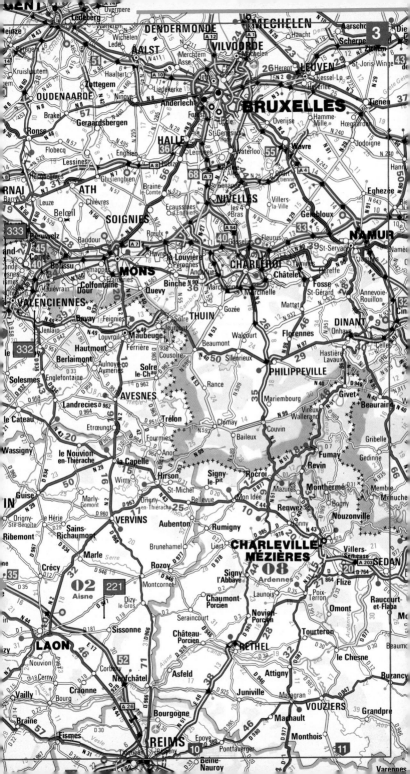

4

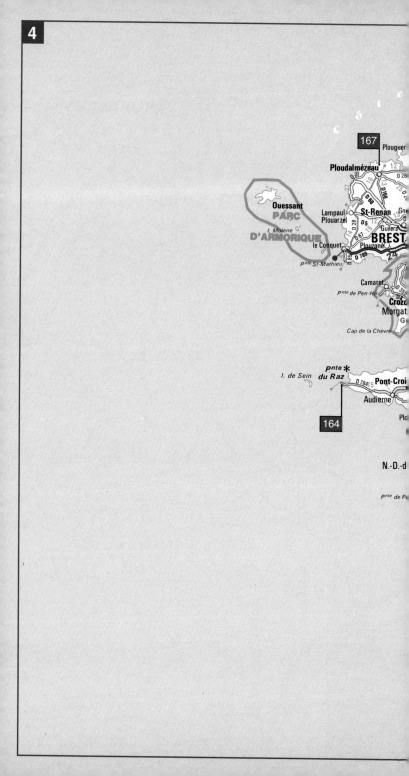

167 Plouguer

Ploudalmézeau

D 28

D 168

Ouessant
PARC
I. Molène
D'ARMORIQUE

Lampaul-   **St-Renan**   Go
Plouarzel
D 28 **D 5**

Guilers
BREST

le Conquet   Plouzané

D 189

Pnte St-Mathieu

24

Camaret

Pnte de Pen-Hir   35

Crozo

Morgat
G

Cap de la Chèvre

I. de Sein   **Pnte** ✱
du Raz   D 784   **Pont-Croi**

Audierne

164   Plo

N.-D.-d

Pnte de Pe

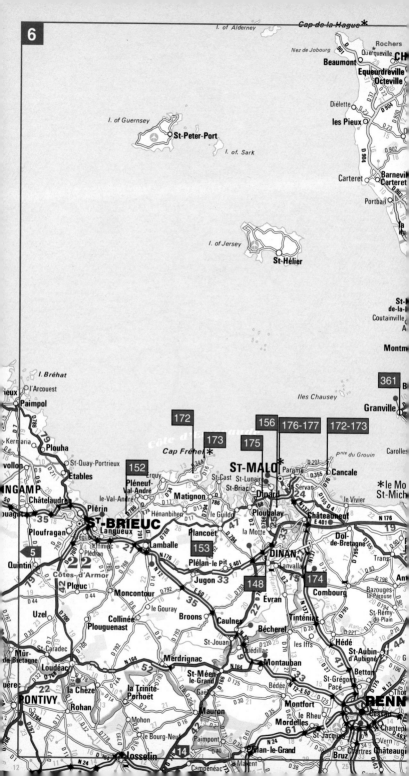

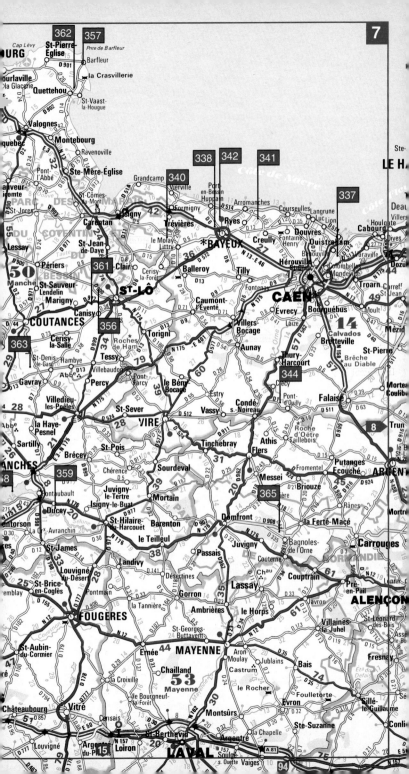

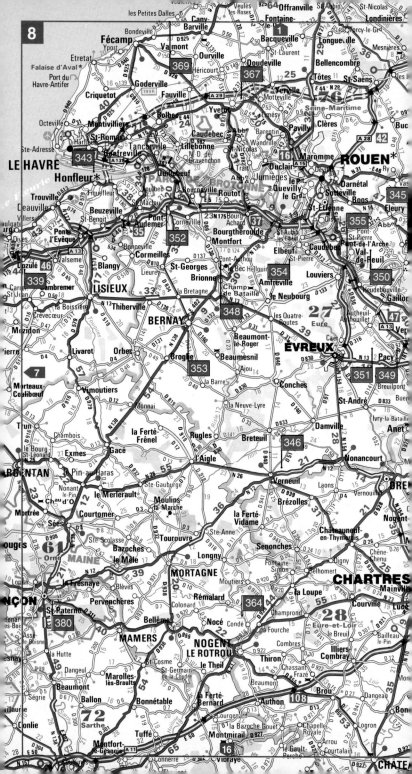

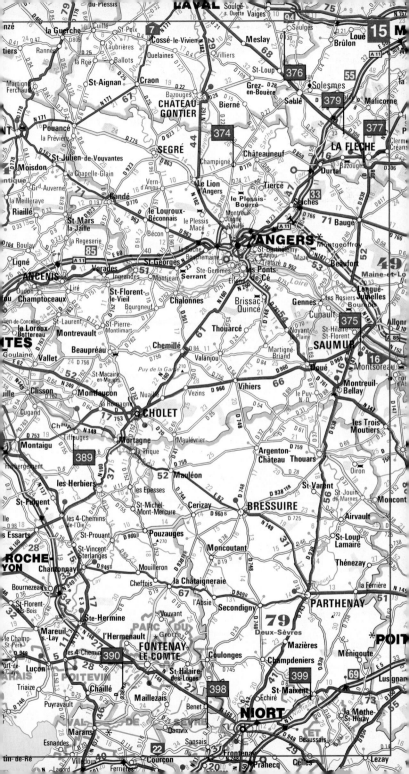

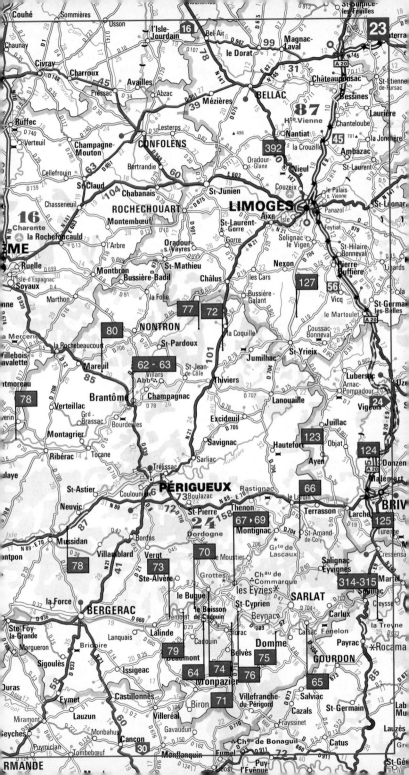

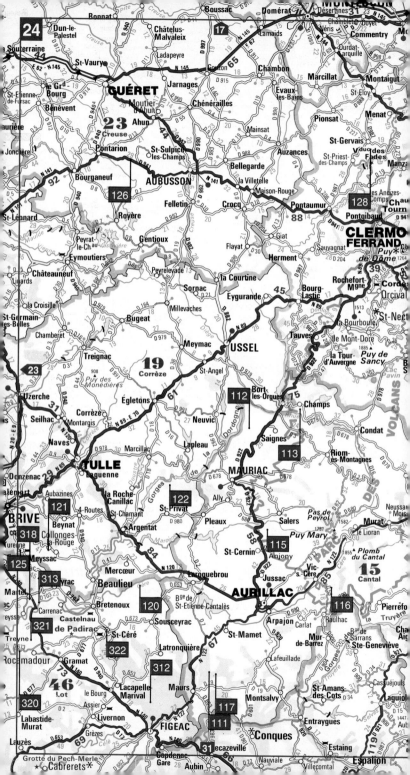

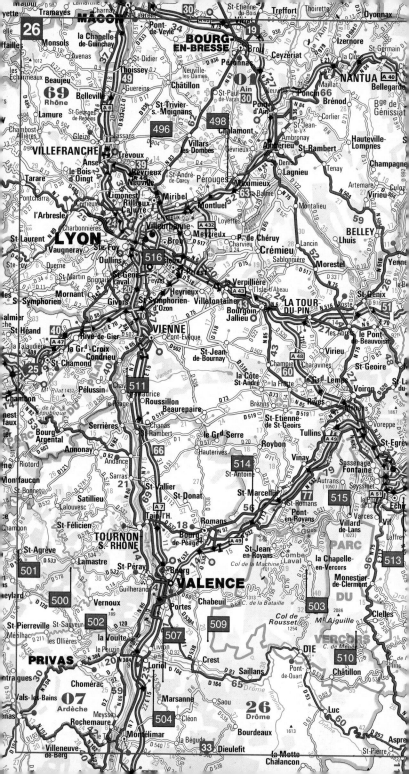

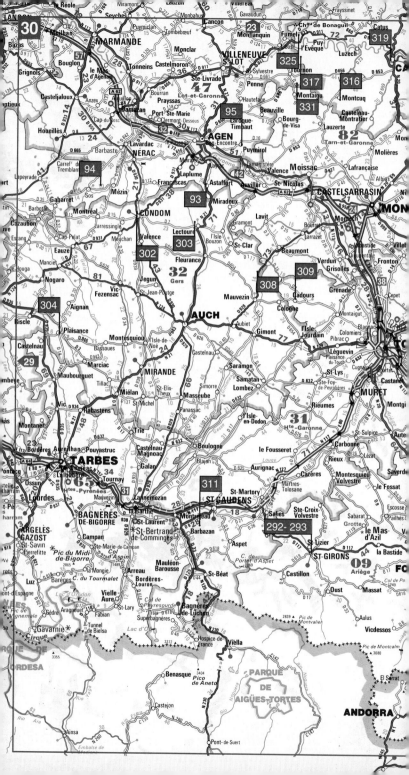

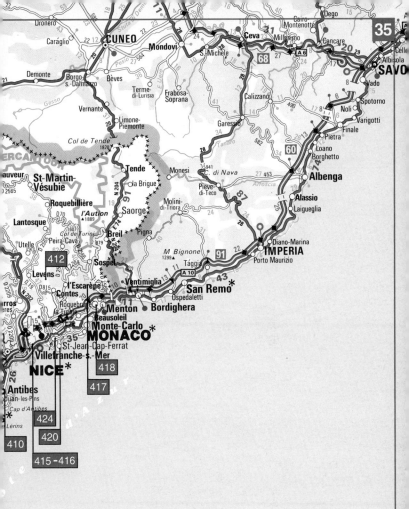

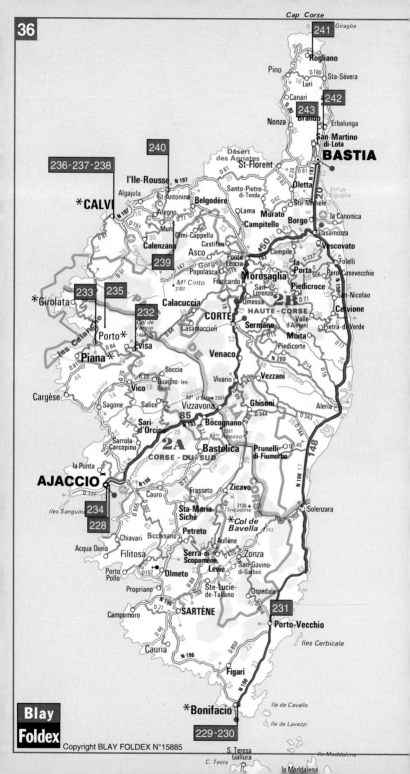

Blay - Foldex
for traveling in France and around the world

15 detailed
regional maps
with index

The easy-to-read
«60kms around»
series

Atlas of France
with alphabetical
listing of towns

More than 130
city maps

maps-plans-guides
40-48, rue des Meuniers
F - 93108 MONTREUIL cedex (FRANCE)
Tél. : (1) 49 88 92 10 - Fax : (1) 49 88 92 09

Hôtel de Notre–Dame★★★

19, rue Maître-Albert
75005 Paris
Tel. (0)1★ 43.26.79.00
Fax (0)1★ 46.33.50.11
M. Fouhety

Rooms 34 with bath or shower and WC, soundproofing, telephone, cable TV, hairdryer, safe, and minibar. **Price** Double 690-790F. **Meals** Breakfast 40F with orange juice, no restaurant. **Credit cards** All major. **Pets** No dogs allowed. **Parking** At 1 rue Lagrange. **Open** All year. **How to get there** (Map 38): Métro Saint-Michel, RER Cluny-Saint-Michel, Bus 21, 24, 27, 38, 47, 85 and 96.

You will have no difficulty in spotting the Hôtel de Notre-Dame, in a small street typical of this old quarter of Paris: its wide frontage was once the window of a shop on the ground floor of the building. In the hotel, which has recently been refurbished, partition walls have been put up without spoiling the original beamed ceilings. A few antiques and a fine tapestry lend a strong period atmosphere to the lobby, bar, and lounges. The bedrooms are attractively furnished and have rather spacious bathrooms. Its position close to Notre-Dame and the quais of the Seine, with their barges and second-hand booksellers, adds to the hotel's many charms.

Les Rives de Notre–Dame★★★★

15, Quai Saint-Michel
75005 Paris
Tel. (0)1★ 43.54.81.16
Fax (0)1★ 43.26.27.09
M. Degravi

Rooms 10 with air-conditioning, telephone, bath or shower, TV, and minibar. **Price** Singles and doubles 950F, 1500F; suite 2350F. **Meals** Breakfast 85F **Credit card** All major. **Pets** Small dogs allowed. **Parking** Square in front of Notre-Dame and 1, rue Lagrange. **Open** All year. **How to get there** (Map 38): Métro Cluny, RER Cluny-Saint-Michel, Bus 21, 24, 27, 47, 63, 67, 86, 87 and 96.

Your windows at Les Rives de Notre-Dame look out over a postcard setting between the Place Saint-Michel and Notre Dame: the quays of the Seine with its bookstalls, and the banks (*rives*) down below where lovers stroll and watch the *bateaux mouches* wending their way upstream. Excellent soundproofing means that you can enjoy this view from a quiet room, of which there are ten. None are is the same but all are handsomely decorated with a tasteful combination of motifs and colors. The rooms are large and include shaped sitting areas with a sofa-bed and pretty bathrooms. On the ground floor, there are three small bedrooms that are equally charming; they are usually for one person, but a couple could stay here if spaciousness is not important. The service is attentive.

Hôtel du Parc Saint-Séverin★★★

22, rue de la Parcheminerie
75005 Paris
Tel. (0)1★ 43.54.32.17
Fax (0)1★ 43.54.70.71
Mme Bonnaffoux

Rooms 27 (air-conditioning in some rooms) with telephone, bath or shower, soundproofing, cable TV, hairdryer and minibar. **Price** Singles and doubles 500F, 600-1500F. **Meals** Breakfast 50F. **Credit cards** All major. **Pets** Dogs not allowed. **Parking** Square in front of Notre-Dame and 1, rue Lagrange. **Open** All year. **How to get there** (Map 38): Métro Cluny, RER Cluny-Saint-Michel, Bus 21, 24, 27, 47, 63, 67, 86, 87 and 96.

Although the Hôtel Parc Saint-Séverin is located in the heart of the Latin Quarter, it is quiet because it is on a pedestrian street away from the crowds. The beautiful spaces of the handsome, airy building have been well preserved. The muted colors and contemporary or 1930s furniture in the lounge further reenforce the sense of spaciousness. The same is true in the large, bright bedrooms which are pleasantly decorated with antique furniture and paintings. For a beautiful view of the rooftops, the Saint-Séverin Cloister, and the gardens of the Cluny Museum, ask for a room on the *cinquième étage* (6th floor) or above; the largest are those on a corner, and on the last floor, you can even have a lovely terrace.

Hôtel des Deux Iles★★★

59, rue Saint-Louis-en-l'Ile
75004 Paris
Tel. (0)1★ 43. 26. 13. 35
Fax (0)1★ 43. 29. 60. 25
Mme Buffat

Rooms 17 with bath or shower and WC, soundproofing, telephone, cable TV and hairdryer. **Price** Single 720F, double 830F. **Meals** Breakfast 45F, snacks available. **Credit cards** Not accepted. **Pets** Dogs not allowed. **Parking** At 2 rue Geoffroy-l'Asnier and square in front of Notre-Dame. **Open** All year. **How to get there** (Map 38): Métro Pont-Marie, Bus 24, 63, 67, 86 and 87.

M. and Mme Buffat have converted two buildings into charming hotels between a former Archbishop's Palace, the Church of Saint-Louis-en-l'Ile, and Bertillot, famous for its ice cream. We have chosen this one for its atmosphere – English with a tinge of exoticism: flowery fabrics and painted cane and bamboo furniture are the main features of the decor. The bedrooms are not very large, but they are delightful. Provençal fabrics replace the chintzes used in the lounge, and the bathrooms are lined with gleaming blue tiles. Everything here is comfortable, including the beautiful vaulted breakfast room. This hotel has a faithful following and often there are no vacancies. If this is the case, you might be able to reserve a room in the Buffat's Hôtel de Lutèce just next door, which is also very charming.

Hôtel du Jeu de Paume★★★★

54, rue Saint-Louis-en-l'Ile
75004 Paris
Tel. (0)1★ 43 26 14 18
Fax (0)1★ 40 46 02 76
Mme Prache

Rooms 32 with bath and shower and WC, telephone, cable TV, hairdryer and minibar. **Price** Double 820-1395F. **Meals** Breakfast 80F, snacks available. **Credit cards** All major. **Pets** Dogs allowed. **Facilities** Sauna, gym. **Parking** At 2 rue Geoffroy-l'Asnier and square in front of Notre-Dame. **Open** All year. **How to get there** (Map 38): Métro Pont-Marie, Bus 24, 63, 67, 86 and 87.

This hotel is an authentic old palm-tennis court. The spacious interior has been entirely and artfully restructured by creating a series of galleries and mezzanines to form a dynamic and very decorative architectural arrangement. Several areas have thus been created: On the ground-floor, there is an intimate lounge-bar and a warm, inviting breakfast room; on the mezzanine, you will find a reading room, and off the galleries are the elegant bedrooms with beautiful baths. The delicious breakfasts include excellent homemade preserves.

Hôtel Relais Christine★★★★

3, rue Christine
75006 Paris
Tel. (0)1★ 43.26.71.80
Fax (0)1★ 43.26.89.38
M. Regnault

Rooms 34 and 17 duplex, with air-conditioning, bath or shower and WC, soundproofing, telephone, cable TV, hairdryer and minibar. **Price** 1630-1800F, suite 2450F, duplex 2450-3000F. **Meals** Breakfast 95F, snacks available. **Credit cards** All major. **Pets** Dogs allowed. **Facilities** Free private parking. **Open** All year. **How to get there** (Map 38): Métro Odéon, Saint-Michel, RER Cluny-Saint-Michel, Bus 24, 27, 58, 63, 70, 86, 87 and 96.

This hotel occupies a former Augustinian convent, entered through a paved courtyard/garden but the interior has nothing monastic about it. On the contrary, it is decorated with a rainbow of warm colors, in both the panelled lounge - which has a handsome collection of portraits - and in the spacious, elegant bedrooms, some of which look onto the garden. Note also the duplexes, which are ideal for long stays. The breakfast room is in one of the most beautiful vaulted rooms of the cloister. The personnel is very attentive, discreet and efficient. Le Relais Christine has become a classic Paris *hôtel de charme*.

Left Bank
Saint-Germain Hôtel★★★

9, rue de l'Ancienne-Comédie
75006 Paris
Tel. (0)1★ 43.54.01.70
Fax (0)1★ 43.26.17.14
M. Teil

Rooms 30 and 1 suite with air-conditioning, bath or shower and WC, soundproofing, telephone, cable TV, safe, hairdryer and minibar. **Price** 895-990F, suite 1400F. **Meals** Breakfast 25F. **Credit cards** All major. **Pets** Dogs not allowed. **Parking** Opposite 21, rue de l'Ecole-de-Médecine and 27, rue Mazarine. **Open** All year. **How to get there** (Map 38): Métro Odéon, RER Cluny-Saint-Michel, Bus 58, 63, 70, 86, 87 and 96.

The Left Bank is in the heart of Saint-Germain-des-Prés, next door to the *Procope* Restaurant, which is steeped in the history of the Revolutionaries, the Encyclopedists and the romantic writers. The small lobby opens onto a pretty lounge which immediately sets the style of the hotel. Oak and walnut panelling and 17th-century-style chairs were made for the hotel and are well coordinated with the antique furniture and Aubusson tapestry. The same style can be seen in the bedrooms, where fabric-upholstered walls enhance the warm and very comfortable atmosphere. (The rooms whose numbers end with 4 and 6 are the largest). All have beautiful, fully equipped bathrooms. The breakfast buffets are delicious and copious.

Hôtel du Lys★★

23, rue Serpente
75006 Paris
Tel. (0)1★ 43.26.97.57
Mme Decharme

Rooms 22 with bath or shower and WC, telephone, hairdryer. **Price** 360-420F. **Meals** Breakfast incl. **Credit cards** Not accepted. **Pets** Dogs allowed. **Parking** Square in front of Notre-Dame. **Open** All year. **How to get there** (Map 38): Métro Saint-Michel, RER Cluny-Saint-Michel, Bus 21, 24, 27, 38, 63, 85, 86, 87 and 96.

This is a very special hotel. In the heart of the Latin Quarter, you can have a room for an undreamed-of price in a small, charming hotel. On arrival, you will be greeted by the charming Mme Decharne. The hotel is simple but the bedrooms are cheerful and have renovated baths. Likewise, the 17th-century staircase has been restored. (There is no elevator). The mansard bedrooms are the largest and some even have small balconies, but you have to climb the stairs. The prices and the friendly personnel have attracted a faithful clientèle, so you should reserve early.

Hôtel Prince de Conti★★★

8, rue Guénégaud
75006 Paris
Tel. (0)1★ 44.07.30.40
Fax (0)1★ 44.07.36.34
Mme Etienne

Rooms 26 with air-conditioning, bath or shower and WC, soundproofing, telephone, cable TV, hairdryer and minibar - Elevator. **Price** Single 750-850F, double 990F, suite 1250F. **Meals** Breakfast 60F. **Credit cards** All major. **Pets** Dogs allowed. **Parking** At rue Mazarine. **Open** All year. **How to get there** (Map 38): Métro Odéon,Saint-Michel, RER Cluny-Saint-Michel, Bus 70, 58, 27, 87, 63 and 96.

The Hôtel Prince de Conti is located in an 18th-Century building in the heart of artistic and literary Saint-Germain-des-Prés. The newly renovated hotel's bedrooms, we must note, are not large, but they are very beautiful. The choice of the various coordinated fabrics is superb and there are modern amenities like double windows, air-conditioning, and beautiful, well-equipped bathrooms. The duplex suites are also charming and are larger, with lounges and upstairs bedrooms. Note that there are two single rooms on the ground floor opening onto the courtyard. There is a refined, British atmosphere here, and the people are very friendly.

Hôtel des Grands Hommes★★★

17, place du Panthéon
75005 Paris
Tel. (0)1★ 46.34.19.60
Fax (0)1★ 43.26.67.32
Mlle Brethous

Rooms 32 with air-conditioning, bath and WC, telephone, cable TV, hairdryer and minibar. **Price** Single 610F, double 770F. **Meals** Breakfast 45F (buffet) with orange juice, no restaurant but snaks available for lunchtime. **Credit cards** All major. **Pets** Dogs allowed. **Parking** At 20, rue Soufflot and Place du Panthéon. **Open** all year. **How to get there** (Map 38): Métro Cardinal-Lemoine, RER Luxembourg, Bus 21, 27, 38, 82, 84, 85 and 89.

The Hôtel des Grands Hommes is named for such great men of France as Mirabeau, Voltaire and Victor Hugo, who are buried in the Panthéon. The reception area, with its ornate moldings, 1930s armchairs and subtle orange-pink color scheme, sets the style for the entire building. The atmosphere is both classic and refined. Delicate colors have also been used in the bedrooms, which have brass beds and bathrooms tiled in beige. The most charming rooms are those located on the top floor of the building, with sloping ceilings and balconies looking out onto the Place du Panthéon.

Hôtel des Trois Collèges★★

16, rue Cujas
75005 Paris
Tel. (0)1★ 43.54.67.30
Fax (0)1★ 46.34.02.99

Rooms 44 with bath or shower and WC, soundproofing, telephone and hairdryer. **Price** Single 360-500F, double 450-600F, suite 750F. **Meals** Breakfast 40F, no restaurant. **Credit cards** All major. **Pets** Dogs not allowed. **Parking** At 20, rue Soufflot. **Open** All year. **How to get there** (Map 38): Métro Saint-Michel, Odeon, RER Luxembourg and Cluny-Saint-Michel, Bus 21, 27, 38, 63, 82, 84, 86 and 87.

This small, discreet hotel is located in the shadow of three famous, ancient seats of learning: La Sorbonne, the prestigious Collège de France, and the 15th-century Collège Sainte-Barbe, the oldest private school in France. The decoration of the hotel is deliberately simple in style, and white is the dominant colour. The bedrooms are comfortable and fully equipped, with pretty bathrooms or shower rooms. The largest rooms are on the top floor and overlook the Sorbonne and the Panthéon. The delicious breakfast here, complete with homemade jam, is served in a pleasant small dining-room.

Résidence Les Gobelins★★

9, rue des Gobelins
75013 Paris
Tel. (0)1★ 47.07.26.90
Fax (0)1★ 43.31.44.05
M. and Mme Poirier

Rooms 32 with bath or shower and WC, telephone, TV. **Price** Single 365F, double 400-455F. **Meals** Breakfast 37F with orange juice, no restaurant. **Credit cards** All major. **Pets** Dogs not allowed. **Parking** At place d'Italie and 1, rue Lagrange. **Facilities** Patio. **Open** All year. **How to get there** (Map 38): Métro Gobelins, RER Port-Royal, Bus 27, 47, 83 and 91.

Close to the Manufacture Royale des Gobelins tapestries after which it is named, this hotel is a haven of peace in a busy, colorful neighborhood. The rue Mouffetard and its popular, bustling market are within a short walking distance, as well as the souks, hammam, cafés and restaurants surrounding the Mosquée de Paris (the city's oldest and most important mosque). The decoration of the hotel is bright and pleasant. In the bedrooms bamboo furniture sets the style and imposes the color scheme. Some of the rooms on the upper floors command pretty views of the courtyard and of a garden, and those on the top floor have sloping ceilings. The breakfast room leads out into a flowery patio with teak furniture. You will receive a friendly welcome.

Hôtel du Parc Montsouris★★★

4, rue du Parc-Montsouris
75014 Paris
Tel. (0)1★ 45.89.09.72
Fax (0)1★ 45.80.92.72
M. Grand and Mme Piguet

Rooms 35 with bath or shower and WC, telephone, TV. **Price** Single and double 310-370F, suite 420-480F. **Meals** Breakfast 35F with orange juice. **Credit cards** Amex, Visa, Eurocard and MasterCard. **Pets** Dogs allowed. **Parking** In private road. **Open** All year. **How to get there** (Map 37): Métro Porte d'Orléans, RER Cité Universitaire. Bus for Orly from Porte d'Orléans, Bus PC, 27, 38 and 47.

The Hôtel du Parc Montsouris is located in a former villa near the beautiful park of that name. It has been fully renovated, and its columns and Art Deco paintings convey something of the original atmosphere of the house. The decoration is classic in style, and the bedrooms and bathrooms are comfortably arranged. The neighbourhood is quiet, and a stay in this part of the 14th *arrondissement* will show you a new side of Paris, with its quiet *cul-de-sacs* and 1930s villas, among them some interesting works of Sauvage, Le Corbusier and Lurçat. But the 14th arrondissement also boasts two large parks: that of the Cité Internationale Universitaire and, of course, the Parc Montsouris.

Hôtel Raspail-Montparnasse★★★

203, boulevard Raspail
75014 Paris
Tel. (0)1★ 43.20.62.86
Fax (0)1★ 43.20.50.79
M. and Mme Branche

Rooms 36 and 2 suites with air-conditioning, bath or shower and WC, soundproofing, telephone, cable TV, minibar and safe. **Price** Single 560-610F, double 860-1210F. **Meals** Breakfast 50F. **Credit cards** All major. **Pets** Dogs not allowed. **Parking** At 116, boulevard du Montparnasse. **Open** All year. **How to get there** (Map 37): Métro Porte Vavin, Raspail, RER Port-Royal. Bus 68, 82, 83 and 91.

Shortly before he died, the famous decorator Serge Pons became fond of this Art Deco hotel. In 1992, he restored the noble, vast and light-filled lobby with its large rounded bay windows and its ceilings outlined with beautiful geometric moldings. He opened up the monumental stairway, brought back the lounge-bar, and restored the superb canopy of the façade. The bedrooms are tastefully decorated with grey tones enhanced with brighter fabrics on the walls. Each bedroom bears the name of, and is decorated with, a fine reproduction of a painting by an artist who lived in Montparnasse. Pierre Branche and his wife are always here, personally ensuring that guests are well taken care of.

Hôtel Danemark★★★

21, rue Vavin
75006 Paris
Tel. (0)1★ 43.26.93.78
Fax (0)1★ 46.34.66.06
M. and Mme Nurit

Rooms 15 with bath and WC, soundproofing, telephone, cable TV, hairdryer and minibar. **Price** Single and double 590-690F, with Jacuzzi 790F. **Meals** Breakfast 50F. **Credit cards** All major. **Pets** Dogs allowed. **Parking** At 116, boulevard du Montparnasse. **Open** All year. **How to get there** (Map 37): Métro Vavin and Notre-Dame-des-Champs, RER Port-Royal, Bus 58, 68, 75, 82, 83 and 91 - Montparnasse station.

The Hôtel Danemark stands just opposite the remarkable *maison à gradins sportive* (house with a tiered facade), which is covered in white ceramic tiles and was built in 1912 by Sauvage. Perhaps as a tribute to that building, or simply as a reminder of Danish enthusiasm for contemporary design, the decoration of this hotel is resolutely modern in style. Bright and strongly contrasting colors have been chosen for the reception area and lounge. A more subdued color scheme prevails in the bedrooms, to match the 1930s furniture. There are few rooms, all extremely comfortable and well soundproofed. You will find a friendly and attentive welcome.

L'Atelier Montparnasse★★★

49, rue Vavin
75006 Paris
Tel. (0)1★ 46.33.60.00
Fax (0)1★ 40.51.04.21
Mme Tible

Rooms 17 with bath or shower and WC, soundproofing, telephone, TV, hairdryer and minibar. **Price** Single and double 700F, "Fujita room" 950F. **Meals** Breakfast 40F. **Credit cards** All major. **Pets** Small dogs allowed. **Parking** At 116, boulevard du Montparnasse. **Open** All year. **How to get there** (Map 37): Métro Notre-Dame-des-Champs and Montparnasse, RER Port-Royal, Bus 68, 82, 83 and 91 - Montparnasse station.

Very near La Coupole restaurant, the Atelier Montparnasse makes the earlier spirit of the quarter come to life. The hotel has kept the 30s style in the entrance, which harmonizes with the carpet-mosaic of the floor. There is a permanent exhibit of paintings, thus renewing the Montparnasse tradition. The bedrooms are sober, pleasant and comfortable, but the bathrooms—with glass mosaics evoking a great painter from the grand days of Montparnasse—are simply splendid. Mme Tible's dynamism and professionalism are everywhere in evidence in this friendly hotel.

Hôtel Ferrandi★★★

92, rue du Cherche-Midi
75006 Paris
Tel. (1) 42.22.97.40
Fax (1) 45.44.89.97
Mme Lafond

Rooms 41 and 1 suite, with air-conditioning, bath or shower and WC, soundproofing, telephone, TV, hairdryer. **Price** Double 460-980F, suite 1280F. **Meals** Breakfast 60F with fresh fruit juices and traditional jams; snacks available. **Credit cards** All major. **Pets** Dogs allowed. **Parking** Garage at hotel (140F per day) and at Bon Marché. **Open** All year. **How to get there** (Map 37): Métro Saint-Placide and Sèvres-Babylone, Bus 39, 48, 84, 89, 94, 95 and 96.

The Hôtel Ferrandi is a classic hotel, with vast reception rooms, Restoration-style mahogany furniture and lavishly draped hangings. The bedrooms are also spacious, and no two are alike. In each one, a different bed creates the style and color scheme. The bathrooms are immaculate. The Hôtel Ferrandi stands just opposite the delightful Hôtel de Montmorency, which now houses the works of the 19th-century French artist Ernest Hébert, whom you might like to discover.

Hôtel Sainte-Beuve★★★

9, rue Sainte-Beuve
75006 Paris
Tel. (0)1★ 45.48.20.07
Fax (0)1★ 45.48.67.52
Mme Compagnon

Rooms 23, with bath and WC, telephone, TV, safe and minibar. **Price** 700-1300F, suite 1550F, apart. 1700F. **Meals** Breakfast 80F, snacks available. **Credit cards** Amex, Visa, Eurocard and MasterCard. **Pets** Dogs not allowed. **Parking** At 116, boulevard du Montparnasse. **Open** All year. **How to get there** (Map 37): Métro Vavin and Notre-Dame-des-Champs, Bus 68, 82, 83 and 91.

The Sainte-Beuve is the model of a charming hotel. For the decoration, David Hicks's Paris ateliers were called in and the spirit of the master is seen in the hotel's comfortable, simple luxury. A great refinement, created by the subtle harmony of colors and materials, distinguishes the neo-Gothic architecture of the lounge. Decoration apart, the amenities are modern and the bedrooms are spacious and bright with delicate colors which are well coordinated with the print wall-fabrics and antique furniture. The breakfasts are delicious and the service impeccable in this beautiful hotel.

Hôtel le Saint Grégoire★★★

43, rue de l'Abbé-Grégoire
75006 Paris
Tel. (0)1★ 45.48.23.23
Fax (0)1★ 45.48.33.95
Mme Agaud and M. Bouvier

Rooms 20 (with air-conditioning in 1996) with bath or shower and WC, soundproofing, telephone, TV and hairdryer. **Price** Double 790-930F, suites and rooms with terrasse: 1390F. **Meals** Breakfast 60F, snacks available. **Credit cards** All major. **Pets** Small dogs allowed. **Parking** At rue de l'Abbé-Grégoire. **Open** All year. **How to get there** (Map 37): Métro Saint-Placide, Bus 48, 89, 94, 95 and 96.

The Saint Grégoire is located halfway between Montparnasse and Saint Germain in a small 18th-century building. The intimate decor beautifully blends a range of colors, subtly mixing shades of orange and mauve in the lounge, and pink and brown in the bedrooms. The rooms are well appointed with period furniture and very functional bathrooms. Some have terraces. You can have breakfast in a beautiful room with a vaulted ceiling, and you will enjoy a warm and pleasant welcome.

L'Abbaye Saint-Germain★★★

10, rue Cassette
75006 Paris
Tel. (0)1★ 45.44.38.11
Fax (0)1★ 45.48.07.86
M. Lafortune

Rooms 42 and 4 suites (duplex with balcony and minibar) with air-conditioning, bath, WC, telephone and TV. **Price** Standard room 900-980F, large room 1500-1600F, duplex or apartment 1800-1950F. **Meals** Breakfast incl., snacks available. **Credit cards** Amex, Visa, Eurocard and MasterCard. **Pets** Dogs not allowed. **Parking** At place Saint-Sulpice. **Facilities** Patio, bar. **Open** All year. **How to get there** (Map 37): Métro Saint-Sulpice and Sèvres-Babylone, Bus 48, 63, 70, 84, 87, 95 and 96.

Recent renovations have made the Hotel de L'Abbaye even more charming. The ground floor now has a broader view onto the flowering patio, where breakfast is served and bar service is provided in good weather. The plush couches around the fireplace in the lounge are ideal for relaxing in cooler weather. All the rooms are very comfortable, refined, and homey; some are air-conditioned. Among the most recently renovated rooms are the largest ones, which are lovely garden-level duplexes with balconies.

Hôtel de Seine★★★

42, rue de Seine
75006 Paris
Tel. (0)1★ 46.34.22.80
Fax (0)1★ 46.34.04.74
M. Henneveux

Rooms 30 with bath, telephone , soundproofing, cable TV and safe. **Price** 880-900F. **Meals** Breakfast 45F. **Credit cards** Visa, Eurocard and MasterCard. **Pets** Dogs not allowed. **Parking** At 27, rue Mazarine. **Open** All year. **How to get there** (Map 37): Métro Mabillon, Saint-Germain-des-Prés, Bus 58, 63, 70, 86, 87, 95 and 96.

After a complete renovation, the Hôtel de Seine has become a very appealing hotel, beginning with the provincial charm of the lounge, where a wood fireplace and panelling are brightened with a prettily colored floral tapestry. The bedrooms are as pleasantly decorated, with Provençal fabrics and patinated painted furniture. Their amenities have also been improved as have their bathrooms thanks to a recent recent renovation. The staff are energetic and welcoming in this hotel, which is under the same management as the Hôtel des Marronniers.

Relais Saint-Germain★★★

9, carrefour de l'Odéon
75006 Paris
Tel. (0)1★ 43.29.12.05
Fax (0)1★ 46.33.45.30
M. Laipsker

Rooms 22 with air-conditioning, bath, WC, telephone, soundproofing, cable TV, hairdryer, safe and minibar. **Price** Single 1280F, double 1530-1700F, suite 1950F, duplex 3200F. **Meals** Breakfast incl., snacks available. **Credit cards** All major. **Pets** Dogs allowed. **Parking** At place Saint-Sulpice, opposite 21, rue de l'Ecole-de-Médecine. **Open** All year. **How to get there** (Map 37): Métro Odéon and RER Cluny-Saint-Michel, Bus 58, 63, 70, 86, 87 and 96.

This is a small hotel of great luxury and charm. The very elegant lobby gives onto a small, luxurious lounge with beautiful 18th-century paintings and a Louis XIV chest of drawers. The Relais Saint-Germain has only 22 bedrooms, all beautiful, spacious and furnished with antiques. All are different, with lovely print or striped fabrics that harmonize with the air individual color schemes. The suite on the top floor is especially attractive. Modern amenities and service are, of course, flawless.

Hôtel de l'Odéon★★★

13, rue Saint-Sulpice
75006 Paris
Tel. (0)1★ 43.25.70.11
Fax (0)1★ 43.29.97.34
M. and Mme Pilfert

Rooms 30 with air-conditioning, bath or shower and WC, soundproofing, telephone, cable TV, hairdryer and safe. **Price** Single 630F, double 760-920F, suite 1080F. **Meals** Breakfast 50F, orange juice 20F, snacks available. **Credit cards** All major. **Pets** Dogs allowed. **Parking** At place Saint-Sulpice and opposite 21, rue de l'Ecole-de-Médecine. **Open** All year. **How to get there** (Map 37): Métro Odéon, Saint-Sulpice and Saint-Germain-des-Prés, RER Cluny-Saint-Michel, Bus 58, 63, 70, 86, 87 and 96.

This handsome 16th–century building incorporates a skilful blend of decorative styles. Thus, in the ground-floor lounges, you find Louis-Philippe armchairs and pedestal tables beside a large church pew, and Persian rugs with a flowery English fitted carpet all creating a warm, intimate atmosphere. The bedrooms are individually decorated: Haute Epoque rooms with canopied beds and romantic rooms with large brass beds or Sicilian painted-iron twin beds. All have small writing or sitting areas. As this is the center of Paris, the rooms overlooking the street are well soundproofed, and the more exposed ones have air-conditioning for the summer. Lavish amounts of care and attention have been devoted to creating a stunning decor.

Relais Médicis★★★

23, rue Racine
75006 Paris
Tel. (0)1★ 43.26.00.60
Fax (0)1★ 40.46.83.39

Rooms 16 with air-conditioning, bath and WC, soundproofing, telephone, cable TV, hairdryer, safe and minibar. **Price** Single 930F, double 995-1495F. **Meals** Breakfast incl. **Credit cards** All major. **Pets** Dogs not allowed. **Parking** At place Saint-Sulpice and opposite 21, rue de l'Ecole-de-Médecine. **Open** All year. **How to get there** (Map 37): Métro Odéon, RER Cluny-Saint-Michel, Bus 58, 63, 70, 86, 87 and 96.

The Relais Médicis appropriately defines itself as a hotel with the colors of Provence and the scent of Italy. This is very much the atmosphere inside, with its warm and sunny decoration. Waxed beamed ceilings, garden furniture, antique paintings and photos decorate the reception rooms downstairs. The bedrooms are fresh, cheerful and delightful with bathrooms as pretty as they are comfortable. The largest are on the street side. There is the same charm in the breakfast room with its checked tablecloths and its vacation atmosphere. This is a hotel where you'll love returning in the evening.

Le Clos Médicis★★★

43, rue de l'Abbé-Grégoire
75006 Paris
Tel. (0)1★ 45.48.23.23
Fax (0)1★ 45.48.33.95
Mme Agaud and M. Bouvier

Rooms 38 with air-conditioning, bath, WC, soundproofing, telephone, cable TV, hairdryer, safe and minibar - 1 room for disabled persons; elevator. **Price** Single 786F, double 886-986F, duplex 1206F. **Meals** Breakfast 60F. **Credit cards** All major. **Pets** Dogs allowed (+60F). **Parking** At rue Soufflet. **Open** All year. **How to get there** (Map 37): Métro Odéon, RER Luxembourg, Bus 21, 27, 38, 58, 82, 84, 85 and 89.

The Clos Médicis, like many hotels in this quarter, is named after the Medici Palace which was built in the Luxembourg Gardens for Marie de Medicis. At Number 54 next door, Blaise Pascal wrote a large part of *Les Provinciales* and *Les Pensées*. It has just been entirely renovated, with a beautiful and inviting reception area brightened by a cheerful fireplace in winter. With the first fine days of spring, breakfasts are served in the leafy courtyard which is just off the breakfast room. The bedrooms are generally spacious, and very comfortable, with modern conveniences and well-designed bathrooms; double windows and air-conditioning ensure that they are quiet. The walls are a pretty yellow, and the draperies and bedspreads are coordinated with lovely prints. The staff is very courteous.

Hôtel Le Régent★★★

61, rue Dauphine
75006 Paris
Tel. (0)1★ 46.34.59.80
Fax (0)1★ 40.51.05.07

Rooms 25 with air-conditioning, bath or shower and WC, telephone, TV, hairdryer and safe. **Price** 750-950F. **Meals** Breakfast 55F. **Credit cards** All major. **Pets** Dogs not allowed. **Parking** At 27, rue Mazarine. **Open** All year. **How to get there** (Map 37): Métro Odéon, RER Cluny-Saint-Michel, Bus 25, 27, 58, 63, 70, 86, 87 and 96.

The Hôtel Le Régent has recently opened in a former 18th-century town house between the boulevard Saint-Germain and the Seine. In the lobby, a mirrored wall reflects the painted beams and old stones of the house. The lounge is classic, and the bedrooms, more fanciful, are light and very cheerful with their assorted printed fabrics. The harmonizing bathrooms have beautiful tiles. The owners of the hotel also own the legendary *Café des Deux Magots*, where you can conveniently have your meals.

Hôtel de Fleurie★★★

32, rue Grégoire-de-Tours
75006 Paris
Tel. (0)1★ 43.29.59.81
Fax (0)1★ 43.29.68.44
Famille Marolleau

Rooms 29 with air-conditioning, bath or shower and WC, soundproofing, telephone, cable TV, hairdryer, safe and minibar. **Price** Single 650-850F, double 850-1200F. **Meals** Breakfast 50F (buffet), snacks available. **Credit cards** All major. **Pets** Dogs not allowed. **Parking** Opposite 21, rue de l'Ecole-de-Médecine. **Open** All year. **How to get there** (Map 37): Métro Odéon, RER Cluny-Saint-Michel and Luxembourg, Bus 58, 63, 70, 86, 87 and 96.

We were immediately attracted by the white façade of this hotel, which is highlighted on each level with a white niche and statue. There are the same light tones inside, with white stones or panelling and 18th-century-style caned chairs in the lounge and breakfast room. The bedrooms, which are not very spacious, are tastefully decorated in the same soft shades, and the bathrooms are comfortably equipped. (The rooms ending in 4 are the largest). The staff is efficient and welcoming.

Hôtel les Marronniers★★★

21, rue Jacob
75006 Paris
Tel. (0)1★ 43.25.30.60
Fax (0)1★ 40.46.83.56
M. Henneveux

Rooms 37 with air-conditioning, bath or shower, WC and TV. **Price** Single 510F, double 700-850F, suite 1020F. **Meals** Breakfast 45F, no restaurant. **Credit cards** Not accepted. **Pets** Dogs not allowed. **Parking** Opposite 169, boulevard Saint-Germain and at place Saint-Sulpice. **Open** All year. **How to get there** (Map 37): Métro Saint-Germain-des-Prés, Bus 39, 48, 63, 68, 69, 86, 87 and 95.

The Hôtel Les Marronniers is truly a delightful place, especially with its lovely garden. An ornate Napoleon III verandah houses the lounge and breakfast room. It is elegantly decorated with white cast-iron garden furniture, flowery carpets and graceful drapes in soft tones of pink and green. The bedrooms and bathrooms are more conventional. For a view of the garden, ask for a room on the *troisième étage* or higher, with a number ending in 1 or 2. The mansard rooms on the *cinquième* and *sixième étages* overlook the courtyard and have a pretty view of the rooftops. The staff is very pleasant.

Hôtel d'Angleterre★★★

44, rue Jacob
75006 Paris
Tel. (0)1★ 42.60.34.72
Fax (0)1★ 42.60.16.93
Mme Soumier

Rooms 24, 3 apartments with bath, WC, telephone and TV. **Price** Single and double 600-1100F, apart.1250F. **Meals** Breakfast 50F with orange juice. **Credit cards** All major. **Pets** Dogs not allowed. **Parking** Opposite 169, boulevard Saint-Germain. **Open** All year. **How to get there** (Map 37): Métro Saint-Germain des Prés, Bus 39, 48, 63, 70, 86, 87, 95 and 96.

This beautiful house is historic, for it was here that the independence of the United States was recognized. It is now a marvelous hotel, with high-ceilinged rooms, ornate panelling, ancient beams and antique furniture. The bedrooms are all individually decorated. In one of the most remarkable rooms, a wall with exposed stonework provides a stunning backdrop for beautiful 17th-century furniture, including a canopy bed. Note that the largest rooms are those overlooking the garden. The service is excellent and the staff will make theatre and restaurant reservations and do everything to make your stay in Paris pleasant.

Hôtel des Saints-Pères★★★

65, rue des Saints-Pères
75006 Paris
Tel. (0)1★ 45.44.50.00
Fax (0)1★ 45.44.90.83

Rooms 39 (air-conditioning in some rooms) with bath or shower and WC, soundproofing, telephone, TV, safe and minibar. **Price** Single and double 500-1620F, suite 1620F. **Meals** Breakfast 55F, snacks available. **Credit cards** Amex, Visa, Eurocard and MasterCard. **Pets** Dogs not allowed. **Parking** Opposite 169, boulevard Saint-Germain. **Facilities** Bar, patio. **Open** All year. **How to get there** (Map 37): Métro Saint-Germain-des-Prés, Bus 39, 48, 63, 70, 84, 86, 87 and 95.

An atmosphere of elegance and comfort prevails in this lovely hotel. The spacious bedrooms and bathrooms have been tastefully decorated with simplicity and refinement. Worthy of special note is the *chambre à la fresque*, which has retained its lovely period ceiling. Most of the rooms overlook the hotel patio, and the ground-floor reception rooms lead out into this delightful courtyard full of flowers, where comfortable cane chairs are set in the shade in summer. The service is extremely efficient and professional.

Hôtel Lenox-Saint-Germain★★★

9, rue de l'Université
75007 Paris
Tel. (0)1★ 42.96.10.95
Fax (0)1★ 42.61.52.83
M. Destouches

Rooms 34 (5 duplex) with bath or shower and WC, telephone and TV. **Price** Single and double with shower 590F, with bath 670-830F, duplex 960F. **Meals** Breakfast 45F, snacks available. **Credit cards** All major. **Pets** Dogs not allowed. **Parking** At 9, rue Montalembert and opposite 169, boulevard Saint-Germain. **Facilities** Bar. **Open** All year. **How to get there** (Map 37): Métro rue du Bac and Saint-Germain-des-Prés, RER Gare d'Orsay, Bus 39, 48, 63, 70, 84, 86, 87 and 95.

Admirably located on the corner of the rue du Pré-aux-Clercs and the rue de l'Université, the Lenox has long attracted a regular young and chic clientele. The 1930s rosewood-panelled bar, which is open late, adds greatly to the atmosphere of the hotel. The bedrooms are pretty but some are small; in general, it is best to ask for a room on the upper floors. They are somewhat larger and, above all, less noisy. (The hotel should be soundproofed.) The Lenox Saint-Germain nevertheless is comfortable and the prices are very reasonable.

Hôtel de l'Université★★★

22, rue de l'Université
75007 Paris
Tel. (0)1★ 42.61.09.39
Fax (0)1★ 42.60.40.84
Mme Bergmann

Rooms 27 with air-conditioning, bath or shower and WC, telephone, TV and safe. **Price** Single 500-700F, double 900-1300F, suite 1100-1500F. **Meals** Breakfast 45F, with fruit juice and cheese; snacks available. **Credit cards** Visa, Eurocard and MasterCard. **Pets** Dogs not allowed. **Parking** At 9, rue de Montalembert and opposite 169, boulevard Saint-Germain. **Facilities** Bar. **Open** All year. **How to get there** (Map 37): Métro rue-du-Bac and Saint-Germain-des-Prés, RER Gare d'Orsay, Terminal Invalides, Bus 24, 27, 39, 48, 63, 68, 69, 70, 87 and 95.

This is an excellent hotel which owes its long-established reputation to an attentive and discriminating management committed to creating the atmosphere and charm of a family house rather than a hotel. The original vaulted ceilings, their oak supporting pillars, the staircase and fireplaces have been preserved. A subtle ochre color scheme has been chosen for the damask and velvet upholstery on the chairs and sofas in the lounges. The comfortable bedrooms are decorated with antique furniture and curios.

Hôtel de l'Académie★★★

22, rue des Saints-Pères
75007 Paris
Tel. (0)1★ 45.48.36.22
Fax (0)1★ 45.44.75.24
M. Chekroun

Rooms 34 with air-conditioning, bath or shower, WC, telephone, cable TV, hairdryer, minibar and safe. **Price** Single 490-790F, double 690-890F, suite 990-1290F. **Meals** Breakfast 50F, served 7:00-11:00; snacks available. **Credit cards** All major. **Pets** Dogs allowed. **Facilities** Bar, private parking. **Open** All year. **How to get there** (Map 37): Métro Saint-Germain-des-Prés, Bus 34, 48, 63, 70, 84, 86, 87 and 95.

The Hôtel de l'Académie is being handsomely refurbished. The reception area, bar, a small lounge and the breakfast room are now quite separate areas. Beautiful 18th-century and Directoire furniture, enhanced by original beams and old stone walls are stunningly highlighted with superb green and red fabrics. The bedrooms, which all have fully equipped bathrooms, are decorated in pastel shades. Ask for a room overlooking the courtyard, as these are quieter. The only reproach is the carpets in the hallways, which are already showing signs of wear.

Hôtel Montalembert★★★★

3, rue de Montalembert
75007 Paris
Tel. (0)1★ 45.49.68.68.
Fax (0)1★ 45.49.69.49
M. Pelletier

Rooms 51 and 5 suites with air-conditioning, bath and WC, telephone, TV, video, hairdryer,safe and minibar. **Price** Single 1625F, double 1960-2080F, suite 2750-3600F. **Meals** Breakfast 100F. Restaurant. **Credit cards** All major. **Pets** Dogs allowed on request. **Parking** Montalembert opposite to the hotel. **Facilities** bar. **Open** All year. **How to get there** (Map 37): Métro rue-du-Bac, Bus 24, 63, 68, 69, 83, 84 and 95.

The new "grand hotels" have changed in style and the Montalembert is one of the most beautiful examples of them. There is no nostalgic reference to the past; instead, modernity is employed to beautiful advantage: Clients of the grand hotels will surely enjoy the Montalembert's discreet luxury. The sobriety of the lobby enhances the interior architecture. The decoration of the lounge, which is both chic and warm, is centered around a fireplace-library at guests' disposal. The bedrooms and their refined baths have every amenity, and the service and welcome are on a par with the hotel's class.

Hôtel Bersoly's★★★

28, rue de Lille
75007 Paris
Tel. (0)1★ 42.60.73.79
Fax (0)1★ 49.27.05.55
Mme Carbonnaux

Rooms 16 with bath or shower and WC, soundproofing, telephone, cable TV, hairdryer and safe. **Price** Single and double 580-680F. **Meals** Breakfast 50F with fruit juice, snacks available. **Credit cards** Amex, Visa, Eurocard and MasterCard. **Pets** Dogs allowed on request. **Parking** At 9, rue de Montalembert and opposite 169, boulevard Saint-Germain. **Facilities** Bar. **Open** All year except 3 weeks in Aug. **How to get there** (Map 37): Métro rue-du-Bac and Solférino, RER Gare d'Orsay. Terminal Invalides, Bus 24, 27, 39, 48, 63, 68, 69, 86, 87 and 95.

Bersoly's is a small hotel with an intimate atmosphere. The Louis XIII furniture in the reception area harmonizes handsomely with the rustic decor of the hotel, while the breakfast room in the vaulted cellars is more exotic. The bedrooms are decorated in a charming country style, and all have large fans for summer. The largest rooms are on the ground floor. You will find a warm and friendly welcome.

Hôtel de Nevers★★

83, rue du Bac
75007 Paris
Tel. (0)1★ 45.44.61.30
Fax (0)1★ 42.22.29.47
Mme Ireland

Rooms 11 with bath or shower and WC, telephone, TV, hairdryer and safe. **Price** Single 380F, double 410-440F. **Meals** Breakfast 30F. **Credit cards** Not accepted. **Pets** Dogs allowed. **Parking** At 30, boulevard Raspail. **Facilities** Bar. **Open** All year. **How to get there** (Map 37): Métro rue-du-Bac, Bus 63, 68, 69, 83, 84 and 94.

This is a small, simple, unpretentious hotel whose charming service and very reasonable prices are rare in Paris. A former outbuilding of the Récolettes Convent, the building still has some of the original architectural details, which adds further charm. The bedrooms are quite simple but have the usual amenities. Those on the top floor even have summery terraces on the roofs. The owner takes very good care of her clients.

Hôtel de Suède★★★

31, rue Vaneau
75007 Paris
Tel. (0)1★ 47.05.00.08
Fax (0)1★ 47.05.69.27
M. Chesnot

Rooms 41 with bath or shower and WC, soundproofing, telephone, cable TV, hairdryer, safe and minibar. **Price** Single 590F, double 650F, triple 860F, suite 1300F. **Meals** Breakfast incl. **Credit cards** Amex, Visa, Eurocard and MasterCard. **Pets** Dogs allowed. **Parking** At 30, boulevard Raspail and square Boucicault. **Open** All year. **How to get there** (Map 37): Métro Saint-François-Xavier and Sèvres-Babylone, Bus 82, 87 and 92.

The Hôtel de Suède enjoys the quiet which prevails in this quarter of embassies and the Musée d'Orsay. The reception and lounge are entirely panelled. The bedrooms are decorated in shades of grey, white and blue and furnished with white Directoire period furniture, with checked bedspreads and curtains in the same tones. Ask for those giving onto the courtyard and on the top floors with a view over the trees of the Matignon Garden.

Hôtel de la Tulipe★★

33, rue Malar
75007 Paris
Tel. (0)1★ 45.51.67.21
Fax (0)1★ 47.53.96.37
M. Fortuit

Rooms 22 with bath or shower and WC, soundproofing, telephone, TV, minibar - Handicap access. **Price** Single 438F, double 518-568F. **Meals** Breakfast 40F with cheese. **Credit cards** Amex, Visa, Eurocard and MasterCard. **Pets** Dogs allowed. **Parking** At Esplanade des Invalides. **Facilities** Patio. **Open** All year. **How to get there** (Map 37): Métro Latour-Maubourg and Invalides, RER Pont de l'Alma. Terminal Invalides, Bus 28, 49, 63, 69, 80, 83 and 92.

A delightful cobblestone courtyard engulfed in greenery is all that remains of the former convent which is now this small hotel. It is rustic in style, with beamed ceilings, Louis XIII furniture and bunches of dried flowers in the reception area. The bedrooms, many of which have exposed stone walls, are very quiet. The management is efficient and welcoming, and there is a friendly, informal atmosphere.

Hôtel Saint-Dominique★★

62, rue Saint-Dominique
75007 Paris
Tel. (0)1★ 47.05.51.44
Fax (0)1★ 47.05.81.28
Mme Petit and M. Tible

Rooms 34 with bath or shower and WC, telephone, TV, hairdryer, safe and minibar. **Price** Single and double 430-515F, executive 600-700F. **Meals** Breakfast 40F with orange juice and cheese. **Credit cards** All major. **Pets** Dogs allowed. **Parking** At Esplanade des Invalides. **Open** All year. **How to get there** (Map 37): Métro Latour-Maubourg and Invalides, RER Pont de l'Alma. Terminal Invalides, Bus 28, 42, 49, 69, 80 and 92.

Its convenient location and reasonable prices make the Saint-Dominique a very popular hotel. There is English-style decor in the lobby, where the pale pine furniture blends with the soft colors of the walls and the pink-beige fabrics. A charming country style has been chosen for the bedrooms, which have well equipped bathrooms. Some rooms are larger, with sitting areas, and most overlook patios full of flowers in summer. Those on the street are soundproofed. This is a lovely place to stay.

Hôtel de Tourville★★★★

16, av. de Tourville
75007 Paris
Tel. (0)1★ 47.05.62.62
Fax (0)1★ 47.05.43.90
M. Bouvier - Mme Agaud
Mlle Maas

Rooms 30 with air-conditioning, bath or shower and WC, telephone, cable TV and hairdryer. **Price** Single and double 690-990F, suite 1390-1990F. **Meals** Breakfast 60F. **Credit cards** All major. **Pets** Dogs allowed (+70F). **Parking** At Esplanade des Invalides. **Open** All year. **How to get there** (Map 37): Métro Ecole-Militaire. Terminal Invalides, Bus 28, 82, 92 and 95.

The Hôtel de Tourville was very recently opened in a beautiful building between the dome of the Invalides and the Rodin Museum. There is an intimate atmosphere in the elegant lounge which was decorated by the David Hicks Atelier. The muted lighting and colors lend softness also to the bedrooms, which are personalized with antique furniture and paintings. The bathrooms are immaculate, with beautiful tiles and veined grey marble, and some open onto pleasant private terraces. This is also a hotel where you will enjoy the charm and quiet of this part of the Left Bank, not to mention the very attractive prices.

Hôtel du Bailli de Suffren★★★

149, av. de Suffren
75015 Paris
Tel. (0)1★ 47.34.58.61
Fax (0)1★ 45.67.75.82
M. and Mme Tardif

Rooms 25 with bath or shower and WC, soundproofing, telephone, TV, hairdryer. **Price** Single 595-636F, double 660-695F, suite 1080-1280F. **Meals** Breakfast 45-70F. **Credit cards** All major. **Pets** Dogs allowed (+50F). **Parking** Garage Bonvin, rue F. Bonvin (90F). **Open** All year. **How to get there** (Map 37): Métro Segur, Sèvres-Lecourbe, Bus 28, 49 and 92.

Located in the UNESCO quarter, the Hôtel du Bailli de Suffren has just been taken over by a dynamic couple who are renovating the hotel reviving the memory of the 18th-century French sailor and member of the Order of Malta called the Bailli de Suffren. They are beginning with very functional, modern bathrooms in most of the bedrooms. Redecoration of some of the bedrooms is not yet complete but the newly redone Versailles room and the Bailli suite are very lovely, while the older rooms also have their charm. The quietest and the lightest rooms look onto the courtyard. In the small lounge, you will find newspapers and magazines. The service is excellent and the owners are very anxious to help you enjoy your stay.

Hôtel Pergolèse ★★★★

3, rue Pergolèse
75116 Paris
Tel. (0)1★ 40.67.96.77
Fax (0)1★ 45 00 12 11
Mme Vidalenc

Rooms 40 with air-conditioning, bath and WC, telephone, cable TV, hairdryer and minibar. **Price** Single and double 960-1220F, "Pergolèse" 1520F. **Meals** Breakfast 75F. **Credit cards** All major. **Pets** Small dogs allowed. **Open** All year. **How to get there** (Map 37): Métro Argentine.

Clients attending conferences at the nearby Palais des Congrès are delighted to stay in this beautiful hotel, very near the Etoile, and to do their morning jogging in the Bois de Boulogne. Artfully restructured by Rena Dumas, the interior design is resolutely contemporary but the materials and colors used lend great gaiety and softness to the decoration. The bedrooms all have the same ash furniture and leather armchairs, which were designed especially for the hotel and which differ in their color schemes. The white marble bathrooms are very modern. In the lounge and dining room, other well-known designers have contributed to the decor, including Philippe Stark for the tables and Hilton McConnico for the wall decoration.

Hôtel de Banville★★★

166, boulevard Berthier
75017 Paris
Tel. (0)1★ 42.67.70.16
Fax (0)1★ 44.40.42.77
Mme Lambert

Rooms 39 with bath or shower and WC, telephone, soundproofing, TV, hairdryer and safe. **Price** Single 635F, double 760F. **Meals** Breakfast 45-80F, snacks available. **Credit cards** Amex, Visa, Eurocard and MasterCard. **Pets** Dogs allowed. **Parking** At 210, rue de Courcelles. **Facilities** Bar. **Open** All year. **How to get there** (Map 37): Métro Péreire and Porte-de-Champerret. Bus for Roissy-Charles-de-Gaulle at Porte Maillot, Bus 83, 84, 92 and 93.

The Hôtel de Banville is a good hotel in a small 1930s building near the Palais des Congrès and the Etoile, on a quiet street lined with plane-trees. The Hôtel de Banville is a hotel of taste: its lounge is elegant, with antique furniture and beautiful Rubelli fabrics. The original elevator leads to the bedrooms, which are bright and spacious and overlook the leafy boulevard. From the *septième étage* up they have panoramic views. Breakfast is served amid the romantic *trompe l'oeil* decor of the dining room.

Le Jardin de Neuilly★★★

5, rue Paul-Déroulède
92200 Neuilly-sur-Seine
Tel. (0)1★ 46.24.51.62
Fax (0)1★ 46.37.14.60
Mme Rouah

Rooms 29 (3 with air-conditioning) with bath or shower and WC, telephone, soundproofing, cable TV, hairdryer and minibar. **Price** Single and double 650-1050F. **Meals** Breakfast incl., snacks available. **Credit cards** Amex, Visa, Eurocard and MasterCard. **Pets** Dogs allowed. **Parking** At 210, rue de Courcelles. **Facilities** Bar. **Open** All year. **How to get there** (Map 37): Métro Sablons, Porte Maillot. Bus for Roissy-Charles-de-Gaulle and Orly at Porte Maillot.

This is an ideal place for those attending meetings at the Palais des Congrès and those who like returning to a charming, quiet hotel in the evening: A lovely garden separates the hotel from the street. The reception area is spacious, though somewhat impersonal, while the bedrooms are more appealing. Some are elegant while others are more rustic, but all are comfortable and decorated with antique furniture. The marble bathrooms are modern and functional. With the first beautiful days of spring, guests can enjoy their breakfast outside, but a verandah opening onto the garden makes this possible in fine weather all year. Note that this hotel is especially quiet on the weekend, when many residents of Neuilly are away.

Hôtel Galileo★★★

54, rue Galilée
75008 Paris
Tel. (0)1★ 47.20.66.06.
Fax (0)1★ 47.20.67.17
M. Mencaroni

Rooms 27 with air-conditioning, bath and WC, telephone, safe, hairdryer and minibar - Elevator, 2 rooms for disabled persons. **Price** Single and double 800-950F. **Meals** Breakfast 50F. **Credit cards** Amex, Visa, Eurocard and MasterCard. **Pets** Dogs not allowed. **Parking** Georges V (70-80F). **Open** All year. **How to get there** (Map 37): Métro and RER Charles-de-Gaulle-Etoile and Georges V, Bus 22, 30, 31, 52 and 73.

Well located between the Champs Elysées and the Avenue Georges V, the Galiléo is truly a *hôtel de charme*. Refinement and modernity are in evidence throughout, from the elegant lounge with its 18th-century fireplace and Aubusson tapestry to the breakfast room with its lovely soft colors and lighting. The elegant bedrooms also have very modern amenities with air-conditioning, good reading lamps, an office area with fax plug and extremely comfortable bathrooms with radio. The most spacious are the two ground-floor rooms and the two on the *cinquième étage* with a lovely verandah, which are our favorites.

Hôtel du Bois★★

11, rue du Dôme
75116 Paris
Tel. (0)1★ 45.00.31.96
Fax (0)1★ 45.00.90.05
M. Byrne

Rooms 41 with bath or shower and WC, soundproofing, telephone, cable TV, minibar and safe. **Price** Single 415-445F, double 495-595F. **Meals** Breakfast 48F. **Credit cards** Amex, Visa, Eurocard and MasterCard. **Pets** Dogs allowed. **Parking** At 34, rue Lauriston. **Open** All year. **How to get there** (Map 37): Métro Kléber and Etoile, RER and bus for Roissy-Charles-de-Gaulle, Bus 22, 30, 31, 52, 73 and 92.

A small stairway from the avenue Victor-Hugo to the small rue du Dôme leads to the Hôtel du Bois, which is very near the Etoile. Managed by an Englishman, the hotel has a British atmosphere. The bedrooms are decorated with prints in pastel colors and Kashmiri designs. They are comfortable and soundproofed to keep out noise from the large avenues around the Etoile. The staff is very courteous and friendly, and the hotel offers excellent value for the price in this very elegant quarter.

Hôtel Raphaël-Paris★★★★

17, avenue Kléber
75016 Paris
Tel. (0)1★ 44.28.00.28
Fax (0)1★ 45.01.21.50
M. Astier

Rooms 55 and 32 suites with air-conditioning with bath or shower and WC, soundproofing, telephone, TV, minibar. **Price** Double "Charme" 1720-1970F, "Boudoir" 2020-2520F, "Alcove" 2220-3520F, "Salon" 3820-4020F. **Meals** Breakfast 120-165F. Restaurant. **Credit cards** All major. **Pets** Dogs allowed. **Parking** At 8, avenue Foch. **Open** All year. **How to get there** (Map 37): Métro Kléber, RER and bus for Roissy-Charles-de-Gaulle. Bus 22, 30, 31, 52, 73, 92.

The Raphaël has its faithful following and we are among them because it remains a model of what great French hotels were and still can be. In the lounges and bedrooms, there is classic decor of wood panelling, ornate mirrors, Louis XV chairs and Persian carpets. The bedrooms are very spacious and comfortable. You will also enjoy the courtesy and attentiveness of a discreet, distinguished staff. The hotel bar is a very chic meeting spot: Have a drink there and you will discover one of the most elegant hotels in Paris.

Hôtel Franklin-Roosevelt★★★

18, rue Clément-Marot
75008 Paris
Tel. (0)1★ 47.23.61.66
Fax (0)1★ 47.20.44.30
Mme Prudhon

Rooms 45 with bath or shower and WC, soundproofing, telephone, TV, hairdryer and minibar. **Price** Single and double 790-890F. **Meals** Breakfast 55F. **Credit cards** Amex, Visa, Eurocard and MasterCard. **Pets** Dogs not allowed. **Parking** At Georges V, opposite 103, avenue des Champs-Elysées and François Ier. **Open** All year. **How to get there** (Map 37): Métro Franklin-Roosevelt and Alma-Marceau, RER Charles-de-Gaulle, Bus 32, 42, 63, 80 and 92.

Hotelkeeping has been a tradition in this family for three generations, and you will find professionalism throughout. The hotel today has been entirely renovated. The bedrooms are romantically exotic, with panoramic scenes above the bedsteads, inspired by the paintings of Zuber. All are different and comfortable, and there are good bathrooms. The lounge and bar are pleasant, as is the breakfast room, which is designed like an interior patio. The staff is charming and attentive and the location is ideal.

Hôtel Queen Mary★★★

9, rue Greffulhe
75008 Paris
Tel. (0)1★ 42.66.40.50
Fax (0)1★ 42.66.94.92
M. Byrne

Rooms 36 with air-conditioning, bath and WC, soundproofing, telephone, cable TV, hairdryer and minibar. **Price** Single 710F, double 810-890F, suite 1175F. **Meals** Breakfast 69F. **Credit cards** Amex, Visa, Eurocard and MasterCard. **Pets** Dogs allowed. **Parking** At place de la Madeleine. **Open** All year. **How to get there** (Map 37): Métro Madeleine and Havre-Caumartin, Opéra, RER Auber, Bus 22, 24, 28, 32, 48, 80, 84 and 94.

Sheltered from the traffic in this busy quarter of large department stores, the Queen Mary has opened following a successful renovation. The light-filled lounge is handsomely decorated with 18th-century French furniture. The colors chosen for the bedrooms are well coordinated with the mahogany furniture, and beautiful striped fabrics are used for the walls, the chairs and the bedspreads. There are, of course, the usual modern conveniences and very thoughtful details like the trouser press and the carafe of sherry awaiting your arrival. The efficient staff will help you make the most of your vacation or business trip.

Hôtel Lido★★★

4, passage de la Madeleine
75008 Paris
Tel. (0)1★ 42.66.27.37
Fax (0)1★ 42.66.61.23
Mme Teil

Rooms 32 with air-conditioning, bath and WC, soundproofing, telephone, cable TV, hairdryer, safe and minibar. **Price** Single 830F, double 980F. **Meals** Breakfast incl. **Credit cards** Amex, Visa, Eurocard and MasterCard. **Pets** Dogs allowed. **Parking** At place de la Madeleine, rue Chauveau-Lagarde. **Open** All year. **How to get there** (Map 37): Métro Madeleine, RER Auber, Bus 24, 42, 43, 52, 84 and 94.

The first hotel in a small group, including the Beau Manoir next door, the Lido remains a good model of personalized hotelkeeping. This is due in large part to Mme Teil, who personally makes sure that her clients are pleased. Haute-Epoque-period carpets, tapestries and chairs add warmth to the reception area and lounge. The bedrooms, which have their original beamed ceilings, are also very tastefully furnished; there are beautiful warm-colored fabrics on the walls and the well-thought-out details include functional closets and elegant toiletries in the comfortable bathrooms. (The rooms with numbers ending with 3 are the most spacious). The good breakfast includes homemade croissants and old-fashioned preserves.

Hôtel Beau Manoir★★★★

6, rue de l'Arcade
75008 Paris
Tel. (0)1★ 42.66.03.07
Fax (0)1★ 42.68.03.00
Mme Teil and Mlle Soudan

Rooms 32 with air-conditioning, bath and WC, telephone, soundproofing, cable TV, hairdryer, safe and minibar. **Price** Single and double 995-1155F, suite 1365F. **Meals** Breakfast incl. **Credit cards** All major. **Pets** Dogs allowed. **Parking** At place de la Madeleine, rue Chauveau-Lagarde. **Open** All year. **How to get there** (Map 37): Métro Madeleine, RER Auber, Bus 24, 42, 43, 52, 84 and 94.

The owners have put their knowhow to good use here and created a lovely small *hôtel de prestige*. In the lounge, antique-style panelling is a beautiful complement to an 18th-century Aubusson tapestry. Damask-covered sofas and armchairs also contribute to the atmosphere, which is both luxurious and intimate. The decoration in the bedrooms includes a tasteful combination of coordinated prints. The rooms are spacious and most have corner sitting areas. (We prefer the rooms ending in 1). Note that you can have a meal brought to your room, prepared by Daniel Metery, who trained with the Troisgros brothers and whose acclaimed restaurant is just across the street.

Hôtel Mansart★★★

5, rue des Capucines
75001 Paris
Tel. (0)1★ 42.61.50.28
Fax (0)1★ 49.27.97.44
M. Dupain

Rooms 57 (air-conditioning in some rooms) with bath and WC, telephone, soundproofing, cable TV, hairdryer, safe and minibar. **Price** Single 526-826F, double 656-960F, suite 1206-1512F. **Meals** Breakfast 50F, snacks available. **Credit cards** Amex, Visa, Eurocard and MasterCard. **Pets** Dogs not allowed. **Parking** At place Vendôme. **Open** All year. **How to get there** (Map 37): Métro Madeleine, RER Auber. Bus Opéra, Madeleine, Concorde, Tuileries, RER Auber-Opéra, Bus 21, 27, 52, 68, 81 and 95.

On the corner of the Place Vendôme and the Rue des Capucines, the Hôtel Mansart has an idyllic location. The refurbishment was conceived in homage to Louis XIV's architect, Jules Mansart. Thus, you will find a tastefully baroque décor in the lobby, with mauve damask-covered 18th-century-style furniture and large paintings inspired by the famous formal gardens of Le Nôtre, Mansart's contemporary. The bold decorative scheme has been carried out tastefully. The spacious bedrooms are marvelously comfortable and decorated in pretty shades of coordinated colors. If you would like to be a neighbor of the Ritz and look out over the Place Vendôme, ask for the Mansart Room, which is superb.

Hôtel de la Place du Louvre★★★

21, rue des Prêtres Saint-Germain-
l'Auxerrois
75001 Paris
Tel. (0)1★ 42.33.78.68
Fax (0)1★ 42.33.09.95
M. Chevalier

Rooms 20 with bath and WC, telephone, cable TV, safe and hairdryer. **Price** Single 496-682F, double 682-812F, duplex 812F. **Meals** Breakfast 40-50F. **Credit cards** All major. **Pets** Dogs allowed. **Parking** At Place du Louvre-Saint-Germain-l'Auxerrois. **Facilities** Bar. **Open** All year. **How to get there** (Map 38): Métro Louvre-Rivoli and Pont-Neuf, RER Châtelet-les-Halles, Bus 21, 24, 27, 67, 69, 74, 76, 81 and 85.

A room with a view awaits you at this hotel. And what a view! You will look out over the famous Louvre itself. A few beautiful vestiges of this ancient building have been preserved and successfully incorporated with modern decorative elements. The lounge and bar are located beneath a glass roof, while breakfast is served in a beautiful vaulted cellar called the *Salle des Mousquetaires,* which once communicated with the Louvre. The bright, sunny bedrooms have up-to-date amenities, and each is named after a painter. The service is efficient.

Le Relais du Louvre ★★★

19, rue des Prêtres-Saint-
Germain-l'Auxerrois
75001 Paris
Tel. (0)1★ 40.41.96.42
Fax (0)1★ 40.41.96.44
Mlle Aulnette

Rooms 18 and 2 suites with bath and WC, telephone, soundproofing, cable TV, safe, hairdryer and minibar. **Price** Single 600-750F, double 800-900F, suite 1280-1450F. **Meals** Breakfast 50F. **Credit cards** All major. **Pets** Small dogs allowed. **Parking** At 2 private locations (65F) and at place du Louvre-Saint-Germain-l'Auxerrois. **Open** All year. **How to get there** (Map 38): Métro Louvre-Rivoli and Pont-Neuf, RER Châtelet-les-Halles, Bus 21, 24, 27, 67, 69, 74, 76, 81 and 85.

From the day it opened, the Relais du Louvre has obviously been a *hôtel de charme.* This is in evident beginning with the reception area, where pretty lighting and warm colors on the walls complement the chairs and antique furniture, all creating a lovely effect. There is the same tasteful décor in the comfortable bedrooms, which can be made into apartments, and in the suites. Here you will live in one of the most prestigious areas of Paris, near the Grand Louvre and in the shadow of the church of Saint-Germain-l'Auxerrois, the former parish of the Kings of France.

Hôtel Brighton★★

218, rue de Rivoli
75001 Paris
Tel. (0)1★ 47.03.61.61
Fax (0)1★ 42.60.41.78
M. Hashimoto

Rooms And suites 70 with bath or shower and WC, telephone, soundproofing, TV and minibar.
Price Single 640-870F, double 660-910F, suite 1300F. **Meals** Breakfast incl. **Credit cards** All major.
Pets Dogs not allowed. **Parking** At place Vendôme and place du Marché-Saint-Honoré. **Open** All year.
How to get there (Map 38): Métro Tuileries and Concorde, Bus 68, 69 and 72.

The Brighton has been refurbished but has nonetheless kept all the features that made it, a grand hotel with charm. Marble, velvets, carpets and crystal create a quiet, refined atmosphere, and the discreet staff are anxious to make your stay a pleasant one. We recommend the bedrooms giving onto the Tuileries Gardens or, better still, those on the top floors (some can be noisy), which have a lovely view. They are vast, with large windows, period furniture and modern bathrooms. (The bath in Room 115 is exceptional). The bedrooms on the courtyard have been partly renovated, and they have the advantage of being quiet.

Hôtel de la Tamise★★★

4, rue d'Alger
75001 Paris
Tel. (0)1★ 42.60.51.54
Fax (0)1★ 42.86.89.97
Mme Bellec

Rooms 20 with bath or shower and WC, telephone. **Price** Single 500F, double 750F, 3 pers. 930F.
Meals Breakfast 40F. **Credit cards** Visa, Eurocard and MasterCard. **Pets** Dogs allowed. **Parking** At
place Vendôme and place du Marché-Saint-Honoré. **Open** All year. **How to get there** (Map 38): Métro
Tuileries and Concorde, Bus 68, 69 and 72.

Very near the Tuileries, the Hôtel de la Tamise occupies a house which once belonged to the Noailles and Mac Mahon families. Its modest size creates an atmosphere of intimacy, which is enhanced by the small, ground-floor lounges; here, lovely English furniture, curios, engravings and paintings lend a personal touch to the interior, as if this were a private home. The bedrooms are classically charming and comfortable. The prices are still reasonable for such a prized quarter, making the Tamise an especially attractive hotel.

Hôtel Louvre Saint-Honoré★★★

141, rue Saint-Honoré
75001 Paris
Tel. (0)1★ 42.96.23.23
Fax (0)1★ 42.96.21.61
M. Gamelon

Rooms 40 with bath and WC, telephone, soundproofing, cable TV, hairdryer, safe and minibar. **Price** Single 496-756F, double 762-862F. **Meals** Breakfast 45F. **Credit cards** Amex, Visa, Eurocard and MasterCard. **Pets** Dogs allowed. **Parking** Louvre des Antiquaires, Croix des Petits-Champs, Forum des Halles. **Open** All year. **How to get there** (Map 38): Métro Louvre-Rivoli, Louvre, RER Châtelet-Les Halles, Bus 21, 67, 69, 74, 75, 76, 81 and 85.

Next to the Louvre and Les Halles, this hotel comprises two buildings connected by a skylight, and the decor and accommodations are modern without being austere. The bedrooms are bright, quiet (20 give onto the courtyard) and the bathrooms are well equipped. The staff are very friendly, and the quarter is extremely picturesque. The open market on the Rue Montorgueil on Sunday morning offers the visitor a chance to revisit the authentic Old Paris. And then, around the Place des Victoires nearby, you will find the fashionable boutiques of the city's leading *créateurs*.

Hôtel de la Bretonnerie★★★

22, rue Sainte-Croix-de-la-Bretonnerie
75004 Paris
Tel. (0)1★ 48.87.77.63
Fax (0)1★ 42.77.26.78
M. and Mme Sagot

Rooms 30 with bath or shower and WC, telephone, soundproofing, TV, safe and minibar. **Price** Single and double 630-750F, suite 900F. **Meals** Breakfast 45F. **Credit cards** Visa, Eurocard and MasterCard. **Pets** Small dogs allowed. **Parking** Hôtel-de-Ville. **Open** All year except in Aug. **How to get there** (Map 38): Métro Hôtel-de-Ville, Bus 29, 38, 47, 58, 67, 69, 70, 72, 74, 75 and 76.

With each season, the Hôtel de la Bretonnerie has pleasant surprises for us. Now, guests can enjoy new bedrooms as well as seven rooms which have been transformed and redecorated. Most are very large and some have a mezzanine. They are decorated in sober tones of beige, brown and burgundy, which harmonize with the exposed beams and antique-style furniture, and with the bathrooms. The suite has been redone in shades of pink. The staff is very welcoming.

Hôtel Saint-Paul-le-Marais★★★

8, rue de Sévigné
75004 Paris
Tel. (0)1★ 48.04.97.27
Fax (0)1★ 48.87.37.04
Mmes Leguide and Marcovici

Rooms 27 with bath and WC, soundproofing, telephone, cable TV, hairdryer and safe. **Price** Single 500F, double 630F. **Meals** Breakfast 45F with fruit juice, cheese and fresh fruit, no restaurant. **Credit cards** All major. **Pets** Dogs not allowed. **Facilities** Patio and bar. **Parking** At 2, rue Geoffroy-l'Asnier and 16, rue Saint-Antoine. **Open** All year. **How to get there** (Map 38): Métro Saint-Paul, Bus 29, 67, 69, 76 and 96.

This hotel is ideal for those who love the Marais quarter with its impressive private mansions, craftsmen's workshops, boutiques and the famous Place des Vosges. Only a few beams and pillars remain of the old building and the rest of the decoration is modern. The reception area, with wide windows onto the street, is light and airy, and it is decorated with black leather armchairs contrasting with pastel-colored walls. The same soft colors are repeated in the bedrooms, which have beamed ceilings and comfortable bathrooms. There is a delicious breakfast and the prices are reasonable.

Hôtel Caron de Beaumarchais★★★

12, rue Vieille-du-Temple
75004 Paris
Tel. (0)1★ 42.72.34.12
Fax (0)1★ 42.72.34.63
M. Bigeard

Rooms 19 with air-conditioning, bath or shower and WC, soundproofing, telephone, cable TV, hairdryer, safe and minibar; elevator. **Price** Single and double 620-690F. **Meals** Breakfast 48-78F. **Credit cards** All major. **Pets** Dogs not allowed. **Parking** Rue Lobeau. **Open** All year. **How to get there** (Map 38): Métro Hôtel-de-Ville, Saint-Paul-le-Marais, Bus 54, 68, 74, 80, 81 and 95.

The Marais quarter now has a new hotel in keeping with its history. This comfortable 18th-century house has been restored in homage to the famous author of *The Marriage of Figaro*, who lived on this street. The decoration was carried out by Alain Bigeard, who researched and took inspiration from documents of the time. Thus, in the lobby, the walls are covered with embroidered fabric reproduced from the original designs, and there are Burgundian stone floors with period furniture. The same elegance is found in the beautifully comfortable bedrooms and the bathrooms, whose tiles are modeled on those of Rouen and Nevers. In addition, the prices are very reasonable.

Pavillon de la Reine★★★★

28, place des Vosges
75003 Paris
Tel. (0)1★ 42.77.96.40
Fax (0)1★ 42.77.63.06
M. Sudre

Rooms 30 with air-conditioning, bath and WC, telephone, cable TV, hairdryer and minibar. **Price** Single 1500F, double 1700F, duplex 1900-2100F, suite 2500-2950F. **Meals** Breakfast 95F. **Credit cards** All major. **Pets** Dogs allowed. **Parking** Private garage. **Open** All year. **How to get there** (Map 38): Métro Bastille, Saint-Paul, Bus 20, 29, 65, 69 and 96.

This is an admirable hotel in an admirably historic place. The hotel consists of two buildings, one dating from the 17th century and the other harmoniously rebuilt around a small courtyard. The Haute Epoque interior reflects the architectural style, with oak panelling on the walls of the very comfortable lounge, chairs upholstered in *petit point* tapestry and canopied beds. The colors and materials are very elegant and the bedrooms, which look out on the garden or the flower courtyard, are comfortable and quiet. The service is discreet, efficient and attentive.

TimHôtel Montmartre★★

11, rue Ravignan
75018 Paris
Tel. (0)1★ 42.55.74.79
Fax (0)1★ 42.55.71.01
Mme Fournier

Rooms 63 with bath or shower and WC, telephone, cable TV and hairdryer. **Price** Single 450F, double 550F, 3 pers. 690F. **Meals** Breakfast 49F. **Credit cards** All major. **Pets** Dogs allowed. **Parking** Impasse Marie-Blanche. **Open** All year. **How to get there** (Map 38): Métro Abbesses, Bus 30, 54, 67 and 80.

The TimHôtel enjoys one of the most charming locations in Montmartre. The rooms with the most beautiful views over Paris are those on the *quatrième* and *cinquième étages*, on the street side. Those on the top floor, on the *place* side, look out over the rooftops and Sacré-Cœur. The decoration of the bedrooms is ordinary but the hotel is comfortable and very functional; there's a baby's bottle-warmer, a diaper-changing table, a crib and even an iron and ironing board for guest use. The breakfast-buffet is a veritable brunch. You will find also that, despite its touristic reputation, Montmartre is still a village, with little squares, tiny stairway-streets which wind down from the Butte and its neighborhood spirit, all in evidence around the TimHôtel.

Hôtel Arnold ★★★

98, route du Vin
67140 Itterswiller (Bas-Rhin)
Tel. (0)3★ 88.85.50.58 – Fax (0)3★ 88.85.55.54 – Mme Arnold

Rooms 28 with telephone, bath or shower, WC, TV and minibar. **Price** Double 270-595F. **Meals** Breakfast 48F, served 8:00-10:00; half board and full board 350-525F (per pers.). **Restaurant** Service 11:30-14:30, 19:30-21:00 (closed Sunday evening and Monday); menus 130-395F, also à la carte. «Menu Oncle Xavier» 35-55F. Specialties: Noisette de chevreuil, civet de sanglier, choucroute, baeckeoffe, foie gras. **Credit cards** Visa, Eurocard and MasterCard. **Pets** Dogs not allowed. **Facilities** Parking. **Nearby** Alsace Wine Route from Marlenheim to Thann, church in Andlau, church of Sainte-Marguerite d'Epfig. **Open** All year.

The Hôtel Arnold lies in the heart of the Alsatian vineyards at the foot of the Vosges Mountains. It is composed of three buildings in the most traditional Alsatian style. Windows and balconies overflow with flowers. The bedrooms, which are decorated in a standard, functional style, are very comfortable, bright and quite large. The great attraction of most rooms is their view over the vineyards and a large balcony. The entrance, corridors, breakfast room and lounge (upstairs) are warm and prettily decorated. On the *Réserve* side, the bedrooms are more attractive but the view looks over less greenery. Intent on maintaining Alsatian traditions, the Arnold family will invite you to try the regional specialties in the restaurant. Or you can buy them in the hotel's shop, which offers wines, *foie gras* and other products from the family estate.

How to get there *(Map 12): 41km south of Strasbourg via A35; Obernai exit; then N422 to Epfig; turn right on D 335 to Itterswiller.*

Hôtel Gilg ★★

1, route du Vin
67140 Mittelbergheim (Bas-Rhin)
Tel. (0)3★ 88.08.91.37 - Fax (0)3★ 88.08.45.17 - M. Gilg

Rooms 15 with telephone, bath, WC and TV. **Price** Single 215-250F, double 360-400F. **Meals** Breakfast 35F, served 7:30-10:00. **Restaurant** Service 12:00-14:00, 19:00-21:00; menus 125-325F, also à la carte. Specialties: Feuilleté chaud du vigneron, sandre à la moutarde de Meaux, émincé d'agneau au curry, cyrano glacé au croquant. **Credit cards** All major. **Pets** Dogs allowed. **Facilities** Parking. **Nearby** Barr, church in Andlau, church of Sainte-Marguerite in Epfig, Mont Sainte-Odile. **Open** Feb 2 – June 24, July 10 – Jan 8 (closed Tuesday evening and Wednesday).

This imposing *winstub* is located on the corner of two small streets in a lovely village whose principal activity is winegrowing. The rooms here are quiet, warm and cozy, with furniture that is somewhat old-fashioned but charming in the oldest rooms. Comfortable and well decorated, those which have just been renovated are truly lovely (it's best to reserve). Meals are served in a large dining room with handsome traditional decor; the excellent cuisine is flavorsome and delicate. The hospitality and the many qualities of this hotel make it a noteworthy place to stay not far from the vineyards and the splendid villages of Alsace.

How to get there (Map 12): 37km north of Colmar via N83 to Sélestat and N422 towards Barr.

 Hôtel A la Cour d'Alsace ★★★★

3, rue de Gaie
67210 Obernai (Bas-Rhin)
Tel. (0)3★ 88.95.07.00 – Fax (0)3★ 88.95.19.21 – Mme Hager and M. Hartleyb

Rooms 43, with telephone, bath or shower, WC, TV and Minibar; elevator. **Price** Single and double 450-760F, 695-800F. **Meals** Breakfast 55F, 75F (Buffet), served 7:00-10:00; half board and full board 530-595F (per pers.,3 nights min.). **Restaurant** Service 12:00-15:00, 19:00-22:00; menus 195-390F, also à la carte. **Credit cards** All major. **Pets** Dogs allowed (+50F). **Facilities** Parking. **Nearby** Alsace Wine Route, church in Andlau, church of Sainte-Marguerite in Epfig, Mont-Saint-Odile; Barr – Wantzenau golf course. **Open** Mid Jan – end Dec.

This magnificent hotel is composed of several adjoining houses grouped around a very old courtyard and built against the ramparts of Obernai. Whether you are in the *Petite France* or the *Petite Suisse*, the bedrooms are elegant, very comfortable and of varying sizes (which justifies the price differences). The style is set by light colors with pale or beige tints, paneling and furniture of natural wood and white eiderdowns, all contributing to a refined ambiance. For lunch or dinner, you have a choice between the gastronomic restaurant or the charming *winstub*. And at any time, you can have a drink in the garden, which has lovely flowers and is niched in the old moats running the length of the hotel. This is an impeccable, genuinely luxurious hotel where you can be assured of a professional, attentive and friendly welcome.

How to get there (Map 12): 24km south of Strasbourg.

Relais des Marches de l'Est ★★

9, rue de la Chapelle
67280 Oberhaslach (Bas-Rhin)
Tel. (0)3★ 88.50.99.60 - Mme Weber

Rooms 9, with telephone, bath or shower, WC and TV. **Price** Single and double 170F, 190-210F. **Meals** Breakfast 25F, served 7:00-10:30; half board 200F (per pers.). **Restaurant** For residents only, by reservation. Service from 19:00; menus 60-160F. Specialties: tarte flambée, choucroute, bacleolle. **Credit cards** Not accepted. **Pets** Dogs allowed. **Facilities** Parking. **Nearby** Alsace Wine Route, Mont Sainte-Odile, Barr, church in Andlau, church of Sainte-Marguerite in Epfig – Wantzenau golf course. **Open** All year.

Sculptors as well as hoteliers, Bénédicte and Sylvain have succeeded in creating a personal, warm atmosphere here. On the street side, however, the hotel is unremarkable; it is certainly pleasant with its pink Alsatian sandstone, but it is nevertheless unobtrusive, as if it were afraid to be discovered too easily. Inside, the rooms on the ground floor have a "refined bistrot" ambiance, with the bread oven as the central element. On weekends, guests can observe as *baeckeoffe* (reserve two days in advance) and flamed tarts come out of the oven. Upstairs, the bedrooms all have old stone walls and the antique beds have been modernized for comfort; an old wardrobe, pretty fabrics and impeccable bathrooms complete the furnishings. The result is simple and charming; only the tiled floors could do with a few carpets. In the morning, you have a choice of two kinds of breakfast, which is served in the garden in good weather. This is a very pleasant hotel, and ideal for discovering the Hasel Valley and the Nideck region. Prices are more than reasonable.

How to get there *(Map 12): 24km south of Strasbourg.*

Hôtel Anthon ★★

40, rue Principale
67510 Obersteinbach (Bas-Rhin)
Tel. (0)3★ 88.09.55.01 – Fax (0)3★ 88.09.50.52 – Mme Flaig

Rooms 9 with telephone, bath (1 with shower) and WC (7 with minibar). **Price** Double 260-290F. **Meals** Breakfast 50F, served 8:00-10:00. **Restaurant** Service 12:00-14:00, 18:30-21:00; menus 260-340F (also 120F weekdays), also à la carte. Specialties: Foie gras frais de canard, game in season. **Credit cards** Visa, Eurocard and MasterCard. **Pets** Dogs allowed. **Facilities** Parking. **Nearby** Lake at Hanau, Châteaux of Lutzelhardt and Falkenstein – 18-hole golf course in Bitche. **Open** Feb – Dec.

The hotel-restaurant Anthon, in a small picturesque village in the heart of the Vosges du Nord Park, has nine pleasant, well-renovated bedrooms, all overlooking the surrounding countryside as far as the wooded slopes of the Vosges. The dining room is spacious; it is circular in shape and its large bay windows give the impression of dining in a garden full of flowers: perfect surroundings for the very high-quality food that is served there. The hotel also has a lively bar and a quiet lounge. The hotel itself, surrounded by extensive grounds, is very quiet.

How to get there *(Map 13): 66km north of Strasbourg via A4 and D44 to Haguenau, then D27 to Lembach, and D3 to Obersteinbach.*

Auberge d'Imsthal ★★

Route Forestière d'Imsthal
67290 La Petite-Pierre (Bas-Rhin)
Tel. (0)3★ 88.01.49.00 - Fax (0)3★ 88.70.40.26 - Michaely Family

Rooms 23 (2 with lounge), with telephone, bath or shower (20 with WC and TV). **Price** Single 200-320F, double 280-600F. **Meals** Breakfast (buffet) 48F, served 8:00-10:00; half board 300-460F, full board 380-540F (per pers., 3 days min.). **Restaurant** Service 12:00-14:00, 19:00-21:00; menus 80-250F, also à la carte. Specialties: Regional cooking. **Credit cards** All major. **Pets** Dogs allowed (+30F). **Facilities** Health center, sauna (50F), parking. **Nearby** Vosges du Nord Regional Park, Neuwiller-les-Saverne, Bouxvillier, Lichtenberg, crystal and glass factory in Wingen-sur-Moder – 18-hole golf course in Bitche. **Open** All year.

The Auberge d'Imsthal is located in the splendid region of the Northern Vosges Mountains. The interior is authentically rustic and warm. We particularly recommend the renovated bedrooms, which are very pleasant with their antiqued wood furniture and colorful fabrics. Some look out onto a small lake and the others face the back, which is much less beautiful but still pleasant. They are comfortable and tasteful. There are many fitness installations such as whirlpools and saunas. The cuisine is good, nourishing and is charmingly served, which compensates for the welcome, which could at times be better.

How to get there *(Map 12): 59km northwest of Strasbourg via A4, Saverne exit, N4, D122, D133 and D178 to the Lake of Imsthal.*

Hôtel Neuhauser ★★

Les Quelles
67130 Schirmeck (Bas-Rhin)
Tel. (0)3★ 88.97.06.81 – Fax (0)3★ 88.97.14.29 – M. Neuhauser

Rooms 14 with telephone, bath or shower and WC (6 with TV). **Price** Single and double 270-310F. **Meals** Breakfast 40F, served 8:00-10:00; half board 310-330F, full board 360-380F (per pers., 3 days min.). **Restaurant** With air-conditioning. Service 12:00-14:00, 19:00-21:00 (closed 10–31 Jan); menus 110-300F, also à la carte. Specialties: Foie gras maison, filet de lapereau farçi, noisette de chevreuil forestière. **Credit cards** Visa, Eurocard and MasterCard. **Facilities** Heated swimming pool and parking. **Nearby** Belvédère de la chatte pendue. **Open** All year.

This hotel, and the few small houses which make up the hamlet, are ringed on all sides by meadows and forests. This isolation guarantees absolute tranquillity. The hotel does not have many rooms, but they are comfortable, well kept up and tastefully decorated in a traditional style (country furniture, beams...). Planned for this year, however, are three small Scandinavian chalets with suites, lounge and terrace which will certainly appeal to families or to those who want more space. The food is varied and well prepared, and meals are served in a vast panoramic dining room decorated like a winter garden. The wine list is worth close attention, as is the list of liqueurs and *eaux de vie*. Reasonably priced, this hotel is well worth a visit and has a heated swimming pool for use in the summer months.

How to get there *(Map 12): 56km southwest of Strasbourg via A35 and A352, then N420 or D392 to Schirmeck, then Les Quelles.*

Hôtel du Dragon ★★★

2, rue de l'Ecarlate - 12, rue du Dragon
67000 Strasbourg (Bas-Rhin)
Tel. (0)3★ 88.35.79.80 - Fax (0)3★ 88.25.78.95 - M. Iannarelli

Rooms 32 with telephone, bath, WC and TV - Wheelchair access. **Price** Single 430-590F, double 475-640F, suite 765-865F. **Meals** Breakfast 56F, served 6:45-10:00. No restaurant. **Credit cards** All major. **Pets** Dogs not allowed. **Nearby** La Wantzenau, Alsace Wine Route – 18-hole golf courses in Illkirch-Graffenstaden and Plobsheim. **Open** All year.

We tend to equate charming with picturesque and old; and yet the 17th-century Hôtel du Dragon, which has been done in a very modern style, certainly has its own charm. The grey tones of the interior decoration and the designer furniture create a somewhat cold atmosphere, but the friendly, welcoming staff and the beautiful contemporary paintings quickly compensate for this. The very comfortable bedrooms face onto one of the quiet streets of the historic quarter. There is no restaurant, but delicious breakfasts are served on pretty china from the Café Coste. (If you admire the paintings, some are for sale.) For restaurants, M. Iannarelli will give you good recommendations, but be sure to visit *Chez Yvonne*, one of the most popular wine bars in the city.

How to get there *(Map 13): in the center of Strasbourg via the Quai Saint-Nicolas and the Quai Ch. Frey.*

Parc Hôtel ★★★

39, rue du Géneral–de–Gaulle
67710 Wangenbourg (Bas–Rhin)
Tel. (0)3★ 88.87.31.72 – Fax (0)3★ 88.87.38.00 – M. Gihr

Rooms 34 with telephone, bath or shower and WC. **Price** Single 253-278F, double 304-412F. **Meals** Breakfast 49F, served 7:30-9:30; half board 331-371F, full board 340-402F (per pers., 3 days min.). **Restaurant** Service 12:00-13:30, 19:00-20:30; menus 115-270F, also à la carte. Specialties: Munster chaud sur canapé, magret de canard. **Credit cards** Visa, Eurocard and MasterCard. **Pets** Dogs not allowed. **Facilities** Covered swimming pool, tennis, mountain bike, sauna (50F), garage. **Nearby** Château de Wangenbourg, Haslach Forest, château and waterfall in Nideck, Château de Saverne, Abbey of Marmoutier. **Open** Mar 20 – Nov 4, Dec 22 – Jan 2.

The hotel lies in the heart of the village and is made up of a number of houses of different periods. It has a lovely park with its own nature trail, and is most attractively decorated, particularly the delightful lounge and the billiard room. All the bedrooms are large and well equipped, some with balconies looking over the garden. With the enjoyment of their guests in mind, the owners (the sixth generation of the same family) have provided facilities for sport and relaxation, including a very charming covered swimming pool giving onto the lawn. Those who want to go on excursions or sightseeing will find all the information they need at the desk. Every Thursday evening in the restaurant food is grilled on an open fire and the atmosphere is very convivial. This is a family hotel to which many guests return every year, creating a vacation–club atmosphere which may not be to everyone's taste.

How to get there (Map 12): 38km west of Strasbourg via A4, Saverne exit, then N4 towards Wasselonne, D224 and D218.

Le Moulin de La Wantzenau ★★

3, impasse du Moulin
67610 La Wantzenau (Bas-Rhin)
Tel. (0)3★ 88.59.22.22 – Fax (0)3★ 88.59.22.00 – Mmes Dametti and Wolff

Rooms 20 with telephone, bath or shower, WC and TV. **Price** Single and double 310-410F, suite 510F. **Meals** Breakfast 50-55F (Buffet). **Restaurant** (Independent but at the hotel) Service 12:15-13:45, 19:15-21:15 (closed Sunday evening and national holidays in the evening); menus 150-250F. **Credit cards** All major. **Pets** Dogs allowed (+40F). **Facilities** Garage (+35F). **Nearby** Strasbourg, Alsace Wine Route – 18-hole golf course in La Wantzenau. **Open** Jan 2 – Dec 24.

Though close to Strasbourg, this hotel is in the quiet countryside. It is a beautifully restored old mill with lovely, comfortable bedrooms decorated with pale wood furniture and Laura Ashley fabrics. Most are spacious and have immaculate bathrooms. We also loved the warm lounge-bar, whose large fireplace and big armchairs invite you to relax, and the library (it also has children's books). The various services are much appreciated: the morning newspaper is brought with your breakfast and the hotel will press your clothes. The Moulin de La Wantzenau is a very friendly hotel with good value for the money. The restaurant is separate but just in front of the hotel. Light meals are served in the bedrooms when the restaurant is open.

How to get there (Map 13): 12km north of Strasbourg via A4, Reichstett exit, D63, and D301 towards Zone Industrielle La Wantzenau, then D468; 1.5km from La Wantzenau.

Hostellerie Saint-Barnabé ★★★

Buhl
68530 Murbach (Haut-Rhin)
Tel. (0)3★ 89.76.92.15 - Fax (0)3★ 89.76.67.80 - M. and Mme Orban

Rooms 27 with telephone, bath or shower, WC, TV and minibar. **Price** Single and double 310-560F, Suite 695-750F. **Meals** Breakfast 55F, 65F (in room), served 7:30-10:30. **Restaurant** Service 12:00-14:00, 19:00-21:00 (closed Sunday evening Nov – Mar); menus 125F-315F, also à la carte. Specialties: Chaud-froid de foie gras au vieux gewurztraminer, langoustines aux morilles, aiguillettes de pigeon au vin d'épice. **Credit cards** All major. **Pets** Dogs allowed (+30F). **Nearby** Lauch Valley, Murbach Abbey, Unterlinden Museum in Colmar, Automobile and Rail Museums in Mulhouse, Alsace Wine Route – 9-hole Rouffach golf course. **Open** Mar 3 – Feb 19.

Now that the Saint-Barnabé has been beautifully refurbished, we are pleased to put it it back into the Guide. The Hostellerie has several dining rooms, lounges, and smoking rooms with beautiful views of its beautiful forest setting. The atmosphere is tranquil and the decoration is classic and pleasant. The bedrooms are attractive and very comfortable, with beautiful bathrooms. (Rooms 11 and 16 can be noisy during meal times). Certain suites are ideal for families, and nature lovers will enjoy the Pavillon Vert rooms on the ground floor. Note also the irresistible Chalet room with a cheerful fireplace. The fabrics throughout have been beautifully chosen. The regional cuisine is excellent - you are served on the terrace in summer - and there is a delightful choice of Alsatian wines. The owners are young and friendly.

How to get there (Map 20): 3km from Guebwiller. Go straight through the center of town to Bulh; then turn left for Murbach.

Hostellerie Le Maréchal ★★★★

4-6, place des Six Montagnes Noires
68000 Colmar (Haut-Rhin)
Tel. (0)3★ 89.41.60.32 - Fax (0)3★ 89.24.59.40 - M. and Mme Bomo

Rooms 30 with air-conditioning, telephone, bath or shower, WC and TV. **Price** Single 450-500F, double 550-1200F, suite 1400-1500F. **Meals** Breakfast 65F, served 7:30-10:00; half board 650F, full board 800F (per pers.). **Restaurant** Service 12:00-14:00, 19:00-22:00; menus 150-380F, also à la carte. Specialties: Terrine de foie de canard servie avec sa gelée au Muscat d'Alsace, esturgeon aux herbes cuit sur le foin avec caviar, râble de lapereau farci aux légumes en feuilleté accompagné d'un beurre aux fines herbes. **Credit cards** All major. **Pets** Dogs allowed (+35F). **Facilities** Parking (+35F). **Nearby** Issenheim altarpiece at the Unterlinden Museum in Colmar, Alsace Wine Route, Neuf-Brisach, Trois-Epis, Munster – 18-hole golf course in Ammerschwihr. **Open** All year.

Well located in the old quarter of Petite Venise (Little Venice) in Colmar, the Hostellerie Le Maréchal occupies four old houses on the edge of the canals. The interior is delightful. Beams and stone go well with the Louis XIII furniture in the lounge and dining room. Each bedroom has its own style, and you can choose between medieval or 18th-century decor. They are elegant, comfortable and well equipped, and though some are rather small, this fits in perfectly with the cozy atmosphere of the hotel. Ask for a room on the canal side. The candlelit dinners in the long dining room beside the Lauch, the specialties offered there, and the warm, solicitous welcome make the Hostellerie Le Maréchal the best hotel in Colmar.

How to get there *(Map 12): in the center of old Colmar.*

Hôtel La Clairière ★★★

50, route d'Illhaeusern
68970 Guémar - Illhaeusern (Haut-Rhin)
Tel. (0)3★ 89.71.80.80 - Fax (0)3★ 89.71.86.22 - M. Loux

Rooms 23, and 2 apartments, with telephone, bath, WC, TV and minibar; elevator.
Price Single 430F, double 560-950F, suite 1250-1600F. **Meals** Breakfast 65F, served
7:30-10:00. No restaurant. **Credit cards** Visa, Eurocard and MasterCard. **Pets** Dogs
allowed. **Facilities** Tennis, swimming pool, parking. **Nearby** Colmar, Alsace Wine
Route from Marlenheim to Thann – 18-hole golf course in Ammerschwihr (25km).
Open Mar 1 – Dec 31.

Somewhat off the *départementale* road, the Hôtel La Clairière
offers 25 bedrooms of varying sizes, many of which are very
well decorated, very comfortable and have a lovely view over the
plain and the Vosges. The excellent breakfasts are served in your
room, enabling you to take further advantage of the view.
Comfortable armchairs and a beautiful fireplace make the lounge
welcoming and restful. There is no restaurant in the hotel, but the
famous, three-star Auberge de L'Ill is nearby. It is one of the great
restaurants of France, and the prices are in keeping with its stature.
The Clairière has its own tennis courts and a small swimming pool
and is also a good starting point for lovely walks. The owners are
very hospitable.

How to get there *(Map 12): 17km north of Colmar via N83 towards Sélestat;
at Guémar D106 towards Marckolsheim.*

Les Hirondelles ★★

33, rue du 25 janvier
68970 Illhaeusern (Haut-Rhin)
Tel. (0)3★ 89.71.83.76 - Fax (0)3★ 89.71.86.40 - Mme Muller

Rooms 14 with telephone, shower, WC and TV. **Price** Double 240-260F.
Meals Breakfast 32F, served 8:00-10:00; half board 235-265F (per pers.).
Restaurant By reservation, service from 19:30 (closed Sunday evening and Nov1 –
Easter). Specialties: Traditional country cooking, Alsatian specialties. **Credit cards**
Visa, Eurocard and MasterCard. **Pets** Small dogs allowed. **Facilities** Parking. **Nearby**
Colmar, Alsace Wine Route from Marlenheim to Thann, Haut-Koenigsbourg – 18-
hole golf course in Ammerschwihr. **Open** Mar – Jan.

Les Hirondelles is an ancient farm of vast dimensions lying near the famous Auberge de l'Ill Restaurant and the lovely Ill River. The bedrooms are located in a large outbuilding which has been entirely refurbished. Decorated for comfort and practicality, they are furnished with new but typically Alsatian wardrobes of polychromed wood. You may choose between rooms giving onto flowery balconies and the courtyard, or a more rural view over small vegetable gardens. There is a welcoming lounge on the ground floor where breakfast is served, along with good dinners based on regional cooking. The welcome is charming and informal at this pleasant hotel near the vineyards, and the prices are very reasonable.

How to get there *(Map 12): 12km north of Colmar via RN83 in the Strasbourg towards.*

Auberge Les Alisiers ★★

5, rue Faude
68650 Lapoutroie (Haut-Rhin)
Tel. (0)3★ 89.47.52.82 – Fax (0)3★ 89.47.22.38 – M. and Mme Degouy

Rooms 10 with telephone, bath or shower and WC. **Price** Single 190F, double 350F. **Meals** Breakfast (buffet) 42F, served 7:30-10:00; half board 280-340F. **Restaurant** Service 12:00-13:00, 19:00-21:00 (closed Monday evening except for guests on half board, and Tuesday); menus 79-189F, also à la carte. Specialties: Pigeonneau rôti, truite saumonée à la crème de lard, cervelas rôti sur salade de choucroute, pommes de terre coiffées de munster fondu. **Credit cards** Visa, Eurocard and MasterCard. **Pets** Dogs allowed. **Facilities** Parking. **Nearby** Colmar, Alsace Wine Route from Marlenheim to Thann – 18-hole golf course in Ammerschwihr. **Open** Feb 1 – Dec 31.

The Auberge Les Alisiers lies 700 meters up in the mountains; the view from it over the Hautes Vosges and the Béhine Valley is stunning, and the hotel itself is very pleasant. The small bedrooms are intimate, comfortable and well kept; one has a small private terrace. A warmly decorated lounge is at your disposal where, in winter, you can enjoy the beautiful fireplace before dinner. The dining room is delightful with several pieces of antique furniture and above all, an admirable panoramic view. You will enjoy excellent, very reasonably priced cuisine. From your table in the evening, you might see several deer grazing at the edge of the woods, a bird of prey circling over the valley and, certainly, the chef's assistant coming in to dip a beautiful trout out of the fishtank. This is a very friendly hotel whose relaxed and informal atmosphere is largely created by the hospitable owners.

How to get there *(Map 12): 19km northwest of Colmar via N415; at Lapoutroie go left in front of the church and follow the signs for 3km.*

Hôtel Le Clos Saint-Vincent ★★★★

Route de Bergheim
68150 Ribeauvillé (Haut-Rhin)
Tel. (0)3★ 89.73.67.65 - Fax (0)3★ 89.73.32.20 - M. Chapotin

Rooms 12, and 3 apartments, with telephone, bath, WC, TV and minibar. **Price** Single 650F, double 700-935F, apart. 1000-1100F. **Meals** Breakfast incl., served 8:15-10:30. **Restaurant** Service 12:00-14:00, 19:00-20:30 (closed Tuesday and Wednesday); menus 260F, also à la carte. **Credit cards** Visa, Eurocard and MasterCard. **Pets** Dogs allowed (+30F). **Facilities** Covered swimming pool, parking. **Nearby** Hunawihr, swan reproduction center, ruins of the Château of St-Ulrich, Riquewihr, Alsace Wine Route from Marlenheim to Thann, Le Haut-Koenigsbourg; local festivities: Wine Festival in July-Aug, Minstrel Festival in Sept, Baroque Music Festival in autumn – 18-hole golf course in Ammerschwihr. **Open** Mar 15 – Nov 15.

In the heart of the Riesling wine country, the three-storey Clos Saint Vincent looks out on the Alsace plateau, the Black Forest, and to the east, the Alps. On the *premier étage* there is a lobby and a pleasant restaurant with a panoramic view. The bedrooms, with Directoire-style or rustic furniture, are bright, very comfortable and totally quiet. The tasteful fabrics lend much to the decoration. There is a very beautiful covered swimming pool, but note that the service is sometimes lacking.

How to get there *(Map 12): 19km north of Colmar via N83 and D106 towards Ribeauvillé, then D1b towards Bergheim (follow the signs).*

Hostellerie des Seigneurs de Ribeaupierre ★★★

11, rue du château
68150 Ribeauvillé (Haut-Rhin)
Tel. (0)3★ 89.73.70.31 - Fax (0)3★ 89.73.71.21 - Mmes Barth

Rooms 10 with telephone, bath or shower and WC. **Price** Doubles 470-540F, suite 560-730F. **Meals** Breakfast 48F, served 8:00-11:00. No restaurant. **Credit cards** Amex, Visa, Eurocard and MasterCard. **Pets** Dogs not allowed. **Nearby** Hunawihr, swan reproduction center, ruins of the Château of Saint-Ulrich, Riquewihr, Alsace Wine Route from Marlenheim to Thann, Le Haut-Koenigsbourg; local festivities: Wine Festival in July-Aug., Minstrel Festival in Sept., Baroque Music Festival in autumn – 18-hole golf course in Ammerschwihr. **Open** All year (Jan and Feb reservation by fax only).

The Hostellerie des Seigneurs de Ribeaupierre is a remarkable small hotel in one of the most beautiful villages of Alsace: There are several delicious rooms in this 18th-century auberge, which is located in a quiet spot outside the center. All are charming and comfortable, with beautiful old regional furniture, soft beds, light-colored woodwork and half-timbering, and ravishing fabrics. The bathrooms are superb and there is a lovely corner sitting area in many rooms. On the ground floor, there is a small lounge where a fireplace is often blazing and, several steps down, you come to the breakfast room. Breakfasts are delicious and copious and you may even ask for a veritable brunch, with cold cuts, eggs and, as this is Alsace, a slice of *foie gras*. This is a magnificent hotel, where you are greeted warmly by two very dynamic sisters. For restaurants, we suggest the gastronomic *La Winstub Zum Pfifferhüs*; and the simpler *La Flammerie* (delicious *jambonneau*) and *L'Auberge Zahnacker*.

How to get there *(Map12): 19km north of Colmar via N83 and D106 towards Ribeauvillé.*

Hôtel de la Rochette ★★

La Rochette
68910 Labaroche (Haut-Rhin)
Tel. (0)3★ 89.49.80.40 – M. Preiss

Rooms 7 with shower and WC. **Price** Double 250F, suite 400F. **Meals** Breakfast (buffet) 45F, served 8:00-9:30; half board 265-300F (child 190F). **Restaurant** Service 12:30-13:30, 19:30-21:00; menus 85-185F, also à la carte. Specialties: Traditional Alsatian cooking, foie gras maison, bouillabaisse (Nov – April). **Credit cards** Amex, Visa, Eurocard and MasterCard. **Pets** Dogs not allowed. **Facilities** Parking. **Nearby** Turckheim, Colmar, Alsace Wine Route from Marlenheim to Thann – 18-hole golf course in Ammerschwihr (5km). **Open** All year (closed Sunday evening and Wednesday).

On a plateau in the heart of the green forests of the Vosges, the Hôtel de la Rochette is to be found a little way from the village. It is difficult not to be charmed by this small house – a hotel for fifty years – with its antique furniture, polished floors, and collections of folk art and local pottery. The bedrooms reflect the spirit of the house: they are all comfortable and number 8 is quite charming, but some could do with new carpets. Note that this is actually a restaurant with rooms, which is why some of the communal areas are not very big, though there is a bar. The welcome here is warm. When the weather is good, drinks and snacks are served on the terrace.

How to get there *(Map 12): 18km northwest of Colmar via D417 to Turckheim, then D11 towards Trois-Epis, Orbay.*

Hôtel Au Moulin ★★

68127 Sainte-Croix-en-Plaine (Haut-Rhin)
Tel. (0)3★ 89.49.31.20 - Fax (0)3★ 89.49.23.11
M. and Mme Wœlffle

Rooms 16 and 1 suite with telephone, bath, WC and TV; elevator - Wheelchair access.
Price Single and double 230-400F, suite 500F. **Meals** Breakfast 45F, served 7:30-10:00. No restaurant. **Credit cards** Visa, Eurocard and MasterCard. **Pets** Dogs allowed (+30F). **Facilities** Parking. **Nearby** Colmar, Neuf-Brisach, Munster, Trois-Epis, Alsace Wine Route from Marlenheim to Thann – 18-hole golf course in Ammerschwihr. **Open** End Mar – Nov 5.

This former flour mill was built in the 16th-century by a colony of Mennonites and was converted into a hotel in 1982. It is a large white building with windows brightened by geraniums. The owners, the Wœlffle family, live in adjoining buildings, the ensemble forming a pretty courtyard with banks of flowers surrounding an old stone well. Spread over three floors, the bedrooms face either west, towards the Vosges, or across the fields. Most are spacious and all have very well equipped bathrooms. (There is no television, as peace and quiet are the main concern). Finally, there are three further rooms in another building facing onto the courtyard, where breakfast can be enjoyed to the sound of water flowing down the Thur River, also called the "canal of the twelve mills" (two still work). This is a hotel with a very friendly atmosphere and very attractive prices. For fine dining, we recommend *Le Caveau d'Eguisheim* and *Hostellerie du Pape* in Eguisheim, and *La Maison des Têtes* and *Au Fer Rouge* in Colmar.

How to get there *(Map 12): 6km south of Colmar via N422, then D1 towards Sainte-Croix-en-Plaine. On motorways exit 27, toward Herrlisheim.*

Auberge La Meunière ★★

30, rue Sainte-Anne
68590 Thannenkirch (Haut-Rhin)
Tel. (0)3★ 89.73.10.47 – Fax (0)3★ 89.73.12.31 – M. Dumoulin

Rooms 15 with telephone, shower and WC (6 with TV). **Price** Double 270-350F, suite 650F. **Meals** Breakfast 30F, served 8:30-9:30; half board 235-295F, full board 305-365F. **Restaurant** Service 12:15-14:00, 19:15-21:00; menus 95-190F, also à la carte. Specialties: Foie gras de canard au gewürztraminer, langue de bœuf à la crème de radis noir, Kouglof glacé. **Credit cards** Amex, Visa, Eurocard and MasterCard. **Pets** Dogs allowed (+20F). **Facilities** Health center and sauna (150F for 2 pers.), mountain bikes, parking. **Nearby** Haut-Koenigsbourg, Ribeauvillé, Riquewihr, Kaysersberg – 18-hole golf course in Ammerschwihr. **Open** Easter – Nov 15.

It is impossible not to notice the typically Alsatian facade of this lovely auberge in the little village of Thannenkirch in the foothills of the Vosges. You will find the same charm in the dining room, with its almond-green table linens and low ceilings and the wooden partitions that create several little intimate corners. The bedrooms, some furnished with antiques and some in more modern style, all have the same cozy and comfortable feel. Instead of numbers, the bedroom doors have enameled plaques inscribed with women's names. We particularly liked the *Sophie* and *Josephine* rooms with their glassed-in balconies looking over the countryside towards the fortress of Haut-Koenigsbourg in the distance. The view is superb from the large terrace, where meals are also served.

How to get there *(Map 12): 25km north of Colmar via N83 to Guémar, N106 and D42.*

Hôtel Les Violettes ★★★

68500 Jungholtz-Thierenbach (Haut-Rhin)
Tel. (0)3★ 89.76.91.19 – Fax (0)3★ 89.74.29.12
M. and Mme Munsch

Rooms 24 with telephone, bath or shower and WC (20 with TV, 12 with minibar).
Price Single 220F, double 540-740F. **Meals** Breakfast 60F, served 8:00-10:00.
Restaurant Service 12:00-14:00, 19:00-21:00 (closed Monday evening and Tuesday
except National Holidays); menus 170-410F, also à la carte. Specialties: Brioche de
foie gras, cassolette de turbot et langouste aux morilles. **Credit cards** All major.
Pets Dogs allowed (+40F). **Facilities** Sauna (150F for 2 pers.), parking.
Nearby Walks, Automobile and Rail Museums in Mulhouse, Unterlinden Museum in
Colmar – 18-hole golf course in Ammerschwihr. **Open** All year.

M. and Mme Munsch have devoted much care and attention
to their small hotel. It is quiet, on the edge of a forest and
has a lovely view over the valley and the little village of Thierenbach
which lies just below. Inside, antique furniture, beautiful carpets,
paintings and *objets d'art* create a warm and cheerful ambience. In
the dining room with its panoramic windows and floral fabrics you
will enjoy M. Munsch's excellent cooking. All the bedrooms,
whether in the main building or the annex, are prettily decorated
with beautiful fabrics, lace, pictures and white lacquered or natural
wood furniture. Some have a terrace looking out on the forest.
This is a charming place to stay.

*How to get there (Map 20): 5km south of Guebwiller in the towards of
Soultz, at Thierenbach go left of the basilica, then 300m to the edge of the
forest.*

Château d'Adoménil ★★★

Rehainviller
54300 Lunéville (Meurthe-et-Moselle)
Tel. (0)3★ 83.74.04.81 - Fax (0)3★ 83.74.21.78 - M. Million

Rooms 8, and 4 dupplex (some with air-conditioning) with telephone, bath, WC, TV and minibar. **Price** Single and double 480-850F, suite 1200F. **Meals** Breakfast 70F, served 8:00-11:00; half board 710F (per pers., 3 days min.). **Restaurant** with air-conditioning. Service 12:15-14:00, 19:30-21:30 (closed Sunday evening and Monday and Tuesday lunchtime Nov 1– April 15, and Monday and Tuesday lunchtime Apr 16 – Oct 31); menus 240-450F, also à la carte. Specialties: Sandre aux lardons, gris de Toul, foie gras poêlé. **Credit cards** All major. **Pets** Dogs allowed. **Facilities** Swimming pool - parking. **Nearby** Château de Lunéville, Crystal Museum in Baccarat, Place Stanislas, School of Nancy Museum and Emile Gallé Museum in Nancy, Saint-Etienne Cathedral in Toul. **Open** All year except Feb 21 – Mar 7 (closed Sunday evening and Monday and Tuesday lunchtime Nov 1– April 15, and Monday and Tuesday lunchtime Apr 16 – Oct 31).

Some ten years ago, M. Million left his restaurant in Lunéville to move into this beautiful château. He has opened a successful restaurant here, and the old stables have been converted into five spacious rooms which open onto the orchard. They all have beautiful tiled floors, modern Italian furniture and decorative objects, and luxurious bathrooms. In the château there are three other rooms of a more classical charm. The château is on a beautiful 17-acre estate, which is disturbed only occasionally by a little railway nearby. The cuisine lives up to its reputation, and you will enjoy delicious breakfasts with croissants and assorted pastries.

How to get there (*Map 12*): *30km southeast of Nancy via N4 to Lunéville; 3km south of Lunéville via D914.*

La Bergerie ★★

15, rue des Vignes
57640 Rugy (Moselle)
Tel. (0)3★ 88.77.82.27 – Fax (0)3★ 87.77.87.07 – Mme Keichinger

Rooms 42 with telephone, bath or shower, WC and TV. **Price** Single and double 300-380F. **Meals** Breakfast 40F, served 6:30-10:30. **Restaurant** Service 12:00-13:30, 19:00-21:30; menus 120-200F, also à la carte. Specialties: Traditional cooking. **Credit cards** Visa, Eurocard and MasterCard. **Pets** Dogs allowed. **Facilities** Parking. **Nearby** Saint-Etienne Cathedral in Metz, Waliby Park (Schtroumpf) – 18-hole golf course in Metz. **Open** All year.

La Bergerie is conveniently placed for the autoroute but nevertheless stands in a green and quiet spot. The hotel consists of several buildings, some of which are very old. The bedrooms are modern, airy and functional and are furnished with lovely country fabrics. We recommend the bedrooms on the garden side: numbers 2 to 6, 14 to 19, and 30 to 39; others look out on the parking lot. Their bathrooms are pleasant and well equipped, but the soundproofing is not always perfect. Buffet-style breakfasts are served in two charming small rooms in the old part of the inn. For lunch and dinner, you will be served in two vast, prettily decorated dining rooms. In good weather, you can enjoy meals beneath the shady trellis outside. This is a useful place for a brief stay.

How to get there (Map 12): 10km north of Metz via A4, Ennery exit.

L'Horizon ★★★

50, route du Crève-Cœur
57100 Thionville (Moselle)
Tel. (0)3★ 82.88.53.65 - Fax (0)3★ 82.34.55.84 - Speck Family

Rooms 10 with telephone, bath, WC and TV. **Price** Single 480F, double 680-780F.
Meals Breakfast 62F, served 7:15-10:30; half board 560-660F (per pers., 3 days
min.), 840-980F (per 2 pers., 3 days min.). **Restaurant** Service 12:00-13:45, 19:00-
21:30 (closed Saturday lunchtime); menus 215-325F, also à la carte. Specialties:
Escargotière de petits gris, sandre en mode lorraine, le mirabellier (dessert).
Credit cards Amex, Visa, Eurocard and MasterCard. **Pets** Dogs allowed (+70F).
Facilities Parking, garage (+70F). **Nearby** St-Etienne Cathedral in Metz, Waliby Park
(Schtroumpf) – 18-hole golf course in Metz. **Open** Mar 1 – Jan 31.

Although it's only a few minutes from the center of Thionville,
L'Horizon is surrounded by greenery, and its hillside location
gives you a panoramic view over the city. When it was built some
thirty years ago, the hotel was a vast family residence. Even though
it is a luxury hotel today, you are very much aware of the family
feeling, which has been maintained. The bedrooms are very
comfortable, and period furniture lends a personal touch to each.
Those on the *deuxième étage* are smaller but pleasant, and obviously
less expensive. On the ground floor, the living room, dining room
(magnificent) and bar are very warm and inviting. Like many of
the bedrooms, they look out over Thionville and the Moselle Plain.
L'Horizon is a half-city, half-country place to stay, offering
renowned cuisine and a warm welcome.

How to get there *(Map 12): 30km south of Luxembourg. 30km north of Metz
via A 31, exit 40. At Thionville, follow the signs "Bel Air," then "Crève-Cœur."*

Auberge du Kiboki **

Route du Donon (D993)
57560 Turquestein (Moselle)
Tel. (0)3★ 87.08.60.65 – Fax (0)3★ 87.08.65.26 – M. Schmitt

Rooms 15 with telephone, bath or shower, WC and TV. **Price** Double 370-400F, suite 550F. **Meals** Breakfast (buffet) 45F, served 8:00-10:00; half board 350F (per pers., 3 days min.). **Restaurant** Service 12:00-14:00, 19:00-21:00; à la carte 130-180F. Specialties: Jambon fumé de gibier, ballotin de saumon au blanc de poireaux, médaillon de biche flambé au whisky, mirabelles flambée sur fleur de vanille. **Credit cards** Visa, Eurocard and MasterCard. **Pets** Dogs not allowed. **Facilities** Covered swimming pool, whirlpool, sauna, tennis, parking. **Nearby** Dabo Rock, crystal factories, potteries in Niderviller. **Open** Mar 1 – Jan 31 (closed Tuesday).

In the middle of the forest in the Turquestein-Blancrupt Valley lies the traditional Auberge du Kiboki. A very cozy atmosphere is created by the warm decor in this hotel. The dining rooms are very appealing: one is bright with checked tablecloths, matching curtains and lampshades; the other is decorated in soft colors and has a handsome, large china cabinet filled with local pottery. The comfortably furnished bedrooms reflect the same style, with warm beige and brown tones, canopied beds and antique wardrobes. This authentic forest inn is an ideal place for a restful stay. The cuisine is excellent and the owners are very hospitable, all making the Kiboki one of the outstanding hotels in this guide.

How to get there (Map 12): 73km west of Strasbourg via A35 and D392 towards Saint-Dié; at Schirmeck D392 towards Donon and D993 towards Turquestein-Blancrupt.

Hostellerie des Bas–Rupts ★★★

Les Bas–Rupts
88400 Gérardmer (Vosges)
Tel. (0)3★ 29.63.09.25 - Fax (0)3★ 29.63.00.40 - M. Philippe

Rooms 32 with telephone, bath or shower, WC and TV. **Price** Single and double 380-780F, suite 900F. **Meals** Breakfast 80F, served 7:00-10:00; half board 540-720F. **Restaurant** Service 12:00-14:00, 19:00-21:30; menus 160-450F, also à la carte. Specialties: Tripes au riesling, aiguillettes de canard, andouille fumée sur choucroute. **Credit cards** Amex, Visa, Eurocard and MasterCard. **Pets** Dogs allowed (+50F). **Facilities** Swimming pool, tennis, garage, parking. **Nearby** Les Cuves Waterfall, Longemer Lake, Retournemer Lake, Epinal – 18-hole golf course in Epinal. **Open** All year.

The Hostellerie des Bas–Rupts, with its flower-bedecked chalet and famous restaurant, is located just outside Gérardmer, once a favorite Alsace-Lorraine resort where the well-heeled enjoyed spending time (and money in the casino). The nostalgic town was almost completely destroyed at the end of World War II. The Hostellerie des Bas–Rupts is a veritable celebration of flowers, which are found painted on beams, doors, bedsteads; and in fresh and dried bouquets throughout, adding much charm to the comfortable bedrooms in the annex. Some rooms in the hotel itself are more ordinary. The service is both professional and extremely courteous.

How to get there (Map 12): 56km west of Colmar via D417 and D486 towards La Bresse.

Hôtel de la Fontaine–Stanislas ★★

Fontaine-Stanislas
88370 Plombières-les-Bains (Vosges)
Tel. (0)3★ 29.66.01.53 - Fax (0)3★ 29.30.04.31 - M. and Mme Bilger

Rooms 19 with telephone, 14 with bath or shower, 11 with WC and 8 with TV.
Price Single 135-200F, double 145-300F. **Meals** Breakfast 36F, served 7:30-
9:30; half board 230-320F, full board 270-360F (per pers., 3 days min.).
Restaurant Service 12:00-13:30, 19:00-20:30; menus 90-270F, also à la carte.
Specialties: Cassolette d'escargots aux cèpes, coupe plombières. **Credit cards** Amex,
Visa, Eurocard and MasterCard. **Pets** Dogs allowed (+25F). **Facilities** Parking.
Nearby Epinal, Augronne and Semouse Valleys, Guéhand Waterfall, la Feuillée
Nouvelle – 18-hole golf course in Epinal. **Open** Apr 1 – Sept 30.

Since 1933, four generations have successively run this hotel which
could do with some improvement. Among its attractions are the
excellent hospitality and a splendid forest setting which you can enjoy
from the sloping terraces and the panoramic bay windows of the dining
rooms. There is a charming, old-fashioned atmosphere here, with
1950s furniture in pale wood, parquet ceilings and beautiful table
linens. You will enjoy the ambiance and the menu prices are
reasonable. We are less enthusiastic about the bedrooms: Old-
fashioned and very sparsely furnished, they nevertheless often have a
pretty view and they are not expensive. But the renovations are
superficial and we would have preferred a more tasteful decor. For
the moment, we recommend the bedrooms in the annex and numbers
2, 3 and ll, which have small terraces.

*How to get there (Map 20): 30km south of Epinal via D434 to Xertigny,
then D3, D63 and D20; at Granges-de-Plombières take the forest road on
the right.*

Auberge de la Cholotte

Les Rouges-Eaux 88600 Bruyères (Vosges)
Tel. (0)3★ 29.50.56.93 – Fax (0)3★ 29.50.24.12
Mme Cholé

Rooms 5 with bath or shower and WC. **Price** Double 400F. **Meals** Breakfast incl.; half board 350F, full board 450F (per pers., 3 days min.). **Restaurant** Service 12:00-14:00, 19:00-21:00 (closed Sunday evening and Monday); menus 150F, also à la carte. Specialties: Jambon cuit au foin, rapées de pomme de terre, tarte aux myrtilles. **Credit cards** Visa, Eurocard and MasterCard. **Pets** Dogs allowed. **Facilities** Parking. **Nearby** Skiing in winter, Cathedral and Cloisters of Saint-Dié, Epinal, Gérardmer Lake – 18-hole golf course in Epinal. **Open** Mar 1 – Dec 31 (closed Sunday evening and Monday).

Nestled in a small valley, the Auberge de la Cholotte is an irresistibly charming 18th-century farmhouse. In the bedrooms, which have been carefully restored, fabric and wall colors are tastefully coordinated in shades of yellow, blue and soft green, with an occasional brighter color. There are permanent art exhibits on view and a collection of regional objects, along with 19th-century furniture and handsome old Alsatian pieces in polychromed wood. All combine to create a cheerful, refined atmosphere in the comfortable lounges and the two small dining rooms. Concerts are often given in a third, larger dining room with 18th-century paneling and a Steinway piano. The simple bedrooms are charming, and one has a whirlpool bath. All have a pretty view of the flower garden and the pines which cover this magnificent countryside. The seasonal cuisine is succulent and healthful, and the welcome is very friendly.

How to get there *(See Map 12): 15km west of Saint-Dié via D420, towards Bruyères.*

Chalets des Ayes ★★★

Chemin des Ayes
88160 Le Thillot (Vosges)
Tel. (0)3★ 29.25.00.09 - Fax (0)3★ 29.25.36.48 - M. Marsot

Rooms 2, and 17 chalets (4-10 pers.), with bath or shower, WC and TV - Wheelchair access. **Price** Double 340-420F. Chalets 1200-4800F. **Meals** Breakfast 55F, served 8:00-10:00. **Restaurant** Open during the vacations, service 19:30-21:00; menu 128F. Specialties: Cooking from Alsace and the Vosges. **Credit cards** Visa, Eurocard and MasterCard. **Pets** Dogs allowed only in the chalets. **Facilities** Swimming pool, tennis (38F), parking. **Nearby** Cross-country and downhill skiing, riding, mountain bikes, walks. **Open** All year.

The Chalets des Ayes calls itself a hotel, though it isn't really one. It does however provide a practical and pleasant solution to the problem of lodging in the wild and seductively beautiful Vosges region, where it is sometimes hard to find a hotel with rural charm. At the Chalets des Ayes, two rooms are available on a bed-and-breakfast basis. These are bright and cheerful, and there are also five small chalets which are well-equipped and attractively presented. Strictly speaking, the chalets are rented by the week, but like the bedrooms, they can be taken for a few nights subject to availability. There is a garden and a swimming pool and the valley is a cheerful place even in bad weather.

How to get there *(Map 20): 51km west of Mulhouse via N66 towards Remiremont and towards Mulhouse to Le Thillot.*

Auberge du Val Joli ★★

88230 Le Valtin (Vosges)
Tel. (0)3★ 29.60.91.37 – Fax (0)3★ 29.60.81.73
M. Laruelle

Rooms 16 with telephone, 6 with bath, 7 with shower, 12 with WC and TV, 6 with balconies, 8 with minibar. **Price** Single and double 150-320F. **Meals** Breakfast 33F, served 8:00-10:00; half board 241-520F, full board 346-660F. **Restaurant** Service 12:30-14:00, 19:30-21:00; menus 60-230F, also à la carte. Specialties: Truite fumée maison, pâté lorrain, tarte aux myrtilles. **Credit cards** Visa, Eurocard and MasterCard. **Pets** Dogs allowed (+20F). **Facilities** Tennis, parking. **Nearby** Saint-Dié Cathedral, Gérardmer Lake – 18-hole golf course in Epinal. **Open** All year (closed Sunday evening and Monday in low season).

The little village of Valtin has only 99 inhabitants, and the mayor is also the owner of this auberge which stands at the bottom of one of the prettiest valleys of the Vosges. You only have to open the door to feel its character: low ceilings, beams, flagstones and fireplace create a completely authentic atmosphere. The dining room is very attractive with its many small windows and particularly its carved wood ceiling is the work of an Alsatian carpenter. The comfort of the bedrooms and their bathroom facilities are very variable. They also would be improved with somewhat more decoration. Fortunately, the bedrooms have just been extensively enlarged: the four new bedrooms with balcony should be reserved, and the most pleasant are those which have just been renovated. Even though the hotel is on the road, there is not much noise; if in doubt reserve a room overlooking the mountain, such as number 16, 5, or 4. This is an unpretentious hotel in a very well preserved village.

How to get there *(Map 12): 40km west of Colmar via D417 (by the Schlucht pass) to le Collet, then right on D23 to Le Valtin.*

Le Chatenet ★★★

Le Chatenet
24310 Brantôme (Dordogne)
Tel. (0)5★ 53.05.81.08 – Fax (0)5★ 53.05.85.52 – M. and Mme Laxton

Rooms 10 with telephone, bath and shower and WC (3 with TV) - 1 for disabled persons. **Price** Double 490-580F, suite 810F. **Meals** Breakfast 60F, served 8:30-10:00. No restaurant. **Credit cards** Visa, Eurocard and MasterCard. **Pets** Dogs allowed. **Facilities** Heated swimming pool, tennis (40F), parking. **Nearby** Bell tower of the abbey church in Brantôme, "Peiro-Levado" dolmen, châteaux of Hierce, Puymarteau and Saint-Jean-de-Côle, Chancelade Abbey, Saltgourde estate, Marsac – 18-hole golf course in Périgueux. **Open** All year.

Le Chatenet, which owner Philippe Laxton describes as "a family house open to friends and to friends of friends" in the pretty countryside of Brantôme, is a very pleasant place to stay. It is composed of two buildings in the beautiful regional architectural style. You will find superb bedrooms with upholstered walls, very tasteful furnishings and modern bathrooms. The lounge and dining room are very inviting but in summer, guests are very fond of the loggia, mainly for the excellent breakfasts served there. There is no restaurant but there are many good ones nearby, including *Le Moulin de l'Abbaye*, *Les Frères Charbonnel* (highly rated in Michelin and Gault-Millau), and *Le Saint Marc*. This is a beautiful and very welcoming hotel.

How to get there *(Map 23): 27km north of Périgueux, 1.5km from Brantôme via D78 towards Bourdeilles.*

Domaine de la Roseraie ★★★

24310 Brantôme (Dordogne)
Tel. (0)5★ 53.05.84.74 - Fax (0)5★ 53.05.77.94
M. Roux

Rooms 7 with telephone, bath or shower, WC and TV - Wheelchair access.
Price Double 300-680F, suite 750F. **Meals** Breakfast 50F, served 7:30-10:30. Tea
room. **Restaurant** "Bistro Gourmand" Service 12:00-15:00, 19:00-21:30; menus 59-
169F, also à la carte. Specialties: Grillades, salades. **Credit carts** All major. **Pets**
Dogs allowed. **Nearby** Bell tower of the abbey church in Brantôme, "Peiro-Levado"
dolmen, châteaux of Hierce, Puymarteau and St-Jean-de-Côle, Chancelade Abbey,
Saltgourde estate, Marsac – 18-hole golf course in Périgueux. **Open** Mar – Jan.

Nestled in the countryside outside Brantôme, La Roseraie is
composed of two buildings set at an angle and a Perigourdine
tower. With the first sunny days, breakfasts and drinks are served
here. Inside, the Roseraie is very inviting. There are two lounges
(one is for television exclusively) which are furnished with pleasant,
comfortable period furniture and decorated with Impressionist-
style paintings. The bedrooms and baths are equally attractive and
they are kept impeccably clean. Families should note the splendid
duplex suite. All rooms are on the ground floor and have
independent entrances. It is beautifully quiet here, the service is
friendly, and while there is no restaurant at the hotel, there are
several excellent ones in the region. Try *Le Moulin de l'Abbaye* and
the *Brasserie Saint-Sicaire* in Brantôme.

How to get there *(Map 23): 27km north of Périgueux via D939; in the
center of the town, 1km in the towards of Angoulême.*

Hôtel du Manoir de Bellerive ★★★

Route de Siorac
24480 Le Buisson de Cadouin (Dordogne)
Tel. (0)5★ 53.27.16.19 - Fax (0)5★ 53.22.09.05 - Mme Huin

Rooms 16 with air-conditioning, telephone, bath or shower, WC, TV and minibar.
Price Single and double 420-750F. **Meals** Breakfast 50-65F, served 8:00-11:00.
Restaurant Service 19:30-22:00 (12:00-15:00 only Sunday and national holidays);
menus 115F, 165F, 185F, also à la carte. Specialties: "Cuisine inventive" and regional
cooking. **Credit cards** Visa, Eurocard and MasterCard. **Pets** Dogs allowed. **Facilities**
Swimming pool, tennis, sauna (100F), parking. **Nearby** Le Bugue, cave of Bara-
Bahau and Proumeyssac chasm, Limeuil, National Museum of Prehistory in Les Eyzies
– 18-hole golf course in la-Croix-de-Mortemart. **Open** Easter – Nov 1.

Situated off the road in beautiful English parklike grounds, this 19th-
century manor borders the Dordogne. It has been delightfully
converted by two interior decorators. On the ground floor, the
lounge, bar and dining room open off a vast central colonnaded hall,
from which a double staircase sweeps up to the *premier étage* bedrooms.
The pervading atmosphere of aestheticism and refinement has been
created by a sensitive and masterly combination of colors, fabrics and
trompe l'œil marble. There are also antiques, beautiful carpets,
engravings... Among the very comfortable bedrooms you have the
choice of those with a view over the park or those overlooking the
river. The bathrooms are luxurious. In good weather breakfast is
served on the terrace, which overlooks the Dordogne. You will find
a very hospitable welcome. The restaurant is inaugurating a new menu
called "Dinner Around a Specialty", which is designed to enhance
authentic food tastes with the use of good fresh products.

*How to get there (Map 23): 47km southeast of Périgueux via N89 to
Niversac, D710 to Le Bugue, and D31.*

Le Relais du Touron **

Le Touron
24200 Carsac-Aillac (Dordogne)
Tel. (0)5★ 53.28.16.70 – Fax (0)5★ 53 28 52 51 – Mme Carlier and M. Amriah

Rooms 12 with telephone, bath or shower and WC. **Price** Double 265-375F, triple 390-485F. **Meals** Breakfast 35F, served 8:00-10:00; half board 288-334F. **Restaurant** Closed at lunchtime and Wednesday diner in low season, Tuesday and Wednesday in high season; menus 90-265F, also à la carte. Specialties: Foie gras d'oie poélé aux pommes caramélisées, feuilleté d'escargots aux cèpes, filet d'agneau au beurre de foie gras, sandre à l'orange. **Credit cards** Visa, Eurocard and MasterCard. **Pets** Dogs allowed. **Facilities** Swimming pool, parking. **Nearby** Walk along the valley of the Enéa from Carsac to Sainte-Nathalène, old town and house of La Boétie in Sarlat, Château de Puymartin – 9-hole golf course in Vitrac. **Open** Apr 1 – Nov 14.

The Relais du Touron is a peaceful country inn which lies at the end of the village. The rustling leaves of the poplar trees and the murmuring of the Enea as it flows tranquilly along create a romantic pastoral atmosphere. Comfortable bedrooms all alike are in the building facing the swimming pool. In the neighboring Périgourdine house, you will find No. 11 and No. 12, which is the most attractive although; it is, for 3 or 4 people. (It has a beautiful high ceiling and exposed beams.) A beautiful swimming pool, surrounded by shade trees and lawns, a terrace where meals and breakfasts are served facing the garden: all contribute to making the Touron a pleasant place to stay.

How to get there (*Map 23*): *75km southeast of Périguex to Sarlat, then D704 towards Gourdon (600m before the village of Carsac).*

Manoir d'Hautegente ★★★

24120 Coly (Dordogne)
Tel. (0)5★ 53.51.68.03 – Fax (0)5★ 53.50.38.52
Mme Hamelin

Rooms 10 and 2 duplex, with telephone, bath, WC, TV and minibar. **Price** Double 500-950F. **Meals** Breakfast 55F, served 8:30-10:00; half board 490-720F (per pers.). **Restaurant** Service from 20:00; menus 195-250F, also à la carte. Specialties: Duo de langoustines au foie gras; pigeon farci au foie gras et sa sauce aux truffes. **Credit cards** Visa, Eurocard and MasterCard. **Pets** Dogs allowed. **Facilities** Heated swimming pool, fishing, parking. **Nearby** Lascaux caves, Abbey of Aubazines, Argentat, Collonges-la-Rouge. **Open** Apr 1 – Nov 11.

Formerly a mill and forge of the warrior monks of Saint Amand-du-Coly and the property of the Hamelin family for almost three centuries, this Perigord manor has been an elegant hotel for several years now. It is in a beautiful valley where graceful old walnut and oak trees line the roads. Ducks roam freely along the banks of the winding, babbling brook in front of the manor. The rooms and lounges have all been tastefully decorated with the family furniture in a perfect blend of style and comfort. The fabrics on the walls and in the curtains are splendid, especially in the *Liserons* room. It is very large and has a private balcony overlooking the river. You will receive a warm and attentive welcome at this very charming hotel.

How to get there *(Map 23): 30km southwest of Brive-la-Gaillarde via N89 towards Périgueux to Le Lardin-Saint-Lazare, then D704 and D62 towards Sarlat-Souillac.*

Hôtel Cro–Magnon ★★★

24620 Les Eyzies-de-Tayac (Dordogne)
Tel. (0)5★ 53.06.97.06 – Fax (0)5★ 53.06.95.45
M. and Mme Leyssales

Rooms 18, and 4 apartments, with telephone, bath or shower and WC (TV on request). **Price** Double 350-550F, suite 600-800F. **Meals** Breakfast 50F, served 8:00-10:00; half board 350-500F (per pers., 3 days min.). **Restaurant** Service 12:00-14:00, 19:00-21:15 (closed Wednesday lunchtime except national holidays); menus 140-350F, also à la carte. Specialties: Ravioles d'escargots au bouillon d'ail doux, mille-feuilles d'agneau sauce poivrade, truffe en croustade. **Credit cards** All major. **Pets** Dogs allowed (+30F). **Facilities** Swimming pool, parking. **Nearby** Le Bugue, Bara-Bahau cave and Proumeyssac chasm, Limeuil, National Museum of Prehistory in Les Eyzies – 18-hole La-Croix-de-Mortemart golf course in Le Bugue. **Open** May – Oct 11.

This old coaching inn has been in the family for many generations. The two reception rooms, whose colors harmonize well with the open stonework and old furniture, are very charming. There is a small museum in one. You can choose between a pretty dining room in local style or another modern one, which has been very well integrated and which opens onto a shady terrace. Excellent regional cuisine is complemented by a well-chosen wine list. The bedrooms are comfortable and charmingly decorated; for peace and quiet, we prefer those in the annex, which all look out onto a very large park with a swimming pool. The staff is very friendly.

How to get there *(Map 23): 45km southeast of Périgueux via N89 and D710, then D47.*

Hôtel Les Glycines ★★★

24620 Les Eyzies-de-Tayac (Dordogne)
Tel. (0)5★ 53.06.97.07 - Fax (0)5★ 53.06.92.19
M. and Mme Mercat

Rooms 25 with telephone, bath and WC. **Price** Single 315-390F, double 360-410F. **Meals** Breakfast 50F, served 8:00-10:00; half board 395-450F (per pers., 3 days min.). **Restaurant** Service 12:00-14:00, 19:30-21:30 (closed Saturday lunchtime except national holidays, July, Aug and Sept); menus 140-190F, also à la carte. Specialties: Pavé de bœuf fourré de son escalope de foie frais et sa sauce truffes, pain perdu à la gelée d'abricot aux amandes. **Credit cards** All major. **Pets** Dogs allowed. **Facilities** Swimming pool, park, parking. **Nearby** Le Bugue, cave de Bara-Bahau and Proumeyssac chasm, Limeuil, National Museum of Prehistory in Les Eyzies – 18-hole La-Croix-de-Mortemart golf course in Le Bugue. **Open** Apr 15 – End Oct.

Dating back to 1862, this old coaching inn is a large house where stone, wood and prolific vegetation blend happily together. As the name indicates, there is a pergola covered with an abundance of wisteria; trimmed lime trees shade the terrace. The lounge and bar have a restful atmosphere and have been furnished and decorated with great care. The lovely dining room opens onto the garden, but meals may also be taken on a new veranda that gives onto the lawn. All the bedrooms are very comfortable and the furnishings have been well selected; fabrics, papers and colors are in a contemporary style. The cuisine makes good use of fresh produce from the garden.

How to get there (Map 23): 45km southeast of Périgueux via N89 and D710, then D47.

68

Moulin de la Beune ★★

24620 Les Eyzies-de-Tayac (Dordogne)
Tel. (0)5★ 53.06.94.33 - Fax (0)5★ 53.06.98.06
M. and Mme Soulié

Rooms 20 with telephone, bath or shower and WC. **Price** Single 260F, double 280-300F. **Meals** Breakfast 40F, served 8:00-10:30; half board 320F, full board 420F (per pers., 2 days min.). **Restaurant** Service 12:00-14:30, 19:00-21:30 (closed Tuesday lunchtime); menus 85-315F, also à la carte. Specialties: Saint-Jacques aux truffes, raviolis de foie gras, écrevisses. **Credit cards** Amex, Visa, Eurocard and MasterCard. **Pets** Dogs allowed. **Facilities** Parking, **Nearby** Le Bugue, cave of Bara-Bahau and Proumeyssac chasm, Limeuil, National Museum of Prehistory in Les Eyzies – 18-hole la-Croix-de-Mortemart golf course in Le Bugue. **Open** Feb 16 – Jan 2.

When you arrive at this old mill, it is hard to believe that you are in one of the most touristic areas of France. The River Beune runs quietly at your feet; the small garden dotted with tables is a peaceful haven. In the lounge, beside the large fireplace, there are armchairs and little tables arranged comfortably for reading and writing. To one side there is a room where drinks and breakfast are served. The decor of the recently refurbished bedrooms has been tastefully chosen. The restaurant, Le Vieux Moulin, occupies another adjacent mill, and is also charmingly decorated. In the large dining room with its exposed stonework and beams, or in the garden at the foot of ancient cliffs, truffle-based Périgourdine specialties are served.

How to get there (Map 23): 45km southeast of Périgueux via N89 and D710, then D47; in the middle of the village.

Au Bon Accueil

24510 Limeuil (Dordogne)
Tel. (0)5★ 53.63.30.97
M. and Mme Palazy

Rooms 10 (5 with shower). **Price** Double 130-160F. **Meals** Breakfast 22F, served 8:00-9:30; half board 175-205F, full board 215-250F (per pers., 3 days min.). **Restaurant** Service 12:00-14:30, 19:30-21:30; menus 65-140F, also à la carte. Specialties: Filet de perche au Monbazillac, civet de lièvre ou sanglier, assiette gabare. **Credit cards** Visa, Eurocard and MasterCard. **Pets** Dogs allowed. **Nearby** Le Bugue, cave of Bara-Bahau and Proumeyssac chasm, Limeuil, National Museum of Prehistory in Les Eyzies – 18-hole La-Croix-de-Mortemart golf course in Le Bugue. **Open** Mar 15 – end Oct.

At the top of the magnificent medieval village of Limeuil M. and Mme Palazy have opened Le Bon Accueil. The charm of this very simple inn is due to its owners' wish to create a "real" place. The welcome is warm and professional, the food plain and good, the atmosphere relaxed and calm. At these very reasonable prices the bedrooms are a bit basic, but they are very quiet. We recommend this inn especially in good weather, when you may take a meal or a cup of tea in the charming pergola. A pleasant terraced garden has been added at the base of an ancient battlement. Finally, weather permitting, you can set out at dawn with M. Palazy to fish in the river, and later dine on your catch at the hotel.

How to get there *(Map 23): 37km south of Périgueux via D710 towards Villeneuve-sur-Lot to Le Bugue, then D31 towards Trémolat.*

La Grande Marque ★★

24220 Marnac-Saint-Cyprien (Dordogne)
Tel. (0)5★ 53.31.61.63 - Fax (0)5★ 53.28.39.55
M. and Mme Devaux d'Hangest

Rooms 16 (4 duplex) with telephone, bath or shower, WC and TV - 1 for disabled persons. **Price** Single and double 286F, duplex 426F. **Meals** Breakfast 38F, served 8:30-9:30; half board 286-426F, full board 355-425F (per pers., 3 days min.). **Restaurant** Service 12:30-13:30, 19:30-21:00; menus 98-200F, also à la carte. Specialties: Papitons de lotte et saumon, local cooking. **Credit cards** Visa, Eurocard and MasterCard. **Pets** Small dogs allowed. **Facilities** Salt-water swimming pool, parking. **Nearby** Châteaux of Veyrignac, Les Milandes and Montfort, Beynac and Cazenac, Domme – 9-hole Rochebois golf course in Vitrac. **Open** Apr – Nov 1 and school vacations.

Surrounded by lush vegetation on the side of a hill, La Grande Marque, on a registered historic site, offers an extraordinary panoramic view of the Dordogne. The bedrooms are in an old tobacco barn that has been completely renovated. You enter a modern, soberly furnished reception room lit by immense picture windows. Exhibitions of paintings are held here. Upstairs, the bedrooms are simple though comfortably appointed. The garden, dotted with sculptures by one of the owners' sons, is a mass of flowers and has many pretty nooks and crannies. On a shady terrace tables are laid for summer breakfasts, while in winter dinner is served in a pleasantly rustic dining room. The creative cuisine is excellent and the people are very friendly.

How to get there (Map 23): 57km southeast of Périgueux via N89 to Niversac, D710 to Le Bugue, D31 to Le Buisson, then Siorac and D703. Turn left in 1km.

Château de Mavaleix ★★★

Mavaleix
24800 Thiviers (Dordogne)
Tel. (0)5★ 53.52.82.01 – Fax (0)5★ 53.62.03.80 – Mme Ruel

Rooms 18 with telephone, bath or shower and WC (10 with TV). **Price** Double 260-410F. **Meals** Breakfast 45F, served 8:00-10:00; half board 410F, full board 490F (per pers., 3 day min.). **Restaurant** Service 12:00-13:45, 19:30-21:00 (closed Jan and Wednesday); menus 85-220F, also à la carte. Specialties: Civet de canard aux pruneaux d'Agen et à l'hysope, sauté de cèpes en coque de Saint-Jacques, foie frais de canard cuit au torchon, tarte Tatin. **Credit cards** Visa, Eurocard and MasterCard. **Pets** Dogs allowed. **Facilities** Swimming pool, jogging path, fishing, parking. **Nearby** Chancelade, Bourdeilles, Brandôme, Saint-Jean-de-Côle, Jumilhac-le-Grand – 18-hole golf course in Périgueux. **Open** Feb – Dec.

A magnificent vault of trees extending out from a side entrance leads into the courtyard of this château, which was built in the 12th-century. This was home to the Knights Templars, and pilgrims stopped here on their way to Compostela. The bedrooms located in the Commanderie—the Knights' apartments—have a somewhat old-fashioned charm, but they are comfortable and well kept. Ask for the *Empire* room and avoid the *Espagnole* room. The bedrooms in the main building are very charming with their old parquet floors and antique furniture but the stairway and the bathrooms should be extensively refurbished. All look out over the countryside. The small dining room, at once rustic and elegant, is very pretty (the large summer dining room is less intimate.) The staff is discreet, elegant and extremely kind, and there is total peace and quiet here.

How to get there (Map 23): 35km north of Périgueux via RN21, in the towards of Limoges.

La Métairie ★★★

24150 Mauzac (Dordogne)
Tel. (0)5★ 53.22.50.47 – Fax (0)5★ 53.22.52.93
Mme Vigneron and M. Culis

Rooms 10 with telephone, bath, WC and TV (6 with minibar). **Price** Double 450-600F (low season), 500-650F (high season), suite 950-1110F. **Meals** Breakfast 60F, served 8:00-10:00, half board 450-550F (per pers., 2 days min.). **Restaurant** Service 12:30-13:45, 19:30-21:00 (closed Tuesday Apr 1 – June 1, and Tuesday lunchtime from July 1); menus 120-300F, also à la carte. Specialties of Périgord. **Credit cards** Visa, Eurocard and MasterCard. **Pets** Dogs allowed (+30F). **Facilities** Swimming pool, parking. **Nearby** Les Eyzies, Limeuil, Le Bugue, Bergerac – 18-hole la-Croix-de-Mortemart golf course in Le Bugue. **Open** Apr 1 – Oct 15.

A few kilometers from the famous horse shoe–shaped Cingle de Trémolat, in a beautiful valley where great loops of the Dordogne River wind through a mosaic of cultivated fields, lies La Métairie. It is a charming and beautiful house converted with comfort, delicacy and good taste. The garden is also very well done. At the same level as the lawn a pleasant terrace runs along the side of the house, and in summer there is a grill near the swimming pool. The cuisine is very appetizing and aromatic. Finally, it is worth noting that the hotel is close to a superb lake where every type of water sport is available.

How to get there *(Map 23): 68km south of Périgueux via N89 and D70 to Le Bugue, then D703 and branch off for Mauzac.*

L'Auberge du Noyer ★★

Le Reclaud-de-Bouny-Bas
24260 Le Bugue (Dordogne)
Tel. (0)5★ 53.07.11.73 – Fax (0)5★ 53.54.57.44 – M. and Mme Dyer

Rooms 10 with telephone, bath and WC. **Price** Single 320F, double 400-480F.
Meals Breakfast 48F, served 8:15-10:00; half board 400-440F (per pers.).
Restaurant Service 19:30-21:00; menu 160F. Specialties: Coussin de truite farcie
aux pleurotes, magret à l'orange, tarte aux noix. **Credit cards** Visa, Eurocard and
MasterCard. **Pets** Dogs not allowed. **Facilities** Swimming pool, parking. **Nearby** Le
Bugue, Proumeyssac chasm, Limeuil, Les Eyzies, Vézère Valley from Limeuil to
Montignac, Lascaux – 18-hole La-Croix-de-Mortemart golf course in Le Bugue.
Open Palm Sunday – Nov 1.

Five kilometers from Le Bugue, this 18th-century Périgourdine
farm has been completely renovated by an English couple, Paul
and Jenny Dyer, who fell in love with the region. The Auberge
du Noyer is a charming, tranquil place to stay, even in August.
The bedrooms are spacious and have impeccable bathrooms: five
have their own private terraces on which to have breakfast; (ask
for number 8). The cooking is simple but refined and meals are
served in a pretty, rustic dining room. Breakfast is a high point,
with home-made jams, freshly squeezed orange juice and toasted
farmhouse bread. The owners are charming, very informal, and
this is an ideal place for a stay of several days, for which the owners
recommend half-board.

How to get there *(Map 23): 37km south of Périgueux via D710 towards
Villeneuve-sur-Lot, then D703 towards Sainte-Alvère.*

La Plume d'Oie
Au Bourg
24250 La Roque-Gageac (Dordogne)
Tel. (0)5★ 53.29.57.05./53.28.94.93 - Fax (0)5★ 53.31.04.81 - M. and Mme Walker

Rooms 4 with telephone, bath and shower, WC, TV and minibar. **Price** Single 275F,double 350-380F. **Meals** Breakfast 55F, served 8:00-9:30. **Restaurant** Service 12:15-13:30, 19:30-21:00; menus 175F, 255F, 395F, also à la carte. Specialties: Cuisse de canard en braisade d'aromates au brouet de noix, gâteau de maïs, à la pomme verte; foie gras de canard cuit au naturel, à la fleur de sel; disques et mousse de chocolat amer, au sorbet de cacao. **Credit cards** Visa, Eurocard and MasterCard. **Pets** Dogs allowed (+25-40F). **Nearby** Old Town and La Boétie's house in Sarlat, châteaux of Puymartin and Commarques, Carsac, Lascaux – 9-hole golf course in Vitrac. **Open** Mar – Jan (closed Monday)

L a Plume d'Oie is a restaurant with an excellent reputation to which four charming bedrooms have just been added. Light and bright, comfortably modern, they are decorated like guest rooms, with pretty chestnut furniture and cream-colored fabrics with occasional splashes of color; the bathrooms are impeccable. Three rooms open onto the river, which is just across the narrow street. Built on the flank of a gigantic cliff right on the Dordogne, La Roque-Gageac is a simply superb site. There's another side to the coin, however: you hear the cars somewhat, which can be a problem in the high season – July and August. If you want complete silence, it's best to reserve the bedroom looking out on the cliff. Breakfasts are served in your room when you wish. The jovial, thoughtful owners will welcome you warmly.

How to get there (Map 23): 8km south of Sarlat-la-Canéda.

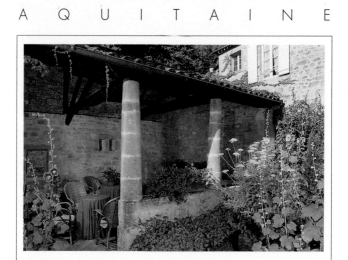

Hôtel de L'Abbaye ★★★

Rue de l'Abbaye
24220 Saint-Cyprien-en-Périgord (Dorgogne)
Tel. (0)5★ 53.29.20.48 - Fax (0)5★ 53.29.15.85 - M. and Mme Schaller

Rooms 24 with telephone, bath or shower and WC (11 with TV and minibar).
Price Single 340-360F, double 550-680F, suite 680-700F. **Meals** Breakfast 50F,
brunch in July and Aug 60F, served 8:00-10:00; half board 390-560F (per pers.).
Restaurant Service 12:00-14:00, 19:30-21:00; menus 140-320F, also à la carte.
Specialties: Foie gras frais, poulet sauté aux langoustines, escargots à la crème de
persil. **Credit cards** Amex, Visa, Eurocard and MasterCard. **Pets** Dogs allowed.
Facilities Swimming pool, parking. **Nearby** Cave of Proumeyssac, Le Bugue, Château
de Campagne, Les Eyzies – 18-hole La-Croix-de-Mortemart golf course in Le Bugue.
Open Apr 15 – Oct 15.

The exterior of this large house in the pretty village of Saint-Cyprien has been left untouched, so that the local stone acts as decoration. The same feeling is echoed in the lounge, with its stone walls and fireplace and the original stone floor. The bedrooms are all comfortably appointed, and some are more luxurious than others. In one of the annexes, some bedrooms can be combined to form a family apartment, and the bedrooms in the new building are really luxurious. A lovely terrace and pleasant gardens with swimming pool add to the charm of L'Abbaye, where the cuisine is very good and the owners warm and welcoming.

How to get there *(Map 23): 54km southeast of Périgueux via N89 and D710 to Le Bugue, then D703 and D35 to St-Cyprien.*

Hostellerie Saint-Jacques ★★★

24470 Saint-Saud-Lacoussière (Dordogne)
Tel. (0)5★ 53.56.97.21 – Fax (0)5★ 53.56.91.33
M. and Mme Babayou

Rooms 22 and 3 apartments, with telephone, bath or shower and WC (10 with TV and minibar). **Price** Single 300F, double 330-450F, suite 750F. **Meals** Breakfast 45F, brunch by the swimming pool; half board 255-385F, full board 335-465F (per pers., 3 days min.). **Restaurant** Service 12:30-13:30, 19:30-21:00, 21:30 in July and Aug (closed Sunday evening and Monday except for residents, and Oct 15 – Easter except Sunday and national holidays); menus 115-290F, also à la carte. Specialties: Terrine de foie gras au magret de canard et pruneaux, croustade de pigeon aux girolles sauce foie gras. **Credit cards** Visa, Eurocard and MasterCard. **Pets** Dogs allowed. **Facilities** Heated swimming pool, tennis, riding (2km), parking. **Nearby** Brantôme Abbey, Villars caves, Saint-Jean-de-Côle – 18-hole Saltgourde golf course in Marsac. **Open** Apr 1 – Oct 15 (closed Sunday evening and Monday in low season).

The Hostellerie Saint-Jacques has the generous proportions of an 18th-century Périgourdine house. The bedrooms all have different fabrics and furniture. They are all comfortable, cheerful, bright and decorated with a great amount of taste and imagination. Some have a small corner lounge and the bookshelves, which are worthy of Arsène Lupin, open up to give access to the (luxurious) bathroom. Downstairs, the dining room has a Provençal air with its elegant yellow and blue decor, but the cuisine is nevertheless authentically Périgourdine. Made with local farm products, it is excellent and light. In the summer, a few tables are set out beneath the maples and the service is extremely pleasant. This is a beautiful hotel which owes its charm to the dynamism of the entire Babayou family.

How to get there (*Map 23): 58km north of Périgueux via N21 to La Coquille, then D79.*

Le Chaufourg en Périgord

24400 Sourzac (Dordogne)
Tel. (0)5★ 53.81.01. 56 – Fax (0)5★ 53.82.94.87
M. Dambier

Rooms 10 (2 suites) with telephone, bath, WC and TV (4 with minibar). **Price** Double 700-1150F, suite 1400F. **Meals** Breakfast 70F, served 8:00-11:00. No restaurant. **Credit cards** Amex, Visa, Eurocard and MasterCard. **Pets** Dogs allowed on request. **Facilities** Heated swimming pool, parking. **Nearby** Périgueux, Echourgnac and forest of la Double, Chancelade Abbey, Saltgourde estate, Marsac – 18-hole golf course in Périgueux. **Open** All year.

This very beautiful and elegant 17th-century family mansion is not really a hotel: Le Chaufourg en Périgord is M. Dambier's childhood home, which he has restored "to create the elegant decor I dreamed of for entertaining." You will, not surprisingly, find everything here you could wish for when you travel: very comfortable accommodations, warm hospitality, and those extra details that make all the difference, the tasteful decoration combines antiques with handsome personal objects, magazines and books. There is a billiard table at your disposal. The garden overlooking the Isle River is heavenly. You can relax around the swimming pool, stroll in the shady park or take a boat ride down the river. There is no restaurant, but on request, M. Dambier will prepare a truly memorable meal of the specialties for which the Périgord is renowned. He will also point out the many good local restaurants. Ask him for his native son's tips on making the most of your visit to this enchanting region.

How to get there *(Map 23): 30km southwest of Périgueux via N 89, towards Mussidan.*

Le Vieux Logis ★★★
24510 Trémolat (Dordogne)
Tel. (0)5★ 53.22.80.06 – Fax (0)5★ 53.22.84.89
M. Giraudel

Rooms 24 with telephone, bath, WC, TV, and minibar. **Price** Single and double 740-1290F, suite 1545F. **Meals** Breakfast 72F, served 8:00-11:00. **Restaurant** Service 12:30-14:30, 19:00-21:30, carte. **Credit cards** All major. **Pets** Dogs allowed. **Facilities** Swimming pool, parking. **Nearby** Tobacco Museum in Bergerac, Lanquais, bastide town of Sainte-Foy-la-Grande. **Open** All year.

For four centuries, the same family has lived on this superb estate, which was made into a hotel by M. Giraudel's mother. The different buildings are all charming: In addition to the main building, there is the tobacco barn, the lodge, the gardener's house... No two bedrooms are alike but they have one point in common: They are extremely comfortable, quiet and elegantly decorated down to the last detail; the antique furniture and the *souleiado* Provençal fabrics go together beautifully. The two dining rooms are magnificent. One is small, with pale wood paneling; the other is immense, overlooked by a balustraded lounge (the former hayloft). Gourmets will love it, and so will those who appreciate interior design.

How to get there *(Map 23): 54km south of Périgueux via N 89 to Niversac. D 710 to Le Bugue and D 81.*

Château de Vieux–Mareuil ★★★

Vieux-Mareuil
24340 Mareuil (Dordogne)
Tel. (0)5★ 53.60.77.15 – Fax (0)5★ 53.56.49.33 – Mme Lefranc

Rooms 14 with telephone, bath, WC, cable TV and minibar. **Price** 500-1000F (2-3 pers.). **Meals** Breakfast 60F, served 8:00-10:00; half board 500-700F (per pers., 3 days min.). **Restaurant** Service 12:00-14:30, 19:00-21:30; menus 130-300F, also à la carte. **Credit cards** Visa, Eurocard, MasterCard and Amex. **Pets** Dogs not allowed. **Facilities** Swimming pool, parking. **Nearby** Brantôme Abbey, château de Bourdeilles et Puyguilhem, St-Jean-de-Côle, Jumilhac-le-Grand – 18-hole golf course in Montbron. **Open** Apr 1 – Oct 31.

Perched on a little hill in 50 acres of woods and fields, this old château has been tastefully converted into a very comfortable hotel. In the main part of the building there are two attractive dining rooms, a small living room with a lovely fireplace, and in the tower of the château three beautiful bedrooms furnished in antique style. The other bedrooms, more modern but also very pleasing, are in a wing overlooking the park. For sunny days there is a swimming pool. The delicious cooking varies according to the season, and the very good *demi-pension* menu changes every day. The pleasant atmosphere created by the owners, and the excellent service, make this an ideal place to stay in one of the loveliest regions of France.

How to get there *(Map 23): 42km northwest of Périgueux via D939 to Vieux-Mareuil.*

◇1996◇ Villa Térésa-Hôtel Semiramis ★★★

33120 Arcachon (Gironde)
4, allée de Rebsomen
Tel. (0)5★ 56.83.25.87 – Fax (0)5★ 57.52.22.41 – Mme Baurès

Rooms 20 with telephone, bath, WC and TV on request. **Price** Double 390F, 580-630F. **Meals** Breakfast 58F; half board 520F. **Restaurant** By reservation. Service 20:00-21:00; menu 180F. Specialties: regional cooking. **Credit cards** Visa, Eurocard and MasterCard. **Pets** Small dogs allowed (+35F) except in the restaurant. **Facilities** Swimming pool, parking. **Nearby** Bassin d'Arcachon: dune du Pyla; Cap Ferret; étangs de Hourtins-Carcans, Lacanau; Bordeaux; Le Bordelais. **Open** All year.

In 1860, the Pereire banking family had the idea of building a vast "urban park" on the dune belt of Arcachon. It was a fabulous ensemble of neo-Gothic, Moorish, colonial, Swiss and other villas which were frequented by the aristocracy, the *haute bourgeoisie* and the medical world. Saved from a seemingly inevitable ruin and classed as a historic monument, Thérésa has been brilliantly restored. In the lobby, wood paneling runs around vast decorative compositions in earthenware tiles, continuing up the stairway and onto a gallery upstairs. The comfortable bedrooms are located in the Villa and a small pavilion near the swimming pool. Those in the Villa are soberly decorated in tones of pearl-grey and pink. (The room in a small turret is surrounded by windows in arcades and enjoys an immense terrrace). The pavilion bedrooms have prettier fabrics and beautiful carpets. There is a pleasant salon decorated with squat armchairs. The dining room is bright and elegant, and each evening on reservation a set menu is served, based on fresh market produce. Elegantly enhanced by pretty dishes and embroidered tablecloths, the breakfasts are outstanding and original.

How to get there *(Map 22): 60 km southwest of Bordeaux. In the winter city.*

Hauterive Hôtel Saint-James ★★★★

3, place Camille-Hostein
33270 Bouliac (Gironde)
Tel. (0)5★ 57.97.06.00 - Fax (0)5★ 56.20.92.58 - M. Amat

Rooms 17 (10 with air-conditioning) with telephone, bath, WC, TV and minibar. **Price** Single 600-800F, double 650-850F, suite 1150-1350F. **Meals** Breakfast 75F, served from 7:00. **Restaurant** Service 12:00-14:00, 20:00-22:00; menus 250F, also à la carte. Specialties: Fondant d'aubergine au cumin, pigeon aux épices et sa pastilla, salade d'huîtres au caviar et sa crépinette. **Credit cards** All major. **Pets** Dogs not allowed. **Facilities** Swimming pool, tennis, sauna, health center, parking. **Nearby** Museum of Contemporary Art, Museum of Fine Art, Port-de-la-Lune Theatre, Cité Mondiale du Vin (25, quai des Chartons) in Bordeaux; Le Bordelais (renowned world-wide for its wines) – 18-hole Cameyrac golf course, 18-hole Bordelais golf course. **Open** All year.

To make an exception and include this ultra-modern place means that it must be out of the ordinary. And so it is, owing to the immense talents of two people: the owner and chef, Jean-Marie Amat, and the architect Jean Nouvel. The result of their combined efforts is amazing. Occupying three buildings, all the bedrooms have picture windows with extensive views over vineyards and the plain of Bordeaux. The decor is in tones of white and cream, broken by brightly-colored carpets or the flash of steel grey. This high-tech approach combines with bunches of flowers, sculpture and books to create the intimacy of a private house: what could have been cold, is warm instead. There is no need to describe the famous cuisine of Jean-Marie Amat. His celebrated restaurant and an excellent bistro adjoin the hotel.

How to get there (Map 22): 5km east of Bordeaux. On "Rocade-road," Bouliac exit (no. 23).

Château du Foulon

33480 Castelnau-de-Médoc (Gironde)
Tel. (0)5★ 56.58.20.18 – Fax (0)5★ 56.58.23.43
M. and Mme de Baritault du Carpia

Rooms 5 with bath and WC. **Price** Double 450F, suite 500-600F. **Meals** Breakfast incl. No restaurant. **Credit cards** Not accepted. **Pets** Dogs not allowed. **Facilities** Parking. **Nearby** Médoc peninsula on the left bank of the Garonne, then the Gironde (day trip, 150km), Mouton-Rothschild Museum in Pauillac – 18-hole Bordelais golf course, 18-hole Bordeaux-le-Lac golf course. **Open** All year.

The very elegant Château du Foulon stands at the end of a long avenue of trees which leads into a wood and then an immense park where you will discover magnificent peacocks and snow-white swans. M. and Mme de Baritault, who will greet you with great hospitality, have tastefully decorated each bedroom with beautiful antique furniture and great comfort. There are also two charming apartments, which are ideal for a long stay. Breakfasts are served at a large table in the magnificent dining room, a model of elegance and refinement. For dinner or for discovering the region, your hosts will give you a wealth of good advice.

How to get there *(Map 22): 28km northwest of Bordeaux via D1 to Le Verdoux, then go south to Foulon.*

Hostellerie du Vieux Raquine ★★★

Lugon
33240 Saint-André-de-Cubzac (Gironde)
Tel. (0)5★ 57.84.42.77 - Fax (0)5★ 57.84.83.77 - Mme de Raquine

Rooms 10 with telephone, bath or shower and WC (5 with TV). **Price** Single 420-450F, double 450-600F, suite 650F. **Meals** Breakfast 50F, served 8:00-10:00. No restaurant. **Credit cards** Visa, Eurocard and MasterCard. **Pets** Dogs not allowed. **Facilities** Parking. **Nearby** Church of Saint-André-de-Cubzac, château de Bouilh, Bourg, Saint-Emilion – 18-hole Bordeaux golf course. **Open** All year.

The ground floor of this hotel covers the whole top of a hill. Completely renovated, it is furnished in an old-fashioned style. The bedrooms are impeccably kept and all are at ground level. There are two reception rooms including the one used as the dining room; it has windows all along one side opening onto a large terrace with an outstanding view of the vineyards of Fronsac, bordered by the Dordogne in the distance. Mme Raquine makes the hotel feel like a family house. Tranquillity and fresh air are guaranteed. For fine dining, try a restaurant near the hotel or *Au Sarment* in Saint-Gervais.

How to get there *(Map 22): 23km northeast of Bordeaux; A10 St-André-de-Cubzac exit, D670.*

Château Lardier ★★

33350 Ruch - Castillon-la-bataille (Gironde)
Tel. (0)5★ 57.40.54.11 - Fax (0)5★ 57.40.70.38
M. and Mme Bauzin

Rooms 9 with telephone, bath or shower and WC (2 with TV). **Price** Double 230-340F. **Meals** Half board 270-330F, full board 340-440F (per pers., 3 days min.). **Restaurant** Service 12:00-13:30, 19:30-21:30; menus 90-240F, also à la carte. Specialties: Croquant de Saint-Jacques, terrine de foie gras, confit de canard, saladine d'aiguillettes de canard avec maïs à l'aigre-doux. **Credit cards** Visa, Eurocard and MasterCard. **Pets** Dogs allowed. **Facilities** Mountain bikes rentals - Parking. **Nearby** Libourne and the Libournais (Pomerol, Château Pétrus, St Emilion), Blasimon, Duras. **Open** Mar – end Nov (closed Sunday evening and Monday except July, Aug and Sept).

This charming country hotel on a little hill overlooking vineyards is very peaceful and you will receive a warm welcome from the young owners, who have furnished it very comfortably and in discreet good taste. The bedrooms vary in size; they are light and airy and have pleasant turn-of-the-century furniture. Ask for the *Green* room as your first choice. The cooking is good traditional fare, with some well meals are prepared specialties, and served in a dining room where a log fire burns in winter. In summer the tables are placed outside on the terrace in the shade of a cedar, facing the view. The hotel is well kept and for guests' amusement there is a billiard table upstairs. This is a good family place from which to visit the vineyards or explore the nearby Romanesque abbeys.

How to get there *(Map 22): 9km south of Castillon-la-Bataille via D15 and D17 towards Sauveterre, then D232 (2km from the town).*

La Closerie des Vignes ★★

Village des Arnauds
33710 Saint-Ciers-de-Canesse (Gironde)
Tel. (0)5★ 57.64.81.90 – Fax (0)5★ 57.64.94.44 – Mme Gladys Robert

Rooms 9 with telephone, bath, WC and TV. **Price** Double 360F. **Meals** Breakfast 35F, served 8:00-10:00; half board 325F (per pers., 3 days min.). **Restaurant** Service 12:00-13:30, 19:30-21:00 (closed Sunday evening and Tuesday in low season); menus 120-170F, also à la carte. Specialties: Gambas flambées au whisky, lamproie bordelaise, magret confit, foie gras. **Credit cards** Visa, Eurocard and MasterCard. **Pets** Dogs allowed. **Facilities** Swimming pool, parking. **Nearby** Citadel in Blaye, Bourg, cave of Pair-non-Pair near Prignac, Château de Bouilh, Church of St-André-de-Cubzac. **Open** Mar 1 – Jan 31

The Closerie des Vignes is not an old building but this small auberge is truly delightful and the ambience so welcoming and friendly that it cries out to be included in this guide. Lying amid vineyards, it is very comfortable and admirably well cared for. Its decor includes modern furniture, soft pastel colors, pretty floral fabrics and comfortable sofas and chairs. The dining room opens onto the vineyards and there is a pleasant swimming pool for summer visitors.

How to get there *(Map 22): 8km southeast of Blaye via D669 to Villeneuve, then D250.*

Le Couvent des Herbes ★★★★

40320 Eugénie-les-Bains (Landes)
Tel. (0)5★ 58.05.06.07 - Fax (0)5★ 58.51.10.10
M. and Mme Guerard - M. Hardy - M. Leclercq

Rooms 8 with telephone, bath, WC, TV and minibar. **Price** Double 1000-1700F, suite 1450-2050F. **Meals** Breakfast 110F, served 7:30-10:15. **Restaurant** "Les Prés d'Eugénie". Service 13:00-14:30, 19:00-22:30 (closed Wednesday and Thursday lunchtime); menus 390-690F, also à la carte. **Credit cards** All major. **Pets** Dogs allowed (+150F). **Facilities** Swimming pool, tennis, sauna, health center, parking. **Nearby** Aire-sur-Adour, Mont-de-Marsan, Samadet, Saint-Sever — 18-hole golf course in Mont-de-Marsan. **Open** Feb 15 – Dec 31.

This village in the heart of Gascony which was made famous in the 19th-century by Empress Eugénie, who came here "to take the waters." Le Couvent aux Herbes is a former 18th-century convent and girls' boarding school lying on the edge of a lovely park lush with magnolias, palms and banana trees. It has been exquisitely restored by Christine Guérard of *Les Prés d'Eugénie* in the village, which is famous for the cuisine of her husband, Michel, as well as for her own gracious hospitality and decorative talents. Mme Guérard has decorated the Couvent aux Herbes with soft, refined, harmonious touches throughout the eight exquisite bedrooms/salons. They are so beautiful we wanted to try them all: *Le Temps des Cerises* for its delicious scent of old roses; *Belle Nonnette* for its magnificent oak beams; or, *Jardin Secret*, which opens onto the luscious herb garden for which Le Couvent aux Herbes is named. If a week's slimming and exercising is part of your vacation plan, this is the place to come.

How to get there *(Map 29): 25km south of Mont-de-Marsan via D124 towards Pau. Pau Airport 45km away, Bordeaux 150km.*

La Maison Rose ★★

40320 Eugénie-les-bains (Landes)
Tel. (0)5★ 58.05.05.05 - Fax (0)5★ 58.51.10.10
M. and Mme Guérard - M. Hardy and M. Leclercq

Rooms 32 and 5 suites, with telephone, bath, WC and TV. **Price** Single 400-500F, double 480-580F, suite with kitchen 550-850F. **Meals** Breakfast 70F (Buffet), served 8:00-9:30; full board 620-850F (per pers., 3 days min.). **Restaurant** "Cuisine minceur" Service 13:00 and 20:00; menu 185F. "Ferme aux Grives" meals 170F. **Credit cards** All major. **Pets** Dogs allowed (+60F). **Facilities** Swimming pool, tennis, sauna, health center, parking. **Nearby** Aire-sur-Adour cathedral and organs, Mont-de-Marsan museums and keep, Samadet pottery museum, Saint-Sever Dominican monastery. **Open** Feb 14 – Dec 4, Dec 23 – Jan 3.

Michel and Christine Guérard have always been successful at combining their respective arts. There is Michel's gastronomic art, of course, which has made his Prés d'Eugénie into one of the greatest restaurants in France. And Christine's art of gracious hospitality has made the couple's three houses in Eugénie into models of charm. While Les Prés has a colonial touch and Le Couvent des Herbes has become one of their prettiest hotels, La Maison Rose is decorated in a more country manner. We especially like this one for its *"Feather Weight, Feather Price"* menu, with five daily thermal treatments and the possibility of following a slimming regime, for a reasonable full room-and-board price. Throughout your stay, you can enjoy the master's famous *Cuisine Minceur*, or a rustic festive meal at *La Ferme aux Grives*, the couple's third auberge. Be prepared for a week-long dream in a decor of charm.

How to get there (Map 29): 25km south of Mont-de-Marsan via D124 towards Pau. Pau Airport 45km away, Bordeaux 150km.

La Ferme aux Grives ★★★

40320 Eugénie-les-Bains (Landes)
Tel. (0)5★ 58.51.19.08 - Fax (0)5★ 58.51.10.10
M. and Mme Guerard - M. Hardy - M. Leclercq

Rooms 4 with telephone, bath, WC, TV and minibar. **Price** Double 550-600F, suite 750F. **Meals** Breakfast in lounge 70F, served 8:30-10:00. **Restaurant** Service 12:00-14:00, 20:00-22:30 (closed Mon. evening, Tues. lunchtime except July 12 – Sep 10); menus 170F. **Credit cards** Visa, Eurocard and MasterCard. **Pets** Dogs allowed (+60F). **Facilities** Swimming pool, tennis, sauna, health center, parking. **Nearby** Aire-sur-Adour, Mont-de-Marsan, Samadet, Saint-Sever. **Open** Fev 10 – Jan 5.

La Ferme aux Grives is yet another of our newly selected hotels in the small village of Eugénie-les-Bains. We have included this rustic auberge because it offers real quality and country charm at affordable prices. This old farmhouse has been entirely restored in the finest regional tradition: its walls of large rocks from the Adour River, its big stone fireplaces and terra cotta floors have all been charmingly renewed. There are two dining rooms: the Café du Village, where you can sample the excellent wines of the region and enjoy the chef's special; and the large auberge dining room where a beautiful menu highlights authentic family recipes of this gastronomic region. Here, plump, farm-raised Landes chickens turn roasting on the spit and hams are hung from the ceilings to cure, while fresh seasonal vegetables and magnificent country breads are displayed on a large butcher block in the center. There are several bedrooms in a small building, which have all the delightful rusticity and charm of the country.

How to get there *(Map 29): 25km south of Mont-de-Marsan towards Pau.*

Pain, Adour et Fantaisie ★★★

7, place des tilleuls
40270 Grenade-sur-Adour (Landes)
Tel. (0)5★ 58.45.18.80 – Fax (0)5★ 58.45.16.57 – M. Garret

Rooms 11 with air-conditioning, telephone, bath (9 with whirlpool), WC, TV, safe and minibar - wheelchair access. **Price** Double 380-700F, apart. 1200F. **Meals** Breakfast 75F; "Week-end de charme" 2500-3000F (per 2 pers.); "soirée fantaisie" 1300F (per 2 pers.). **Restaurant** Service 12:00-14:15, 19:45-22:30 (closed Sunday evening and Monday; Monday lunchtime in July and Aug); menu 175-300F, also à la carte. **Credit cards** All major. **Pets** Dogs allowed (+50F). **Facilities** Parking, garage (+50F). **Nearby** Landes de Gascogne Regional Park, Bastides tour– 9- and 18-hole golf courses in Mont-de-Marsan. **Open** All year.

On the village side, this superb, half-timbered 17th–century auberge looks out onto the arcades of the large public square. On the river side, a cool, shady terrace (a summer dining room), the large traditional balconies and certain bedrooms look out directly onto the river Adour. Here is a place of peace and pleasure. The bedrooms, with evocative names from nature, are vast and bright. Decorated with great talent, they all have charm and character; and the bathrooms are very well equipped. The original old wood paneling graces the dining room. Henceforth, guests will enjoy the cuisine prepared by Philippe Garret, who has taken over the hotel and who was long Didier Oudill's second in the kitchen; (the well-known M. Oudill is today at the Café de Paris in Biarritz). This is yet another very good auberge, and is reason enough to make the trip to the Landes staying here.

How to get there (Map 29): 15km south of Mont-de-Marsan via N 124.

La Vieille Auberge ★★★

Port-de-Lanne
40300 Peyrehorade (Landes)
Tel. (0)5★ 58.89.16.29 - Fax (0)5★ 58.89.12.89 - M. and Mme Lataillade

Rooms 10 with telephone, bath or shower and WC (2 with TV). **Price** Single and double 230-450F, suite 500-600F. **Meals** Breakfast 40-50F, served 8:30-10:30; half board 320-450F (per pers.). **Restaurant** Service 12:00-13:30, 19:30-21:00; menus 120-235F, also à la carte. Specialties: Magret, mousseline de saumon, saumon frais, confits de canard et de porc à l'ail. **Credit cards** Not accepted. **Pets** Dogs allowed. **Facilities** Swimming pool, fishing, parking. **Nearby** Biarritz, Peyrehorade, abbey of Arthous, Sorde-l'abbaye, Romanesque church in Cagnotte, Bonnat and Basque museums in Bayonne – 18-hole Hossegor golf course. **Open** May 1 – Oct 21 (closed Monday).

Both M. Lataillade and his father were born in this old coaching inn whose rustic beams, walls and floors bear the imprint of time. The inviting reception rooms are disturbed only by the slow rhythm of an antique pendulum clock or occasional music from an old piano. The bedrooms, located in the former stables and barns, are charming and comfortable, and there is a lovely garden with a swimming pool. M. Lataillade has built up an interesting museum, which is in the old hay barn. It contains objects retracing the history of the port of Lanne and its seafarers, who were known as *Gabariers*. La Vieille Auberge is a friendly Gascon inn, where you will enjoy Mme Lataillade's homemade preserves at breakfast, and her excellent cuisine.

How to get there *(Map 29): 30km northwest of Bayonne via N117; on the church square.*

Auberge des Pins ★★

Route de la Piscine
40630 Sabres (Landes)
Tel. (0)5★ 58.07.50.47 – Fax (0)5★ 58.07.56.74 – M. and Mme Lesclauze

Rooms 24 with telephone, bath or shower and WC (21 with TV). **Price** Single and double 230-450F, suite 600F. **Meals** Breakfast 40-50F, served 7:30-10:00; half board 320-450F (per pers., 3 days min.). **Restaurant** Service 12:00-14:00, 19:30-21:00; menus 100-320F, also à la carte. Specialties: Foie gras poêlé pointe d'asperges, filets de rouget, langoustines aux cèpes, pigeon en croûte. **Credit cards** Visa, Eurocard, MasterCard and Amex. **Pets** Dogs not allowed. **Facilities** Parking. **Nearby** Church in Sabres, local history museum in Marquèze, Les Landes de Gascogne Regional park. **Open** All year (closed Sunday evening and Monday in low season).

You will be enchanted by this hotel amid the pines on the way out of the village of Sabres. Generations of good hotel keeping ensure high-quality service and a faultless welcome. The bedrooms in the main building have every comfort and an old-fashioned charm, but the bedrooms in the newer building, which blend very well with the old ones, are our favorites. They are large, light, airy and elegantly modern, with lovely fabrics, superb bathrooms and a small terrace. The dining room, with its antique furniture, copperware, ceramics and fireplace laden with a collection of rare old Armagnacs, is a place to linger in over the beautiful cooking of Michel Lesclauze, who uses the best local produce to make truly memorable meals,. We strongly recommend the Auberge des Pins.

How to get there (Map 29): 40km east of Mimizan via D44.

Le Square ★★★

5, place de la Craste
47220 Astaffort (Lot-and-Garonne)
Tel. (0)5★ 53.47.20.40 - Fax (0)5★ 53.47.10.38 - M. Cabrel

Rooms 8 with air-conditioning, telephone, bath, WC, TV and minibar - 1 wheelchair access room. **Price** Single 295F, double 350F. **Meals** Breakfast 32F, served 8:00-10:00. **Restaurant** Closed Sunday evening and Monday. Service 12:00-14:00, 19:30-22:00; menu 92F, also à la carte. Specialties: Regional cooking. **Credit cards** All major. **Pets** Dogs allowed. **Nearby** Agen, bastides of Villeneuve-sur-Lot and of Beauville, Prades, Auvillar, Nérac, market "fermier" Monday in Astaffort. **Open** All year (except 2-3 weeks in Jan; Sunday evening and Monday).

The pretty pink and blue façade of Le Square seems to beckon you to this brand-new village hotel which is surprisingly refined and comfortable. The ravishing bedrooms are decorated with tasteful combinations of colors and prints, while the bathrooms, in the same color schemes, are superb. There are two dining rooms where you are served the delicious cuisine of the Southwest, which is both traditional and inventive. One dining room opens onto a small terrace where you can have meals in summer; in the other, which is cool and informal, you are served on warmly colored enameled-lava tables. Guests enjoy the friendly atmosphere of Le Square, a charming hotel very near Agen.

How to get there *(Map 30): 16km south of Agen via RN 21. Via A62, number 7 Agen exit.*

A la Belle Gasconne

47170 Poudenas (Lot-et-Garonne)
Tel. (0)5★ 53.65.71.58 - Fax (0)5★ 53.65.87.39
M. and Mme Gracia

Rooms 7 with telephone, bath or shower and WC (3 with TV). **Price** Single 380F, double 530-670F, suite 630F. **Meals** Breakfast 55F; half board 570-750F (per pers.) **Restaurant** Service 12:00-14:15, 19:30-21:30; menus 185-290F, also à la carte. Specialties: Foie gras frais, civet de canard au vin vieux de Buzet. **Credit cards** All major. **Pets** Dogs allowed. **Facilities** Swimming pool. **Nearby** Beauville, Auvillar (pottery museum), Nérac – 18-hole golf courses in Albret and Barbaste. **Open** Mar 1 – Dec 31 (closed Sunday evening and Monday in low season).

Who hasn't dreamed of spending a few romantic days in an old mill lulled by the sound of water trickling beneath the window? Lying at the foot of a stunningly beautiful medieval village, A la Belle Gasconne offers comfortable, beautifully appointed bedrooms whose colors are tastefully coordinated with the elm furniture; the bathrooms are decorated with Salernes tiles and even the dressing gowns are changed daily. The dining room still has the original beams, stones and old machinery of the original mill. Further atmosphere is lent by a log fire, a large bay window overlooking the water, and elegant table linens. The esthetic pleasures are enhanced by those of the table, for the cuisine is one of the finest in France, and each dish is a veritable enchantment. Mme Gracia is the chef, oversees the dining room and her kindness adds a lovely touch to the meal. In good weather, you can relax on the leafy island, enjoy the swimming pool and have breakfast by the waterside. A la Belle Gasconne is truly marvelous.

How to get there (Map 30): 47km southwest of Agen via D656 towards Nérac.

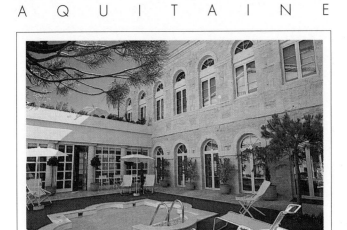

Les Loges de l'Aubergade ★★★★

47270 Puymirol (Lot-et-Garonne)
5, place de la Craste
Tel. (0)5★ 53.95.31.46 – Fax (0)5★ 53.95.33.80 – M. Trama

Rooms 11 with air-conditioning, telephone, bath, WC, TV, safe and minibar - 1 for disabled persons. **Price** Double 750-1410F. **Meals** Breakfast 90F, served 8:00-10:00; half board 2000F (2 pers., 3 days min.). **Restaurant** Service 12:00-13:30, 19:30-21:30 (closed Sunday evening and Monday); menus 180-580F, also à la carte. Specialties: Papillottes de pommes-de-terre à la truffe, hamburger de foie gras chaud aux cèpes, double corona trama et sa feuille de tabac au poivre. **Credit cards** All major. **Pets** Dogs allowed (+100F). **Facilities** Swimming pool, jacuzzi, mountain bikes - Parking (70F). **Nearby** Agen, Villeneuve-sur-Lot, Beauville; Prades, Auvillar (pottery museum), Nérac – 9-hole Saint-Ferréol golf courses. **Open** Mid Mar – mid Feb (closed Sunday evening and Monday in low season).

First and foremost here, we are in the restaurant of the great chef Michel Trama, whose outstanding cuisine is given top ratings throughout France. His taste for beautiful things inspired him, with the help of Mme Trama, to decorate eleven spacious, light bedrooms in an old house which belonged to the Counts of Toulouse in the 13th-century. All enjoy the most elegant modern conveniences and bathrooms where the slightest detail is provided for relaxation and pleasure. The rooms are arranged around a patio, the center of which is occupied by a large outdoor jacuzzi. In the heart of the fortified village of Puymirol, this is a welcoming place, as renowned for its rooms as for its cuisine.

How to get there *(Map 30): 20km east of Agen. Via A62 exit Valence-d'Agen, towards Golfech le Magistère, turn right, follow signs.*

Chez Chilo ★★

64130 Barcus (Pyrénées–Atlantiques)
Tel. (0)5★ 59.28.90.79 – Fax (0)5★ 59.28.93.10
M. and Mme Chilo

Rooms 14, 10 with telephone, bath or shower, 10 with WC and 9 with TV. **Price** Single 165-350F, double 185-450F. **Meals** Breakfast 35F; half board 290-670F, full board 495-830F (2 pers., 3 days min.). **Restaurant** Service 12:00-14:00, 19:30-22:00 (closed Sunday and Monday in low season); menus 85-260F, also à la carte. Specialties: Galette tiède de daurade aux piments "Piquillos", carré d'agneau de lait "Axuria" aux raviolis de fromage de brebis, pêche blanche farcie à la glace pistache au sabayon de Jurançon mœlleux. **Credit cards** All major. **Pets** Dogs allowed. **Facilities** Swimming pool, parking. **Nearby** Châteaux of Moumour and Aven, Saint-Blaise-Hospital, Pau – Golf course in Artiguelouve. **Open** Feb 4 – Jan 14 (closed last week in Mar, Sunday evening and Monday in low season).

You have to have an adventurous spirit to turn off onto this tiny winding road in the heart of the green Béarn mountains. Yet it's only a few kilometers from the villages of Aramits and Lanne, immortalized in Alexandre Dumas's *The Three Musketeers*. You won't regret your detour. Awaiting you in this beautiful countryside is a restaurant offering sumptuous cuisine and a hotel worthy of the most discriminating tastes. This family auberge has recently been enlarged and redecorated with taste and originality by young Mme Chilo, whose husband is the chef. The most recent bedrooms are the most luxurious; those in the old part are simpler but still comfortable and have been newly carpeted. So there is a room for everyone's taste. And the welcome is extremely courteous.

How to get there *(Map 29): 16km west of Oloron-Sainte-Marie via D24; towards Mauléon-Licharre.*

Hôtel Laminak ★★★

Route de Saint-Pée
64210 Artonne (Pyrénées-Atlantiques)
Tel. (0)5★ 59.41.95.40 – Fax (0)5★ 59.41.87.65 – M. and Mme Cauderlier

Rooms 10 with telephone, 6 with bath, 4 with shower, WC, TV and minibar - Wheelchair access. **Price** Double 350-560F. **Meals** Breakfast 50F, served 8:00-11:00. No restaurant. Snacks available in evening on request. **Credit cards** Amex, Visa, Eurocard and MasterCard. **Pets** Dogs allowed. **Facilities** Parking. **Nearby** Biarritz, Anglet and the forest of Chiberta, Arcangues, Bidart, Saint-Jean-de-Luz – 18-hole golf courses in Arcangues and Bussussary. **Open** All year.

Perched on a hilltop on the edge of Biarritz between the Atlantic and the Pyrenees, this old 18th-century Basque farmhouse has just been entirely converted into a charming small hotel. Surrounded by hilly countryside, the Laminak is calm and peaceful. The bedrooms have been carefully decorated, combining the latest amenities with original touches which lend an individual character to each. Some are larger and have corner sitting areas, but all are in exquisite taste. You can enjoy a copious, elegant breakfast in the colonial-style winter garden, which also serves light snacks if you don't want to go out. There are many good restaurants nearby, including *L'Epicerie d'Ahetze* and *Les Frères Ibarboure* in Bidart, and *La Tantine de Burgos* in Biarritz.

How to get there *(Map 28): 4km south of Biarritz. On A 63 exit Biarritz-La Négresse, then D 255 towards of Arbonne.*

Le Château du Clair de Lune ★★★

48, avenue Alan-Seger
64200 Biarritz (Pyrénées-Atlantiques)
Tel. (0)5★ 59.41.53.20 - Fax (0)5★ 59.41.53.29 - Mme Beyrière

Rooms 16 with telephone, bath, WC, TV and minibar. **Price** Double 430-680F. **Meals** Breakfast 50F, served 8:00-11:00. No restaurant. **Credit cards** All major. **Pets** Dogs allowed (+35F). **Facilities** Parking. **Nearby** Rock of the Virgin, Museum of the Sea in Biarritz, Anglet and the Forest of Chiberta, Arcangues, Bidard — 18-hole Biarritz golf course, 18-hole Chiberta golf course in Anglet. **Open** All year.

This turn-of-the-century house above Biarritz is very peaceful and stands in a serene garden of roses, flower beds, trees and lawns. It is the sort of house which conjures up nostalgic memories of childhood. The bathrooms and bathtubs have the huge proportions of another era, and the floor tiles and basins are antique. The large lounge on the ground floor opens onto and merges with the garden: cheerful, airy and bright, it is furnished with yellow sofas and a grand piano. The dining room, where guests breakfast together around a large table, makes you wish that you could dine here as well. This lovely family house on the Basque coast, though a hotel, begins to feel as if it were your own. You should note however that the owners are often away and the lack of supervision during their absence is noticeable. For restaurants, we recommend *La Tantina de Burgos* and *Le Calejon* (Spanish specialties), *La Bodega* and *les Trois Salsas* (surfers' favorite), and *Chez Albert* (fish and shellfish).

How to get there *(Map 28): 4km south of the town center via the Pont de la Négresse and D255 (Arbonne route).*

Le Saint-Charles ★★

47, avenue Reine-Victoria
64200 Biarritz (Pyrénées-Atlantiques)
Tel. (0)5★ 59.24.10.54 - Fax (0)5★ 59.24.56.74 - A. Faget-Marc

Rooms 13, 9 with telephone, 3 with bath, 10 with shower, WC and cable TV. **Price** 250-420F. **Meals** Breakfast 35F, served 7:30-11:00; half board 480-560F, full board 610-700F (per 2 pers.). **Restaurant** For residents only. Service 12:30-13:00, 19:30-20:00; menu 90F. Specialties: Regional cooking. **Credit cards** Visa, Eurocard and MasterCard. **Pets** Dogs allowed. **Nearby** Biarritz, Anglet and the Forest of Chiberta, Arcangues, Bidart, Saint-Jean-de Luz – 18-hole Biarritz golf course, Le Phare; 18-hole Chiberta golf course in Anglet. **Open** Feb 16 – Nov 30.

Don't be misled: Behind the old-fashioned façade of this charming family *pension* is hidden a small hotel which is quite comfortable. The simply decorated bedrooms are all well equipped with newly redone baths or showers. The small lounge and the dining room have an atmosphere of the past. In the garden, where your breakfast is served in summer, there are lush geraniums, hydrangeas, plumbagos and pink oleander. The only drawback is the traffic in the street, which can be quite noisy in the summer. It's the price you pay when you're just a few steps from the center of town, the beach, and the Louison Bobet Thassalotherapy Center!

How to get there *(Map 28): Signs in the center of Biarritz.*

Hôtel Villa L'Arche ★★★

64210 Bidart (Pyrénées-Atlantiques)
Chemin Camboénéa
Tel. (0)5★ 59.51.65.95 - Fax (0)5★ 59.51.65.99 - Mme Salaignac

Rooms 8 with telephone, bath or shower, WC, TV and minibar – Wheelchair access. **Price** Double 450-750F. **Meals** Breakfast 50F, served to 12:00. No restaurant. **Credit cards** Visa, Eurocard and MasterCard. **Pets** Dogs allowed (+30F). **Facilities** Parking. **Nearby** Biarritz, Anglet and the Forest of Chiberta, Arcangues, Bidart, Saint-Jean-de-Luz – 18-hole Arcangues golf course, 18-hole Bussussary golf course. **Open** All year.

This small hotel alone is worth making long detours. For how is it possible to find a more enchanting location than this flower-covered cliff with a stairway leading directly to the beach? When Bernadette Salaignac transformed her house into a hotel, she might have been content with simply the location, but she also put an enormous amount of talent into decorating the comfortable bedrooms. A bay window opens onto each terrace where you can have breakfast (delicious) and, from six terraces, there is a view of the ocean. Those who prefer breakfast in the salon enjoy the same view with, in addition, classical music in the background. Here too, the decoration is very tasteful, with blue and white checkered sofas, chairs painted in pearl grey, old paintings, collector's objects, all slyly observed through the window by a pig and a saddle horse. This very homey atmosphere is echoed at the reception and you will certainly leave the Villa with a promise to return. There is no restaurant in the hotel, but there are good addresses nearby, including *La Tantina della Playa*, *Les Frères Ibarboure*, *La Ferme de l'Ostalapia* and *La Cucaracha*.

How to get there *(Map 28): 4km south of Biarritz. On A 63, exit Biarritz-La Négresse, then D 255 towards Arbonne.*

Lehen Tokia

64500 Ciboure (Pyrénées–Atlantiques)
Tel. (0)5★ 59.47.18.16 – (0)5★ Fax 59.47.38.04
M. Taboulet

Rooms 6 with telephone, bath or shower, WC and TV. **Price** Single and double 500-800F, suite 1200F. **Meals** Breakfast 50F, served 8:30-10:00. **Restaurant** Only for residents and by reservation. Menu. Specialties: Turbot, foie gras, paëlla. **Credit cards** Visa, Eurocard and MasterCard. **Pets** Dogs not allowed. **Facilities** Swimming pool, sauna, parking. **Nearby** Saint-Jean-Baptiste church in Saint-Jean-de-Luz, coast road, Ciboure, Bayonne, Biarritz – 18-hole Nivelle and Chantaco golf courses. **Open** All year.

Built in 1925, this splendid Basque villa has recently been classed as a Historic Monument, notably because of its remarkable stained glass. The original owner used to come here on vacation with his family. Today, two of his grandchildren have opened Lehen Tokia to guests. The interior has been refurbished, but the original splendid decoration is intact. There is a subtle combination of magnificent objects and Art Déco furniture with antique regional furniture and family paintings (which explains why young children, are not admitted), and the rooms are of superb size. You enter the vestibule, then go up several steps to the salon, which in turn is surrounded by an elegant curving stairway leading to the bedrooms. Ravishingly beautiful and very comfortable, they have a marvelous view out over the Atlantic. In the foreground, you also see the garden which slopes down to the swimming pool and the charming small pavilion. In summer, several pretty dining tables are set out here for residents. You will enjoy good home cooking with Basque specialties at this very beautiful hotel.

How to get there *(Map 28): 2km from Saint-Jean-de-Luz. On A 63, exit Saint-Jean-de-Luz south.*

Artzaïn Etchea★★

Route d'Iraty
64220 Esterençuby (Pyrénées–Atlantiques)
Tel. (0)5★ 59.37.11.55 – Fax (0)5★ 59.37.20.16 – M. Arriaga

Rooms 22 with telephone, bath or shower and WC (8 with TV) - Wheelchair access to 2 rooms. **Price** Single 180F, double 220F, suite 290F. **Meals** Breakfast 36F; half board 200-240F, full board 226-272F (per pers., 2 days min.). **Restaurant** Service 12:30-14:00, 19:30-21:00; menus 94-190F (child 60F), also à la carte. Specialties: Foie de canard chaud aux raisins, saumon frais au champagne, salmis de palombe. **Credit cards** Not accepted. **Pets** Dogs allowed (+20F). **Facilities** Parking. **Nearby** Saint-Jean-Pied-de-Port (Pilgrim's Route), Saint-Etienne-de-Baïgorry, Saint-Jean-le-Vieux. **Open** Dec 20 – Nov 11 (closed Wednesday in low season).

A small road lined with low walls, trees and streams brings you to the crossroads where Artzaïn Etchea stands. As its Basque name indicates, this was once a shepherd's dwelling which has been converted into a simple but good country hotel. The bedrooms are comfortable but you will do well to choose one of the more recent ones, some of which have wonderful views of the valley. The pleasant dining room also has beautiful prospects. In summer tables are placed outside, and you can hear the sound of the stream which runs below. The owners are very welcoming.

How to get there (Map 28): 52km southeast of Bayonne via D918 to Saint-Jean-Pied-de Port, then D301.

Hôtel Arcé ★★★

64430 Saint-Etienne-de-Baïgorry (Pyrénées-Atlantiques)
Tel. (0)5★ 59.37.40.14 - Fax (0)5★ 59.37.40.27
M. Arcé

Rooms 22 with telephone, bath or shower, WC and TV. **Price** Single and, double 420-680F, suite 1030F. **Meals** Breakfast 47F, served 7:45-10:30; half board 400-540F, 730F in suites (per pers., 3 days min.). **Restaurant** Service 12:30-13:45, 19:30-20:30 (closed Monday lunchtime in low season); menus 110-260F, also à la carte. Specialties: Truite au bleu du vivier, tête de veau vinaigrette, carré d'agneau à la fleur de thym, foie chaud aux goldens. **Credit cards** Visa, Eurocard and MasterCard. **Pets** Dogs allowed. **Facilities** Heated swimming pool, tennis, parking. **Nearby** Aduldes valley, Saint-Jean-Pied-de-Port, dolmens, Cromlechs – 18-hole Souraïde golf course. **Open** Mid Mar – mid Nov.

This old inn, typical of the region and luxuriously restored, has been managed by the same family for the last five generations. The large picture windows are in keeping with the beautiful proportions of the dining room, and outside, long terraces are laid out at the water's edge. The bedrooms are extremely comfortable, newly decorated and overlook the river and the Pyrenees; a variety of reading matter is supplied. Bouquets of flowers are placed all over the hotel. The little annex is a pleasing addition, with its balconies overhanging the river: you can fish without even leaving your bedroom! You will enjoy good classic regional cooking and a very friendly welcome.

How to get there (Map 28): 50km southeast of Bayonne via D932 and D918 to Saint-Martin d'Arossa, then D948 to St-Etienne-de-Baïgorry.

La Devinière ★★★

5, rue Loquin
64500 Saint-Jean-de-Luz (Pyrénées-Atlantiques)
Tel. (0)5★ 59.26.05.51 - Fax (0)5★ 59.51.26.38 - M. Carrère

Rooms 8 with telephone, bath and WC. **Price** 500-650F. **Meals** Breakfast 50F, served all morning. No restaurant. **Credit cards** Visa, Eurocard and MasterCard. **Pets** Dogs allowed on request (+50F). **Nearby** Saint-Jean-Baptiste Church in Saint-Jean-de-Luz, Basque coast road, Ciboure, Bayonne, Biarritz – 18-hole Nivelle and Chantaco golf courses. **Open** All year.

There is no obvious reason why M. and Mme Carrère should have taken on and renovated this residential family hotel – he is a lawyer and she an antiques dealer – other than the pleasure of opening a charming place in the heart of Saint-Jean-de-Luz. Good taste and discernment are apparent everywhere. The eight bedrooms are ravishingly pretty and are furnished with beautiful antiques, as are the music room and library, which are open for the use of the guests. The pedestrian street and the garden ensure quiet nights even in the heart of the town. The welcome is warm. Breakfast is served in the tea room, which offers homemade pastries, teas and old-fashioned hot chocolate. For fine dining, try *Chez Pablo* (*piperades* and *chipirons*), *Kaïku* (*sole aux cèpes*) or *Tourasse* in town, or *La Ferme Penzia* in Ascain (open only in the summer) and *Chez Mattin* in Ciboure for its special *ttorro*.

How to get there (*Map 28*): *15km southwest of Biarritz via A63.*

Hôtel Arraya ★★★

Place du village
64310 Sare (Pyrénées–Atlantiques)
Tel. (0)5★ 59.54.20.46 - Fax (0)5★ 59.54.27.04 - M. Fagoaga

Rooms 20 with telephone, bath or shower, WC and TV. **Price** Single 395-400F, double 480-540F, suite 755-855F. **Meals** Breakfast 50F, served 8:00-10:00. **Restaurant** Service 12:00-14:00, 19:30-22:00; menus 120-198F, also à la carte. Specialties: Méli-mélo de gambas et ris d'agneau aux girolles, chipirons entiers poêlés et marmelade de crabe sur feuilles d'épinards, gratin de fraises et framboises au sabayon à l'orange. **Credit cards** Amex, Visa, Eurocard and MasterCard. **Pets** Dogs not allowed. **Facilities** Parking. **Nearby** Villa Arnaga in Cambo, Espelette, Ascain, Saint-Jean-de-Luz, Bonnat and Basque museums in Bayonne – 18-hole La Nivelle and Chantaco golf courses. **Open** May 1 – Nov 6.

Do not be put off by the Arraya's somber facade, which is typical of the region. This superb Basque hotel, set on the corner of two streets in the center of the village, is made up of three old houses; the garden, invisible from the street, effectively screens out the noise. On the ground floor, the lovely lounges and the comfortable dining room are charming with patinated rustic furniture and bright bowls of flowers. The bedrooms are all different but are furnished equally attractively: the prettiest is on the garden side. There is a boutique selling regional delicacies which you can eat on the spot or take away. The restaurant menu is long and varied, but regional dishes remain the specialties of the house.

How to get there *(Map 28): 28km south of Bayonne via A63, Saint-Jean-de-Luz exit, D918 to Ascain and D4 to Sare.*

Hôtel La Patoula ★★★

64480 Ustaritz (Pyrénées-Atlantiques)
Tel (0)5★ 59.93.00.56 – Fax (0)5★ 59.93.16.54
M. Guilhem

Rooms 9 with telephone, bath and WC. **Price** Double 350-470F. **Meals** Breakfast
60F, served 8:00-10:00; half board 350-410F, full board 450-510F (per pers.).
Restaurant Service 12:00-14:00, 20:00-22:00; menus 130-250F (child 90F), also à
la carte. Specialties: Alose grillée, saumon sauvage, gibier, agneau de lait. **Credit
cards** Visa, Eurocard and MasterCard. **Pets** Dogs allowed (+35F). **Facilities** Parking.
Nearby Villa Arnaga in Cambo, Biarritz, Bonnat and Basque museums in Bayonne
– 18-hole Biarritz golf course, 18-hole Chantaco golf course in Saint-Jean-de-Luz.
Open Feb 15 – Jan 5 (closed Sunday evening and Monday in low season).

This hotel is set back from the road in a park bordered by the
tranquil waters of the River Nive. This romantic view can be
enjoyed either from the dining room, from the pergola where
breakfast tables are laid in summer, or from the *chaise longues* in the
garden. In the winter, when there are fewer tourists, the dining
room with its open fire provides an intimate setting, and people
come for the cooking from all over the region. The bedrooms are
spacious, comfortable and very prettily decorated. We preferred
the two which overlook the river and the four which overlook
the garden. The modest number of rooms and Mme Guilhem's
friendliness give La Patoula a very pleasant atmosphere.

*How to get there (Map 28): 11km south of Bayonne via A10, Bayonne-
sud exit number 5, towards Cambo-les-Bains, then D982; in the center of
Ustaritz, opposite the church.*

Grand Hôtel Montespan Talleyrand ★★

03160 Bourbon L'Archambault (Allier)
2/4, place des Thermes
Tel. (0)4★ 70.67.00.24 - Fax (0)4★ 70.67.12.00 - M. Livertout

1996

Rooms 59 with telephone, bath or shower, WC and TV; elevator - 1 for disabled persons. **Price** Single 163-173F, double 280-330F. **Meals** Breakfast 38F, served 7:30-10:30; half board 295F, full board 325F (per pers., 3 days min.). **Restaurant** Service 12:30-13:30, 19:30-21:00; menus 105-220F, also à la carte. Specialties: Filet d'agneau en croûte, poêlée de langoustines aux pâtes fraîches, délice glacé au chocolat, crème de miel. **Credit cards** Amex, Visa, Eurocard and MasterCard. **Pets** Dogs allowed. **Facilities** Swimming pool, parking. **Nearby** Bourbon; Souvigny priory, châteaux of the Besbre Valley and of Lapalisse in Dompierre (half day's journey), triptych of the Maître de Moulins at Notre Dame cathedral in Moulins – 9-hole Avenelles golf course in Moulins. **Open** Beg Apr – end Oct.

This hotel derives its name from the illustrious guests who came here for the famous thermal baths. It is made up of four adjoining town houses with well appointed bedrooms. The *Sévigné* and *Talleyrand* rooms are vast, decorated with antique furniture and some have a balcony. The *Capucine* room, with a view over the gardens, is decorated with rattan furniture and elegant floral fabrics. The *Montespan* bedroom is reserved for guests taking the waters. On the ground floor, comfortable reception rooms and a large dining room (good family cooking) look out onto the greenery where in summer you can have breakfast. Another attractive feature of the Grand Hôtel is its immense terrace-garden built against the wall and surrounded by a medieval tower. It has a swimming pool, several flower-covered rock gardens, and tables and chaises-longues. This is a very pleasant hotel with extremely reasonable prices.

How to get there *(Map 18): 20km west of Moulins.*

Le Chalet ★★★

03000 Coulandon (Allier)
Tel. (0)4★ 70.44.50.08 – Fax (0)4★ 70.44.07.09
M. Hulot

Rooms 28 with telephone, bath or shower, WC and TV. **Price** Single 290-340F, double 360-460F. **Meals** Breakfast 45F, served 7:00-11:00; half board 430-380F, full board 440-485F (per pers., 3 days min.). **Restaurant** Service 12:30-13:30, 19:30-21:00; menus 110-240F, also à la carte. Specialties: Fresh local produce. **Credit cards** All major. **Pets** Dogs allowed. **Facilities** Lake, fishing, swimming pool, parking. **Nearby** Souvigny priory, châteaux of the Besbre Valley and of Lapalisse in Dompierre (half a day's journey), triptych of the Maître de Moulins at Notre Dame cathedral in Moulins – 9-hole Avenelles golf course in Moulins. **Open** Feb 1 – Dec 15.

This turn-of-the-century hotel is set in the hilly Bourbonnais countryside. The bedrooms are located in the main house and the outbuildings: numbers 8, 3 and 4, which still have the charm of the past, are beautifully spacious and they have a pretty balcony. Numbers 16, 17 and 19, which have been renovated, are comfortable and well-decorated. Avoid number 1, which is too close to the parking lot. The other rooms have varying amenities but they are all pleasant, with prettily coordinated wallpapers and fabrics. The restaurant is in a building somewhat too new for our taste. In summer, tables are set out on the terrace, and you can dine with a beautiful view past the swimming pool below to a landscape of fields and trees all around. The staff is very courteous, but an additional person would perhaps improve the service. This is a lovely country setting just several minutes from Moulins.

How to get there (Map 18): 6km west of Moulins via D945.

Château de Boussac

Target
03140 Chantelle (Allier)
Tel. (0)4★ 70.40.63.20 – Fax (0)4★ 70.40.60.03 – M. and Mme de Longueil

Rooms 5 with bath and WC. **Price** Single and double 600-800F, suite 950-1100F.
Meals Breakfast 55F, served 8:00-10:00; half board 1100F (per pers., 5 days min.).
Restaurant Set meal in the evening only and on reservation; menu 260-320F incl.
wine and alcohol. **Credit cards** Amex, Visa, Eurocard and MasterCard. **Pets** Dogs
allowed (fee). **Facilities** Parking. **Nearby** Church of Sainte-Croix and museum of the
Vine in Saint-Pourçain-sur-Sioule, priory in Souvigny, triptych of the Maître de
Moulins at Notre Dame cathedral in Moulins – 18-hole golf course in Montluçon.
Open Apr 1 – Nov 15.

The many faces of this beautiful château blend medieval austerity
with the grace of the 18th-century. The owners receive you
like friends and spontaneously include you in their aristocratic
country life. Each very comfortable bedroom is superbly furnished
with antiques (often Louis XV or Louis XVI), family mementos,
and beautiful fabrics. The lounges have been charmingly restored.
Finally, the large dining room table sets the scene for festive dinner
parties which are very popular with sportsmen in the hunting
season. The elegant silverware, the conversation, and the cuisine
all contribute towards making each evening a lovely and
memorable event.

How to get there *(Map 25): 40km south of Moulins via A71, number 11*
Montmarault exit, then D42 to Boussac (between Chantelle and
Montmarault).

Le Tronçais ★★

Avenue Nicolas-Rambourg
Tronçais - 03360 Saint-Bonnet-Tronçais (Allier)
Tel. (0)4★ 70.06.11.95 - Fax (0)4★ 70.06.16.15 - M. and Mme Bajard

Rooms 12 with telephone, bath or shower, WC and TV. **Price** Single 204F, double 260-344F. **Meals** Breakfast 35F, served 8:00-10:30; half board 244-286F, full board 297-340F (per pers., 3 days min.). **Restaurant** Service 12:00-13:30, 19:30-21:00; menus 98-180F, also à la carte. Specialties: Terrine d'anguille aux mûres, sandre au gratin, côte de veau aux cèpes, game. **Credit cards** Visa, Eurocard and Mastercard. **Pets** Dogs allowed only in bedrooms. **Facilities** Tennis, parking. **Nearby** Oak forest of Tronçais, château d'Ainay-le-Vieil, Château Meillant – 18-hole Nassigny golf course. **Open** Mar 15 – Dec 15 (closed Sunday evening and Monday in low season).

Once the private house of a forge owner, the Tronçais is located at the edge of the forest in a garden bordered by a lake. From the entrance steps to the bedrooms, the hotel is calm, comfortable and civilized. The bedrooms are very tastefully arranged, comfortable, and many are very large. Several are also located in a small annex but we find them small, less pleasant and we especially advise you to avoid number 8. The graveled garden in front of the two buildings serves as the terrace and bar in the summer. The cuisine is excellent, light and appetizing, and meals are served in a charming dining room. The hotel grounds stretch all the way to the banks of the lake, in which you can fish.

How to get there *(Map 17): 45km north of Montluçon. On A71 Forêt-de-Tronçais exit, then N144 and D978A to Tronçais.*

Auberge de Concasty ★★★

15600 Boisset (Cantal)
Tel. (0)4★ 71.62.21.16 – (0)4★ Fax 71.62.22.22
Mme Causse

Rooms 16 with telephone, bath, WC and TV. **Price** Single 270-305F, double 315-490F. **Meals** Breakfast 45F, brunch 80F, served 9:00-11:30; half board 340-450F (per pers., 2 days min.). **Restaurant** By reservation; closed Wednesday except for residents. Service 12:30-13:30, 20:00-21:30; menus 140-200F. Specialties: Fresh local produce. **Credit cards** All major. **Pets** Dogs allowed (+35F). **Facilities** Heated swimming pool, whirlpool, Turktish bath, parking. **Nearby** Audillac, valleys of the Lot and the Truyère, Champollion museum in Figeac. **Open** All year (on reservation).

The Auberge de Concasty is an old family mansion surrounded by its farm and fields. It has been completely restored and equipped with a swimming pool and whirlpool. The inn nonetheleess looks like a traditional family vacation house. It is very comfortable, the rooms have again been improved, and the reception rooms are pleasantly decorated. At Concasty, Mme Causse will delight you with fine seasonal cuisine featuring local specialties, (*cèpe* mushrooms, *foie gras*). You can also enjoy a good Auvergnat breakfast in this lovely vacation spot.

How to get there *(Map 24): 25km southwest of Aurillac. In Aurillac via Cahors/Montauban by N122 for 20km; then in Manhes, turn left on D64 and follow signs.*

Château de Lavendès ★★★

15350 Champagnac (Cantal)
Tel. (0)4★ 71.69.62.79 – Fax (0)4★ 71.69.65.33
M. and Mme Gimmig

Rooms 8 with telephone, bath or shower, WC and TV. **Price** Double 420-560F.
Meals Breakfast 52F, served until 10:00; half board 415-515F (per pers, 3 days min.).
Restaurant Service 12:30-13:45, 19:30-21:00; menus 165-260F, also à la carte.
Specialties: Filet de bœuf gergoire, volailles fermières, fromages au lait cru, glacé à
la chicorée, tarte aux pruneaux, crème brulée, fondant au miel de pays et sa glace.
Credit cards Visa, Eurocard and MasterCard. **Pets** Dogs not allowed. **Facilities**
Swimming pool, sauna (100F), parking. **Nearby** Bort-les-Orgues, Bort dam and château
de Val, gorges of the Dordogne from Bort to the Aigle dam (2 hours) – 9-hole Mont-
Dore golf course. **Open** Mar 1 – Nov 15 (closed Monday in low season).

This 17th–century manor house is set in the middle of a 2 1/2-
acre park. In the lobby, which has an imposing fireplace,
afternoon tea is also served. In the two dining rooms, one furnished
in Louis XV style and the other in Louis XIII, you will dine on
the *specialités de la maison* and modernized regional cuisine prepared
by Mme Gimmig, a professional chef. A splendid staircase (on
which you will find many curiosities including old wooden
mechanisms and children's toys) leads to the comfortably furnished
bedrooms. The only sound you will hear is the tinkling of cow
bells in the surrounding meadows. (Salers beef is a prized regional
specialty).

*How to get there (Map 24): 78km north of Aurillac via D922 to Ydes via
Mauriac, then left on D12 or D112 to Champagnac; (the château is on D15).*

Auberge du Vieux Chêne ★★

34, route des Lacs
15270 Champs-sur-Tarentaine (Cantal)
Tel. (0)4★ 71.78.71.64 – Fax (0)4★ 71.78.70.88 – Mme Moins

Rooms 15 with telephone, bath or shower, WC and TV. **Price** Double 320-420F.
Meals Breakfast 45F, served 8:00-10:00; half board 280-300F, full board 320-380F
(per pers., 3 days min.). **Restaurant** Service 12:00-13:30, 19:00-20:30; menus 130-
230F, also à la carte. Specialties: Foie gras d'oie maison, ris de veau aux morilles,
escalope de saumon à l'oseille. **Credit cards** Visa, Eurocard and MasterCard.
Pets Dogs allowed. **Facilities** Parking. **Nearby** Bort-les-Orgues, Bort dam and
château de Val, gorges of the Dordogne from Bort to the Aigle dam (3 hours)– 9-hole
Mont-Dore golf course. **Open** Mar 15 – Nov 15 (closed Sunday evening and Monday
except July and Aug).

This old stone and timber farmhouse, which is set well away
from the road, has been charmingly restored and enlarged.
The bedrooms have been beautifully renovated with cheerful,
refined colors, coordinated fabrics and wallpapers and many
charming decorative details. At one end of the ground floor, there
is a pleasant bar, while the rest of the area is occupied by a salon
and a vast dining room whose end wall is one immense fireplace.
Outside, a garden-terrace is set for breakfast. The hospitality is
warm and the cuisine is excellent.

How to get there *(Map 24): 93km north of Aurillac via D922 to Bort-les-Orgues, then D979.*

Auberge du Pont de Lanau ★★

Lanau
15260 Chaudes-Aigues (Cantal)
Tel. (0)4★ 71.23.57.76 - Fax (0)4★ 71.23.53.84 - M. Cornut

Rooms 8 with telephone, bath, WC and TV. **Price** Single and double 270-350F.
Meals Breakfast 35F; half board 270-300F, full board 350-400F (per pers., 3 days
min.). **Restaurant** Service 12:30-14:00, 19:30-21:30; menus 95-300F, also à la
carte. **Credit cards** Visa, Eurocard and MasterCard. **Pets** Dogs allowed (+35F).
Facilities Parking. **Nearby** Saint-Flour, gorges of the Truyère. **Open** All year except
in Jan (closed Tuesday evening and Wednesday in low season).

Courtesy is the tradition in this old farmhouse–auberge built in
1855. In the past, clients were served meals on the left (today
the restaurant) and horses were stabled on the right (today the
lounge, breakfast room and bar). The beautifully decorated rustic
restaurant has stone walls and is dominated by an immense fireplace.
Guests once slept in bed recesses close to the fireplace to keep
warm, and you can still see traces of the original wooden partitions.
Today the inn is primarily a restaurant serving very good, refined
regional cooking. M. Cornut often prepares specialties which are
little known today, or delicious new versions of traditional regional
dishes. The eight bedrooms are pleasant, some decorated in floral
motifs while others are drenched in salmon pink. They have fabric-
covered walls and are well insulated with double windows. The
auberge is located beside a country road and is a lovely place to
stay.

How to get there *(Map 25): 20km south of Saint-Flour via D921.*

Hostellerie de la Maronne ★★★

Le Theil
15140 Saint-Martin-Valmeroux (Cantal)
Tel. (0)4★ 71.69.20.33 – Fax (0)4★ 71.69.28.22 – Mme Decock

Rooms 21 with telephone, bath, WC and minibar (6 with TV). **Price** Single and double 350-600F, suite 700F. **Meals** Breakfast 40-50F, served 8:30-10:00; half board 365-500F. **Restaurant** Service 19:30-21:00; menus 140-300F, also à la carte. Specialties: Escalope de sandre aux mousserons, foie gras chaud au caramel de porto, gâteau tiède aux marrons et chocolat amer. **Credit cards** Visa, Eurocard and MasterCard. **Pets** Dogs allowed. **Facilities** Swimming pool, tennis, parking. **Nearby** Medieval city of Salers, basilica of Notre-Dame-des-Miracles in Mauriac, Puy Mary. **Open** April 3 – Nov 5.

M. and Mme Decock have marvelously transformed this 19th-century Auvergnat house into a hotel. Everything has been provided for guests' rest and recreation. The living room, reading room and bar have been elegantly decorated with comfortable armchairs and some antique furniture. The modern, very comfortable bedrooms are done in pale colors and they have splendid views (except for rooms 6 and 7); the finest views are offered by the rooms with large terraces and balconies. (There is also an apartment which is ideal for families). The four rooms in the annex are quite far away and are used only when the hotel is full. The cuisine is increasingly renowned and the dining room is beautiful, with a lovely view over the countryside. Walking in the area is a pleasure here, and there are tennis courts and a swimming pool. Last but not least, the hospitality and service are charming.

How to get there *(Map 24): 33km north of Aurillac via D922 to Saint-Martin Valmeroux, then D37 towards Fontanges.*

Auberge des Montagnes ★★

15800 Pailherols (Cantal)
Tel. (0)4★ 71.47.57.01 - Fax (0)4★ 71.49.63.83
M. Combourieu

Rooms 26 with telephone, bath or shower, WC (7 with TV and minibar). **Price** Single 198F double 198-260F, suite 260F. **Meals** Breakfast incl., served 8:00-9:30; half board 230-260F (per pers., 2 days min.). **Restaurant** Service from 12:30, from 19:30; menus 78-118F, also à la carte. Specialties: Truite saumonée feuilletée, chou farci, truffade, noisettes sous la neige, croustine au praliné. **Credit cards** All major. **Pets** Dogs allowed. **Facilities** Swimming pool, courses in cross-country skiing and horse-drawn mountain carriages, parking. **Nearby** Medieval city of Salers, basilica of Notre-Dame-des-Miracles in Mauriac, Puy Mary. **Open** Dec 21 – Oct 14.

The Auberge is located in the center of this village which lies between the mountains of Les Puys and L'Aubrac. A countryside of holes and hollows, low stone walls, cropped grass and woods, the Pailherois plateau has a wild kind of beauty, seeming to belong to its Salers cows and a few houses with roofs of lauze, the regional volcanic stone. The hotel consists of several buildings fairly far apart. The main building includes the restaurant, a bar-lounge and bedrooms which we do not recommend. Across the street, you will find two swimming pools, one of which is heated and is installed in a barn adjacent to a game room. Finally, 200 meters farther on, the Clos des Gentiannes annex has just been built, offering vast, very comfortable bedrooms decorated in a modern, cheerful style. They offer unbeatable value for the money and all overlook a sublime landscape; some are ideal for families. M. and Mme Cambourieu are especially friendly and turn out regional cuisine whose reputation is known throughout the valleys. You will enjoy a family-style, informal atmosphere here.

How to get there *(Map 24): 21km east of Aurillac via Vic-sur-Cère.*

Auberge de la Tomette ★★
15220 Vitrac (Cantal)
Tel. (0)4★ 71.64.70.94 – Fax (0)4★ 71.64.77.11
M. and Mme Chausi

Rooms 21 with telephone, bath or shower, WC and TV. **Price** Single 230-260F, double 280-310F, suite 390-460F. **Meals** Breakfast 40F; half board 228-305F, full board 318-395F (per pers., 3 days min.). **Restaurant** Service 12:00-14:00, 19:00-20:30; menus 65-178F, also à la carte. Specialties: Truite paysanne aux noix, caille forestière, ris de veau crémaillère, tartes maison. **Credit cards** Amex, Visa, Eurocard and MasterCard. **Pets** Dogs allowed in bedrooms only. **Facilities** Swimming pool, sauna (45F). **Nearby** Conques, Salers, monts du Cantal, château d'Anjony, Vic-sur-Cère. **Open** Apr 1 – Dec 31.

Vitrac, surrounded by chestnut plantations, is a beauty spot in the south of the Cantal, and the Auberge de la Tomette is right in the heart of the village. Several bedrooms open onto a delightful little garden in the back, but the greater part of the hotel is a few steps away in a vast flowery park with a very beautiful view of the countryside. The bedrooms are comfortable, impeccably kept and decorated in a sober, modern style, brightened with pretty fabrics. Note the duplex, which is ideal for families. The atmosphere in the rustic dining room, with its exposed beams and wood paneling, is very friendly, and the cuisine is excellent. Mme Chausi will greet you charmingly and advise you on what to do and where to go in the region. This is a picturesque place to stay, where you become part of the village life.

How to get there *(Map 24): 25km south of Aurillac via N122 towards Figeac; at Saint-Mamet-La Salvetat take D66.*

Hôtel de l'Echo et de l'Abbaye ★★

Place de L'Echo
43160 La Chaise-Dieu (Haute-Loire)
Tel. (0)4★ 71.00.00.45 - Fax (0)4★ 71.00.00.22 - Mme Chirouzé

Rooms 11 with telephone, bath or shower and 9 with TV. **Price** Single 250-300F, double 300-350F **Meals** Breakfast 42F, served 7:30-9:30; half board 300-330F (per pers., 3 days min.). **Restaurant** Service 12:00-14:00, 19:30-21:00; menus 90-250F, also à la carte. Specialties: Flan aux cèpes sauce forestière, mignon de porc à la crème de myrtilles, tournedos de saumon aux lentilles vertes du Puy, entrecôte à la fourme d'Ambert, tarte aux fruits des bois. **Credit cards** All major. **Pets** Dogs not allowed. **Nearby** Basilica of Notre-Dame du Puy, church of Saint-Laurent and Aiguille au Puy, Mont Mezenc, Mont Gerbier-de-Jonc, village of Arlempdes. **Open** Easter – Nov 1.

This auberge is part of the enclave formed by the splendid La Chaise Dieu Abbey, and is the ideal place for visiting the historic village. Its name refers to the "Room of Echoes" nearby, which is known for its strange acoustical phenomenon. The hotel is a very old house, beautifully maintained by Mme Chirouzé, who is always warm and welcoming. The small bedrooms are charming and comfortable, and some have a view of the cloister. There is always a contemporary painting exhibit on view in the restaurant dining room, which is decorated in Haute Epoque style. Often complimented in the guest book, the regional Auvergnate cuisine is excellent. Cocktails and refreshments can be served outside on the terrace, which is reserved exclusively for the hotel.

How to get there *(Map 25): 35km north of Le Puy-en-Velay.*

Le Pré Bossu ★★★

43150 Moudeyres (Haute-Loire)
Tel. (0)4★ 71.05.10.70 – Fax (0)4★ 71.05.10.21
M. Grootaert and Mme Moreels

Rooms 10 with telephone, bath or shower and WC. **Price** Double in half board 430-590F (per pers.). **Meals** Breakfast incl., served 8:00-10:00. **Restaurant** In low season closed lunchtime except Saturday and Sunday. Service 12:00-13:30, 19:30-21:00; menus 170-360F (child 65F), also à la carte. Specialties: Ecrevisses aux petits légumes, andouillette d'escargot au coulis de céleri. **Credit cards** All major. **Pets** Dogs allowed in bedrooms (+35F). **Facilities** Parking. **Nearby** Basilica of Notre-Dame-du-Puy in Puy-en-Velay, Gerbier-des-Joncs, Mézenc forest – 9-hole Chambon-sur-Lignon golf course in Romières. **Open** Palm Sunday – Nov 11.

Located in the lovely village of Moudeyres, this old thatched cottage built in local stone is named for the meadow which surrounds it. The atmosphere is cozy and welcoming. To one side there is a reception room with a large fireplace, TV and library. In the beautiful stone dining room with its smartly set tables, you will be served outstanding regional gourmet specialties, which are made with fresh produce from the kitchen garden. The bedrooms are very comfortable and attractively furnished, and the garden and terrace overlook the countryside. If you wish to go out for the day, picnic baskets can be prepared, and the welcome is very friendly.

How to get there *(Map 25): 25km east of Le Puy via D15 to Les Pandreaux, then D36 to Moudeyres via Laussonne.*

Hôtel Le Turenne ★★

19120 Beaulieu-sur-Dordogne (Corrèze)
1, boulevard Saint-Rodolphe-de-Turenne
Tel. (0)5★ 55.91.10.16 - Fax (0)5★ 55.91.22.42 - M. Cave

Rooms 15 with telephone, bath or shower and WC; elevator. **Price** Double 260-280F; half board 260F. **Meals** Breakfast 35F. **Restaurant** Service 12:15-13:30, 19:30-21:00 (closed Sunday evening and Monday in low season); menus 80F(lunch)-320F, also à la carte. Specialties: Croustillant de foie gras et cèpes sauce banuyls, lotte piquée à l'aïl et crème de fenouil, rôti d'agneau du lot, assiette aux noix. **Credit cards** All major. **Pets** Dogs allowed. **Facilities** Parking. **Nearby** Collonges, Turenne, church in Beaulieu-sur-Dordogne, Argentat – 18-hole Coiroux golf course in Aubazines. **Open** Mid Feb – mid Jan (closed Sunday evening and Monday in low season).

There are so many superb houses in Beaulieu because in the 13th century a powerful abbey was built here. This hotel occupies a part of its venerable walls, 100 meters from the banks of the Dordogne River. Inside, various vestiges are reminders of the ancient age of the building: many monumental fireplaces, a superb spiral staircase, parts of age-old doors...all confer special charm to the place. Pascal Cavé, the chef, respects the Quercy culinary traditions while lending them a lighter and more delicate touch. His cuisine is marvelous. In winter, there is always a fire crackling in the immense fireplace of the restaurant, while in summer the large ogival French doors open onto a leafy terrace with a few tables. The bedrooms are being renovated in pastel colors with classic furniture. Some look out on the medieval city, others onto the square and all are very quiet. Overall, the hotel is simple, family-style and the prices are very reasonable.

How to get there *(Map 24): 39km south of Tulle via D940.*

Relais de Saint-Jacques-de-Compostelle ★★

19500 Collonges-la-Rouge (Corrèze)
Tel. (0)5★ 55.25.41.02 - Fax (0)5★ 55.84.08.51
M. Guillaume

Rooms 24 (14 in the annex) with telephone, 10 with bath or shower and WC and 4 with TV. **Price** Double 170-300F. **Meals** Breakfast 38F. **Restaurant** Service 12:30-13:30, 19:30-21:30; menus 100-250F, also à la carte. Specialties: Feuilleté de Saint-Jacques, filet de bœuf fourré au foie gras, terrine de cèpes au coulis de jambon de pays, marquisette aux deux chocolats. **Credit cards** All major. **Pets** Dogs allowed. **Facilities** Parking. **Nearby** Collonges, Turenne, church in Beaulieu-sur-Dordogne, Argentat – 18-hole Coiroux golf course in Aubazines. **Open** Mid-Mar – mid-Jan.

Its fascinating medieval houses in red sandstone make Collonges-la-Rouge a very beautiful and much visited place. Located in the heart of the village, the hotel has just been very tastefully restored; the general effect is light and flowery. On the ground floor are two dining rooms, a small reception room furnished with amusing "toad" armchairs, and an intimate bar. The small bedrooms are all very attractive. Excellent cooking is served with a smile. In summer, tables are laid on three lovely shaded terraces. M. and Mme Guillaume's welcome even in this highly tourist-ridden town, is reason enough for a visit.

How to get there (Map 24): 45km south of Tulle via N89 to Brive, then towards Collonges-la-Rouge. The hotel is in the village.

Au Rendez–Vous des Pêcheurs ★★

Pont du Chambon
19320 Saint-Merd-de-Lapleau (Corrèze)
Tel. (0)5★ 55.27.88.39 – Fax (0)5★ 55.27.83.19 – Mme Fabry

Rooms 8 with telephone, bath or shower, WC and TV. **Price** Single and double 235F, 265F. **Meals** Breakfast 35F, served 8:00-9:30; half board 250F, full board 290F (per pers., 3 days min.). **Restaurant** Service 12:15-13:30, 19:45-21:00; menus 75-195F, also à la carte. Specialties: Sandre au beurre blanc, ris de veau aux cèpes, mousse de noix glacée. **Credit cards** Visa, Eurocard and MasterCard. **Pets** Dogs allowed. **Facilities** Parking. **Nearby** Merle, château of Sédières, viaduc des Rochers Noirs. **Open** Dec 20 – Nov 11 (closed Friday evening and Saturday evening Oct 1 – Mar 30).

Built on the banks of the Dordogne, this large house has a backdrop of wooded hills; it owes much of its appeal to its exceptional location. On the ground floor, a light, large and well-decorated dining room with flowered curtains and pretty tables has beautiful views across the river. At one side, a small lounge and bar give access to a lovely terrace overlooking the river. The bedrooms have been refurbished but, again, it is the view that makes them special; though they are comfortable, they would be improved with soundproofing. There is good fishing here, and you can try the local perch, pike and trout cooked by Elise. Pedalboats are for rent at the hotel, and you can also cruise on the Dordogne in a traditional *gabare*. This is a good hotel, and very moderately priced.

How to get there *(Map 24): 45km east of Tulle via D978 to Saint-Merd-de-Lapleau via Marcillac-la-Croisille, then D13 to Pont-du-Chambon.*

La Maison Anglaise

Saint-Robert – 19310 Ayen (Corrèze)
Tel. (0)5★ 55.25.19.58 – Fax (0)5★ 55.25.23.00
Mlle Aurore Clarke - M. Chouzenoux

Rooms 6 with shower and WC. **Price** Double 220-350F. **Meals** Breakfast 45-65F, served 8:00-10:00; half board 280-520F (per pers., 3 days min.). **Restaurant** Service 12:00-14:00, 19:30-21:30; menus 70-295F, also à la carte. Specialties: Feuilleté de turbot, noix de saint-jacques aux pommes, magret de canard au coulis de ceps, tournedos à la périgourdine. **Credit cards** Amex, Visa, Eurocard and MasterCard. **Pets** Dogs allowed. **Facilities** Swimming pool, parking. **Nearby** Château de Hautefort, abbey of Tourtoirac, Brive-la-Gaillarde, Périgueux. **Open** Mid Dec – mid Nov.

The Maison Anglaise was opened four years ago in this lovely little village perched on a green hill. The hotel, whose charm and quality have added much to the village, occupies a small, ancient house. It has a real country-style bar with wooden furnished a handsome dining room and, adjoining it, a comfortable lounge, beautifully furnised, with paintings and *objets d'art*. The fireplaces are huge and fires are always lit in winter. There are six bedrooms on the *premier étage*, some of them large. We liked their white walls, their curtains and thick quilts, all enhanced by the lovely pale wooden furniture, wide floorboards and pink-skirted tables. The bathrooms are simple and well kept. Some are partitioned off in the rooms but this has been done discreetly. In summer there is a grill by the swimming pool and tables are set on the terrace, where the view is superb.

How to get there *(Map 23): 30km northwest of Brive-la-Gaillarde towards Objat, then Ayen, to Saint-Robert.*

Auberge des Prés de la Vézère **

19240 Saint-Viance (Corrèze)
Tel. (0)5★ 55.85.00.50 - Fax (0)5★ 55.84.25.36
M. Parveaux

Rooms 11 with telephone, bath, WC and TV. **Price** Single and double 250-350F. **Meals** Breakfast 35F, served 7:30-10:00; half board 310-350F (per pers.). **Restaurant** Service 12:00-14:00, 19:30-21:00; menus 105-220F, also à la carte. Specialties: Saumon fumé maison, dorade à l'ail et au thym, civet de canard tradition. **Credit cards** Visa, Eurocard and MasterCard. **Pets** Dogs allowed. **Facilities** Parking. **Nearby** Abbey of Aubazines, Uzerches, Argentat, Collonges-la-Rouge, Pompadour stud farm, Beaulieu-sur-Dordogne – 18-hole Coiroux golf course in Aubazines. **Open** All year except in Jan.

Saint-Viance is a very well-preserved small town, with its old houses and the lovely bridge that spans the Vézère, a river very popular with fishermen. The hotel is at the entrance to the village beside a quiet road. There is a large dining room which extends onto a beautiful shaded terrace. On the *premier étage*, although the corridor is somewhat dark, you will be agreeably surprised by the bedrooms, which have lovely pale wallpapers and pretty curtains matching the bedcovers. The rooms are cheerful and well-kept and all have well-equipped bathrooms. This is a good place for a family holiday.

How to get there *(Map 23): 11km northwest of Brive-la-Gaillarde, towards Objat then Allassac.*

La Maison des Chanoines

19500 Turenne (Corrèze)
Route de l'église
Tel. (0)5★ 55.85.93.43 – M. and Mme Cheyroux

Rooms 3 with bath and WC. **Price** Double 300F and 370F. **Meals** Breakfast 35F, served 7:30-10:00; half board 330F. **Restaurant** Service 12:00-14:00, 19:30-21:00; menus 140-195F, also à la carte. Specialties: Escalope de foie gras de canard, escalope de saumon à l'étuvé de comcombres, médaillon de veau du limousin sauce quercycoise. **Credit cards** Visa, Eurocard and MasterCard. **Pets** Dogs allowed. **Nearby** Abbey of Aubazines, Uzerches, Argentat, Collonges-la-Rouge, Pompadour stud farm, Beaulieu-sur-Dordogne – 18-hole Coiroux golf course in Aubazines. **Open** Mar 1 – Nov 14 (closed Tuesday evening and Wednesday except July 1 – Sept 20).

Turenne is one of the most beautiful villages of France and this old house is a good illustration of the architectural richness of the town. La Maison des Chanoines is basically a small restaurant to which three bedrooms have been added. Totally renovated, the rooms are elegant and tastefully decorated with antiques. To the great pleasure of their dinner guests, M. and Mme Cheyrou have given quality priority over quantity. There is a reasonable number of dishes on the menu, a maximum of 16 diners in the beautiful vaulted dining room, and no more than 25 when meals are served outdoors beneath the honeysuckle trellis. Strictly fresh products, reliable gastronomic quality and very friendly service are guaranted. We will long remember the *foie gras* simply marinated with truffle and *girolle* vinegar.

How to get there *(Maps 23 and 24): 14km south of Brive-la-Gaillarde.*

Domaine des Mouillères **

Les Mouillères
Saint-Georges-la-Pouge - 23250 Pontarion (Creuse)
Tel. (0)5★ 55.66.60.64 - Fax (0)5★ 55.66.68.80 - M. and Mme Thill

Rooms 7 with telephone (3 with bath, 4 with WC). **Price** Single 110F, double 200-370F. **Meals** Breakfast incl., served 8:00-9:30. **Restaurant** For residents only. Service 20:00-20:30; menus 90-150F, also à la carte. Specialties: Filet de truite rose au beurre blanc, feuilleté aux cèpes, tournedos forestier cépes. **Credit cards** Visa, Eurocard and MasterCard. **Pets** Dogs not allowed. **Facilities** Parking. **Nearby** Hôtel de Moneyroux and Guéret Museum, abbey church of Moutier-d'Ahun – 18-hole la Jonchère golf course in Montgrenier-Gouzon. **Open** Mar 20 – Oct 1.

This old farmhouse is set in an absolutely magnificent countryside of valleys, pastures, small rivers, birch groves, conifer-covered hills and large trees. The lovely small lounge has a mixture of furniture and old-fashioned objects. We prefer the bedrooms with bathrooms, but the others have been totally refurbished and are equipped with basins. They are all pretty and pleasant, many with satin bedcovers and small, round, skirted tables. Dinners are served in a rustic dining room and feature good first courses, salads and excellent meats (ask for the meat dishes with little sauce.) The owners rent bikes for exploring the superb surrounding countryside. Drinks and meals can be served on the lovely garden terrace. The staff is very courteous.

How to get there (Map 24): *34km south of Guéret via D942 towards Limoges to Pontarion; then towards La Chapelle-Saint-Martial, D3.*

Au Moulin de la Gorce ★★★

87800 La Roche l'Abeille (Haute-Vienne)
Tel. (0)5★ 55.00.70.66 - Fax (0)5★ 55.00.76.57
M. Bertranet

Rooms 9 and 1 apartment, with telephone, bath, WC and TV. **Price** Single 350F, double 700-900F, suite 1300F. **Meals** Breakfast 75F, served from 8:00; half board 1400-1500F, full board 1850-1950F (2 pers., 3 days min.). **Restaurant** Service 12:00-13:30, 19:30-21:00; menus 180-480F, also à la carte. Specialties: Œufs brouillés aux truffes dans leur coque, foie poêlé aux pommes, lièvre à la royale. **Credit cards** All major. **Pets** Dogs allowed. **Facilities** Parking. **Nearby** Saint Etienne cathedral and Adrien-Dubouché ceramics museum in Limoges, abbey of Solignac, church of Saint-Léonard-de-Noblat – 18-hole Porcelaine golf course in Limoges. **Open** Mar 1 – Dec 31 (closed Sunday evening and Monday Sept 20 – Apr 30).

Converted into a sumptuous hotel-restaurant by a family of pastry cooks/caterers from Limoges, this flour mill dates back to 1569. Today entirely renovated, it consist of several buildings set around a beautiful lake with a stream that tumbles down into the garden. The interior decoration is very tasteful, intimate and comfortable. The bedrooms are pleasant and elegantly furnished. Drinks are served on the terrace overlooking the lake and garden, and there is fine, gourmet cuisine with an interesting "Saint Jacques de Compostelle" menu. This is a luxurious, professionally run hotel which has nevertheless retained its family-style hospitality.

How to get there *(Map 23): 30km south of Limoges via D704 then D17.*

Castel–Hôtel 1904 ★★

Rue du Castel
63390 Saint-Gervais-d'Auvergne (Puy-de-Dôme)
Tel. (0)4★ 73.85.70.42 – Fax (0)4★ 73.85.84.39 – M. Mouty

Rooms 17 with telephone, bath or shower, WC and TV (3 with minibar). **Price** Single and double 260-280F. **Meals** Breakfast 38F, served 7:30-10:00; half board 225-235F, full board 290-300F (per pers., 3 days min.). **Restaurant** Service from 12:30 and 19:30; menus 69-300F, also à la carte. Specialties: Tournedos roulé aux pieds de porc, sandre, crêpe Célina. **Credit cards** Visa,Eurocard and MasterCard. **Pets** Dogs not allowed. **Facilities** Parking. **Nearby** Gorges of the Sioule, church in Ménat, Fades viaduct, Mandet museum and museum of the Auvergne in Riom – 9- and 18-hole Volcans golf course in Orcines. **Open** Easter – Nov 11.

This ancient château, built in 1616, was converted into a hotel in 1904 and has been run by the same family ever since. All the charm of an old French hotel is to be found in its warm and welcoming rooms, the bar and above all the large dining room, whose parquet floors gleam. The fireplaces, the antique furniture and the ochre tones of the walls and curtains all contribute to the old-fashioned but very charming character of the hotel. The comfortable bedrooms are all different and in keeping with the spirit of the hotel. You have the choice of two restaurants: the *Castel,* which has an inventive menu, and the *Comptoir à Moustache,* an authentic country bistro. The Castel is welcoming and friendly – the kind of place you become attached to.

How to get there *(Map 24): 55km northwest of Clermont-Ferrand via N9 to Châtelguyon, then D227 to Saint-Gervais-d'Auvergne via Manzat.*

Hôtel Clarion ★★★

21420 Aloxe-Corton (Côte-d'Or)
Tel. (0)3★ 80.26.46.70 - Fax (0)3★ 80.26.47.16
M. and Mme Voarick

Rooms 10 with telephone, bath, WC, TV and minibar. **Price** Single 500F, double 600-800F. **Meals** Breakfast 75F, served 8:00-13:00. No restaurant. **Credit cards** Visa, Eurocard and MasterCard. **Pets** Dogs allowed. **Facilities** Parking. **Nearby** Hôtel-Dieu, basilica of Notre Dame in Beaune, Hôtel de la Rochepot and Bourgogne Wine museum in Beaune, Côte de Beaune between Serrigny and Chagny, château du Clos-Vougeot, Nolay, Rochepot – 18-hole Beaune-Levernois golf course. **Open** All year.

At the Clarion, behind the village of Aloxe-Corton, only two miles from Beaune, the Voaricks have successfully blended natural beauty and modern comfort. The former mansion is surrounded by a large lawn which extends down to a vineyard. But behind this traditional appearance, there is a tastefully decorated contemporary interior, which combines old exposed beams and fireplaces with the clean lines of a simple modern design. The result is a warm, intimate atmosphere. The rooms have soft lights, antiqued furniture, comfortable armchairs and magnificent bathrooms. The breakfasts are marvelous, and you can have brunch anytime next to the fireplace or under the linden trees in the garden. The service is attentive and discreet in this truly lovely hotel. For local restaurants, we recommend *Le Benaton* in Beaune and *Les Coquines* in Ladoix-Serrigny.

How to get there *(Map 19): 5km north of Beaune via N74.*

Chez Camille ★★★

1, place Edouard-Herriot
21230 Arnay-le-Duc (Côte-d'Or)
Tel. (0)3★ 80.90.01.38 - Fax (0)3★ 80.90.04.64 - M. and Mme Poinsot

Rooms 14 with telephone, bath and TV. **Price** Double 395F, suite 500F (free for children under 11 years). **Meals** Breakfast 50F, served 7:00-12:00; half board 400F (per pers.). **Restaurant** Service 12:00-14:30, 19:30-22:00; menus 100-450F, also à la carte. Specialties: Rissoles d'escargots aux pâtes fraîches et champagne, le charolais. **Credit cards** All major. **Pets** Dogs allowed. **Facilities** Garage. **Nearby** Basilica of Saint-Andoche in Saulieu, château de Commarin, Châteauneuf – 18-hole Château de Chailly golf course. **Open** All year.

This charming hotel is peaceful and quiet despite its town location in small Arnay-le-Duc. There is a large, comfortable lobby with a piano, and a lovely 17th-century stairway leads to the bedrooms. They are restful, comfortable and beautifully decorated, some with antique furniture. We especially liked Number 17. (Reserve ahead of time.) Not only an excellent hotel, Chez Camille is also a famous restaurant. The ravishing dining room is set in a winter garden with a glass roof: a perfect setting for trying the fine specialties of Burgundy, which are made with products from the Poinsots' farm. The regional cuisine is light and inventive, making Chez Camille a Burgundian must.

How to get there (Map 19): 28km northeast of Autun via N81.

Hôtel Le Home ★★

138, route de Dijon
21200 Beaune (Côte-d'Or)
Tel. (0)3★ 80.22.16.43 - Fax (0)3★ 80.24.90.74 - Mme Jacquet

Rooms 23 with telephone, bath or shower and WC (8 with TV). **Price** Single and double 325-450F. **Meals** Breakfast 32F. No restaurant. **Credit cards** Visa, Eurocard and MasterCard. **Pets** Dogs allowed. **Facilities** Garage. **Nearby** Hôtel Dieu, basilica of Notre-Dame in Beaune, Côte de Beaune between Serrigny and Chagny, château du Clos-Vougeot, Nolay, Rochepot – 18-hole Beaune-Levernois golf course. **Open** All year.

The inspiration for this small hotel, at the entrance to Beaune, is definitely English. The Virginia-creeper –covered house is surrounded by a flowery garden where breakfast is served. Well-chosen antiques, lamps and carpets give a personal touch to every room. The bedrooms are pretty, comfortable and quiet; the living room inviting. The proximity of the road is noticeable only from outside and the interior is well-insulated from noise. The hospitable Mme Jacquet loves her house, which explains the care that is evident; you will be received here as a friend. For restaurants see page 133.

How to get there *(Map 19): In Beaune, on the Dijon road; beyond the church of Saint-Nicolas.*

Hôtel Le Parc ★★

Levernois – 21200 Beaune (Côte-d'Or)
Tel. (0)3★ 80.22.22.51/(0)3★ 80.24.63.00 – Fax (0)3★ 80.24.21.19
Mme Oudot

Rooms 25 with telephone and TV (19 with shower, 6 with bath and 22 with WC).
Price Double 200-460F. **Meals** Breakfast 34F, served 7:30-9:30. No restaurant.
Credit cards Visa, Eurocard and MasterCard. **Pets** Dogs allowed (fee).
Facilities Parking. **Nearby** Hôtel Dieu, basilica of Notre-Dame in Beaune, Côte de
Beaune between Serrigny and Chagny, château du Clos-Vougeot, Nolay, Rochepot –
18-hole Beaune-Levernois golf course. **Open** All year except a few days in Dec.

The Hôtel Le Parc is an old, ivy-covered Burgundian house on
the doorstep of the charming international wine capital of
Beaune. It has a flowery courtyard where breakfast is served, and
a garden with huge, ancient trees. Hôtel Le Parc has the feel of a
much smaller hotel despite the number of bedrooms. The
atmosphere of every bedroom is different, created in one by the
wallpaper, in another by a chest of drawers and in yet another by
a quilt. M. and Mme Oudot refurbish the rooms regularly. Those
which have just been redecorated have pretty floral-bordered
English wallpapers coordinated with the curtains and bedspreads.
Some of them are very large and luxurious, and always in good
taste. Although not far from the town, you will feel as if you are
in the country, and, most importantly, you will be charmingly
welcomed. For restaurants, try the famous *Hostellerie de Levernois*,
or in Beaune the elegant *Jardin des Remparts*, the charming *Le
Bénaton*, or *Le Gourmandin*.

How to get there *(Map 19): 4km southeast of Beaune via D970, towards
Verdun.*

Château de Challanges ★★★

Rue des Templiers
Challanges 21200 Beaune (Côte-d'Or)
Tel. (0)3★ 80.26.32.62 - Fax (0)3★ 80.26.32.52 - Mme Battisti

Rooms 9 and 5 suite with telephone, bath or shower, WC and TV. **Price** Single 390-440F, double 430-480F, suite 690-750F. **Meals** Breakfast 50F (buffet), served 8:00-11:00. No restaurant. **Credit cards** Amex, Diner's, Visa, Eurocard and MasterCard. **Pets** Dogs not allowed. **Facilities** Tennis (80F), parking. **Nearby** Hôtel Dieu, basilica of Notre-Dame in Beaune, Côte de Beaune between Serrigny and Chagny, château du Clos-Vougeot, Nolay, Rochepot – 18-hole Beaune-Levernois golf course. **Open** Apr 1 – Nov 30.

When you arrive at the Château de Challanges, don't worry about the proximity of the autoroute because it is hidden by a large 17-acre park. The noise of the cars sounds only like a faraway murmur; ask for the bedrooms overlooking the entrance to the park. The hotel is decorated in classical, tasteful style with straw–yellow walls, a great amount of blue, sober contemporary furniture. The breakfast buffet is prettily presented in a pleasant, bright dining room. The bedrooms and suites are all attractive, each with their own color and handsome fabrics in the same tones. The adjoining bathrooms all have white tiles with a coordinated frieze. The bedrooms are not all very large; ask for those with a king-size bed (160 centimeters wide). This is a very comfortable hotel from which to visit Beaune and its environs.

How to get there *(Map 19): On A6, take the Beaune exit towards Dole; turn right in 2km to Challanges.*

Le Manassès

21220 Curtil-Vergy (Côte-d'Or)
Tel. (0)3★ 80.61.43.81 – Fax (0)3★ 80.61.42.79
M. Chaley

Rooms 7 (5 with air-conditioning) with telephone, bath, WC, TV and minibar. **Price** Single and double 400F. **Meals** Breakfast 50F, served 7:45-10:00. No restaurant. **Credit cards** Visa, Eurocard and MasterCard. **Pets** Small dogs allowed. **Facilities** Parking. **Nearby** Abbey of Saint-Vivant in Curtil-Vergy, abbey of Cîteaux, château du Clos-Vougeot, Côte de Nuits – 18-hole Dijon-Bourgogne golf course. **Open** Mar – Nov 31.

To reach this small, quiet hotel you go under a little porch and then across an inner courtyard. M. Chaley is a wine grower and as a jovial host, he well upholds the profession's reputation! His house has been totally renovated and transformed into a hotel. References to wine abound: in the barn which houses an interesting wine museum, in the big room where breakfast is served and in the corridors and bedrooms – each picture is a reminder. From the cellars close by comes the faint aroma of casks in which the wine is aging. The communal rooms are furnished with beautiful old furniture, while the comfortable bedrooms are more modern, with pretty color combinations and marble-lined bathrooms. The view over the wild green valley is superb. Good restaurants include *L'Orée du Bois* in Quémigny-Poisot and *La Gentilhommière* in Nuits-Saint-Georges.

How to get there (Map 19): 24km northwest of Beaune. A31, Nuits-Saint-Georges exit, D25 and D35.

Hostellerie du Val-Suzon ★★★

R.N. 71 - 21121 Val-Suzon (Côte-d'Or)
Tel. (0)3★ 80.35.60.15 - Fax (0)3★ 80.35.61.36
M. and Mme Perreau

Rooms 17 with telephone, of which 16 with bath and WC, 1 with shower, 10 with TV and minibar. **Price** Single 300-350F, double 400-500F, suite 600-800F. **Meals** Breakfast 55F, served 7:30-9:30; half board 442-517F, full board 632-707F (per pers., 3 days min.). **Restaurant** Closed Thursday noon in low season. Service 12:00-14:00, 19:30-21:45; menus 128-400F, also à la carte. Specialties: Œufs coque homard et foie gras, millefeuille d'escargots au beurre de persil. **Credit cards** All major. **Pets** Dogs allowed (+50F). **Facilities** Parking. **Nearby** Château de Vantoux-lès-Dijon, Dijon, Carthusian monastery in Champmol, Côte de Nuits – 18-hole Dijon-Bourgogne golf course. **Open** All year (closed Wednesday Oct – Apr).

The Hostellerie is composed of two houses separated by a ravishing, vast garden laid out on a slight rise. The restaurant is located in the main house; a fireplace, a few prettily set tables and thick draperies make a pleasant decor, which adds to the pleasure of tasting delicious, creative cuisine of Yves Perreau. The other house resembles a chalet and overlooks the garden. The bedrooms are located here. All are comfortable (some beds have been replaced), bright and decorated in a somewhat strict modern style, with a traditional note added by 19th-century-style armchairs or antique tables. The staff in the hotel could be somewhat more attentive.

How to get there (Map 19): 15km northwest of Dijon via N71 towards Troyes.

Manoir de Sornat ★★★

Allée de Sornat
71140 Bourbon-Lancy (Saône-et-Loire)
Tel. (0)3★ 85.89.17.39 - Fax (0)3★ 85.89.29.47 - M. Raymond

Rooms 13 with telephone, bath or shower, WC, TV and minibar. **Price** Single and double 350-650F, suite 700F. **Meals** Breakfast 55-60F, served 7:30-11:00; half board 450-700F, full board 550-850F (per pers., 3 days min.). **Restaurant** Closed Monday lunchtime. Service 12:00-14:00, 19:30-21:30; menus 160-400F, also à la carte. Specialties: Galette d'escargots de Bourgogne, filet de bœuf. **Credit cards** All major. **Pets** Dogs allowed (+30F). **Facilities** Parking. **Nearby** Château de Saint-Aubin-sur-Loire, church in Ternant, abbey at Paray-le-Monial. **Open** All year (closed Sunday evening in low season).

This house was built in the 19th-century at the whim of an affluent Lyonnais who was fond of horse racing at Deauville. He chose a pure Anglo-Norman style of architecture which, though common in Deauville, is unusual here. Adjoining the Manoir are the remains of a racecourse where up to World War II the Bourbon Lancy stakes race was run. The bedrooms are spacious, light, airy and tastefully decorated. If you reserve a room with a terrace looking out over the park, you can enjoy your hearty breakfast while watching the squirrels playing in the century-old trees. In the evenings you can walk down the beautiful carved staircase to enjoy Gérard Raymond's cuisine, which combines traditional dishes with modern presentation. The dining room has large bay windows that look out over the beautiful park. The owners are efficient and kind, and you may find it hard to leave.

How to get there (Map 18): 30km northeast of Moulins via N79 towards Chevagnes.

Hostellerie du Château de Bellecroix ★★★

RN 6 – 71150 Chagny (Saône-et-Loire)
Tel. (0)3★ 85.87.13.86 – Fax (0)3★ 85.91.28.62
Gautier-Crinquant Family

Rooms 21 with telephone, bath or shower, WC, TV and minibar. **Price** Single and double 580-1000F. **Meals** Breakfast 65F, served 7:30-10:30; half board 590F, full board 690-950F (per pers., 3 days min.). **Restaurant** Closed Wednesday. Service 12:00-14:00, 19:30-21:00; menus 250-350F, also à la carte. Specialties: Escargots en cocotte lutée, filet de charollain et foie gras chaud. **Credit cards** All major. **Pets** Dogs allowed (+50F). **Facilities** Swimming pool, parking. **Nearby** Hôtel-Dieu in Beaune, Côte de Beaune between Serrigny and Chagny, château du Clos-Vougeot, Nolay, Rochepot – 18-hole Beaune-Levernois golf course. **Open** Feb 15 – Dec 18 (closed Wednesday except July and Aug).

Built in the 12th-century and modified in the 18th, the Hostellerie, which is just out of the town, was once the *commanderie* of the Knights of Malta. At the entrance, a large, beautifully decorated panelled room serves as reception hall and dining room. It is decorated with lovely flowered draperies, comfortable Louis XV-style chairs around, elegantly laid tables, and reproductions of Old Master paintings on the walls. Next to it in a turret, there is a small intimate lounge. The comfortable bedrooms, located in two buildings, all look out onto the lovely five-acre park with swimming pool, shady terraces and lawns. The rooms in the first building are small but well designed; many are done in a handsome 18th-century style. Those in the other building, which is magnificent, with old walls and mullioned windows, are vast, superbly Haute Epoque in decor, but of course more expensive. Some open directly onto the garden. The staff is very courteous.

137

Hôtel de Bourgogne ★★★

Place de l'Abbaye
71250 Cluny (Saône-et-Loire)
Tel. (0)3★ 85.59.00.58 – Fax (0)3★ 85.59.03.73 – Mme Gosse

Rooms 15 with telephone, bath or shower, WC and TV. **Price** Single and double 390-490F, suite 890-920F. **Meals** Breakfast 55F, served 7:30-9:30; "Soirée étape gourmande" 900-1000F (2pers.). **Restaurant** Service 12:00-14:00, 19:30-21:00; menus 82-420F (lunchtime)–195-420F, also à la carte. Specialties: Foie gras frais de canard, volaille de Bresse à la vapeur de truffes. **Credit cards** All major. **Pets** Dogs allowed (+60F). **Facilities** Garage (+40F). **Nearby** Abbey and Ochier museum in Cluny, caves in Azé, arboretum in Pézanin, château de Chaumont – 18-hole Château de la Salle golf course in Lugny. **Open** Mar 5 – Nov 18 (closed Tuesday evening).

This hotel was built on part of the site of the ancient abbey of Cluny, the pride of the little town which attracts many visitors every summer. But, the reasonable number of bedrooms and the arrangement of the rooms around a small inner garden ensure peace and quiet. There is a pleasantly proportioned living room, where several styles are nicely combined; a large dining room, and gourmet cooking that lives up to its excellent reputation. The bedrooms are comfortable and well-decorated, and there is a bar where breakfast is served when the weather makes it impossible to use the garden. Everything, including the welcome, contributes to the pleasure of your stay. Lamartine enjoyed the charm of the house, and after him, a number of famous people have signed the visitors' book over the past thirty years.

How to get there (Map 19): 24km northwest of Mâcon via N79 and D980.

Moulin de Bourgchâteau ★★

Route de Chalon
71500 Louhans (Saône-et-Loire)
Tel. (0)3★ 85.75.37.12 – Fax (0)3★ 85.75.45.11 – M. Gonzales

Rooms 21 with telephone, bath or shower, WC and TV. **Price** Single 220-260F, double 240-300F, suite 400-650F. **Meals** Breakfast 40F, served 7:30-9:30. **Restaurant** Service 12:00-13:30, 19:30-21:00; menus 100-230F, also à la carte. Specialties: Poulet de Bresse. **Credit cards** All major. **Pets** Dogs allowed. **Facilities** Parking. **Nearby** Côte Chalonnaise around Mercurey, Rully, château de Germolles, church in Givry, Buxy, Hôtel-Dieu in Louhans – 18-hole Lons-le Saunier golf course. **Open** Jan 15 – Dec 18.

Louhans is a large town in the part of the Bresse region that lies between Burgundy and the Jura. Once a month on big market days, when the streets and arcades are full of live poultry and farm produce, it is not unusual to hear the local patois spoken. The hotel occupies an old grain mill which was still working less than fifteen years ago; you can see the impressive cog wheels in the bar. The huge building gives the impression of a rock standing on the water. The bedrooms are all similar in comfort and appearance. Their windows look out over the water and sometimes the mist gives you the feeling of being on a ship. You will have the same view from the restaurant, where you can enjoy the wines and food of Bresse and Burgundy. This is a good place to stay in a relatively unknown region of France.

How to get there *(Map 19): 33km southeast of Chalon-sur-Saône via A6, Chalon Sud exit (then D978), or Tournus exit (then D971).*

Moulin d'Hauterive ★★★

Saint-Gervais-en-Vallière
71350 Chaublanc (Saône-et-Loire)
Tel. (0)3★ 85.91.55.56 – Fax (0)3★ 85.91.89.65 – M. and Mme Moille

Rooms 22 with telephone, bath or shower, WC, TV and minibar. **Price** Single 300F, double 530-600F, suite 700-850F. **Meals** Breakfast 70F, served to 10:00; half board 600F, full board on request (per pers., 3 days min.). **Restaurant** Service 12:00-14:00, 19:00-21:00 (closed Monday and Tuesday lunchtime); menus 85-160F (lunchtime)–240-300F, also à la carte. Specialties: Croustade d'escargots, foie gras poêlé à la purée de pomme de terre. **Credit cards** All major. **Pets** Dogs allowed (+35F). **Facilities** Swimming pool, tennis, sauna, hammam, health center, parking. **Nearby** Château de Germolles, château de Rochepot, Buxy, valley of Les Vaux – 18-hole Chalon-sur-Saône golf course, Saint-Nicolas leisure park. **Open** All year except in Jan (closed Monday and Tuesday in low season).

Located in the heart of the countryside, this old mill lies in 7 1/2 acres of grounds through which the Dheune River runs. It's an attractive house with two lovely dining rooms, in one of which armchairs are arranged around the fireplace in an inviting little group. The bedrooms are exquisite and have all been decorated and furnished with care and good taste. Outside there are plenty of places to relax: beside the swimming pool, around the house, and on a more private terrace reached by crossing a little wooden bridge over the river. In summer, food and drink are served outdoors. Christiane Moille has a passion for cooking which adds to the enormous pleasure of staying in this very hospitable place.

How to get there (Map 19): *15km southeast of Beaune via D970, then D94.*

La Montagne de Brancion ★★★

Brancion
71700 Tournus (Saône-et-Loire)
Tel. (0)3★ 85.51.12.40 - Fax (0)3★ 85.51.18.64 - M. and Mme Million

Rooms 20 with telephone, bath or shower (hairdryer), WC, TV and minibar. **Price** Single 450-610F, double 450-750F. **Meals** Breakfast 60F, served 8:00-9:30. **Restaurant** Service 12:00-13:30, 19:15-21:00; menus 200-380F, also à la carte. Specialties: regional. **Credit cards** All major. **Pets** Dogs allowed (+50F). **Facilities** Swimming pool, parking. **Nearby** Church of Saint-Philibert in Tournus, church in Chapaize, Blanot, Cluny, Taizé, château de Cormatin – 9- and 18-hole Château-la-Salle golf course. **Open** Mar 15 – Nov 1.

Located in very well-preserved countryside, this recently built hotel is perched on a hilltop and enjoys a sweeping view over the vineyards and the pretty village of Martilly-les-Brancion. The interior is modern. The bedrooms are regularly redecorated and are pleasant and simple with coordinated fabrics. They are exposed to the morning sun over the countryside and four have a small balcony. The most recent rooms with warmer colors are especially cheerful, and the bathrooms have modern conveniences. While the dining room is somewhat too modern, the service there is professional and pleasant, featuring gourmet cuisine made with local farm products. You will also enjoy the swimming pool and the overall peaceful setting. The staff is hospitable and friendly and the countryside is beautiful.

How to get there (Map 19): 35km south of Chalon via A6, Tournus exit; 13 km of Tournus via D14 (it's 1km from Brancion).

La Fontaine aux Muses ★★

89116 La Celle-Saint-Cyr (Yonne)
Tel. (0)3★ 86.73.40.22 – Fax (0)3★ 86.73.48.66
Pointeau-Langevin Family

Rooms 17 with telephone, bath or shower and WC (4 with TV). **Price** Single 340F, double 390F, suite 550-650F. **Meals** Breakfast 36F, served 8:00-10:00; half board 370-520F (per pers., 3 days min.). **Restaurant** Service 12:30-13:45, 20:00-21:15; menu 185F, also à la carte. **Credit cards** Visa, Eurocard and MasterCard. **Pets** Dogs not allowed. **Facilities** Swimming pool, golf (50F), tennis (35F), parking. **Nearby** Joigny, Othe forest, St-Cydroine, church of St-Florentin, cathedral of St-Etienne in Auxerre. **Open** All year.

The charm of certain hotels is largely due to their owners and that is certainly the case with the Fontaine aux Muses, which was created by a family of artists. Today son Vincent is the dynamic spirit of the place. Obviously in love with this tiny hamlet, he decided to indulge his passion for the country and to share it with his clients. He loves wine and has his own vineyard; he loves to hunt, with the exception of Toto the wild boar who is a great favorite of city children. Vincent also loves music and often invites his musician friends to enliven weekend dinners with ballads and bossa-novas during the meal, finishing with a veritable professional jazz session. Comfortable armchairs await you beside the fire in the bar-lounge, and whether your beautiful bedroom is on the *premier étage* or at ground level opening onto the garden. More bedrooms have just been opened in a small house at the entrance to the golf course. We are delighted that this traditional auberge spirit is being maintained.

How to get there *(Map 18): 36km northwest of Auxerre via N6 to Joigny, D943 for 7km, then D194. By A6, Courtenay/Sens exit.*

Château de Prunoy

Prunoy
89120 Charny (Yonne)
Tel. (0)3★ 86.63.66.91 – Fax (0)3★ 86.63.77.79 – Mme Roumilhac

Rooms 13 and 6 suites with telephone, bath and WC. **Price** Double 500-700F, suite 850-900F. **Meals** Breakfast 50F, served 8:00-10:30. **Restaurant** Service 12:00 and 20:00; menus 190-220F, also à la carte. Family cooking. **Credit cards** Amex, Visa, Eurocard and MasterCard. **Pets** Dogs allowed. **Facilities** Swimming pool, tennis, health center, parking. **Nearby** Saint-Fargeau, Boutissaint animal park, château de Ratilly, cathedral of Saint-Etienne d'Auxerre – 18-hole de Roncemay golf course in Chassy. **Open** Mar 16 – Jan 1.

Surrounded by a 250-acre park on which there are two lakes, the Château de Prunoy is built in the purest 17th-century architectural style. The owner, a former antiques dealer in Paris, will greet you like a member of the family and will point out the lovely walks you can take around her estate. The cuisine is both simple and refined, and meals are served in a charming dining room whose family objects remind you that you are in a private home. Breakfast is served either in the dining room or in your bedroom. There are 16 rooms all together, and all are remarkable because of their splendid decoration, as well as their spaciousness and comfort. Note also the small living room library, which is ideal for having a cup of tea and reading in winter. This is fabulous place to stay, midway between a hotel and a bed and breakfast.

How to get there *(Map 18): 45km northwest of Auxerre via A6, exit towards Montargis, then D943 for 4km and D16 to Prunoy (towards Charny then Vézelay).*

Le Castel ★★

Place de l'église
89660 Mailly-le-Château (Yonne)
Tel. (0)3★ 86.81.43.06 - Fax (0)3★ 86.81.49.26 - M. and Mme Breerette

Rooms 12 with telephone, of which 8 with bath, 3 with shower and 8 with WC.
Price Single 160F, double 230-340F. **Meals** Breakfast 36F, served 8:00-9:30; 1 meal
a day obligatory in high season. **Restaurant** Service 12:15-13:30, 19:15-20:30;
menus 75-170F, also à la carte. Specialties: Escargots aux noisettes, pavé de
charolais, pétoncles à la bretonne, gratin de framboises. **Credit cards** Visa, Eurocard
and MasterCard. **Pets** Dogs allowed (+25F). **Nearby** Basilica of Sainte-Madeleine
in Vézelay, Saussois rocks, cathedral of Saint-Etienne in Auxerre, Arcy caves – 18-
hole Roncemay golf course in Chassy. **Open** Mar 16 – Nov 14 (closed Wednesday).

A pretty garden with a lime-shaded terrace awaits you in front
of this late 19th-century house. The arrangement of the
ground floor means that the lounge lies between the two dining
rooms, the whole forming a single area. Around the fireplace are
Empire tables and armchairs, and although the furniture in the
dining rooms is in a different style, the ensemble is tasteful and
effective. Several bedrooms have been renovated and until the
others follow suit, we recommend rooms 6, 9 and especially
number 10, which is very handsome with its blue Jouy fabric and
corner lounge. Despite several new carpets, the others are still too
lackluster for our taste. Located in a historically preserved site in
front of the church of this tiny, typical village, Le Castel is a quiet
hotel with a very good restaurant, and a bar on the terrace. The
owners and friendly and informal.

How to get there *(Map 18): 30km northwest of Avallon via N6 to Voutenay-
sur-Cure, then D950 towards Courson-les-Carrières; at the top of the village.*

Auberge du Château
3, rue du Pont
89580 Val-de-Merey (Yonne)
Tel. (0)3★ 86.41.60.00 - Fax (0)3★ 86.41.69.70 - M. Ramos

Rooms 4 and 1 suite with telephone, bath or shower, WC and TV. **Price** Double 350-490F, suite 550-650F. **Meals** Breakfast 50F. **Restaurant** Service 12:00-14:00, 19:30-22:00 (closed Wednesday); menus 170-1350F, also à la carte. Specialties: Sablé à l'éffilochée de crabe coulis de jeunes carottes au cerfeuil anisé, rosace de pomme de terre et hachi de bœuf épicé, fondue aux cépes à l'estragon, lotte truffée au filet d'agneau fumé en croûte de riz sauvage. **Credit cards** Amex, Visa, Eurocard and MasterCard. **Pets** Dogs allowed. **Nearby** Cathedral Saint-Etienne and abbey of Saint-Germain in Auxerre; Cure valley; Ouanne valley. **Open** Mar 22 – Jan 1 (closed Wednesday except reservation).

This lovely inn recently opened in the quiet Burgundian village of Val-de-Mercy. It is made up of several exposed-stone buildings which are connected by a flowery courtyard, extending into a pleasant garden. The bedrooms are upstairs and are very tastefully decorated with parquet floors (in all but one), white walls which show off the old-pink of the drapes and bedcovers, and some antique furniture. In good weather, the room with an immense terrace is especially in demand. The restaurant is located in two small lounges and the dining tables are set with rare elegance. M. Ramos prepares extremely delicious, inventive dishes, occasionally combining excellent local products with more exotic seasonings. Breakfasts are served either in a lovely corner bar, the garden, or beneath the beautiful roof beams of a room which serves as an art gallery and tea room. This is a charming inn offering reasonable prices and friendly service.

How to get there *(Map 18): 18km south of Auxerre via A6, Auxerre Sud exit; then N6 towards Avallon, D85 towards Coulanges-la-Vineuse, D165 to Val-de-Mercy.*

La Lucarne aux Chouettes

14, Quai Bretoche
89500 Villeneuve-sur-Yonne (Yonne)
Tel. (0)3★ 86.87.18.26 – Fax (0)3★ 86.87.22.63 – M. Marc Daniel

Rooms 4 with telephone, bath and WC. **Price** Double 490F, suite 720F, loft and Duplex 830F. **Meals** Breakfast 50F,served 8:30-10:30. **Restaurant** Closed Sunday evening and Monday in winter. Service 12:00-14:30, 19:30-22:30; menu 98F (weekday lunch)-158F, also à la carte. Specialties: Terrine de chévre aux artichauts, navarin de lotte au curry, truffier praliné à l'orange. **Credit cards** Amex, Visa, Eurocard and MasterCard. **Pets** Dogs allowed. **Facilities** Parking. **Nearby** Cathedral and Synod Palace, the municipal greenhouses in Sens, Joigny: church of Saint-Florentin, cathedral Saint-Etienne d'Auxerre, Avarollais museum. **Open** Mar 16 – Feb 14.

Originally four village houses, the Lucarne aux Chouettes has recently been converted into a very charming auberge by Leslie Caron herself. On the ground floor, there is a bar-veranda and a superb dining room whose beams and half-timbering create the essential part of the decoration. The cuisine is delicious, inventive, light and refined. (Marc Daniel used to be the chef at Paris' famous restaurant Lasserre). The service is attentive and in summer, meals are served on the lovely terrace overlooking the quay. The bedrooms are upstairs and all have a beautiful view over the river. Priority has been given to spaciousness, modern amenities and charm in the bedrooms, where there are antique-style beds, pretty fabrics, family furniture and paintings. The welcome is very hospitable and friendly, making the Lucarne aux Chouettes a delightful place to stay.

How to get there *(Map 10): 15km south of Sens. Via A6 exit Courtenay/ Sens, then D15 towards Piffonds and Villeneuve-sur-Yonne.*

Château Hôtel de Brélidy ★★★

Brélidy - 22140 Bégard (Côtes-d'Armor)
Tel. (0)2★ 96.95.69.38 - Fax (0)2★ 96.95.18.03
Mme Pémezec and M. Yoncourt

Rooms 14 with telephone, bath and WC (4 with TV). **Price** Single 380-430F, double 420-755F, suite 1080-1155F. **Meals** Breakfast 50F, served 8:00-10:00; half board 400-605F. **Restaurant** Service 19:30-21:00; menus 135-175F. Specialties: Panaché de poissons, aiguillettes de canard aux pommes caramélisées. **Credit cards** All major. **Pets** Dogs allowed. **Facilities** Fishing, Mountain bikes, jacuzi, parking. **Nearby** Saint-Tugdual cathedral in Tréguier, basilica of Notre-Dame-de-Bon-Secours in Guingamp, château de Tonquedec, Kergrist, Rosambo – 18-hole Ajoncs d'or golf course in Saint-Quai-Portrieux. **Open** Easter – Nov 1.

From this old Breton château buried in the countryside you can see woods, wild hedgerows and deep lanes criss-crossing the hills. The granite walls rise out of banks of hydrangeas. The bedrooms are as comfortable as those of a good hotel. A set menu is served in one of two beautiful dining rooms, featuring cuisine which, like the welcome and the service, is friendly and family-style. After dinner you can retire to the lounge or take advantage of the billiard room. Both are vast and, though a little bare, welcoming nonetheless. The bedrooms are named after flowers and the suite has a canopied bed and beautiful views; but for less money you might prefer the *Jasmine* or *Iris* rooms. This is a place to treasure in the most unspoiled Breton countryside.

How to get there *(Map 5): 6km west of Bégard via D15, towards Pontrieux.*

Hôtel d'Avaugour ★★★

1, place du Champ-Clos
22100 Dinan (Côtes-d'Armor)
Tel. (0)2★ 96.39.07.49 – Fax (0)2★ 96.85.43.04 – Mme Quinton

Rooms 27 with telephone, bath, WC and TV. **Price** Single 340-450F, double 480-560F. **Meals** Breakfast (Buffet) 48F, served 7:00-10:00. No restaurant. **Credit cards** All major. **Pets** Dogs allowed. **Nearby** Léhon, Pleslin, Pleslin, Pléven, château de la Hunaudaie – 18-hole Dinard golf course in Saint-Briac-sur-Mer. **Open** All year.

The beautiful grey stone façade of the Avaugour overlooks the ramparts in the middle of the town. Inside, you will find the comfortable, intimate atmosphere of a family home. All the bedrooms are charming and some look out onto a beautiful garden. They are comfortable but we prefer those which have been recently redecorated, which are more attractive, brighter and have pretty fabrics. The hotel is very pleasant throughout and it is lovely to stroll in the garden, which is laid out on the old cannon emplacement on the ramparts, and to enjoy the beautiful view out over the château of Duchess Anne. Last but not least, Mme Quinton is a very warm hostess. At the back of the garden, in the constable's tower, there is the restaurant *La Poudrière*. In the center of town, try *La Caravelle, Les Grands Fossés,* or *Chez la Mère Pourcel*.

How to get there *(Map 6): 29km south of Saint-Malo (in the center of the town).*

Manoir du Cleuziou ★★

22540 Louargat (Côtes-d'Armor)
Tel. (0)2★ 96.43.14.90 – Fax (0)2★ 96.43.52.59
M. and Mme Costan

Rooms 28 with telephone, bath (1 with shower) and WC. **Price** Single 320-380F, double 400-420F. **Meals** Breakfast 40F, served 8:00-10:00; half board 335F (per pers.). **Restaurant** Service 12:00-13:30, 19:00-21:30; menus 95-210F, also à la carte. **Credit cards** Amex, Visa, Eurocard and MasterCard. **Pets** Dogs allowed. **Facilities** Swimming pool, Tennis (30F), parking. **Nearby** Basilica of Notre-Dame-de-Bon-Secours in Guingamp, Menez-Bré – 18-hole Saint-Samson golf course in Pleumeur-Bodou. **Open** Mar 1 – Jan 31.

The oldest part of the manor dates back to the 15th century. It is a beautiful building, the interior a match for its elegant façade. There are magnificent carved stone fireplaces, lovely doors and tapestries. The small bedrooms have less character but they are quite comfortable and offer families good value for the money. Many of them have bunk beds or a mezzanine. The cuisine is now under the direction of a new chef, Joseph Traon; guests will surely enjoy it, along with the guidance of the new *maître sommelier, Nöel Constan*. They can also enjoy the bar which has been attractively installed in the old wine cellars. We should point out the presence of a small deluxe camping site a little way away which belongs to the manor and has the use of its leisure facilities.

How to get there *(Map 5): 14km west of Guingamp via N12; in the village follow signs.*

Le Repaire de Kerroc'h ★★★

29, quai Morand
22500 Paimpol (Côtes-d'Armor)
Tel. (0)2★ 96.20.50.13 - Fax (0)2★ 96.22.07.46 - M. Broc

Rooms 13 with telephone, bath, WC, TV and minibar. **Price** Single and double 290-480F, suite 580-990F. **Meals** Breakfast 45F, served 8:00-12:00; half board 395F, full board 495F (per pers., 3 days min.). **Restaurant** Service 12:15-14:00, 19:15-21:30; menus 95-350F, also à la carte. Specialties: Dorure de saumon breton au vinaigre balsamique, caneton rôti au miel et aux épices, homard en 3 services. **Credit cards** Visa, Eurocard and MasterCard. **Pets** Dogs allowed. **Facilities** Ocean fishing (150F per pers.). **Nearby** Abbey of Beauport, Guilben Point, l'Arcouest Point, Lanieff, Kermaria-an-Iskuit chapel, Lanloup, Plouézec, Bilfot Point. **Open** All year.

Bréhat and Plougescant are only a few kilometers from the small town of Paimpol. On the quayside stands this very charming hotel, built in 1793 in typical St. Malo style. The pretty bedrooms are named after islands off the Brittany coast and are well furnished in old-fashioned style. The hotel has been enlarged by the acquisition of an other part of this former pirate's house. There the bedrooms are larger and decorated with wallpapers and chintzes in bright, cheerful colors. The windows are double , which together with the thick walls of the old house ensures a peaceful night's sleep. Kerroc'h'Kitchen is famous for its excellent fish, unequalled in Paimpol. This is a very pleasant town hotel, full of the spirit of the sea and of Brittany.

How to get there (Map 5): 33km east of Lannion via D786 to Paimpol.

Le Manoir du Sphinx ★★★

67, chemin de la Messe
22700 Perros-Guirec (Côtes-d'Armor)
Tel. (0)2★ 96.23.25.42 – Fax (0)2★ 96.91.26.13 – M. and Mme Le Verge

Rooms 20 with telephone, bath, WC and TV; elevator - Wheelchair access.
Price Double 490-550F. **Meals** Breakfast 44F, served 7:30-10:00; half board 500-
550F (per pers.). **Restaurant** Closed Monday lunchtime except holidays. Service
12:30-14:00, 19:30-21:30; menus 125-270F, also à la carte. **Credit cards** Amex,
Visa, Eurocard and MasterCard. **Pets** Dogs not allowed. **Facilities** Direct access to
the sea, parking. **Nearby** Footpath to Ploumanac'h, pink granite coast (chapel of
Notre-Dame-de-la-Clarté), Sainte-Anne-de-Trégastel, boat excursions to the Sept
Iles (Ile aux Moines) – 18-hole Saint-Samson golf course in Pleumeur-Bodou.
Open Feb 15 – Jan 3.

Located on a small road along the pink granite coast, overlooking
the Bay of Trestrignel, this hotel has an exceptional site with
a garden going all the way down to the sea, a warmly decorated
bar-lounge and adjoining dining room jutting out over the
Channel; the owners are very hospitable. The rooms are always
comfortable and well kept, although a bit impersonal. They all
have a splendid view of the bay. Some have been recently built
and are very pleasant with their English-style furniture and bay
windows right over the sea. They are modern but elegant and
cheerful. M. Le Verge's savory cuisine is excellent.

How to get there *(Map 5): 11km of Lannion, along the coast.*

Domaine du Val ★★★

22400 Planguenoual (Côtes-d'Armor)
Tel. (0)2★ 96.32.75.40 – Fax (0)2★ 96.32.71.50
M. Hervé

Rooms 38 and 2 apartments (4-6 pers.) with telephone, bath, WC and TV. **Price** Single and double 450-900F, apart. 760-1050F. **Meals** Breakfast 45-55F; half board 480-660F. **Restaurant** Service 12:30-14:00, 19:30-21:30; menus 140-340F, also à la carte. Specialties: Saumon fumé maison, homard breton à l'armoricaine, pigeonneau à la Valoise, foie gras poêlé aux pommes. **Credit cards** Visa, Eurocard and MasterCard. **Pets** Dogs allowed. **Facilities** Covered and heated swimming pool, sauna, squash, covered tennis, covered and heated balnéo, parking. **Nearby** Château de Bienassis, stud farm and church of Saint-Martin in Lamballe – 18-hole Val d'Armor golf course. **Open** All year.

Set in large grounds stretching down to the sea, the Château du Val is well camouflaged. The covered tennis courts, squash courts, gymnasium and covered swimming pool are virtually hidden from sight. Amidst the greenery only a pretty Renaissance style building is visible. There is also a row of little granite houses, surrounded by shrubs. In these, every bedroom is at ground level and has its own terrace: they are peaceful and comfortable. The bedrooms in the château are a bit more expensive and classic, and their bathrooms, with Plancoët tiles, deserve a special mention. On the ground floor the dining room is comfortable and decorated in Neo-Gothic style. Beside it is an attractive verandah where in summer you can dine under bunches of grapes hanging from the vine. In all, the pleasant welcome and the many leisure activities available make the Domaine du Val a good place to stay.

How to get there *(Map 6): 27km northeast of Saint-Brieuc, exit autoroute at Le Val-André; 1km from Planguenoual.*

Manoir du Vaumadeuc ★★★★
22130 Pleven (Côtes-d'Armor)
Tel. (0)2★ 96.84.46.17 - Fax (0)2★ 96.84.40.16
M. O'Neill

Rooms 14 with telephone, bath or shower and WC. **Price** Single 490F, double 490-950F, suite 950F. **Meals** Breakfast 50F, served 8:00-10:00; half board 450-680F (per pers., 3 days min.). **Restaurant** Diner by reservation 195F. **Credit cards** All major. **Pets** Dogs allowed (+50F). **Facilities** Fishing in the lake, parking. **Nearby** Château de la Hunaudaie, Dinan, Saint-Malo, Léhon – 9-hole Pen Guen golf course, 18-hole Briac-sur-Mer golf course. **Open** Easter – Jan 5.

Dating from the end of the 15th century, this manor house has survived unscathed. In the main building are the dining room, a huge lounge and delightful bedrooms, immaculately decorated and furnished. To one side there are two small houses in the same style, also comfortably arranged. In front of the manor in the 16th-century dovecote is the bar. Set in woods, but only 18km from the sea, this is an excellent place to stay. As the restaurant is open only in season, it is difficult for us to comment on the cuisine. Note however that in the low season you can order a seafood platter (the day before).

How to get there *(Map 6): 37km east of Saint-Brieuc via N12 to Lamballe; in the village, D28 to Pléven via La Poterie and the Hunaudaie Forest.*

Le Fanal ★★

Route du Cap Fréhel
Plévenon - 22240 Fréhel (Côtes-d'Armor)
Tel. (0)2★ 96.41.43.19 - M. and Mme Legros

Rooms 9 with telephone, shower and WC. **Price** Single 240F, double 320F.
Meals Breakfast 33F. **Restaurant** Crêperie, service 18:00-21:00 weekends and
school holidays. **Credit cards** Visa, Eurocard and MasterCard. **Pets** Dogs not allowed.
Facilities Parking. **Nearby** Cap Fréhel, Fort La Latte, rock of la Grande Fauconnière,
market in Matignon (Wednesdays) – 18-hole Sables-d'Or-les-Pins golf course in Cap
Fréhel. **Open** Apr 1 – Sept 30.

Surrounded by the Fréhel moors between Plévenon and the
cape, Le Fanal with its wooden architecture might come as a
surprise but it blends perfectly with the environs: Go inside and
you will understand its secret charm. Antique furniture, classical
music, books about Brittany: everything contributes to peace and
relaxation. The tastefully decorated bedrooms are modern and
comfortable, and all have views over the moor and the sea. They
are all pleasant but number 6, with its beautiful spaciousness, roof
beams and 18th-century wardrobe, as well as rooms 7, 8 and 9,
deserve special mention. Nature lovers will enjoy the bird reserve
and the walks, or they can relax in the garden. The welcome is
informal and friendly.

How to get there (Map 6): 40km west of St-Malo via D786, then D16.

Relais de Fréhel *
Route du cap Fréhel
22240 Le Fréhel (Côtes-d'Armor)
Tel. (0)2★ 96.41.43.02 – Mme Lemercier

Rooms 13, 2 with bath, 7 with shower and 7 with WC. **Price** 237-287F.
Meals Breakfast 33F, served 8:00-11:00, half board 287F, full board 367F (per pers.,
3 days min.). **Restaurant** Service 12:30-14:00, 19:30-21:00; menus 82-265F, also
à la carte. Specialties: Seafood, lobster, grillades au feu de bois. **Credit cards** Visa,
Eurocard and MasterCard. **Pets** Dog not allowed. **Facilities** Tennis, parking.
Nearby Cape Fréhel, La Latte Fort, Grande Fauconnière rock, Matignon market on
Wednesday – 18-hole Sables-d'Or-les-Pins golf course. **Open** Apr – Nov 2

The Relais de Fréhel is an old farm which has been restored;
its long low façade of pink stone is surmounted by large slate-
covered mansard roofs and faces a lovely garden of hydrangeas and
a very lush and verdant park. Inside, the warm wood of the window
and ceiling joists softens the stark but beautiful exposed stones
which frame doors and windows, and the white stucco of the walls.
The bedrooms are small, rustic and very simple, but the prices are
in keeping. The dining room is charming; the cuisine,
unfortunately, is nothing to write home about, but the meals grilled
in the fireplace are good. The atmosphere is very family-style, calm
and restful. The Côte Sauvage (Wild Coast) and the bird sanctuary
at Cape Fréhel are several kilometers away, attracting lovers of the
sea as well as bird watchers.

How to get there *(Map 6): 40km west of Saint-Malo via D786, then D16;
follow the signs in the towards of Cap Fréhel.*

Manoir de Rigourdaine *
22290 Plouër-sur-Rance (Côtes-d'Armor)
Tel. (0)2★ 96.86.89.96 - Fax (0)2★ 96.86.92.46
M. Van Valenberg

Rooms 17 with telephone, bath or shower, WC and TV - Wheelchair access. **Price** Double 290-390F, suite 420F. **Meals** Breakfast 38F, served 8:30-10:30. No restaurant. **Credit cards** Visa, Eurocard and MasterCard. **Pets** Dog allowed. **Facilities** Parking. **Nearby** Saint-Malo; Dinan; Léhon; Pays de Rance and Aguenon – 18-hole Saint-Cast golf course, 18-hole Ormes golf course. **Open** Apr – Nov 15

The location of this old, extensively renovated farmhouse combines the charms of the country with a sweeping view over the blue waters of the Rance Valley 200 meters below. The bedrooms, all of which enjoy this panorama, are new, with English-style wallpaper and a pleasant decor. An old wardrobe here, a chest-of-drawers there and paintings lend a personal touch. Those on the ground floor have a private terrace and are perfect for summer; for families, we recommend the suites, which are especially well-suited to groups. Breakfast is served in a large, rustic-style dining room or on the leafy terrace. Despite decoration which is still somewhat stiff (and which we are sure will improve with time), the general ambiance is very pleasant, as is M. Van Valenberg's youthful and attentive hospitality.

How to get there *(Map 6): 15km southeast of Dinan. On N176 between Dol and Dinan, take the Plouer exit towards Langrolay. Signposted.*

Ti Al-Lannec ★★★

Allée de Mezo-Guen
22560 Trébeurden (Côtes-d'Armor)
Tel. (0)2★ 96.23.57.26 – Fax (0)2★ 96.23.62.14 – M. and Mme Jouanny

Rooms 29 with telephone, bath, WC and cable TV. **Price** Single 400-450F, double 630-1050F. **Meals** Breakfast 65-90F, served 7:15-10:30; half board 565-775F, full board 735-945F. **Restaurant** Service 12:30-14:00, 19:30-21:30; menus 105-390F, also à la carte. Specialties: Noix de coquilles Saint-Jacques dorées sauce curry, caneton rôti aux baies de cassis, la tentation de l'écureuil. **Credit cards** All major. **Pets** Dogs allowed (+45F). **Facilities** Fitness-beauty center, parking. **Nearby** Le Castel, Bihit point, the Breton corniche from Trébeurden to Perros-Guirec – Saint-Samson golf course in Pleumeur-Bodou. **Open** Mid-Mar – mid-Nov.

Ti Al-Lannec is exceptionally well decorated and the hotel has a wonderful view of the sea (which is easily accessible by a small path) and terraced gardens. The very comfortable bedrooms are beautifully furnished and decorated, some with English fabrics and wallpaper; most have a sitting area, a charming verandah or terrace. The same care in decoration is evident in the lounges and in the dining room, which extends onto a large verandah overlooking the bay. The service here is perfect and the cuisine excellent. Also worthy of note is the fitness center.

How to get there *(Map 5): 9km northwest of Lannion via D65.*

Manoir de Crec'h-Goulifen

Beg Leguer-Servel
22300 Lannion (Côtes-d'Armor)
Tel. (0)2★ 96.47.26.17 – Mme Droniou

Rooms 7 with telephone, bath or shower and WC. **Price** Single 280-300F, double 350-420F. **Meals** Breakfast incl., served 8:00-10:30. No restaurant. **Credit cards** Not accepted. **Pets** Dogs allowed (+40F). **Facilities** Tennis, parking. **Nearby** Chapel of Kerfons, châteaux de Tonquédec, de Kergrist and de Rosambo, chapel of the Sept-Nains – Saint-Samson golf course in Pleumeur-Bodou. **Open** All year.

The manor of Crec'h-Goulifen, originally an 18th-century farm, has been lovingly renovated. The main room on the ground floor is arranged with regional country furniture, and breakfast is served here or on the terrace. The bedrooms are also in country style, small and comfortable although somewhat dark. We recommend the two which have bathrooms, (The third room, called The Studio, is less pleasant). The Manoir is a pleasing and peaceful place, in a good location. For fine dining, try *Le Serpolet,* which is located in a pretty house in a small street behind the post office.

How to get there *(Map 5): 6km northwest of Lannion via D21, then towards Servel.*

Kastell Dinec'h ★★★

22200 Tréguier (Côtes-d'Armor)
Tel. (0)2★ 96.92.49.39 - Fax (0)2★ 96.92.34.03
M. and Mme Pauwels

Rooms 15 with telephone, bath and WC (6 with TV). **Price** Double 420-490F.
Meals Breakfast 55F, served 8:00-10:00; half board 425-480F. **Restaurant** Service
19:30-21:30; menus 130-300F, also à la carte. Specialties: Bar en croûte de sel,
cassolette de moules aux mousserons, crêpes de seigle au homard. **Credit cards** Visa,
Eurocard and MasterCard. **Pets** Dogs allowed (+25F). **Facilities** Heated swimming
pool May 15 – Sept 15, parking. **Nearby** Cathedral of Saint-Tugdual and the house
of Ernest Renan in Tréguier, Pleubian, chapel of Saint-Gonéry in Plougescrant,
château de la Roche-Jagu – 9-hole Saint-Samson golf course in Pleumeur-Bodou.
Open Mar 15 – Oct 11 and Oct 27 – Dec 31 (closed Tuesday evening and Wednesday
in low season).

In the countryside 2km from Tréguier stands this 17th-century
manor-farm. The main building – housing a beautiful dining
room, a small comfortable lounge and some of the bedrooms – has
two annexes containing the other bedrooms. Together they look
onto a lovely garden where drinks and breakfast are served in
summer. The bedrooms are small but tastefully decorated, some
with antique furniture. The overall effect is simple and elegant.
Mme de Pauwels' is very hospitable, and her husband's cooking is
delicious.

How to get there *(Map 5): 16km east of Lannion via D786, 2km before
Tréguier; follow the signs.*

Le Minaret ★★

Corniche de l'Estuaire
29950 Bénodet (Finistère)
Tel. (0)2★ 98.57.03.13 – Fax (0)2★ 98.66.23.72 – Mme Kervran

Rooms 20 with telephone, bath or shower, WC and TV; elevator. **Price** Double 260-420F **Meals** Breakfast 40F, served 8:00-10:00; half board (obligatory in high season) 275-390F. **Restaurant** Closed Tuesday in Apr and May. Service 12:30-14:00, 19:30-21:00; menus 90-210F, also à la carte. Specialties: Gigot de lotte au poivre vert, pavé de poisson grillé à la façon des îles, homard grillé. **Credit cards** Visa, Eurocard and MasterCard **Pets** Dogs allowed except in the restaurant. **Facilities** Parking. **Nearby** Quimper, boat trip on the Odet from Quimper to Bénodet, Breton museum and villages, Notre-Dame de Quilinen chapel. **Open** Easter – Oct 1.

An oasis in the midst of traditional Brittany: That is what Le Minaret looks like! It is a large white house designed in the 1920s by the architect Laprade; from the top of its real minaret, there's a breathtaking view out over the estuary of the River Odet, where sailboats pass regularly on their way in or out of the port. Even more than the exterior, the interior of the house reminds you discreetly of its Oriental character. The bright rooms, three of which have a small terrace, have a view of the sea or the charming small inlet bordering the town of Sainte-Marine. The great curiosity of the house is the *Pacha* bedroom, decorated in pure Moroccan style with wide windows opening onto the estuary. The mixture of the styles is attractive and lends unusual charm to the hotel. A pretty garden surrounds the house, and the terrace on the seafront also affords a superb view.

How to get there *(Map 5): 16km south of Quimper.*

Domaine de Kéréven ★★

29950 Bénodet (Finistère)
Tel. (0)2★ 98.57.02.46 – Fax (0)2★ 98.66.22.61
Mme Berrou

Rooms 16 with telephone, bath or shower and WC. **Price** Double 280-375F.
Meals Breakfast 38F, served 8:30-10:00; half board 310-345F. **Restaurant** Closed
Sept 25 – May 20. Service 19:30-20:30; menu 120F. Specialties: Seafood.
Credit cards Not accepted. **Pets** Dogs not allowed. **Facilities** Parking. **Nearby** Boat
trip on the Odet from Quimper to Bénodet, chapels of Gouesnac'h and le Drennec,
châteaux of Bodinio and Cheffontaines, Quimper, îles de Glénan – 18-hole l'Odet
golf course in Bénodet. **Open** Easter – Oct 14 (by reservation Easter – May 20 and
Sept 22 – Oct 15).

Surrounded by fields and farmland, the vast Domaine de Kéréven
and its contiguous old farm buildings are eloquent examples of
the unspoiled traditional charm you will still find in this part of the
Breton countryside (and yet it is still near the sea and beaches). The
family atmosphere and the hospitality of the domaine are very
pleasant. The bedrooms have comfortable, modern amenities; they
are well-kept and very quiet, but greater effort should be made with
respect to the decor to make them more personal and cheerful.
However the *demi-pension* is certainly a good value. Dinner is served
in a large, rustic dining room which opens onto a terrace, a pleasant
place to have drinks before dinner. One of the buildings has
apartments with kitchens, which is very convenient if you are a
family or a group. The Domaine de Kéréven is truly a haven of
comfort and tranquillity.

How to get there *(Map 5): 16km south of Quimper via D34.*

Hôtel Ty Mad ★★

Plage Saint-Jean
29100 Douarnenez (Finistère)
Tel. (0)2★ 98.74.00.53 - Fax (0)2★ 98.74.15.16 - Mme Martin

Rooms 23 with telephone, bath or shower and WC (TV on request). **Price** Single and double 230-320F. **Meals** Breakfast 36F, served 8:00-11:00. **Restaurant** Service 12:30-14:00, 19:30-21:30; menus, also à la carte. Specialties: fish, seafood. **Credit cards** All major. **Pets** Dogs allowed (+25F). **Facilities** Parking. **Nearby** Douarnenez (port-musée), coast paths of Plomarc'h and Roches Blanches, Beuzec point, Cap Sizun, Quimper, Locronan, church of Confort, Pont-Croix and Sainte-Anne-la-Palud – 18-hole l'Odet golf course in Bénodet. **Open** Easter – Nov 1.

What famous guests for such a small hotel! Many renowned people in search of peace and quiet have sought refuge in this house, including Christopher Wood and Max Jacob, who lived here for more than two years. Located twenty minutes from the house of Françoise Gilot, Picasso's companion, Ty Mad has bedrooms which, from its three upper floors, look out over a countryside beautiful enough to be painted. Meals are served in a large, bright room with white tablecloths and a glossy parquet floor, which gives onto a terrace. Nearby, there is a small 17th-century chapel and a beach for the clients of the hotel. The Ty Mad is right out of a Jacques Tati film, – an excellent small hotel.

How to get there *(Map 5): 18km northwest of Quimper via D765; at the Tréboul Yacht Harbor, the hotel is signposted.*

Manoir de Moëllien **

29550 Plonévez-Porzay (Finistère)
Tel. (0)2★ 98.92.50.40 – Fax (0)2★ 98.92.55.21
M. and Mme Garet

Rooms 10 with telephone, bath, WC and TV. **Price** Double 345-360F. **Meals** Breakfast 40F, served 8:00-9:30; half board 355-365F, full board 430-450F (per pers.). **Restaurant** Closed Wednesday in low season. Service 12:30-14:00, 19:30-21:00; menus 120-250F, also à la carte. Specialties: Fish and shellfish. **Credit cards** All major. **Pets** Dogs allowed (+30F). **Facilities** Parking. **Nearby** Saint-Corentin cathedral and art museum in Quimper, Locronan, Sainte-Anne-la-Palud, church in Ploéven – 18-hole l'Odet golf course in Bénodet. **Open** Mar 20 – Jan 2.

Invisible from the little road leading to it, this château is hidden by a pine forest. The dining room is on the ground floor of the main building, built of stone in the 17th century. It is very Haute Epoque in style and is pleasantly decorated with antique Breton furniture, fresh flowers, pale table linens, and pictures. Next door is a small, intimate bar. In the relaxing first-floor lounge a stone fireplace is pride of the place. Opposite the noble façade of the manor is a building housing bedrooms at ground-floor level. They are comfortable, pretty, quiet and well-kept, with a beautiful view of the surrounding countryside. This is an excellent hotel just several minutes from the superb Finistère coastline.

How to get there (*Map 5*): *20km northwest of Quimper via D63 to Locronan at the first traffic circle, take Plonévez-Porzay exit.*

Hôtel de L'Iroise

29770 Pointe-du-Raz (Finistère)
Tel. (0)2★ 98.70.64.65
Mme Le Coz

Rooms 10 with shower (3 with WC). **Price** Double 150-200F. **Meals** Breakfast 22F, served 8:30-10:30. No restaurant. **Credit cards** Not accepted. **Pets** Dogs allowed. **Facilities** Parking. **Nearby** Route de la Pointe du Raz, Saint-Tugen chapel, cape Sizun ornithological reserve. **Open** All year.

Whipped by the wind, thrust out in the wild moor of the Pointe du Raz, this small white house struggles all alone against the terrible storms which blow in from the Atlantic Ocean. The ten small, simply decorated rooms all have a view of the Baie des Trépassés, an extraordinary, apocalyptic landscape where there is not a single tree growing and where the earth and stones prevent any kind of plants from thriving. The only vegetation that survives in this austere climate is a few clumps of broom. At the Iroise, you can peruse the photos which several great photographers have given Mme Le Coz in gratitude for the combat she has waged for so long for the survival of this magic place. In fact, it is planned to demolish the house in 1997. So you have only a short time left in which to discover this strange and mysterious site, where fairy tales and goblins are still alive. If you love strong emotions, don't miss it. You can have dinner 1km away in Lescaf, at *La Brochette*, or in Audierne at *La Goélette*.

How to get there *(Map 4): 14km northwest of Audierne via D784.*

Moulin de Rosmadec ★★

Venelle de Rosmadec
29930 Pont-Aven (Finistère)
Tel. (0)2★ 98.06.00.22 - Fax (0)2★ 98.06.18.00 – Sébilleau Family

Rooms 4 with telephone, bath, WC and TV. **Price** Double 470F. **Meals** Breakfast 40F.
Restaurant Service 12:30-14:00, 19:30-21:30; menu 165F, 300F, 400F with lobster,
also à la carte. Specialties: Fish, homard grillé Rosmadec. **Credit cards** All major.
Pets Dogs allowed (+25F). **Facilities** Parking. **Nearby** Gauguin Museum in Pont-
Aven, Saint-Corentin cathedral and museum fine arts in Quimper, Tremal chapel,
Nizon, Kérangosquer, the enclosed city of Concarneau, boat ride down Odet River –
18-hole Odet golf course in Bénodet **Open** Mar 1 – Nov 15 (closed Wednesday and
Sunday exept mid-June – beg-Sep).

You will find the Moulin de Rosmadec at the end of a small
lane in the charming village of Pont Aven, immortalized by
Paul Gauguin. Nestling between two branches of a pretty river,
this 15th-century mill is an ideal place to stay in order to explore
this marvelous Breton village with fifteen mills. The Moulin's four
small rooms are all comfortable, and from them you will hear the
peaceful sound of water tumbling through the wheel, which is still
in operation. The hotel's Michelin-starred restaurant, which is run
by the owners' son, has been here for more than sixty years,
specializing in grilled lobster and other succulent Breton fish dishes.
You can have breakfast on the patio, in the center of which stands
a charming old moss-covered well. In short, you will love this
special place to stay!

How to get there *(Map 5): 32km southeast of Quimper via D783, towards*
Concarneau.

Château de Kernuz **

29120 Pont-L'Abbé (Finistère)
Tel. (0)2★ 98.87.01.59 - Fax (0)2★ 98.66.02.36
M. and Mme du Chatellier

Rooms 19 with telephone, bath and WC. **Price** Single 350F, double 350-450F and 600F. **Meals** Breakfast 35F, served 8:00-10:00; half board 360-410F, full board 510-560F (per pers.). **Restaurant** Service 12:00-13:30, 19:30-21:30; menu 150F (diner), also à la carte. **Credit cards** All major. **Pets** Dogs not allowed. **Facilities** Swimming pool, tennis and parking. **Nearby** Cathedral Saint-Corentin and fine arts museum in Quimper, Breton villages, Pont-Aven, Concarneau, boat ride down Odet River – 18-hole Odet golf course in Bénodet. **Open** Apr – Sept.

This is a family home and a beautiful château which became a hotel out of necessity but which has maintained itself proudly and nobly in its park, surrounded by a dovecote, a chapel and a watchtower. There is a very charming lounge whose beautiful dark woodwork is brightened by beige-grey sofas, and farther on a very handsome bar with two Renaissance pillars of painted sculpted wood. The bedrooms are also striking, although not so alluring as the rooms on the main floor. These are very charming, each with different colors and decor. Everything here is in good taste, and the welcome is friendly.

How to get there (Map 5): 20km south of Quimper; 1km south of Pont-L'Abbé, take D785, towards Plomeur, then the road for Penmarc'h.

La Demeure Océane

29830 Portsall (Finistère)
Tel. (0)2★ 98.48.77.42 – Fax (0)2★ 98.80.52.64
M. and Mme Richard

Rooms 6 and 2 duplex with shower and WC. **Price** Double 250-350F, duplex 400F.
Meals Breakfast 35F, served 8:30-12:00; half board 360-410F, full board 510-560F
(per pers.). No restaurant but evening meal for residents only on reservation. Service
from 21:00; menu 120-140F. **Credit cards** Visa, Eurocard and MasterCard. **Pets**
Dogs allowed. **Facilities** Parking. **Nearby** "Côte des abers" from Conquet to
Brignognan (120km); Guiligui Dolmen. **Open** Mar – Oct except Public Holidays.

This large, somewhat ordinary village house is surrounded by a
garden and is very well-located a hundred meters from a small
bridge. You will find family-style hospitality, half-way between that
of a bed-and-breakfast and a hotel. Recently renovated, the bedrooms
are simple, pleasant, impeccably maintained and very bright. On the
premier étage upstairs, they are classic and decorated with period
furniture. On the *second étage*, there is a younger ambiance and some
duplex rooms which are ideal for families. A dinner menu is posted
in the lobby every day (on reservation). The cuisine is traditional and
of course regularly features fish and shellfish. A great wine lover, M.
Richard has built up a very interesting cellar of estate-bottled wines
and *grands crus*. This is an occasion to make interesting discoveries,
although it is a shame that the decoration of the dining room is not
of the same distinction as the wines. Larger tables with more space
between them and pretty tablecloths would fill the bill. Apart from
that, the "Ocean Residence" is pleasant, the prices are reasonable and
you shouldn't miss a walk to the highly poetic port.

How to get there *(Map 4): 30km north of Brest towards Saint-Renan. In*
Ploudaimézeau, take the road to Portsall. Signposted.

Le Brittany ★★★

Boulevard Sainte–Barbe
29681 Roscoff (Finistère)
Tel. (0)2★ 98.69.70.78 – Fax (0)2★ 98. 61. 13. 29. – Mme Chapalain

Rooms 25 and 1 studio with telephone,bath or shower,WC and TV; elevator. **Price** Single 390-440F, double 460-630F, studio 650-950F. **Meals** Breakfast 58F, served 7:00-10:30; half board 390-590F. **Restaurant** "Le Yachtman" Service 12:15-14:00, 19:15-21:30 (closed Monday noon); menus 120-320F, also à la carte. Specialties: Fish and shellfish. **Credit cards** Amex, Visa, Eurocard and MasterCard. **Pets** Dogs allowed except in restaurant. **Facilities** Covered and heated swimming pool, sauna, parking. **Nearby** Balz island (15 min. by boat), Saint-Pol-de-Léon, tour of châteaux of Léon (château of Kérouzéré, manoir of Tronjoly, château of Kerjéan). **Open** Apr – Oct.

In the delightful small town of Roscoff, the Brittany Hotel is the last rampart against the winds that beat in from the Atlantic. The bedrooms are decorated with beautiful old furniture and white fabric wall coverings; they are calm and pleasant, with well equipped bathrooms. You might want to have breakfast in your room because the breakfast room near the swimming pool can be noisy. The dining room, which is located in a 17th-century manor house, is the most charming and pleasant part of the hotel: Facing due west, it looks out over the sea and its large bay windows bathe the room with light. The hospitality is very British, and the cuisine is typical of the region, with lots of fresh fish; and there is a very good wine list. The bar has the discreet atmosphere of a great hotel. The last stop on the way to Ireland and England, this auberge combines the pleasures of a comfortable stopover with the tranquillity of an old Breton house.

How to get there *(Map 5): 25km north of Morlaix.*

Hotel de la Plage ★★★★

Boulevard Sainte-Barbe
29550 Sainte-Anne-la-Palud (Finistère)
Tel. (0)2★ 98.92.50.12 - Fax (0)2★ 98.92.56.54 - M. and Mme Le Coz

Rooms 30 with telephone, bath or shower, WC, TV and minibar; elevator. **Price** Single 400-450F, double 750-1350F, suite 1000-1350F. **Meals** Breakfast 75F, served 8:00-10:00; half board 400F (obligatory in summer), full board 550F (per pers., 2 days min.). **Restaurant** Service 12:30-13:30, 19:30-21:00; menus 220-400F, also à la carte. Specialties: Fish and shellfish. **Credit cards** All major. **Pets** Dogs allowed except in restaurant. **Facilities** Swimming pool, tennis, sauna, parking. **Nearby** Saint-Corentin cathedral and art museum in Quimper; Locronan; church in Ploéven – 18-hole l'Odet golf course in Bénodet. **Open** End-Mar– beg-Nov.

The small road that leads to this hotel goes right up to the sandy beach facing a superb bay. The hotel thus well deserves its name, "The Beach". Luxurious without being stuffy, it takes maximum advantage of its exceptional location. The comfortable bedrooms are classically decorated overall, with beautiful period furniture, paintings, and carpets. Others have been recently appointed in an especially elegant seaside style; they overlook the garden or the ocean. You can enjoy a marvelous panorama from the salon-bar and the restaurant. Spacious bay windows give you the impression that the hotel is right on the beach: you definitely feel as if you're on vacation. The restaurant service is attentive and pleasant and the famous gastronomy of course gives a place of honor to seafood.

How to get there *(Map 5): 17km northwest of Quimper via D63 to Locronan at the first traffic circle, take Plonévez-Porzay exit.*

Les Grandes Roches ★★★

Route des Grandes-Roches
29910 Trégunc (Finistère)
Tel. (0)2★ 98.97.62.97 – Fax (0)2★ 98.50.29.19 – M. and Mme Henrich

Rooms 22 with telephone, bath or shower and WC. **Price** Single 250F, double 300-400F, suite 550F. **Meals** Breakfast 45F, served 8:00-9:30; half board 300-450F (per pers., 3 days min.). **Restaurant** Closed mid. Nov – mid. Mar. Service 12:30-14:30 (only Saturday, Sunday and National Holidays), 19:15-21:15 (every night); menus 98-250F, also à la carte. Specialties: Seafood, saumon à la peau, poissons fumés à l'auberge, filets de canard, nougat glacé maison. **Credit cards** Visa, Eurocard and MasterCard. **Pets** Dogs not allowed. **Facilities** Parking. **Nearby** Pont-Aven, Nizon, Kérangosquer, Concarneau, Nevez – 18-hole l'Odet golf course in Bénodet and Queven. **Open** Jan 15 – Dec 15.

This old farmhouse, which has been renovated and is very comfortable, stands in a large and well-shaded garden. There is a bar with a terrace, two dining rooms and a lounge with television. The thatched cottages, an unusual and interesting feature, have been very well restored and turned into apartments furnished in traditional style. A *menhir* can be found in the grounds – evidence of prehistoric occupation – and in the countryside around there are more dolmens, menhirs and monoliths. A number of beaches are close by. The owner's husband is German, which makes this a popular spot for visitors from beyond the Rhine.

How to get there *(Map 5): 28km southeast of Quimper via D783 to Trégunc via Concarneau; (the auberge is just outside the village).*

Hôtel Ménez ★★

Saint–Antoine
29252 Plouézoc'h (Finistère)
Tel. (0)2★ 98.67.28.85 – Mme Ménez

Rooms 8 with telephone, bath or shower and WC. **Price** Single 170F, double 250-290F. **Meals** Breakfast 25F, served 8:00-10:00. No restaurant. **Credit cards** Not accepted. **Pets** Dogs not allowed. **Facilities** Parking. **Nearby** Morlaix River, Plougonyen, parish enclosures of Saint-Thegonnec, Guimiliau and Lampaul-Guimiliau – 18-hole Saint-Samson golf course in Pleumeur-Bodou. **Open** June 1 – Sept 1 only by reservation.

This is another recently built hotel, but this one adheres scrupulously to the Breton style. Standing in a park with countryside around, it has ten very well-furnished bedrooms with every modern facility. On the ground floor the light and cozy living room is peaceful and relaxing. The proprietors are kind and welcoming. In Morlaix, try the small restaurant *L'Auberge Saint-Antoine* and *La Marée Bleue*.

How to get there (Map 5): 9km north of Morlaix via D46.

Hôtel Richeux

35260 Cancale (Ille-et-Vilaine)
Tel. (0)2★ 99.89.25.25 - Fax (0)2★ 99.89.88.47
M. and Mme Roellinger

Rooms 11 and 2 suites with telephone, bath, WC, TV and minibar; elevator - 1 for disabled persons. **Price** Double 750-1550F. **Meals** Breakfast 85F, served 8:00-10:00. **Restaurant** Closed Monday and Tuesday noon in low season. Service 12:30-14:00, 19:30-21:30; menu shellfish from 100F, also à la carte. **Credit cards** All major. **Pets** Dogs allowed (+50F). **Facilities** Parking. **Nearby** Saint-Malo, Côte d'Emeraude, Mont Saint-Michel – 18-hole Dinard golf course in Saint-Briac. **Open** All year.

In this beautiful, spacious house, Olivier and Jeanne Roellinger have just opened a luxurious auberge on the seafront whose discreet charm, comfort and refinement will delight you. In each bedroom, with a view over the Bay of Mont Saint-Michel or the Breton countryside, you will find a different atmosphere, with beautiful old furniture and a bouquet of fresh flowers. All the bathrooms are bright and very pleasant. In the dining room, which opens onto the garden, you will savor the chef's fish specialties, along with fresh vegetables from the garden and fruit from the orchard. This is a very high-quality hotel which will surely satisfy the most demanding guests.

How to get there *(Map 6): 12km east of Saint-Malo; in Cancale, turn towards of Mont Saint-Michel.*

Hôtel Les Rimains

1, rue Duguesclin
35260 Cancale (Ille-et-Vilaine)
Tel. (0)2★ 99.89.64.76 – Fax (0)2★ 99.89.88.47 – M. and Mme Roellinger

Rooms 6 with telephone, bath, WC, TV and minibar. **Price** Double 750-850F.
Meals Breakfast 85F, served 8:00-10:00. **Restaurant** (600 m from hotel) Closed
Tuesday and Wednesday in low season. Service 12:30-14:00, 19:30-21:00; menu,
also à la carte. **Credit cards** All major. **Pets** Dogs allowed (+50F). **Facilities** Parking.
Nearby Saint-Malo, Côte d'Emeraude, Mont Saint-Michel – 18-hole Dinard golf
course in Saint-Briac. **Open** Mar 1 – Dec 31.

On the edge of a wild and unspoiled cliff overlooking the Bay
of Mont Saint Michel, Les Rimains has six small, bright
bedrooms which are tastefully decorated and have up-to-date
amenities. From the ground floor and the upstairs rooms, the
grandiose panoramic view dominates the hotel. There is no lounge
here but the garden of this authentic Breton house is a lovely place
in which to relax and enjoy the view of the beautiful countryside.
You can also have a delicious breakfast in the garden. There is no
restaurant but the owners will welcome you to their Relais
Gourmand Olivier Roellinger and ply you with the tempting local
specialties and the fresh products of the region. The welcome is
charming and discreet.

How to get there *(Map 6): 12km east of Saint-Malo; hotel signposted
beginning at the church.*

Château de la Motte Beaumanoir ★★★

35720 Pleugueneuc (Ille-et-Vilaine)
Tel. (0)2★ 99.69.46.01 - Fax (0)2★ 99.69.42.49
M. Bernard

Rooms 6 and 2 suites with telephone, bath and WC (TV on request). **Price** Double 900F, suite 1000F. **Meals** Breakfast incl., served 8:00-10:00; half board 560F (per pers.). **Restaurant** Closed Tuesday and Nov 15 – Mar 15. Service 12:00-13:00, 20:00-22:00; menus 140-250F, also à la carte. Specialties: Traditional cooking. **Credit cards** Amex, Visa, Eurocard and MasterCard. **Pets** Dogs allowed (+60F). **Facilities** Heated swimming pool, boating, fishing, parking. **Nearby** Dinan, Léhon, Pleslin, château de la Hunaudaie – 18-hole Dinard golf course in Saint-Briac-sur-Mer. **Open** Jan 3 – Dec 22.

A landscape of forests, lakes and fields surrounds this tranquil 15th-century château. Most of the rooms are very spacious, furnished with antique or period furniture and have a superb view of the lake. These attractions and the beautiful swimming pool surrounded by a carefully tended garden, however, are not enough to make you forget the final bill. La Motte Beaumanoir thus is still a good place for a short visit, but we hesitate to recommend it for a longer stay.

How to get there *(Map 6): 12km southeast of Dinan via N137; then north of Pleugeuneuc turn right at first crossroads from Dinan, toward Plesder.*

Manoir de la Rance ★★★

Château de Jouvente
35730 Pleurtuit (Ille-et-Vilaine)
Tel. (0)2★ 99.88.53.76 - Fax (0)2★ 99.88.63.03 - Mme Jasselin

Rooms 10 with telephone, bath, WC and TV. **Price** Single 400-450F, double 450-800F, suite 800-1200F (-20% Oct – Apr). **Meals** Breakfast 50F, served 7:00-11:00. No restaurant. **Credit cards** Visa, Eurocard and MasterCard. **Pets** Dogs allowed (+40F). **Facilities** Parking. **Nearby** Banks of the river Rance, castle and walled town of Saint-Malo, Cézembre island, Chausey island, côte d'Emeraude from Dinard to Le Val André – 27-hole Saint-Malo golf course. **Open** Mar – Dec.

Facing the Rance and surrounded by trees and flowers, this 19th-century manor stands in large and lovely grounds. The big lounge is pleasantly furnished in a mixture of styles. The bar and the small living room, where tea is served, have a very homey atmosphere. Refreshments are served outside in the charming gardens and terraces, which have reclining chairs. Located on three floors, all the bedrooms are very comfortable and quiet, and all have a stunning view of the sea, the cliffs and the countryside. Mme Jasselin, the owner, is very friendly. For dining, you will find *Le Petit Robinson* in La Richardais (3km), and many restaurants in Saint-Malo.

How to get there *(Map 6): 15km southeast of Saint-Malo via D168, then left after the Rance Dam on D114 to La Jouvente (via La Richardais). The manor is to the left on the way out of the village.*

La Korrigane ★★★

39, rue Le Pomellec - Saint-Servan
35400 Saint-Malo (Ille-et-Vilaine)
Tel. (0)2★ 99.81.65.85 - Fax (0)2★ 99.82.23.89 - M. Marchon

Rooms 10 with telephone, bath or shower, WC and TV. **Price** Single and double 400-800F. **Meals** Breakfast 55F, served 8:00-10:00; brunch 120F. No restaurant. **Credit cards** All major. **Pets** Dogs allowed (+50F). **Facilities** Parking. **Nearby** Ramparts, castle and walled town of Saint-Malo, Chaussey islands, Cézembre island, Jersey, England, Saint-Samson cathedral in Dol-de-Bretagne. **Open** Feb 1 – Dec 31.

This is without doubt one of the most charming little hotels in France. It lies within a turn-of-the-century house which from the outside looks like an old holiday retreat turned into a family *pension*. The atmosphere is so comfortable that you feel quite at home, and the welcome is warm, discreet and courteous. Everything is restful, exquisitely tasteful and unpretentious. Each bedroom has its own color scheme, with perfectly harmonized colors and fabrics, and lovely furniture and paintings. Behind the house is a small garden where you can have breakfast or enjoy the sunshine. The large, book-lined living room is an invitation to relax as are the tea-room and bar. La Korrigane is better than a hotel: it is your own special *pied-à-terre* in Saint-Malo. *Le Saint Placide* is one of the best restaurants in this part of Saint Malo; note also the *Métairie de Beauregard*, *La Corderie* and *La Duchesse Anne* in the town.

How to get there *(Map 6): In the center of town, on N137 take the Saint-Servan road.*

L'Ascott Hôtel ★★★

35, rue du Chapitre – Saint-Servan
35400 Saint-Malo (Ille-et-Vilaine)
Tel. (0)2★ 99.81.89.93 – Fax (0)2★ 99.81.77.40 – M. and Mme Hardouin

Rooms 10 with telephone, bath, WC and TV. **Price** Single 350-400F, double 400-600F. **Meals** Breakfast 50F, served all morning. No restaurant. **Credit cards** Visa, Eurocard and MasterCard. **Pets** Dogs allowed. **Facilities** Parking. **Nearby** Ramparts, castles and walled town of Saint-Malo, Chaussey and Cézembre islands, Jersey, England, Saint-Samson cathedral in Dol-de-Bretagne. **Open** All year.

In an elegantly renovated 19th-century mansion surrounded by a tiny garden, this small hotel is a charming new address in Saint Malo. The hospitality and the atmosphere are very refined. No detail has been overlooked. The bedrooms, which are named after racetracks, are snug and quiet. The walls are covered with prettily colored fabrics, which are coordinated with the bedspreads and curtains. Some rooms have a small balcony where you can have breakfast. On the ground floor, there is the lounge, as appealing as the rest of the house, and which opens onto the small, lush garden where drinks are served. Near the hotel, you will find *Le Saint Placide*, one of the best restaurants in this part of Saint Malo; note also the *Métairie de Beauregard*, *La Corderie* and *La Duchesse Anne* in the town.

How to get there *(Map 6): Via N137, take the towards Saint-Servan, then Boulevard Douville and the second street to the left (signposted).*

Hôtel Village La Désirade ★★★

56360 Belle-Ile-en-Mer (Morbihan)
Tel. (0)2★ 97.31.70.70 - Fax (0)2★ 97.31.89.63
Mme Mulon

Rooms 26 with telephone, bath, WC and TV. **Price** Double 390-560F. **Meals** Breakfast 60F, served 8:00-11:00. No restaurant but evening meal April 1 – Nov 11. **Credit cards** All major. **Pets** Dogs allowed (+30F). **Facilities** Heated swimming pool, parking. **Nearby** Vauban fortifications, cave of l'Apothicairerie, port Donnan, les Aiguilles de Port-Coton – 18-hole Sauzon golf course in Belle-Ile-en-Mer. **Open** March 15 – Jan 6.

Facing the Côte Sauvage 1500 meters from the sea in a hamlet typical of Belle-Ile-en-Mer where Monet painted "Les Aiguilles de Port-Coton," La Désirade is composed of five small houses built around a heated swimming pool. Each of these has four bedrooms, giving a family or group of friends a place entirely to themselves. The decor is simple but in good taste, with brightly colored chintzes creating a cheerful effect all year round. In the morning a breakfast buffet is set out by the swimming pool, allowing everybody to keep his own pace. This is a relaxed place where privacy is respected. There is a restaurant adjoining the hotel.

How to get there *(Map 5): By car, take the Quiberon-Le Palais ferry; by air from Lorient by Finist-Air (20 min. flight); 7km southwest of Le Palais via D190 through Bangor; (the hotel is 2km from Bangor).*

Petit Hôtel Les Pougnots

Rue du Chemin-Neuf - Le Sauzon
56340 Belle-Ile-en-Mer (Morbihan)
Tel. (0)2★ 97.31.61.03 - Mme Guillouët

Rooms 5 with telephone, shower and WC. **Price** Single 450F, double 530F.
Meals Breakfast incl., served 8:30-12:00. No restaurant. **Credit cards** Not accepted.
Pets Dogs not allowed. **Nearby** Vauban fortifications, cave of l'Apothicairerie, Port
Donnan, les Aiguilles de Port-Coton – 18-hole Sauzon golf course in Belle-Ile-en-
Mer. **Open** All year.

The Hôtel des Pougnots is in Sauzon is in a little port surrounded
by whitewashed cottages with colored shutters. Set high up
in the village, this friendly small hotel looks rather like a chalet and
has only five bedrooms to offer. Inside, the decoration is simple,
even somewhat monastic in style, but tasteful and comfortable.
Breakfast can be served on a small balcony overlooking the harbor.
This delightful hotel, until recently known by word of mouth only,
it is superbly located on wild, romantic Belle-Ile with its ocean-
swept cliffs, gorse and heaths. In Le Sauzon, the friendly restaurant
Roz-Avel serves delicious cuisine made with fresh ingredients.

How to get there *(Map 5): By car, take the Quiberon-Le Palais ferry; by
air from Lorient by Finist-Air (20 min. flight); 5km from Le Palais, at the
port of Le Sauzon.*

Domaine de Rochevilaine ★★★★

Pointe de Pen Lan
56190 Billiers-Muzillac (Morbihan)
Tel. (0)2★ 97.41.61.61 - Fax (0)2★ 97.41.44.85 - M. Cotillard

Rooms 26 and 1 suite with telephone, bath, WC and TV - Wheelchair access.
Price Double 750-1150F, suite 1400-1600F. **Meals** Breakfast 60F, served 7:00-
10:30; half board 780F, full board 1030F (per pers., 3 days min.). **Restaurant** Service
12:15-14:00 and 19:30-21:15; menu 250-375F (with lobster), also à la carte.
Specialties: Lobster and seafood. **Credit cards** All major. **Pets** Dogs allowed (+50F).
Facilities Heated swimming pool, parking. **Nearby** Rochefort-en-Terre, Morbihan
gulf– 18-hole Kerver golf course. **Open** March 16 – end Jan.

Built on the majestic site of the Pointe de Pen Lan, a former
lookout post, the Domaine de Rochevilaine looks like a small
village. Its several buildings follow the geographic contours of the
Point and face the sea, taking maximum advantage of the
breathtaking view over the Atlantic. This is a luxurious hotel whose
bedrooms are well located and spacious, elegantly classic and
comfortable. The most attractive are the ones with antique
decoration; the more modern rooms are unremarkable. Note also
the suite with a beautiful private terrace. The panoramic restaurant
offers one of the finest cuisines of Brittany (try the lobster menu),
but it is a shame that the tables are so close together. The
Rochevilaine is a superb hotel for a very special weekend.

*How to get there (Map 14): 20km southeast of Vannes via the express route
(towards Nantes) to Muzillac; then to Billiers and Pointe de Pen Lan.*

Les Chaumières de Kerniaven

Route de Port-Louis
56700 Hennebont (Morbihan)
Tel. (0)2★ 97.76.29.04 - Fax (0)2★ 97.76.82.35 - M. de La Sablière

Rooms 11 with telephone, bath, WC and TV (10 with minibar). **Price** Single and double 380-680F. **Meals** Breakfast 68F, served 7:45-10:30; half board 780F, full board 1030F (per pers., 3 days min.). **Restaurant** In the château of Locguénolé. **Credit cards** All major. **Pets** Dogs allowed (+50F). **Facilities** Swimming pool, sauna, tennis (4km), parking. **Nearby** La Cie des Indes museum in Port-Louis; haras nationaux d'Hennebont; Saint-Cado island; la Barre d'Etel; Groix island– 18-hole Val Queven golf course. **Open** Mar – Nov.

These two charming thatched-roof cottages are part of the Château of Locguénolé. They are located 3km away in the heart of the countryside but all enjoy the advantages of the hotel: a superb swimming-pool, sauna, tennis courts, and innumerable private paths along the seafront. You can alternate your stay between the luxurious atmosphere of the château and the calm countryside of your cottage. In the main *chaumière*, the bedrooms are vast and decorated in a style which is both rustic and elegant, with several pieces of smartly waxed antique furniture and exposed-stone walls. On the *premier étage*, the bedrooms have a mezzanine which families will enjoy, while on the ground floor, beautiful log fires crackle in imposing fireplaces (except for one, which we like somewhat less). In the other *chaumière*, the bedrooms are somewhat smaller, decorated in the same spirit and are somewhat less expensive. You can ask for your breakfast there, unless you prefer having it outdoors. Lunches and dinners are served in the château dining room, which has elegant yellow or blue tablecloths and an 18th-century Aubusson tapestry on one wall. You will enjoy famous cuisine and the especially friendly hospitality refutes the notion that luxury is always stuffy.

How to get there *(Map 5): 5km of Hennebont, via Port-Louis.*

Logis Parc er Gréo ★★★

Mané-Guen-Le Gréo
56610 Arradon (Morbihan)
Tel. (0)2★ 97.44.73.03 - Fax (0)2★ 97.44.80.48 - M. Bermond

Rooms 12 with telephone, bath or shower, WC and TV - Wheelchair access. **Price** Single 224-420F, double 280-450F. **Meals** Breakfast 30-45F, served 8:00-12:30 (11:00 in room); half board 245-560F (per pers., 3 days min.). No restaurant but evening meal for residents only, by reservation in the morning; service from 20:00; menus 115-320F. Specialties: Fish, seasonal cuisine. **Credit cards** All major. **Pets** Dogs allowed (+40F). **Facilities** Swimming pool, monutain bikes rentals. **Nearby** Morbihan Gulf, Ile de Gravinis, Ile aux Moines, Carnac – 18-hole Baden golf course. **Open** Feb 1 – Dec 31.

Even though the Logis Parc er Gréo has been built recently, this small hotel is indeed one of "character and charm," beginning with the welcome you receive. The decoration combines shapes and colors beautifully, with antique furniture here and there, a boat model, or a painting done by an artist friend. Finally, there is the beautiful island setting itself. From the terrace as well as the bedrooms, you have a lovely view of the swimming pool, the fields and trees and, just behind them, one of the small inlets that so charmingly dot the Morbihan Gulf. The bedrooms, which look due south, are a model of taste and comfort. On the ground floor, the living room is also a dining room where excellent breakfasts and dinners are served. When it's sunny, meals are also served on the pretty flowery terrace. There is a small winter garden with luxuriant bougainvillia where you can enjoy a view of the countryside whether it rains or shines.

How to get there *(Map 14): 10km southwest of Vannes via D101 to Le Moustoir, on left, then 6ᵗʰ turn on right.*

Hôtel de la Marine ★★

7, rue du Général-de-Gaulle
56590 Ile-de-Groix (Morbihan)
Tel. (0)2★ 97.86.80.05 - Fax (0)2★ 97.86.56.37 - Mme Hubert

Rooms 22 with telephone, bath or shower and WC. **Price** Single 186-215F, double 217-440F. **Meals** Breakfast 35F, served 8:00-10:00; half board 218-341F, full board 292-420F (per pers., 2 days min.). **Restaurant** Service 12:00-13:30, 19:30-21:30; menus 70-150F, also à la carte. Specialties: Feuilleté de Saint-Jacques, barbecue de poisson, marquise au chocolat. **Credit cards** Visa, Eurocard and MasterCard. **Pets** Dogs allowed (+20F). **Facilities** Parking. **Nearby** Museum in Groix, L'Enfer point, Saint-Nicolas seaport, Pen-Mer. **Open** Feb 1 – Dec 31.

This is a real find, because many of the hotels on the islands are neglected and seem to count on their isolation (and the necessity of catching the last boat) to keep their clientele. There is none of that attitude here. Mme Hubert, the owner, has lovingly designed and arranged this hotel, and we are certain that you will appreciate her taste. The reception room has pretty, old-fashioned furniture; the dining room, where you can eat very well at reasonable prices, has attractive colored table linens; on the fireplace and the shelves is a collection of pottery; in a corner, a shell-encrusted clock is the only reminder of the passage of time. The bedrooms are simple, painted white and brightened with colored curtains and bedspreads. Ask for those facing the sea (especially No. 1), but all are very pleasant and comfortable. Outside in a paved garden, drinks are served in the shade of the oldest tree on the island. An unreservedly kind welcome awaits you here.

How to get there *(Map 5): boat from Lorient (45 min., tel. 97.21.03.97).*

Le San Francisco ★★

56780 Ile aux Moines (Morbihan)
Tel. (0)2★ 97.26.31.52 – Fax (0)2★ 97.26.35.59
M. Vérien

Rooms 8 with telephone, bath or shower, WC and TV. **Price** Double 315-525F.
Meals Breakfast 40-55F, served 8:00-9:30; half board 285-380F (per pers.).
Restaurant Closed Thursday in winter. Service 12:00-14:00, 19:00-20:30; menu 135-230F, also à la carte. Specialties: Fish and shellfish, sauté de langoustines sauce crustacés, mousse de saumon sur crème de courgettes. **Credit cards** Amex, Visa, Eurocard and MasterCard. **Pets** Dogs allowed (+30F). **Nearby** Morbihan Gulf – 18-hole La Bretesche golf course. **Open** Dec 19 – Nov 16.

The San Francisco enjoys the most beautiful location on the island: facing the port, with the dramatic, jagged coast of the Gulf of Morbihan in the distance. Today a spot that tourists love, the small hotel nevertheless is beautifully quiet. The ambience is refined but not stiff, and the overall decoration is very pleasant. All the rooms are quiet, comfortable and brightened with elegant color schemes. Reserve in advance and ask for a room with a superb view over the sea. One room has a small terrace facing the port. There is a pleasant reception area, a charming dining room and, above all, as soon as it's fine weather, you can relax on a delicious terrace where you can have meals and admire the magnificent view. You will always be warmly welcomed to this charming hotel on "Monks' Island".

How to get there *(Map 14): 14km south of Vannes; on Autoroute E60, exit Vannes-Ouest; then follow signs for Ile aux Moines to boat landing. 5 min. crossing; in winter, 7 AM to 8 PM; in summer, 7 AM to 10 PM.*

Au Vieux Chêne **

Kerault
56690 Landévant (Morbihan)
Tel. (0)2★ 97.56.90.01 – M. and Mme Bouteloup

Rooms 7 with telephone (3 with bath, 2 with shower and 3 with WC). **Price** Single and Double 150-230F. **Meals** Breakfast 35F, served until 10:20; half board 270-350F, full board 370-450F. **Restaurant** Closed Tuesday evening and Wednesday in low season. Service 12:15-14:00, 19:15-21:30; menus 75-170F, also à la carte. Specialties: Salade de crevettes tiède au vinaigre de framboise, saumon fumé maison, escargots en croûte, caramel de crème, fondant au chocolat. **Credit cards** All major. **Pets** Dogs allowed (+20F). **Facilities** Parking. **Nearby** Ile de Groix, Hennebont, Citadel of Port-Louis – 18-hole Ploemem golf course. **Open** All year (closed Tuesday evening and Wednesday in low season).

In a small park planted with 300-year-old trees, set between the countryside and the spectacular coastline of the Morbihan, the Vieux Chêne offers seven comfortable rooms where you can enjoy the areas peace, quiet and lush green beauty. While the decoration of the bedrooms is simple, and not all have bathrooms, the cuisine is outstanding in both originality and finesse. In the atmosphere of a country inn, the owners will greet you like a member of their family; they do their job with love and professionalism, and you will reap the benefits of their devotion. This is very good quality for the price, and every effort is made so that children are neither a burden for their parents nor a nuisance for other guests. We're sure you will love "The Old Oak" for its simplicity and courtesy.

How to get there *(Map 5): 20km southeast of Lorient via N165, exit Landevant interchange; then follow signs.*

Moulin de Lesnehué ★★

Lesnevé
56890 Saint-Avé (Morbihan)
Tel. (0)2★ 97.60.77.77 - Mme Cheval

Rooms 12 with telephone, bath or shower and WC. **Price** Single 170F, double 240-260F. **Meals** Breakfast 32F, served 8:00-10:00. No restaurant but "crêperie". **Credit cards** All major. **Pets** Dogs allowed. **Facilities** Parking. **Nearby** Chapel of Notre-Dame-du-Loc in Saint-Avé, ramparts and Saint-Pierre cathedral in Vannes, Conleau peninsula, fortress of Largoët, château du Plessis-Jossot – 18-hole Kerver golf course in Saint-Gildas de Rhuys.**Open** Jan 15 – Dec 15.

This 15th-century stone mill has a lovely location in the middle of the countryside on the banks of a stream. The bedrooms are arranged in the two buildings which form the hotel. All of them are simple and modern, with contemporary furnishings, but charming and comfortable. The hotel has no restaurant, but there is a *crêperie* in one of the buildings. Ferns, flowers, the sound of water and birdsong provide nature's backdrop to this lovely welcoming place.

How to get there *(Map 14): 5km north of Vannes via D126; turn right on the way out of the village of Lesnehué.*

Hôtel des Trois Fontaines ★

56740 Locmariaquer (Morbihan)
Tel. (0)2 97.57.42.70 – Fax (0)2 97.57.30.59
Mme Orain

Rooms 18 with telephone, bath, WC, TV, 17 with minibar and safe. **Price** Double 295-550F.
Meals Breakfast 45F, served 7:30-12:00. No restaurant. **Credit cards** All major. **Pets** Dogs
allowed (+30F). **Facilities** Parking. **Nearby** Menhirs of Carnac and Erdeven, church in
Plouhinec, Belle-Ile – 18-hole Saint-Laurent-Ploëmel golf course. **Open** Beg April – Nov 15.

When you arrive at this hotel, don't worry about the proximity
of the small road (it goes only to the village) or about the walls
which are still new: The hospitality and the interior decoration of the
"Three Fountains" largely compensate for this drawback. You will
surely admire, as we did, the tastefully modern and pleasant decoration
of the small lounge which forms a half-circle around the fireplace, as
well as the bedroom designs. The floors are of terra-cotta or parquet,
and the mahogany furniture is reminiscent of boat furniture; other
main features are the white walls with elegant drapes coordinated with
courtepointe bedcovers and beautiful bathrooms. Reserve in advance
for a room with a pretty view over a small natural port. Of course,
the prices vary with the room, the most beautiful room (for families)
is in the center of the hotel and has a bow window which is ideal for
watching the tides. The breakfasts are good and are served on the
terrace with the first nice weather. For dinner, there are two excellent
restaurants in La Trinité: *L'Azimuth* and *L'Ecallier*. Locqmariaquer
itself occupies a kind of peninsula at the tip of the Gulf of Morbihan.
The location is superb, apart from its vast beaches, jagged creeks and
mooring coves, the village has large megalithic vestiges.

How to get there *(Map 5): 15km south of Auray towards La-Trinité-
sur-Mer and Locmariaquer.*

Hôtel de Kerlon ★★

56680 Plouhinec (Morbihan)
Tel. (0)2 97.36.77.03 – Fax (0)2 97.85.81.14
M. and Mme Coëffic

Rooms 16 with telephone and WC, (15 with bath or shower and 15 with TV).
Price Single 240-265F, double 270-300F. **Meals** Breakfast 38F, served 8:00-10:00;
half board 265-300F (per pers.). **Restaurant** Service 19:30-21:00; menus 82-155F,
also à la carte. Specialties: Fish, seafood. **Credit cards** Visa, Eurocard and
MasterCard. **Pets** Dogs not allowed. **Facilities** Parking. **Nearby** Quiberon, Morbihan
Gulf, île de Groix, Port-Louis – 18-hole Queven golf course, 18-hole Ploemeur-Océan
golf course in Saint-Jude. **Open** Mar 16 – Oct 31.

This hotel is set in the middle of the countryside, 5km from the
sea and midway between Lorient and Carnac. It is a farmhouse
which has been completely renovated. The beams, exposed
stonework and two fireplaces give a rustic air to the dining room,
which has a small terrace where drinks are served or where you
can relax beside the garden. The bedrooms are plainly decorated
and quiet. Being close to the beaches and resorts does not spoil this
hotel's tranquil, rural atmosphere, and you can enjoy biking
everywhere.

How to get there *(Map 5): 30km southeast of Lorient. Leave N165 at
Hennebont, Carnac-Quiberon-Port-Louis exit, then follow signs Carnac-
Quiberon.*

Hostellerie Les Ajoncs d'Or ★★

Kerbachique
56340 Plouharnel (Morbihan)
Tel. (0)2★ 97.52.32.02 – Fax (0)2★ 97.52.40.36 – Mme Le Maguer

Rooms 17 with telephone, bath or shower and WC (10 with TV). **Price** Double 280-380F, suite 650F (4 pers.). **Meals** Breakfast 36F, served 8:00-9:30; half board 290-350F (per pers.). **Restaurant** Service 19:00-21:30; menus 96-145F, also à la carte. Specialties: Regional cooking, seafood. **Credit cards** Visa, Eurocard and MasterCard. **Pets** Small dogs allowed (+20F) **Facilities** Parking. **Nearby** Menhirs of Carnac and Erdeven, church in Plouhinec, Belle-Ile – 18-hole Saint-Laurent-Ploëmel golf course. **Open** Mar 15 – Nov 2.

Les Ajoncs d'Or is a pink granite Breton farmhouse made up of three adjoining buildings and situated outside the village. On the ground floor, a large restaurant with a lovely fireplace happily combines beams, exposed stonework, flowered curtains and pictures. Next door is another very pleasant room for breakfasts. The bedrooms are simple and comfortable. We recommend those above the restaurant, which are well-renovated, light and cheerful. Thanks to the hostess, the hotel has a family atmosphere. And the warmth of the welcome makes Les Ajoncs d'Or a very special place to stay.

How to get there *(Map 5): 52km of Lorient via N165 to Auray, then D768 and D781 (between Carnac and Plouharnel).*

Domaine de Bodeuc ★★★

Nivillac - 56130 La Roche-Bernard (Morbihan)
Tel. (0)2★ 99.90.89.63 - Fax (0)2★ 99.90.90.32
M. and Mme Grandpierre

Rooms 8 with telephone, bath or shower, WC and TV; elevator - Wheelchair access.
Price Double 550F, 250F (1 small room for 1 pers.). **Meals** Breakfast 45F, served
8:00-12:30. **Restaurant** Residents only, by reservation. Service 19:00-21:00; menu
170F. **Credit cards** Amex, Visa, Eurocard and MasterCard. **Pets** Dogs allowed.
Facilities Heated swimming pool, Parking. **Nearby** La Baule, tour of La Brière and
the Guérande marshes, Morbihan Gulf– 18-hole La Bretesche golf course. **Open** All
Year.

Charming M. and Mme Grandpierre will welcome you to this
pretty hotel, which is hidden in the Breton countryside but
is only 20 minutes from the beach. The lovely little manor house
stands in a large 37–acre park, its façade so covered with ivy that
you can see only the white shutters and slate roof. The eight
bedrooms are spacious, each with its own style, and all are decorated
with antique furniture and pretty fabrics. The bathrooms, which
have been tiled by a specialized craftsman, are comfortable and
bright. As a final touch, a basket of fruit is placed in your bedroom.
On the ground floor, there is a large lounge where drinks and
coffee are served, and downstairs, there is a billiard table for guests.
If you wish, M. Grandpierre will make you dinner of simple but
delicious family dishes. He also makes his own jams, which are
served with hot croissants for breakfast.

How to get there (Map 14): 40km south of Vannes via E60. At La Roche-
Bernard, turn towards Redon for 5km, then follow the signs.

Auberge du Moulin de Chaméron ★★★

18210 Bannegon (Cher)
Tel. (0)2★ 48.61.83.80 – Fax (0)2★ 48.61.84.92
M. Candore

Rooms 13 with telephone, bath or shower, WC and TV. **Price** Single 330F, double 500F, suite 670F. **Meals** Breakfast 50F, served 7:30-10:00. **Restaurant** Service 12:15-14:00, 19:30-21:00; menus 145-195F, also à la carte. Specialties: Seasonal cooking. **Credit cards** Amex, Visa, Eurocard and MasterCard. **Pets** Dogs allowed (+30F). **Facilities** Swimming pool, parking. **Nearby** Basilica and château of Châteauneuf-sur-Cher, church of Saint-Amand-Montrond, abbey of Noirlac, châteaux of Meillant and Ainay-le-Vieil, Bourges – 18-hole Val-de-Cher golf course in Montluçon. **Open** Mar 1 – Nov 15. (closed Tuesday in low season).

This renovated 18th-century mill lies deep in the countryside. The old mill machinery has been kept intact in the middle of the building and a museum displays a collection of tools and objects used by millers in the past. The bedrooms located in an annex are attractive enough and vary in spaciousness; some have a small ground-floor terrace (where you can have breakfast.) They still have their old flowery wallpaper and rustic furniture; all could do with refurbishing. In good weather, lunch and dinner are served in the garden near the millpond; otherwise, service takes place in a beautiful and intimate small room with fireplace in the old mill. The cuisine is excellent and the staff are very pleasant. The Auberge is particularly charming in good weather.

How to get there *(Map 17): 42km southeast of Bourges via N76 towards Moulins, then D953 and D41.*

La Solognote ⋆⋆

18410 Brinon-sur-Sauldre (Cher)
Tel. (0)2⋆ 48.58.50.29 - Fax (0)2⋆ 48.58.56.00
M. and Mme Girard

Rooms 13 with telephone, bath or shower, WC and TV. **Price** Double 310-420F, suite 500F. **Meals** Breakfast 55F; half board 840-940F (per 2 pers., 3 days min.). **Restaurant** Service 12:30-14:00, 19:30-20:30 (closed Tuesday lunchtime, Wednesday lunchtime except in July and Aug); menus 160-330F, also à la carte. Specialties: Gibier en saison. **Credit cards** Visa, Eurocard and MasterCard. **Pets** Dogs not allowed. **Facilities** Parking. **Nearby** Orléans Cathedral, La Source flower gardens in Olivet, châteaux on the Jacques-Coeur road, Aubigny-sur-Nère, the Berry from La Chapelle d'Angillon to Saint-Martin-d'Auxigny, Sancerre – 18-hole Sully golf course in Viglains, 18-hole Marcilly golf course. **Open** Mar 16 – May 27, June 6 – Sept 16, Sept 27 – Feb 14 (closed Tuesday and Wednesday in winter).

This pink brick inn, located in a small village in Sologne just fifteen minutes from the National Route 20, is famous for its excellent cuisine and beautiful rooms. The restaurant is warm, elegant, and very charming. The rooms are lovely, each one decorated in a different style, with one or two antique pieces, beautiful fabrics, and polished wooden floors. They are comfortable and very quiet, their bathrooms are well equipped, and many look out on a small flower garden. There are apartments available for families. M. and Mme. Girard's gracious welcome and commitment to quality have made this one of our favorite hotels in France.

How to get there (Map 17): 60km southeast of Orléans via N20 to Lamotte-Beuvron, then D923 towards Aubigny-sur-Nère.

Auberge des Meaulnes ★★★

Route de Vierzon
18330 Nançay (Cher)
Tel. (0)2★ 48.51.81.15 - Fax (0)2★ 48.51.84.58 - M. and Mme Bisson

Rooms 10 with telephone, bath or shower, WC, TV and minibar. **Price** Singles 450F, double 500F. **Meals** Breakfast 50F. **Restaurant** Service 12:00-14:00, 19:30-21:30; menus 130-180F, also à la carte. Specialties: Foie gras frais de canard, brouillade d'écrevisses, ris de veau aux morilles, pigeon au miel d'acacias, tarte Tatin. **Credit cards** All major. **Pets** Dogs allowed. **Facilities** Parking. **Nearby** Imaginary Museum of Le Grand Meaulnes (souvenirs of Alain Fournier) and the Villâtre barn in Nançay; Bourges, Aubigny-sur-Nère, Sancerre – 9-hole Meaulnes golf course. **Open** End Apr – Jan 15 (closed Monday and Tuesday).

Recently taken over by a new owner and redecorated, the delightful Auberge des Meaulnes has several very comfortable rooms. Located in the main building as well as in a charming small house, they are attractively decorated with antique furniture and pretty *objets d'art*. On the main floor the inviting gourmet restaurant, specializing in succulent regional dishes, is decorated with beautiful furniture, colorful *faïences* and a large fireplace, all combining to create an elegant, traditional ambiance. The auberge is the perfect reflection of this superb region of the Loire hunt country, known for its excellent quality of life. You will find a charming terrace in the small garden outside where it's delightful to read or have drinks in the shade of a large willow. The hospitality at the auberge is very warm.

How to get there *(Map 17): 36km north of Bourges. On A71, exit Salbris, then D944.*

Château de la Beuvrière ★★

18100 Saint-Hilaire-de-Court (Cher)
Tel. (0)2★ 48.75.14.63 - Fax (0)2★ 48.75.47.62
M. and Mme de Brach

Rooms 15 with telephone, bath or shower and WC (4 with minibar). **Price** Single 270F, double 350-480F, duplex 460F, suite 600F. **Meals** Breakfast 38F, served 7:30-10:00. **Restaurant** Closed Sunday evening and Monday. Service 12:00-14:00, 19:30-21:00; menus 140-198F, gastronomic menu 250F, also à la carte. Specialties: Saumon fumé maison, foie gras frais maison, sandre braisé au beurre de truffes, ris de veau braisé à l'orange. **Credit cards** All major. **Pets** Dogs allowed. **Facilities** Swimming pool, tennis, parking. **Nearby** Saint-Etienne cathedral, hôtel Jacques-Coeur in Bourges, Aubigny-sur-Nère – 18-hole La Picardière golf course. **Open** Mar 16 – Dec 14 (closed Sunday evening).

The château has kept its 2,562–acre estate intact since the Middle Ages. Inherited by the present owners, it is a very charming hotel today. The family furniture is authentic and dates from the 15th to the 19th-century – the overall effect is one of excellent quality arranged with perfect taste. Lovely and very well-kept, the bedrooms overlook the grounds. Those on the *premier étage* are almost sumptuous, and if their bathrooms are a bit on the small side this allows room for the wood–panelled bed alcoves. The *deuxième étage* bedrooms have original beams and some have a mezzanine. You will dine sitting on Empire armchairs at a beautifully laid table. The food is as excellent as the decor, and the welcome is informal and cordial.

How to get there *(Map 17): 39km northwest of Bourges via A71, Vierzon-Nord exit, then N20 towards Châteauroux.*

Hostellerie Saint-Jacques ★★★

Place du Marché-aux-Œufs
28220 Cloyes-sur-le-Loir (Eure-et-Loir)
Tel. (0)2★ 37.98.40.08 - Fax (0)2★ 37.98.32.63 - M. Thureau

Rooms 22 with telephone, bath or shower, WC and TV. **Price** Single and double 320-480F, suite 680F. **Meals** Breakfast 50F, served 8:00-10:30; half board 420F, full board 570F (per pers.). **Restaurant** Service 12:00-13:30, 19:30-21:00; menus 169F. Specialties: Fricassée de poulet fermier à l'ail doux, poêlée de rascasse au romarin. **Credit cards** Visa, Eurocard and MasterCard. **Pets** Dogs´allowed. **Facilities** Boats, table tennis, parking. **Nearby** Chapel of Yrou at Châteaudun, Vendôme, valley of the Loir (Montoire-sur-le-Loir, Lavardin, Troô, manoir de la Possonnière) – 9-hole la Bosse golf course in Oucques. **Open** Mar 1 – Nov 20.

Located on the village square, l'Hostellerie Saint-Jacques is an old 16th-century coaching inn. Here you may go boating on the Loire, which crosses the shady 1 1/2-acre gardens. The bedrooms are comfortable and quite pretty, with printed cotton fabrics, period furniture (occasionally a beautiful antique wardrobe), and they are well-soundproofed, a detail so rare that it deserves mention. The tasteful and intimate dining room overlooks the garden. The Hostellerie is well known for its gastronomy and in good weather, when lunch is served on the·flowery terrace, the pleasures of the table are enhanced by the charm of the site. Note also the *Petit Bistrot,* which serves excellent, reasonably priced meals.

How to get there *(Map 16): 53km north of Blois via D957 to Vendôme, then N10 (going north) to Cloyes-sur-le-Loir.*

Château du Vivier

Le Vivier
36200 Argenton-sur-Creuse (Indre)
Tel. (0)2★ 54.24.22.99 – Fax (0)2★ 54.01.12.87 – M. and Mme Longin

Rooms 9 with telephone, bath, WC and TV. **Price** Single and double 300-580F.
Meals Breakfast 65F, served until 12:00; half board 500-650F, full board 650-900F
(per pers., 3 days min.). **Restaurant** Service 12:00-14:00, 19:00-23:00; menus 135-
380F, also à la carte. Specialties: Fish, foie gras, rare mushrooms. **Credit cards** All
major. **Pets** Dogs allowed (+60F). **Facilities** Parking. **Nearby** Pont-Vieux and Saint-
Benoît chapel in Argenton, château de Nohant-Vic, Georges Sand museum in La
Châtre, abbey church of Fontgombault – 18-hole Dryades and Pouligny-Notre-Dame
golf courses. **Open** All year.

There is a romantic air about this small château, built in the
17th-century and renovated in the early 19th. Anxious to keep
the family character of the place and to welcome their guests as
friends, M. and Mme Longin have decorated it delightfully. In the
dining room there are antique furniture, paintings, old
photographs, curios and dried-flower arrangements. The *premier
étage* bedrooms are large, with lovely materials used as wall or bed-
hangings, as well as antique furniture. On the *deuxième étage* the
bedrooms are smaller but very charming, with long windows
reaching to the floor. In good weather tables are set outside under
the big trees. There you can have tea, read Proust or lose yourself
in the maze of greenery in the garden.

How to get there (*Map 16*): *30km southwest of Châteauroux, on the way
out of Argenton-sur-Creuse, at "Le Vivier."*

Manoir de Boisvillers ★★

14, rue du Moulin de Bord
36200 Argenton-sur-Creuse (Indre)
Tel. (0)2★ 54.24.13.88 – Fax (0)2★ 54.24.27.83 – M. and Mme Nowakowski

Rooms 14 with telephone, bath or shower, 13 with WC and TV. **Price** Single 180-280F, double 230-380F. **Meals** Breakfast 40F, served 7:30-10:00. No restaurant. **Credit cards** Amex, Visa, Eurocard and MasterCard. **Pets** Dogs allowed (+30F). **Facilities** Swimming pool, parking. **Nearby** Pont-Vieux and Saint-Benoît chapel in Argenton, château de Nohant-Vic, Georges Sand museum in La Châtre, abbey church of Fontgombault – 18-hole Dryades and Pouligny-Notre-Dame golf courses. **Open** Jan 16 – Dec 14.

This welcoming hotel in the center of town enjoys an excellent location with its large garden and the immediate proximity of the Creuse River. Taken over by Isabelle and Christophe Nowakowski, it has been rejuvenated with pleasant bedrooms, which are simply decorated in bright colors and located in the hotel and an outbuilding. (The bathrooms need some improvement but are still recommendable.) All the rooms are different, with some overlooking the river; others overlook the garden or the courtyard. Room 5 is very beautiful with its wood paneling and vast proportions. On the ground floor, there is a small modern lounge and the breakfast room. In good weather, you can enjoy a pleasant garden with swimming-pool and, if you prefer not to go out to dinner, you can have a meal platter brought to you. The young owners are hospitable and very pleasant.

How to get there (Map 16): 30km southwest of Châteauroux, Argenton-sur-Creuse exit.

Domaine de l'Etape ★★★

Route de Bélâbre
36300 Le Blanc (Indre)
Tel. (0)2★ 54.37.18.02 - Fax (0)2★ 54.37.75.59 - Mme Seiller

Rooms 35 with telephone, bath or shower and WC (20 with TV). **Price** Single 210-390F, double 220-440F. **Meals** Breakfast 48F, served 7:00-11:00. **Restaurant** Residents only. Service 19:30-21:30; menus 125-140F, also à la carte. Specialties: Sandre au beurre blanc, coq au vin, pâté berrichon. **Credit cards** Visa, Eurocard and MasterCard. **Pets** Dogs allowed. **Facilities** Riding, fishing, hunting, boating, parking. **Nearby** Museum of local history in Le Blanc, châteaux of Azay-le-Ferron, le Guillaume and le Bouchet, Benedictine abbey of Fontgombault. **Open** All year.

You will be delighted by the kind welcome in this 19th-century house standing in a 320-acre estate. Everything is charming and a bit old-fashioned. The lounge, with Louis Philippe furniture, is ideal for reading or watching television. The pale wood-panelled dining room is often brightened by an open fire. There is a small garden terrace with a bar. The bedrooms are simple, comfortable, and all different. Country-lovers will enjoy the bedrooms in the farmhouse, which are rustic but also comfortable. The farm provides fresh produce for the kitchen. Fishermen can try their luck in the lake and horse lovers can go riding and inspect the foals in the fields.

How to get there *(Map 16): 59km west of Châteauroux via N20 and N151 to Le Blanc, then D10 towards Bélâbre.*

Château de Bouesse

36200 Bouesse (Indre)
Tel. (0)2★ 54.25.12.20 - Fax (0)2★ 54. 25.12.30
M. and Mme Courtot-Atterton

Rooms 11 with telephone, bath or shower and WC. **Price** Single 350F, double 480F, suite 720F. **Meals** Breakfast 55F, served 8:00-10:00; half board 395-455F (per pers., 3 days min.). **Restaurant** Service 12:00-14:00, 19:30-21:30; menus 145-190F, also à la carte. Specialties: Fish, foie gras, rognons de veau à l'ancienne, scallops. **Credit cards** Amex, Visa, Eurocard and MasterCard. **Pets** Dogs not allowed. **Facilities** Parking. **Nearby** Pont-Vieux and Saint-Benoît chapel in Argenton, château de Nohant-Vic, Georges Sand museum in La Châtre, abbey church of Fontgombault – 18-hole Dryades and Pouligny-Notre-Dame golf courses. **Open** Feb 1 – Dec 31 (closed Monday in low season).

M onsieur and Mme Courtot-Atterton love history and have focused their enthusiasm on the restoration of this superb 13th- and 15th-century château. The bedrooms' names refer to the château's history: *Jeanne d'Arc, Raoul VI de Gaucourt*, etc. The bedrooms are all very large, and often have stone fireplaces bearing coats of arms. Some rooms have been redecorated recently in the style of the Middle Ages, using furniture specially made for the château. Others are in the romantic style of the English 19th century. The hotel is totally comfortable and peaceful. The view cannot have changed for centuries. We particularly admired the dining room, which has pale blue and grey panelling and a 17th-century painting on the ceiling. In summer an excellent breakfast is served outside on the terrace.

How to get there (Map 17): *33km south of Châteauroux, on D927 between Argenton-sur-Creuse and La Châtre.*

Château de la Vallée Bleue ★★★

Saint-Chartier
36400 La Châtre (Indre)
Tel. (0)2★ 54.31.01.91 - Fax (0)2★ 54.31.04.48 - M. Gasquet

Rooms 13 with telephone, bath or shower, WC, TV and minibar. **Price** Single 200-390F, double 325-550F. **Meals** Breakfast 47F; half board 425-450F, full board 500-600F (per pers., 3 days min.). **Restaurant** Service 12:00-13:30, 19:30-21:00; menus 125-325F, also à la carte. Specialties: Home-smoked produce, tartare de langoustines et de crabe, agneau aux pignons de pin et jus anisé, croustillants aux poires épicées. **Credit cards** Visa, Eurocard and MasterCard. **Pets** Dogs allowed (+50F). **Facilities** Swimming pool, health center, parking. **Nearby** Georges Sand museum in La Châtre, château des Maître-Sonneurs in Saint-Chartier, château de Nohant-Vic – 18-hole Dryades golf course. **Open** Mar – Jan (closed Sunday evening and Monday Oct – Mar).

The ghosts of George Sand and Chopin float over this small château, which was built by that couple's doctor in a 10-acre park. The entrance hall is lovely, and M. and Mme Gasquet are very welcoming. Everywhere there are pictures and memorabilia to do with the writer and the musician. The bedrooms are identified by small glass plaques with reproduction signatures of George Sand's artist friends. The bedrooms are comfortable, stylishly furnished and pleasantly decorated with Laura Ashley papers and fabrics, and they have lovely views over the park and the countryside. The English-style lounge is warm and a glass of old cognac or liqueur beside the fire is a pleasure. The list of *eaux-de-vie* is amazing. Off the lounge there are two very attractive dining rooms opening onto the park with its two-hundred-year-old oak tree. The cuisine is delicious.

How to get there (Map 17): 27km southeast of Châteauroux via D943 to Saint-Chartier. The hotel is outside the village on the Verneuil road.

200

Hôtel du Bon Laboureur et du Château ★★★

6, rue du Docteur Bretonneau
37150 Chenonceaux (Indre-et-Loire)
Tel. (0)2★ 47.23.90.02 - Fax (0)2★ 47.23.82.01 - M. Jeudi

Rooms 33 with telephone, bath or shower and WC (24 with cable TV). **Price** Single 280-500F, double 320-600F, suite 900-1000F. **Meals** Breakfast 45F, served 7:30-10:30; half board 400-650F. **Restaurant** Service 12:00-14:00, 19:30-21:30; menus 160-300F, also à la carte. Specialties: Tartare de saumon, poêlée de saint-jacques, magret de canard au bourgueil, croustillant d'agneau, millefeuilles sablé aux fraises. **Credit cards** All major. **Pets** Dogs allowed. **Facilities** Swimming pool, parking. **Nearby** Château de Chenonceaux, Loire Valley (châteaux de la Loire), Montlouis-sur-Loire via the Cher Valley– 18-hole Touraine golf course in Ballan-Miré. **Open** Dec 16 – Nov 14 and Feb 16 – Jan 1.

Like a field regularly tended by a «good laborer», this hotel, which has been in the same family for four generations, is constantly being improved. Located 200 meters from the Château de Chenonceaux, it consists of several buildings on either side of the street, gardens and a swimming pool. The bedrooms are all different, comfortable, prettily decorated and those which have just been renovated are, of course, the most attractive. Some are especially well-designed for families. You will also enjoy three pleasant, restful lounges. The first is English-style and has a bar; the two others are more modern, with their armchairs reflected in the beige lacquer of the ceilings. There is a bright, large dining room where guests greatly enjoy the owner's excellent regional cuisine. Note too that in summer several tables are set out on the terrace in the shade of a large tree. The staff are efficient and very friendly.

How to get there (Map 16): 35km southeast of Tours; on A10 Tours exit, then via D410, or N76 to Bléré, then D40 to Chenonceaux; (the hotel is in the center of the town).

Hostellerie du Château de l'Isle ★★

Civray-en-Touraine
37150 Chenonceaux (Indre-et-Loire)
Tel. (0)2★ 47 23 80 09 - Fax (0)2★ 47 23 82 91 - M. Gandon

Rooms 10 with telephone, bath or shower, WC and minibar (4 with TV). **Price** Single and double 290-400F, suite 500F. **Meals** Breakfast 48F, served 8:15-11:00; half board 350F, full board 448F (per pers.). **Restaurant** Service 12:00-14:00, 19:30-21:00; menus 98F (lunch), 145-195F, also à la carte. Specialties: Regional cuisine. **Credit cards** Amex, Visa, Eurocard and MasterCard. **Pets** Dogs allowed. **Facilities** Parking. **Nearby** Loire Valley (châteaux de la Loire), Château de Chenonceaux, Montlouis-sur-Loire via the Cher Valley — 18-hole Touraine golf course in Ballan-Miré. **Open** Dec 12 – Nov 14.

Monsieur Gandon describes his small Hostellerie du Château de l'Isle as "the friends' house"; given his hospitality and the relaxed atmosphere here, the description is fully justified. The bedrooms are all different, simple, comfortable and quite pretty, offering you a pleasant view out over the garden and the gentle countryside of the Loire Valley in the distance. There are two inviting rooms on the garden, whose amenities are more basic but which have a private terrace. A ravishing double-spiral wooden staircase leads to the other rooms. On the main floor, you will find a series of charming small dining rooms, where there is often a cracking fire in the fireplace. Traditional old furniture and paintings provide the decor for the excellent meals here: good, traditional Loire Valley cuisine made with fresh ingredients from the region. This is truly a hotel of character and charm on the doorstep of exquisite Chenonceaux.

How to get there (*Map 16*): *35km southeast of Tours. On A10, Tours exit, then D 140 and D 40 to Civray-en-Touraine.*

Hôtel Diderot ★★

4, rue Buffon
37500 Chinon (Indre-et-Loire)
Tel. (0)2★ 47.93.18.87 – Fax (0)2★ 47.93.37.10 – M. Kazamias

Rooms 28 (4 in annex) with telephone, bath or shower and WC (TV on request). **Price** Single 250-320F, double 300-400F. **Meals** Breakfast 40F, served 7:30-10:00. No restaurant. **Credit cards** All major. **Pets** Dogs not allowed. **Facilities** Parking. **Nearby** Château de Chinon, château d'Ussé, château d'Azay-le-Rideau, Saché, Richelieu, Rabelais country (La Devinière), château du Coudray-Montpensier, Lerné, château de la Roche-Clermanet – 18-hole Touraine golf course in Ballan-Miré. **Open** Jan 15 – Dec 15.

Its location close to the Place Jeanne D'Arc in the center of Chinon does not spoil the appeal or the tranquillity of this hotel. In the garden courtyard, Monsieur Kazamias has planted trees and herbs of his native Mediterranean: olive, fig and even banana trees, rosemary, all upholding the region's much-vaunted reputation for its microclimate! On the ground floor, a corner bar has just been added; it could do with softer lighting and a few deep armchairs, but that will certainly come in time. Adjoining the bar is the breakfast room, where you will enjoy excellent homemade preserves (the proceeds go to aid Chad). There is often a log fire in the old fireplace, and the beamed ceiling and antique furniture all lend authentic charm to the room. For the time being, we recommend the bedrooms which have been renovated: numbers 1, 3, 5, 9, 10, 15, 22, 23, 24 and 25. For plentiful meals in a medieval setting, try *L'Hostellerie Gargantua*; or *Au Plaisir Gourmand* for its delicate, savory cuisine.

How to get there *(Map 16): 48km southwest of Tours via D751. Go along the Vienne to the Place Jeanne-d'Arc; on the corner of the Rue Diderot.*

Hôtel George Sand ★★★

39, rue Quintefol
37600 Loches (Indre-et-Loire)
Tel. (0)2★ 47.59.39.74 - Fax (0)2★ 47.91.55.75 - Mme and M. Fortin

Rooms 20 with telephone, bath or shower, WC and TV. **Price** Single and double 260-650F. **Meals** Breakfast 35F, served 7:00-9:30; half board 490-680F, full board 690-890F (per pers., 3 days min.). **Restaurant** Service 12:00-14:00, 19:30-21:30; menus 85-245F, also à la carte. Specialties: Géline de touraine, pavé de carpe au vin du Lohois, croustillant de pommes au vieux marc de Touraine et framboises. **Credit cards** Visa, Eurocard and MasterCard. **Pets** Dogs allowed (+25F). **Nearby** Château and keep of Loches, Carthusian monastery of Le Liget in the Loches forest, abbey church of Beaulieu-les-Loches, Montrésor, Indre valley, Cormery, Montbazon, Monts, Saché —18-hole Touraine golf course in Ballan-Miré. **Open** All year.

Standing at the foot of the impressive Château de Loches, this ancient 15th-century house once marked the boundary of the medieval town. M. Loiseau will welcome you with great kindness. Entering from the street you will be pleasantly surprised to find that the dining room and its large terrace are on the edge of the river Indre, which at this point forms a large waterfall. With access via an antique spiral staircase, many of the bedrooms still have their original beams and some a beautiful stone fireplace. All have just been fully renovated with new wallpaper, carpets, double-glazing windows and bathrooms. Some are especially convenient for families. The rustic furniture is nothing out of the ordinary but a few pieces of antique furniture are slowly being added. The delicate, traditional cuisine is excellent, perfectly prepared, culminating with delicious desserts. The staff is as friendly as always.

How to get there (Map 16): 42km southeast of Tours via N143.

Domaine de la Tortinière ★★★
Route de Ballan-Miré - Les Gués de Veigné
37250 Montbazon-en-Touraine (Indre-et-Loire)
Tel. (0)2★ 47.26.00.19 - Fax (0)2★ 47.65.95.70
Mme Olivereau-Capron and M. Olivereau

Rooms 21 (1 with air-conditioning) with telephone, bath, WC and TV -1 for disabled persons. **Price** Double 455-890F, suite 990-1200F. **Meals** Breakfast 70F, served 8:00-11:00; half board 550-900F (per pers., 3 days min.), 590-955F (per pers., 1-2 days). **Restaurant** Service 12:15-13:45, 19:30-21:00; menus 195-350F, also à la carte. Specialties: Chausson d'asperges et de foie gras truffé, civet de homard et dorade au bourgueil, chibouste aux framboises et citron vert. **Credit cards** Visa, Eurocard and MasterCard. **Pets** Dogs not allowed. **Facilities** Heated swimming pool, tennis, boat, mountain bikes on request, parking. **Nearby** Keep of Fouques Nerra in Montbazon, Indre valley, Cormery, Monts, Saché, Tours cathedral, château d'Azay-le-Rideau – 18-hole Touraine golf course in Ballan-Miré. **Open** Mar 1 – Dec 19.

A Renaissance-style château built in 1861, the Tortinière is set in a 37-acre park dominating the Indre valley, although it is only 10km from Tours. The two restaurants, the salon and most of the bedrooms are in the château. The bedrooms are all different, superbly decorated, and very comfortable; the ones in old pavillions outside are as beautiful and recommendable as those in the château. There is a beautiful restaurant with a terrace where meals are served in good weather. In autumn, the park is carpeted with cyclamen, and in good weather you can still enjoy the heated swimming pool.

How to get there *(Map 16): 10km south of Tours via A10, Nr. 14 exit, then N10 towards Montbazon; via route of Ballan-Miré it's at Les Gués de Veigné.*

Château de la Bourdaisière

25, rue de la Bourdaisière
37270 Montlouis-sur-Loire (Indre-et-Loire)
Tel. (0)2★ 47.45.16.31 - Fax (0)2★ 47.45.09.11 - M. de Broglie

Rooms 13 (2 suites) with bath or shower and WC (TV on request); elevator.
Price Double 550-1100F, suite 750-1050F. **Meals** Breakfast 50F. No restaurant.
Credit cards Visa, Eurocard and MasterCard. **Pets** Dogs allowed. **Facilities** Heated
swimming pool, tennis, riding, parking. **Nearby** Tours, grange de Meslay, Vouvray
wine cellars, Loire valley (châteaux de la Loire) – 18-hole Touraine golf course in
Ballan-Miré. **Open** Feb 16 – Feb 1.

Built on the foundations of a 14th-century citadel by order of
François I, the Château de la Bourdaisière was a gift from the
king to his mistress, Marie Gaudin. Less than a century later, it was
the birthplace of the beautiful Gabrielle d'Estrée, with whom Henri
IV fell in love. It is no wonder, therefore, that the hotel's bedrooms
and two suites are named after women who had an influence on
French history. The bedrooms are superb: large and all different,
their decoration is bright and colorful while respecting the age of
the building. Throughout the house there is a wealth of period
furniture, with some truly sumptuous pieces in the lounge. This
room is dedicated to the Princesse de Broglie, whose young
descendants will welcome you like old friends. The hotel has
splendid and extensive grounds, with formal gardens, a kitchen
garden, an arboretum, a rose garden and an animal park. For
restaurants, we recommend: *Jean Bardet* (one of France's top chefs),
Le Canotier, Les Tuffeaux in Tours; and *L'Oubliette* in Rochecorbon.

How to get there *(Map 16): 11km east of Tours via D152.*

Hostellerie Les Perce-Neige ★★

37210 Vernou-sur-Brenne (Indre-et-Loire)
Tel. (0)2★ 47 52 10 04 – Fax (0)2★ 47 52 19 08
Mme Chemin

Rooms 15 with telephone, bath or shower (14 with WC) and TV. **Price** Double 200-280F. **Meals** Breakfast 32F, served 8:00-10:00; half board 410F, full board 630F (2 pers., 3 days min.). **Restaurant** Service 12:00-14:00, 19:30-22:00; menus 98-147F (children 50F), also à la carte. Specialties: Traditional cuisine. **Credit cards** Amex, Visa, Eurocard and MasterCard. **Pets** Dogs allowed. **Facilities** Parking. **Nearby** Tours, grange de Meslay, Vouvray wine cellars, Loire valley (châteaux de la Loire) – 18-hole Touraine golf course in Ballan-Miré. **Open** Feb 16 – Jan 1 (closed Sunday evening and Monday in low season).

Now that the management has changed, we are happy to be able to put the Perce-Neige ("Snow Drops") back in this guide because the little hotel is truly one of character and charm. Located in a lovely small winegrowing village in the Loire Valley, it is comfortable and tastefully decorated. On the ground floor, there is a small lounge decorated in warm tones, an inviting bar and two charming dining rooms (the small non-smoking dining room is the prettiest). Apart from two bedrooms which are located in an adjacent building and which give directly onto the park, the others are upstairs in the hotel. Comfortable and charming, many have retro furniture which is painted in the dominant color of the room. In summer, you can have dinner in the park, which is shaded with beautiful trees: a veritable invitation to a romantic stroll before or after dinner. Last but not least, the hospitality is delightful.

How to get there *(Map 16): 11km east of Tours, towards Amboise-Blois; in Vouvray, take towards Vernou.*

La Croix Blanche de Sologne ★★★

41600 Chaumont-sur-Tharonne (Loir-et-Cher)
Tel. (0)2★ 54 88 55 12- Fax (0)2★ 54 88 60 40
M. and Mme Goacolou

Rooms 18 with telephone, bath, WC, TV and minibar - Wheelchair access.
Price Single 250-400F, double 300-500F, suite 580-680F. **Meals** Breakfast 45F,
served 7:30-11:00; half board 420-520F, full board 620-820F (per pers., 2 days
min.). **Restaurant** Service 12:00-13:45, 19:30-21:30; menus 118-250F, also à la
carte. Specialties: Sologne and Périgord cooking. **Credit cards** All major. **Pets** Dogs
allowed. **Facilities** Bicycle, parking. **Nearby** Saint-Viâtre, Marcilly, route des Etangs
to La Ferté-Saint-Aubin (château), châteaux de la Loire (Chambord, Cheverny),
Sologne aquarium – 27-hole Aisses golf course. **Open** All year.

The very old Croix Blanche auberge is located in a ravishing
village in the Sologne forest. Since the 18th century, thirteen
generations of women chefs have presided over the kitchen,
gradually winning a solid gastronomic reputation. The dining room
is tastefully decorated with hunting trophies, antique country
furniture, and the smartly laid tables of a good old-fashioned
restaurant. In the summer, you can have dinner in the pretty flower
garden. Service throughout is both friendly and efficient. The
bedrooms are very comfortable and some have small sitting areas
with rustic, warm decoration (though it is somewhat heavy on
fabric and carpet motifs). The breakfasts are especially pleasant. The
Croix Blanche is a friendly, professionally run old inn, and a long-
time favorite in the Loire Valley.

How to get there *(Map 17): 34km south of Orléans via N20 to La Ferté-
Saint-Aubin, then D922 to Chaumont. Via A71, exit Lamotte-Beuvron.*

Château de Chissay ★★★★

Montrichard
41400 Chissay-en-Touraine (Loir-et-Cher)
Tel. (0)2★ 54.32.32.01 - Fax (0)2★ 54.32.43.80 - M. Savry

Rooms 31 with telephone, bath and WC. **Price** Single 390F, double 550-910F, suite or apartment 950-1600F. **Meals** Breakfast 65F, served 7:30-10:30; half board 490-680F, full board 670-860F (per pers.). **Restaurant** Service 12:00-14:00, 19:30-21:30; menus 185-295F, also à la carte. Specialties: Marbré de sandre et langoustines, feuilleté de noix de Saint-Jacques, pigeonneau rôti au jus de truffes, aumônière de fraises au rosé de Touraine. **Credit cards** All major. **Pets** Dogs allowed (+45F). **Facilities** Swimming pool, parking. **Nearby** Tours, grange de Meslay, Vouvray wine cellars, Loire valley (châteaux de la Loire) – 18-hole Touraine golf course in Ballan-Miré. **Open** beg. Mar – mid. Nov.

This ancient fortified château is full of historic memories: Charles VII, Louis XI and the Duke of Choiseul all stayed here. More recently, General de Gaulle spent several days here in June 1940 before going to England. Entirely renovated in 1986, it has 31 luxurious bedrooms; those in the turrets are especially charming (Nos. 12, 22, 10, 30). The restaurant is elegant, and there are pleasant walks in the surrounding garden and woods, and in the Touraine countryside.

How to get there *(Map 16): 35km east of Tours via D40 to Chenonceaux, then D76; 4km before Montrichard.*

Hôtel Les Charmilles **
Route de Pierrefitte-sur-Sauldre
41600 Nouan-le-Fuzelier (Loir-et-Cher)
Tel. (0)2★ 54.88.73.55 - Mme Sené

Rooms 14 with telephone, bath or shower, WC and TV. **Price** Single 310F, double 340-380F, suite 460F. **Meals** Breakfast incl., served 7:30-9:00. No restaurant. **Credit cards** Visa, Eurocard and MasterCard. **Pets** Dogs allowed in the ground-floor bedrooms. **Facilities** Parking. **Nearby** Church of Saint-Viâtre, château du Moulin, lake road from Saint-Viâtre to Romorantin via Selle Saint-Denis, La Source flower garden in Olivet – 12-hole Rivaulde golf and country club in Sallris. **Open** Mar 16 – Dec 14.

This big, comfortable family house, built at the beginning of the century, has been converted into a hotel. The decoration is old-fashioned, particularly the wallpapers and some pieces of furniture. However, the bedrooms and baths are comfortable and well kept. Breakfast is served in the bedrooms – just hang your breakfast order on the doorknob the evening before. The grounds are delightful. The large garden has a lake, cool shady areas under very old trees, comfortable garden furniture, and a beautiful lawn. The owners are very hospitable. There is no restaurant, but you can picnic on the grounds. For dinner, *Le Lion d'Or* in Pierrefitte and *Le Raboliot* in Nouan are pleasant addresses.

How to get there *(Map 17): 44km south of Orléans via N20 towards Vierzon; on the way out of the village D122.*

Hôtel Château des Tertres ★★★
Route de Monteaux
41150 Onzain (Loir-et-Cher)
Tel. (0)2★ 54.20.83.88 – Fax (0)2★ 54.20.89.21 – M. Valois

Rooms 14 with telephone, bath or shower and WC. **Price** Double 390-500F. **Meals** Breakfast 42F, served 8:00-10:00. No restaurant. **Credit cards** Amex, Visa, Eurocard and MasterCard. **Pets** Dogs not allowed. **Facilities** Bicycles, parking. **Nearby** Châteaux of Chaumont, Blois, Amboise, Chambord, Beauregard and Chenonceaux – 9-hole la Carte golf course in Onzain, 18-hole château de Cheverny golf course. **Open** Apr 1 – Nov 12.

This 19th-century château is a beautiful building and charmingly decorated. On the ground floor overlooking the garden and the countryside, the reception area adjoins a lounge with 19th-century furniture. To one side is a very attractive room where a delicious breakfast is served. The overall effect is that of a family house. The bedrooms are very comfortable and pretty. They are regularly redecorated with beautiful fabrics and the latest conveniences. Although in a popular tourist area, the château is quiet and reasonably priced. The welcome is very warm. The hotel does not serve meals but there are some good restaurants in the village, notably *Le Pont d'Ouchet* and *Le Domaine des Hauts de Loire*, which is more elegant and more expensive.

How to get there *(Map 16): 44km northeast of Tours via N152 to the bridge of Chaumont-sur-Loire, then D1 to Onzain.*

Relais des Landes ★★★

Ouchamps
41120 Les Montils (Loir-et-Cher)
Tel. (0)2★ 54.44.03.33 – Fax (0)2★ 54.44.03.89 – M. Badenier

Rooms 28 with telephone, bath, WC, TV and minibar. **Price** Single and double 495-745F. **Meals** Breakfast 55F, served 7:30-10:00; half board 580-660F. **Restaurant** Service 12:30-13:30, 19:00-21:30; menus 175-295F, also à la carte. Specialties: Foie gras de canard maison à la mignonnette de poivre, fricassée d'anguille Rabelais au beurre d'herbe, éventail de filet de canard aux épices et miel toutes fleurs. **Credit cards** All major. **Pets** Dogs allowed (+35F). **Facilities** Bicycle rent, parking. **Nearby** Châteaux of Chaumont, Blois, Amboise, Chambord, Beauregard and Chenonceaux – 9-hole la Carte golf course in Onzain, 18-hole château de Cheverny golf course. **Open** Apr 1 – Nov 15.

L ying in the middle of the countryside in a 24-acre park, the Relais de Landes is a 17th-century house which has been restored and is well-kept. The lounge/reception area also houses the bar and offers corners for conversation or reading. The furniture is comfortable in these rooms and in the dining room, where a fire is lit in winter. Next to it there is a winter garden leading to the lawn where dining tables are also set. In summer, you can have meals in the flower garden beside its small streams. The bedrooms are very comfortable, prettily decorated and they have beautiful bathrooms. The staff is friendly and helpful.

How to get there (Map 16): *15km east of Blois towards Montrichard; follow the signs from Les Montils.*

Château de la Voûte

Troo
41800 Montoire-sur-le-Loir (Loir-et-Cher)
Tel. (0)2★ 54.72.52.52 - Fax (0)2★ 54.72.52.52 - MM. Clays and Venon

Rooms 5 with bath or shower and WC. **Price** Double 370-470-550F. **Meals** Breakfast incl., served 8:00-10:00. No restaurant. **Credit cards** Not accepted. **Pets** Dogs not allowed. **Facilities** Parking. **Nearby** Benedictine abbey of la Trinité and church of Rhodon in Vendôme, valley of the Loir, chapel of Saint-Gilles in Montoire, Gué-du-Loir, Lavardin, Saint-Jacques-des-Guérets, manoir de la Possonnière – 9-hole La Bosse golf course in Oucques. **Open** All year.

Here is a place for the discerning. The rooms in this old manor are full of beautiful things, reflecting the owners' passion for antiques. The bedrooms are furnished and decorated with some of their finds. Every room is different and has its own style and charm; even the smallest is lovely. Some are suites (named *Pompadour, Louis XIII* and *Empire*) and even apartments *(Les Tours)*. The view is worthy of a 17th-century painting. This is an ideal place for exploring the Tours region and the valleys of the Loir and the Loire. This is a well managed hotel of great quality. For restaurants, we recommend *Le Cheval Blanc* in Troo, *Le Cheval Rouge* in Montoire and *Le Relais d'Antan* in Lavardin.

How to get there *(Map 16): 48km north of Tours via D29 to La Chartre-sur-le-Loir, then right on D305 and D917 to Troo.*

Manoir de la Forêt **

Fort-Girard
41160 La Ville-aux-Clercs (Loir-et-Cher)
Tel. (0)2★ 54.80.62.83 – Fax (0)2★ 54.80.66.03 – Mme Autebon

Rooms 19 with telephone, bath or shower, WC and TV. **Price** Single and double 290-340F, suite 390-480F. **Meals** Breakfast 45F; half board 500F, full board 550F. **Restaurant** Service 12:15-14:00, 19:30-21:00; menus 145-270F, also à la carte. Specialties: Foie gras frais au Muscat, grenadin de lotte et langoustines au sabayon de champagne, poêlée de ris de veau, fish. **Credit cards** Amex, Visa, Eurocard and MasterCard. **Pets** Dogs allowed. **Facilities** Fishing, parking. **Nearby** Benedictine abbey of la Trinité and church of Rhodon in Vendôme, Loire Valley (châteaux de la Loire), valley of Loir, chapel of Saint-Gilles in Montoire, Gué-du-Loir, Lavardin, Saint-Jacques-des-Guérets, manoir de la Possonnière – 9-hole la Bosse golf course in Oucques. **Open** All year (closed Sunday evening and Monday Oct – Mar).

The former hunting lodge of the Château de la Gaudinière, which dates from the 18th century, the Manoir de la Forêt stands in five acres of wooded grounds with a lake. The lounge/reception sets the scene with its restful atmosphere, fresh flowers and pleasant furniture. Two living rooms with deep armchairs and sofas are the ideal place for a drink, morning coffee or afternoon tea. The dining room, whose eleven windows open onto the garden, offers an excellent menu. Throughout, the choice of colors and fabrics is good. The bedrooms overlook the grounds or the forest and number 6 has a pretty terrace. In good weather drinks and meals are served outside.

How to get there (Map 16): 72km northeast of Tours via N10 to 6km beyond Vendôme, then left on D141 to La Ville-aux-Clercs.

Hôtel de l'Abbaye ★★★

2, quai de l'Abbaye
45190 Beaugency (Loiret)
Tel. (0)2★ 38.44.67.35 – Fax (0)2★ 38.44.87.92 – M. Aupetit

Rooms 18 with telephone, bath, WC and TV. **Price** Single 420-480F, double 510-560F, suite 560-700F. **Meals** Breakfast 42F, served 7:00-10:00. **Restaurant** Service 12:00-14:00, 19:00-21:30; menu 185F, also à la carte. Specialties: Traditional cooking. **Credit cards** All major. **Pet** Dogs allowed (+50F). **Facilities** Parking. **Nearby** Medieval and Renaissance quarters of Beaugency, château de Meung-sur-Loire, basilica and chapel of Saint-Jacques in Cléry-Saint-André – 18-hole Saint-Laurent-Nouan golf course. **Open** All year.

A discreet nameplate announces that this 17th-century former Augustine convent built on the banks of the Loire opposite the old bridge in Beaugency is... a hotel. You will be charmingly welcomed in an immense but comfortable hall. Adjacent to it is a very inviting bar, which is next to the dining room. A tall fireplace, very tasteful rustic furnishings and windows overlooking the Loire all make it very pleasant, particularly as the cuisine is extremely good (the prices are somewhat high but the very reasonable wine list compensates for this when the bill comes). In the summer, several tables are set out on the extraordinary, whose splendid austerity would not be out of place in an Italian palace. The bedrooms on the *premier étage* upstairs have a mezzanine, thus making good use of the high ceilings. They are comfortable, very elegant and the beautiful Louis XIII period furniture contributes to the authenticity of this truly exceptional hotel.

How to get there *(Map 17): 25km southwest of Orléans via A10, Meung-sur-Loire exit, then N152.*

Hôtel de la Sologne ★★

Place Saint-Firmin
45190 Beaugency (Loiret)
Tel. (0)2★ 38.44.50.27 – Fax (0)2★ 38.44.90.19 – Mme Rogue

Rooms 16 with telephone, bath or shower, WC and TV. **Price** Single and double 250-410F. **Meals** Breakfast 38F, served 7:00-9:30. No restaurant. **Credit cards** Visa, Eurocard and MasterCard. **Pet** Dogs not allowed. **Nearby** Medieval and Renaissance quarters of Beaugency, château de Meung-sur-Loire, basilica and chapel of Saint-Jacques in Cléry-Saint-André – 18-hole les Bordes golf course in Saint-Laurent-Nouan. **Open** All year except Christmas and New Year.

This charming hotel in the heart of old Beaugency is very courteously managed by Mme Rogue. The bedrooms are plain but comfortable, and she has equipped them with television sets with headphones (so as not to disturb the neighbors), wall lamps with pretty shades, hairdryers, and, in as many as possible, electric trouser presses. The living room is rustic and welcoming, with a fireplace, old beams and a huge selection of magazines. There is a pleasant verandah, which is also a lounge and winter garden. There is a good restaurant in the Hôtel de L'Abbaye.

How to get there *(Map 17): 29km southwest of Orléans via A10, Meung-sur-Loire exit, then N152.*

L'Auberge de Combreux ★★

45530 Combreux (Loiret)
Tel. (0)2★ 38.46.89.89/(0)2★ 38.59.47.63 – Fax 38.59.36.19
Mme Gangloff

Rooms 20 with telephone, bath or shower, WC and cable TV (2 with whirlpool). **Price** 315-495F. **Meals** Breakfast 33F, served 8:00-10:00; half board 335-495F (per pers., 2 days min.). **Restaurant** Service 12:00-14:00, 19:15-21:15; menus 90-200F, also à la carte. Specialties: Mousseline de chèvre chaud au cresson, filet de brochet aux échalotes confites, navarin d'agneau, tarte au citron. **Credit cards** Visa, Eurocard and MasterCard. **Pets** Dogs allowed (+30F). **Facilities** Heated swimming pool, tennis (30F), bicycles (50F half-hour), parking. **Nearby** Orléans, arboretum and museum in Châteauneuf-sur-Loire, La Source flower gardens in Olivet – 18-hole Orléans golf course. **Open** Jan 20 – Dec 20.

This is a lovely, simple inn with white walls, white beds, bunches of reeds, and wood everywhere: beams, rustic furniture, mantelpieces. Throughout there is a gentle harmony between the colors of the curtains, the lampshades and, to add brighter tones, bouquets of flowers. The bedrooms too are very attractive, though some of them are in the annex on the other side of the street. In summer the arbor is perfect for a lazy breakfast or uplifting aperitifs. The cuisine is rustic and delicious – real French family cooking. The warmth of the welcome is worth mentioning and so is the pleasure of excursions on the bicycles you can rent at the hotel.

How to get there *(Map 17): 35km east of Orléans via N60, Châteauneuf-sur-Loire and Vitry-aux-Loges exit.*

Domaine de Chicamour ★★

45530 Sury-aux-Bois (Loiret)
Tel. (0)2★ 38.55.85.42 – Fax (0)2★ 38.55.80.43
M. Merckx

Rooms 12 with telephone, bath or shower, and WC. **Price** Single 325F, double 365F. **Meals** Breakfast 45F, served 8:00-10:00; half board 380F, full board 485F. **Restaurant** Service 12:00-14:00, 19:30-21:00; menus 95-350F, also à la carte. Specialties: Foie gras, noisettes d'agneau. **Credit cards** Visa, Eurocard and MasterCard. **Pets** Dogs allowed (+25F). **Facilities** Tennis, riding, bicycles, boules and parking. **Nearby** Orléans, arboretum and museum in Châteauneuf-sur-Loire, La Source flower gardens in Olivet – 18-hole Orléans golf course. **Open** Mar 1 – Nov 30.

Set in a 20-acre park in the heart of the Orléans National Forest, the small château of Chicamour has been turned into a hotel with the accent on simplicity and elegance. The result is remarkable. The lovely lounge has deep sofas surrounding the fireplace and beautifully chosen curtains and fabrics. The superb collection of paintings and decorative objects helps to make this a special place you will not want to leave. The bedrooms also are beautiful, with pale wood furniture and Laura Ashley fabrics matching the wallpapers and lampshades. They are all comfortable, overlook the park and have beautiful bathrooms. In the elegant dining room, you will enjoy refined cuisine based on regional produce. The cellar includes a great variety of Loire wines, which are available for purchase.

How to get there *(Map 17): 39km west of Montargis on N60, between Bellegarde and Châteauneuf-sur-Loire.*

Hôtel de l'Abbaye ★★

8, rue des Tourelles
02600 Longpont (Aisne)
Tel. (0)3★ 23.96.02.44 – Fax (0)3★ 23.96.02.44 – M. Verdun

Rooms 12 with telephone, (5 with bath or shower and 6 with WC). **Price** Double 175-320F. **Meals** Breakfast "campagnard" 40F, served any time; half board 290-390F, full board 360-460F (per pers., 3 days min.). **Restaurant** Service 12:00-14:00, 19:30-21:00; menus 98-220F, also à la carte. Specialties: Wood grills, canard aux cerises, game and mushrooms in season. **Credit cards** All major. **Pets** Dogs allowed. **Facilities** Bicycle rent. **Nearby** Abbey and château of Longpont, château, Hôtel de Ville and Alexandre Dumas museum in Villers-Cotterêts, château de Vierzy, forest of Retz – 9-hole Valois golf course in Barbery. **Open** All year.

This fine old house is located in a village in the heart of the Forest of Retz. Its large, heavy dining tables and its fireplace are the scene of warm and friendly gatherings for walkers and sports enthusiasts. The delicious home cooking owes a great deal to the proprietor, who does everything to make you feel at home. The few bedrooms vary in quality; five have full bathroom facilities, and all have a peaceful atmosphere and look out on the forest or the abbey. Their decoration is somewhat basic and old-fashioned but the overall effect is quite pleasant. Other amenities of the hotel are a reading room, a TV room, a delightful garden and a wealth of tourist information about the region.

How to get there *(Map 10): 20km south of Soissons via N2 towards Villers-Cotterêts, then D2.*

Hostellerie Le Château ★★★

Neuville–Saint-Amand
02100 Saint-Quentin (Aisne)
Tel. (0)3★ 23.68.41.82 – Fax (0)3★ 23.68.46.02 – M. Meiresonne

Rooms 15 with telephone, bath, WC and TV (6 with minibar). **Price** Single and double 330-390F. **Meals** Breakfast 45F, served from 7:30. **Restaurant** Service 12:00-13:30, 19:00-21:00; menus 125-350F, also à la carte. Specialties: Cassolette d'escargots crème d'ail et poivrons, mélange de ris et rognon au genièvre de Houlles, assiette gourmande. **Credit cards** All major. **Pets** Dogs not allowed. **Facilities** Parking. **Nearby** Antoine Lécuyer Museum (pastels by Quentin de la Tour), college and Hôtel de Ville of Saint-Quentin – 9-hole le Mesnil golf course. **Open** All year (closed Saturday noon and Sunday evening, 3 weeks in Aug).

This château lies in the heart of a beautiful wooded park. The ground floor rooms are occupied by its famous restaurant, while other pleasantly furnished rooms extend into a modern wing with bay windows and a view of the park. Viewed from the outside, however, the architectural effect is disappointing. The comfortable, pleasantly furnished bedrooms are very attractive, with pastel wall fabrics. The bathrooms are lovely. At the Hostellerie, you will enjoy a restful stay and welcoming hospitality.

How to get there *(Map 2): 120km south of Lille via A26, exit Saint-Quentin-Gauchy or Saint-Quentin-Center; Rue du General-Leclerc and D12; in the centre 200m from the church.*

Château de Barive ★★★★

Sainte-Preuve
02350 Liesse (Aisne)
Tel. (0)3★ 23.22.15.15 – Fax (0)3★ 23.22.08.39 – M. Bergman

Rooms 15 with telephone, bath or shower, WC and TV. **Price** Single 380F, double 480-580F, Apart. 780F. **Meals** Breakfast 55F, served from 7:30; half board from 400F (per pers.). **Restaurant** Service 12:00-14:00, 19:00-21:30; menus 150-310F, also à la carte. Specialties: Ravioles de crustacés servis dans leur nage, filet de Saint-Pierre aux truffes et poireaux. **Credit cards** All major. **Pets** Dogs not allowed. **Facilities** Swimming pool, sauna, tennis. **Nearby** Laon cathedral, abbey of Prémontrés, forest of Saint-Gobain, ruins of abbeys of Le Tortoir and Saint-Nicolas-aux-Bois. **Open** All year.

Surrounded by countryside, this 17th century château was first a hunting lodge, then a boarding house, and has now been fully restored and opened as an impeccable hotel. The bedrooms are large and extremely comfortable, with thick eiderdowns and luxuriously fitted bathrooms. There is no period furniture, but some fine copies recreate something of the historic atmosphere of the château. The big breakfast room opens onto the surrounding greenery and is arranged rather like a winter garden. The lounge and dining room are still a little formal, but both rooms are comfortable, and the gourmet cuisine served in the latter certainly contributes much to the atmosphere. Hotel facilities include a large heated indoor swimming-pool, a sauna and a tennis court, so a stay here provides the perfect opportunity to get back into shape. The hospitality is friendly and attentive.

How to get there *(Map 3 and 10): 18km east of Laon via D977.*

Auberge de la Scierie ★★★

La Vove - 10160 Aix-en-Othe (Aube)
Tel. (0)3★ 25.46.71.26 - Fax (0)3★ 25.46.65.69
M. and Mme Gayina-Taillandier

Rooms 15 with telephone, bath or shower, WC and TV. **Price** Single and double 390-490F. **Meals** Breakfast 42F, served 8:00-11:00; half board 590F (per 1 pers.), 790F (per 2 pers.). **Restaurant** Service 12:00-14:00, 19:30-21:15 (closed Feb, Sunday evening and Monday Oct 15 – Apr 15) ; menus 130-240F, also à la carte. Specialties: Regional cooking. **Credit cards** All major. **Pets** Dogs allowed. **Facilities** Heated swimming pool, parking. **Nearby** Saint-Urbain Basilica, Cathedral of Saint Pierre and Saint Paul, Modern Art Museum in Troyes – 18-hole la Cordelière golf course in Chaource. **Open** All year except Feb.

This inn, lying in unspoiled countryside, is in an old sawmill. The main structure has been so well restored and refurbished that it seems as if the Auberge has always been a hotel. The beautiful surroundings provide lovely places for al fresco meals and walks in the beautiful 5-acre park which also was pretty stream. The bedrooms, which surround the swimming pool, are quiet and comfortable; some are traditionally furnished. The lounge is pleasant and has a beautiful fireplace and a library. The food is excellent and guests are sure of a warm welcome.

How to get there *(Map 10): 33km west of Troyes via N60 towards Sens, then D374 or via A5 Vulaines exit or Touvilliers exit; on the way out of the village in the Villemoiron-en-Othe towards.*

Château d'Etoges

4, rue Richebourg – 51270 Etoges by Montmort (Marne)
Tel. (0)3★ 26.59.30.08 - Fax (0)3★ 26.59.35.57
Mme Filliette-Neuville

Rooms 20 with telephone, bath or shower and WC (TV on request). **Price** Single 400F, double 550-700F, suite 1050F. **Meals** Breakfast 70F, served 8:00-11:00; half board 505-580F, full board 665-740F (per pers., 2 days min.). **Restaurant** By reservation. Service 12:00-14:00, 19:30-21:30; menu 180F. Specialties: Poisson au champagne, pintade vigneronne, Charlotte au marc de champagne. **Credit cards** All major. **Pets** Dogs allowed (+40F). **Facilities** Parking. **Nearby** Champagne Museum in Epernay, abbey of Hautvillers (where Dom Perignon invented champagne) – 18-hole La Vitarderie golf course in Dormans, 18-hole Val-Secret golf course in Château-Thierry. **Open** Feb 24 – Jan 28.

The splendid Château d'Etoges dates from the 17th century. It is set against a low hill beneath where springs emerge as elegant fountains. The interior of the château is equally enchanting; it has been refurbished with good taste to retain the building's character and provide modern amenities. (The bathrooms are beautiful). There is a grand staircase, as well as spacious lounges with decorative panels, delightful percale tablecloths in the dining room, and superb bedrooms. Some are big and sumptuous, others more intimate, but in each there is a delightful blend of antique furniture and pretty materials and romantic views over the moat. A warm, personal welcome at the Château d'Etoges, evokes a way of life in a more graceful age. It is an ideal base for exploring the Champagne vineyards.

How to get there *(Map 10): 40km west of Châlons-sur-Marne via D33.*

Le Prieuré ★★★

Chevet de l'Eglise
60440 Ermenonville (Oise)
Tel. (0)3★ 44.54.00.44 - Fax (0)3★ 44.54.02.21 - M. and Mme Treillou

Rooms 11 with telephone, bath or shower, WC, TV and minibar. **Price** Double 450-500F. **Meals** Breakfast 50F. No restaurant. **Credit cards** All major. **Pets** Small dogs allowed. **Nearby** Châalis abbey, Ermenonville forest, Astérix park, Eurodisneyland. **Open** All year except in Feb.

You will feel right at home at Le Prieuré, a true gem hidden in an English garden just next to the church. M. and Mme Treillou love polished antique furniture, paintings, knick-knacks, and rugs. The fabrics they have selected for the curtains and bedspreads reflect the atmosphere of each room. The bedrooms are very large and comfortable, and certain attic rooms have beautiful exposed beams. They are all quiet (the road to Ermenonville is not too far but it is not busy on weekends). On the ground floor, the reception rooms open directly onto the garden. Each one has a fireplace, but when it's nice outside, the sun warms the polished tile floors all over the house and you can have breakfast in a charming country dining room. You can dine very pleasantly at *L'Ermitage*, about 100 yards from the hotel. Le Prieuré is enchanting.

How to get there *(Map 9): 45km northeast of Paris via A1, exit Survilliers, then D104 towards Villepinte, then Ermenonville.*

A la Bonne Idée ★★★

3, rue des Meuniers
60350 Saint-Jean-aux-Bois (Oise)
Tel. (0)3★ 44.42.84.09 - Fax (0)3★ 44.42.80.45 - M. Drieux

Rooms 23 with telephone, bath, WC and TV - 1 wheelchair access room. **Price** Single and double 385-430F, suite 430F. **Meals** Breakfast 55F, served 7:30-10:30; half board 360-460F, full board 590F (per pers.). **Restaurant** Service 12:15-14:00, 19:15-21:00; menus 100-385F, also à la carte. Specialties: Escalopine de foie gras chaud, ragôut de homard, tarte fine chaude aux pommes. **Credit cards** Amex, Visa, Eurocard and MasterCard. **Pets** Dogs allowed (+25F). **Facilities** Parking. **Nearby** Château and forest of Compiègne, archery museum in Crépy-en-Valois — 18-hole golf course in Compiègne. **Open** All year.

This hotel, a former 18th-century hunding lodge, is located in a charming little village in the heart of the Forest of Compiègne. In the entrance hall and the bar and the large dining room with beamed ceiling, exposed stones, fireplaces and Louis XIII-style chairs create a rustic, very countrified atmosphere. In summer, tables are elegantly set under a vast tent, allowing you to enjoy the garden. The cuisine here is good, invariably based on fresh products, and while the à la carte menu and set meals might seem somewhat expensive, the weekend *forfaits* (fixed prices) are very good value. The bedrooms are beginning to age somewhat but certain renovations are planned. The rooms in the annex have already been renovated; located on the ground floor overlooking the garden, they are very pleasant. Visitors will appreciate its hospitable welcome and its calm ambience, ensured by the fact that the hotel's proximity to the forest paths.

How to get there (*Map 9*): *75km northeast of Paris via A1, number 9 exit in Chevrières towards Verberie, then D200 to La-Croix-Saint-Ouen and D85 through the Forest of Compiègne to Saint-Jean-aux-Bois.*

A l'Orée du Bois ★★

Futeau - 55120 Clermont-en-Argonne (Meuse)
Tel. (0)3★ 29.88.28.41 - Fax (0)3★ 29.88.24.52
M. and Mme Aguesse

Rooms 7 with telephone, bath, WC and TV. **Price** Single 295F, double 340-360F.
Meals Breakfast 48F, served 7:30-11:00; half board 420F, full board 520F (per pers.,
3 days min.). **Restaurant** Closed Tuesday and Sunday evening in low season. Service
12:00-13:30, 19:00-20:30; menus 115F (in week), 190-360F, also à la carte.
Specialties: Pigeonneau des Hauts de Chée, fricassée d'écrevisses, rognons de lapin
aux champignons, bourgeon de sapin glacé. **Credit cards** Visa, Eurocard and
MasterCard. **Pets** Dogs allowed (+40F). **Facilities** Parking. **Nearby** Argonne Forest,
Butte de Vauquois, Varennes-en-Argonne, Lachalade Abbey, Verdun, Rarécourt
Museum, Les Islettes pottery factory (open July 1 – Aug 30). **Open** All year (closed
Jan,Nov 1, school holidays, Sunday evening and Tuesday in low season).

With a beautiful forest at the back, the small Orée du Bois
looks out over a beautiful, peaceful countryside. The
interior decoration is pleasant and is lent character by traditional
old furniture. Located in a recently built wing, the bedrooms are
on the ground floor facing the lawn and all have a very beautiful
view. They are large and decorated in a classically rustic style, but
the pretty fabrics give the rooms warmth. The dining room with
large bay windows has the most beautiful view. M. Aguesse turns
out such regional specialties as fricassée of crayfish, while his wife,
who oversees the dining room, will advise you very competently
on wines. Both M. and Mme will see to it that your stay at "The
Edge of the Woods" is memorable.

*How to get there (Map 11): 40km west of Verdun via A4, exit Sainte-Menehould.
Then take N3 towards Verdun to Islettes, then D2 on the right, towards Futeau.*

Auberge Le Fiacre

Rue des Pommiers
Routhiauville 80120 Quend (Somme)
Tel. (0)3★ 22.23.47.30 – Fax (0)3★ 22.27.19.80 – M. Masmonteil

Rooms 11 with telephone, bath, WC and TV – Wheelchair access. **Price** Double 350-380F. **Meals** Breakfast 40F, served 8:00-10:00; half board 360-380F (per pers., 3 days min.). **Restaurant** Service 12:00-14:00, 19:00-21:30; menus 98-210F, also à la carte. Specialties: Poissons cotiens, agneau de pré salé de la baie de Somme, gibier an automne. **Credit cards** All major. **Pets** Dogs not allowed. **Facilities** Mountainbike rentals, parking. **Nearby** Beaches of Quend and Fort-Mahon (3km); parc ornithologique de Marquenterre; Le Crotoy; Le Touquet – 18-hole Belle Dune golf course. **Open** Feb 4 – Jan 14.

Standing in the midst of the Picardie countryside, this old auberge is located in a hamlet which is quiet day and night. The buildings, which have been very well restored, surround a charming dovecote and a beautifully tended garden. Well known in the region for their excellent restaurant, the owners have opened eleven bedrooms, half of them downstairs on the garden. All are comfortable, quite spacious, and decorated without ostentation; care is given to small details (like the high-quality water faucets and the excellent radio acoustics in the bathroom). However, the delicious homemade pastries and the good morning coffee, served in pretty thermos bottles, deserve a more attractive breakfast room, especially as the restaurant has a very beautiful old-farm decor, with a fireplace and period furniture. M. Masmonteil himself is the excellent chef and his elegant and discreet wife, a great wine connoisseur, will guide you in your choice of wines. In good weather, the owners plan to set up several tables outside as well as chaises-longues on the lawn.

How to get there *(Map 1): 30 south of Le Touquet; in Quend-ville, take towards Fort-Mahon. Turn at the Routhiauville traffic circle.*

Hôtel Dolce Vita ★★★

Route des Sanguinaires
20000 Ajaccio (Corse-du-Sud)
Tel. (0)4★ 95.52.00.93 - Fax (0)4★ 95.52.07.15 - M. Federici

Rooms 32 with telephone, bath, WC, TV and minibar. **Price** Single and double 435-970F. **Meals** Breakfast 60F, served 7:00-10:00; half board and full board (obligatory in July and Aug) 665-945F. **Restaurant** Service 12:30-13:45, 19:30-21:30; menu 200F, also à la carte. Specialties: Raviolis au broccio, fricassée de langouste. **Credit cards** All major. **Pets** Dogs allowed (+60F). **Facilities** Swimming pool, water skiing, beach. **Nearby** Gulf of Ajaccio via the Route des Iles Sanguinaires, Les Milelli, Château de la Punta, Bastelica. **Open** Easter – Nov 1.

The Dolce Vita is a modern hotel whose superb location compensates for the functional style of its architecture and its rather flashy interior decor. All the rooms face the sea. They are located on two levels; the lower give direct access to a small beach built on the rocks. The hotel is very comfortable and the bathrooms have all the usual facilities. There are flowers everywhere and it is a pleasure to stroll among the bougainvillea, oleanders and palm trees. The dining area is composed of a large interior room, which is used in winter, and a spacious shaded terrace which overlooks the sea. At night, with the swimming pool floodlit, the twinkling lights in the trees and the glimmer of lights across the bay, the scene is reminiscent of Hollywood.

How to get there (Map 36): 8km west of Ajaccio via the Route des Sanguinaires. Ajaccio-Campo dell'Oro Airport 15km away, tel. (0)4★ 95.21.03.64.

Hôtel Genovese ★★★

Quartier de la Citadelle
20169 Bonifacio (Corse-du-Sud)
Tel. (0)4★ 95.73.12.34 - Fax (0)4★ 95.73.09.03

Rooms 14 with air-conditioning, telephone, bath, WC, TV and minibar. **Price** Double 700-1500F, suite 950-1700F. **Meals** Breakfast 70-80F, served 7:30-11:00. No restaurant. **Credit cards** All major. **Pets** Dogs allowed. **Facilities** Parking. **Nearby** Boat trip to marine grottoes, cave of Sdragonato and tour of the cliffs, gulf of Santa-Manza – 18-hole golf course in Sperone. **Open** All year.

Set out along the walls of the Bonifacio ramparts, this hotel is in an old naval building and has a beautiful view of the sea, the town and the harbor. It is luxuriously and elegantly furnished. The rooms are set around a delightful courtyard and are decorated in pastel shades with flowered curtains. The bathrooms are faultless and there is a whirlpool bath in every suite. Room 2 also has a balcony which overlooks the port. There is no restaurant but the ground floor has a breakfast area and a lounge where a handsome white settee blends delightfully with the stone walls. An additional asset is that the hotel is fully air conditioned. *La Caravelle* is the popular fish restaurant; *Le Voilier* and *Le Stella d'Oro* (upstairs), are favorites with the region's famous people; and *La Cantina Doria* serves the best authentic Corsican specialties.

How to get there *(Map 36): In Bonifacio, turn right immediately on leaving the road to the Citadelle. Figari Airport 21km away, tel. (0)4★ 95.71.00.22.*

Résidence du Centre Nautique ★★★

Quai Nord
20169 Bonifacio (Corse-du-Sud)
Tel. (0)4★ 95.73.02.11 – Fax (0)4★ 95.73.17.47 – M. Lantieri

Rooms 10 with air-conditioning, telephone, shower, WC, TV and minibar. **Price** Double 450-950F. **Meals** Breakfast 50-60F. No restaurant. Snacks available. **Credit cards** All major. **Pets** Dogs allowed. **Facilities** Parking. **Nearby** Boat trip to the marine grottoes, Sdragonato Cave and tour of the cliffs, Santa-Manza Gulf – 18-hole golf course in Sperone. **Open** All year.

This hotel on Bonifacio harbor lies below the upper town and looks out over the moored boats. Despite its name it is a place that gives a cordial welcome to tourists as well as to sailing enthusiasts. The high ceilings have made it possible to convert the rooms into small duplexes. On the lower level there is a small living room and on the mezzanine the bedroom and bathroom. It is more like a studio than a conventional hotel bedroom and perfect for inviting your neighbors in for cocktails. Some units have a view over the garden and others over the port, which is quiet and peaceful at night. You can have breakfast on the terrace overlooking the sailboats and yachts.

How to get there (Map 36): On the port. Figari Airport 21km away, tel. (0)4★ 95.71.00.22

Grand Hôtel Cala Rossa ★★★★
Cala Rossa - 20137 Porto-Vecchio (Corse-du-Sud)
Tel. (0)4★ 95.71.61.51 - Fax (0)4★ 95.71.60.11
M. Canarelli and Mme Biancarelli

Rooms 50 with air-conditioning, telephone, bath, WC and TV. **Price** Single 500-2000F, double 640-2700F, suite 1500-2700F. **Meals** Breakfast incl., served 7:30-11:30; half-board obligatory in high season. **Restaurant** Service 12:30-14:30, 19:45-22:00; menus, also à la carte. Specialties: Mesclun de seiches à l'origan, craquant de loup aux aubergines, filet d'agneau à la choucroute de fenouil. **Credit cards** All major. **Pets** Dogs not allowed. **Facilities** Private beach, water skiing, windsurfing, boat trips, parking. **Nearby** Palombaggia beach and Piccovaggia Peninsula, Ospedale Forest – 18-hole golf course in Sperone. **Open** Apr 15 – Dec 31.

The success of the Grand Hôtel Cala Rossa is due mainly to the enthusiasm of proprietor Toussaint Canarelli and his loyal and hard-working team. The hotel is very well located on the edge of the sea, and the restaurant, which is one of the best in Corsica, has become the summer haunt of famous politicians and actors from the Cala Rossa residential area. The bedrooms are all comfortable, but the suites decorated in Mediterranean style are especially luxurious as are the reception and the salon. The surroundings are magnificent: the garden with its shady pines, oleanders and plumbagos extends as far as the private beach. It is essential to reserve very early for the summer season, but in spring and autumn you can enjoy the pleasures of the maquis and the Ospedale Forest as well as the sea. Note the very attractive low-season rates.

How to get there (Map 36): 10km northeast of Porto Vecchio via N198, D568 and D468. Figari Airport 33km away, tel. (0)4★ 95.71.00.22.

L'Aïtone ★★

20126 Evisa (Corse-du-Sud)
Tel. (0)4★ 95.26.20.04 – Fax (0)4★ 95.26.24.18
M. Ceccaldi

Rooms 32 with telephone, bath or shower, WC and cable TV. **Price** Single 150-400F, double 200-550F. **Meals** Breakfast 35-38F, served 8:00-9:30; half board 250-450F, full board 380-550F (per pers, 3 days min.). **Restaurant** Service 12:00-14:00, 19:30-22:00; menus 85-160F, also à la carte. Specialties: Terrine de sanglier aux châtaignes, omelette broccio et menthe, charcuterie corse, truite. **Credit cards** Amex, Visa, Eurocard and MasterCard. **Pets** Dogs allowed. **Facilities** Swimming pool, garage, parking. **Nearby** Waterfall and pool in the forest of Aïtone, gorges of the Spelunca, forest of Aïtone, calanques of Piana, villages of Ota and Vico, Girolata. **Open** Jan – Nov.

The Aïtone auberge is 850m above sea level on the edge of the spectacular forest of pines and larches of Aïtone and the Valdo-Niello. Toussaint Ceccaldi, the proprietor, has taken over from his parents and is constantly refurbishing and enlarging the hotel. The building is not particularly attractive but it has a superb location, with its large swimming pool overlooking the beautiful Spelunca Valley. The bedrooms – some, with balconies are more luxurious than others – have a magnificent view of the Gulf of Porto. You will enjoy very good cuisine.

How to get there *(Map 36): 23km east of Porto via D84. Ajaccio Airport 70km away, tel. (0)4★ 95.21.03.64.*

Les Roches Rouges ★★

20115 Piana (Corse-du-Sud)
Tel. (0)4★ 95.27.81.81 - Fax (0)4★ 95.27.81.76
Mme Dalakupeyan

Rooms 30 with telephone, shower and WC. **Price** Double 265-280F. **Meals** Breakfast 40F, served 7:30-11:00; half board 320F (per pers.). **Restaurant** Service 12:00-14:00; menus 100-360F, also à la carte. Specialties: Fish, lobster. **Credit cards** All major. **Pets** Dogs allowed. **Facilities** Parking. **Nearby** Calanques of Piana, boat to Girolata (dep. Porto), villages of Ota, Evisa and Vico, Lava peak, route de Ficajola. **Open** Apr 1 – Oct 30.

This turn-of-the-century Corsican house, on the edge of the village of Piana and three kilometers from the famous creeks, has been refurbished. There is a spacious, well-lit, handsome restaurant which extends onto a terrace, and from here as well as from the bedrooms there are superb views. The rooms themselves are rather simple and could do with improvement, but this is made up for by the cordial welcome given by Mady and the very reasonable prices.

How to get there *(Map 36): 71km north of Ajaccio via D81. Ajaccio Airport, tel.(0)4★ 95.21.03.64.*

Le Maquis ★★★★

20166 Porticcio (Corse-du-Sud)
Tel. (0)4★ 95.25.05.55 – Fax (0)4★ 95.25.11.70
Mme Salini

Rooms 19 with air-conditioning, telephone, bath, WC, TV and minibar. **Price** Not communicated for 1996 - 840F in low season, Half board only, double 1780-2480F. **Meals** Breakfast incl., served 8:00-10:30. **Restaurant** Service 12:30-14:00, 19:30-22:00; à la carte 300-450F. **Credit cards** All major. **Pets** Dogs allowed (+60F). **Facilities** Heated swimming pool, tennis, gym, private beach, parking. **Nearby** Gulf of Ajaccio via the Route des Iles Sanguinaires, Les Milelli, Château de la Punta, Bastelica. **Open** All year.

The Maquis is one of the outstanding hotels in this guide. It is splendidly located on a small inlet off the Gulf of Ajaccio, two kilometers from Porticcio. Its pretty private beach, the elegant decor and the comfort of its communal rooms and bedrooms (ask for a room with a terrace facing the sea) make it ideal for a relaxing, comfortable vacation. The terrace, the covered swimming pool and a tennis court complete the picture. At noon, there is a delicious buffet lunch on the terrace and in the evenings an excellent menu, changed every day, is served. What more could we want? Mme Salini has made Le Maquis a veritable oasis on a coast that unfortunately has been rather spoiled. But if you do want to leave the hotel, you can explore the beautiful interior of Corsica. However, we hope that customers will be welcomed more courteously than we were when we asked for the new rates.

How to get there (Map 36): 18km southeast of Ajaccio via N196, D55 along the coast. Ajaccio-Campo dell'Oro Airport, tel. (0)4★ 95.21.03.64.

Hôtel L'Aiglon ★★

20147 Serriera (Corse-du-Sud)
Tel. (0)4★ 95.26.10.65 - Fax (0)4★ 95.26.14.77
M. Colonna-Ceccaldi

Rooms 18 with telephone, bath or shower (8 with WC). **Price** 210-360F.
Meals Breakfast 35F, served 8:00-9:30; half board 200-300F, full board 250-360F
(per pers., 3 days min.). **Restaurant** Service 12:30-14:00, 20:00-21:30; menus 90-
150F, also à la carte. Specialties: Omelette au broccio, daube de sanglier, cannellonis
à la corse. **Credit cards** All major. **Pets** Dogs allowed. **Facilities** Parking.
Nearby Waterfall and pool in the Forest of Aïtone, Gorges of the Spelunca, Forest of
Aïtone, calanques of Piana, boat to Girolata, villages of Ota and Vico. **Open** May 1 –
end Sept.

The Hôtel L'Aiglon, built about thirty years ago out of Porto
stone, is a place for lovers of peace and tranquillity. It is set in
the heart of the maquis. To reach the hotel, you take a winding
road across hilly countryside; but it is not as isolated as this might
suggest for the sea is only five kilometers away. Because it is
patronized by a regular clientele, the bedrooms have not been
updated. They are quite simple and the furniture is very 1950s.
The bathrooms are behind rather thin partitions. To one side of
the building there are six rooms in bungalows, each one with its
own terrace. The moderate rates are interesting if you wish to
explore the interior of Corsica or want inexpensive proximity to
the sea.

How to get there *(Map 36): 5km north of Porto via D81; follow signs. Calvi
Airport 80km, tel. (0)4★ 95.65.08.09.*

Hôtel Balanéa ★★★
6, rue Clémenceau
20260 Calvi (Haute-Corse)
Tel. (0)4★ 95.65.00.45 - Fax (0)4★ 95.65.29.71 - M. Ceccaldi

Rooms 37 with air-conditioning, telephone, bath, WC and TV (32 with minibar).
Price Double 300-1200F, suite 700-1200F. **Meals** Breakfast 60F, served 7:30-10:30.
No restaurant. **Credit cards** All major. **Pets** Dogs allowed (+100F). **Nearby** Citadel
of Calvi, tour of the villages of Balagne (Calenzana, Zilia, Montemaggiore,
Sant'Antonino, church of the Trinity in Aregno, convent of Corbara), Scandola national
park – 9-hole Lumio golf course. **Open** All year.

Located on the harbor in Calvi, the Balanéa is the most pleasant
hotel in the center of town. The bedrooms, which are very
comfortable, are spacious and well decorated; they have large
bathrooms with all the amenities, including hair-dryers. Most have
balconies and some have real terraces from which there are
marvelous views of the fort and citadel. All the rooms are air-
conditioned, making for pleasant sleeping in the hot summer. The
Balanéa is the only hotel open in Calvi during the winter. For an
unforgettable evening, we recommend dinner on the marvelous
terrace of *La Signoria* and the piano-bar of *Chez Tao*.

How to get there *(Map 36): on the port in Calvi. Calvi Airport 7km, tel.
(0)4★ 95.65.08.09*

Auberge de la Signoria ★★★
Route de forêt de Bonifato
20260 Calvi (Haute-Corse)
Tel. (0)4★ 95.65.23.73 - Fax (0)4★ 95.65.38.77 - MM. Ceccaldi

Rooms 10 with telephone, bath, WC, TV and minibar. **Price** Single and double 450-1100F, suite 1000-1500F, apart. 1200-2000F. **Meals** Breakfast 70F, served 8:00-11:00; half board 1150-1800F (per 2 pers., 2 days min.). **Restaurant** Service 12:00-13:30, 19:30-22:30 (closed lunchtime in July and Aug except weekend and National Holidays); menu 320F (child 130F), also à la carte. Specialties: Carpaccio de saumon aigre doux, salade de pigeonneau, noisettes d'agneau à la croute d'herbes du maquis. **Credit cards** Amex, Visa, Eurocard and MasterCard. **Pets** Dogs allowed. **Facilities** Swimming pool, tennis, team bath, parking. **Nearby** Citadel of Calvi, tour of the villages of Balagne (Calenzana, Zilia, Montemaggiore, Sant'Antonino, church of the Trinity in Aregno, convent of Corbara), Scandola national park – 9-hole Lumio golf course. **Open** End Mar – Oct 15.

La Signoria is the kind of hotel that dreams are made of. It is in a beautiful old house on a large estate with eucalyptus and palm trees and a beautiful swimming pool in the garden. The owners have converted the house into a hotel, without spoiling any of its charm. The rooms in the main building are the most pleasant and comfortable ones, but you will not feel deprived if you have one in the annex. Dinner by candlelight under the canopy of palm trees on the terrace is one of the many lovely moments you will spend here. This beautiful hotel is perfectly quiet even in the middle of August.

How to get there *(Map 36): 5km from Calvi on the airport road. Calvi Airport 7km, tel. (0)4★ 95.65.08.09.*

Marina d'Argentella

L'Argentella
20260 Calvi (Haute-Corse)
Tel. (0)4★ 95.65.25.08 – M. Grisoli

Rooms 25 with bath and WC. **Price** Double room with half board 350-450F (per pers.), reduced rate for children. **Meals** Breakfast incl. **Restaurant** Service 12:30-14:30, 20:00-22:00; menu 120F, also à la carte. Specialties: Fish and Corsican dishes. **Credit cards** Visa, Eurocard and MasterCard. **Pets** Dogs allowed. **Facilities** Parking. **Nearby** Citadel of Calvi, tour of the villages of Ballagne (Calenzana, Zilia, Montemaggiore, Sant 'Antonino, church of the Trinity in Aregno, convent of Corbara), Scandola regional park – 9-hole Lumio golf course. **Open** May 1 – Oct 1.

The Argentella is a very special place, not only because it is so beautifully located on the beach of Crovani Bay, but also because of Pierre and Dorine's friendly hospitality. The bedrooms, which are in small bungalows in a eucalyptus grove, are simple but charming, and all have comfortable bathrooms. Chef Dhair prepares new recipes regularly. At noon, meals are light and fresh, while in the evening the fare is more ambitious. Swimming, windsurfing, picnics and boat excursions are offered by the hotel. At seven in the evening, you can join in the traditional volleyball game and then enjoy a drink as you admire the wonderful sunset. The Argentella is ideal for a family vacation; note the special slimming week in June.

How to get there *(Map 36): 22km south of Calvi towards Porto by coast road. Calvi Airport 25km away, tel. (0)4★ 95.65.08.09.*

Hôtel Mare e Monti ★★

20225 Feliceto (Haute-Corse)
Tel. (0)4★ 95.61.73.06 – Fax (0)4★ 95.61.78.67
M. Renucci

Rooms 18 with telephone, (14 with shower and 2 with bath and WC). **Price** Single
252-265F, double 283-297F. **Meals** Breakfast 30F, served 8:00-10:00; half board
276F, full board 385F (per pers., 3 days min.). **Restaurant** Service 12:00-14:00,
19:30-22:00; menus 80-180F, also à la carte. Specialties: Truite à la Calamenti,
agneau de lait à la mode corse. **Credit cards** All major. **Pets** Dogs allowed.
Facilities Parking. **Nearby** Citadel of Calvi, tour of the villages of Ballagne
(Calenzana, Zilia, Montemaggiore, Sant 'Antonino, church of the Trinity in Aregno,
convent of Corbara). **Open** May 1 – Sept 30.

This lovely house, which lies between the sea and the
mountains, was built in 1870 and is still lived in by the same
family. Behind the hotel there are steep rocky cliffs, and in the
distance one can see the sea behind Ile Rousse. On one side of the
hotel is a lovely terrace where meals are served. Nearby are two
magnificent cedar trees, and an orchard of apple trees provides fruit
for breakfast. The *deuxième étage* bedrooms, with high ceilings,
simple decor and old paintings, are preferable to those on the
troisième étage, where the linoleum-covered floor is not attractive.
M. Renucci gives a cordial welcome to all his guests and the
traditional, delicious cuisine provided by his chef is an attraction
for people who want to know a more authentic Corsica than that
found in its seaside resorts.

How to get there *(Map 36): 26km northeast of Calvi via N197 to beyond
Alcajola, then right on D13 to Feliceto via Santa Reparata. Calvi Airport,
Tel. (0)4★ 95.65.08.09.*

La Bergerie *

Route de Monticello
20220 L'Ile-Rousse (Haute-Corse)
Tel. (0)4★ 95.60.01.28 – Fax (0)4★ 95.60.06.36 – M. Caumer

Rooms 19 with telephone, bath or shower, WC and TV. **Price** Single and double 250-450F. **Meals** Breakfast 35F, served 8:00-10:00; half board 400-460F (per pers., 5 days min.). **Restaurant** Service 12:00 and 19:30; also à la carte. Specialties: Brochettes de liche, araignées farcies, omelette aux oursins, sardines farcies, mérou à la juive. **Credit cards** Visa, Eurocard and MasterCard. **Pets** Dogs allowed. **Facilities** Swimming pool, parking. **Nearby** Citadel of Calvi, tour of the villages of Ballagne (Calenzana, Zilia, Montemaggiore, Sant 'Antonino, church of the Trinity in Aregno, convent of Corbara). **Open** Mar 15 – Dec 1 (closed Monday in low season).

L a Bergerie is an old sheep farm converted into a small hotel 800 meters from Ile Rousse and the beach. It is famous as a restaurant throughout Ile Rousse and Calvi, and bedrooms have been added in the quiet garden. The owner is an enthusiastic fisherman and delights his guests with dishes he creates using his catch of the day. These might include such refined dishes as sea-urchin omelette and sea-anemone fritters. The atmosphere is relaxed and friendly.

How to get there *(Map 36): 24km northeast of Calvi via N197 to L'Ile Rousse. Calvi Airport, tel. (0)4★ 95.65.08.09.*

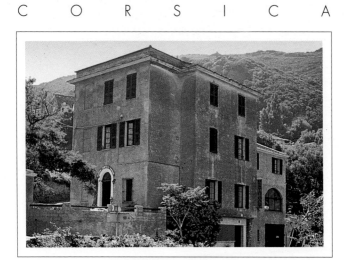

U Sant' Agnellu

20247 Rogliano (Haute-Corse)
Tel. (0)4★ 95.35.40.59 - Fax (0)4★ 95.35.40.59
M. and Mme Albertini

Rooms 9 with bath and WC. **Price** Double 220-320F. **Meals** Breakfast 30F; half board 250-300F (per pers.). **Restaurant** Service 12:00-15:00, 19:30-23:00; menu 90F, also à la carte. Specialties: Brandade, boulettes au broccio, cannelonis, tourte Sant Agnellu, cabri. **Credit cards** Visa, Eurocard and MasterCard. **Pets** Dogs allowed. **Facilities** Parking. **Nearby** Romanesque Cathedral of la Canonica and San Parteo Church, villages of Cap Corse from Bastia to Saint-Florent. **Open** Easter – Oct.

Young M. and Mme Albertini set up a restaurant in this old town hall in 1984 and three years later converted it into a hotel. They deserve encouragement for their delicious cuisine at unbeatable prices, as well as for the charming bedrooms. With white stucco walls and solid wooden furniture, the accomodations are simple but very comfortable and the tiled bathrooms are impeccable. Five bedrooms look out onto the sea and the others onto the mountains. In good weather, meals are served on the panoramic terrace: the spacious indoor dining room with its semicircle of large windows also has beautiful views. Visitors who enjoy old buildings will find much to interest them in this picturesque 12th-century village, which has two churches, a convent and the ruins of a château as well as various Genoese towers.

How to get there *(Map 36): 42km north of Bastia via D80 towards Macinaggio (free bus from port of Macinaggio to the hotel). Bastia Airport, tel. (0)4★ 95.54.54.54.*

Hôtel Castel Brando ★★★

20222 Erbalunga (Haute-Corse)
Tel. (0)4★ 95.30.10.30 – Fax (0)4★ 95.33.98.18
M. and Mme Pieri

Rooms 10 and 6 apartments with air-conditioning, telephone, bath, WC and TV, kitchenette. **Price** Double 380-530F, apart. 530-830F (per 3-4 pers). **Meals** Breakfast incl., served 8:30-10:00. No restaurant. **Credit cards** All major. **Pets** Dogs allowed. **Facilities** Swimming pool, parking. **Nearby** Bastia, romanesque cathedral of La Canonica and San Parteo church, villages of Cap Corse from Bastia to Saint-Florent. **Open** Apr 1 – Oct 30.

Joëlle and Jean-Paul Piéri, who were born in this picturesque fishing village, have restored a beautiful and charming house here, lending it comfort and personality. You can live here at your own pace and the apartments with kitchenette are especially recommendable for long stays. The shady park has a swimming pool, but if you prefer the sea, the pebble beaches in Erbalunga or Piétracorba are nearby. Fairly new to the hotel business, M. and Mme Piéri have quickly become real professionals. They are very enthusiastic and will give you a warm welcome – as well as tips for discovering and enjoying the real Corsica. Erbalunga itself is classed as a preserved site and has inspired numerous painters. For dinner, the owners will give you their special addresses. We recommend *La Citadelle* and *Le Romantique* in Bastia; and in Erbalunga, overlooking the sea, *Le Pirate*.

How to get there (Map 36): 9km north of Bastia. Bastia-Poretta Airport tel.: (0)4★ 95 54 54 54.

Hôtel de la Corniche ★★

San-Martino-di-Lota
20200 Bastia (Haute-Corse)
Tel. (0)4★ 95.31.40.98 – Fax (0)4★ 95.32.37.69 – Mme Anziani

Rooms 19 with telephone, bath or shower and WC (10 with TV). **Price** Single 250-300F, double 300-450F. **Meals** Breakfast 30-35F, served 7:30-10:00; half board 280-360F (per pers.). **Restaurant** Service 12:00-14:00, 19:30-21:30 (closed Sunday evening and Monday, Oct – end Mar); menus, also à la carte. Specialties: Raviolis au broccio et aux herbes, Pageot du golf en étuvée de fenouil confit olives vertes, grenadins de veau sautés au gingembre et citron vert et ses canellonis de courgette au basilic, pastizzu du Cap Corse et son coulis d'orange caramélisé. **Credit cards** All major. **Pets** Dogs not allowed. **Facilities** Swimming pool. **Nearby** Romanesque cathedral of La Canonica and San Parteo church, villages of Cap Corse from Bastia to Saint-Florent. **Open** Feb 1 – Dec 20.

This hotel at San Martino-di-Lota lies along a winding road ten minutes' drive from Bastia. It has been owned by the same family since 1935 and has incomparable views of the sea. The first thing you will notice is the beautiful terrace and its splendid plane trees. Meals are served here in beautiful weather and on clear days you can see as far as the Italian coast. Home cuisine and Corsican specialties are the keynotes of the menu. The bedrooms are excellent for their price range; they are tastefully and comfortably decorated with classic wooden furniture and attractive bathrooms, and all look out to the sea. You will find a cordial welcome here.

How to get there *(Map 36): 6km north of Bastia via D80, then D131 at Pietranera. Bastia Airport, tel. (0)4★ 95.54.54.54.*

Auberge Le Moulin du Plain ★★

25470 Goumois (Doubs)
Tel. (0)3★ 81.44.41.99 – Fax (0)3★ 81.44.45.70
M. Choulet

Rooms 22 with telephone, bath or shower and WC. **Price** Single and double 204-295F. **Meals** Breakfast 34F, served 8:00-9:30; half board 228-244F, full board 290-312F (per pers., 3 days min.). **Restaurant** Service 12:00-13:30, 19:00-21:30; menus 95-194F, also à la carte. Specialties: Truite à l'échalote, feuilleté aux morilles, jambon du pays, coq au savagnin. **Credit cards** Visa, Eurocard and MasterCard. **Pets** Dogs allowed. **Facilities** Parking. **Nearby** Circuit from Maîche (D437) to Gière and Indevillers, Corniche of Goumois via the gorges of the Doubs to the Echelles de la Mort, art and clock making museums in Besançon – 18-hole Prunevelle golf course. **Open** Feb. 25 – Nov 2.

This hotel is a great favorite with fishermen. It stands on the banks of the Doubs River with its sand and pebble beach, at the foot of the mountains facing Switzerland. The emphasis here is on calm and simplicity: the steep roof of the building is a typical feature of farmhouses in the Haut-Jura, and the bedrooms are attractively unpretentious. The Auberge du Moulin du Plain is ideal for those seeking a peaceful retreat. It has a small lounge, several fireplaces and a bar area. Its exceptional location has a lot to offer not only to fishermen but also to those in search of simple pleasures: bathing in crystal-clear waters, stunning walks and excursions (Switzerland is within easy reach). The cuisine is of the same calibre as the hotel.

How to get there (Map 20): 53km south of Montbéliard via D437 towards Maîche, at Maison Rouge D437b to Goumois; 4km before Goumois beside the River Doubs.

Hôtel Taillard ★★★

25470 Goumois (Doubs)
Tel. (0)3★ 81.44.20.75 - Fax (0)3★ 81.44.26.15
M. Taillard

Rooms 17 with telephone, bath or shower, WC and TV (6 with minibar).
Price Double 280-350F, suite 430-440F. **Meals** Breakfast 50F, served 8:00-9:30;
half board 370-420F (per pers., 3 days min.). **Restaurant** Service 12:00-14:00,
19:15-20:45; menus 135-370F, also à la carte. Specialties: Escalope de foie gras
aux griottes de Fougerolles. **Credit cards** All major. **Pets** Dogs allowed (+30F).
Facilities Swimming pool, parking. **Nearby** The Maîche road (D437) to Gière and
Indevillers, Goumois (coastal road) via the Doubs gorges to Les Echelles de la
Mort, art and clock making museums in Besançon – 18-hole Prunevelle golf
course. **Open** Mar – Nov (closed Wednesdays in Mar and Oct).

You will appreciate the innkeeping and gastronomic knowhow of four generations of Taillards in this hotel. It is in the middle of the Jura countryside on a hillside overlooking a small valley. You can see the blue foothills of the Swiss Alps on the horizon. The rooms are comfortable and most of them have a balcony facing the mountains. The pastures of the Haut-Doubs are soft green, and you can still hear the tinkling of cow bells there, the Doubs river is great for trout fishing and kayaking. Everything is simple and quiet here. We especially liked M. Taillard's cuisine, which features regional specialties with a local flavor. The menu is imaginative and the "light" dishes will satisfy many a gourmet. The service is also outstanding.

How to get there *(Map 20): 53km south of Montbéliard via D437 towards Maîche, at Maison Rouge D437b to Goumois; near the church.*

Hôtel de la Vouivre ★★

39 bis, rue Gédéon-David
39300 Champagnole (Jura)
Tel. (0)3★ 84.52.10.44 - Fax (0)3★ 84.52.04.07 - Mme Pernot

Rooms 20 with telephone, bath or shower, WC and TV. **Price** Single 300-360F, double 370-460F. **Meals** Breakfast 40F, served 7:00-9:30; half board 280-350F, full board 370-430F (per pers.). **Restaurant** Closed Wednesday noon. Service 12:00-14:00, 19:30-21:30; menus 110-170F, also à la carte. Specialties: Truite au vin jaune, filet de bœuf aux morilles. **Credit cards** Visa, Eurocard and MasterCard. **Pets** Dogs allowed. **Facilities** Swimming pool, tennis, parking. **Nearby** Lake of Chalain, cirque of Beaume-les-Messieurs, château of Syam, Billaude waterfall, Langouette and Malvaux gorges – 18-hole Val-de-Sorne golf course in Lons-le-Saunier. **Open** May 1 – Oct 30.

The Vouivre is a beautiful hotel somewhat on the outskirts of Champagnole. Comfortable bedrooms, a swimming pool, tennis courts and a quiet location make it a restful place to stay in this beautiful region of the Jura. It is very near the La Joux Forest with its famous President fir tree (132 feet high, 12 feet in diameter), which is unfortunately difficult to get to. The lake, which is surrounded by a ten-acre park, provides good fishing. Champagnole itself is a dynamic small town there toys and furniture are made.

How to get there (Map 20): 43km southwest of Pontarlier via D471.

Le Moulin de la Mère Michelle ★★★

Les Planches
39600 Arbois (Jura)
Tel. (0)3★ 84.66.08.17 - Fax (0)3★ 84.37.49.69 - M. Delavenne

Rooms 22 with telephone, bath or shower, WC, TV and minibar; elevator. **Price** Double 380-680F. **Meals** Breakfast 55F, served 8:00-10:30; half board 450-600F (per pers.). **Restaurant** Closed Thursdays in low season. Service 12:00-13:30, 19:30-21:00; menus 65-298F, also à la carte. Specialties: Poularde aux morilles et au vin jaune, pochouse de truite. **Credit cards** Amex, Visa, Eurocard and MasterCard. **Pets** Dogs allowed (+60F). **Facilities** Swimming pool, tennis, parking. **Nearby** Wine and vineyard Museum, Pasteur's house, Planches cave, Hôtel-Dieu pharmacy in Poligny – 18-hole Val-de-Sorne golf course in Lons-le-Saunier. **Open** All year.

The Moulin de la Mère Michelle stands well off the beaten track on the way to Switzerland and not far from Arbois, a town that delights visitors with the opulent provincial charm of prosperous businesses and vineyards. Formerly a mill where walnuts were ground for oil, the building has been carefully restored by its current owner, who has transformed it into a small fortress with an elevator in its tower. The bedrooms have been modernized and are very comfortable with their warm colors, stone walls, and beamed ceilings. Rooms 10 and 11 each have the added luxury of a four-poster bed. All these improvements and enlargements have nevertheless taken away from the charm of both the site and the hospitality. This is a good hotel in a peaceful and superb setting near a spectacular waterfall. Note that half-board is compulsory in summer, particularly for guests staying for one night only.

How to get there *(Map 19): 42km northeast of Lons-le-Saunier via N83 to Arbois via Poligny, D107 to Mesnay then D247.*

Hôtel de France ★★

39220 Les Rousses (Jura)
Tel. (0)3★ 84.60.01.45 – Fax (0)3★ 84.60.04.63
Mme Petit

Rooms 33 with telephone, bath or shower, (31 with WC) and TV. **Price** Double 285-515F. **Meals** Breakfast 49F; half board 325-445F, full board 415-535F (per pers., 2 days mim.). **Restaurant** Service 12:15-14:00, 19:15-22:00, menus 145-430F. Specialties: Œufs brouillés aux morilles, aiguillettes de sole au champagne, crépinette de pigeon aux foies pochés forestière, moelleux de chocolat amer infusé au cognac. **Credit cards** All major. **Pets** Dogs not allowed. **Nearby** Ski: 200m from the ski lift – 18-hole Rochat golf course. **Open** Dec 15 – Nov 20 (closed June 10 – 28).

The Petit family has been running this hotel for more than thirty years. It is a large chalet whose balconies overflow with flowers in summer. Once you're inside the front door, you will love the Hôtel de France; the large lounge with its wood paneling and beautiful exposed ceiling beams beckons you to take a seat by the large stone fireplace. On the left, the dining room is bright and welcoming. The chef, Jean-Pierre Durcrot, who was Roger Petit's apprentice and trained with famous Paris chefs, puts all his considerable talent in the service of the hotel's clientele. Meals are served on the large shady terrace in summer. All the bedrooms are simply and comfortably decorated and have a view of the forest. You can enjoy total relaxation here after a vigorous day of cross-country or downhill skiing. Mme Petit is very friendly and hospitable.

How to get there *(Map 20): 85km southwest of Pontarlier via D72 to Chaffrois; D471 to Champagnole and N5 via Morez.*

Auberge de Courpain ★★★

Courpain
91690 Fontaine-la-Rivière (Essonne)
Tel. (0)1★ 64.95.67.04 – Fax (0)1★ 60.80.99.02 – Mme Tewe

Rooms 18 with telephone, bath or shower and WC (7 with TV). **Price** Single and double 350F, suite 450-700F. **Meals** Breakfast 40F. **Restaurant** Service 12:30-14:00, 19:30-21:00; menus 130 (in week)-180F, also à la carte. Specialties: Filet Waldorff, blanquette de lotte aux morilles, nougat glacé, Pithiviers chaud. **Credit cards** Amex, Visa, Eurocard and MasterCard. **Pets** Dogs allowed. **Facilities** Helicopter pad, parking. **Nearby** Château promenade des parfums in Chamerolles, Juine Valley in Méréville, aérodrome Jean Salis in La Ferté-Alais, Jeurre Park in Morigny-Etampes. **Open** All year except in Feb.

Although the small road beside the hotel has been widened, this former coachmen's inn and its several adjacent buildings are set in the middle of a large garden. A path leads from the inn to a delightful valley where you can stroll along the banks of its trout streams. You will enjoy reading or relaxing in the lounge or by the fireplace of the hotel, where a warm and cozy atmosphere prevails. There are three dining rooms, all spacious and pleasantly furnished. (Our favorite is the summer dining-room, its vast windows looking out onto the garden). The bedrooms are all different and have been tastefully decorated, and the same amount of care and attention to detail has been devoted to the bathrooms (ask for those which do not overlook the road). The cuisine is good and the owner is warm and hospitable.

How to get there *(Map 9): 58km south of Paris via N20 to Etampes, then N191 Malhesherbes-Pithiviers to the roundabout, on your right D721 towards Pithiviers.*

Auberge de l'Ile du Saussay ★★★

Route de Ballancourt
91760 Itteville (Essonne)
Tel. (0)1★ 64.93.20.12 - Fax (0)1★ 64.93.39.88 - M. Lebrun

Rooms 7, 2 apartments (4 pers.), 13 suites with telephone, bath or shower, WC, TV, minibar and safe. **Price** Double 350F, apart. 900F, suite 450F. **Meals** Breakfast 45F, served 7:00-10:30. **Restaurant** Closed Monday. Service 12:00-14:30, 19:00-22:00; menus 145-195F, also à la carte. **Credit cards** All major. **Pets** Dogs allowed. **Facilities** Parking. **Nearby** Dourdan, Arpajon and Renarde Valley, château of Farcheville. **Open** All year except in Aug (closed Monday).

M. and Mme Lebrun fell in love with the beautiful setting of the Auberge de l'Ile du Saussay at first sight. Although the Auberge is very contemporary in design, the surrounding lakes and trees make it perfectly charming. Three different categories of accommodations are proposed, but all share beautiful decor and modern conveniences. Large bay windows open onto a terrace with a view of the lake or, in the back, trees and a small inlet. You have a choice of bedrooms; suites with a small living room and bedroom on the mezzanine; or apartments with two bedrooms and a living room. The overall effect is lovely. The restaurant also enjoys a splendid view of these small lakes, created centuries ago when the River Essonne filled up old quarries which had been duy by monks to extract peat for heating Parisian homes. At the Auberge, you will enjoy very friendly service and hospitality on the part of a couple who want to share their enthusiasm for this very special setting.

How to get there (Map 9): 40km south of Paris via N 20 to Etampes; then, after Arpajon, take towards La Fertais-Alais.

Hostellerie de la Clé d'Or ★★★

73, Grande-Rue
77630 Barbizon (Seine-et-Marne)
Tel. (0)1★ 60.66.40.96 – Fax (0)1★ 60.66.42.71 – M. Gayer

Rooms 16 with telephone, bath or shower, WC, cable TV and minibar. **Price** Single 280F, double 420-480F, suite 850F. **Meals** Breakfast 45F, served 7:45-11:00. **Restaurant** Service 12:00-14:00, 19:30-21:00; menus 160-230F, also à la carte. **Credit cards** All major. **Pets** Dogs allowed. **Facilities** Parking. **Nearby** Museum of Théodore Rousseau, forest and palace of Fontainebleau – 18-hole Fontainebleau golf course. **Open** All year (closed Sunday evenings in low season).

Located on the edge of the forest in Barbizon, the Hostellerie de la Clé d'Or is a traditional hotel, evocative of opulence and comfort. Formerly a coaching inn, it is the oldest establishment in a village whose peace and beauty have inspired many artists. The cuisine certainly constitutes the highlight of a visit. Skillfully prepared gourmet cuisine is served here, admirably complemented by an interesting wine list. The hotel has much to offer: a beautiful dining-room with a fireplace, a terrace looking out across the garden where meals can be served in summer, and fully-equipped bedrooms with access to the lawn. The elegant atmosphere is enhanced by beautiful antique furniture, copperware, pottery and tastefully-hung paintings.

How to get there *(Map 9): 57km southeast of Paris via A6, Fontainebleau exit; then N37 and D64 to Barbizon.*

Hostellerie Les Pléiades *

21, Grande-Rue
77630 Barbizon (Seine-et-Marne)
Tel. (0)1* 60.66.40.25 - Fax (0)1* 60.66.41.68 - M. Karampournis

Rooms 23 and 1 apartment with telephone, bath (1 with shower), WC and TV. **Price** Double 320-550F, 420F, apart. 620F (per 4 pers.). **Meals** Breakfast 45F; half board 390-490F, full board 650F. **Restaurant** Service 12:30-14:30, 19:30-21:30; menus 145-280F, also à la carte. Specialties: Fresh local produce. **Credit cards** All major. **Pets** Dogs allowed. **Facilities** Parking. **Nearby** Museum of Théodore Rousseau, Museum of Auverge Ganne; Milly-la-forêt; forest and palace of Fontainebleau – 18-hole Fontainebleau golf course. **Open** All year.

Located in the large street lined with old houses which leads directly into Fontainebleau Forest, the Hostellerie Les Pléiades was frequented between the two wars by illustrious representatives of politics, the arts and literature. But it is above all the memory of Millet, Théodore Rousseau, Ziem and their landscape-artist friends which lingers in this ravishing village. (Note that the auberge-museum of Père Ganne has reopened after five years of closure). In the bedrooms of Les Pléiades, the atmosphere of a vacation house reigns; all are unigne and have modern conveniences. The large dining room, which opens onto the shady terrace in summer, the inventive cuisine and the friendly, generous hospitality all contribute to making this an excellent hostelry.

How to get there *(Map 9): 57km southeast of Paris via A6 to Fontainebleau exit, then N37 and D64 to Barbizon.*

Château des Bondons ★★★

47/49, rue des Bondons
77260 La Ferté-sous-Jouarre (Seine-et-Marne)
Tel. (0)1★ 60.22.00.98 - Fax (0)1★ 60.22.97.01 - M. Busconi

Rooms 14 with telephone, bath, WC, TV and minibar. **Price** Double 400-550F, suite 650-900F, apart. 500-800F. **Meals** Breakfast 60F. No restaurant. **Credit cards** All major. **Pets** Dogs allowed (+30F). **Facilities** Parking. **Nearby** Jouarre, Eurodisneyland. **Open** All year.

Set in a vast park, this small 19th-century château was sinking into oblivion before the Busconis thoroughly renovated and resuscitated it. The reception rooms on the ground floor look out onto the surrounding gardens. The entrance hall has an elaborate marble mosaic floor and the same geometrical patterns can be seen in the ivory inlay of the paneling. In the dining-room there is delightful paneling inlaid with small landscape pictures. You will find a wealth of 18th-century style furniture – modern copies, but elegant. The lounge is vast and light, but the tiled floor could do with a few rugs. A beautiful wooden staircase leads up to the bedrooms which are extremely warm and cozy, with thick carpets and lovely flowered fabrics. The bedrooms are individually decorated and have luxuriously equipped bathrooms. Rooms 4 and 8 are particularly noteworthy (albeit more expensive). You will enjoy an friendly welcome and excellent, hearty breakfasts. *L'Auberge de Condé* is the best restaurant in the city; another good choice is *L'Auberge du Petit Morin* in Mourette.

How to get there *(Map 10): 65km east of Paris via A4, Ferté-sous-Jouarre exit, then N3; in the village Chalons-sur-Marne and Montménard towards.*

Au Moulin ★★★

2, rue du Moulin
77940 Flagy (Seine-et-Marne)
Tel. (0)1★ 60.96.67.89 - Fax (0)1★ 60.96.69.51 - M. and Mme Scheidecker

Rooms 10 with telephone, bath and WC. **Price** Single 250-320F, double 310-500F. **Meals** Breakfast 48F, served 7:45-11:00; half board 380-461F, full board 540-621F (per 2 pers., 4 days min.). **Restaurant** Service 12:15-14:15, 19:15-21:15; menus 180-230F, also à la carte. **Credit cards** All major. **Pets** Dogs allowed. **Facilities** Parking. **Nearby** Palace and forest of Fontainebleau, Moret-sur-Loing – 18-hole La Forteresse golf course. **Open** Jan 20 – Sept 15 and Sept 18 – Dec 17 (closed Sunday evenings and Mondays except Easter, May 23: Monday evening and Tuesday).

This 13th-century flour mill has been well restored. Beneath the stucco façade the ancient masonry was discovered in a remarkable state of preservation. The original half-timbering, the cob walls, the ground-floor stonework and the beautiful vaulted gable have all been stripped bare and greatly contribute to the strong period atmosphere of the building. The hotel accommodates guests in ten fully equipped and carefully decorated bedrooms. The dining-room looks out onto the river, and there is also a terrace and a garden. Dinner is served by candlelight in the evening and log fires are lit in winter. You are assured of a comfortable stay in this hotel where a quiet rural setting and beautiful architecture combine to create an ambience of warmth and well-being only an hour away from Paris.

How to get there *(Map 9): 88km southeast of Paris via A6, Fontainebleau exit, then N6 for 18km; at the traffic lights turn right onto D403 and immediatly on your left D120.*

Hostellerie Aux Vieux Remparts ★★★

3, rue Couverte - Ville Haute
77160 Provins (Seine-et-Marne)
Tel. (0)1★ 64.08.94.00 - Fax (0)1★ 60.67.77.22 - M. Roy

Rooms 25 with telephone, bath or shower, WC, TV and minibar. **Price** Single 340-470F, double 395-650F. **Meals** Breakfast 50F, served 7:00-11:00; half board 420-590F, full board 570-800F (per pers.). **Restaurant** Service 12:00-14:30, 19:30-21:30; menus 170-350F, also à la carte. Specialties: Petite salade de langouste tiède en crudité, gapacho de tomates, lasagnes de homard breton et ragoût de coquillages, pomme de ris de veau piquée, foie gras braisée au beurre mousseux, confiture de vieux garçon. **Credit cards** All major. **Pets** Dogs allowed (+60F). **Facilities** Parking. **Nearby** Ramparts, tower of César, church of Saint-Quiriace in Provins, spectacle de fauconnerie, tournoi de chevalerie, church of Saint-Loup-de-Naud — 18-hole Fontenaille golf course. **Open** All year.

Located in the most beautiful part of medieval Provins, the Hostellerie Aux Vieux Remparts has twenty-five bedrooms in an adjoining modern building. It successfully blends in with the town's splendid medieval architecture. In the comfortable, quiet bedrooms, the modern decor includes quilted bedcovers, carpets, and many white-lead pieces of furniture. In the restaurant, you will have the choice between a highly reputed gastronomic menu or the bistrot fare, which is served in a beautiful half-timbered 16th-century house, or on the terrace in summer. The decoration is in strict keeping with the traditional character of the village and tables are also set up in a very charming small courtyard in good weather. The Hostellerie is very lovely and you will be warmly welcomed.

How to get there *(Map 10): 86km southeast of Paris via A4, then D231 to Provins.*

La Louveterie ★★★★

77515 Saint-Augustin (Seine-et-Marne)
10, route de Faremoutiers
Tel. (0)1★ 64.03.37.59 - Fax (0)1★ 64.03.89.00 - Mme Lucia Di-Meo

Rooms 8 with telephone, bath, WC and TV. **Price** Double 500F, apart. 700F. **Meals** Breakfast 65-95F, served 7:30-10:30; half board 550-750F (per pers., 3 days min.). **Restaurant** Service 12:00-14:30, 19:30-21:00 (Closed Feb 1 – 20.and Nov 1 – April 30).; menus 175-250F, also à la carte. Specialties: Parmentier de queue de bœuf, gigot de lapin cuit au foin, raviolis de l'océan au consommé de volaille, agrumes grillés aux écorces d'oranges confites. **Credit cards** All major. **Pets** Dogs allowed. **facilities** Swimming pool, sauna, parking. **Nearby** Meaux, Provins, Jouarre, Grand Morin Valley, Eurodisneyland – Crécy-la-Chapelle golf course. **Open** All year except Feb 1 – 20.

L a Louveterie was a private residence before the present owner, a decorator, converted it into a hotel. So it is not surprising that it is so beautifully decorated, and as pleasant to live in as to look at. It is modern, warm, spacious and flooded with light from its bay windows. Several steps lead to the lounge and the dining room, which are furnished with contemporary paintings, comfortable furniture - antique as well as designer pieces - and shimmering rugs. The bedrooms and baths reflect the same intimate, tranquil beauty. There is also an indoor swimming pool whose sliding bay windows open onto a vast terrace; in the summer, several dining tables are set out here. The final touch is the excellent cuisine; the service and hospitality are very friendly.

How to get there *(Map 10): 70km east of Paris via A 4, exit Provins, towards Coulommiers; 8km south of Coulommiers, on the edge of the Malvoisine Forest.*

Hostellerie Le Vieux Logis

5, rue Sadi-Carnot
77810 Thomery (Seine-et-Marne)
Tel. (0)1★ 60.96.44.77 – Fax (0)1★ 60.70.01.42 – M. Plouvier

Rooms 14 with telephone, bath, WC and TV. **Price** Single and double 400F.
Meals Breakfast 50F, served 7:15-10:00. **Restaurant** Service 12:15-14:45, 19:45-
21:30; menus 145-240F, also à la carte. **Credit cards** Amex, Visa, Eurocard and
MasterCard. **Pets** Dogs allowed (+35F). **Facilities** Heated swimming pool, tennis,
parking. **Nearby** Palace and forest of Fontainebleau, Barbizon, Milly-la-Forêt (chapel
of Saint-Blaise, decorated by Cocteau, and covered market), Moret-sur-Loing – 18-
hole Fontainebleau golf course. **Open** All year.

Having restored and opened the beautiful Moulin de Flagy, M.
and Mme Plouvier decided to apply all their energy and flair
to this handsome late 18th-century house, set in a village once
famous for its vineyards and close to Fontainebleau Forest. The
fourteen fully equipped bedrooms are decorated in a muted
contemporary style combining painted wood and pastel fabrics.
The chef's inspired efforts in the kitchen result in exquisite dishes,
which are served in a magnificent dining-room. In the
conservatory, white tables, a white piano and potted plants create
an elegant modern atmosphere which is carried through to the
pleasant bar area. The hotel has just added a magnificent heated
swimming pool and a beautiful garden where meals are served in
good weather. Mme Plouvier is energetic and hospitable and will
welcome you like a friend.

How to get there *(Map 9): 71km southeast of Paris via A6, 9km west of
Fontainebleau via N6 towards Sens, then D137 towards Champagne.*

Hostellerie Le Gonfalon

2, rue de l'Eglise
77910 Germigny-L'Evêque (Seine-et-Marne)
Tel. (0)1★ 64.33.16.05 - Fax (0)1★ 64.33.25.59 - Mme Colubi

Rooms 10 with telephone, bath or shower, WC, TV and minibar. **Price** Single and double 280-360F. **Meals** Breakfast 45F, served 7:30-10:30. **Restaurant** Service 12:00-13:30, 19:30-21:00; menus 250-330F, also à la carte. **Credit cards** All major. **Pets** Dogs allowed. **Facilities** Parking. **Nearby** Forest of Montceaux. **Open** All year except in Jan (closed Sunday evening and Monday).

In the heart of Brie country and right on the Marne River, an unremarkable village auberge in 1977 was transformed into a beautiful country inn by Mme Line Colubi, already a reputable Cordon Bleu chef. Behind the plain façade of the Gonfalon, you discover a cool terrace out of a summer's dream, shaded by enormous century-old linden trees and surrounded by luxuriant vegetation overlooking the banks of the Marne. Bons vivants come here especially for Mme Colubi's delicately sauced specialties, which are served either on the delicious terrace or in the elegant Louis XIII dining room with its warm woodwork and beautiful log fires in winter. There are ten comfortable, very quiet bedrooms upstairs and on the *second étage*; ask for those with a large private terrace-conservatory overlooking the trees and the river (especially number 2). For a more youthful, brighter decoration, request the mansard rooms on the second floor. The delicious breakfasts, with hot homemade brioches and fruit juice, are served either in your room, the dining room or on the terrace in good weather. The friendly waitresses are discreet and professional. Less than an hour from Paris, this is a beautiful place for your gastronomic weekends.

How to get there *(Map 9): 60km east of Paris via A4 to Meaux, then N3*

Dame Carcas ★★★

15, rue Saint-Louis - La Cité
11000 Carcassonne (Aude)
Tel. (0)4★ 68.71.37.37 - Fax (0)4★ 68.71.50.15
M. Faidherbe and M. Luraschi

Rooms 30 with air-conditioning, telephone, bath or shower, WC and TV - Wheelchair accessible. **Price** Single and double 380-750F. **Meals** Breakfast 60F, served 7:00-11:00. **Restaurant** "Les Coulisses du Théatre". Service 12:00-14:00, 19:00-22:00 (closed Wednesday in Sept – Mar); menus 80-180F, also à la carte. Specialties: Regional cooking. **Credit cards** All major. **Pets** Dogs allowed. **Facilities** Parking. **Nearby** La Cité, churches of Saint-Vincent and Saint-Nazaire in Carcassonne, château de Pennautier – 9-hole Auriac golf course in Carcassonne. **Open** All year.

Formerly an annex of the Hôtel de la Cité, the Dame Carcas is now a hotel in its own right, and a very pleasant one, too. It has been entirely refurbished with as much flair and attention to detail as its neighbor, but is more sober in style. The bedrooms are all comfortable, with cherrywood beds and beautiful furniture, and their decor is charming and fresh. Rooms 215 to 219 are resolutely rustic in character with floor tiles and a flowery decor, whereas rooms 201 to 210, lavishly equipped with marble bathrooms, are the epitome of elegance. The hotel doesn't have a restaurant of its own, but a footbridge allows easy access to the restaurant in the Hôtel de la Cité which is under the same management.

How to get there *(Map 31): Inside the ramparts.*

Château Haut-Gléon
11360 Durban (Aude)
Tel. (0)4★ 68.48.85.95 – Fax (0)4★ 68.48.46.20
M. Duhamel

Rooms 6 with bath, 5 with WC. **Price** Double 350-450F. **Meals** Breakfast incl. No restaurant. **Credit cards** Not accepted. **Pets** Dogs allowed. **Facilities** Parking. **Nearby** Saint-Just Cathedral in Narbonne; mountain of la Clape; African reserve of Sigean; abbey of Fontfroide; Lagrasse – 9-hole Auriac golf course in Carcassonne. **Open** All year.

Located in the heart of the Corbières countryside only 15km from the sea, this winemaking château has just been renovated. Six simple, tasteful bedrooms have been arranged in the old Shepherds' House and Winemakers' House. Breakfast is served at a communal table in the dining room, and the adjacent lounge is at your disposal. There is no restaurant but the owners will invite you to taste the wine from the vineyards, and they will indicate good restaurant addresses nearby, such as Le Moulin (8km away) or the Restaurant de la Berre (4km away).

How to get there *(Map 31): 25km south of Narbonne. On A9 take Sigean exit, towards Portel, then towards Durban. Follow signs.*

Hostellerie du Grand Duc ★★

2, route de Boucheville
11140 Gincla (Aude)
Tel. (0)4★ 68.20.55.02 - Fax (0)4★ 68.20.61.22 - M. and Mme Bruchet

Rooms 10 with telephone, bath or shower, WC, TV and hairdryer. **Price** Single 225-250F, double 260-320F. **Meals** Breakfast 38F, served 8:00-11:00; half board 270-300F, full board 370-400F (per pers., 3 days min.). **Restaurant** Closed Wednesdays in low season. Service 12:15-14:00, 19:30-21:00; à la carte. Specialties: Baignades de sépiole au Fitou, cailles au muscat, faux-filet au foie gras et aux griottes, duo de lotte et saumon sur fondue de poivrons. **Credit cards** Visa, Eurocard and MasterCard. **Pets** Dogs allowed. **Facilities** Parking. **Nearby** Forest of Fanges, Saint-Paul-de-Fenouillet, Belvianes, Saint-Paul-de-Fenouillet, gorges of Galamus. **Open** Mar 25 – Nov 15.

This hotel of great charm – a carefully restored family mansion – is set in a small village. Their guests' well-being is the friendly owners' chief concern and they pride themselves on their warm hospitality. The bedrooms are all individually designed and decorated in a wide range of styles. Whitewashed walls, exposed stonework and beamed ceilings highlight the rustic character of the pleasant dining room. The lounge and the bar area are particularly cozy. In summer, breakfast and dinner can be served in the garden, with candles on the tables in the evening.

How to get there *(Map 31): 63km northwest of Perpignan via D117 to Lapradelle, then D22 to Gincla.*

Relais du Val d'Orbieu ★★★

11200 Ornaisons (Aude)
Tel. (0)4★ 68.27.10.27 – Fax (0)4★ 68.27.52.44
M. and Mme Gonzalvez

Rooms 20 with telephone, bath, WC, TV and minibar. **Price** Single and double 490-790F, suite 890-1590F. **Meals** Breakfast 70F, served 7:30-10:30; half board 635-815F (per pers.). **Restaurant** Service 12:15-13:45, 19:30-21:00; menus 165-295F, also à la carte. Specialties: Langoustines rôties, magret au rancio, gratin de fruits. **Credit cards** All major. **Pets** Dogs allowed (+80F). **Facilities** Swimming pool, tennis, golf practice, parking. **Nearby** Cathedral of Saint-Just in Narbonne, mountain of la Clape, African reserve of Sigean, abbey of Fontfroide, Lagrasse – 9-hole Auriac golf course in Carcassonne. **Open** Feb 7 – Nov 23, Dec 7 – Jan 24 (closed lunchtime Nov – Feb except Sunday, Sunday evening).

Facing the stunningly picturesque Montagne Noire, the Relais couldn't have a better location. The building itself, formerly a mill, has been carefully restored: the rooms are elegantly decorated and an atmosphere of calm and coziness prevails. The bedrooms at garden level are all very comfortable and in the morning delicious and ample breakfasts are served there, with fresh fruit juices, cheese, *pâtisseries* and home-made jams, as well as a large choice of teas and coffees. The Relais' much-praised cuisine has earned it a reputation as one of Languedoc's leading restaurants, and it is admirably set off by J.P. Gonzalvez's remarkable selection of regional wines. Guests will find the hospitality attentive.

How to get there *(Map 31): 47km east of Carcassonne via A61, Lézignan exit then D611 to Lézignan and D24 (eastward) to Ornaisons; signposted.*

Hameau de Foussargues La Buissonnière

30700 Aigaliers (Gard)
Tel. (0)4★ 66.03.01.71
Mme Hanotin and M. Zandstra

Rooms 6 and 2 apartments with kitchen, telephone, bath or shower and WC, TV on request. **Price** Double 500F, apart. 600-850F. **Meals** Breakfast 40-50F, served 8:00-10:00; half board 292-355F (per pers., 3 days min.). Evening meals 1 day by week. Service 20:00, menus 100-150F. **Credit cards** Visa, Eurocard and MasterCard. **Pets** Dogs not allowed. **Nearby** Le Duché, Church of Saint-Etienne and Saint-Théodorit in Uzès; pont du Gard; Nîmes; Avignon – 9-hole golf course in Uzès, 18-hole glof course (20km). **Open** All year.

A Franco-Dutch couple have put great enthusiasm into restoring this old *mas* a few kilometers from Uzès. While authenticity was their major concern, comfort and decoration have not been overlooked. The bedrooms are spacious, some with a fireplace and others with a mezzanine. The apartments have a small kitchen in addition. Mediterranean decoration lends a personal touch to each room, but all have a small terrace where breakfast is served, unless you prefer to enjoy it in the cool inner courtyard. The flowers and plants are young and not yet luxuriant but the owners take such good care of everything that the garden will surely be beautiful.

How to get there *(Map 31): 7km from Uzès, towards Arles; in 6km towards Aigaliers, go 800m, turn right at the intersection, then left immediately, and follow signs.*

Hôtel Les Arcades

23, bd Gambetta
30220 Aigues-Mortes (Gard)
Tel. (0)4★ 66.53.81.13 - Fax (0)4★ 66.53.75.46

Rooms 6 with air-conditioning, telephone, bath and WC. **Price** Double 460-550F.
Meals Breakfast incl. **Restaurant** With air-conditioning. Closed Monday and Tuesday.
Menus 120-200F, also à la carte. Specialties: Gardiane de taureau à l'ancienne,
huîtres chaudes, filet de taureau grillé, croustillant aux fruits. **Credit cards** All major.
Pets Small dogs allowed. **Nearby** The Camargue, Arles, Saintes-Maries-de-la-Mer
(gypsies' pilgrimage May 24 – 25), Tarascon, Nîmes, Montpellier. **Open** All year except
Feb 13 – 28 and Nov 12 – 28.

We loved this 16th-century house set in a quiet street in the
old town. Inside, everything is neat and charming. A lovely
aged and patinated paint effect, in colors ranging from lime green
to brown, enhances the corridors and the bedrooms, where
curtains, bedspreads and antique furniture are in perfect harmony.
The bedrooms are vast, with high, elaborate ceilings and tall
mullioned windows, and fully equipped bathrooms provide all the
modern comforts. Breakfast and dinner – which are excellent – are
served in a pleasant dining-room with an ancient terra-cotta tiled
floor. It opens on one side into a little garden, and on the other
into an arcade where a few tables are set up. A warm, family
atmosphere prevails.

How to get there *(Map 32): 48km west of Arles towards Saintes-Maries-
de-la-Mer, then D58.*

Hôtel Les Templiers ★★★

23, rue de la République
30220 Aigues-Mortes (Gard)
Tel. (0)4★ 66.53.66.56 - Fax (0)4★ 66.53.69.61 - M. Berdin

Rooms 11 with air-conditioning, telephone, bath or shower, WC and cable TV - Wheelchair access. **Price** Double 450-750F, suite 600-800F. **Meals** Breakfast 50F, served from 7:30. No restaurant. **Credit cards** All major. **Pets** Dogs allowed. **Facilities** Garage. **Nearby** La Camargue, Arles, Les Sainte-Marie-de-la-Mer (gypsies' pilgrimage May 24 – 25), Tarascon, Nîmes, Montpellier. **Open** Mar 1– Jan 15.

Over the last four years, the present owners have made an elegant hotel in the center of Aigues-Mortes out of what was once a dilapidated 17th-century merchants' house. The Polvaras are in love with the region, the city, the hotel, and their work – which is a very recent discovery for them – and they are anxious to share their enthusiasm in every way with their guests. After their tasteful restoration of the house, the couple searched the region for Provençal furniture, which lends each bedroom a personal touch, as do the family portraits on the walls. Some rooms look out onto the street but are nevertheless very quiet except on holidays: Aigues-Mortes is a pedestrian town. We liked other rooms for their view onto the interior courtyard and a cool fountain. There is no restaurant but the hotel serves pleasant snacks and will provided list of good restaurants. We like *Le Minos*, *La Goulue* and *Les Arcades*.

How to get there *(Map 32): 48km west of Arles, towards Saintes-Maries-de-la-Mer, then D 58.*

Hostellerie Le Castellas ★★★

Grand' Rue
30210 Collias (Gard)
Tel. (0)4★ 66.22.88.88 - Fax (0)4★ 66.22.84.28 - M. and Mme Aparis

Rooms 15 and 1 suite with air-conditioning, telephone, bath or shower, WC, TV and minibar. **Price** Single 400-440F, double 500-590F, suite 800-1000F. **Meals** Breakfast 60F, served 7:30-11:00; half board 495-750F. **Restaurant** Service 12:00-14:00, 19:00-21:15; menus 160-300F, also à la carte. Specialties: Foie gras poêlé et plateau de pommes de terre à la truffe, suprême de pigeon rôti à la provençale, champignons et jus de ses abats. **Credit cards** All major. **Pets** Dogs allowed (+50F). **Facilities** Swimming pool, parking. **Nearby** Pont du Gard, Uzès, Nîmes – 9-hole golf course in Uzès. **Open** Mar 10 – Jan 6.

In a little street in the center of Collias, two venerable 17th-century dwellings house the Hostellerie Le Castellas. The layout of the buildings forms an enclosed courtyard which makes the perfect location for a beautiful swimming-pool, the terrace of the restaurant, and a delightful little garden *à la Monet*. A favorite haunt of artists and sculptors, the second house has remarkable interior decoration and extraordinary bathrooms. The bedrooms in the main building are also very pleasant, but more classical in style. A friendly welcome and a restaurant serving refined and imaginative cuisine add to the many attractions of the hotel.

How to get there *(Map 33): 26km northeast of Nîmes via A9, Remoulins exit; at Remoulins D981 then D112 to Collias.*

La Bégude Saint-Pierre

D 981
30210 Vers – Pont du Gard (Gard)
Tel. (0)4★ 66.22.10.10 – Fax (0)4★ 66.22.73.73 – M. Griffoul

Rooms 28 with air-conditioning, telephone, bath, WC, TV, safe and minibar - Wheelchair access. **Price** Double 415-680F, suite 800-1300F. **Meals** Breakfast 60F, served 7:00-10:30; half board 230F, full board 420F (per pers., 3 days min.). **Restaurant** Service 12:00-14:00, 19:30-22:00; menus 150-360F, also à la carte. Specialties: Foie gras poêlé, saumon fumé par la maison. **Credit cards** All major. **Pets** Dogs allowed (+40F). **Facilities** Swimming pool, parking. **Nearby** Pont du Gard, Uzès, Nîmes, Avignon. **Open** All year except in Nov.

A *bégude* used to be a postal relay station with a twin farmhouse next door. The owner of an auberge in a village near Uzès, M. Griffoul has extensively restored this pretty Provençal *bégude*, creating a comfortable, luxurious hotel with a swimming pool, bedrooms with large terraces, a bar, a restaurant and a grill for the summer. We especially liked room 31 for its unusual spaciousness, and number 15 for its charming mezzanine. All are decorated with the simplicity which is appropriate to Provençal houses, including Souleïado fabrics and regional furniture. The lounges and dining rooms are decorated with similar traditional charm, conferring homogeneity to the style of this recently inaugurated hotel. Special attention is given to the cuisine because M. Griffoul is first and foremost a chef! He even smokes his own salmon on the premises.

How to get there *(Map 33): 25km northeast of Nîmes via A9, exit Remoulins, then D981 towards Uzès.*

La Vieille Fontaine ★★★

30630 Cornillon (Gard)
Tel. (0)4★ 66.82.20.56 – Fax (0)4★ 66.82.33.64
M. Audibert

Rooms 8 (4 with air-conditioning) with bath, WC, TV and minibar. **Price** Double 550-850F. **Meals** Breakfast 55F, from 8:00; half board 550-700F (per pers., 3 night min.). **Restaurant** Service 12:00-13:30, 19:30-21:30; menus from 195F, also à la carte. Specialties: SMoules farçies à la Diable, soupe au pistou, gratiné de langoustines, civet de porcelet. **Credit cards** Amex, Visa, Eurocard and MasterCard. **Pets** Dogs allowed (+50F). **Facilities** Swimming pool. **Nearby** Avignon, Orange, Modern Art Museum in Bagnols-sur-Cèze, village of Roque-sur-Cèze, Goudargues Abbey Church, gorges of the Cèze. **Open** Mar 1 – Dec 31.

Restaurant owners for more than twenty years, M. and Mme Audibert have discovered a new calling as hotel keepers. Within the walls of the former medieval castle of Cornillon, they have integrated a very modern structure with eight bedrooms decorated by Mme Audibert. There are two bedrooms per floor. Upstairs, the original small medieval apertures have been kept, providing lovely cool air in the summer. Your climb up to the last floor is rewarded with the view from pleasant balconies, which look out over the château walls and the valley. To reach the swimming pool, you must climb up a terraced garden which is not advisable for people who have difficulty walking. Those who do stroll through the beautiful, carefully arranged garden, however, do not regret it!

How to get there *(Map 33): 45km northwest of Avignon via A9, exit Tavel to Bagnols-sur-Cèze; then D980 towards Barjac. On A7, take Bollène exit.*

L'Hacienda ★★★

30320 Marguerittes - Mas de Brignon (Gard)
Tel. (0)4★ 66.75.02.25 - Fax (0)4★ 66.75.45.58
M. and Mme Chauvin

Rooms 12 with telephone, bath or shower, WC, TV and minibar. **Price** Single 400-450F, double 450-550F. **Meals** Breakfast 70-80F, served 8:00-10:00; half board 450-550F (per pers.). **Restaurant** Service 12:00-13:30, 19:30-21:30; menus 140-340F, also à la carte. Specialties: Feuillantine de bravadade de Nîmes aux arômes de provence, pigeonneau désossé rôti à l'ail confit. **Credit cards** Visa, Eurocard and MasterCard. **Pets** Dogs allowed (+50F). **Facilities** Swimming pool, tennis (70F), archery, pétanque, bicycles, sauna (70F), parking. **Nearby** Nîmes, Maison Carrée, Art Museum in Nîmes, Pont du Gard, château de Villevieille in Sommières, chapel of Saint-Julien-de-Salinelles – 18-hole Hauts-de-Nîmes and Nîmes Campagne golf course. **Open** All year.

The Hacienda is set in a quiet park enclosed by walls. In the center of the house, we were pleasantly surprised to find a beautiful patio with a few tables where drinks and dinner are served around a magnificent swimming pool. Next to the patio is the dining room, where you will be served by candlelight and enjoy delicious cuisine, which M. Chauvin and his young assistant prepare with the freshest farm products. The bedrooms are comfortable and furnished in rustic English style. Some are lighted by large, half-moon windows and others, on the ground floor, have a terrace on the garden. Not far away, you will find a *pétanque* court set among pink oleanders and roses, and a small Scandinavian chalet which houses a sauna. This is a friendly, lovely place to stay.

How to get there (Map 33): 6km east of Nîmes via A9, Nîmes-Est exit; then N86 and D135; go through Marguerittes and follow signs.

Auberge de la Paillère

Avenue du Puits-Vieux
30121 Mus (Gard)
Tel. (0)4★ 66.73.78.79 – Fax (0)4★ 66.73.79.28 - M. Terol

Rooms 7 with telephone, bath or shower, WC, TV, VCR and minibar. **Price** Double 350F (spacial price during Féria). **Meals** Breakfast incl., from 8:30. **Restaurant** Closed Monday and Tuesday noon. Service 12:00-13:30, 20:00-21:30; menus 110-230F (65F lunchtime), also à la carte. Specialties: Provençale cooking. **Credit cards** Amex, Visa, Eurocard and MasterCard. **Pets** Dogs allowed. **Nearby** Nîmes, Saint-Gilles, Sommières, château de Villevieille – 18-hole Hauts-de-Nîmes golf course. **Open** All year (except Jan).

When you've gone through one of the first gates of the village, you will be beneath the trellis of La Paillère's restaurant, where meals are served as soon as the weather is good. In winter, two intimate dining rooms inside, complete with traditional straw hats on the walls, serve up the aromatic specialties of Provence. Fires blaze in the fireplaces in both dining rooms as well as in the small, carefully decorated lounge. A stairway leads from the lounge to the most beautiful bedrooms: number 6, with a large sandstone bathroom; and number 7, with a balcony overlooking the graceful Virginia creeper vine. Several more functional and somewhat less charming bedrooms are located in a building of much more recent construction, which is nevertheless quite pleasant. For reasonable prices, the Auberge is lovely for festivals, vacations or even for a rainy weekend: the owner gives you a choice of l50 video cassettes to enjoy on the VCR in your bedroom.

How to get there *(Map 32): 15km southwest of Nîmes via A9, exit Gallargues, towards Les Plages, then N113 towards Codognan.*

Hôtel Impérator Concorde ★★★★

Quai de la Fontaine
30900 Nîmes (Gard)
Tel. (0)4★ 66 21 90 30 - Fax (0)4★ 66 67 70 25 - M. Creac'h

Rooms 62 with air-conditioning, telephone, bath or shower, WC, TV, minibar; elevator.
Price Single and double 250-480F. **Meals** Breakfast 40F, served 7:00-11:00.
Restaurant Service 12:30-13:45, 19:30-21:45; menu 100F; also à la carte.
Specialties: Mediterranean cooking, fish. **Credit cards** All major. **Pets** Dogs allowed
(+60F). **Nearby** Arènes, Maison Carrée, art museum and Carré d'Art in Nîmes, Pont
du Gard, château de Villevieille in Sommiéres, chapel of Saint-Julien-de-Salinelles –
18-hole Haut-de-Nîmes golf course. **Open** All year.

Well located in the town center very near the beautiful Jardin
de la Fontaine gardens, the Impérator is an institution in
Nîmes: It is here that the most famous toreros and bullfight
aficionados stay during the *féria*. The hotel, which has undergone
renovation, has lost some of its sparkle, but the bedrooms, especially
those on the *troisième étage*, are more spacious and more
comfortable. It is preferable to have a room on the garden side,
even if the air-conditioning insulates the other rooms from the
noise of the quay. The pleasantly decorated bar and restaurant
overlook the walled garden behind the hotel. Meals are served
either on the modern veranda or the large shady terrace. The cuisine
is inventive and subtly seasoned, and the set menu at lunch offers
a large number of specialities. The staff is very courteous.

How to get there *(Map 32): In the town center, between the Jardin de la
Fontaine and the Maison Carrée.*

Royal Hôtel ★★★

3, Boulevard Alphonse-Daudet
30000 Nîmes (Gard)
Tel. (0)4★ 66.67.28.36 – Fax (0)4★ 66.21.68.97 – Mmes Riera and Morel

Rooms 23 with telephone, bath or shower, WC and TV. **Price** Single and double 250-480F. **Meals** Breakfast 40F, served 7:00-12:00. **Restaurant** Service 12:00-15:00, 19:30-23:30; menu 100F. Specialties: Mediterranean cooking, fisch. **Credit cards** Amex, Visa, Eurocard and MasterCard. **Pets** Dogs allowed (+40F). **Nearby** Maison Carrée, art museum in Nîmes, Pont du Gard, château de Villevieille in Sommiéres, chapel of Saint-Julien-de-Salinelles – 18-hole Haut-de-Nîmes golf course. **Open** All year.

This small hotel is located close to the Quai de la Fontaine and the Maison Carrée, and looks out onto the Place d'Assas renovated by Martial Raysse. The hotel has a clientele of artists and designers and the atmosphere is relaxed and informal. The hotel has been entirely renovated, with white walls and sparse decoration including several 1950s and '60s pieces of furniture; it is quite unusual but attractive. A tempting restaurant serves salads and brunches; in summer tables are set up outside in the square. It is better to take a room at the back of the hotel to avoid hearing the clattering of forks deep into the night. During the *férias* the atmosphere is animated and festive, and the bar and restaurant stay open late. There are jazz sessions held on some evenings.

How to get there *(Map 32): In the town center.*

Le Mas d'Oléandre

Saint-Médiers
30700 Uzès (Gard)
Tel. (0)4★ 66.22.63.43 – Eva and Carl-Heinz Törschen

Rooms 3, 2 apartments and 1 studio, with bath or shower and WC. **Price** Single 180F, double 260F, apart. 380-500F(per 1-2 pers.) 420-600F (per 2-5 pers.). **Meals** Breakfast 45F, served 9:00-10:00. No restaurant. **Credit cards** Not accepted. **Pets** Dogs not allowed. **Facilities** Swimming pool, parking. **Nearby** le Duché, churches of Saint-Etienne and Saint-Théodorit in Uzès, Pont du Gard, Nîmes, Avignon – 9-hole golf course in Uzès. **Open** Mar 16 – Oct 31.

A secluded location and a stunning view are the main features of this hotel tucked away at the end of a peaceful little village. All around it cypresses, vineyards and hills combine to create a beautifully harmonious landscape and that may be what kept the owners from returning to their native Germany once they had set eyes on it. This doesn't feel like a hotel at all. The farmhouse has been carefully restored to make your stay as pleasant as possible. The bedrooms are comfortable and welcoming, two practical small apartments enable you to accommodate relatives and children, and there is a studio with a small kitchen. The hotel is an ideal base for exploring the beautiful Uzès area, and the swimming-pool proves an irresistible invitation to laze in the sun. In the evening your hosts will gladly indicate the best local restaurants, including *L'Auberge de Cruvier*, or *Le Fou du Roi* in Pougnadoresse, and dinner *L'Auberge Saint-Maximin* in Saint-Maximin.

How to get there *(Map 33): 40km west of Avignon via N100 and D981 to Montaren, then D337 to Saint-Médiers; (the Mas is on the edge of the hamlet).*

Auberge du Pont Romain ★★★

2, rue Emile-Jamais
30250 Sommières (Gard)
Tel. (0)4★ 66.80.00.58 – Fax (0)4★ 66.80.31.52 – Mme Michel

Rooms 18 with telephone, bath or shower (16 with WC). **Price** Single 260-400F, double 260-445F. **Meals** Breakfast 45F, served 7:45-10:00; half board 410F. **Restaurant** Service 12:15-13:15, 20:15-21:30 (closed Wednesdays in winter); menus 160-240F, also à la carte. Specialties: Petit gris des garrigues au roquefort, foie gras maison. **Credit cards** All major. **Pets** Dogs allowed. **Facilities** Swimming pool, parking. **Nearby** Château de Villevieille, chapel of Saint-Julien-de-Salinelles, church of Notre-Dame-des-Pommiers in Beaucaire, Pont du Gard, Nîmes – 18-hole Nîmes-campagne golf course. **Open** Mar 15 – Jan 15.

The façade that looks out onto the street is austere and barracks-like, betraying something of the history of the building. It was a carpet factory in the 19th-century, then a laundry, then, until 1968, a distillery. But as soon as you walk through the porch you enter a different world. A garden full of trees and flowers (all the more marvelous for its unlikely location) provides a pleasant setting for a terrace and a swimming-pool, and leads down to the Vidourle River. The vastness of the bedrooms can prompt memories of dormitories; the best rooms are those on the garden. The cuisine is traditional and generous, but the service can be a bit casual. This is the only hotel in France which is surmounted by a factory chimney.

How to get there (Map 32): 28km southwest of Nîmes via D40.

Hostellerie du Seigneur

30126 Tavel (Gard)
Place du Seigneur
Tel. (0)4★ 66.50.04.26 – Mme Bodo

Rooms 7. **Price** Double 170F. **Meals** Breakfast 30F, served 8:00-9:30; half board 240F. **Restaurant** Service 12:15-14:00, 19:15-20:30 (closed evening Oct – March); menus 90-135F. Specialties: Cuisse de canard au vin de pays, langue de porcelet au poivre vert, charlotte maison. **Credit cards** Visa, Eurocard and MasterCard. **Pets** Dogs allowed. **Nearby** Avignon; Villeneuve-lez-Avignon; le Lubéron. **Open** Mid Jan – mid Dec (closed Thusday).

The Hostellerie du Seigneur was installed more than thirty years ago in the former town hall of the village, which lends it a special charm. Dating from the 18th-century, the hostelry has cool, tastefully appointed rooms and the beautiful stone of the stairway bears witness to the generations who have come through here. M. Bodo is mainly known for his good regional cooking but you will also enjoy the hotel even if the bathrooms and toilets are separate from the bedrooms, as in a private house. The seven rooms are quiet and decorated *à l'ancienne*. This is an excellent, friendly hostelry, located off the main roads in the small village of Tavel, which has given its name to one of the heady, beautifully colored *rosés* of the Côtes du Rhône vineyards.

How to get there *(Map 32): 12km north of Avignon. On A9, Roquemaure exit, towards Tavel.*

Demeures du Ranquet ★★★★

Tornac
30140 Anduze (Gard)
Tel. (0)4★ 66.77.51.63 – Fax (0)4★ 66.77.55.62 – M. and Mme Majourel

Rooms 10 with air-conditioning, telephone, bath, WC, TV and minibar - Wheelchair access. **Price** Single 480-680F, double 580-860F. **Meals** Breakfast 75F, served from 8:00; half board 520-650F (per pers., 3 days min.). **Restaurant** Service 12:00-13:30, 19:30-21:30; menus 150-360F, also à la carte. Specialties: Daurade rose en croûte de sel, fenouille braisé à l'huile d'olive, épaule d'agneau au four, gratin de pommes de terre à l'ancienne, beignets d'aubergines sucrées avec glace au miel. **Credit cards** Visa, Eurocard and MasterCard. **Pets** Dogs allowed (except in the restaurant). **Facilities** Swimming pool, golf practice green, cooking lessons, parking, helicopter pad. **Nearby** Prafance, Bamboo Grove, Générargues, Luziers, Mas-Soubeyran (Desert Museum), Trabuc Cave, Saint-Jean-du-Gard. **Open** Mar 11 – Nov 10.

The distinguished people who have long been coming here are still faithfully returning. If you're not immediately charmed by the bungalows scattered in the woods, you will soon fall under the spell of the original ambiance of the Ranquet. The beautiful cuisine adds a great deal to the appeal of the place. The breakfasts are fabulous, the lunch and dinner menus are varied, and new recipes (Mediterranean red fish with preserved lemons) are often created. Everything is made on the premises and wine lovers will also be enchanted. Then too, you will sense the Majourels' love of a difficult job, which they handle with skill. If you enjoy painting and gardening, you will want to discuss both with them.

How to get there *(Map 32): 47km northwest of Nîmes, towards Alès; 6km south of Anduze on D982, on the road to Sainte-Hippolyte-du-Fort.*

Hôtel Marie d'Agoult ★★★

Château d'Arpaillargues
30700 Uzès (Gard)
Tel. (0)4★ 66.22.14.48 – Fax (0)4★ 66.22.56.10 – Mme and M. Savry

Rooms 28 (22 with air-conditioning) with telephone, bath, WC, TV and minibar. **Price** Single and double 400-850F, suite 900-1150F. **Meals** Breakfast 55F, served 7:30-10:30; half board 440-790F (per pers.). **Restaurant** Service 12:30-14:00, 19:30-21:00; menus 125-210F, also à la carte. Specialties: Filets de rougets au basilic. **Credit cards** All major. **Pets** Dogs allowed (+60F). **Facilities** Swimming pool, tennis, parking. **Nearby** Le Duché, churches of Saint-Etienne and Saint-Théodorit in Uzès, Pont du Gard, Nîmes, Avignon – 9-hole golf course in Uzès, 18-hole golf course at 20km. **Open** Apr 1 – Nov 2.

This hotel is in the beautiful 18th-century Château d'Arpaillargues, once the home of Marie de Flavigny, Franz Liszt's companion. The bedrooms are comfortably furnished and tastefully decorated. Eleven bedrooms have a terrace, either at ground level on the garden, or on the rooftop. A small duplex in the annex enjoys a covered terrace. Elegance and professional service are also among the star qualities of this hotel. The extremely high standards of everything here make up for the somewhat formal atmosphere that prevails. A pleasant bar area, lunch by the swimming-pool, and breakfast and dinner in the garden in summer make a stay here a delightful prospect. The cuisine is light and refined.

How to get there *(Map 33): 40km west of Avignon via N100 to Remoulins (on A9, Remoulins exit), then D981 to Uzès and D982 (westward) to Arpaillargues (4km).*

Hôtel d'Entraigues ★★★

8, rue de la Calade
30700 Uzès (Gard)
Tel. (0)4★ 66.22.32.68 – Fax (0)4★ 66.22.57.01

Rooms 36 (26 with air-conditioning) with telephone, bath, WC, TV and minibar; elevator. **Price** Single 185-195F, double 290-650F. **Meals** Breakfast 45F, served 7:15-11:00; half board +160F (per pers.). **Restaurant** With air-conditioning. Service 12:15-13:30, 19:30-21:30; menus 135-185F, also à la carte. **Credit cards** All major. **Pets** allowed (+35F). **Facilities** Swimming pool, garage (+50F). **Nearby** Le Duché, churches of Saint-Etienne and Saint-Théodorit in Uzès, Pont du Gard, Nîmes, Avignon – 9-hole golf course in Uzès and 18-hole golf course at 20km. **Open** All year.

The Hôtel d'Entraigues is a beautiful 15th–century mansion in the center of Uzès, just opposite the ancient seat of the barons of Castille and the Bishop's Palace. The rooms are all attractive and pleasant although different in style and size: some nestle under the eaves; others are much bigger (rooms 14, 15, 16, 18). A small lounge close to the reception area and a vaulted breakfast room provide all the comfort guests can wish for. The gastronomic restaurant *Les Jardins de Castille* is just across the street. and upstairs there is a large flowery terrace with a superb view. This is a hotel and a town full of charm and character.

***How to get there** (Map 33): 40km west of Avignon via N100 to Remoulins (on A9, Remoulins exit), then D981 to Uzès.*

Hôtel de l'Atelier ★★

5, rue de la Foire
30400 Villeneuve-lès-Avignon (Gard)
Tel. (0)4★ 90.25.01.84 - Fax (0)4★ 90.25.80.06 - M. and Mme Gounaud

Rooms 19 with telephone, bath or shower and WC (11 with TV). **Price** Double 240-420F. **Meals** Breakfast 36-40F, served 7:00-10:00. No restaurant. **Credit cards** All major. **Pets** Dogs allowed. **Nearby** "The Crowning of the Virgin" by Enguerand Quarton in the Musée Municipal in Villeneuve, Carthusain monastery of the Val-de-Bénédiction, fort Saint-André in Villeneuve, chapel of Notre-Dame-de-Belvezet, Avignon – 18-hole Châteaublanc-les-Plans golf course in Avignon. **Open** Beg-Dec – beg-Nov.

The Hôtel de l'Atelier is in Villeneuve-lès-Avignon, a small town at the foot of the Fort Saint-André which faces Avignon across the Rhône river. Avignon was once the City of the Popes; Villeneuve was home to the cardinals. Outwardly a quiet village house, the building has many hidden charms: a sequence of flower-filled patios where fig-trees provide welcome shade, a roof terrace – the perfect setting for a cup of tea or an evening drink – and delightful bedrooms. The latter have all been carefully and individually designed, and their shape and size vary, as do the pieces of period furniture they contain. Our favorite is room 42 on the top floor: it has all the character of attic rooms (with air-conditioning!), and if you stand on the little platform you can see Avignon through the high window. The hotel doesn't have a restaurant of its own but Avignon is just on the doorstep and in Villeneuve itself there are some very good restaurants. Try *La Magnaneraie* or *Le Saint-André* (less expensive).

How to get there *(Map 33): 3km west of Avignon via N100; if on A6, Avignon-Nord exit.*

Château de Madières ★★★★

Madières
34190 Ganges (Hérault)
Tel. (0)4★ 67.73.84.03 - Fax (0)4★ 67.73.55.71 - M. and Mme Brucy

Rooms 10 with telephone, bath or shower, WC, TV and minibar. **Price** Double 615-1090F, suite 980-1260F. **Meals** Breakfast 75F, served 8:30-10:30; half board 630-935F (per pers., 3 days min.). **Restaurant** Service 12:30-14:00, 19:30-21:00; menus 190-350F, also à la carte. Specialties: Foie gras chaud au banyuls, noix d'agneau farcie, médaillons de lotte rotie sur coulis. **Credit cards** All major. **Pets** Dogs allowed (+supp.). **Facilities** Heated swimming pool, fitness room, parking. **Nearby** Gorges of the river Vis, cirque de Navacelles, La Couvertoirade, cave of the Demoiselles, church of Saint-Guilhem-le-Désert. **Open** Apr 1 – Nov 4.

Set on the southern slopes of the Cévennes among the gorges of the River Vis, this 14th-century fortified house juts out like a balcony on the side of the mountain, only 40 minutes away from the Cirque de Navacelles. The Château has been carefully restored to become a hotel of great character. The bedrooms are luxuriously equipped and look out onto a patio. They are extremely comfortable and pleasant, and their individual decoration shows great attention to detail. The elegant lounge still has a Renaissance fireplace and leads out onto a terrace overlooking the river and the village. There are two dining-rooms (one with panoramic views) in which to enjoy Mme Brucy's excellent cooking. In summer, meals can be served by the swimming-pool which has just been completed on a terrace below the hotel.

How to get there *(Map 32): 60km northwest of Montpellier via D986 towards Le Vigan to Ganges, then D25 towards the Cirque de Navacelles, Lodève (18km from Ganges).*

Relais Chantovent
34210 Minerve (Hérault)
Tel. (0)4★ 68.91.14.18 - Fax (0)4★ 68.91.81.99
Mme Evenou

Rooms 7 with shower (1 with bath) and WC. **Price** Single 180F, double 220F.
Meals Breakfast 28F, served 8:00-10:00; half board 320F (per pers., 3 days min.).
Restaurant Service 12:30-14:00, 19:30-21:00; menus 95-230F. Specialties:
Croustillant aux deux saumons sur coulis de poivrons doux. **Credit cards** Visa,
Eurocard and MasterCard. **Pets** Dogs not allowed. **Nearby** Lagrasse, château de
Gaussan, abbey of Fontfroide, African reserve of Sigean, gorges of the Tarn. **Open** Mar
15 – Jan 1 (closed Mondays in July and Aug).

Minerve is a village high up between the gorges of the rivers
Cesse and Briand, and the hotel buildings are scattered in its
narrow alleys. The annex is a tastefully restored old village house
next to the "post-office library" and the rooms are as charming as
the ones in the main building. Two of them share a terrace, and
the one in the attic has kept its original layout, with the bathroom
more or less in the room; all have charm and character. The rooms
facing the restaurant have been redecorated and renovated, with
fabrics and contemporary lithographs brightening the decor. The
restaurant, with a view over the limestone Briand Valley, serves
good regional cuisine (on the terrace in good weather.) The village
and its surroundings are splendid and the welcome is very friendly.

How to get there *(Map 31): 45km northwest of Carcassonne via N113 and
D160 to Homps, then D910 to Olonzac and D10 to Minerve (northward).*

Domaine de Rieumégé ★★★

Route de Saint-Pons
34390 Olargues (Hérault)
Tel. (0)4★ 67.97.73.99 - Fax (0)4★ 67.97.78.52 - M. Sylva

Rooms 14 with telephone, bath or shower and WC. **Price** Single 318-478F, double 350-518F, suite (4 pers.) 619-774F. **Meals** Breakfast (buffet) 55F, served 8:30-10:00; half board 398-509F, full board 493-604F (per pers., 2 days min.). **Restaurant** Service 12:00-14:00, 19:00-21:30; menus 100F (lunchtime)-135-220F, also à la carte. **Credit cards** Amex, Visa, Eurocard and MasterCard. **Pets** Dogs allowed (+40F). **Facilities** 2 swimming pools, tennis, parking. **Nearby** Abbey of Fontcaude, mountains of l'Espinouse, cave of la Devèze. **Open** Apr – Dec .

The mountains of the Haut-Languedoc provide an impressive backdrop for the Domaine de Rieumégé, a pleasant place to stay in an area where good hotels are few and far between. This is an old 17th-century house which has been restored by the owners with great taste and a feeling for comfort. The terraces, lounges and kitchen have been improved this year. The interior decoration skillfully combines country-style antiques with more modern pieces of furniture, exposed stonework, and well-chosen colors on the walls. Despite the nearby road the hotel is quiet. A luxury accommodation is also possible, offering a bedroom and a suite giving onto a private swimming pool with a tropical garden, which is reserved exclusively for the occupants. The price is 100F extra per person.

How to get there *(Map 31): 50km northwest of Béziers via D14, then D908 towards Olargues; 3km from Olargues in the Saint-Pons-de-Thomières towards.*

Château d'Ayres ★★★

48150 Meyrueis (Lozère)
Tel. (0)4★ 66.45.60.10 - Fax (0)4★ 66.45.62.26
M. de Montjou

Rooms 26 with telephone, bath or shower, WC and TV (18 with minibar). **Price** Double 360-800F, suite 830-930F. **Meals** Breakfast 62F; half board 390-580F, full board 490-680F (per pers.). **Restaurant** Service 12:30-13:45, 19:30-22:00; menus 153-300F, also à la carte. Specialties: Feuilleté aux deux saumons, croustillant de magret au foie gras. **Credit cards** All major. **Pets** Dogs allowed (+45F). **Facilities** Swimming pool, tennis, parking. **Nearby** Gorges of the Tarn, Aven d'Armand, gorge of Dargilan, Cévennes national park. **Open** Apr 1 – Nov 15.

The Château d'Ayres has not been spared the many vicissitudes of history. Rebuilt in the 18th-century by the Nogaret family, it was later sold and turned into a hotel. But the woman who inherited it, Miss Roussel, married one of the Nogarets' cousins, thus bringing the castle back into the family. We can easily understand why the family is so attached to it. Set amidst 12 acres of beautiful parkland planted with age-old oaks and gigantic sequoias, it is lovely. The lounges, bedrooms and library are decorated with beautiful period furniture and attractive paintings. Exquisite taste is in evidence throughout the house, including the lovely dining room, which is more rustic in style. This is truly a special place.

How to get there *(Map 32): 55km south of Mende via N88, and D986 to Meyrueis via Sainte-Enimie.*

Hôtel Chantoiseau ★★★

48220 Vialas (Lozère)
Tel. (0)4★ 66.41.00.02 - Fax (0)4★ 66.41.04.34
M. Patrick Pagès

Rooms 15 with bath or shower, WC, TV and minibar. **Price** Single and double 400-480F. **Meals** Breakfast 50F, served 8:00-10:00; half board 420F, full board 480F (per pers., 3 days min.). **Restaurant** Service 12:00-13:30, 19:00-20:30; menus 130-750F, also à la carte. Specialties: Ravioles au pélardon, carré d'agneau, suprême au chocolat. **Credit cards** All major. **Pets** Dogs not allowed. **Facilities** Swimming pool, parking. **Nearby** Ridgeway to Alès via Portes; La Garde, Guérin, Florac. **Open** Apr 8 – Nov 15 (closed Tuesday evenings and Wednesdays).

The Chantoiseau is one of the best hotels in the region. This former 17th-century coaching inn, set 600 meters up on the steep Mediterranean slopes of the Cévennes, provides a sunny stopping place on the doorstep of the Cévennes National Park. The bedrooms are comfortable and look out onto peaceful valleys and mountains. The dining room retains the austere character of houses in the area: walls built from large slabs of granite, deep embrasures, the warm presence of wood. It commands beautiful views over the valley. The menu features specialties of the Cévennes only, prepared by the owner whose talent has earned wide recognition, and who has chosen the finest wines to accompany them. The wine list is outstanding, ranging from modest but charming *vins de pays* to great vintages.

How to get there (Map 32): Northwest of Alès via D906, towards Genolhac; in Belle-Poèle, D998 to Vialas.

La Terrasse au Soleil ★★★★

Route de Fontfrède
66400 Céret (Pyrénées-Orientales)
Tel. (0)4★ 68.87.01.94 - Fax (0)4★ 68.87.39.24 - B. and P. Leveillé-Nizerolle

Rooms 27 with air-conditioning, telephone, bath, WC, TV, minibar and safe. **Price** Single and double 595-795F. **Meals** Breakfast 80F, served 7:00-12:00; half board 578-678F, full board +100F (per pers.). **Restaurant** Service 12:00-14:00, 19:30-22:00; menus 160-380F, also à la carte. Specialties: Rosée des Pyrénées poêlés, étuvée de girolles à la catalane, pigeon fermier rôti aux tagliatelles fraîches. **Credit cards** Visa, Eurocard and MasterCard. **Pets** Dogs allowed. **Facilities** Heated swimming pool, tennis, par-3 golf course, parking, helicopter pad. **Nearby** Museum of modern art and church of Saint-Pierre in Céret, Cabestany, Prats-de-Mollo, château de Quéribus, Quilhac and the château de Peyrepertuse, Perpignan – 27-hole Saint-Cyprien golf course, 7-hole Amélie-les-Bains golf course, 18-hole Falgos golf course. **Open** Feb 4 – Jan 3.

La Terrasse au Soleil is an old farmhouse which has been completely restored. It occupies an enviable position crowning the village among cherry trees. The bedrooms have all the modern comforts. The largest and best are the upstairs ones with a terrace and views of the mountains. The La Cerisaie restaurant will delight you with its excellent cuisine; for lunch, it also proposes a simpler *brasserie* menu, in addition to the dessert menu: don't miss the superb *mille-feuille* pastry. In good weather meals can be served in the garden. A heated swimming-pool, tennis court and par-3 golf course add to the many assets of this hotel, where a friendly and informal atmosphere encourages guests to relax.

How to get there (Map 31): *31km southwest of Perpignan via A9, Le Boulou exit, then D115 towards Céret; it's 2km from the center of the village via D13f in the Fontfrède towards.*

Le Mas Trilles ★★★
66400 Céret-Reynès (Pyrénées-Orientales)
Tel. (0)4★ 68.87.38.37 - Fax (0)4★ 68.87.42.62
M. and Mme Bukk

Rooms 10 with telephone, bath, WC and TV - 1 room for disabled persons. **Price** Double and suite 440-975F. **Meals** Breakfast 65F, served 8:30-10:30; half board 440-710F. **Restaurant** Service 20:00; menus 175-220F. Specialties: Seasonal cooking. **Credit cards** Visa, Eurocard and MasterCard. **Pets** Dogs allowed (+supp.). **Facilities** Heated swimming pool, parking. **Nearby** Museum of modern art and church of Saint-Pierre in Céret, Cabestany, Prats-de-Mollo, château de Quéribus, Quilhac and the château de Peyrepertuse, Perpignan – 27-hole Saint-Cyprien golf course, 7-hole Amélie-les-Bains golf course, 18-hole Falgos golf course. **Open** Easter – Nov 1.

The Mas Trilles is an old house surrounded by a garden with fruit trees. From the swimming-pool, when there is a lot of traffic and the wind is blowing in the wrong direction, the rumble of cars on the road above the hotel can sometimes be heard. The bedrooms, however, are quiet at all times. Inside, the house has been fully refurbished and decorated with exquisite taste: there are terra-cotta floors, the walls in some rooms have been sponge painted and in others whitewashed, and each fabric has been carefully chosen by Mme Bukk to blend in with, and round off, the decor. The bedrooms have lovely bathrooms and many of them also have a private terrace where breakfast (which always includes fresh fruit) can be served. Dinner (for residents only) is in a charming dining-room or on the terrace. Friendly hospitality adds to the pleasant homey atmosphere that prevails. This is a beautiful, comfortable hotel.

How to get there *(Map 31): 31km southwest of Perpignan via A9, Le Boulou exit, then D115 towards Céret; 3km from the center, in Amélie-les-Bains towards.*

Hôtel Casa Païral ★★★

Impasse des Palmiers
66190 Collioure (Pyrénées-Orientales)
Tel. (0)4★ 68.82.05.81 – Fax (0)4★ 68.82.52.10
Mmes De Bon and Lormand

Rooms 28 some with air-conditioning, telephone, bath or shower, WC, cable TV and minibar. **Price** Single 300-600F, double 350-690F, suite 670-900F. **Meals** Breakfast 45-50F. No restaurant. **Credit cards** Amex, Visa, Eurocard and MasterCard. **Pets** Dogs allowed (+30F). **Facilities** Swimming pool, parking (+40F). **Nearby** The Vermeille coast between Argelès-sur-Mer and Cerbère, Balcon de Madeloc, mountain road between Collioure and Banyuls, Château de Salses, museum of modern art in Céret – 27-hole Saint-Cyprien golf course. **Open** Apr – Oct.

A real gem, Casa Païral is hidden in a small *cul-de-sac*, right in the center of Coullioure, just a few minutes from the beach, restaurants, and cafés. It is perfectly quiet. This luxurious 19th-century town house was built in a Moorish style with wrought ironwork, marble, and ceramic tilework. On the patio, lush vegetation grows in the shade of a stately palm tree and a hundred-year-old magnolia tree. All the rooms are comfortable, but ask for the ones in the main house, which are nicer. The very pleasant breakfast room and lounges open onto the walled garden and swimming pool. This hotel is very much in demand, so you will need a reservation. For dinner, try the fish at *Pa i Trago* or at *Le Puits* in the old town, or at *La Marinade*, for its pretty terrace on the town square.

How to get there (Map 31) 26km southeast of Perpignan via N114.

Auberge L'Atalaya ★★★

Llo – 66800 Saillagouse (Pyrénées-Orientales)
Tel. (0)4★ 68.04.70.04 – Fax (0)4★ 68.04.01.29
M. and Mme Toussaint

Rooms 13 with telephone, bath or shower, WC, cable TV, safe and minibar. **Price** Single and double 490-650F, suite 750F. **Meals** Breakfast 60F, served 7:30-10:30; half board 470-600F, full board 620-740F (per pers., 3 days min.). **Restaurant** Closed Mondays and Tuesday noon in low season. Service 12:30-14:30, 19:30-21:30; menus 165-390F, also à la carte. **Credit cards** Visa, Eurocard and MasterCard. **Pets** Dogs allowed in the bedrooms. **Facilities** Swimming pool, solarium, parking. **Nearby** Ski in Eyne, Odeillo solar furnace, lake of Les Buoillouses north of Mont-Louis, gorges of the river Aude, château de Quérigut – 18-hole Real Club de Cerdana golf course, 9-hole golf course in Font-Romeu, 18-hole Fontanals golf course (15km). **Open** Apr 1– Jan 10.

Llo is the most typical pastoral village of the Cerdagne region on the border between Andorra and Spain, which can be seen from some of the bedrooms. Clustered around its watchtower – called an *atalaya* in old Castilian – and the ruins of its 11th-century castle, the village stands above the gorges of the River Sègre. Needless to say, its location is one of the memorable features of the Auberge. But the building itself is well worth the stay. The magnificent house has been tastefully decorated throughout and the bedrooms are comfortable and attractive. In summer, meals are served outside on a terrace among geraniums and hollyhocks, and there is now also a swimming-pool. In winter, the closest ski stations are Eyne and Err-Puigmal, and there are at least eight others within easy reach. The food is delicious.

How to get there (Map 31): 90km west of Perpignan via N116 to Saillagouse, then D33.

Lou Rouballou

66210 Mont-Louis (Pyrénées-Orientales)
Tel. (0)4★ 68.04.23.26 – Fax (0)4★ 68.04.14.09
M. and Mme Duval

Rooms 14 with bath or shower and 8 with WC. **Price** Double 150-300F.
Meals Breakfast 35F; half board 230-280F, full board 270-320F (per pers., 3 days
min.). **Restaurant** Service 12:30-13:30, 19:30-20:30; menus 125-195F, also à la
carte. Specialties: Catalan cooking. **Credit cards** Visa, Eurocard and MasterCard.
Pets Dogs not allowed. **Nearby** Romanesque church of Planès, lake of Les
Bouillouses, gorges of the river Aude, château de Quérigut, pass of Saint-Georges.
Open All year except in Oct., Nov. and May (closed Wednesdays in low season).

You will find this auberge among the village houses. Its façade
is inconspicuous, but as soon as you walk through the door
you will feel at ease. Inside, the decor is rustic, cozy and genuine.
Some of the bedrooms are more comfortable than others: we
recommend rooms 3, 18, 19, 20, 21, which Christiane Duval has
lovingly arranged with antique furniture, extremely comfortable
beds and pleasant bathrooms. But Lou Raballou is also renowned
for the gourmet cuisine turned out by Pierre Duval. The menu
features excellent traditional dishes, prepared with only the freshest
products. In the autumn, Pierre will take you hunting for
mushrooms, and then prepare the mushrooms in a delicious dish
for dinner. This is a charming, friendly and unpretentious inn.

How to get there *(Map 31): 10km east of Font-Romeu via N116 (in the*
old part of the town).

Château de Camon

09500 Camon (Ariège)
Tel. (0)5★ 61.68.28.28 - Fax (0)5★ 61.68.81.56
M. du Pont

Rooms 7 with bath or shower and WC. **Price** Single and double 600-1000F, suite 1500F. **Meals** Breakfast incl. **Restaurant** Evening meals on reservation; menu 300F. **Credit cards** All major. **Pets** Dogs not allowed. **Facilities** Swimming pool, parking. **Nearby** Mirepoix, châteaux of Lagarde and of Caudeval, Montségur and Foix. **Open** Easter – Dec.

At the château Camon, in the beautiful region of Ariège on the wooded road into Spain, you will be treated more like a guest than a customer. The château has been in the family of M. du Pont for two centuries: "Only two hundred years," he says as if to apologize for so recent an acquisition. The château is closed to the public unless, of course, you are a guest, but there is an abbey next to it which can be visited; they both overlook the village below. A colorful terraced garden descends to a lawn with a swimming pool. The bedrooms have been admirably decorated by the owner, (who is an interior decorator) with antique furniture. You will be delighted with every aspect of this château, which feels like a private home.

How to get there *(Map 31): 59km southwest of Carcassonne via D119 to Mirepoix, then D7 towards Chalabre. If on A61, Castelnaudary exit.*

La Maison des Consuls ★★★

09500 Mirepoix (Ariège)
Tel. (0)5★ 61.68.81.81/83.84 – Fax (0)5★ 61.68.81.00/81.15
M. Garcia

Rooms 7 (1 with air-conditioning) with telephone, bath or shower, WC, TV and minibar. **Price** Double 450F, 650F. **Meals** Breakfast 40-62F, served 7:15-12:00. No restaurant. **Credit cards** Visa, Eurocard and MasterCard. **Pets** Dogs allowed (+40F). **Facilities** Parking (50F). **Nearby** Cathedral of Mirepoix; tour Sainte-Foy; châteaux of Lagarde and of Caudeval, Montségur and Foix; caves of mas d'Azil. **Open** Easter – Dec.

L a Maison des Consuls is a historic residence located on the medieval square for which Mirepoix is famous. The hotel's letterhead reads "Panoramic view of the 18th century;" this is a figurative way of saying that four of the seven bedrooms recently decorated with antique furniture look out over the magnificently preserved square. All the bedrooms are very comfortable and have beautiful bathrooms. Breakfast is served in a small salon upstairs. For dinner, try *La Flambée*, just next door, or other small restaurants in the village during the summer season. M. Garcia is a jovial host.

How to get there *(Map 31): 59km southwest of Carcassonne via D119.*

Hôtel Eychenne ★★★

8, avenue Paul Laffont
09200 Saint-Girons (Ariège)
Tel. (0)5★ 61.66.20.55 – Fax (0)5★ 61.96.07.20 – M. and Mme Bordeau

Rooms 42 with telephone, bath or shower, WC, 30 with cable TV and 35 with minibar.
Price Single and double 290-550F. **Meals** Breakfast 46F, served 7:00-10:30; half
board 367-427F, full board 497-557F (per pers., 3 days min.). **Restaurant** Closed
Sunday evening and Monday Nov – Mar. Service 12:15-13:30, 19:45-21:30; menus
130-320F, also à la carte. Specialties: Foie de canard frais aux raisins , pigeonneau
au fitou, gigot de lotte safrané, soufflé au grand marnier. **Credit cards** All major.
Pets Dogs allowed. **Facilities** Swimming pool, parking. **Nearby** Saint-Lizier, Montjoie,
Romanesques churches at the valley of Couserans in Oust and Cominac, Ercé Chapel
in Garbet Valley, Castillon, Audressein, Sentein, Ayet, Ourtjou-les Bordes. **Open** Feb
2 – Dec 21 (closed Sunday evening and Monday Nov – Mar).

Managed by the Bordeau family for generations, the Eychenne
has preserved its atmosphere of the past while offering the
latest in modern amenities. In the two lounges, small bar, and dining
room, the furniture, family objects and pictures create a friendly
atmosphere. Most of the comfortable bedrooms, which are not
very large, are furnished with antiques. Some have a beautiful view
out over the Pyrénées. The cuisine – savory specialties of the
Southwest – warrants a visit here. In summer, meals are served in
the dining room which looks onto a garden, or lighter fare is
available by the swimming pool. Breakfasts are generous. The staff
is friendly and attentive.

How to get there *(Map 30): In Saint-Girons, head towards Foix and follow
the signs.*

Château de Seignan ★★★
Montjoie
09200 Saint-Girons (Ariège)
Tel. (0)5★ 61.96.08.80 – Fax (0)5★ 61. 96.08.20 – M. de Bardies

Rooms 9 with telephone, bath or shower, WC, TV and minibar. **Price** Double 320-850F. **Meals** Breakfast 42F, served 7:00-11:00; half board 395-580F (per pers., 3 days min.). **Restaurant** Service 12:00-14:30, 19:30-22:00; menus 98-380F, also à la carte. Specialties: Brochette de poisson à l'indienne, panaché de foies gras, pigeon désossé sauce forestière, clafoutis au caramel de pommeau. **Credit cards** All major. **Pets** Dogs allowed. **Meals** Swimming pool, tennis, parking. **Nearby** Saint-Lizier, Montjoie, Romanesque churches in the Couserans Valleys in Oust and Cominac, Ercé Chapel in the Garbet Valley, Castillon, Audressein, Sentein, Ayet, Ourtjou-les Bordes. **Open** Dec 16 – Oct 31.

At the foot of the Pyrénées, on the edge of the mysterious valleys of the Couserans and scarcely 1km from Saint-Girons, this family château was opened to guests several years ago by M. de Bardies. There are nine large, comfortable bedrooms furnished with antiques, while the bathrooms are very modern. The dining room is welcoming, as is the small lounge, where a pianist plays during cocktail hour. In summer, meals are served in the garden, which is shaded by century-old chestnut trees along the edge of the River Baup. A tennis court and swimming pool lend further appeal to the site. The staff is kind and courteous.

How to get there *(Map 30): 1km east of Saint-Girons. In Saint-Girons, take D117 in the towards of Foix, on the right.*

Château de Castelpers ★★

Castelpers
12170 Ledergues (Aveyron)
Tel. (0)5★ 65.69.22.61 - Fax (0)5★ 65.69.25.31 - Mme Tapié de Celeyran

Rooms 8 with telephone, bath or shower, WC and 6 with TV. **Price** Single and double 285-485F. **Meals** Breakfast 48F, served 8:00-9:30; half board 235-345F, full board 300-420F (per pers., 3 days min.). **Restaurant** Only for guests. Service 12:30-14:00, 19:30-21:00; menu 135F, also à la carte. Specialties: regional cooking. **Credit cards** Amex, Visa, Eurocard and MasterCard. **Pets** Dogs allowed (+20F). **Facilities** Parking. **Nearby** Châteaux of Le Bosc and Taurines, Sauveterre, Viaduct and Valley of Le Viau, Pareloup Lakes – 18-hole golf course in Albi. **Open** Apr 1 – Oct 1.

The Château de Castelpers is tucked away in a verdant corner of Rouergue, in the peaceful Viaur Valley, a region where inns are scarce. The rustic dry-stone building adjoins another with Gothic arches where the main lounge has a ceiling resembling a ship's hull. The terrace overlooks a large park with centuries-old trees bordered by a trout stream. Handsome old furniture gives character to the dining room, the lounge and the comfortable bedrooms. Room 5 has leaded windows and a canopied bed; the other rooms are more modern, as are number 9 and its neighbor on the ground floor, which open onto the garden.

How to get there *(Map 31): 40km from Rodez and Albi via N88, then take D80 at Les Peyronnies, 3km from Nancelle-Gare.*

Hôtel Longcol ★★★

La Fouillade
12270 Najac (Aveyron)
Tel. (0)5★ 65.29.63.36 – Fax (0)5★ 65.29.64.28 – Luyckx Family

Rooms 17 with telephone, bath or shower, WC, TV and minibar. **Price** Double 550-850F. **Meals** Breakfast 70F, served 7:30-10:30; half board 540-690F (per pers., 2 days min.). **Restaurant** Service lunchtime (guests only), 19:45-21:30; menus 135-390F, also à la carte. Specialties: Seasonal cuisine, home-made foie gras,salade Longcol. **Credit cards** Amex, Visa, Eurocard and MasterCard. **Pets** Dogs allowed. **Facilities** Swimming pool, tennis, fishing, helicopter landing pad, parking. **Nearby** Château of Najac, Gorges of the Aveyron, Carthusian Monastery, Pénitents Noirs chapel and Place of Cornières in Villefranche-de-Rouergue. **Open** Easter – Nov 15.

This old Rouergue country house is like a miniature village sitting on a wild mountain pass with the Aveyron flowing below. Recently restored and decorated beautifully, each room is furnished with Oriental objects, antique rugs and furniture and old studded doors – all elegantly arranged and comfortable. The lounge and billiards rooms are particularly gracious, a corner fireplace and large leather armchairs creating a convivial atmosphere. The bedrooms are all individually decorated, bright and cheerful. All have views of either the swimming pool or the valley. In summer you can fish in the river that runs through the property and can enjoy lunch by the pool, looking out over the beautiful countryside. The staff is courteous in keeping with the beauty of this hotel.

How to get there *(Map 31): 19km south of Villefranche-de-Rouergue via D922, at La Fouillade (between La Fouillade and Najac, on D638).*

L'Oustal del Barry **

Place du Bourg
12270 Najac (Aveyron)
Tel. (0)5★ 65.29.74.32 – Fax (0)5★ 65.29.75.32 – Mme Miquel

Rooms 24 with telephone, bath or shower, WC and TV. **Price** Single 220-300F, double 315-450F. **Meals** Breakfast 48F, served 8:00-10:30; half board 305-335F, full board 385-420F (per pers., 2 days min.). **Restaurant** Service 12:30-14:00, 19:30-21:00; menus 100-320F, also à la carte. **Credit cards** Amex, Visa, Eurocard and MasterCard. **Pets** Dogs allowed. **Facilities** Parking. **Nearby** Château of Najac, Gorges of the Aveyron, Carthusian Monastery, Pénitents Noirs chapel and Place of Cornières in Villefranche-de-Rouergue. **Open** Apr – Oct (closed Monday, except public holidays, from Apr – June and Oct).

Five generations of the same family have presided over the Oustal del Barry, which has all the charms of a traditional French hotel. On the whole the bedrooms are rustic but with a curious mixture of other styles, principally Art Deco. The dining room has a panoramic view of the flowers and greenery of the l5–acre grounds. A vegetable garden cultivated by Mme Miguel grows several types of herbs used in the excellent cuisine, which also incorporates other local produce. The kindness of your hosts will make you regret leaving this simple and charming hotel. Hotel rates include free admission to the swimming pool at Najac, one hour of tennis a day and the use of bicycles.

How to get there (Map 31): 24km south of Villefranche-de-Rouergue via D922, then D239.

Grand Hôtel de la Muse et du Rozier ★★★

La Muse
12270 Peyreleau-le-Rozier (Aveyron)
Tel. (0)5★ 65.62.60.01 – Fax (0)5★ 65.62.63.88 – Mme Rigail

1996

Rooms 35, 5 apartments, with telephone, bath or shower, WC and TV; elevator - 1 for disabled persons. **Price** Single 350-430F, double 410-650F, apart. 710-810F (per 2 pers.), 795-880F (per 3 pers.). **Meals** Breakfast 60-65F, served from 8:00; half board 555-635F (obligatory in high season), full board 720-800F (per pers., 2 nights min.). **Restaurant** Service 12:30-14:15, 19:30-21:30; menus 165-220F, also à la carte. Specialties: Truite farcie au bleu des Causses, ravioles de Roquefort aux trompettes des bois, côtes d'agneau et son tripoux aux blettes et noix, gratin de chocolat et son jus d'orange au safran. **Credit cards** All major. **Pets** Dogs allowed (+50F). **Facilities** Swimming pool, tennis, parking, garage (50F). **Nearby** Gorges of Tarn; gorges of the Jonte; gorges of the Dourbie; Montpelier-le-Vieux; the Aven Armand; caves of Dargilan; Batelier de la Malène; caves of Roquefort. **Open** Mar 16 – Nov 14.

Located at the entrance to the gorges of the Tarn, this large hotel, decorated in a resolutely modern and somewhat flashy style, is like a great ocean liner docked at the river's edge.

Thirty-five bedrooms, all different and equipped with beautiful bathrooms, look out over the river. Several lounges and a large terrace where meals are served in summer enable you also to enjoy the superbly unspoiled site. At the hotel, you can swim in the pool, canoe or fish, and there are innumerable sports and touristic activities nearby. The hotel is ideal for a stopover or a restful stay, and the staff is friendly.

How to get there *(Maps 31 and 32): 19km northeast of Millau, take towards Clermont-Ferrand to Aguessac, then road to Florac, CD907. Then go about 13km.*

Hostellerie Les Magnolias

12550 Plaisance (Aveyron)
Tel. (0)5★ 65.99.77.34 – Fax (0)5★ 65.99.70.57
M. and Mme Roussel

Rooms 6 with telephone, bath, WC and TV. **Price** Single and double 250-350F.
Meals Breakfast 48F (buffet); half board 250-300F (per pers.). **Restaurant** Service
12:15-14:00, 20:00-21:30; menus 68-300F, also à la carte. Specialties: Cuisine
based on traditional local products. **Credit cards** Amex, Visa, Eurocard and
MasterCard. **Pets** Dogs allowed (+25F). **Nearby** Churches in Plaisance, Abbey of
Sylvanes, Château du Bosc, Toulouse-Lautrec Museum in Albi – 18-hole golf course
in Albi. **Open** Apr – Dec.

This is one of the outstanding hotels in this guide. A beautiful
14th-century dwelling once owned by Paul Valéry's brother,
the property will enchant you at first glance. Carefully chosen,
delicate decor has transformed this village house into a hotel of
charming intimacy and character. The cuisine is truly a labor of
love. M. Roussel speaks with real passion about the sauces and
stocks that go into the succulent dishes he serves; all the produce
is local, fresh and home made. It is with the same enthusiasm that
he has collected the materials and furnishings to decorate and restore
his hotel. The already beautiful bedrooms at the top of a lovely
staircase are to be renovated to further enhance the charm and
comfort of this superb hotel. The Hostellerie is a place where the
staff goes to great pains to ensure that you are content.

How to get there *(Map 31): 42km east of Albi via D999 to Alban, then
after 4km take D127.*

Hôtel du Midi–Papillon ★★

12230 Saint-Jean-du-Bruel (Aveyron)
Tel. (0)5★ 65.62.26.04 - Fax (0)5★ 65.62.12.97
M. and Mme Papillon

Rooms 19 with telephone, (13 with bath, 3 with shower and 17 with WC). **Price** Single 79F, double 125-195F, suite 320F. **Meals** Breakfast 23,50F, served 8:00-10:00; half board 185-220F, full board 218-282F (per pers., 3 days min.). **Restaurant** Service 12:30-14:00, 19:30-21:30; menus 72-200F, also à la carte. Specialties: Petite galette de sarrasin aux langoustines sauce iodée, filet de canard dans un chou farci aux blettes sauce aux baies de giroflier, cuisses de grenouilles fraîches sautées au beurre persillé, croquant de nougatine à la crème légère pailleté au cidre pomme écrasée. **Credit cards** Visa, Eurocard and MasterCard. **Pets** Dogs allowed. **Facilities** Heated swimming pool, whirlpool. **Nearby** Millau Belfry, Montpellier-le-Vieux, Gorges of the Tarn. **Open** Palm Sunday – Nov 11.

On the road to Mont Aigoual, the highest point in the Cévennes, Saint-Jean-du-Bruel is a good stopping place in the gorges of the Dourbie. The hotel is an old coach inn and has been run by the same family for four generations. Well situated on an outcrop above the river, it offers an outstanding picture-postcard view of the old village houses and a stone bridge. You'll find a friendly atmosphere and good cuisine prepared with homemade ingredients (poultry, *confits, foie gras, charcuteries*). Our favorite rooms are those which have just been renovated and have terraces overlooking the river. The breakfasts are excellent. The prices are surprisingly reasonable.

How to get there (Map 32): *99km northwest of Montpellier via N109 and N9 in the towards of Le Caylar to La Cavalerie, then D999as you enter the village).*

Château Saint Saturnin

12560 Saint-Saturnin-de-Lenne (Aveyron)
Tel. (0)5★ 65.70.36.00 – Fax (0)5★ 65 70 36 19
M. and Mme Lenton

Rooms 12, with telephone, bath, WC and TV (11 for non-smokers, 1 for smokers).
Price 600-980F **Meals** Breakfast 35F, served 8:00-10:00; half board 450-650F, full
board 550-700F (per pers., 3 days min.). **Restaurant** Service 20:00-21:30 (closed
Sunday evening); menus 145-190F. Specialties: Tournedos à la causse, râbles de lapin
à l'estragon, gâteau-mousse aux quatre chocolats. **Credit cards** Amex, Visa, Eurocard
and MasterCard. **Pets** Dogs allowed. **Facilities** Heated swimming pool, parking.
Nearby Cathedral of Rodez, abbey of Conques, Séverac-le-château, Gorges du Tarn,
Valley of Lot; markets at Saint-Geniez and Séverac-le-château. **Open** Apr 1 – Jan 14.

A château in name only, the Saint-Saturnin is more like a vast
mansion with beautifully large rooms offering panoramic
views over an ancient sheep-herding village. The owners have
successfully combined British hospitality with the American taste
for modern amenities – all done in a very French style. They make
every effort to make their guests feel at home and happy in this
authentic French country house. Upon request, M. and Mme
Lenton are pleased to serve meals - either around a large communal
dining table or even in the immense kitchen. After dinner, coffee
is served in the library, which is the only room (along with one
bedroom) where guests are allowed to smoke. Some of the rooms
are very large and all are as comfortable as those you would find
in the best hotels. The tastefully decorated bathrooms are supplied
with dressing gowns and toiletries.

How to get there *(Map 31): A75, exit Campagnac. 46km east of Rodez, take*
N88 to Laissac. D28 to Pont-de-Palmas and D45 to Saint-Saturnin-de-Lenne.

Le Sénéchal ★★★

12800 Sauveterre-de-Rouergue (Aveyron)
Tel. (0)5★ 65.71.29.00 - Fax (0)5★ 65.71.29.09
M. Truchon

Rooms 11 with air-conditioning, telephone, bath, WC, TV and minibar; elevator – 1 wheelchair access room. **Price** 450-550F, duplex 650-750F, suite 850-950F. **Meals** Breakfast 70F; half board 450-550F, full board 520F (per pers., 3 days min.). **Restaurant** Service 12:00-14:00, 19:30-21:30 (closed Monday and Tuesday except public holidays, July and Aug); menus 135-400F, also à la carte. Specialties: Terrine de queues de bœuf en gelée à l'orange, tournedos de pied de porc en écailles de truffes, mousse de verveine fraîche et son sorbet. **Credit cards** All major. **Pets** Dogs allowed. **Facilities** Heated swimming pool. **Nearby** Rodez, Plateau Le Ségala, lakes of Levézou and villages of Saint-Beauzély, Combéroumal, Castelnau-Prégayrols, Montjaux, Chestnut Festival on Nov 1, Saint-Christophe's Feast Day in July, Light Festival in Aug. **Open** All year except Feb.

In a former royal fortified village in the heart of the lovely Avéyron countryside, the big, brand-new Sénéchal is a haven of refinement and hospitality. The bedrooms, decorated in pale lemon colors, are very spacious, and look out over gentle hillsides. Spacious, too, are the bathrooms, the lounge and the dining room. Decor is modern and comfortable, with some antique furniture. The cuisine here is renowned; breakfast is outstanding. Across the street are 15 inexpensive rooms in the Sénéchal's old auberge, but they do not have the charm of the new rooms. You will want to visit the village, which has beautifully preserved medieval arcades, fortifications, and a church-dungeon with a small museum.

How to get there (Map 31): 32km southwest of Rodez.

Hôtel des Trois Lys ★★★

38, rue Gambetta
32100 Condom (Gers)
Tel. (0)5★ 62.28.33.33 – Fax (0)5★ 62.28.41.85 – Mme Manet

Rooms 10 with telephone, bath or shower, WC and TV. **Price** Single 280F, double 380-550F. **Meals** Breakfast 38F, served 7:30-10:00. No restaurant. **Credit cards** Visa, Eurocard and MasterCard. **Pets** Dogs allowed. **Facilities** Swimming pool, parking. **Nearby** Armagnac Museum in Condom, châteaux, churches and bastides of Armagnac; Flaran, Larresingle, Fourcès, Tillac, Bassoues, Lavarders, Collegiate Church of La Romieu, Jazz festival in Marciac (August) – 18-hole Guinlet golf course in Eauze. **Open** All year except in Feb.

When they converted this 18th-century manor house into a hotel, the Manets decorated it with their own fine taste. The ten rooms are done in coordinated colors and furnished with antiques or excellent reproductions finished in splendid fabrics. The rooms are big – some very big – and some retain their wood paneling and Louis XV alcoves; double doors, thick carpeting and double windows ensure absolute silence. The bathrooms are also beautiful, with gleaming taps, colored tiles and soft lighting. A monumental stone staircase leads from the bedrooms to the ground floor. Pleasingly decorated in pastel tones, the dining room and the lounge wind to the back of the house where a swimming pool tempts you to plunge into its refreshing depths, especially in the height of summer. Needless to say the hospitality stems from Mme Manet's kindness. A small meal can be served for those who do not wish to go out for dinner; other guests can dine at *La Ferme de Flarans*, which belongs to the hotel and is five minutes away; or at *Le Moulin du Petit Gascon*, which serves regional cuisine.

How to get there *(Map 30): 40km south of Agen.*

Hôtel de Bastard ★★

Rue Lagrange
32700 Lectoure (Gers)
Tel. (0)5★ 62.68.82.44 - Fax (0)5★ 62.68.76.81 - M. Arnaud

Rooms 28 and 1 suite with telephone, bath or shower, WC and TV. **Price** Single 190-280F, double 220-320F. **Meals** Breakfast 35-40F; half board 270-320F, 460F for the suite (per pers., 3 days min.). **Restaurant** Closed Friday, Saturday noon and Sunday evening Oct 1 – Apr 30. Service 12:15-13:30, 19:30-21:30; menus 80-240F, also à la carte. Specialties: Foie frais, carpaccio de magret. **Credit cards** All major. **Pets** Dogs allowed (+15F). **Facilities** Swimming pool, parking. **Nearby** Château de Gramont; châteaux, churches and bastides of Armagnac; Flaran, Larresingle, Fourcès, Tillac, Bassoues, Lavarders; Collegiate Church of La Romieu; jazz festival ih Marciac (August) – 9-hole Fleurance golf course. **Open** Mar 1 – Jan 7.

Lectoure is a magnificent small fortified town overlooking the undulating countryside of the Gers. Setting out to explore the narrow streets lined with old houses, you will come across a large carved stone gateway which is the entrance to this 18th-century house. A large paved terrace with a swimming pool overlooks the village rooftops and open countryside. This view can be seen from the reception rooms, which are beautifully decorated, with pretty fabrics, high ceilings and handsome 18th-century style furniture. The bedrooms are small but comfortable; choose a room on the *premier étage* and make sure that the hotel is not giving a wedding party if it is a weekend! The Hôtel de Bastard is a charming place to stay.

How to get there *(Map 30): 35km north of Auch via N21.*

Le Ripa Alta ★★

3, place de l'église
32160 Plaisance (Gers)
Tel. (0)5★ 62.69.30.43 – Fax (0)5★ 62.69.36.99 – M. and Mme Cosculluela

Rooms 13 with telephone, bath or shower, 3 with WC, 8 with TV and minibar. **Price** Single 170F, double 275F, suite 450F. **Meals** Breakfast 33F; half board from 175F, full board from 240F (per pers., 3 days min.). **Restaurant** Service 12:00-13:30, 20:00-22:00, menus 80-248F, also à la carte. Specialties: Foie gras, écrevisses mousquetaire, fricassée de poulet à l'armagnac, croustade gasconne. **Credit cards** All major. **Pets** Dogs allowed (+30F). **Facilities** Parking. **Nearby** Châteaux, churches and bastides of Armagnac; Flaran, Larresingle, Fourcès, Tillac, Bassoues, Lavarders, Collegiate Church of La Romieu, Jazz festival in Marciac (Aug) – 18-hole Guinlet golf course in Eauze. **Open** All year.

People have been coming here for a long time just for Maurice Cosculluela's cuisine. His dishes of course are based on the traditions of Gascony, but he is also very inventive in his choice of products and his way with tastes, textures, and spices of all kinds. In addition to a very good cellar of Bordeaux wines, you will find the best regional wines and Armagnacs. To prolong the gastronomic pleasure or if you are a jazz fan (the famous Marciac Festival is only 10km away), you can stay over in bedrooms which are unremarkable but comfortable. Irénée Cosculluela will greet you with polite, attentive hospitality. In summer, breakfasts and meals are served beneath the arcades of this pleasant hostelry.

How to get there (Map 30): 45km north of Tarbes.

Château de Projan

Projan 32400 Riscles (Gers)
Tel. (0)5★ 62.09.46.21 - Fax (0)5★ 62.09.44.08
J. and C. Vichet

Rooms 11 (5 with shower). **Price** 180-410F. **Meals** Breakfast 40-60F, served 8:00-10:30; half board 340F (per pers., 5 days min.). **Restaurant** Service from 13:00, 20:00 (closed Sunday in hight season, Sunday and Monday in low season); menus 75-185F. Specialties: Regional cooking. **Credit cards** All major. **Pets** Dogs allowed on request (+40F). **Nearby** Landes and Gascony Regional Parks; bastides; Lourdes (1hr); Château of Mascaraas, Museum of Vic-Bilh, the ocean 1 1/2 hr., jazz festival in Marciac (August). **Open** Mar – Nov 19.

The beautiful, ancient Château de Projan is located in a 7-1/2-acre park on a rocky spur overlooking the two Valleys of the Lees. The present owners, who are veritable patrons of the arts, have gathered an impressive collection of contemporary art, which is exhibited throughout the château; combined with several imposing 17th- and 18th-century pieces of furniture, the overall effect is warm and inviting. The bedrooms, impeccably renovated and tastefully decorated, vary from vast to tiny. Some ultra-modern designer baths were cleverly integrated into the château, where space was available. Don't be horrified if you have to use the communal showers: the owners have transformed the ancient thermal baths into modern and beautiful facilities. This hotel, with its reasonable prices, is a true find: It deserves a detour!

How to get there *(Map 29): A 64, exit Pau. 40km north of Pau via N134 to Sarron, and D646 in the towards of Riscles.*

Auberge du Bergeraye *
32110 Saint-Martin d'Armagnac (Gers)
Tel. (0)5★ 62.09.08.72 - Fax (0)5★ 62.09.09.74
Mme Sarran

Rooms 13 with telephone, bath or shower, WC, 7 with TV. **Price** 300-425F. **Meals** Breakfast 35F; half board 225-310F (obligatory in july and Aug), full board 335-400F (per pers.). **Restaurant** Service 12:00-14:30, 19:30-21:00 (closed Wednesday); menus 80-200F, also à la carte. Specialties: Foie gras de canard sur le grill, magret fourré de foie sur lit de cèpes et pommes de terre, pastis gascon. **Credit cards** Diner's, Visa, Eurocard and MasterCard. **Pets** Dogs allowed. **Facilities** Parking. **Nearby** Landes and Gascony Regional Parks; bastides; Lourdes (1hr); Château of Mascaraas, Museum of Vic-Bilh, jazz festival in Marciac (Aug) – 18-hole Quintet golf course, 18-hole Bigone golf course. **Open** All year.

The Auberge du Bergeraye is a typical house of the Gers *département:* simple, solid, and planted in the midst of vineyards and fields. At the foot of the auberge is a lake, and in the distance the Pyrénées appear, splendid and mysterious. You will find fourteen bedrooms here, some in the old auberge, others around the swimming pool, and the most recent in another building which has just been renovated. Each decorated individually, the rooms are quiet and comfortable. A discreet garden shades a large swimming pool, which the guests love. Pierrette Sarran, who is a cooking teacher from November to April, turns out a generous *cuisine de terroir*, employing products from neighboring farms and confering on this delicious auberge the charm of the past.

How to get there (Map 29): 35km southeast of Mont-de-Marsan towards Aire-sur-l'Adour, then towards Riscle; at the traffic circle, take towards Nogaro and follow signs.

Domaine de Bassibé *
32400 Ségos(Gers)
Tel. (0)5★ 62.09.46.71 - Fax (0)5★ 62.08.40.15
M. and Mme Lacroix

Rooms 11, 7 suites with telephone, bath, WC and TV. **Price** Double 650F, suite 980F.
Meals Breakfast 75F; half board 640-805F, full board 850-1015F (per pers.).
Restaurant Service 12:00-14:00, 19:30-22:00 (closed Tuesday and Wednesday in
low season); menus 180-240F, also à la carte. Specialties: Salade de joue de bœuf
aux deux pommes et ciboulette, foie chaud petites pommes aux épices, bonne poule
au pot d'autrefois, craquant de noisette. **Credit cards** All major. **Pets** Dogs allowed.
Facilities Swimming pool, bicycle, parking. **Nearby** Landes and Gascony Regional
Parks; bastides; jazz festival in Marciac (August) – 18-hole Mont-de-Marsan golf
course, 18-hole golf course in Pau. **Open** Mid-Mar – Jan (closed Tuesday and
Wednesday lunchtime except June – Oct).

The Domaine de Bassibé was built in the old family mansion of a
large farming estate. The ancient trees in the park and the carefully
tended garden confer it with the reassuring atmosphere of tradition.
Modern conveniences and elegance are also the key words in the
bedrooms and bathrooms in the *Maison Vieille* as well as in the more
recent *Maison des Champs* facing it. The rooms overlook the fragrant
honeysuckle garden or, as far as the eye can see, the gentle hills of the
Gers. There is no set time for breakfast, which you can enjoy in the
flower garden in summer. Elegant meals accompanied by well-chosen
wines are served around the large swimming pool shaded by great oak
trees or in the pleasant dining room installed in the old wine press.
The hospitality is friendly and attentive, too, making the Domaine de
Bassibé, without reservation, a very charming hotel.

How to get there *(Map 29): 35km southeast of Mont-de-Marsan towards
Aire-sur-l'Adour, then towards Riscle; at the traffic circle, towards Nogaro and
follow signs.*

Auberge d'Enrose

32120 Solomiac (Gers)
Tel. (0)5★ 62.65.01.42 – Fax (0)5★ 62.65.02.93
R. Ryan and P. Cuff

Rooms 6 and 1 apartment with shower, WC and TV. **Price** From 300F, apart. 400-450F (per 2 pers.). **Meals** Breakfast incl., served until 10:00. **Restaurant** By reservation. Service 12:00-14-30, 20:00-21:30; menus (lunch) 135F. Specialties: Regional cooking and English cooking. **Credit cards** Visa, Eurocard and MasterCard. **Pets** Small dogs allowed. **Facilities** Heated swimming pool. **Nearby** Auch, bastides tour: Mauvezin, Beaumont-de-Lomagne, Gimont, Mirande, Fleurance; Lectoure, Vic-Fezensac (bullfights on Whit Sunday). **Open** Feb – Dec.

Perched on a lush, green hilltop, the Auberge d'Enrose is a vast, quiet and comfortable country house in the heart of traditional Gascony. Several bedrooms and a small, well-equipped apartment for two to four people (note that because of the owner's dogs, children are not admitted in the hotel) have been elegantly decorated. All are on the ground floor and open onto the lovely countryside. Thoughtful small details include an electric tea kettle in each room and a laundry room at guests' disposal. With the first beautiful days of spring, you can swim in the heated pool and have drinks in the garden while waiting for your hosts' delicious meal and your choice of wines and spirits. (Don't miss the Armagnac of the region, or the more rustic Pousse Rapière.) The hosts are very welcoming and friendly.

How to get there *(Map 30): 30km northeast of Auch via N 124 in the towards of Gimont. In Aubet, go in the towards of Mauvezin and Solomiac. As you leave Solomiac, take the towards of Montfort (road on the right indicated).*

Le Demeure d'en Jourdou ★★

31480 Cadours (Haute-Garonne)
Tel. (0)5★ 61.85.77.77
M. Lachambre

Rooms 7 with telephone, bath or shower, WC, TV on request and minibar. **Price** Single 250-390F, double 280-420F. **Meals** Breakfast 37-47F, served 8:00-10:00; half board 380-500F, full board 480-600F (per pers., 3 days min.). **Restaurant** By reservation(dinner). **Credit cards** Amex. **Pets** Dogs allowed. **Facilities** Swimming pool, parking. **Nearby** Châteaux of Laréole, Larra and Launac; abbey of Sainte-Marie-du-Désert; bastide of Grenade – Saint-Gabriel, La Ramée, Toulouse-Seih Golf Course near Toulouse. **Open** All year on request.

This elegant pink brick house, somewhat set back from the road, is surrounded by beautiful countryside and fields as far as the eye can see. Skillful restoration has preserved its traditional charm. The large, comfortable bedrooms on the *premier étage* retain their original flooring and beautiful Louis XIV doors. They are comfortable, with tasteful furnishings and well-appointed bathrooms. The other bedrooms, smaller but well-designed, are in the attic; soft blue carpeting and cane furniture lend these rooms an intimate charm. In the dining room, with its pastel fabrics and dark blue walls, an elegant table setting awaits you. The cuisine is in keeping with the rest of the hotel: refined and creative, with classical touches. The hosts are informal and pleasant.

How to get there *(Map 30): 39km west of Toulouse via D1.*

Auberge du Poids Public ★★★

31540 Saint-Félix-Lauragais (Haute-Garonne)
Tel. (0)5★ 61.83.00.20 – Fax (0)5★ 61.83.86.21
M. and Mme Taffarello

Rooms 13 with telephone, bath or shower, WC, TV and minibar. **Price** Double 250-300F. **Meals** Breakfast 42F, served 8:00-10:00; half board 540-590F (per 2 pers.). **Restaurant** Closed Sunday evening Oct – Apr. Service 12:00-13:15, 19:30-21:15; menus 135-300F, also à la carte. Specialties: Terrine de foie gras aux poireaux, gigotin d'agneau de lait des Pyrénées, croustillant aux fruits rouges. **Credit cards** Amex, Visa, Eurocard and MasterCard. **Pets** Dogs allowed. **Facilities** Parking. **Nearby** Cathedral of Saint-Papoul, Toulouse-Lautrec museum in Albi, Toulouse, Pastel road, Midi Canal road – 9 and 18-hole golf courses in Toulouse. **Open** Feb – Dec.

Located on the outskirts of the village, this old inn makes a pleasant stopping place. The bedrooms are fairly large and simply furnished with some antique pieces; six of them enjoy a beautiful view. Most are quiet; the few that look onto the street are only used if the others are full. There is a private bar-lounge. Depending on the time of year lunches and dinners are served either in the large, bright and prettily decorated dining room or in the shade of wide umbrellas on the lovely terrace. In either case the marvelous view is enhanced by outstanding cuisine, some of the best in the region.

How to get there *(Map 31): 40km southeast of Toulouse via D2 towards Revel.*

Hostellerie des 7 Molles ★★★

31510 Sauveterre-de-Comminges (Haute-Garonne)
Tel. (0)5★ 61.88.30.87 - Fax (0)5★ 61.88.36.42
M. Ferran

Rooms 19 with telephone, bath, WC, TV and minibar. **Price** Single 405-580F, double 760F, suite 900-1100F. **Meals** Breakfast 70F, served 8:00-11:00; half board 560-675F, full board 750-900F (per pers., 3 days min.). **Restaurant** Service 12:00-13:30, 19:30-21:30; menus 195-300F, also à la carte. Specialties: Pastis gersois de foie gras à la pomme reinette, agneau de lait des Pyrénées et sa moulinade de haricots. **Credit cards** All major. **Pets** Dogs allowed. **Facilities** Swimming pool, tennis, parking. **Nearby** Saint-Bertrand-de-Comminges, Montréjeau, Gallo-Roman villa of Montmaurin – 18-hole Lannemezan golf course, 9-hole golf course in Luchon. **Open** Mid-Mar – end Oct.

The seven watermills have disappeared but the millstones remain and lend their name to the hotel. The immediate surroundings are superb: meadows, vines and groves of trees surround the house. The spacious, luminous bedrooms are furnished in traditional style. There is a warm ambience in the dining room and reception rooms. The cuisine, both traditional and modern, is made largely from homemade products, including sausages from the hotel's own pig farm, trout from the fish tank, *foie gras* and pastries. The staff is welcoming and friendly.

How to get there *(Map 30): 74km southeast of Tarbes via N117 to Saint-Gaudens, then D8 to Valentine and D9 (follow signs).*

311

Chez Marcel

Rue du 11 mai 1944
46100 Cardaillac (Lot)
Tel. (0)5★ 65.40.11.16 – M. Marcel

Rooms 6. **Price** Double 140F. **Meals** Breakfast 30F, served all morning; half board 190F, full board 235F (per pers., 3 days min.). **Restaurant** Closed Monday except in July and Aug. Service 12:00-13:30, 19:00-20:30; menus 78-175F, also à la carte. Specialties: Foie gras, omelette aux cèpes ou aux truffes, tripoux, agneau du causse, fromage de Rocamadour, gâteau aux noix, clafoutis, profiteroles à la menthe et à la crème. **Credit cards** Visa, Eurocard and MasterCard. **Pets** Dogs allowed in restaurant. **Facilities** Parking. **Nearby** "Musée Eclaté" in Cardaillac, Valleys of the Lot and the Célé (Figeac-Cahors-Figeac). **Open** All year (closed Monday in low season).

In tiny Cardaillac, the grocery store is also the tobacco shop and the picturesque village restaurant Chez Marcel has several rooms for visitors. You will enjoy delicious regional dishes as well as a friendly staff here. The bedrooms are furnished in traditional style and while not very large, they are charming – but there is only one shower for the six rooms. Still, the price is right. Chez Marcel is located in a beautiful village which still has many vestiges of the Middle Ages and the time when it was a Protestant refuge. Today, the community takes pride in what is voted "one of the most beautiful villages of France."

How to get there *(Map 24): 9km northwest of Figeac via N140, then D15 on the right.*

Hôtel Les Falaises ★★
Gluges
46600 Martel (Lot)
Tel. (0)5★ 65.37.33.59 - Fax (0)5★ 65.37.34.19 - M. Dassiou

Rooms 17 with telephone, bath or shower and WC. **Price** Single 165F, double 210-320F. **Meals** Breakfast 38F, served 8:00-10:00; half board 220-270F, full board 290-350F (per pers., 3 days min.). **Restaurant** Service 12:30-14:00, 19:30-21:00; menus 100-250F, also à la carte. Specialties: Magret de canard au vert jus et raisins confits. **Credit cards** Visa, Eurocard and MasterCard. **Pets** Dogs not allowed. **Facilities** Parking. **Nearby** Quercy region of the Dordogne from Souillac to Saint-Céré, Rocamadour, Padirac, Lacave, Car museum in Souillac – 9-hole Mas del Teil golf course in Souillac. **Open** Mar 1 – Nov 30.

At the foot of the cliffs bordering the Dordogne, this old residence has been converted into a hotel. A large terrace with an ornamental pool separates it from the main building, and in summer meals are served here in the shade of the trees. The dining room has just been renovated; predominantly blue, its large windows open out onto the terrace. The bedrooms are comfortable and sensibly furnished, and we particularly recommend numbers 10 or 12, all of which have terraces. The hotel has just purchased a 2 1/2-acre park so that guests may enjoy a peaceful stroll before dinner. The beautiful location, warm welcome, excellent cooking and particularly good breakfasts are the trump cards of this family hotel.

How to get there *(Map 24): 70km south of Brive-la-Gaillarde via N140 towards Martel (on the banks of the Dordogne).*

Château de la Treyne ★★★★

La Treyne
Lacave 46200 Souillac (Lot)
Tel. (0)5★ 65.27.60.60 - Fax (0)5★ 65.27.60.70 - Mme Gombert

Rooms 12, 2 apartments with air-conditioning, telephone, bath, WC and TV. **Price** Double 700-1600F, apart. from 1600F. **Meals** Breakfast 80F, served all the morning; half board and full board 840-1250F (per pers., obligatory in summer). **Restaurant** Service 12:30-14:00, 19:30-22:00, menus 180F (lunchtime) 220-380F; à la carte. Specialties: Agneau des Causses, foie gras, soufflés sucrés. **Credit cards** All major. **Pets** Dogs allowed. **Facilities** Swimming pool, tennis, parking. **Nearby** Quercy region of the Dordogne from Souillac to Saint-Céré, Rocamadour, Padirac – 9-hole Rochebois golf course in Vitrac. **Open** Easter – mid-Nov.

The Château de la Treyne enjoys an exceptional location. Surrounded by a 297-acre forest, it has a formal garden and a park with age-old trees in which a crystalline swimming pool and tennis courts are nestled. This is a château on a human scale. The owner has elegant taste and has skillfully combined the respect for authenticity with the most modern conveniences. All the bedrooms are different and attractive in their own way. With names like *Soleil Levant, Prison Dorée, Enfant Modèle* and *Turenne*, each has an individual atmosphere. Here, luxury and charm blend marvelously, making this a very special and delightful place to stay.

How to get there *(Map 23): 37km south of Brive-la-Gaillarde via N20 to Souillac, then D43 for 5km to La Treyne. Toulouse-Blagnac Airport.*

Le Pont de L'Ouysse ★★★

46200 Lacave (Lot)
Tel. (0)5★ 65.37.87.04 – Fax (0)5★ 65.32.77.41
M. and Mme Chambon

Rooms 13 with telephone, bath, WC, TV and minibar. **Price** Single 350F, double 600F, suite 750F. **Meals** Breakfast 60F, served 8:00-10:00; half board 600-650F (per pers.). **Restaurant** Service 12:30-14:00, 19:30-21:00; à la carte. Specialties: Ecrevisses, foie gras, pigeon aux cèpes, poulette rôtie aux truffes. **Credit cards** All major. **Pets** Dogs allowed. **Facilities** Swimming pool, parking. **Nearby** Quercy region of the Dordogne from Souillac to Saint-Céré, Rocamadour, Padirac – 9-hole Rochebois golf course in Vitrac. **Open** Mar 1 – Dec (closed Monday in low season).

The same family has always run this hotel, which is perched on the side of a rock surrounded by lush vegetation. The large, light bedrooms are very comfortable, with an attractive decor based on English wallpapers and coordinated fabrics. The bathrooms are equally pleasant. The road which goes over the river and up to the hotel is a dead end, ensuring peace and quiet. The charm of this place is enhanced by its lovely terrace, which is shaded by a horse chestnut and a linden tree, and provides outdoor dining in summer. The menu is not extensive but changes often, and the excellent cooking is a result of the imagination and skill of M. Chambon. Mme Chambon will give you a very friendly welcome.

How to get there (Map 23): 37km south of Brive-le-Gaillarde via N20 to Souillac, then D43.

La Petite Auberge

46800 Lascabanes (Lot)
Domaine de Saint-Géry
Tel. (0)5★ 65.31.82.51 – Fax (0)5★ 65.22.92.89 – M. and Mme Duler

Rooms 4, 1 apartment with telephone, bath, WC. **Price** Double 290-450F, 500F, apart. 580-680F. **Meals** Breakfast 60F, served 8:30-10:00; half board 340-420F (per pers., 3 days min., the night, obligatory in July and Aug). **Restaurant** Service 20:00-21:00 (closed Monday and Tuesday except in July and Aug), menus 120-350F. Specialties: Marcassin à la broche, salaisons de porc noir gascon maison, pruneaux de Cahors, marquise au chocolat. **Credit cards** Visa, Eurocard and MasterCard. **Pets** Dogs allowed (+25F). **Facilities** Swimming pool, parking. **Nearby** Cathedral of Saint-Etienne in Cahors, Cahors wine route (château de Bonaguil), valley of the Lot. **Open** Mar 16 – Jan 9 (closed Monday and Tuesday).

This is an auberge but it is above all Patrick and Pascale Duler's home where you will share with them the atmosphere of the past. The beautiful farm buildings surrounding the auberge are used for the farm. Acres of grain, a wild-boar farm, several black Gascon pigs, ducks and a vegetable garden provide the basis for hearty meals prepared and served with discreet charm by Pascale. The dinners served at a communal table, in the lounge or on the adjoining terrace in summer, are moments of great pleasure. (For proof, you only need to see the smiles when guests gather around the dessert buffet.) Five guest rooms with country furniture have been tastefully arranged, offering you space, quiet and comfort. At the Petite Auberge, you know what hospitality means.

How to get there (Map 31): 8km north of Cahors via D653, towards Saint-Géry.

Hostellerie Le Vert ★★

Le Vert
46700 Mauroux (Lot)
Tel. (0)5★ 65.36.51.36 – Fax (0)5★ 65.36.56.84– M. and Mme Philippe

Rooms 7 with telephone, bath or shower, WC and TV. **Price** Single 230-270F, double 360F. **Meals** Breakfast 38F, served 7:30-10:30; half board 295-340F, full board 385-430F (per pers., 3 days min.). **Restaurant** Closed Thursdays and Friday lunchtime. Service 12:00-13:15, 19:30-20:30; menus 100-150F, also à la carte. Specialties: Foie gras frais aux fruits frais, agneau du Quercy, poêlée de cèpes aux petits gris. **Credit cards** Amex, Visa, Eurocard and MasterCard. **Pets** Dogs allowed (+25F). **Facilities** Swimming pool, parking. **Nearby** Cathedral of Saint-Etienne in Cahors, Cahors wine route (château de Bonaguil), valley of the Lot. **Open** Feb 14 – Nov 12.

The Hostellerie Le Vert is an old converted farmhouse. Its windows shed a soft and gentle light on the spacious, comfortable and refined interior. A lovely terrace looks out over the surrounding countryside – a pleasant spot for a summer breakfast. The cuisine is very good. In summer, ask for the bedroom that has been made in the old vaulted cellar (No. 6), which is cool and unusual. Above it a large, bright new bedroom has just been added, with a beamed ceiling, stone floor, a beautiful fireplace and a piano. The bedrooms in the main hotel are not so original but are no less inviting and comfortable.

How to get there *(Map 30): 37km west of Cahors via D911 to Puy-l'Evêque, then D5 in the towards of Mauroux.*

Relais Sainte-Anne ★★★

Rue du Pourtanel
46600 Martel (Lot)
Tel. (0)5★ 65.37.40.56 – Fax (0)5★ 65.37.42.82 – Mme Lachèze

Rooms 10 with telephone, bath or shower, WC, TV and 8 with minibar. **Price** Single and double 220-700F. **Meals** Breakfast 55F, served 8:00-12:00. No restaurant. **Credit cards** All major. **Pets** Dogs allowed (+50F). **Facilities** Swimming pool, parking. **Nearby** Rocamadour, Padirac, caves of Lacave, Dordogne Valley, Collonges-la-Rouge, abbey of Aubazines - Music festival in summer. **Open** Nov 6 – Easter.

Don't be surprised to find a chapel here: The Relais Sainte-Anne was once a boarding house for nuns. There are ten lovely bedrooms located in several recently renovated buildings. All have very modern conveniences but each room is individually decorated in sober, elegant fabrics and colors. The largest room has a fireplace and a terrace; smaller rooms are less expensive. There is a walled-in, old garden with a lovely terrace, small paths and a beautiful swimming pool surrounded by a lawn. Breakfast can be served in your room, in the breakfast room which has a fireplace or, in good weather, on the terrace. In summer, classical music concerts are performed in the chapel. The Relais Sainte-Anne radiates with turn-of-the-century charm.

How to get there (Map 23 and 24): 30km south of Brive.

Claude Marco ★★★

Lamagdelaine 46090 Cahors (Lot)
Tel. (0)5★ 65.35.30.64 - Fax (0)5★ 65.30.31.40
Mme and M. Marco

Rooms 4 with telephone, bath, WC and cable TV. **Price** Double 480F, 550F, 580F; suite 680F. **Meals** Breakfast 50F, served 8:00-11:00. **Restaurant** Service 12:00-14:00, 19:30-21:30 (closed Sunday evening and Monday except June 15 – Sep 15), menus 120F (lunchtime) 195-295F; also à la carte. Specialties: Foie gras au sel, tatin de foie gras, pot-au-feu de canard, filet de bœuf aux morilles. **Credit cards** Amex, Visa, Eurocard and MasterCard. **Pets** Dogs allowed. **Facilities** Swimming pool, parking. **Nearby** Cahors; Cahors Wine Route from Mercues to Montcabrier; Lot and Célé valley. **Open** Mar 9 –Jan 7 (closed Sunday evening and Monday in low season).

Claude Marco is well known and highly rated in all the French gastronomic guides. The addition of several bedrooms now gives us the opportunity to include his address in our guide and to suggest, a true gourmet's stay in an inn of character and charm. This beautiful old Quercy building and balcony are covered in greenery; inside, the lounges and dining room are located in superb barrel-vaulted rooms of pale-yellow stone, while the bedrooms have been installed in the garden, around the swimming pool. They are fresh, cheerful, elegant, and very comfortable, as are the the bathrooms with whirlpool bathtubs. In the restaurant, you may choose between the Menu Quercynois if you wish to discover the regional specialties; the Menu Surprise, which is made up depending on the best products from the market that day, and the chef's inspiration; and finally the Carte des Saisons, for seasonal specialties. The delicious cuisine aside, remember that you are in a very beautiful region, which has many natural and touristic sites of interest.

How to get there *(Map 3): 7km from Cahors via D653.*

Hôtel Les Vieilles Tours ★★

Lafage
46500 Rocamadour (Lot)
Tel. (0)5★ 65.33.68.01 – Fax (0)5★ 65.33.68.59 – M. and Mme Zozzoli

Rooms 18 with telephone, bath or shower and WC. **Price** Double 210-460F.
Meals Breakfast 40-60F, served 8:00-11:00; half board 280-425F. **Restaurant** Lunch
Sunday and National holiday,19:30-21:00; menus 115-300F, children 56F, also à la
carte. Specialties: Magret au miel, foie gras aux trois parfums. **Credit cards** Visa,
Eurocard and MasterCard. **Pets** Dogs allowed except in the restaurant (+30F).
Facilities Swimming pool, parking. **Nearby** Old town, Francis Poulenc museum in
Rocamadour, Padirac chasm, Lascaux caves – 9-hole Saint-Céré golf course. **Open**
Apr 1 – Nov 4.

This hotel is only 2 kilometers from Rocamadour. It has been
well restored using beautiful local stone and enjoys exceptional
views and tranquillity. The reception and dining room have their
original stone walls and the tables are tastefully laid. There are
bedrooms in both the old building and its modern annex, which
was built in the local style. Pleasantly furnished, with some 19th-
century pieces, the bedrooms are all different and have comfortable
amenities, as do the bathrooms. M. Zozzoli is a painter, engraver
and lithographer and you will find frequent examples of his work,
which is inspired by the region. The menu offers delicious regional
dishes, which change according to the season and Mme Zozzoli's
inspiration.

How to get there *(Map 24): 53km south of Brive-la-Gaillarde via N20 to
Cressensac, then N140 and D673; 3km from Rocamadour, in the towards of
Payrac/Gourdon.*

Domaine de la Rhue ★★★

La Rhue
46500 Rocamadour (Lot)
Tel. (0)5★ 65.33.71.50 – Fax (0)5★ 65.33.72.48 – M. and Mme Jooris

Rooms 12 with telephone, bath or shower, WC and 4 with TV. **Price** Single 370F, double 370-570F, apart. (4 pers.) 680F. **Meals** Breakfast 45-65F, served 8:00-10:00. No restaurant. **Credit cards** Visa, Eurocard and MasterCard. **Pets** Dogs allowed (+30F). **Facilities** Swimming pool, parking. **Nearby** Old town, Francis Poulenc museum in Rocamadour, Dordogne valley, Lascaux caves, Padirac chasm – 9-hole Montal golf course in Saint-Céré. **Open** Easter – Oct 15.

This hotel is located in the splendid stables of a château which is surrounded by beautiful rolling countryside. The Domaine is tastefully and comfortably furnished throughout. The vast entrance hall still has its original paving and traces of the stalls. Pleasantly furnished in a rustic style, the bedrooms are named after horse breeds, and are all spacious, quiet and attractive, with some antique furniture, elegant fabrics and many original beams. Some of the rooms on the ground floor are like small houses with a private terrace. The Domaine has all the modern amenities, mixed with the charm of the past. For excellent cuisine try the *Sainte-Marie* Restaurant.

How to get there *(Map 24): 55km south of Brive-la-Gaillarde via N20 towards Cressensac, then N140; 1km before junction with D673, take the road on the right.*

Hôtel Ric ★★★
Route de Leyme
46400 Saint-Céré (Lot)
Tel. (0)5★ 65.38.04.08 – Fax (0)5★ 65.38.00.14 – M. Ric

Rooms 6 with telephone, bath, WC and TV. **Price** Double 300-350F. **Meals** Breakfast 45F, served until 9:00 (in room); half board 350-380F (per pers.). **Restaurant** Closed Monday in low season except national holidays. Service 12:00-14:00, 19:30-21:30; menus 110-250F, also à la carte. Specialties: Parmentier de foie gras aux oignons frits, fleurs de courgettes farcies aux écrevisses, taboulé de langoustines, fondant au chocolat aux framboises et fraises des bois. **Credit cards** Visa, Eurocard and MasterCard. **Pets** Dogs allowed. **Facilities** Swimming pool, parking. **Nearby** Quercy region of the Dordogne from Souillac to Saint-Céré – 9-hole Saint-Céré golf course. **Open** Mar –Jan (closed Monday in low season except national holidays).

Surrounded by beautiful foliage, this small hotel has a magnificent view over the hills of Saint-Céré. The accommodations are modern, as is the decor. All the bedrooms are comfortable, but we prefer those on the front. In the pale-green dining room or on the terrace in summer, you will enjoy the inventive cuisine of the owner, M. Ric, who serves such specialties as fresh squash blossoms stuffed with crayfish. The staff is young and friendly.

How to get there *(Map 24): 55km south of Brive-la-Gaillarde via D 702, in the towards of Saint-Céré. At 2.5km from Saint-Céré, Leymé road by D48.*

Hôtel de la Pelissaria ★★★

46330 Saint-Cirq-Lapopie (Lot)
Tel. (0)5★ 65.31.25.14 – Fax (0)5★ 65.30.25.52
Mme Matuchet

Rooms 10 with telephone, bath, WC and TV - 1 wheelchair access room. **Price** Double 410-610F, suite 650F. **Meals** Breakfast 50F, served 8:00-10:00. **Restaurant** Closed Thursday and Friday. Service 20:00-21:00; à la carte. Specialties: home-made pasta and sorbets, confit de canard. **Credit cards** Visa, Eurocard and MasterCard. **Pets** Dogs allowed (+15F). **Facilities** Small swimming pool. **Nearby** Lot and the Célé valleys. **Open** Apr 1 – Nov 15.

There is something magical about the village of Saint-Cirq-Lapopie. It is one of the most beautiful medieval villages in France, and has been classified as a historic monument. Hôtel de la Pelissaria, one of the most beautiful hotels listed on this book, was built in the 13th-century in local stone, and has been carefully and tastefully restored by its cordial owners. Our favorite bedroom is number 4, with its little window opening onto the village and the Lot Valley. Two small cottages nestled in a garden house two charming rooms. In the dining room, which has a piano and a lovely fireplace, you will enjoy very good cuisine (and excellent value for money). The number of seats in the restaurant is limited, so reservations are a must.

How to get there *(Map 31): 33km east of Cahors via D653 towards Saint-Géry, then D662.*

Auberge du Sombral ★★

46330 Saint-Cirq-Lapopie (Lot)
Tel. (0)5★ 65.31.26.08 - Fax (0)5★ 65.30.26.37
M. and Mme Hardeveld

Rooms 8 with telephone, 5 with bath, 5 with shower. **Price** Single 300F, double 400F. **Meals** Breakfast 48F, served until 9:30. **Restaurant** Service 12:00-14:00, 19:30-21:00; menus 100-280F, also à la carte. Specialties: Truite au vieux Cahors, feuilleté d'asperges aux morilles, escalope de foie chaud aux pommes, terrine de foie de canard confit. **Credit cards** Visa, Eurocard and MasterCard. **Pets** Dogs allowed. **Nearby** Valleys of the Lot and the Célé. **Open** Apr 1 – Nov 11 (closed Tuesday evening and Wednesday).

This auberge is in an old house which has been perfectly restored. It faces the town square in the heart of this village, now classed as a historic monument. The village is on an escarpment overlooking the Lot Valley. The atmosphere is calm, the surroundings exceptional. The bedrooms are pleasant and comfortable. You can explore the village with its alleys and picturesque houses, as well as the auberge itself, which has its own museum with a permanent display of paintings by local artists. The restaurant offers excellent cuisine and emphasizes regional specialties.

How to get there *(Map 31): 33km east of Cahors via D653 towards Saint-Géry, then D662.*

Hostellerie La Source Bleue ★★★

Touzac
46700 Puy-l'Evêque (Lot)
Tel. (0)5★ 65.36.52.01 – Fax (0)5★ 65.24.65.69 – M. and Mme Bouyou

Rooms 16 with telephone, bath, WC and 7 with TV. **Price** Single 290F, double 290-450F. **Meals** Breakfast 35F, served 7:30-9:30; half board from 275F, full board from 385F (per per., 2 days min.). **Restaurant** Service 12:00-13:30, 19:30-21:15 (closed Tuesday lunchtime); menus 105, 140, 220F, also à la carte. Specialties: Saint-Jacques au safran, magret aux pêches, feuilleté de foie gras, agneau du Quercy. **Credit cards** Amex, Visa, Eurocard and MasterCard. **Pets** Dogs allowed (+20-30F). **Facilities** Swimming pool, sauna (100F), health center, boat, parking. **Nearby** Marguerite-Moréno museum, Cahors wine route (château de Bonaguil) – 18-hole La Chapelle golf course in Auzac, 18-hole Castelnaud-de-Gratecambe golf course. **Open** Apr 26 – Dec 31.

La Source Bleue, in a converted 14th-century paper mill on the left bank of the Lot, has been tastefully restored by its owners. The bedrooms, some with modern furniture, are comfortable, and the bathrooms are impeccable. Four new bedrooms have been added in the tower and decorated with antique furniture. The cooking is refined and served in a beautiful dining room. The service is attentive but discreet, and there is soft background music. The gardens and park of "The Blue Spring" are beautiful with their many species of trees, including an impressive bamboo forest.

How to get there *(Map 30): 48km west of Cahors via D911 towards Fumel; at Touzac, cross the Lot.*

Hostellerie Saint-Antoine ★★★★

17, rue Saint-Antoine
81000 Albi (Tarn)
Tel. (0)5★ 63.54.04.04 - Fax (0)5★ 63.47.10.47 - MM. Rieux and fils

Rooms 48 with air-conditioning, telephone, bath, WC, TV and minibar. **Price** Single 360-450F, double 450-750F, suite 850-950F. **Meals** Breakfast 60F; half board 420-720F (per pers.). **Restaurant** Closed Saturday and Sunday lunchtime. Service 12:00-14:00, 19:00-21:30; menus 150-280F, also à la carte. Specialties: Foie gras, salade de homard, daube de bœuf à l'albigeoise, tournedos Périgueux, tarte à l'ancienne, glace aux noix. **Credit cards** All major. **Pets** Dogs allowed (+55F). **Facilities** Parking. **Nearby** Cathedral of Sainte-Cécile, Toulouse-Lautrec museum in Albi, Viaur viaduct, Ambialet, Gaillac, Cordes – 18-hole golf course in Albi. **Open** All year.

Founded in the 18th-century and run by the same family for five generations, this inn was restored in 1960. Elegantly modernized, each room is enhanced by antique furniture – including Directoire and Louis-Phillippe pieces, and bright fabrics. The bedrooms are extremely comfortable, quiet, well-designed and many have a view of the flower garden. Some of the larger ones have a lounge area. On the ground floor the dining room opens onto the garden. You will enjoy good traditional cooking, attentive service and warm hospitality.

How to get there *(Map 31): In the town center.*

Cuq-en-Terrasse

Cuq-le-Château - 81470 Cuq-Toulza (Tarn)
Tel (0)5★ 63.82.54.00 - Fax (0)5★ 63.82.54.11
M. and Mme Whitmore

Rooms 7 and 1 apartment (duplex), bath or shower, WC and TV. **Price** 400-500F, suite 700F, apart. 900F. **Meals** Breakfast 55F. **Restaurant** By reservation. Service 12:00-14:30, 19:30-21:30; menus 130F (lunch), 150F (dinner). Specialties: Vichyssoise, gazpacho, mousse de saumon fumé, filet mignon de veau à l'estragon et aux baies roses, noisettes d'agneau aux deux poivrons. **Credit cards** Diner's, Visa, Eurocard and MasterCard. **Pets** Dogs allowed. **Facilities** Swimming pool. **Nearby** Albi, Carcassonne, Castres market in Revel – 18-hole Fiac Golf Course. **Open** All year.

This ancient house spreads out over an enchanting terraced hillside. From the terraces and the garden swimming pool, you will have a superb view over the patchwork of rich valleys the locals call *Le Pays de Cocagne*, the land of abundance. Le Cuq en Terrasse has been magnificently restored and decorated by an English architect and his wife. Tasteful decoration in the bright bedrooms and baths make this a very beautiful hotel, in which traditional decor has been skillfully combined with the most modern amenities. You will enjoy the sheer serenity of the place, from the terrace to the shady nooks around the swimming pool. Breakfasts are generous and elegant and Zara Whitmore serves delicious regional cuisine. There is an excellent choice of wines, and the owners are friendly and considerate.

How to get there *(Map 31): 35km east of Toulouse, towards Castres. In Cuq, take direction Revel for 2km. On A61, exit number 17.*

Demeure de Flore ★★★
106, Grande rue
81240 Lacabarède (Tarn)
Tel. (0)5★ 63.98.32.32. – Fax (0)5★ 63.98.47.56 – Mme Tronc

Rooms 12 and 1 suite with telephone, bath, WC and TV - Wheelchair access.
Price Single 350F, double 460F, suite 730F. **Meals** Breakfast 54F. **Restaurant** Service
19:30-21:30; menus 130-200F, also à la carte. **Credit cards** Visa, Eurocard and
MasterCard. **Pets** Small dogs allowed (+70F). **Facilities** Swimming pool, parking.
Nearby Goya museum in Castres, le Sidobre and the Monts Lacaune de Castres in
Mazamet – 18-hole La Barouge golf course in Pont-de-l'Arn. **Open** All year except in
Feb.

This small hotel is hidden from the road by lush vegetation.
Indoors, the decor is elegant; antique furniture, paintings and
curios combine to create a warm and cozy atmosphere. The
comfortable bedrooms are all individually decorated with colorful
designer fabrics and antiques bought locally. The bathrooms are
modern and luxuriously equipped. Our favorite rooms are those
with a small terrace and access to the garden and swimming pool.
Evening meals, based on fresh local produce, are served in the
lovely dining room. This is a marvelous place to stay.

How to get there (Map 31): 15km east of Mazamet via N112.

Château de Montlédier ★★★
Route d'Anglès
81660 Pont-de-L'Arn (Tarn)
Tel. (0)5★ 63.61.20.54 – Fax (0)5★ 63.98.22.51 – Mme Thiercelin

Rooms 9 with telephone, bath, WC, TV and minibar. **Price** Single 330-360F, double 450-590F. **Meals** Breakfast 50F; half board 360-440F, full board 480-560F (per pers., 3 days min.). **Restaurant** Closed Sunday evening and Monday except July – Aug. Service 12:00-13:30, 19:30-21:30; menus 120-180F, also à la carte. Specialties: Foie gras maison, carré d'agneau, magret de canard, soufflé léger à la poire. **Credit cards** All major. **Pets** Dogs allowed. **Facilities** Swimming pool, parking. **Nearby** Goya museum in Castres, le Sidobre and the Monts Lacaune de Castres in Mazamet – 18-hole La Barouge golf course in Pont-de-l'Arn. **Open** Feb 1 – Dec 31.

You enter the château through the grand courtyard. Inside there are a number of small lounges, equipped so that there is something to please everyone. The bedrooms are spacious and beautifully decorated, and each is extremely comfortable. The smallest and least expensive rooms (*Victoria* and *Alexandra*) are as charming as the others, and the *Raymond IV* bedroom has a particularly charming bathroom – it is huge and from it you can see through the trees into the ravine. Meals are served in the small dining room or on a shady terrace which forms an extension to the lounge.

How to get there *(Map 31): 19km southeast of Castres via N112 towards Mazamet, then D65 at Bout-du-Pont-de-l'Arn.*

Le Métairie Neuve ★★★

81660 Pont-de-L'Arn (Tarn)
Tel. (0)5★ 63.61.23.31 - Fax (0)5★ 63.61.94.75
Mme Tournier

Rooms 11 with telephone, bath, WC, TV and 9 with minibar. **Price** Single 310-500F, double 290-550F. **Meals** Half board 300-550F, full board 450-680F (per pers., 3 days min.). **Restaurant** Closed Saturday and Sunday Oct 1 – Mar 1. Service 19:30-21:00; menus 85-110F, also à la carte. Specialties: Regional cooking. **Credit cards** Diners, Visa, Eurocard and MasterCard. **Pets** Dogs allowed. **Facilities** pool, parking. **Nearby** Goya museum in Castres, le Sidobre and the Monts Lacaune de Castres in Mazamet – 18-hole La Barouge golf course in Pont-de-l'Arn. **Open** Jan 20 – Dec 13.

This lovely old farmhouse is on the outskirts of a village which is expanding with commercial developments, but the hotel remains in a leafy, quiet area. The bedrooms are all well equipped and elegantly furnished; the colors are harmonious and the old furniture blends perfectly with the more modern pieces. The hotel has a beautiful courtyard, a large garden with a terrace, and a swimming pool. One of the restaurant's two rooms is reserved for non-smokers. But the cuisine itself needs improvement.

How to get there *(Map 31): 19km southeast of Castres via N112 towards Mazamet.*

Château de l'Hoste **
Saint-Beauzeuil
82150 Montaigu-de-Quercy (Tarn-et-Garonne)
Tel. (0)5★ 63.95.25.61 - Fax (0)5★ 63.95.25.50 - M. Poumeyrau

Rooms 32 with telephone, bath and WC. **Price** Single and double 210-260F.
Meals Breakfast 40F, served 8:00-10:00; half board 280F, full board 380F (per pers.,
3 days min.). **Restaurant** Closed Sunday evening and Monday in low season. Service
12:00, 19:45; menus 115-265F, also à la carte. Specialties: Lamproie bordelaise,
trilogie de bœuf, cassoulet d'antan. **Credit cards** Visa, Eurocard and MasterCard.
Pets Dogs allowed (+20F). **Facilities** Swimming pool, parking. **Nearby** Agen
museum, Port-Sainte-Marie, Villeneuve-sur-Lot, Beauville – 18-hole Castelneau golf
course. **Open** All year.

M. Poumeyrau has just acquired this 18th-century mansion. You will be charmed by its pale stone walls, lovely interior courtyard, and the proximity of the swimming pool. The decoration has been less successful in the bedrooms where the antique-style furniture is disappointing. They are nevertheless large, well kept rooms with comfortable beds and impeccable bathrooms. We recommend rooms 204 and 210, which are smaller but charming. In summer avoid the rooms that overlook the terrace where dinner is served; the enthusiasm of the diners enjoying the chef's excellent cooking (especially the *lamproie à la bordelaise*) may disturb you if you want to retire early.

How to get there *(Map 30): 40km northeast of Agen via D656; between Agen and Cahors – 8km west of Montaigu.*

Le Jardin Fleuri ★★

23, rue du Moulin
59990 Sebourg (Nord)
Tel. (0)3★ 27.26.53.31 – Fax (0)3★ 27.26.50.08 – Mme Delmotte

Rooms 13 with telephone, bath or shower, 9 with WC and 8 with TV. **Price** Double 200-300F. **Meals** Breakfast 30F, served 7:00-10:00; half board 260-320F, full board 360-420F (per pers., 4 days min.). **Restaurant** Closed Wednesday. Service 12:00-13:00, 19:00-22:00; menus 130-250F, also à la carte. Specialties: Langue Lucullus, saumon à l'unilatérale, tarte aux pommes. **Credit cards** Visa, Eurocard and MasterCard. **Pets** Dogs allowed. **Facilities** Parking. **Nearby** Art museum in Valenciennes, Bavay, Le Quesnoy, glass museum in Sars-Poterie – 9-hole golf course in Valenciennes. **Open** All year (closed Sept 15 – 30).

In the small rue du Moulin, you first come to the restaurant and then, behind it, the hotel's colorful and charming garden; the little stream with its wooden bridge and the beautiful fir trees are lovely. Beyond it is the hotel, a small brick house. It contains 13 bedrooms on two floors; cozy and comfortable, they look out over the garden and two have a balcony. The Jardin Fleuri is notable for its good cooking and very reasonable prices.

How to get there *(Map 3): 9km east of Valenciennes via A2, Curgies exit, then D8.*

Auberge du Bon Fermier ★★★★

64-66, rue de Famars
59300 Valenciennes (Nord)
Tel. (0)3★ 27.46.68.25 - Fax (0)3★ 27.33.75.01 - M. and Mme Paul

Rooms 16 with telephone, bath or shower WC, TV and minibar. **Price** Single 400-600F, double 480-700F. **Meals** Breakfast 45F, all the morning. **Restaurant** Service 12:00-14:30, 19:00-22:30; menus 120-200F, also à la carte. Specialties: Langue Lucullus, cochon de lait à la broche, tarte au maroilles (goyère). **Credit cards** All major. **Pets** Dogs allowed. **Facilities** Parking (+50F). **Nearby** Remains of the ancient abbey in Saint-Amand-les-Eaux, fortifications of Le Quesnoy, the Helpe valley; Watteau museum in Valence – 9-hole golf course in Valenciennes. **Open** All year.

Stop off at the Auberge du Bon Fermier for a comfortable evening in what used to be a royal carriage house in the17th-century, on the road from the Tuileries to Brussels. It has been an inn since 1840, and is now registered a historic monument, scrupulously restored by its present owners. The red bricks of the outer walls and many inner ones, the exposed beams, and the oak floors all help recreate the atmosphere of that era. The rooms are all spacious and enchanting, and each has a sitting area. The quietest ones are on the park. Modern conveniences have been carefully blended into the decor. The restaurant serves regional specialties but also features fresh lobster and a wide range of spit-roasted meats. The atmosphere is somewhat theatrical, but this is nonetheless a place not to be missed.

How to get there *(Map 3): In the town center, between the Place du Canada and the town hall.*

Chartreuse du Val Saint-Esprit ★★★

1, rue de Fouquières
62199 Gosnay (Pas-de-Calais)
Tel. (0)3★ 21.62.80.00 - Fax (0)3★ 21.62.42.50 - M. and Mme Constant

Rooms 56 with telephone, bath, WC, TV and minibar. **Price** Single 330-600F, double 400-900F. **Meals** Breakfast 50F, served 6:30-10:00. **Restaurant** Service 12:00-14:30, 19:00-22:00; menus 210-365F, also à la carte. Specialties: Poêlée de langoustines et girolles aux oignons nouveaux, homard breton aux petits légumes sauce corail, filet de bar cuit sur sa peau aux spaghettis de courgette et infusion d'ail, blanc de turbot en écailles de pomme de terre au coulis de petits pois, tournedos poêlée aux truffes d'été sauce bordelaise. **Credit cards** Amex, Visa, Eurocard and MasterCard. **Pets** Dogs allowed (+45F). **Facilities** Parking. **Nearby** Golf course at Aa. **Open** All year.

At first sight this splendid brick and stone edifice, with its great courtyard and large park, may seem rather austere. This first impression is, however, immediately dispelled by a warm and friendly welcome and the refinement of the interior decoration. Most of the rooms are vast, and the *premier étage* bedrooms with impressive high-ceilings are extremely comfortable, with beautiful bathrooms. Lavish amounts of attention have been devoted to features such as bedspreads, curtains and wallpapers, which all blend to perfection. The *deuxième étage* rooms tend to be less bright, but this makes them more cozy and intimate. The breakfast room is delightful, with a row of arched windows overlooking the gardens. The hotel has added new bedrooms which match the charm of the older ones. A recent *brasserie* service has been added for simple meals.

How to get there *(Map 2): 5km south of Béthune via A26, number 6 exit, in the direction of Chartreuses.*

Château de Cocove ★★★

62890 Recques-sur-Hem (Pas-de-Calais)
Tel. (0)3★ 21.82.68.29 - Fax (0)3★ 21.82.72.59
François Wibaut

Rooms 24 with telephone, bath or shower, WC and TV. **Price** Single and double 435-690F. **Meals** Breakfast 45F, served 7:30-10:30; "weekend gastronomic" 2250F (per pers.). **Restaurant** Service 12:00-14:00, 19:30-21:30; menus 120-350F, also à la carte. Specialties: Fricassée de soles et langoustines, foie gras maison. **Credit cards** All major. **Pets** Dogs allowed (+45F). **Facilities** Sauna (25F), parking. **Nearby** Basilica of Notre-Dame and Sandelin museum in Valenciennes, blockhouse in Eperlecques, church of Saint-Eloi and museum in Hazebrouck, the 'Bourgeois de Calais', art and lace museum in Calais – 27-hole Saint-Omer golf course in Lumbres. **Open** All year (closed Dec 25).

Only a few minutes from Calais, this 18th-century château is deep in the countryside surrounded by an extensive English-style park. You will enjoy youthful and charming hospitality here. The interior has been beautifully restored in keeping with the age of the building. In the same spirit the dining room has been converted from the old stables, its wide doors replaced by bay windows; pale subdued decor adds to the elegance of the room. The cuisine is good, attractively presented and offers excellent value for money. The bedrooms are bright and quiet and some are very large; there are occasional antiques. Renovation of the rooms is being completed and we are already very satisfied with the result as regards the cheerful, elegant decoration as well as the modern amenities(only two rooms in the annex are less recommendable.) Before leaving, wine lovers can visit the cellars and buy from a large selection of excellent wines at reasonable prices.

How to get there *(Map 2): 17km southeast of Calais: from Calais by A26, number 2 Ardres-Licques exit. Or via N43 towards Saint-Omer.*

Hôtel Cléry ★★★

62360 Hesdin-l'Abbé (Pas-de-Calais)
Tel. (0)3 21.83.19.83 - Fax (0)3 21.87.52.59
Catherine and Didier Legros

Rooms 20 with telephone, bath or shower, WC and TV. **Price** Single 330F, double 450-590F, pavillon 1100F (5 pers.). **Meals** Breakfast 50F, served 7:00-10:00. No restaurant but snacks available in the evening (except weekends and National Holidays) for residents only. **Credit cards** All major. **Pets** No dogs allowed. **Facilities** Tennis, mountain bike rentals, parking. **Nearby** Castle-museum and national marine center in Boulogne-sur-Mer, pottery museum in Desvres, Opal coast, Cap Gris-Nez, Cap Blanc-Nez – 18-hole golf course in Hardelot. **Open** Feb 1 – Dec 14.

Legend has it that Napoleon stayed at this small château. There are three rooms on the ground floor: a large, light room where breakfast is served, a bar and a beautiful room where you can sit in deep leather armchairs by an open fire. An elegant staircase with a Louis XV style wrought iron banister leads to the *premier étage*. The bedrooms are comfortable and the decor simple. The rooms on the *deuxième étage* have gently sloping mansard roofs, but whether they look out on the chestnut trees in the park or on the drive, all the bedrooms are quiet. Behind a courtyard with old stone paving and geraniums, there are seven other bedrooms in the former stable block. Room eight is on the ground floor and among the others, on the *premier étage*, are two pretty small bedrooms. Finally, in a pretty corner of the park, there is a pavilion offering two bedrooms with bathrooms and a small lounge with fireplace. Not far from the national highway, the hotel is located on the road to England. The outstanding restaurants in Boulogne are *La Matelote* and *La Liégeoise*. In the Centre National de la Mer, you can also enjoy delicious shellfish lunches at *Le Grand Pavois*.

How to get there (Map 1): *9km southeast of Boulogne via N1.*

336

Hostellerie du Moulin du Pré **

14860 Bavent (Calvados)
Tel. (0)2★ 31.78.83.68 – Fax (0)2★ 31.78.21.05
Hamchin-Holtz Family

Rooms 10 with telephone, bath or shower and 5 with WC. **Price** Double 220-340F.
Meals Breakfast 40F, served 8:00-10:00. **Restaurant** Service 12:30-13:30, 19:30-
21:00; menus 250-280F, also à la carte. Specialties: Pommes de terre en millefeuille
au saumon à la crème de ciboulette, tartelette de sardines fraîches au beurre de
safran, papillottes de poisson fin aux pommes at au curry. **Credit cards** All major.
Pets Dogs not allowed. **Facilities** Parking. **Nearby** Deauville, Caen, Normandy
landing beaches, Houlgate – 18-hole Le Home Varaville golf course in Cabourg. **Open**
All year except Mar 1-15 and Oct (closed Sunday evening and Monday except July,
Aug and national holidays).

On the borders of the Auge region, this renovated country
farmhouse stands on a large property with a small lake. The
sea is only 4 km away. The interior of the hotel is comfortable.
The small bedrooms are delightful, some in a rustic style, and all
of them look out on the peaceful countryside. The bathroom
facilities and soundproofing vary from room to room. The large
dining room and lounge on the ground floor are very welcoming
and mealtimes provide an opportunity to discover excellent French
home cooking.

*How to get there (Map 7): 14km northeast of Caen via D513 towards
Cabourg, then D95 towards Gonneville-en-Auge.*

Hôtel d'Argouges ★★

21, rue Saint-Patrice
14400 Bayeux (Calvados)
Tel. (0)2★ 31.92.88.86 – Fax (0)2★ 31.92.69.16 – M. and Mme Auregan

Rooms 25 with telephone, bath or shower, WC, minibar and 18 with TV. **Price** Single 190-350F, double 190-420F. **Meals** Breakfast 38F, served 7:30-10:30. No restaurant. **Credit cards** All major. **Pets** Dogs allowed (+35F). **Facilities** Parking. **Nearby** Bayeux cathedral, Port-en-Bessin, beach of debarquement – 27-hole Omaha Beach golf course in Bayeux (10km). **Open** All year.

You will feel at home in this old private hotel run by the Argouges family. It is on the quiet outskirts of the old town and within walking distance of all points of interest. The hotel's rooms, all very quiet and plainly but comfortably furnished, are in two buildings and have high ceilings and exposed beams. Most are quite large. Rooms 23 and 25, built in old barns, are actually small, well designed apartments, each one with a large main bedroom and a small bedroom for children. At the rear of the hotel, behind an 18th-century facade, there is an extensive garden where you can have breakfast, unless you prefer the delightful dining room. This is a beautiful hotel; and a good deal. *Le Lion d'Or* is a charming restaurant, while *L'Amaryllis* is simpler.

How to get there *(Map 7): 27km west of Caen via N13.*

Auberge de la Boule d'Or

14430 Beuvron-en-Auge (Calvados)
Tel. (0)2★ 31.79.78.78
M. and Mme Duval

Rooms 3 with bath or shower and WC. **Price** Double 230F. **Meals** Breakfast 35F, served 7:00-10:00; half board 230F, full board 300F (per pers., 7 days min.). **Restaurant** Closed in Jan. Service 12:00-13:30, 19:00-21:30; menus 98-155F, also à la carte. Specialties: Norman cuisine. **Credit cards** All major. **Pets** Small dogs allowed. **Nearby** Lisieux, pays d'Auge from Lisieux to Deauville and Lisieux to Cabourg. **Open** All year (closed Sunday evening and Monday except July – Aug).

In summer, every street and square in Beuvron-en-Auge seems to be in bloom, and the houses are so decked out with geraniums that their ancient half-timbering itself seems to be blossoming. The Boule d'Or is a small, modest inn well known for its traditional cuisine. There is no reception area as such, so you should go straight into the dining room, which is rustic in style, with pink table cloths striking a note of simplicity. A small staircase leads up to the hotel's three bedrooms, which are small but comfortable, bright and neat, and have pleasant bathrooms. This is a friendly, unpretentious address in one of the most beautiful villages in Normandy. Special mention should be made of the excellent traditional cuisine.

How to get there *(Map 8): 25km west of Lisieux via A13, exit Dozulé for 7km.*

Hostellerie du Château de Goville ★★★

14330 Le-Breuil-en-Bessin (Calvados)
Tel. (0)2★ 31.22.19.28 - Fax (0)2★ 31.22.68.74
M. Vallée

Rooms 12 with telephone, bath or shower, WC and minibar. **Price** Double 425-695F, suite 795F. **Meals** Breakfast 55F, served 8:30-11:30; half board 445-625F (per pers., 2 days min.). **Restaurant** "Le Baromètre". Closed Tuesday in low season except by reservation. Service 12:30-14:00, 19:30-21:30; menus 140-245F, also à la carte. Specialties: Traditional cuisine. **Credit cards** All major. **Pets** Dogs allowed (+75F). **Facilities** Parking. **Nearby** Bayeux tapestry and cathedral, châteaux of Vaulaville and of Fontaine-Henry, beach of debarquement, church of Saint-Loup-Hors, abbey of Mondaye – 27-hole Omaha Beach golf course. **Open** All year.

This château, owned by the Vallée family since 1813, has retained the charm of a private house. The interior decor is elegant: there is hardly a piece of furniture, objêt d'art or picture which is not an original. There is something of the atmosphere of an English country house here. The spacious dining room is lit by a huge crystal chandelier, and you will be enchanted by the lounge while you enjoy your aperitif or perhaps a glass of Calvados. Your hospitable hosts will ensure your enjoyment of a stay at one of the most charming hotels in Normandy.

How to get there *(Map 7): 38km northwest of Caen via N13 to Bayeux, then D5 towards Molay-Littry.*

Ferme Hôtel La Rançonnière ★★
Route d'Arromanches - 14480 Crépon (Calvados)
Tel. (0)2★ 31.22.21.73 - Fax (0)2★ 31.22.98.39
Mmes Vereecke and Sileghem

Rooms 35 with telephone, bath or shower, WC and TV. **Price** Single and double 295-420F. **Meals** Breakfast 42F, served 7:45-10:00; half board 205-315F (per pers.). **Restaurant** Service 12:00-14:00, 19:00-21:30; menus 60-235F, also à la carte. Specialties: Homard frais flambé, salade champêtre. **Credit cards** All major. **Pets** Dogs allowed. **Facilities** Parking. **Nearby** Bayeux tapestry and cathedral, châteaux of Creullet and of Creully, church of Saint-Loup-Hors, abbey of Mondaye – 27-hole Omaha Beach golf course. **Open** All year.

The Bessin region is full of old manor houses and Crépon has more than its share in terms of both numbers and quality. You enter this old farm through a crenellated carriage gate into a vast courtyard around which are the reception, restaurant and the bedrooms of the hotel. The interior is decidedly rustic with wooden furniture and exposed timbers everywhere. Comfortable bedrooms have small windows and old furniture whose dark tones are at times a little heavy. We particularly like rooms 2, 3, 5, 6, 7, 9, 18, 24, 28, 29 and for families we like rooms 8, 23, 25, 31 and 32. The rooms above the restaurant are a little small but very pleasant. The food is good and abundant and served in a vast hall, often brightened by a cheerful wood fire. In summer you can dine in the courtyard. The cordial staff will make you feel at home.

How to get there (Map 7): 21km northwest of Caen via D22 towards Arromanches, then D112 towards Couseulles.

La Chenevière ★★★★

Escures–Commes
14520 Port-en-Bessin (Calvados)
Tel. (0)2★ 31.21 47 96 - Fax (0)2★ 31 21 47 98 - M. Neutelings

Rooms 19 with telephone, bath, WC, TV and minibar; elevator - Wheelchair access.
Price Double 700-1100F. **Meals** Breakfast 80F. **Restaurant** Menus 130-350F, also
à la carte. Specialties: Fricassée de langoustines aux girolles, agneau de prés-salés
au jus de truffes, feuillantine de pommes au caramel de cidre. **Credit cards** Amex,
Visa, Eurocard and MasterCard. **Pets** Dogs allowed (+100F). **Facilities** Parking,
garage. **Nearby** Epaves museum in Commes, Port-en-Bessin, cathedral of Bayeux
– 27-hole Omaha Beach golf course. **Open** Feb 29 – Nov 30.

Very near Port–en–Bessin, Arromanches and Omaha Beaches,
this is an elegant mansion surrounded by a beautifully kept
park. The interior resembles a private home which has been
furnished to please the eye as well as to provide the comfort you
crave after a tiring drive. You will find a succession of very pretty,
bright rooms which are generously decorated with light fabrics,
collections of paintings (old seals, architectural drawings) and
handsome objects. The bedrooms, with efficient soundproofing,
are furnished in the same tasteful style; bathrooms are luxurious.
All the windows look out on the lawn and flowers.

How to get there *(Map 7): 8km north of Bayeux via D6, in the towards of*
Port-en-Bessin.

Hôtel l'Ecrin ★★★

19, rue Eugène–Boudin
14602 Honfleur (Calvados)
Tel. (0)2★ 31.14.43.45 – Fax (0)2★ 31.89.24.41 – Mme Blais

Rooms 22 with telephone, bath or shower, WC, TV and minibar. **Price** Double 370-900F, suite 950F. **Meals** Breakfast 50F, served 8:00-11:00. No restaurant. **Credit cards** All major. **Pets** Dogs not allowed. **Facilities** Sauna (65F), parking. **Nearby** Old dock, church of Sainte-Catherine, Eugène Boudin museum in Honfleur, Deauville, Trouville – 27-hole New-Golf, 18- and 9-hole Saint-Gatien golf courses in Deauville. **Open** All year.

You can truly relax in the courtyard and lovely gardens of this elegant Napoleon III mansion. Although in the center of the town, the hotel is out of the way of the hordes of tourists who head for Honfleur when summer begins. The ground floor rooms still retain their original layout and much of the style of their period. In the Proustian lounge the gilt of the plasterwork echoes the gilt on the armchairs, and the delicate tints of the numerous paintings are repeated in the silks, the curtains and the carpets; there's even an adjoining conservatory. The bedrooms are a little overdone (number 2 is extraordinary) but very comfortable. Avoid the ones on the *deuxième étage* but do not reject the ones in the front pavilions where the cheaper rooms are not necessarily the least pleasant. Breakfast is served in a room full of paintings, many in the style of the school of Honfleur, or in the glassed-in veranda which opens onto the pretty garden. For restaurants we recommend: *La Lieutenance* and *La Taverne de la mer* for fish and shellfish and *L'Assiette Gourmande*.

How to get there *(Map 8): 97km west of Rouen via A13, Beuzeville exit, then D22(in the town center).*

343

Auberge Saint-Christophe ★★

14690 Pont-d'Ouilly (Calvados)
Tel. (0)2★ 31.69.81.23 - Fax (0)2★ 31.69.26.58
M. Lecoeur

Rooms 7 with telephone, bath or shower, WC and TV. **Price** Double 270F. **Meals** Breakfast 40F, served 8:00-9:30; half board 285F, full board 390F (per pers., 2 days min.). **Restaurant** Service 12:00-13:30, 19:30-21:00; menus 95-250F, also à la carte. Specialties: Nonnettes de saumon au beurre de cidre, salade tiède de queues de langoustines, crème brûlée. **Credit cards** Amex, Visa, Eurocard and MasterCard. **Pets** Dogs allowed (+25F). **Facilities** Parking. **Nearby** Castle of Falaise, 'La Suisse Normande', Thury-Harcourt, Clécy (châteaux of La Pommeraye and Placy), Oëtre rock, gorges of Saint-Aubert, château de Pontécoulant – 18-hole Clécy-Cantelou golf course. **Open** All year, except Nov 1 holidays and Feb 2– Mar 13 (closed Sunday evening and Monday).

This hotel is in an elegant house in the Suisse Normande. Its interior has been carefully designed to provide every comfort. Plants and flowers adorn every corner. There is a small lounge, a breakfast room which becomes a bar in the evening, and many places to sit, talk and read. The bedrooms are small but charming and have recently been renovated in a modern style. They look out over peaceful gardens, but the soundproofing in the hotel could be better. During the summer, lunch can be enjoyed on the terrace. The cuisine is excellent and the young owners will make you feel at home.

How to get there *(Map 7): 26km south of Caen via D562 towards Flers, or N158 towards Falaise, then D1; 1.5km from Pont-d'Ouilly via D23 towards Thury-Harcourt.*

La Chaîne d'Or ★★★

27, rue Grande
27700 Petit Andelys (Eure)
Tel. (0)2★ 32.54.00.31 – Fax (0)2★ 32.54.05.68 – M. and Mme Foucault

Rooms 10 with telephone, bath or shower, WC and TV. **Price** Single and double 395-740F. **Meals** Breakfast 65F, served 8:00-9:30. **Restaurant** Closed Sunday evening and Monday. Service 12:00-14:00, 19:30-21:30; menus 140-298F, also à la carte. Specialties: Raviolis de langoustines à la crème d'étrilles, caille farcie de foies de volailles et amandes fraîches, sorbet à l'estragon, plaisir au chocolat chaud et sirop de jasmin. **Credit cards** Amex, Visa, Eurocard and MasterCard. **Pets** Dogs not allowed. **Facilities** Parking. **Nearby** Church of Notre-Dame and Château Gaillard in Les Andelys, Giverny – 18-hole Vaudreuil golf course. **Open** Feb 1 – Dec 31.

This friendly hostelry was founded in 1751. From the wing in the inner courtyard there is a stunning view of the Seine. Most of the bedrooms are large and light. The ones overlooking the river have just been entirely refurbished; very elegant and refined, they have gained in comfort what they have lost in traditional style. The rooms looking out over the church or the courtyard have period furniture, rugs and engravings; foreign guests prefer them for their "old France" atmosphere. The breakfast room has a high ceiling with polished beams, and is sometimes used in the evening as a lounge. In the dining room, half timbering, paintings and flowers combine to create a warm and cozy ambience, while the pink tablecloths compliment the silvery green of the Seine. The traditional cuisine is delicious.

How to get there *(Map 8): 92km northwest of Paris via A13, Gaillon exit, then D316.*

Relais Moulin de Balisne **

Baline
27130 Verneuil-sur-Avre (Eure)
Tel. (0)2★ 32.32.03.48 - Fax (0)2★ 32.60.11.22 - M. Gastaldi

Rooms 10 and 2 suites with telephone, bath, WC, 10 with TV and minibar. **Price** Double 350-450F. **Meals** Breakfast 50F, served 8:00-11:00; half board 380F, full board 480F (per pers., 2 days min.). **Restaurant** Closed Monday noon in winter. Service 12:00-15:00, 19:30-22:00; menus 150-280F, also à la carte. Specialties: Duo de sole et langouste, cassolette d'escargots et gambas aux petits lardons, œuf d'autruche farci. **Credit cards** All major. **Pets** Dogs allowed. **Facilities** Lake and river fishing, supervised parking. **Nearby** Senonches forest, châteaux de Beauménil and d'Anet – 9-hole golf course in Coulonges. **Open** All year.

When you first see this hotel you may worry about its proximity to the road, but as soon as you enter, you will be reassured by the beautifully quiet surroundings. The only sound is that of the waters converging here from the Rivers Avre and Iton. The Moulin is surrounded by 25-acres of land with a small lake; boats are available for fishing enthusiasts. The bar dining room is furnished with antiques, Persian tablecloths and a splendid fireplace. The bedrooms are just as appealing. Some of them in the attic seem to be "perched in the trees." You will be warmly welcomed at the Relais and its proximity to Paris makes it an appealing place to stay.

How to get there *(Map 8): 75km west of Paris via Autoroute-Ouest (in the towards of Dreux), Bois d'Arcy exit, then N12 to Dreux, Alençon. 45km southwest of Evreux via N154 to Nonancourt, then N12 toward Verneuil-sur-Avre.*

Château de la Rapée ★★★

27140 Bazincourt-sur-Epte (Eure)
Tel. (0)2★ 32.55.11.61 - Fax (0)2★ 32.55.95.65
M. Bergeron

Rooms 14 with telephone, bath or shower, WC and 8 with TV. **Price** Single and double 410-510F, suite 680F. **Meals** Breakfast 50F, served 8:00-10:00; half board 700F, full board 1000F (per 2 pers., 3 days min.). **Restaurant** Service 12:30-14:00, 19:30-21:00; menus 160-215F, also à la carte. Specialties: Tarte légère au livarot, douillons, anguille en matelote au cidre brut. **Credit cards** All major. **Pets** Dogs not allowed. **Facilities** Parking. **Nearby** Châteaux of Harcourt and Gisors, A.G. Poulain museum in Vernon and Nicolas-Poussin in Andelys, Monet museum in Giverny – 18-hole Bertichère Golf Course. **Open** All year except Feb 1 – 24 and Aug 16 – 31.

This 19th-century Norman mansion is less than an hour from Paris and a few kilometers from Gisors. Lost in the midst of woods and fields, with a stud farm its only neighbor, it is ideal for those who love tranquillity in a beautiful setting. The bedrooms are comfortable (the largest are on the *premier étage* and number 15 has a terrace) and there are two dining rooms: one for summer and another with a large fireplace for the winter months. M. Bergeron is a good cook and Mme will make you feel like one of the family. Tables in the garden allow you to have breakfast and drinks there, weather permitting.

How to get there *(Map 9): 70km northwest of Paris via A15, Pontoise exit, then D915 to Gisors. 4km north of Gisors via D915.*

Auberge de l'Abbaye ★★★

27800 Le Bec-Hellouin (Eure)
Tel. (0)2★ 32.44.86.02 – Fax (0)2★ 32.46.32.23
Mme Sergent

Rooms 10 with telephone, bath and WC. **Price** Double 380-420F, suite 580F. **Meals** Breakfast 40F, served from 8:30; half board 380-400F. **Restaurant** Service 12:15-14:30, 19:15-21:30; menus 130-250F, also à la carte. Specialties: Cassolette de homard, lapin au cidre, ris de veau aux morilles, tarte aux pommes. **Credit cards** Visa, Eurocard and MasterCard. **Pets** Dogs allowed. **Facilities** Parking. **Nearby** In Bec-Hellouin: abbey, Piano museum; châteaux of Harcourt and of Champ-de-Bataille; insect collection at the Canel museum in Pont-Audemer – 18-hole Champ-de-Bataille golf course in Neubourg. **Open** All year (closed Monday evening and Tuesday in low season).

This hotel is in an 18th-century building close to the abbey and in the center of a very pretty village. There is an interior courtyard blooming with flowers, a small terrace on the front where you can enjoy the fresh air and watch the life of the village square. The bedrooms are rustic, small, quite comfortable and quiet, with complete bathroom facilities. We can recommend only those on the *premier étage* (thus avoiding numbers 9, 10 and 11). The dining room is decorated in the same rustic style. Guests enjoy good cuisine here but we nevertheless regretted that the fireplace was not lit in winter. In good weather, several tables are set out in the courtyard. This is a simple, genuine auberge where you will be courteously welcomed.

How to get there *(Map 8): 40km southwest of Rouen via A13, number 24 Maison Brulée exit, in the towards of Alençon/Le Mans then N138 toward Bec-Hellouin.*

La Ferme de Cocherel

Route de la vallée d'Eure
Cocherel 27120 Paçy-sur-Eure (Eure)
Tel. (0)2★ 32.36.68.27 - Fax (0)2★ 32.26.28.18 - M. and Mme Delton

Rooms 3, 1 with bath, 2 with shower and WC. **Price** Double 350-400F **Meals** Breakfast incl. **Restaurant** Closed Tuesday and Wednesday. Service 12:00-14:00, 19:30-21:15; menu 195F, also à la carte. Specialties: Flan de foie gras à la crème de calvados, chausson de homard crème safranée, rognons de veau au cassis et au cidre. **Credit cards** All major. **Pets** Dogs allowed **Facilities** Parking. **Nearby** Historique village of Cocherel, château of Bizy, Monet museum in Giverny, château of Anet – 18-hole Vaudreuil golf course. **Open** All year except in Jan, 1 week in Sept (closed Tuesday and Wednesday).

There is only a small country road between the Ferme de Cocherel and the peaceful Eure River. The Ferme consists of several picturesque Norman houses with old tile roofs. The largest is reserved for the acclaimed gastronomic restaurant, where the tables are set in a room decorated like an elegant winter garden. You will enjoy succulent meals made with fresh products bought in the local market or from nearby farms. The three bedrooms, opening onto a carefully tended flower garden, are on the ground floor in separate houses; they are decorated with several pieces of rustic or lacquered cane furniture, floral fabrics and a few engravings. The breakfasts are excellent. This is truly a beautiful country inn, located in the peaceful hamlet where Bertrand Du Guesclin won a historic victory over Anglo–Navarre troops in 1364.

How to get there *(Map 8): 7km northwest of Pacy-sur-Eure via D836, towards Louviers. On A 13, number 16 exit towards Vernon, then Cocherel.*

Le Moulin de Connelles ★★★★

40, route d'Amfreville-sur-les-Monts
27430 Connelles (Eure)
Tel. (0)2★ 32.59.53.33 – Fax (0)2★ 32. 59 21 83 – M. and Mme Petiteau

Rooms 7 and 6 suites with telephone, bath, WC, TV and minibar. **Price** Single and double 600-800F, suite 800-950F. **Meals** Breakfast 60F, served 7:30-10:30. **Restaurant** Closed Sunday evening and Monday. Service 12:00-14:30, 19:30-21:00; menus 135-280F (child 70F), also à la carte. Specialties: Foie de canard au vieux calvados, saumon soufflé en portefeuille, rognons de veau sauce Meaux, délice noix de coco et chocolat chaud. **Credit cards** All major. **Pets** Dogs allowed. **Facilities** Heated swimming pool, tennis, Mountain bikes, boad, parking. **Nearby** Centre de loisirs Lery Poses (water skiing, golf, sailing...), church of Notre-Dame in Louviers; cathedral of Rouen; Monet museum in Giverny – 18-hole Vaudreuil golf course. **Open** All year except Jan (closed Sunday evening and Monday Oct – May).

A beautiful lawn and flower gardens on the banks of the Seine surround the Moulin de Connelles, an old mill which was converted into a lovely home and, then, into a luxurious hotel. The Moulin is extremely comfortable, with thick carpets, a handsome decor of soft green and gold–yellow tones, coordinated fabrics, and superb bathrooms. Many bedrooms and the restaurant look out on an enchanting river scene, where the Seine winds in and out of its course and finally forms several lush green islands. It's a lovely place for strolling or having a drink before dinner, and the hotel will happily lend you a boat to explore it all up close, including the resident moorhens.

How to get there *(Map 1 and 8): 30km south of Rouen via A13, exit Louviers. 100km from Paris.*

Château de Brécourt ★★★★

Douains - 27120 Pacy-sur-Eure (Eure)
Tel. (0)2★ 32.52.40.50 - Fax (0)2★ 32.52.69.65
M. Savry and Mme Langlais

Rooms 29 with telephone, bath, shower and WC. **Price** Single 410-495F, double 670-1040F, suite 1155-1680F. **Meals** Breakfast 69F, served 6:30-12:00; half board 490-1100F, full board 710-1300F. **Restaurant** Service 12:00-14:00, 19:30-21:30; menus 225-350F, also à la carte. Specialties: Vinaigrette de langoustines royales, galette de riz de basmati au curry, dos de bar cuit à la vapeur aux belles de Fontenay safranées, pigeonneau de la ferme roti au gingembre pommes dauphine. **Credit cards** All major. **Pets** Dogs allowed (+55F). **Facilities** Swimming pool, whirlpool, tennis, parking. **Nearby** A.G. Poulain museum and church of Notre-Dame in Vernon, château de Gaillon, Monet museum in Giverny – 9-hole golf course in Gaillon. **Open** All year.

The Château de Brécourt is an ideal place for a weekend; it is a Louis XIII building only 60km from Paris on the borders of Normandy. The lovely 17th-century moated château has a 55-acre park where it is a pleasure to stroll at any time of the year. More active guests will enjoy the swimming pool and tennis courts. There are two dining rooms, both with a beautiful view of the woods and the countryside and both with a menu featuring good Normandy specialties. The decor is in keeping with the elegant and comfortable atmosphere of the château.

How to get there (Map 8): 21km east of Evreux via N13, Pacy-sur-Eure exit, then D181 and D533. 70km west of Paris via A13, number 16 Vernon exit.

Auberge du Vieux Puits ★★

6, rue Notre-Dame-du-Pré
27500 Pont-Audemer (Eure)
Tel. (0)2★ 32.41.01.48 - Fax (0)2★ 32.42.37.28 - M. and Mme Foltz

Rooms 12 with telephone, bath or shower, 10 with WC and 6 with TV - 2 wheelchair access. **Price** Single 170-370F, double 270-420F. **Meals** Breakfast 44F, served 8:00-9:30. **Restaurant** Service 12:00-14:00, 19:30-21:00; menus 198F (weekday lunch only)-300F, also à la carte. Specialties: Canard aux griottes, truite 'Bovary'. **Credit cards** Visa, Eurocard and MasterCard. **Pets** Dogs not allowed. **Facilities** Parking. **Nearby** Insect collection in the Canel museum in Pont-Audemer, Risle valley, bridge of Normandie, abbey of Le Bec-Hollouin – 18-hole Champ-de-Bataille golf course in Neubourg. **Open** Jan 27 – Dec 16 (closed Monday evening and Tuesday in low season).

This inn in Pont-Audemer is easily accessible by the highway and is perfect for travelers who want to get aquainted with Normandy. The buildings, in typical 17th-century Norman timbered style, surround a flower garden, with an old well and two impressive willows, where you can have cocktails, coffee, and excellent afternoon snacks in summer. Inside, there are several cozy little lounges where you can have tea or read by the fireplace. The dining room is slightly larger and is decorated with antique china and gleaming copper. The savory cuisine is innovative yet based on traditional Norman recipes. You can choose between the simple, rustic, charming bedrooms in the old houses, or the modern comfort of those in another building, which is built in the same style.

How to get there (Map 1 and 8): 52km west of Rouen via A13, Pont-Audemer exit, then D139 and N182 (300m from the town center).

Hostellerie du Moulin Fourest

27300 Saint-Aubin-le-Vertueux (Eure)
Tel. (0)2★ 32.43.19.95 - Fax (0)2★ 32.45.55.50
M. and Mme Deduit

Rooms 8 with telephone, shower and WC. **Price** Double 235F. **Meals** Breakfast 41F, served 7:30-9:30. **Restaurant** Service 12:00-14:00, 19:30-21:30; menus 98-270F, also à la carte. Specialties: Lapereau à la crème camembert, escalope de foie gras chaud sur pain d'épice, grand dessert Gustave Chauvel. **Credit cards** Amex, Visa, Eurocard and MasterCard. **Pets** Dogs allowed (+51F). **Facilities** Parking. **Nearby** Lisieux, Bernay – 18-hole Champ-de-Bataille golf course. **Open** All year (closed Sunday evening and Monday May 1 – Aug 31).

The small river flowing past the foot of the mill winds in and out, creating small spurs of land perfect for fishing or simply relaxing. Inside the hotel the rustic decor of the bar and the dining room combines beautiful pieces of furniture, ancient beams and paintings to create a warm and cozy atmosphere. François Deduit, who is both the chef and the owner of the hotel, is a promising young cook, and his traditional cuisine has gained him a solid reputation throughout the region. The comfortable bedrooms command beautiful views of the surrounding countryside. Their modern furnishings, however, are a disappointment after the charm and authenticity of the period furniture in the reception rooms and on the landings. In the spring, parasols are set up on a neat and flowery terrace which becomes the ideal setting for breakfast and dinner, enhanced by the distant babble of water gushing through the floodgates.

How to get there *(Map 8): 3km south of Bernay via D833.*

Le Manoir des Saules

2, place Saint-Martin
27370 La Saussaye (Eure)
Tel. (0)2★ 35.87 25 65 - Fax (0)2★ 35 87 49 39 - M. Monnaie-Metot

Rooms 4, 2 apartements with telephone, 1 with bath, 3 with shower, WC and TV - 1 for disabled persons. **Price** Double 450-650F, apart. 850-1150F. **Meals** Breakfast 65F. **Restaurant** Closed Sunday evening and Monday. Service 12:00-14:00, 20:00-21:30; menu 175-350F, also à la carte. Specialties: Foie gras, ragoût de homard frais, fish. **Credit cards** Amex, Visa, Eurocard and MasterCard **Pets** Dogs allowed. **Meals** Parking. **Nearby** Château of Champ-de-Bataille, château and arboretum of Harcourt, collégiale de La Saussaye, Abbey of Bec-Hellouin – 18-hole Champ-de-Bataille golf course. **Open** All year (closed Sunday evening and Monday except public holidays).

With its half-timbering, turrets and recessed walls, the Manoir is as Norman as they come. The associates who run it have named the bedrooms after their grandmothers: Marie, Germaine, Albertine and Joséphine (We especially like the first three). These are very delightful rooms decorated with a mixture of antiques and Louis XV copies, amusing old objects and heavy drapes which are coordinated with silky bedspreads. All the rooms are beautifully kept, including the bathrooms. A lovely lounge in blue and cream colors is an intimte, cozy place for a drink. Adjacent to it, the dining room with its smartly set tables serves excellent cuisine which is based on fresh, seasonal products. In charming weather, you can of course have meals outside on the terrace amidst the flowers. You will always receive very friendly and attentive service.

How to get there (Map 8): South of Rouen, 4km from Elbeuf via D840, towards Le Neubourg. On A13, Pont-de-l'Arche exit.

Hôtel du Golf ★★

Golf du Vaudreuil
27100 Le Vaudreuil (Eure)
Tel. (0)2★ 32.59.02.94 - Fax (0)2★ 32.59.67.39 - Mme Launay

Rooms 20 with telephone, bath or shower, 17 with WC and TV, 10 with minibar.
Price Single 160-225F, double 225-350F. **Meals** Breakfast 30-45F, served 7:00-
11:00. No restaurant. **Credit cards** Amex, Visa, Eurocard and MasterCard. **Pets** Dogs
allowed (+20F). **Facilities** Parking, 18-hole golf course. **Nearby** Rouen, Château
Gaillard. **Open** All year.

The Château de Vaudreuil was destroyed during the Revolution
and all that remains of it are two buildings beside an avenue
that leads nowhere. The château's large park is now a golf course
and one of the buildings is a hotel. It is quiet here, and you can
enjoy views over the greens from the breakfast room and the living
room. The bedrooms, with big windows and almond-green
wallpaper, are simply furnished but pleasant. The rooms on the
premier étage are small but those on the second are considerably
larger. The decor is modern but elegant. There is no restaurant at
the hotel but golfers can eat at the golf club.

*How to get there (Map 8): 15km southeast of Rouen via A13, exit 18 or
19; then D77 to the entrance of Le Vaudreuil.*

Hôtel du Château d'Agneaux ★★★

Avenue Sainte-Marie
50180 Saint-Lô – Agneaux (Manche)
Tel. (0)2★ 33.57.65.88 – Fax (0)2★ 33.56.59.21 – M. and Mme Groult

Rooms 12 with shower, WC, TV and 10 with minibar. **Price** Double 370-700F, suite 850F. **Meals** Breakfast 57-67F. **Restaurant** Service 19:30-21:00; menus 133-182F, 326F, also à la carte. Specialties: Fish and the chef's desserts. **Pets** Dogs allowed (+50F). **Facilities** Tennis (30F), sauna (80F), parking. **Nearby** Church and museum in Saint-Lô, château de Torigni-sur-Vire – 9-hole golf course in Courtainville. **Open** All year.

Leaving the ugly suburbs of Saint-Lô, you'll find that the Château d'Agneaux has escaped the town planners. A narrow gravel lane leads away from the main road to the old chapel, the château and the watchtower which look out over the unspoiled and peaceful valley, with nothing in view but trees and the River Vire flowing gently through the green countryside. M. and Mme Groult owned a farmhouse inn for many years, and now Agneaux is their dream come true; they have refurbished it with love. The bedrooms are very comfortable and prettily though not overwhelmingly decorated, with some four-poster beds and lovely parquet floors. Room 4, with it's five windows, is well-lit all day.

How to get there *(Map 7): 1.5km west of Saint-Lô via D900.*

Hôtel Le Conquérant ★★

16/18 rue Saint-Thomas-Becket
50760 Barfleur (Manche)
Tel. (0)2★ 33.54.00.82 - Fax (0)2★ 33. 54 65 25 - Mme Delomenède

Rooms 16 with telephone, 11 with bath or shower, 5 with cabinet de toilette, 10 with WC and TV. **Price** Double 200-360F. **Meals** Breakfast 25-45F, served 8:00-10:00. **Crèperie** Service 19:00-21:00; menus 80-100F, also à la carte. Specialties: Galette camembert sur beurre d'escargot, galette manchotte, crêpe Le Conquérant. **Credit cards** Visa, Eurocard and MasterCard. **Pets** Dogs not allowed. **Facilities** Parking (30F). **Nearby** Ile Tatihon, Valognes, Thomas-Henry museum in Cherbourg – 9-hole golf course in Fontenay-en-Cotentin. **Open** Feb 1 – Nov 14.

If you are one of the surprisingly few tourists who appreciate the beauty of this splendid region, the Conquérant will be an ideal place for you to stay. Located at the road's edge, this very simple hotel reveals a charming garden behind its walls, where there is direct access to the port. As the modern conveniences of its rooms are variable, we recommend numbers 9, 10, 11, 16 and 17. (The latter has a vast terrace overlooking the garden.) The overall decoration is unremarkable but the prices are reasonable, the people are very friendly, and the breakfasts are delicious. (This is also a very good *crêperie*). From the sea, you can admire the lovely Norman farms dotted with manor houses along the coast between Querqueville and "Jobourg's Nose." The charming Conquérant is, of course, named after William the Conqueror.

How to get there *(Map 7): 30km east of Cherbourg via D901.*

Manoir de Roche Torin ★★★

50220 Courtils (Manche)
Tel. (0)2★ 33.70.96.55 – Fax (0)2★ 33.48.35.20
Mme Barraux

Rooms 12 with telephone, bath or shower, WC, TV, 1 with whirlpool bath and 3 with minibar. **Price** Single and double 450-800F, suite 850F. **Meals** Breakfast 55F, served 8:00-10:30. **Restaurant** Service 12:00-13:00, 19:15-21:00 (closed Monday and Tuesday noon), menus 100-250F, also à la carte. Specialties: Agneau de pré salé, homard de Chaussey grillé. **Credit cards** All major. **Pets** Dogs allowed (+42F). **Facilities** Parking. **Nearby** Jardin des Plantes in Avranches, Mont Saint-Michel. **Open** March 15 – Nov 15.

This turn of the century gentleman's residence combines old and contemporary styles. Flowered fabrics brighten the lounge, and in the dining room there is a splendid fireplace where the chef grills lobsters, beef and salt-meadow lamb. The bedrooms reflect the style of the rest of the house, mixing modern furniture with cane chairs and period pieces. They are all very comfortable. The terrace and garden are very pleasant and in good weather a bar and meal service is provided there. Between the hotel, its lovely 5-acre park and Mont Saint-Michel, which can be seen in the distance, there is nothing but fields crossed by small inlets and dotted with sheep.

How to get there *(Map 7): 12km southwest of Avranches via N175, then towards Mont Saint-Michel via D43.*

Auberge de la Sélune ★★

2, rue Saint-Germain
50220 Ducey (Manche)
Tel. (0)2★ 33.48.53.62 - Fax (0)2★ 33.48.90.30 - M. Girres

Rooms 19 with telephone, bath and WC. **Price** Double 270-295F. **Meals** Breakfast 38F, served 7:30-9:30; half board 300-312F (obligatory in July and Aug), full board 425-435F (per pers., 3 days min.). **Restaurant** Service 12:00-14:00, 19:00-21:00; menus 80-210F, also à la carte. Specialties: Pie au crabe, paupiettes de saumon au poiré, rable de lapereau farci au vinaigre de cidre. **Credit cards** Visa, Eurocard and MasterCard. **Pets** Dogs not allowed. **Facilities** Parking. **Nearby** Jardin des Plantes in Avranches, Mont Saint-Michel. **Open** All year.

The Auberge de la Sélune is a former almshouse of spacious proportions. It is set in the country on the edge of the village in a large garden by the River Sélune (where you might be lucky enough to catch a salmon). The hotel has vast rooms with high ceilings. Well kept, decorated with simple rattan furniture and pretty fabrics. The small bedrooms are pleasant. A number of them afford a tranquil view over the river and the flower garden, while on the side there is a small pavillion which is practically on the riverbank (several of the bedrooms here give directly onto the garden.) Several other rooms look out over the small street, but they are the last to be rented. The restaurant has been enlarged, with the choice of materials and colors giving a half-classic, half-contemporary result; the principal decorative element is provided by wide bay windows opening onto the terrace (where dinner is served in summer) and the garden. The Auberge offers family-style cuisine at reasonable prices and the hospitality is pleasant.

How to get there *(Map 7): 10km southeast of Avranches via N175, then N176 towards Saint-Hilaire-du-Harcouët (follow signs as you enter Ducey).*

Hôtel des Bains ★★★
50400 Granville (Manche)
Tel. (0)2★ 33.50.17.31. - Fax (0)2★ 33 50 89 22
Mme Robbe

Rooms 47 with telephone, 32 with bath, with 6 whirlpool bath, 15 with shower, WC and TV. **Price** Single and double 250-650F, suite 850F. **Meals** Breakfast 40F, served 7:00-10:00; half board 370F (per pers., 3 days min.). **Restaurant** Service 19:30-22:00; menu 98-188F. **Credit cards** Amex, Visa, Eurocard and MasterCard. **Pets** Dogs allowed. **Facilities** Parking. **Nearby** Mont Saint-Michel, îles anglo-normandes, Avranches, La Lucerne abbey, cathedral of Coutances – 9-hole and 18-hole Bréhal golf course. **Open** Mar – Dec.

This town hotel dramatically overlooks the English Channel, very near a long quay where you can take a lovely walk and watch the waves crash onto the shore. The interior has just been very elegantly and imaginatively renovated. The bedrooms are bright and cheerful and decorated with contemporary furniture and fabrics. On the ground floor, there is a small tea room next to the dining room, which also has a corner lounge. The traditionally Norman cuisine, featuring lots of fresh fish and local cheeses, is succulent and the service is efficient and courteous. The tables are well spaced, and here too, the decoration is attractive. Ask for a room facing the sea, for a view of spectacular sunsets. Service with a smile adds a final positive note to this excellent hotel.

How to get there (Map 6): 25km north of Avranches via D973.

Château de la Roque

50180 Hébécrevon (Manche)
Tel. (0)2★ 33.57.33.20 – Fax (0)2★ 33.57.51.20
M. and Mme Delisle

Rooms 15 with telephone, bath or shower, WC and TV - Wheelchair access.
Price Single 240F, double 330F, suite 520F. **Meals** Breakfast incl.; half board 520F
(per 2 pers., 3 days min.). **Restaurant** Evening meals. Service 20:00; menus 95F
(wine incl.). Specialties: Regional cuisine. **Credit cards** All major. **Pets** Dogs allowed.
Facilities Bicycle rentals, fishing, hunting, tennis, parking. **Nearby** Church and
museum (Tenture des Amours de Gombault and Macé) in Saint-Lô, château of Torigni-
sur-Vire – 9-hole golf course in Couttainville. **Open** All year.

In the midst of the gentle Norman countryside, this very pretty
château has been opened to guests by Raymond Delisle of cycle
racing fame. It's a great success: All the rooms are comfortable and
beautiful, with special attention paid to the choice of fabrics, which
are complemented by antique furniture. Bread is made every day
in an old oven here; it is served at the breakfasts which guests enjoy
at a large communal table in the charming dining room. Meals are
by reservation.

How to get there *(Map 7): 6km northwest of Saint-Lô. Before Saint-Lô,
take D972, towards Coutances, to Saint-Gilles, then towards Pont Hébert
(D77) for 3km.*

Hôtel de France et des Fuchsias ★★
20, rue du Maréchal-Foch
50550 Saint-Vaast-la-Hougue (Manche)
Tel. (0)2★ 33.54.42.26 - Fax (0)2★ 33.43.46.79 - M. and Mme Brix

Rooms 33 and 1 suite with telephone, 29 with bath or shower, WC and TV. **Price** 290-400F. **Meals** Breakfast 42F, served 8:00-10:30; half board 290-345F, full board 365-410F (per pers., 3 days min.). **Restaurant** Closed Monday except in June – mid. Sept; Tuesday lunchtime Nov – end March. Service 12:00-14:00, 19:00-21:15; menus 76-250F, also à la carte. Specialties: Choucroute de la mer au beurre blanc, ravioles de homard et son coulis, salade tiède de queues de langoustines. **Credit cards** All major. **Pets** Dogs allowed (+40F). **Facilities** Bicycle rental. **Nearby** Ile Tatihon, Valognes, Barfleur, Thomas Henry museum in Cherbourg – 9-hole golf course in Fontenay-en-Cotentin. **Open** Mar – Jan 5 (closed Monday in low season).

At Saint Vaast-la-Hougue on the eastern side of the Cotentin Peninsula the climate is so mild that mimosas flourish. The bedrooms in this old coachman's inn are simple but elegant, with muted colors and handsome furniture (Room 14 is a bit small, however). Those at the back of the garden, in the *Les Feuillantines* house, are decorated in the same spirit and most are more spacious. The last two weeks of August, chamber-music concerts are given in the pleasant small lounge (and the garden). They are very popular with guests, who attend them at no charge. Meals are served on a veranda opening onto the garden and feature seafood along with produce from the nearby farm at Quettehou. In addition, this beautiful hotel is in a part of Normandy where the climate is especially clement more, near a small fishing port, a sandy beach, and hedgerows and woods.

How to get there *(Map 7): 37km southeast of Cherbourg via N13 to Valognes, then D902 and D1 to Saint-Vaast-la-Hougue (it's in the town center).*

La Verte Campagne ★★
50660 Trelly (Manche)
Tel. (0)2★ 33.47.65.33 - Fax (0)2★ 33.47.38.03
M. and Mme Bernou

Rooms 7 (4 with bath and 3 with WC). **Price** Single 150F, double 220-380F. **Meals** Breakfast 35F, served 8:30-10:00; half board +170F, full board +270F (per pers., 3 days min.). **Restaurant** Closed Monday in low season. Service 12:30-14:00, 19:30-21:00; menus 140-350F, also à la carte. Specialties: Filet de canette aux épices et aux figues, vinaigrette tiède de rougets aux artichauds, moelleux au chocolat et mousse chicorée. **Credit cards** Visa, Eurocard and MasterCard. **Pets** Dogs not allowed. **Facilities** Parking. **Nearby** Mont Saint-Michel, valley of the Vire (G.R. 221) – 18-hole Granville golf course in Bréhal. **Open** Feb 1 – Dec 1 and Dec 7 – Jan 6 (closed Sunday evening and Monday in low season).

This hotel is in an authentic Normandy farmhouse of the 18th-century and, as it is in the heart of wooded countryside, it deserves its name: "Green Countryside." This is not a large place but its size gives it an intimate atmosphere. The stone walls, beams and furniture, antique ceramics and copperware create an ambience which is rustic yet civilized, comfortable and welcoming. All the bedrooms are different, but whether large or small they are furnished with an eye to harmony and comfort. There is an air of English elegance in the delightful fabrics used and the charming furniture. When they took over the hotel, M. and Mme Bernou preserved the charming features which we found so attractive. And they have added a big plus: gastronomy. The *Verte Campagne* has become a leading restaurant in the area.

How to get there *(Map 7): 42km southwest of Saint-Lô via D972 to Coutances, then D971 towards Bréhal to Quettreville-sur-Sienne, then D35 and D49.*

Moulin de Villeray ★★★★

61110 Condeau (Orne)
Tel. (0)2★ 33.73.30.22 - Fax (0)2★ 33.73.38.28
M. Eelsen

Rooms 16 and 2 apartments with telephone, bath or shower, WC, TV and minibar. **Price** Single and double 390-950F; suite 850-1250F. **Meals** Breakfast 65F; half board 960-1150F. **Restaurant** Service 12:00-14:00, 19:00-22:00; menus 145-330F, also à la carte. Specialties: Regional cuisine. **Credit cards** All major. **Pets** Dogs allowed (+50F). **Facilities** Swimming pool, parking. **Nearby** Hills of the Perche (about 150km), museum of the philosopher Alain in Mortagne-au-Perche – 18-hole Perche golf course. **Open** All year.

The Moulin de Villeray is an old mill on the banks of the peaceful River Huisne in a charming hamlet of the Perche region. It is surrounded by a large and carefully tended park with lovely flower gardens. The bedrooms in two newly added, charming houses are individually decorated with terra-cotta floors, thick carpets, stunning cotton fabrics, and glossy pine furniture. In the mill itself, the rooms are more classic but have equally modern amenities; it's now their turn to be redecorated. There is a pleasant lounge off the terrace, and a delightfully rustic dining room built around the large paddle wheel of the mill. The regional cuisine is delicious and the young owners are especially pleasant and attentive.

How to get there *(Map 8): 9km north of Nogent-le-Rotrou; on A11, Chartes-Est exit, Luigny or La Ferté-Bernard.*

Manoir du Lys ★★★

La Croix Gauthier
61140 Bagnoles-de-l'Orne (Orne)
Tel. (0)2★ 33.37.80.69 – Fax (0)2★ 33.30.05.80 – M. and Mme Quinton

Rooms 23 with telephone, bath or shower, WC, TV and minibar; elevator - Wheelchair access. **Price** Single and double 300-650F, suite 650-1000F. **Meals** Breakfast 55F; half board 350-550F, full board 500-680F (per pers., 3 days min.). **Restaurant** Service 12:30-14:30, 19:30-21:30; menus 130-350F, also à la carte. Specialties: Raviolis de grenouilles, duo de boudin, carré d'agneau de pré-salé. **Credit cards** All major. **Pets** Dogs allowed (+35F). **Facilities** Tennis, golf (3 greens), parking. **Nearby** Andaine forest, Bonvouloir lighthouse, château de Carrouges, Sées cathedral – 9-hole golf course in Bagnoles-de-l'Orne. **Open** Mar 1 – Jan 6 (closed Sunday and Monday Mar 1 – Easter and Nov 1 – Jan 6).

Lying in the midst of the Andaine Forest very near the Bagnoles-de-l'Orne spa, the Manoir du Lys is beautifully quiet. The bedrooms are light and very well equipped. Special mention should be made of the most recent, which are large and feature antiqued or lacquered furniture, prettily colored fabrics and magnificent bathrooms. They are perfectly soundproofed. Some have terraces and those under the mansard eaves have a lovely view of the orchard. Throughout the hotel, you will find contemporary paintings, which add to the charm. Meals are occasionally served in the lovely garden, or you might prefer to dine in the very pretty dining room with a panoramic view. M. Quinton and his son Franck preside over the excellent Norman cuisine.

How to get there *(Map 7): 53km west of Alençon via N12 to Pré-au-Pail, then N176 and D916.*

Château du Landel ★★★

76220 Bézancourt (Seine-Maritime)
Tel. (0)2★ 35.90.16.01 - Fax (0)2★ 35.90 62 47
M. Cardon

Rooms 17 with telephone, bath or shower, WC and 4 with TV. **Price** Double 470-750F. **Meals** Breakfast 55F. **Restaurant** Service 12:30-13:30, 20:00- 21:30, menus 155-250F, also à la carte 180F. Specialties: Regional cuisine and game. **Credit cards** All major. **Pets** Dogs allowed (+70F). **Facilities** Heated swimming pool, tennis (70F/hr), Parking. **Nearby** Le Pays de Bray: church of Gournay-en-Bray, church of Aumale, abbaye of Beaubec in Forges-les-Eaux, château of Mesnières-en-Bray, Forêt de Lyons; abbey of Moretmer – Golfs courses at Chaumont-en-Vexin, Saint-Saens, Vivier Danger. **Open** Mar 15– Nov 15.

This is a former 18th-century glass factory on the edge of the glorious Forest of Lyons. The Château du Landel is a superb family mansion which has been converted into a hotel and where the members of the Cardon family work in various capacities. Mme Cardon is at the reception desk while one of her sons is in the kitchen preparing refined dishes which will be served to you in a very elegant salon (with a fireplace in winter). The bedrooms are all furnished with antiques. The château has recently been soundproofed. With the first sunny days of spring, drinks are served on the terrace overlooking the peaceful park.

How to get there *(Map 1 and 9): 90km northwest of Paris, towards N14 Rouen; 5km after Pontoise, towards D53 Dieppe, then D915; in Neufmarché, towards Bézancourt.*

Auberge du Val au Cesne

Le Val au Cesne
76190 Croix-Mare (Seine-Maritime)
Tel. (0)2★ 35.56.63.06 – Fax (0)2★ 35.56.92.78 – M. Carel

Rooms 5 with telephone, bath, WC and TV. **Price** Double 350F. **Meals** Breakfast 50F, served 8:00-11:00; half board 550F, full board 700F (per pers.). **Restaurant** Service 12:00-14:00, 19:00-21:00; menu 150F, also à la carte. Specialties: Terrine de raie, tête et fraise de veau, sole farcie à la mousse de langoustines, escalope de dinde 'Vieille Henriette', feuilleté aux pommes. **Credit cards** Visa, Eurocard and MasterCard. **Pets** Dogs allowed. **Facilities** Parking. **Nearby** Rouen cathedral, church and museum in Yvetot, abbey of Saint-Wandrille – 18-hole golf course in Etretat. **Open** All year.

The Auberge was initially a restaurant with an excellent reputation, consisting of two charmingly furnished rooms separated by a fireplace. At his customers' request, M. Carel opened five comfortable bedrooms in a house very near the Auberge. In a charming small valley, it has an elegant, welcoming atmosphere which is created by a very tasteful decoration, faithful to the regional style, as well as by the basic architecture which makes you feel very much at home. Part of the garden is home to various animals: you can admire a family of parrots, rare species of hens and doves... The five bedrooms are pleasant, but we like the Rose Room less. The small country road nearby will not disturb you as it happily is quiet before nightfall in the heart of the *Pays de Caux*.

How to get there *(Map 1 and 8): 30km northwest of Rouen via A15 towards Yvetot, then D5 for 3km in the towards of Duclair.*

Auberge du Clos Normand ★★

22, rue Henri IV
76370 Martin–Eglise (Seine–Maritime)
Tel. (0)2★ 35.04.40.34 – Fax (0)2★ 35.04.48.49 – M. and Mme Hauchecorne

Rooms 7 with telephone, bath or shower, WC and TV. **Price** Double 270-370F, suite 460F. **Meals** Breakfast 38F, served 8:00-10:00; half board 347-397F (per pers., 3 days min.). **Restaurant** Service 12:15-14:00, 19:30-21:00; menu 160F, à la carte. Specialties: Tarte aux moules, filets de sole dieppoise, turbotin sauce crème estragon, tarte aux pommes chaude. **Credit cards** All major. **Pets** Dogs allowed (+50F). **Nearby** Castle and museum in Dieppe, church and graveyard in Varengeville, château de Mesnières-en-Bray, Saint-Säens, valley of the Varenne and Eawy forest – 18-hole golf course in Etretat. **Open** Dec 18 – Nov 18 (closed Monday evening and Tuesday).

This is a beautiful little hotel dating back to the 15th century; it is on the edge of the Forest of Arques a few kilometers from the sea. From the pretty, rustic dining room you can watch the chef at work. You can have lunch in the garden that borders the river. There are seven bedrooms in the annex at the bottom of the garden, all of them individually decorated, with floral wallpaper, and views over the green landscape. They are very quiet (ask for those with bathrooms). Their overall decoration is unremarkable and somewhat dull and so their main attraction is the view over the river. In this part of the auberge, there is also a lounge which is entirely at guests' disposal. As is often the case with overnight stops, you will be asked to dine in the hotel.

How to get there *(Map 1): 5km southeast of Dieppe via D1 towards Neufchâtel-en-Bray.*

Château de Sassetot-le-Mauconduit

Sassetot-le-Mauconduit
76540 Valmont (Seine-Maritime)
Tel. (0)2★ 35.28.00.11 – Fax (0)2★ 35.28.50.00 – M. Touzard

Rooms 30 with telephone, bath or shower, WC and TV. **Price** Double 470-730F.
Meals Breakfast 50F, served 8:00-9:30; half board from 880F (2 pers.). **Restaurant**
Service 19:30-21:30 (closed Sunday evening and Monday); menus 110-300F, also
à la carte. Specialties: Foie gras and home-smoked salmon. **Credit cards** Amex,
Visa, Eurocard and MasterCard. **Pets** Dogs allowed (+60F). **Facilities** Parking.
Nearby Church of the Trinité and Benedictine museum in Fécamp, Saint-Valéry-en-
Caux, Châteaux of Valmont and Bailleul, church and château of Cany-Barville – 18-
hole golf course in Etretat. **Open** All year.

This elegant classical château once welcomed Empress Sissi of
Austria. The interior is composed of charming, beautifully
proportioned rooms overlooking the vast English-style park. The
bedrooms, reached via a double wooden staircase, have green or
pink upholstery and have been thoroughly and comfortably
refurbished. The furniture – antique and reproduction – varies
from room to room. You will enjoy refined, creative cuisine, which
is served in a beautiful panelled dining room or, in summer, on
the terrace. In the evenings you can enjoy the bar with its billiard
table.

How to get there *(Map 8): 74km northwest of Rouen via N15 to Valliquerville,
then D926 and D17.*

Hôtel de la Terrasse ★★
Route de Vastérival
76119 Varengeville (Seine-Maritime)
Tel. (0)2★ 35.85.12.54 – Fax (0)2★ 35.85.11.70 – M. and Mme Delafontaine

Rooms 22 with telephone, bath or shower and WC. **Price** Double 240-310F.
Meals Breakfast 36F, served 7:45-9:30; half board 240-265F (per pers.).
Restaurant Service 12:00-13:30, 19:00-20:15; menu 85-180F, also à la carte.
Specialties: Shellfish and fish. **Credit cards** Visa, Eurocard and MasterCard. **Pets** Dogs
allowed. **Facilities** Tennis (35F), parking. **Nearby** Château and museum of Dieppe,
church and cemetery of Varengeville, château de Mesnières-en-Bray, Saint-Saëns,
vallée de la Varenne and forêt d'Eawy – 18-hole golf course. **Open** March 14 – Oct 14.

The views from this hotel's dining room and the flower-covered
terrace (which is opened or covered depending on the
temperamental Norman weather) stretch over the English Channel
to the horizon. Half of the bedrooms also offer this beautiful view;
the others look onto the back but they have the advantage of being
sunnier. All are pleasant and decorated with cheerful fabrics, and
the renovated rooms have elegant rattan furniture. The young
owners are friendly and the prices alone are enough to make you
want to stay.

How to get there (Map 1): 15km west of Dieppe. In Varengeville, take D75
towards Vastérival.

Hôtel Sud-Bretagne ★★★★

42, Bd de la République
44380 Pornichet (Loire-Atlantique)
Tel. (0)2★ 40.11.65.00 - Fax (0)2★ 40.61.73.70 - M. Bardouil

Rooms 30 with telephone, bath, WC and TV. **Price** Single 450F, double 600-800F, suite 1000-1500F. **Meals** Breakfast 60F; half board 500-850F, full board 750-1050F. **Restaurant** Menus 130-270F, also à la carte. **Credit cards** All major. **Pets** Dogs allowed. **Facilities** Swimming pool, tennis, parking. **Nearby** La Baule, La Brière and La Guérande marshes – 18-hole La Baule golf course in Saint-Denac. **Open** All year.

Ideally located not far from the beaches at La Baule, the Hôtel Sud-Bretagne has been in the same family since 1912, and to this day every member of the family joins in running and improving the hotel. Their contributions range from interior decoration to the organization of excursions aboard *La Orana*, a 17-meter teak-and-mahogany ketch. You will feel at home here. And a magnificent home it is, where each room has its own style. There is a lounge with a cozy fireplace, a billiard room, and several dining rooms over looking an indoor swimming pool. Outside, garden furniture invites you to relax in the sun. Each bedroom has a different theme reflected in the choice of fabrics, furniture and objects. There are some small apartments, with a lounge, a terrace, and typical Breton box beds for children. The Sud-Bretagne is one of a few luxury hotels which has retained all its charm and character.

How to get there (Map 14): 5km east of La Baule.

Auberge de Kerhinet **

Le Kerhinet - 44410 Saint-Lyphard (Loire-Atlantique)
Tel. (0)2★ 40.61.91.46 - Fax★ (0)2 40.61.97.57
M. and Mme Pebay-Arnauné

Rooms 7 with bath and WC. **Price** Single 250F, double 270F. **Meals** Breakfast 40F, served 8:00-11:00; half board 300F. **Restaurant** Closed Tuesday evening and Wednesday except July and Aug. Service 12:00-15:00, 19:00-23:00; menus 85-210F, also à la carte. Specialties: Emincés de pimpenneaux, anguilles au roquefort, persillade de cuisses de grenouilles fraîches, petits foies de canard aux pleurotes, matelote d'anguille à la Brièronne. **Credit cards** All major. **Pets** Dogs allowed. **Facilities** Parking. **Nearby** Medieval town of Guérande, marshes, La Brière regional park, Croisic aquarium – 18-hole La Bretesche golf course, 18-hole La Baule golf course in Saint-Denac. **Open** All year.

This lovely little auberge lies in a historically classified village which has been immaculately rebuilt and restored. Thatched roofs and stone walls add special beauty to the Auberge are all done in a rustic style. The bar, dining room and the bedrooms, which are in a separate and quiet pavilion.

How to get there (Map 14): 23km north of Saint-Nazaire via D47 to Saint-Lyphard via Saint-André-des-Eaux. In the village of Kerhinet (follown signs on D47).

Abbaye de Villeneuve ★★★★

Route des Sables-d'Olonne
44840 Les Sorinières (Loire-Atlantique)
Tel. (0)2★ 40.04.40.25 - Fax (0)2★ 40.31.28.45 - M. James

Rooms 24 with telephone, bath and WC (12 with TV). **Price** Single and double 390-935F, suite 1150-1310F. **Meals** Breakfast 70F, served 6:45-10:30; half board 430-970F, full board 645-1190F. **Restaurant** Service 12:00-13:30, 19:00-21:30; menus 163-344F, also à la carte. Specialties: Nage de homard aux salicornes des marais, foie gras chaud aux pruneaux et armagnac, giboulée de fruits flambés. **Credit cards** All major. **Pets** Dogs allowed. **Facilities** Swimming pool, parking. **Nearby** Art museum and Jules Verne museum in Nantes, valley of the Erdre, Clisson – 18-hole golf course in Nantes. **Open** All year.

This former cistercian abbey was founded in 1201 by Constance of Brittany, was partially destroyed during the French Revolution and then restored in 1977 as a hotel only ten minutes from the center of Nantes. The great hall of the monastery is now the restaurant and the bedrooms retain the magnificent timbers of the building's frame. In the lounges, plaster ceilings and stone fireplaces give the room a grand air, but they are comfortable spots to relax – surely less forbidding then the austerity of the original abbey. The cuisine is classic and you will be looked after in grand style.

How to get there *(Map 14): 10km south of Nantes via A83 towards Bordeaux, then Challans.*

Château des Briottières ★★★★

49330 Champigné (Maine-et-Loire)
Tel. (0)2★ 41.42.00.02 – Fax (0)2★ 41.42.01.55
M. and Mme de Valbray

Rooms 10 with telephone, bath. **Price** Double 550-750F, suite 900F. **Meals** Breakfast 45F; Half board 1340-1590F (per 2 pers.). **Restaurant** Evening meals at 20:00 (on reservation); menu 300F (all incl.). **Credit cards** All major. **Pets** Dogs allowed (+50F). **Facilities** Heated swimming pool, bicycle, parking. **Nearby** Abbey of Solesmes, abbey of Fontevrault, château of Angers (tapisserie), Loire Valley (châteaux de la Loire) – 18-hole Anjou country club golf course. **Open** All year (by reservation in winter).

Off the beaten path and surrounded by an immense English-style garden, the Château des Briottières is a private château which hosts guests. It alone is worthy of a trip to the Loire. The young owners are warm and friendly. On the ground floor, a vast gallery leads to the reception areas. The lounges are furnished in 18th-century style, and the large dining room is brightened by pearl-grey woodwork and pink drapes. The owners join you for the excellent, friendly dinners, which are served on a magnificently set dining table. There is a library with a French billiard table. Upstairs, the comfortable bedrooms are all tastefully decorated with lovely fabrics and very beautiful antique furniture. Some rooms are intimate, while others are vast. The bathrooms are luxurious, and all have a view of the park. The swimming pool is located in a beautiful garden. And if you stay on, the sixth night is free!

How to get there *(Map 15): 32km north of Angers via A11, Durtal exit, then D859 and D770 in the towards of Le Lion-d'Angers.*

374

Hôtel Anne d'Ajou ★★★

32, quai Mayaud
49400 Saumur (Maine- et-Loire)
Tel. (0)2★ 41.67.30.30 - Fax (0)2★ 41.67.51.00 - M. and Mme Touzé

Rooms 50 with telephone, bath or shower, WC and TV - 1 wheelchair access. **Price** Single 280F, double 450F, suite 650F. **Meals** Breakfast 48F, served 7:00-10:00; half board 425-475F. **Restaurant** "Les Ménestrels". Closed Sunday and Monday afternoon in low season. Service 12:15-13:30, 19:30-21:30, also à la carte. **Credit card** All major. **Pets** Dogs not allowed. **Facilities** Parking. **Nearby** Notre-Dame church of Nantilly, Horse Museum in Saumur, Château of Montsoreau, abbey of Fontevraud, Montreuil-Bellay (château), Mushroom Museum in Saint-Hilaire-Saint-Florent, Château of Boumois. **Open** All year except Dec 23 – Jan 3.

The Anne d'Anjou is a beautiful 18th-century mansion which is ideally located between the Loire and the imposing medieval Château of Saumur. A magnificent Louis XVI stairway surmounted by a stunning *trompe l'oeil* ceiling leads to the bedrooms. Those on the *premier étage* still have much of their original charm, particularly the room with Empire *bas-reliefs* covered with gold leaf. The rooms are beautifully decorated with elegant fabrics, many with antique furniture or rugs. The price of the rooms varies according to their size and the floor they are on. (We are less enthusiastic about those on the *troisième étage*). Some rooms have a view on the garden and the château rising in the immediate background; others look out over the immense span of the Loire. Double-windows successfully muffle the noise of the traffic. With the first warm days of spring, tables are set out in the beautiful garden for breakfast.

How to get there *(Map 15): 66km west of Tours.*

Hôtel L'Ermitage ★★★

53340 Saulges (Mayenne)
Tel. (0)2★ 43.90.52.28 - Fax (0)2★ 43.90.56.61
M. and Mme Janvier

Rooms 36 with telephone, bath or shower, WC, TV and minibar - Wheelchair access.
Price Single 270-330F, double 310-450F, suite 520F. **Meals** Breakfast (buffet) 52F,
served 8:00-10:30; half board 300-450F, full board 390-550F (per pers., 3 days
min.). **Restaurant** Service 12:00-14:00, 19:15-21:00; menus 98-260F, also à la
carte. Specialties: Salade de gambas sauce orange, foie gras maison, coquilles
Saint-Jacques au vin de Jasnières, rognonnade de lapereau à la sarriette, fricassée
de volaille "pomme d'abeille", comté du maine. **Credit cards** All major. **Pets** Dogs
allowed (+40F). **Facilities** Heated swimming pool, sauna (40F), health center,
parking, garage (+suppl.). **Nearby** Caves of Roquefort and Margot in Saulges,
basilica of Evron, fortified town of Sainte-Suzanne, château of Rocher, abbey of
Clermont, abbey of Solesmes – 27-hole golf courses in Laval and Sablé. **Open** Apr
16 – Sept 23.

L'Ermitage is in the region of the Evre and Vegre, two charming
fishing rivers in the heart of the Mayenne. It is a modern
building in the center of the small and quiet market town of Saulges.
Major refurbishment has done much to improve the comfort of
this hotel. The bedrooms have been completely renovated and all
look out onto the countryside. The garden has been enlarged by
the addition of a meadow, and the restaurant with its views of the
park has also been refurbished to celebrate the arrival of chef Thierry
Janvier, the son of the family, who trained with the best chefs in
Paris.

How to get there (Map 15): 37km east of Laval via A81, number 2 Vaiges
exit, then D24 in the towards of Sablé for 4km, then CD554.

Relais Cicéro ★★★

18, boulevard d'Alger
72200 La Flèche (Sarthe)
Tel. (0)2★ 43.94.14.14 – Fax (0)2★ 43.45.98.96 – Mme Levasseur

Rooms 21 with telephone, bath or shower, WC and TV. **Price** Single 380-425F, double 495-675F. **Meals** Breakfast 45F, served from 7:00. No restaurant. **Credit cards** Amex, Visa, Eurocard and MasterCard. **Pets** Small dogs allowed. **Nearby** Chapel of Notre Dame-des-Vertus, Tertre Rouge zoological park, château de Lude, Solesmes abbey. **Open** Jan 7 – Dec 20.

This hotel isn't really a country hotel since it is in the small, pretty town of La Flèche, yet the Relais Cicéro has various advantages that make it a first-class place to stay. It is on a peaceful tree-lined street away from the bustle and noise of the town. Its large garden is tranquil and the beautiful 16th- and 18th-century building is both comfortably and elegantly furnished. There is a bar, a reading room and a television room. In the dining room a very good breakfast is served – in winter to the warmth of a blazing fire in the fireplace. The bedrooms are comfortable and tastefully furnished. Our favorite rooms are those in the main building. Try the traditional *Fesse d'Ange* and *Le Vert Galant,* two restaurants in the village.

How to get there *(Map 15): 52km northwest of Angers via A11, Durtal exit, then N23 to La Flèche.*

Auberge du Port-des-Roches ★★

72800 Luché-Pringé (Sarthe)
Tel. (0)2★ 43.45.44.48 – Fax (0)2★ 43.45.39.61
Mme and M. Lesiourd

Rooms 13 with telephone, bath or shower (9 with WC, 4 with TV). **Price** Double 230-300F. **Meals** Breakfast 32F, served 8:00-9:30; half board 250-290F, full board 310-360F (per pers., 4 days min.). **Restaurant** Service 12:00-13:30, from 19:30; menus 110-185F, also à la carte. Specialties: Blanquette de sandre aux noix et jasnières, ris de veau braisé aux oreilles de cochon, crème caramélisée au cidre en coque de pomme. **Credit cards** Visa, Eurocard and MasterCard. **Pets** Dogs allowed (+30F). **Facilities** Parking. **Nearby** Châteaux of Montmirail, Courtanvaux and Saint-Calais, château of Lude, château of Bazouges – 18-hole Le Mans golf course in Mulsanne. **Open** All year (closed Sunday evening and Monday).

By the side of a pretty road in the valley of the Loir, this comfortable, unpretentious hotel has a lovely terrace (on the other side from the road) which overlooks the Loir. Mme Martin will make you feel at home. Her husband is the chef, specializing in traditional regional dishes made with fresh produce from the market. The bedrooms are cozy, comfortable and well kept; six have a view of the river. The lounge and dining room are decorated in rustic style. There is a pretty, shady terrace with flowers on the riverbank. This is a marvelous, reasonably priced hotel in a region full of touristc attractions.

How to get there *(Map 16): 40km southwest of Le Mans in the towards of La Flèche, then D13 to Luché-Pringé and D214 to "Le Port-des-Roches".*

Haras de la Potardière

La Portardière
72200 Crosmières (Sarthe)
Tel. (0)2★ 43.45.83.47 – Fax (0)2★ 43.45.81.06 – M. and Mme Benoist

Rooms 17 with telephone, 16 with bath, 1 with shower, WC, TV, 16 with minibar - Wheelchair access. **Price** Single 450F, double 550F. **Meals** Breakfast 40F, served 7:00-11:00. No restaurant but snacks available in winter. **Credit cards** Visa, Eurocard and MasterCard. **Pets** Dogs allowed. **Facilities** Heated swimming pool, billiards, 3-hole compact golf, tennis, horseback trips by reservation. **Nearby** Notre-Dame-des-Vertus chapel, Malicorne pottery, Rairies terra cotta, Tertre Rouge zoological park, château de Lude, abbey of Solesmes – 27-hole Sablé-Solesmes golf course. **Open** All year (by reservation Nov – March).

A countryside of forests and large green valleys surrounds this horse farm, a large part of which has been transformed into a hotel. *Haras* means "stud farm," so it is not surprising that the architecture of the stables is as handsome as that of the château. The bedrooms are beautifully furnished, with beautiful fabrics, antiques, lovely lighting and outstanding bathrooms. The suites, ideal for families, offer unbeatable quality for the price. The young owners are friendly and informal, making the Potardière a place as lovely and gentle as the Loire Valley itself. For restaurants, try *La Petite Auberge* in Malicorne, or *Le Vert Galant* and *La Fesse d'Ange* in La Flèche.

How to get there *(Map 15): 10km northwest of La Flèche. On A11, exit La Flèche/Sablé, Crosmières, then towards Bazouges to La Potardière.*

Château de Saint Paterne *
Saint-Paterne - 72610 (Sarthe)
Tel. (0)2★ 33.27.54.71. - Fax (0)2★ 33.29.16.71
M. de Valbray

Rooms 7 with telephone, bath and WC. **Price** Double 450-650F, suite 750F. **Meals** Breakfast 45F, served 7:30-12:00; half board 370-400F, full board 450-480F (per pers., 3 days min.). **Restaurant** Closed Sunday evening and Monday in low season. Service 12:15-14:00, 20:00-21:30; menus 100-220F, also à la carte. Specialties: Feuilleté de langoustines, foie gras chaud, fish. **Credit cards** Amex, Visa, Eurocard and MasterCard. **Pets** Dogs allowed. **Facilities** Parking. **Nearby** Châteaux of Montmirail, Courtanvaux and Saint-Calais; Carrouges, Bazouges, Ludes; haras du Pin; Alençon; Perche – 18-hole Mans golf course in Luisanne, Arconnay golf course (2km). **Open** Mar 1 – Jan 14.

Alençon is on the doorstep of the village of Saint Paterne but this château remains sheltered in its vast walled-in park. With all the enthusiasm of youth, the owner has restored it throughout and will greet you very warmly. On the ground floor, there is a superb salon with extremely elegant antique furniture, a beautiful dining room and a bedroom. There are other bedrooms upstairs, each with their own special style, including the *Henri IV* with its superb French polychrome ceilings. The bathrooms are faultless. You may have dinner at the château dining table with Charles-Henri or at a small independent table. There is a set menu based on excellent products, particularly the vegetables raised in the garden. This is a superb place to stay with the charm of a private home and the amenities of a luxurious hotel.

How to get there *(Map 8): 3km east of Alençon, towards Chartres-Mamers.*

Hôtel du Martinet **

Place de la Croix-Blanche
85230 Bouin (Vendée)
Tel. (0)2★ 51.49.08.94 – Fax (0)2★ 51.49.83.08 – Mme Huchet

Rooms 21 with telephone, bath or shower, WC and TV. **Price** Single 195-230F, double 265-330F. **Meals** Breakfast 35F; half board 250-290F (per pers.). **Restaurant** Service 12:30-13:30, 19:30-21:30 (closed Oct – Mar), menus 95-130F (60F chlid), also à la carte. Specialties: Fish and shellfish. **Credit cards** All major. **Pets** Dogs allowed (+20F). **Facilities** Bicycles, swimming pool, parking. **Nearby** Church of St-Philbert-de-Grand-Lieu, Machecoul, oyster beds, Ile d'Yeu – 18-hole golf courses in Saint-Jean-de-Monts and in Pornic. **Open** All year.

Y ou will be enchanted by this late 18th-century residence where the smell of wax mingles with that of bowls of cut flowers. The furniture in the bedrooms on the ground floor and *premier étage* is plain but very comfortable. There are two other bedrooms under the eaves which are ideal for families of four. In a small wing of the hotel, five beautiful bedrooms have just been added. They are prettily decorated, and are on the ground floor, looking onto a large garden at the rear of the house; the swimming pool is also here, from where there is a beautiful view over the countryside and marshes of the Vendée. In the restaurant, the owner's oyster-farmer husband will be delighted to serve you oysters from his beds and other seafood. For fine dining, try *Le Courlis*.

How to get there *(Map 14): 51km southwest of Nantes via D751 and D758 in the towards of Noirmoutier.*

Château de la Vérie ★★★

Route de Saint-Gilles-Croix-de-Vie
85300 Challans (Vendée)
Tel. (0)2★ 51.35.33.44 – Fax (0)2★ 51.35.14.84 – M. Martin

Rooms 19 with telephone, bath, WC, TV and minibar. **Price** Single and double 350-880F. **Meals** Breakfast 60-90F, served 7:30-10:30. **Restaurant** Service 12:00-14:00, 19:30-21:30; menus 100-320F, also à la carte. Specialties: Pommes de terre de Noirmoutier farcies aux langoustines, canard de Challans aux sang en deux services, brioche vendéenne dorée aux framboise. **Credit cards** Visa, Eurocard and Mastercard. **Pets** Dogs allowed (+50F). **Facilities** Swimming pool, tennis, parking. **Nearby** Château of Apremont, church of Sallertaine, château and market in Clisson, church of Saint-Philbert-de-Grand-Lieu, Machecoul, Saint-Gilles-Croix-de-Vie, la Fromentine (boats for Ile d'Yeu). **Open** All year.

Recently converted into a hotel, the château boasts exquisite bedrooms, both comfortable and well renovated. Japanese wickerwork, vivid colors, charming little engravings and antique furniture – nothing is lacking: even the mirrors in the bathrooms have china frames. The dining room and lounge have been decorated in the same spirit; they are welcoming rooms, feel very much like a private house, and look out onto a large terrace where breakfast is served and you can view the lush park. There is a swimming pool not far away, useful because this is the second-sunniest part of France. The sea used to come this far but has retreated, leaving behind lush marshland.

How to get there (Map 14): 60km south of Nantes via D65 to Saint-Philbert, then D117 to Machecoul, then D32 to Challans; it's 2.5km from the town hall in the towards of Saint-Gilles-Croix-de-Vie.

Hôtel de l'Antiquité ★★

14, rue Galliéni
85300 Challans (Vendée)
Tel. (0)2★ 51.68.02.84 – Fax (0)2★ 51.35.55.74 – Mme Flaire

Rooms 16 with telephone, bath or shower, WC and TV. **Price** Singles 220-360F, double 260-400F. **Meals** Breakfast 30F, served 7:30-10:00. No restaurant. **Credit cards** All major. **Pets** Dogs not allowed. **Facilities** Swimming pool, parking. **Nearby** Château of Apremont, church of Sallertaine, le marais breton, château and market of Clisson, church of Saint-Philbert-de-Grand-Lieu, Machecoul, Saint-Gilles-Croix-de-Vie, Fromentine (boat for Ile d'Yeu). **Open** Jan 4 – Dec 23.

On the street side, the Hotel de l'Antiquité doesn't look like much. Thus our surprise when we went into the reception area and first saw the lovely dining room with a handsome old china cabinet and charming tables, a lounge/winter garden which opens onto a flower-filled patio, and an inviting swimming pool. Friendly Mme Flaire is also an antiques dealer, which explains the beautiful furniture and tasteful decoration. She is gradually renovating each bedroom, carefully coordinating fabrics, wallpapers and antique furniture. The most beautiful rooms are the four large bedrooms on the other side of the patio, which are very well furnished and have luxurious bathrooms. (Reserve well ahead of time.) This is a very welcoming small hotel in the farm town of Challans, which is famous for its ducks, and it is only a few minutes from the coast of Noirmoutier. In Challans, two good restaurants are *La Gite de Tourne Pierre* and *Le Pavillon Gourmand*.

How to get there *(Map 14): 60km south of Nantes via D65, Saint-Philbert, then D117, Machecoul, D32 to Challans.*

Flux Hôtel ★★

27, rue Pierre-Henry, Port Joinville
85350 Ile-d'Yeu (Vendée)
Tel. (0)2★ 51.58.36.25 Fax (0)2★ 51.59.44.57 – Mme Cadou

Rooms 16 with telephone, bath or shower and TV. **Price** Double 280F. **Meals** Breakfast 35F, served 8:30-9:00; half board 310F, full board 340F (per pers., recommended in July, Aug.). **Restaurant** Closed Sunday evening in low season. Service 12:00-14:00, 19:30-21:00; menus 80-160F. Specialties: Fish, shellfish, tarte aux pruneaux. **Credit cards** Visa, Eurocard and MasterCard. **Pets** Dogs allowed (+30F). **Facilities** Parking. **Nearby** Ker-Chalon beach, lighthouse, Saint-Sauveur church, ruins of the old château. **Open** Jan 15 – Nov 22.

Somewhat on the outskirts of Port-Joinville, the Flux Hôtel has an exceptional location, its garden giving onto a small coastal path overlooking the immense blue ocean. To take advantage of this beautiful view, the owners constructed a building twenty years ago whose *premier étage* bedrooms look out on this magnificent seascape. Those on the ground floor do not enjoy the same panorama but they all have a small garden just in front of the door. There are also two other guestrooms in the main hotel. Room 15 is immense and perfect for families, and number 16 has a vast terrace looking out over the superb landscape. The interior decoration is unremarkable but comfortable. The shellfish you catch in the afternoon are cooked and served to you in the evening. (The dishes in a sauce are disappointing). In summer, the island is irresistible and you should thus reserve well in advance and take half-board in July and August.

How to get there (Map 14): Steamer connections with Port-Joinville (tel. 51.58.36.66) and Fromentine (tel. (0)2★ 51.68.52.32).

Hôtel du Général d'Elbée ★★★
Place d'Armes
85330 Noirmoutier-en-l'Ile (Vendée)
Tel. (0)2★ 51.39.10.29 - Fax (0)2★ 51.39.08.23 - M. Savry

Rooms 29 with telephone, bath and WC. **Price** Single and double 350-715F, suite 825-1600F. **Meals** Breakfast 60-65F, served 7:30-11:30. No restaurant. **Credit cards** All major. **Pets** Dogs allowed (+65F). **Facilities** Swimming pool. **Nearby** Art and folk museum in La Guérinière, L'Herbaudière, salt marshes. **Open** Apr 1 –Oct 1.

The Hôtel du Général d'Elbée is in a large old building on the edge of a small canal. It is named after the leader of the Vendée uprising who died on the Place d'Armes, where you will see *l'arbre de la liberté* (the tree of liberty). The hotel has 29 bedrooms, all with old furniture. The rooms in the main building are very spacious, with high ceilings and a good amount of character; nowever we prefer the bedrooms in the side building, which are less expensive. They give onto the garden and the swimming pool and despite their somewhat smaller size, they are very pleasant. Note too that there are several bedrooms on the *second étage*, beneath the beautiful roof beams. They are truly charming with their small windows and, here too, fine old furniture. Some are arranged in suites and are ideal for families. Several carpets are beginning to show signs of wear and the bathrooms, even though they are irreproachably clean, should be renovated. Nevertheless, the hotel overall is quite handsome and the breakfast buffet, served in a room giving onto the swimming pool, will leave you with a good memory of the hotel. For good seafood, try the *Coté Jardin*.

How to get there *(Map 14): 82km southwest of Nantes via D751 and D758. Access by the bridge from Fromentine. The hotel is in the center of the town.*

Fleur de Sel ★★★

85330 Noirmoutier-en-L'Ile (Vendée)
Tel. (0)2★ 51.39.21.59 – Fax (0)2★ 51.39.75.66
M. and Mme Wattecamps

Rooms 35 with telephone, bath, WC, TV, 22 with minibar - Wheelchair access. **Price** Single 325-520F, double 375-620F. **Meals** Breakfast 48F, served 8:00-9:30 in lounge, 10:30 in room; half board 370-525F (per pers., 2 days min.). **Restaurant** Service 12:00-14:00, 19:00-21:00/22:00; menus 128-168F, also à la carte. Specialties: Seafood, shellfish and fish, homards du vivier. **Credit cards** Amex, Visa, Eurocard and MasterCard. **Pets** Dogs allowed (+40F). **Facilities** Swimming pool, tennis (30-50F in hight season), sauna (60F), uva (50F). **Nearby** Château and museum of Noirmoutier, passage du Gois and the woods of la Chaize, Saint-Phibert church, salt marshes, oyster beds; 18-hole Golf Course in Saint-Jean-de-Monts, 18-hole golf course in Pornic. **Open** Mid. Feb – Nov 1.

Fleur de Sel is a large white house built around a turquoise swimming pool and a pretty garden. It is located somewhat outside the lovely island village of Noirmoutier. The bedrooms are bright and very pleasant. (Those on the ground floor have small private terraces). The furniture is of English pine, mahogany, and colored rattan, which is complemented by matching fabrics and attractive watercolors on the walls. The large dining room is bright and opens onto the sea in summer. Two small lounges decorated in blue and white lend a warm touch to the hotel. This is a beautiful, friendly hotel and the cuisine is excellent.

How to get there (Map 14): 82km southwest of Nantes via D751 and D758. Road bridge as you leave Fromentine, 1/2 km behind the church.

Hôtel Les Prateaux ★★★

Bois de la Chaize
85330 Noirmoutier-en-l'Ile (Vendée)
Tel. (0)2★ 51.39.12.52 - Fax (0)2★ 51.39.46.28 - M. Blouard

Rooms 22 with telephone, bath or shower, WC and TV. **Price** Single and double 305-760F. **Meals** Breakfast 60F; half board 346-615F, full board 410-690F (per pers.). **Restaurant** Service 12:30-13:30, 19:30-20:30; à la carte. Specialties: Fish and shellfish. **Credit cards** All major. **Pets** Dogs not allowed. **Facilities** Parking. **Nearby** Church of Saint-Philbert-de-Grand-Lieu, Machecoul, oyster beds, Ile d'Yeu – 18-hole golf courses in Saint-Jean-de-Monts and Pornic. **Open** Feb 18 – Nov 11.

L es Prateaux has been entirely renovated and nothing has been spared to make the new and old bedrooms beautifully comfortable. The newest rooms are larger, and one even has a private 144-square-foot terrace over looking the park. The other rooms have balconies. The principal building is composed of the dining rooms (which open onto a vast terrace) the lounge and some of the bedrooms. The other rooms are located nearby in the garden. The hotel is very attractively located; built in 1939 on the end of the Ile du Noirmoutier in the middle of the forest of La Chaize, it is very quiet. The sea is only about 300 meters away and a walk through the woods will bring you to a pretty beach. The atmosphere is very summery and there is a scent of the pines and mimosas is reminiscent of the Côte d'Azur.

How to get there (Map 14): 82km southwest of Nantes by D751 and D758. Access by road bridge from Fromentine, 1.5km from Noirmoutier to Bois de la Chaize, then follow signs.

Logis de la Couperie **
85000 La Roche-sur-Yon (Vendée)
Tel. (0)2★ 51.37.21.19 - Fax (0)2★ 51.47.71.08
Mme Oliveau

Rooms 7 with telephone, bath or shower, WC and TV. **Price** Single 265-420F, double
295-480F, suite 420-480F. **Meals** Breakfast 39F, served 7:30-10:00. No restaurant.
Credit cards Amex, Visa, Eurocard and MasterCard. **Pets** Dogs not allowed.
Facilities Lake, bike, parking. **Nearby** History museum and château of Chabotterie,
Saint-Sulpice-le-Verdon, Tiffauges, military Vendée. **Open** All year.

The Logis de la Couperie is a former manor house which was
rebuilt at the end of the 18th-century. It is located in open
countryside, five minutes from the center of town, and surrounded
by a 5-acre park with a small lake. Nature lovers will find peace
here. In the large entrance hall there is a magnificent staircase which
leads to the upper floors. The bedrooms are all comfortable and
tastefully furnished with antiques and regional furniture. There is
a well-stocked lounge/library, where a cheerful log fire burns in
winter. The excellent breakfast, which can include homemade
apple juice and the local brioche, is served in the dining room or
your room. *L'Halbran, l'Auberge de Noiron* and *Le Rivol* are among
the very good restaurants in La Roche-sur-Yon.

How to get there *(Map 14): On D80, five minutes from the town center,
via the Route Nationale from Cholet.*

Hôtel La Barbacane **
2, place de l'Eglise
85130 Tiffauges (Vendée)
Tel. (0)2★ 51.65.75.59 - Fax (0)2★ 51.65.71.91 - Mme Bidan

Rooms 16 with telephone, bath or shower, WC and TV. **Price** Double 280-355F. **Meals** Breakfast 30-45F. No restaurant. **Credit cards** All major. **Pets** Dogs allowed. **Facilities** Swimming pool, billiards, garage. **Nearby** Ruins of château of Gilles de Retz ('Blue Beard'), spectacle of Puy-du-Fou, military Vendée – 18-hole golf course in Cholet. **Open** All year.

This charming little hotel is in a village the mention of whose name made the entire surrounding region tremble in the 15th-century. The fortress of Gilles de Retz, alias Blue Beard, is located here. You will go past its imposing ruins to get to La Barbacane, where you'll find the friendly welcome of Mme Bidan. The hotel is also her home, which is why each room has travel souvenirs and family furniture. On the ground floor there is a billiards room and a dining room where you can have generous breakfasts. The bedrooms are on several floors and in a ground-floor wing which opens onto the main garden; they are charming, often with exotic wicker furniture and pretty bathrooms (terracotta and blond wood), and are reasonably priced. Behind the hotel, there is another garden, with a beautiful terrace around a swimming pool. For dinner, the village restaurant, *L'Auberge du Donjon*, is right next door. If you don't mind going a little further, visit the castle at Clisson and the market before having dinner at *La Bonne Auberge*.

How to get there *(Map 15): 20km west of Cholet via D753 towards Montaigu.*

Auberge de la Rivière ★★

85770 Velluire (Vendée)
Tel. (0)2★ 51.52.32.15 - Fax (0)2★ 51.52.37.42
M. and Mme Pajot

Rooms 11 with telephone, bath and WC (6 with TV). **Price** Single 350F, double 410F. **Meals** Breakfast 60F, served 8:00-10:30; half board 370-400F, full board 450-480F (per pers., 3 days min.). **Restaurant** Closed Sunday evening and Monday in low season. Service 12:15-14:00, 20:00-21:30; menus 100-220F, also à la carte. Specialties: Feuilleté de langoustines, foie gras chaud, fish. **Credit cards** Visa, Eurocard and MasterCard. **Pets** Dogs allowed (+30F). **Nearby** Church of Notre-Dame and museum of the Vendée in Fontenay-le-Comte, Poitou marshes – 9-hole golf course in Niort. **Open** Feb 21 – Jan 9 (closed Monday in low season).

This hotel is in the little village of Velluire on the banks of the Vendée and is only a few kilometers from Fontenay-le-Comte. The place is very peaceful and there are various types of bedrooms. All are very pleasant; those in the main building are decored with several beautiful pieces of antique furniture, while those in the house next door are more functional, elegant, bright and very comfortable. All except one look out on the river. In the large, beautiful dining room, Mme Pajot serves excellent seafood and regional specialities. This is a pleasant and unpretentious place to stay, far from the tourist hordes. It is near the Ile de Ré, famous for is salt marshes and network of canals called "Venise Verte," Green Venice.

How to get there *(Map 15): 45km northwest of Niort via N148 towards Fontenay-le-Comte, then D938 to Nizeau and D68 to Velluire*

Les Pigeons Blancs

110, rue Jules Brisson
16100 Cognac (Charente)
Tel. (0)5★ 45.82.16.36 – Fax (0)5★ 45.82.29.29 – Tachet Family

Rooms 7 with telephone, bath or shower, WC and TV. **Price** Singles 290-390F, double 350-450F. **Meals** Breakfast 45F, served 8:00-10:00. **Restaurant** Service 12:00-14:00, 19:30-21:00; menus 130-275F, also à la carte. Specialties: Poêlée de petits gris aux pleurotes, fricassée de morue charentaise, ris de veau au foie gras frais, voiture gourmandises. **Credit cards** All major. **Pets** Dogs not allowed. **Nearby** In Cognac: museum of Cognac, Chais of Cognac, festival du film policier; Romanesque churches of Cherves and Saint-Hérie in Matha, Le Marestay, Châtres, châteaux of Saint-Sauvan, Richemont and Garde-Epée; Randonnées en roulotte à partir de Matha; Road along the banks of the Charente de Jarnac in Angoulême, cruises on the Charente from June to Sept. **Open** All year.

In the same family since the 18th century, the Pigeons Blancs is a former postal relay station which is set in a quiet private park. The hotel is renowned for its restaurant, which is considered one of the finest in the region and is where merchants from the famous cognac houses often come for business lunches. But the Pigeons Blancs can also be proud of its lovely, comfortable bedrooms. They are decorated with elegant antique furniture, pretty coordinated fabrics and wallpaper. And they are kept immaculate, as are the bathrooms. There is a small, comfortable lounge with deep sofas, books and games which provide pleasant relaxation as you enjoy one of the region's famous brandies. Next to the lounge are two warmly decorated dining rooms with handsome family furniture.

How to get there *(Map 22): 40km west of Angoulême via N141; road to Saint-Jean-d'Angély, Matha.*

Château de Nieuil *

16270 Nieuil (Charente)
Tel. (0)5 45.71.36.38 – Fax (0)5 45.71.46.45
Mme and M. Bodinaud

Rooms 11 (6 with air-conditioning) with telephone, bath, WC, TV and minibar - Wheelchair access. **Price** Singles 630-800F, double 700-1200F, suite 1400-2000F. **Meals** Breakfast 75F, served 8:00-11:00; half board 735-980F, full board 895-1140F (per pers., 3 days min.). **Restaurant** Service 12:00-14:00, 20:00-21:30; menus 185F (lunch), 240-320F, also à la carte. **Credit cards** All major. **Pets** Dogs allowed. **Facilities** Swimming pool, tennis parking. **Nearby** Forest of Braconn, château of Rochebrune and Peyras, romanesque churches in Angoumois country (Cellefrouin, Lichères, Diran, Dignac, Villebois-Lavalette, Mouthiers-sur-Boëme, Saint-Michel, Saint-Armand de Boixe). **Open** Apr 28 – 2 Nov.

In the 14th century, the Château de Nieul was a fortress; and in the 16th century, turrets, crenalations, balusters and watchtowers were added to keep in step with the fashion. In 1937, the present owner's grandparents transformed it into a hotel. The château today is a romantic ensemble lying behind the volutes of a formal garden surrounded by semi-circular moats and an immense park with a lake. *Haute Epoque* interior decoration is predominant in the reception rooms. Each bedroom has its special style, recreated by means of precise and often superb decoration. Throughout, the antique furniture and paintings are of fine quality. But for us, more important still is M. Bodineau's hospitality and that of his staff. Warm and very attentive, it is very far from the stuffy "château" atmosphere we often find. Last but not least, Luce Bodineau's excellent cuisine and the many sports and leisure activities available (you can even rent equipment) make the Château de Nieul a luxurious hotel in which to stay and relax. Note that in winter the country restaurant of the château, the *Grange aux Oies*, offers a more rustic but equally savory version of the château's cuisine.

How to get there *(Map 23): 40km northwest of Angoulême via N141 toward Chasseneuil, Fontafie and Nieul on D739.*

392

Hôtel l'Ecailler ★★★

65, rue du Port
Ile d'Oléron - 17310 La Cotinière (Charente-Maritime)
Tel. (0)5★ 46.47.10.31 - Fax (0)5★ 46.47.10.23 - M. Rochard

Rooms 8 with air-conditioning, telephone, bath, WC, TV and minibar. **Price** Single and double 335-410F. **Meals** Breakfast 40F, served 8:00-9:30, until 11:30 in room; half board 365-420F, full board 450-510F (per pers.). **Restaurant** Service 12:00-14:00, 19:00-22:00. Specialties: Boudin de Saint-Jacques, escargots charentais. **Credit cards** All major. **Pets** Dogs allowed (+35F). **Facilities** Parking (21F). **Nearby** Beachs of Le Coureau and La Giraudière, Aliénor d'Aquitaine Museum in Saint-Pierre-d'Oléron; from Boyardville, boat for Islands of Aix and Fouras; beach of Les Saumonards facing Fort Boyard – 9-hole Oléron golf course. **Open** Feb 7 – Nov 14.

L'Ecaillier is an ideal place from which to enjoy this delightful island fishing village. There is only a small street between the hotel and the picturesque fishing boats, and half the bedrooms have a view over this scene. The other rooms look out on a small garden and have the advantage of being quieter. All are well equipped. On the ground floor, you can enjoy a winter garden where there are a few tables covered with pretty floral cloths. In the adjacent large restaurant, there is a permanent exhibit of bright paintings and watercolors by local artists. The delicious fish on your plate (the *boudin* of scallops is special) is caught each morning. The atmosphere is relaxed and friendly at the Ecaillier, which means "oyster merchant".

How to get there *(Map 22): 10km west of Marennes via the viaduct bridge. 3km west of Saint-Pierre-d'Oléron.*

Hôtel Le Chat Botté ★★

Ile de Ré
17590 Saint-Clément-des-Baleines (Charente-Maritime)
Tel. (0)5★ 46.29.21.93 – Fax (0)5★ 46.29.29.97– Melles Massé

Rooms 19 with telephone, 7 with bath, 12 with shower and WC - Wheelchair access. **Price** Single 300F, double 380-500F. **Meals** Breakfast 42-55F, served 8:15-10:30. No restaurant. **Credit cards** Visa, Eurocard and MasterCard. **Pets** Dogs allowed (+35F). **Facilities** Small health center, parking. **Nearby** Museum and citadel of Saint-Martin-de-Ré, Baleines Lighthouse – 9-hole Trousse golf course. **Open** All year except Dec 1 – 15 and Jan 5 – Fev 15.

The Chat Botté ("puss in boots") is an adorable village house with a patio and a large flower garden on the delightful Ile de Ré. Bright wood paneling harmonizes with elegant terra cotta floors and fabrics. Everything is impeccably kept and decorated, including the bedrooms. Breakfast is served in a pretty room which opens onto the garden. There is also a small, well-equipped exercise room. The young owners and staff are very friendly and informal. There is no restaurant in the hotel but the excellent seafood restaurant *Le Chat Botté* is just next door; and in Portes-en-Ré, there is *L'Auberge de la Rivière* (try the langoustine ravioli). Both are run by other members of the Massé family. And there are many other good restaurants on this delightful island.

How to get there (Map 22): 28km west of La Rochelle via the Pallice Bridge.

Hôtel de Bordeaux **

1, rue Gambetta
17800 Pons (Charente-Maritime)
Tel. (0)5★ 46.91.31.12 - Fax (0)5★ 46.91.22.25- M. Jaubert and Mlle Muller

Rooms 16 with telephone, bath, WC, TV. **Price** Single 220F, double 260F. **Meals** Breakfast 35F, served 7:30-10:30. Restaurant Service 12:00-14:00, 19:30-21:30, menus 85-230F, also à la carte. Specialties: Fumage minute de langoustines, turbot rôti, minestrone de homard, hachis de basilic. **Credit cards** Amex, Visa, Eurocard and MasterCard. **Pets** Dogs allowed. **Facilities** Parking. **Nearby** Dungeon of Pons, château of Usson; romanesque churches of Saintonges; Colombiers, Montils, Jazennes, Belluire; Rétaud, Rioux, Thaims, Corme-Ecluse; Aulnay; château of Damierre; Saintes – 18-hole Saintes golf course. **Open** Apr –Oct (closed Sunday).

From the street, this hotel is like many establishments in the center of town, but inside, pleasant surprises abound. First, there is a small, quite British bar (reserved for hotel guests except on Saturday morning); a lounge decorated with true elegance; and finally the patio, which is the very charming prolongation of the two dining rooms. Sheltered from the wind, bordered by shrubs and hollyhocks, it is a perfect setting for dinner and relaxation in the gentle climate of the southern Charente-Maritime. In the kitchen, young M. Jaubert turns out masterful specialties and the prices are right. After having apprenticed with the greatest chefs, he has returned to his native town to open his own business, and his reputation is growing still. As for the bedrooms, the conveniences and decoration are very ordinary but not unpleasant. Four look out onto the patio and the others onto a quiet street at night; all are perfectly maintained. Let us add that the atmosphere is very welcoming, youthful and informal, and you will understand why the Hôtel de Bordeaux is the delight of all who stay there.

How to get there (Map 22): 22km south of Saintes.

Hôtel France et Angleterre et Champlain ★★★

20, rue Rambaud
17000 La Rochelle (Charente-Maritime)
Tel. (0)5★ 46.41.23.99 - Fax (0)5★ 46.41.15.19 - Mme Jouineau

Rooms 36 with telephone, bath or shower, WC, cable TV, 5 with air-conditioning and 28 with minibar; elevator. **Price** Single and double 310-535F, suite 655F. **Meals** Breakfast 45F, served 7:15-11:30. No restaurant. **Credit cards** All major. **Pets** Dogs allowed (+30F). **Facilities** Garage (35-48F). **Nearby** New World museum, Lafaille museum, Protestant and arts museum in La Rochelle, Ile de Ré, Esnandes, church portal and dungeon in Vouvant, Poitou marshes – 18-hole La Prée golf course in La Rochelle. **Open** All year.

This 17th-century former convent hides a beautiful garden behind its walls, which is a good place for breakfast. To get to the garden you cross a large hall and some lovely reception rooms. Period woodwork, antique statues and lovely old furniture create a warm and elegant ambience. The bedrooms, reached by elevator or by the splendid stone staircase, offer you the choice of a comfortable modern style or the charm and elegance of an earlier era. They are different in decor but all are comfortable, though you will probably prefer those with a view overlooking the garden; the rooms on the street have double glazing and all will soon be air-conditioned. There is no restaurant but the hotel has a *demi-pension* arrangement with the adjacent restaurant. The staff is very pleasant, adding further to the hotel's many attractive features. For the best seafood in La Rochelle, try *La Marmite,* or the bustling bistrot *La Marée,* for its giant platters of shellfish.

How to get there *(Map 22): In the center of La Rochelle.*

Résidence de Rohan ★★★

Parc des Fées
17640 Vaux-sur-Mer (Charente-Maritime)
Tel. (0)5★ 46.39.00.75 – Fax (0)5★ 46.38.29.99 – M. and Mme Seguin

Rooms 41 with telephone, bath or shower, WC and TV. **Price** Single and double 300-700F. **Meals** Breakfast 51F, served 7:30-13:00. No restaurant. **Credit cards** Amex, Visa, Eurocard and MasterCard. **Pets** Dogs allowed. **Facilities** Tennis (+50F), parking. **Nearby** Lighthouse of Cordouan, La Rochelle, Sablonceaux abbey, Talmont-sur-Gironde, zoo of La Palmyre – 18-hole Côte de la Beauté golf course in Royan. **Open** Easter – Nov 13.

This pretty little family house is in a little wood which runs behind the beach at Nauzan. The pink and white 19th-century building has lawns sloping gently down to the beach, with chaises longues scattered among the pines. Inside, the decor is quite different from what you might expect to find in a seaside house; the velvet-covered armchairs in the lounge, the mahogany Charles X-style furniture in the bar, the carpets and rugs create a rather opulent ambience. All the bedrooms have their own style and beautiful fabrics; many are furnished with antique furniture. Some rooms, notably those in the annex, are very spacious, while others open onto the garden where you can have breakfast. The hosts are friendly and hospitable. *Le Chalet, Les Trois Marmites, Les Filets Bleus* and *La Sabotière* are good restaurants which will compensate for the hotel's lack of one.

How to get there *(Map 22): 3km northwest of Royan via D25, which follows the coast in the towards of Saint-Palais-sur-Mer.*

Au Marais ★★★

46-48, quai Louis-Tardy
79510 Coulon (Deux-Sèvres)
Tel. (0)5★ 49.35.90.43 - Fax (0)5★ 49.35.81.98 - M. and Mme Nerrière

Rooms 18 with telephone, bath, WC and TV. **Price** Double 250-600F. **Meals** Breakfast (buffet) 40F, served 7:30-10:00 No restaurant. **Credit cards** Visa, Eurocard and MasterCard. **Pets** Dogs allowed (+35F). **Nearby** Poitou marshes, museums and church of Notre-Dame in Niort – 18-hole golf course in Maziéres-en-Gatine. **Open** All year.

All the magic of the Poitou marshland is here in front of the hotel: the Sèvre River is directly in front of the hotel and the cruise boats are nearby. The hotel is built in classic Poitou style and has been totally restored without being spoiled. The interior decoration is very tasteful. In the bedrooms, there is a beautiful assortment of fresh colors and handsome furniture and fabrics. They are all remarkably well kept and the bathrooms are immaculate. The hotel is quiet despite the numbers of tourists in July and August. This is an excellent small hotel which is ideal for visiting "Green Venice" and where you will find a young, very friendly staff. Note that there is no longer a restaurant in the hotel but you can enjoy a range of local specialties at the pleasant *Les Mangeux de Lumas* three kilometers away.

How to get there *(Map 15): 10km west of Niort via D9 and D1 (beside the Sèvre niortaise).*

Le Logis Saint-Martin ★★★

Chemin de Pissot
79400 Saint-Maixent-l'Ecole (Deux-Sèvres)
Tel. (0)5★ 49.05.58.68 – Fax (0)5★ 49.76.19.93 – Mme and M. Heintz

Rooms 10 with telephone, bath or shower, WC and TV. **Price** Single and double 360-460F. **Meals** Breakfast 55F, served 8:00-10:30; half board 390-440F (per pers., 3 days min.). **Restaurant** Service 12:15-14:00, 19:30-21:30; menus 95F (lunch), 140-160F, also à la carte. Specialties: Foie gras de canard cuit au torchon, carré d'agneau de lait, côte de bœuf Parthenaise. **Credit cards** All major. **Pets** Dogs allowed (+60F). **Facilities** Parking. **Nearby** Local history museum, arts museum, Notre-Dame church in Niort, church in Melle, Tumulus of Bougon museum, Futuroscope in Poitiers – 9-hole golf courses in Mazières-en-Gatine, Sainte-Maxire and Les Forges. **Open** Jan 29 – 31 Dec.

This large 17th-century stone house, so cool when it is hot outside, and so warm in the winter, is a great place to spend a weekend. From here you can walk along the Sèvre River which runs in front of the hotel, and through the countryside described by René Bazin in *L'Église Verte*. You can also enjoy the local architecture in this region rich in Romanesque art and buildings. The comfortable rooms look out on the river. They are all light, quiet, and very pleasant. The cuisine is very good and the hosts are warm and welcoming.

How to get there *(Map 15): 24km northeast of Niort via N11.*

Le Roumanin

Chemin des Plèches
04550 Esparron-de-Verdon (Alpes-de-Haute-Provence)
Tel. (0)4★ 92.77.15.91 - Mme Tellier

Rooms 10 with telephone, bath, shower, WC and 1 with TV. **Price** Double 320F.
Meals Breakfast 40F, served 8:30-10:30; half board (obligatory in July and Aug) 310F
(per pers.). **Restaurant** Only for residents.Service 19:30, menu. **Credit cards** Not
accepted. **Pets** Dogs not allowed. **Facilities** Swimming pool, parking. **Nearby** Gorges
du Verdon, lakes route – 18-hole golf course in Pierrevert. **Open** March – Oct (closed
Nov 1).

Here is a charming simple hotel for lovers of nature and beautiful
landscapes. It was built recently and has a marvelous view of
the turquoise waters of Lake Esparon. Because of the many nooks
and crannies of its architecture, you'll feel as though you are in a
private house. The interior of the building is uncluttered, almost
austere; the white walls, old furniture and blue Provençal fabrics
are delightful. The bedrooms are in the same simple style but are
very comfortable and well cared for. Each has a private terrace. Six
overlook the delightful garden of aromatic plants which slopes
down to the swimming pool, and in the distance are the lake and
the mountains. The other four do not have a view but are cooler.
In any of them you will enjoy perfect quiet. You will also appreciate
Mme Tellier's courtesy and kindness. This pleasant hotel has
reasonable prices.

How to get there *(Map 34): 60km north of Aix-en-Provence via A51, exit
Gréoux-les-Bains, then D952 to Gréoux-les-Bains and D82 (1km from the
village).*

400

Auberge Charembeau ★★

Route de Niozelles
04300 Forcalquier (Alpes-de-Haute-Provence)
Tel. (0)4★ 92.75.05.69 - Fax (0)4★ 92.75.24.37 - M. Berger

Rooms 12 with telephone, bath or shower and WC. **Price** Single 270F, double 350F. Rooms with kitchenette 1700-2700F per week. **Meals** Breakfast 42F, served 8:00-9:30. No restaurant. **Credit cards** All major. **Pets** Dogs allowed (+20F). **Facilities** Swimming pool, tennis (+60F), mountain bikes, parking. **Nearby** Lure mountain, Salagon priory, Ganagobie priory, château de Sauvan, Saint-Michel-l'Observatoire. **Open** Feb 1 – Nov 30.

This little hotel in the middle of the lovely countryside of the Forcalquier region is run by a friendly couple who have given the old restored house a charming family atmosphere. The bedrooms, are simple and in good taste. Some of them have cooking facilities, which may be useful for families. In front of the house is a terrace which is perfect for those who want nothing more than to enjoy the Provençal landscape. For good Provençal country cooking, we recommend *L'Hostellerie des Deux Lions* in Forcalquier or *Le Bois d'Asson* in Sainte-Jaime.

How to get there *(Map 34): 39km south of Sisteron via N85 (or A51, exit La Brillanne), then D12 towards Forcalquier. It's 4km from Forcalquier via N100 towards Niozelles.*

La Fare ★

Pierrerue 04300 Forcalquier (Alpes-de-Haute-Provence)
Tel. (0)4★ 92.75.20.28 - Fax (0)4★ 92.72.71.02
M. Baussan

Rooms 3 with Telephone, bath or shower, WC, TV and minibar. **Price** Single 650F, double 800F, suite 950F. **Meals** Breakfast incl., served from 7:30; half board 550F (per pers.). **Restaurant** Evening meals only for residents. Service 20:00, menu 150F. Specialties: Regional cooking. **Credit cards** All major. **Pets** Dogs not allowed. **Facilities** Swimming pool, hammam, mountain bikes, parking. **Nearby** Lure mountain, Salagon priory, Ganagobie priory, château of Sauvan, Saint-Michel-l'Observatoire. **Open** All year except in Feb

We are happy to be able to suggest a new hotel in the Haute Provence beloved of Jean Giono, which is so beautiful and yet less known than southern Provence. Dating from 1789, this house has just been entirely restored and the owners have taken advantage of the occasion to create two guest bedrooms and a suite with salon in one part of the building. The services available are half-way between those of an auberge and those of a bed-and-breakfast. The decoration of the bedrooms during our visit was not yet finished but we were able to enjoy their modern conveniences. Physical fitness is also a consideration: a hammam, SPA (boiling baths), an exercise room and mountain bikes are at your disposal. For those with a lazy streak, there is a large, beautiful swimming pool. La Fare should live up to all our expectations.

How to get there *(Map 34): 39km south of Sisteron via N85 (or A51, La Brillanne exit); then D12 towards Forcalquier; 3km from Forcalquier.*

Bastide de Moustiers ★★★★

04360 Moustiers-Sainte-Marie (Alpes-de-Haute-Provence)
Tel. (0)4★ 92.70.47.47 - Fax (0)4★ 92.70.47.48
M. Ducasse

Rooms 7 with air-conditioning, Telephone, Fax, bath, shower, WC, TV, safe and minibar. **Price** Double 800-1300F. **Meals** Breakfast 75F. **Restaurant** Service 12:00-14:30, 19:30-21:45, menus 195-260F. Spacialties: Regional cooking. **Credit cards** Amex, Eurocard and MasterCard. **Pets** Dogs not allowed. **Facilities** Heated swimming pool, parking. **Nearby** Church and Pottery Museum in Moustiers, the Grand Canyon of the Gorges of the Verdon via the road or GR4; Lake of Sainte-Croix. **Open** Mar 16 – Jan 3

Great names in French gastonomy are regularly mentioned in this guide. Far from changing our criteria for selection, we have included the great chefs who have opened a charming hotel or inn along with their prestigious restaurant. This year, three-star chef A. Ducasse has opened a Provençal auberge in Moustiers which reflects the loveliest tradition of this region. It is a tradition of hospitality, and you will be received as friends. The kitchen is open to you; you can have dinner at the same table or enjoy a romantic *tête à tête* in one of the dining rooms; and you can browse quietly through the books in the library. You will also find tradition in the decor, with its elegant and comfortable furnishings, antique Provençal furniture. There is tradition, too, in the environment in this part of Provence, where cypresses intermingle with poplars, oaks with olive trees, chestnut with almond trees, and of course, there is the traditional country vegetable garden. Simplicity, charm and the outstanding Ducasse quality are so many reasons you will be enchanted with the Bastide de Moustiers.

How to get there *(Map 34): 50km from Manosque (A51), towards Gréoux-les-Bains, Riez, Moustiers. From Nice (A8) Le Luc exit.*

La Ferme Rose

04360 Moustiers-Sainte-Marie (Alpes-de-Haute-Provence)
Tel. (0)4★ 92.74.69.47 – Fax (0)4★ 92.74.60.76
M. Kako Vagh

Rooms 7 with telephone, shower and WC. **Price** Double 350-380F. **Meals** Breakfast 45F or brunch à la carte. **Restaurant** Service 20:00-22:00, menu 110F, also à la carte. Specialties: Provençal cooking with market produce. **Credit cards** Amex, Visa, Eurocard and MasterCard. **Pets** Dogs allowed. **Nearby** Church and Pottery Museum in Moustiers, the Grand Canyon of the Gorges of the Verdon via the road or GR4; Lake of Sainte-Croix. **Open** All year.

From the terrace of "The Pink Farm," you will have a beautiful view over the lovely village of Moustiers, which seems suspended between two cliffs. The hotel is charming. The owner has decorated it in a very personal style, combining his collection of l950s objects, paintings done by his grandfather – a well-known Provençal painter – and amusing pieces of furniture. Note the tables, chairs and bar banquettes which came from the old Brasserie Noailles in Marseilles. The bedrooms are very pleasant, bright and cheerful, with shower rooms decorated in pretty Salernes tiles from the region. The very helpful owner, Kako, will reserve a mattress for you on a private beach on Sainte Croix Lake, rent you an electric boat to ascend the Verdon Falls, or give you tips insider's for visiting this endearing village in the spectacular Alps of Haute Provence.

How to get there *(Map 34): 50km from Manosque, then D6 towards Valensole. In Moustiers, take the towards of Sainte-Croix for 1km.*

Auberge du Clos Sorel ★★★
Les Molanès
04400 Pra-Loup (Alpes-de-Haute-Provence)
Tel. (0)4★ 92.84.10.74 - Mme Mercier

Rooms 10 with telephone, bath, WC and TV. **Price** Single 400F, double 520-650F. **Meals** Breakfast 50F, served 8:00-10:30; half board +200F (per pers., 3 days min.). **Restaurant** Service 12:30-14:30; menu 165F, also à la carte. Specialties: Morilles, ravioles, gigots. **Credit cards** Visa, Eurocard and MasterCard. **Pets** Dogs allowed (+35F). **Facilities** Swimming pool. **Nearby** Skiing from hotel, Colmars, route de la Bonette. **Open** Dec 15 – Sept 5 and June 30 – Apr 11.

Well located on a hillside, an old farmhouse has been converted into the Auberge du Clos Sorel. The building has lovely stone walls and an entranceway built of logs, and blends in perfectly with the surrounding chalets. Inside, original features such as beams, an impressive fireplace and sloping ceilings have been retained, and these combine with the polished furniture to create the kind of warm and cozy atmosphere one looks forward to after a long day spent skiing or walking. In the evening, dinner is served by candlelight in what used to be the main room of the farmhouse. The tables are pretty and the cuisine is refined. In summer, a swimming-pool and tennis courts add to the many attractions of the inn. A relaxed and informal atmosphere prevails. Clos Sorel is a hamlet which time truly seems to have passed by, although it is on the ski slopes of Pra-Loup.

How to get there *(Map 34): 70km southwest of Gap via D900B and D900 to Barcelonnette, then D902 and D109 to Pra-Loup. (Les Molanès is just before the resort.)*

Auberge de Reillanne

04110 Reillanne (Alpes-de-Haute-Provence)
Tel. (0)4★ 92.76.45.95
M. Bellaiche

Rooms 7 with telephone, bath, WC and minibar. **Price** Single 260F, double 360F.
Meals Breakfast 45F; half board 360F (per pers.). **Restaurant** Closed Wednesday
except for residents. Service 19:00-21:00; menus 125-170F, also à la carte.
Specialties: Piccata de fois gras aux navets confits, soliman d'agneau à la menthe
et au miel, home-smoked fish and duck breast. **Credit cards** Visa, Eurocard and
MasterCard. **Pets** Dogs allowed. **Facilities** Parking. **Nearby** Manosque, priories of
Salagon and Ganagobie, château de Sauvan. **Open** All year.

Located in a part of the Luberon which has remained unspoiled,
this hotel is surrounded by greenery. The few bedrooms are
large, plainly furnished, but warm and comfortable, with an
emphasis on natural materials: light-colored wood or cane,
unbleached wool and flowery fabrics. All the bedrooms have
pleasant views and lovely bathrooms with terracotta floor tiles.
There is no charge to use the minibars in the rooms, guests decide
how much they want to pay for the drinks – obviously trust is the
keyword here. Maurice Bellaiche chose the hotel business because
he enjoys it, and has created a peaceful and above all friendly
atmosphere. He does the cooking himself, and his good seasonal
cuisine is based on fresh local produce, with a touch of exoticism.
You will find it all the more delectable in the charming dining
room where meals are served.

How to get there *(Map 33): 15km northwest of Manosque towards Apt,
then N100 and D214 towards Reillanne.*

Le Pyjama ★★★

04400 Super-Sauze (Alpes-de-Haute-Provence)
Tel. (0)4★ 92.81.12.00 - Fax (0)4★ 92.81.03.16
Mme Merle

Rooms 10 with telephone, bath, WC, TV and minibar. **Price** Single 250-310F, double 300-420F, suite 450-550F. **Meals** Breakfast 39F. No restaurant. **Credit cards** All major. **Pets** Dogs allowed. **Nearby** Skiing from the hotel, village of Colmars, Beauvezer, gorges of Saint-Pierre, Guillaumes via the col des Champs, route de la Bonette. **Open** Dec 15 – Sept 10 and June 25 – Apr 25.

Having spent twenty years running another hotel in the resort, Geneviève Merle (ski champion Carole Merle's mother) has recently had this small hotel built, using materials and designs which blend perfectly with the surroundings. Eight of the ten bedrooms face south, their terraces overlooking a field of larch trees. They are tastefully decorated, with very pleasant bathrooms. M. Merle owns an antique shop nearby, and it has provided the hotel furniture. Four rooms have a mezzanine which can accommodate two extra people. In the annex there are four studios complete with kitchen areas which are very convenient for families. The hotel doesn't have its own restaurant, but there are many in the resort, or higher up. *L'Optraken* which is run by Mme Merle's children, is next door; otherwise, try *Les Deux Mazots*. This is an extremely comfortable establishment, at the foot of the slopes, offering a friendly and informal atmosphere.

How to get there *(Map 34): 79km southeast of Gap via D900B and D900 towards Barcelonnette, then D9 and D209 to Super-Sauze.*

Le Clos de Chantemerle ★★

33, rue du centre Chantemerle
05330 Serre-Chevalier – Saint-Chaffrey (Hautes-Alpes)
Tel. (0)4★ 92.24.00.13 – Fax (0)4★ 92.24.09.51 – Mme Loubier

Rooms 31 with telephone, WC ,16 with bath and 1 with shower. **Price** Double 200-450F. **Meals** Breakfast 35-60F; half board 240-450F (per pers.). **Restaurant** Service from 19:00; menu 90-159F, also à la carte. **Credit cards** Visa, Eurocard and MasterCard. **Pets** Dogs allowed (+35F). **Facilities** Swimming pool in summer. **Nearby** Ski: 60m from the ski lift – 9-hole Montgenèvre Golf Course (18km), 9-hole Clavière Golf Course (21km). **Open** Dec – Sept (closed in May).

This old farmhouse dates from 1732 and was transformed into a hotel in the 1940s, becoming a favorite spot for celebrities who came here for its bohemian atmosphere. Denise Loubier and her husband have now given a new start to this large, very charming hotel whose antique furniture creates an intimate, traditional atmosphere. The bar and lounge, decorated with Provençal fabrics and Austrian-style painted paneling, are favorite gathering places, especially when there is a bright fire in the fireplace. Next to it is the large dining room with a panoramic view of the mountains and ski trails; self-service buffet breakfasts are served in the rear part with a skylight. The bedrooms have their original size and thus vary greatly in spaciousness and bathroom amenities. Antique furniture, engravings and old doors lend personality to the bedrooms. We particularly recommend those which have been recently renovated: they have lost none of their charm and gain considerably in their amenities. The hotel now has a very pleasant swimming pool for the summer.

How to get there *(Map 27): 4km northwest of Briançon via N91; in the village, next to the ski lift.*

La Boule de Neige ★★

15, rue du Centre
05330 Serre-Chevalier - Saint-Chaffrey (Hautes-Alpes)
Tel. (0)4★ 92.24.00.16 – Fax (0)4★ 92.24.00.25 – Mme Maury

Rooms 10 with telephone, bath or shower and WC. **Price** Double 270-440F, 435-630F in winter. **Meals** Breakfast 40F served 8:00-10:00; half board 280-315F, 360-480F in winter (per pers.). **Restaurant** Service 19:30-21:00; menu 115-165F, also à la carte. **Credit cards** Amex, Visa, Eurocard and MasterCard. **Pets** Dogs not allowed. **Facilities** Swimming pool in summer. **Nearby** Ski – 9-hole Montgenèvre Golf Course (18km), 9-hole Clavière Golf Course (21km). **Open** All year except in May, Oct and Nov.

This village house has just been entirely renovated with great taste and good practical sense. On the ground floor, a small curved bar stands next to a room tiled in Burgundian stones and prettily decorated with elegant wooden tables, an imposing piece of Indian furniture and several sprays of dried flowers on the walls. The room extends into a charming barrel-vaulted dining room and, three steps down, there is a pleasant small lounge with fireplace. The bedrooms, comfortable and impeccably kept, have been designed in a modern style, making them less charming than the rest of the hotel. Except for the two bedrooms located on the street side of the *premier étage*, all are very bright. Four rooms have a balcony and look out over the old rooftops of the village and a bumpy field beyond, where skiers can get a final bit of practice before heading out for the slopes.

How to get there *(Map 27): 5km northwest of Briançon via N91.*

Mas de la Pagane

15, avenue du Mas-Ensoleillé
06600 Antibes (Alpes-Maritimes)
Tel. (0)4★ 93.33.33.78 – Fax (0)4★ 93.74.55.37 – Mme Ott

Rooms 5 with telephone, bath, shower, WC and TV. **Price** Single and double 550F. **Meals** Breakfast 35F. **Restaurant** Closed Sunday evening. Service 12:00-14:30, 20:00-22:30; menu 130F, also à la carte. Specialties: Poisson à l'apicius, beignets de cervelle sauce safran, poivron braisé et fondant d'aubergine. **Credit cards** Amex, Visa, Eurocard and MasterCard. **Pets** Dogs allowed. **Facilities** Parking. **Nearby** Picasso museum in Antibes, Cap d'Antibes, Villa Thuret, chapel of La Garoupe, Fernand Léger museum in Biot – 18-hole Opio golf course in Valbonne. **Open** All year.

This is the kind of address one likes to find in the Provence that has charmed so many artists. Close to the yacht harbor, this old house is tucked away from the rest of the town in beautiful grounds. Inside, contemporary works of art, lovely fabrics and antique furniture have been combined with consummate skill. In the bedrooms, the decor is very elegant. The cuisine is far from second-rate: it is light, innovative – in short, delectable. In summer, meals can be served on the flowery terrace. The bar opens out into the garden, and provides the perfect setting for an evening drink. The Mas is a friendly place.

How to get there *(Map 35): Take Avenue du Mas-Ensoleillé at crossroads at entrance to Antibes, then signs for hotel.*

Hôtel de Paris ★★★

34, boulevard d'Alsace
06400 Cannes (Alpes-Maritimes)
Tel. (0)4★ 93.38.30.89 - Fax (0)4★ 93.39.04.61 - M. Lazzari

Rooms 45 and 5 suites, with telephone, bath or shower, WC and TV. **Price** Single 500-650F, double 550-750F, suite 900-1600F. **Meals** Breakfast 50F, served 7:00-11:00. No restaurant. **Credit cards** All major. **Pets** Dogs not allowed. **Facilities** Parking (80F). **Nearby** Massif du Tanneron, Auribeau-sur-Siagne, Mougins, Vallauris, îles de Lérins – 27-hole Cannes golf course in Mandelieu. **Open** Dec 17 – Nov 15.

This hotel is in a large white house near the highway. Its facade is decorated with columns and pediments in typical turn of the century Côte d'Azur style. Although the hotel is in the center of Cannes it has a garden (a bit noisy) with palms and cypresses around a very pleasant swimming pool. The interior is very smart. The bedrooms are decorated with prints. The suites are luxurious and have a private lounge. All the rooms are air-conditioned and soundproofed and some have a balcony on which you can have breakfast. For restaurants, try *Gaston et Gastounette* for bourride or bouillabaisse; *Côté Jardin, Au Bec Fin* or *La Brouette de Grand-mère* for fresh cuisine and good chef's-special menu; and a interesting menu; *Chez Franco* for Italian cooking; *Le Café Carlton* on the beach of the Carlton Hotel, for an informal and chic buffet lunch; and *Le Rado-Plage* under the parasols on the Croisette.

How to get there *(Map 34): In the town center.*

411

Auberge du Soleil *

Quartier Porta-Savel
06390 Coaraze (Alpes–Maritimes)
Tel. (0)4★ 93.79.08.11 – Fax (0)4★ 93.79.37.79 – M. and Mme Jacquet

Rooms 8 and 2 suites in annex with telephone, bath or shower, WC and TV on request. **Price** Single 330-390F, double 350-495F, suite 495-940F. **Meals** Breakfast 45F, served 8:00-12:00; half board 360-440F, (per pers., 3 days min.). **Restaurant** Service 12:00-14:00, 19:30-21:00; menu 142F, also à la carte. Specialties: Tourte maison, gibelotte de lapin, caille aux raisins. **Credit cards** Amex, Visa, Eurocard and MasterCard. **Pets** Dogs allowed (+35F). **Facilities** Swimming pool, boules, table tennis. **Nearby** Mercantour reserve, valley of the Merveilles, Turini forest, villages of Lucéram, Peille and Peillon – 18-hole Agel golf course in La Turbie. **Open** Mar 15 – Nov 15.

This hotel is only half an hour from Nice and not far from the magnificent nature reserve of Mercantour. It is splendidly located in a medieval village 640 meters up on a rocky outcrop. The maze of narrow village streets ensures total peace and calm: you may need to call on the hotel to help with your luggage up the steep slopes. You will find an informal, almost bohemian atmosphere in the hotel but it is all in elegant taste. There is a summer lounge located in a cool vaulted cellar and an attractive dining room which extends out over a covered terrace with panoramic views of the valley. The cuisine is simple and good. The garden slopes down in steps to the swimming pool and orchard, where you can pick the fruit without feeling guilty.

How to get there *(Map 35): 2km north of Nice via A8 exit Nice-Est, then "voie rapide" (highway) towards Drap-Sospel. At the Pointe des Contes, left towards Contes-Coaraze.*

La Tour de l'Esquillon ★★★

Miramar
06590 Théoule-sur-Mer (Alpes-Maritimes)
Tel. (0)4★ 93.75.41.51 – Fax (0)4★ 93.75.49.99 – M. and Mme Dérobert

Rooms 25 with telephone, bath, WC, TV and minibar. **Price** Single and double 400-800F. **Meals** Breakfast 60F, served 8:00-10:00; half board 520-720F. **Restaurant** Service 12:00-14:00, 19:00-21:00; menus 120-145F, also à la carte. Specialties: Fish, bouride, aïoli. **Credit cards** All major. **Pets** Dogs allowed. **Facilities** Private beach, parking. **Nearby** Château of Napoule, Estérel Mountains, point of l'Esquillon, bight of Napoule – 18-hole Cannes-Mandelieu golf course. **Open** Feb 1 – Oct 14.

At the edge of the winding road overlooking the deep-red Esterel Mountains, the Tour de L'Esquillon is perched like a bird's nest. Brilliant yellow broom, pink oleander, hydrangeas and fruit trees covering the terraced garden lie between the hotel and its private beach which you can reach by minibus, and where you can enjoy light meals. The Esquillon has a kind of old-fashioned charm, which is accented by its 1950s furniture and its discreet, friendly service. The 25 bedrooms are large and cool, and they face the Mediterranean. Some more expensive rooms have a balcony, which is a pleasant place to have breakfast. In the restaurant, you will enjoy the savory, spicy specialties of Provence. From the dining room, you will have a panoramic view over Cannes. It's a shame that the background music somewhat spoils this lovely place; at least it covers the sound of the traffic on the road, which certainly can be disturbing.

How to get there (Map 34): Between Saint-Raphael and Cannes, on A7, exit Mandelieu, then in the towards of Théole Miramar.

413

Le Manoir de l'Etang ★★★

66, allée du Manoir
06250 Mougins (Alpes-Maritimes)
Tel. (0)4★ 93.90.01.07 - Fax (0)4★ 92.92.20.70 – Gridaine-Labro Family

Rooms 15 with telephone, bath or shower, WC, TV and minibar. **Price** Double 600-900F, suite 1300-1500F. **Meals** Breakfast 55F, served 8:00-10:30. **Restaurant** Service 12:00-14:00, 20:00-22:00; menus 150F (lunchtime), 145-190F, also à la carte. Specialties: Canelloni de homard au jus de favouilles, lapereau mijoté à la niçoise, millefeuille de framboise et chocolat, nougat glacé au miel du manoir. **Credit cards** Amex, Visa ,Eurocard and MasterCard. **Pets** Small dogs allowed. **Facilities** Swimming pool, parking. **Nearby** The Riviera and her villages – 18-hole Cannes-Mougins golf course. **Open** All year except Nov and Feb.

This superb 19th-century house, surrounded by cypresses and oleander, overlooks a lake in a rolling 17-acre park. On the ground floor there is a warmly decorated lounge with a terra-cotta floor and a bright dining room overlooking the pool; which is framed by olive trees. Beyond the pool there are extensive views over the Provençal landscape. The comfortable bedrooms are brightened by cheerful materials printed with flowers and fruits. You will enjoy delicious regional cuisine which is light and inventive. Enjoy the tranquil atmosphere and the good humor of the owners, who will give you a real family welcome. This is a delightful and charming place to stay.

How to get there *(Map 34): 5km north of Cannes via "voie rapide" (highway).*

Hôtel La Pérouse ★★★★
11, quai Rauba-Capeu
06300 Nice (Alpes-Maritimes)
Tel. (0)4★ 93.62.34.63 – Fax (0)4★ 93.62.59.41 – M. Mercadal

Rooms 64 with air-conditioning, telephone, bath or shower, WC, TV and minibar. **Price** Single 395-1300F, double 650-1300F, suite 1600-2150F. **Meals** Breakfast 80F, served 6:30-11:00. **Restaurant** Closed Sept 15 – May 15. Service 12:00-15:00, 19:30-22:00; à la carte. Specialties: Grills in the hotel gardens. **Credit cards** All major. **Pets** Dogs allowed. **Facilities** Swimming pool, sauna, whirlpool, solarium. **Nearby** Turini forest, valley of La Tinée (Roure, Roubron), valley of La Vésubie, villages of Utelle, Belvédère, le Boréon, Venanson – 18-hole Opio golf course in Valbonne, 18-hole Bastide-du-Roy golf course in Biot. **Open** All year.

La Pérouse is in a large Mediterranean-style mansion at the foot of the château that dominates old Nice and the Baie des Anges. It is surrounded by aloe plants and lemon trees; to reach it you have to take one of the two elevators from the quayside. The bedrooms are spacious and quiet, and prices vary according to whether you have a view of the garden or the sea; some have a terrace with deck chairs. In summer you might take advantage of the barbecue, swimming pool, and solarium, and enjoy a drink on the terrace.

How to get there *(Map 35): In the town center.*

Hôtel Windsor ★★★

11, rue Dalpozzo
06300 Nice (Alpes-Maritimes)
Tel (0)4★ 93.88.59.35 – Fax (0)4★ 93.88.9457 – M. Redolfi-Strizzot

Rooms 60 with telephone, bath or shower, WC, TV and minibar; elevator. **Price** Single 300-525F, double 400-670F. **Meals** Breakfast 40F, served 7:00-10:30; half board 390-495F (per pers.). **Restaurant** Closed Saturday noon and Sunday. Service 12:00-14:00, 19:00-22:30, also à la carte. **Credit cards** All major. **Pets** Dogs allowed. **Facilities** Swimming pool, sauna (70F), parking (60F). **Nearby** Turini forest, valley of La Tinée (Roure, Roubron), valley of La Vésubie, villages of Utelle, Belvédère, le Boréon, Venanson – 18-hole Opio golf course in Valbonne, 18-hole Bastide-du-Roy golf course in Biot. **Open** All year.

From the street, the Windsor seems like a classic mid-town hotel. Once you step inside, however, this impression soon fades. In the modern reception area, there is an ornate Oriental bed encrusted with mother-of-pearl and an ancient gilt shrine with a seated Buddha in the center. Just outside, you will also discover a luxuriant exotic garden with an aviary in the hollow of an old tree; here, a few tables are hidden away not far from a small swimming pool. In the bedrooms, the furniture is deliberately 1950s-60s hotel style. Many are large, all are comfortable and some have interesting frescos on the walls. If you have avant-garde taste, ask for the "Numéro" room. There is a well-equipped gym and a hammam with a skylight. Finally, while there is no restaurant as such, you can enjoy the chef's special at the bar: It, too, is often exotic!

How to get there (Map 35): In the center of town.

Auberge de la Madone ★★★
06440 Peillon (Alpes-Maritimes)
Tel. (0)4★ 93.79.91.17 – Fax (0)4★ 93.79.99.36
Millo Family

Rooms 20 with telephone, bath, shower and WC. **Price** Double 430-780F, suite 850-1100F. **Meals** Breakfast 55F, served 8:00-10:00; half board 460-700F (per pers.). **Restaurant** By reservation. Service 12:30-14:00, 19:30-20:30; menus 140-280F, also à la carte. Specialties: Bouillabaisse froide, carré d'agneau aux petits légumes fondants. **Credit cards** Visa, Eurocard and MasterCard. **Pets** Dogs not allowed. **Facilities** Tennis, parking. **Nearby** Nice, valleys of La Tinée and La Vésubie – 18-hole Mont-Agel golf course. **Open** All year except 20 Oct – 20 Dec and 7 Jan – 24 Jan (closed Wednesday).

The Auberge is a good place for those with a taste for adventure. All around it are deep ravines and rocky summits which you would hardly suspect existed only twenty minutes from Nice. From the hotel's sunny terraces you will have all the time in the world to look out on Peillon, one of the most spectacular villages in the Niçois hinterland, perched on a steep crag and with superb views all around. You can explore it on foot, up the steep stairways which lead up to the Chapel of the Pénitents Blancs. The hotel has an attractive decor with all the refinements for a comfortable stay. The excellent regional cooking is reasonably priced and encourages visitors who prefer the tranquillity of Peillon to the tourist frenzy of the Nice coast.

How to get there *(Map 35): 19km north of Nice via D2204 towards L'Escarène, then on the Peille bridge D21 towards Peillon. On the left as you enter the village.*

Hôtel Les Deux Frères ★★

Place des Deux-Frères
Roquebrune Village, 06190 Cap-Martin (Alpes-Maritimes)
Tel. (0)4★ 93.28.99.00 - Fax (0)4★ 93.28.99.10 - M. Inthout

Rooms 10 with telephone, bath or shower, WC and TV. **Price** Single 385F, double 495F. **Meals** Breakfast 45F. **Restaurant** Service 12:00-14:00, 19:30-22:00; à la carte. Specialties: Fish, duck, foie gras. **Credit cards** Amex, Visa, Eurocard and MasterCard. **Pets** Dogs allowed (+40F). **Nearby** Rue Moncolet in Roquebrune, La Turbie church, footpath to Cap Martin – 18-hole Monte-Carlo Golf Course in La Turbie. **Open** Dec 15 – Nov 15 (closed Thursday).

The two brothers of the hotel's name are actually the two rocks that gave their name to the village of Roquebrune. The square named for them is one of the best sites in the medieval village, protected by its Carolingian castle. Here a school was built; 15 years after its closing a Dutch architect transformed it into a hotel. The classrooms were turned into pretty white-walled bedrooms, and the courtyard into a restaurant. Around the great fireplace comfortable leather covered sofas are grouped, creating a place that most guests find difficult to tear themselves away from in the evenings. The decor is delightful, there are always plenty of flowers, and you will receive a warm welcome.

How to get there *(Map 35): 5km south of Menton via A8 or N98.*

418

Auberge du Colombier ★★★

06330 Roquefort-les-Pins (Alpes-Maritimes)
Tel. (0)4★ 93.77.10.27 - Fax (0)4★ 93.77.07.03
M. Wolff

Rooms 18, 2 suites with telephone, bath, shower, WC and TV **Price** Single 200-350F, double 350-550F, suite 450-800F. **Meals** Breakfast 50F; half board +170F, full board +340F. **Restaurant** Closed Tuesday in low season. Service 12:00-14:30, 19:00-22:00; menus 125-190F, also à la carte. Specialties: Salade gourmande de caille tiède au foie gras, chariot de patisseries maison. **Credit cards** All major. **Pets** Dogs allowed (+40F). **Facilities** Swimming pool, tennis (+50F), parking. **Nearby** Nice, Grasse, gorges of Le Loup and Gourdon – 18-hole Opio golf course in Valbonne. **Open** All year except Jan 10 – Feb 10.

This old stagecoach stop on the route from Nice to Grasse (once a two-day journey) still makes a good overnight halt or a pleasant base from which to explore the many attractions of the French Riviera. The auberge was modernized in 1980 but preserves its old charm. Today it has a beautiful swimming pool, a tennis court and some more recently built bedrooms in which, however, some of the atmosphere has been lost. You will find a pleasant welcome here and a restaurant which is renowned for its cuisine and its *spécialités de la maison*.

How to get there *(Map 34): 25km west of Nice via A8, exit Villeneuve-Loubet, then D2085 towards Grasse.*

Hôtel Brise Marine ★★★

58, avenue Jean–Mermoz
06230 Saint-Jean-Cap-Ferrat (Alpes-Maritimes)
Tel. (0)4★ 93.76.04.36 – Fax (0)4★ 93.76.11.49 – M. Maîtrehenry

Rooms 16 with air-conditioning, telephone, bath or shower, WC, TV and safe. **Price** Double 640-695F. **Meals** Breakfast 55F, served 8:00-10:00. No restaurant. **Credit cards** Visa, Eurocard and MasterCard. **Pets** Dogs allowed. **Nearby** Saint-Pierre chapel (Cocteau) in Villefranche, Villa Ephrussi-de-Rothschild in Saint-Jean-Cap-Ferrat, Villa Kerylos in Beaulieu – 18-hole La Bastide-du-Roy golf course in Biot. **Open** Feb 1 – Oct 30.

Located among the luxurious villas, grand hotels and noble residences in Saint-Jean-Cap-Ferrat, this is a little Italian house built in the 19th century. The Hôtel Brise Marine has a delightful garden with flowers, palm trees, espaliers, stone balustrades, fountains and terraces. The owner has personally looked after the hotel and its sixteen elegant and comfortable little bedrooms for forty-five years. All of them look out on the gardens of an inaccessible château and the surrounding sea. You will enjoy a very friendly welcome here as well as excellent breakfasts. *La Voile d'Or* and *Le Provençal* are among the chic, expensive restaurants of Saint Jean. *Le Sloop* is a simpler, reasonably priced fish restaurant.

How to get there *(Map 35): 15km east of Nice via N98.*

Hôtel Le Hameau★★★

528, route de La Colle
06570 Saint-Paul-de-Vence (Alpes-Maritimes)
Tel. (0)4★ 93.32.80.24 - Fax (0)4★ 93.32.55.75 - M. Huvelin

Rooms 12 and 3 apartments with air-conditioning, telephone, bath or shower, WC, safe and minibar. **Price** Single 390F, double 440-600F, suite 700F. **Meals** Breakfast 53F, served 8:00-10:00. No restaurant. **Credit cards** Visa, Eurocard and MasterCard. **Pets** Dogs allowed. **Facilities** Swimming pool, garage (35F), parking. **Nearby** Chapel of Le Rosaire (Matisse), perfume museum, Maeght Foundation, church of Saint-Charles-Borromée in Saint-Paul-de-Vence, les Clues de Haute-Provence – 18-hole Opio golf course in Valbonne. **Open** All year except Jan 8 – Feb 15 and Nov 15 – Dec 22.

This white 1920s house looks over the valley and the village of Saint-Paul-de-Vence, and is up a path bordered by lemon trees in a flowering garden. The hotel has terraces and arcades and is almost hidden by honeysuckle, fig trees and climbing vines. The bedrooms are large and prettily decorated, and the furniture is traditionally Provençal. Numbers 1, 2 and 3 have a loggia and an impressive view of Saint-Paul. The old iridescent green tiles of some of the bathrooms are superb. In the adjoining 18th-century farmhouse there are other smaller attic rooms but they all have a lovely view. The friendly welcome you will find here will explain why so many guests return. There is no restaurant but apart from a gastronomic pilgrimage to the famous *Colombe d'Or*, you can enjoy delicious Provençal cuisine at *La Brouette*.

How to get there *(Map 34): 20km west of Nice via A8, exit Cagnes-sur-Mer, then D7 towards Vence via La Colle-sur-Loup; it's 1km before Saint-Paul-de-Vence.*

Auberge des Seigneurs et du Lion d'Or ★★

Place du Frêne
06140 Vence (Alpes–Maritimes)
Tel. (0)4★ 93.58.04.24 – Fax (0)4★ 93.24.08.01 – M. and Mme Rodi

Rooms 10 with telephone, shower and WC. **Price** Single 290F, double 324-354F. **Meals** Breakfast 50F, served 7:30-10:30. **Restaurant** Service from 12:30 and 19:30; menus 210-230F, also à la carte. Specialties: Carré d'agneau à la broche, tian vençois. **Credit cards** All major. **Pets** Dogs allowed. **Nearby** Chapel of Le Rosaire (Matisse), perfume museum, Carzou museum in Vence, Maeght Foundation, church of St-Charles-Borromée in Saint-Paul-de-Vence, les Clues de Haute Provence – 18-hole Opio golf course in Valbonne. **Open** All year except July 1 – 10 and Nov 15 – Dec 12.

This is a lovely, almost timeless auberge. Some parts of it date from the 14th century and some from the 17th century. In its day it has welcomed many famous guests such as King Francis I and, more recently, Renoir, Modigliani, Dufy, and Soutine. M. Rodi knows the exact dates of their visits and will enjoy telling you about them. The hotel is situated in a wing of the Château des Villeneuve de Vence, which is mostly occupied by the Carzou Museum. It is on the square where the ash tree planted by Francis I still flourishes. The reception rooms contain an eclectic collection of objects (a 16th-century washstand, an olive oil press, modern lithographs, etc.) all of which have a history. The bedrooms are large, furnished plainly but appropriately for the building, and there is always a basket of fruit and flowers awaiting every guest. The most attractive rooms look out on the square, the quietest over the rooftops. The whole Auberge is full of character and is very welcoming.

How to get there (Map 34): 10km north of Cagnes-sur-Mer via D36.

La Roseraie ★★

Avenue Henri-Giraud
06140 Vence (Alpes-Maritimes)
Tel. (0)4★ 93.58.02.20 - Fax (0)4★ 93.58.99.31 - M. and Mme Ganier

Rooms 12 with telephone, bath or shower, WC, TV and minibar. **Price** Single 390F, double 410-550F. **Meals** Breakfast 50F, served 8:30-12:00. No restaurant. **Credit cards** Amex, Visa, Eurocard and MasterCard. **Pets** Dogs allowed. **Facilities** Swimming pool, bike, parking. **Nearby** Chapelle du Rosaire (Matisse), fondation Maeght, Saint-Charles church, Borromée in Saint-Paul-de-Vence, les Clues de Haute-Provence – 18 hole Opio golf course in Valbonne. **Open** All year.

Dating from the turn of the century, the "Rose Garden" is a beautiful old Mediterranean-style residence in the heart of picturesque Vence. Graceful palm trees, magnolias, yucca, eucalyptus, banana trees, and roses, combined with a spectacular view over Vence and Baou Hill, create a veritable oasis of beauty and charm here. There are only twelve bedrooms, all decorated in the loveliest Provençal style; although all have a beautiful view, the best is to be enjoyed from rooms 4, 5, 8 (which have balconies), and from number 12, which has a terrace. The bathrooms are comfortable and prettily decorated with the famous Provençal tiles from nearby Salernes. The breakfasts are carefully prepared, with homemade croissants and traditional preserves. M. and Mme Ganier make every effort to please you. *La Farigoule*, a small restaurant near the hotel, offers good Provençal cuisine, and the *Auberge de Seigneurs* serves an outstanding rack of lamb grilled in the fireplace.

How to get there *(Map 34): 10km north of Cagnes-sur-Mer via D36.*

Hôtel Welcome ★★★

1, quai Courbet
06230 Villefranche-sur-Mer (Alpes-Maritimes)
Tel. (0)4★ 93.76.76.93 - Fax (0)4★ 93.01.88.81 - M. and Mme Galbois

Rooms 32 with air-conditioning, telephone, bath or shower, WC, TV and minibar. **Price** Single and double 580-890F. **Meals** Breakfast 40F, served 7:30-10:00; half board 440-595F (per pers.). **Restaurant** Service 12:30-14:00, 19:30-22:30; menus 155-195F, also à la carte. Specialties: Fish. **Credit cards** All major. **Pets** Dogs allowed (+25F). **Nearby** The Lower Corniche, St-Jean-Cap-Ferrat (Villa Ephrussi de Rothschild), Beaulieu (Villa Kerylos) – 18-hole Opio golf course in Valbonne. **Open** Dec 19 – Nov 17.

On the quayside of the old port of Villefranche you will find colorful fishing boats, a chapel decorated by Jean Cocteau and a hotel in the pedestrian area which is built on the site of a 17th-century monastery. The hotel is modern with many balconies and large, comfortable, sunny rooms, all of them air-conditioned. The balconies have *chaise longues* and small tables on which you can enjoy your breakfast. On the top story the rooms are outfitted in a nautical style with copper fittings and exotic woodwork. They are smaller than the other rooms but still lovely and warm.

How to get there (Map 35): 6km from Nice via N559.

Villa Gallici ★★★★

Avenue de la Violette
13100 Aix-en-Provence (Bouches-du-Rhône)
Tel. (0)4★ 42.23.29.23 - Fax (0)4★ 42.96.30.45 - M. Gil Dez

Rooms 19 with air-conditioning, telephone, bath, WC, cable TV, safe and minibar.
Price 880-2450F. **Meals** Breakfast 65-95F. **Restaurant** Only for residents. Also à la
carte. Specialties: Regional cooking. **Credit cards** All major. **Pets** Dogs allowed
(+50F). **Facilities** Swimming pool, parking. **Nearby** Place d'Albertas, Hôtel de Ville,
Saint-Sauveur Cathedral (burning bush triptych by N. Froment) in Aix-en-Provence,
Roquefavour aqueduct – 18-hole Club des Milles golf course, 18-hole Fuveau Golf
Course. **Open** All year.

In the Villa Gallici, Gil Dez found a bastide in which to exercise
his talents as an interior decorator and create an elegant *hôtel de
charme*. The villa has been decorated with exquisite style, and
designed like a home rather than a hotel. The bedrooms are
spacious, comfortable and individually decorated. *Toile de Jouy* and
gingham have been used in one, while another boasts a flowery
cotton canopied bed along with boldly striped fabrics. In each room
styles, colors and materials have been subtly and successfully
combined. In the immaculate bathrooms, earthenware tiles,
Carrara marble and glossy white wood panelling create an elegant
decor. Breakfast beneath the plane trees is a delight. The cuisine
at *Le Clos de la Violette*, the restaurant next door, is probably the
best in Aix. This is a truly charming place.

How to get there *(Map 33): near the Archbishop's Palace.*

Hôtel des Quatre-Dauphins ★★

54, rue Roux-Alphéran
13100 Aix-en-Provence (Bouches-du-Rhône)
Tel. (0)4★ 42.38.16.39 - Fax (0)4★ 42.38.60.19- MM. Darricau and Juster

Rooms 12 with telephone, bath or shower, WC, TV and minibar. **Price** Single 280-320F, double 320-380F, suite 480F (3 pers.). **Meals** Breakfast 38F, served 7:00-10:00. No restaurant. **Credit cards** Visa, Eurocard and MasterCard. **Pets** Dogs allowed. **Nearby** Place d'Albertas, Hôtel de Ville, Saint-Sauveur Cathedral (burning bush triptych by N. Froment) in Aix-en-Provence, Roquefavour aqueduct – 18-hole Club des Milles golf course, 18-hole Fuveau golf course. **Open** All year.

This three-story family house in a quiet side street near the famous Place des Quatre Dauphins in Aix has recently been converted into a hotel. On the ground floor there is a small reception area and a lounge which also serves as a breakfast room. The bedrooms are on the upper floors. The decor is in the Provençal style, with pretty fabrics and painted wooden furniture. The rooms are not very large and the furnishings are simple but they are functional. The bathrooms are well-equipped. Everything is in good taste in this charming small hotel. For restaurants, try *Maxime, Côté Cour* on the cours Mirabeau, *Le Bistro Latin,* or *Chez Gu,* and don't forget to have a drink *Aux Deux Garçons.*

How to get there (Map 33): In the center of the town.

Hôtel d'Arlatan ★★★

26, rue du Sauvage
13200 Arles (Bouches-du-Rhône)
Tel. (0)4★ 90.93.56.66 - Fax (0)4★ 90.49.68.45 - M. Desjardin

Rooms 41 with air-conditioning, telephone, bath, WC, cable TV and minibar. **Price** Double 455-695F, suite 795-1350F. **Meals** Breakfast 60F, served 7:00-11:00. No restaurant. **Credit cards** All major. **Pets** Dogs allowed. **Facilities** Garage (+60F). **Nearby** Saint-Trophime church, les Aliscamps, Réattu museum in Arles, abbey of Montmajour, the Camargue – 18-hole Servanes golf course in Mouriès. **Open** All year.

This hotel, like Arles itself, is almost a museum of the past and contains traces of many different eras. It was built on the site of the basilica and baths of Constantine and is a patchwork of architectural styles. This is a very unusual hotel, owned for three generations by the same family, who refurbish and restore the bedrooms constantly. It would take a whole book to describe the bedrooms. In suite 43 there are fragments of a 4th-century wall and 17th-century wooden beams. In suite 41 there is a monumental 17th-century fireplace. We recommend that you ask for the recently refurbished bedrooms, among them rooms 23 and 27 which have a view of the Rhône; or number 34, one of the least expensive which has beautiful stone walls. Whichever you choose you will love this charming hotel hidden away in a little street facing the gardens. The most popular restaurants in Arles are *L'Olivier* and *Le Vaccarès*. For a very fashionable spot, try the restaurant or bar of the famous Hôtel Nord-Pinus or *Le Café de la Nuit*.

How to get there *(Map 33): In the center of the town, signposted.*

Grand Hôtel Nord-Pinus ★★★★

Place du Forum
13200 Arles (Bouches-du-Rhône)
Tel. (0)4★ 90.93.44.44 - Fax (0)4★ 90.93.34.00 - Mme Igou

Rooms 23 with air-conditioning, telephone, bath, WC, TV and minibar. **Price** Single and double 700-900F, suite 1500F. **Meals** Breakfast 65F, served 7:00-11:00. **Restaurant** Service 12:00-14:00, 19:30-22:00; menus 120-180F, also à la carte. Specialties: Provençal cooking. **Credit cards** All major. **Pets** Dogs allowed. **Nearby** Saint-Trophime church, les Aliscamps, Réattu Museum in Arles, abbey of Montmajour, the Camargue – 18-hole Servanes golf course in Mouriès. **Open** Mar 1 – Dec 31.

Like Giono, you might wonder; "Why Pinus? Nord, I understand, but Pinus? It was simply the name of the founder. Nothing is more logical. I now realize that I have entered the land of the imagination and fantasy." Picasso, Cocteau, Dominguez are just some of the famous names in the visitors' book. The hotel was run for some time by Germaine, a chanteuse, and Nello, a famous clown, both of whom were well-known characters in Arles. When they died the hotel lost its soul. It has returned under the care of Anne Igou, whose love for the place has brought back the magic and atmosphere, aided by a skillful restoration combining sensitivity and good taste. The bedrooms are large, with pretty furniture and Provençal fabrics, and the bathrooms have every facility. It is worth remembering to ask for suite 10 or the bedrooms looking onto the courtyard; these are recommended for people who are concerned about the noise on the Place du Forum in summer. This is truly a charming hotel.

How to get there (Map 33): In the town center.

Hôtel Castel-Mouisson ★★

Quartier Castel Mouisson
13570 Barbentane (Bouches-du-Rhône)
Tel. (0)4★ 90.95.51.17 – Fax (0)4★ 90.95.67.63 – Mme Mourgue

Rooms 17 with telephone, bath and WC. **Price** Double 280-330F, suite 395F.
Meals Breakfast 35F, served 8:00-10:30. No restaurant. **Credit cards** Not
accepted. **Pets** Dogs not allowed. **Facilities** Swimming pool, tennis, parking.
Nearby Barbentane, Avignon, Villeneuve-lès-Avignon, abbey of Saint-Michel-de-
Frigolet – 18-hole Châteaublanc golf course, 18-hole Vedène golf course in Grand
Avignon, 4-hole Lou Compact golf course in Barbentane. **Open** Mar 15 – Oct 15.

This peaceful and reasonably priced hotel is at the foot of the
Montagnette Mountain not far from Avignon. It was built
twenty years ago in the style of a Provençal farmhouse and is
surrounded by tranquil countryside. There are cypresses and fruit
trees growing beneath the grey cliffs of the Montagnette, which
overlooks the valley. Brightened with Provençal fabrics, the
bedrooms are simple but reasonably comfortable. In hot weather
you will enjoy cooling off in the pretty swimming pool. In
Avignon, there are numerous good small restaurants such as *La
Fourchette, L'Entrée des Artistes*, as well as charming places for lunch
such as the *Les Félibres* tearoom and bookshop, *Le Bain Marie* and
Simple Simon. For a lovely dinner, try the restaurant in the Mirande
Hotel or *La Vieille Fontaine* in the Hôtel d'Europe.

How to get there *(Map 33): 8km southwest of Avignon via N570, then
D35 towards Tarascon along the Rhône.*

Hôtel Le Benvengudo ★★★

Route d'Arles D78
13520 Les Baux-de-Provence (Bouches-du-Rhône)
Tel. (0)4★ 90.54.32.54 - Fax (0)4★ 90.54.42.58 - M. Beaupied

Rooms 20 with telephone, bath, WC and TV. **Price** Double 520-680F, suite 780-900F. **Meals** Breakfast 58F, served 8:15-10:15; half board 1060-1230F (per 2 pers., 3 days min.). **Restaurant** Closed Sunday. Service 19:30-21:00; menu 225F. Specialties: Soupe de poissons de roche, loup grillé sauce béarnaise, carré d'agneau à la crème de romarin. **Credit cards** Amex, Visa, Eurocard and MasterCard. **Pets** Dogs allowed (+50F). **Facilities** Swimming pool, tennis, parking. **Nearby** Contemporary art museum at the Hôtel des Porcelets in Les Baux, Queen Jeanne's pavilion, Alphonse Daudet's windmill in Fontvieille, the Val d'enfer – 9-hole golf course in Les Baux, 18-hole Servanes golf course in Mouriès. **Open** Feb 1 – Nov 1.

The Benvengudo hides at the foot of a small range of mountains. The hotel was built twenty-one years ago but has the air of always having been there. The bedrooms, some of which are air-conditioned, are very comfortable; each one has individual style and some have small private terraces. There is a rustic touch to the lounge and dining room. In summer you can dine outdoors by the swimming pool under the olive trees. The jagged outline of the Alpilles recalls some of the highest mountain ranges in the world, and their white rocks and dry vegetation in this part of Provence recall Greece.

How to get there (Map 33): 30km south of Avignon via A7, Cavaillon exit, then D99 to Saint-Rémy and D5.

Le Mas d'Aigret ★★★

13520 Les Baux-de-Provence (Bouches-du-Rhône)
Tel. (0)4★ 90.54.33.54 – Fax (0)4★ 90.54.41.37
M. Phillips

Rooms 16 (6 with air-conditioning) with telephone, bath, WC, cable TV and minibar.
Price Double 450-1000F. **Meals** Breakfast 70F, served 8:00-11:00; half board 595-870F (per pers., obligatory in higt season). **Restaurant** Closed Wednesday lunchtime. Service 12:15-13:30, 19:15-21:00; menus 90-130F (lunch), 190-350F. Specialties: Escalope de foie gras chaud, marjolaine de blinis et saumon fumé par nos soins au chèvre frais et sariette, nage de homard et rouget gratin au safran, tarte fondante au chocolat noir, feuilleté à l'orange et crème légére au grand-marnier. **Credit cards** All major. **Pets** Dogs allowed (+40F). **Facilities** Swimming pool, parking. **Nearby** Contemporary art museum at the Hôtel des Porcelets in Les Baux, Queen Jeanne's pavilion, the Val d'enfer, Alphonse Daudet's windmill in Fontvieille – 9-hole golf course in Les Baux, 18-hole Servanes golf course in Mouriès. **Open** Feb 25 – Jan 5.

This farm, built in 1730 and recently restored, stands in an old cave dwelling. All the bedrooms have their own terrace and TV with three satellite channels. Room 16 and Apartment 15 are the most attractive. There is a vaulted lounge and library with large tables. The dining room with its stone walls is built into the rock, as are the lounge bar and music room. The furniture is a pleasant blend of old and new with Provençal fabrics. The restaurant serves excellent cuisine at very affordable prices. The hotel also offers golfers a special package rate. The Mas d'Aigret is truly a charming place to stay.

How to get there (Map 33): 30km south of Avignon via A7, Cavaillon exit, then D99 to Saint-Rémy and D5.

Les Roches Blanches ★★★★

Route des calanques
13260 Cassis (Bouches-du-Rhône)
Tel. (0)4★ 42.01.09.30 – Fax (0)4★ 42.01.94.23 – M. Dellacase

Rooms 25 with telephone, bath, WC, TV and minibar; elevator. **Price** Single 450F, double 900F, suite 1150F. **Meals** Breakfast 75F, served 7:15-11:00; half board 716F, full board 836F (per pers., 3 days min.). **Restaurant** Service 12:00-14:00, 19:30-22:30; menus 95-140F, also à la carte. Specialties: Provençal cooking. **Credit cards** All major. **Pets** Dogs allowed. **Facilities** Swimming pool, parking. **Nearby** The Calanques: Port-Miou, Port-Pin and Envau – 18-hole La Salette Golf Course in Marseille-La Valentine. **Open** May 1 – Oct 3.

Les Roches Blanches is a former town house built in 1885 and then transformed into a hotel in 1930. Built on the rocks next to the rocky inlets *(calanques)* of Cassis, this large house combines the charm of a beach hotel–the terraced garden slopes down directly to the water, where you can swim–with the charm of a family house whose large dining-room windows overlook the sea. The bedrooms are all comfortable, and some have terraces looking out over pine trees and either the sea or Cape Canaille. In their concern for preserving the old charm of the house, the owners have kept several pieces of 1930s furniture, the door and the vast stairway in Art Déco wrought iron, and the pretty *faïence* mosaic tables of the garden. There is a very beautiful overflow swimming pool with a view of the sea.

How to get there (Map 33): 23km east of Marseille via A50 towards Toulon, Cassis exit; in Cassis, take the Le Bestouan beach road.

Le Clos des Arômes ★★

10, rue Paul-Mouton - Rue Agostini
13260 Cassis (Bouches-du-Rhône)
Tel. (0)4★ 42.01.71.84 - Fax (0)4★ 42.01.31.76 - Mme and M. Bonnet

Rooms 8 with telephone, soundproofing, bath or shower and WC. **Price** Double 295-570F. **Meals** Breakfast 45F, served 8:00-12:00. **Restaurant** Service 12:00-14:00, 19:30-22:30; menus 95-140F, also à la carte. Specialties: Provençal cooking. **Credit cards** Amex, Visa, Euracard and MasterCard. **Pets** Dogs allowed (+35F). **Facilities** Garage (+50F). **Nearby** The Calanques: Port-Miou, Port-Pin and Envau – 18-hole La Salette Golf Course in Marseille-La Valentine. **Open** May 1 – Oct 3.

Though located in a little street in the village, this dollhouse of a hotel is surrounded by a garden that is a riot of blue and white with lavender, peonies, arum lilies and marguerites. In beautiful weather this makes a fragrant setting for breakfast and for dinners of delicious Provençal dishes. Indoors the ambience is just as delightful, with lavender-painted furniture, flowered tablecloths and a large fireplace. The bedrooms, with blue and yellow Provençal fabrics, all look out on the garden. The hotel is very quiet though in the middle of the village and only a few meters from the old port.

How to get there *(Map 33): 23km east of Marseille via A50 towards Toulon, Cassis exit.*

Auberge Provençale ★★★

Place de la Mairie
13810 Eygalières (Bouches-du-Rhône)
Tel. (0)4★ 90.95.91.00 Fax (0)4★ 90.90.60.92 - M. Pézevil

Rooms 7 with telephone, bath or shower, WC and TV. **Price** Double 285-500F. **Meals** Breakfast 40F, served 8:30-10:30; half board 350-450F (per pers., 2 days min.). **Restaurant** Service 12:00-13:30, 19:30-21:30; menus 145F(lunchtime)-185F, also à la carte. Specialties: Plateau de hors d'œuvre, cabillaud rôti aux 15 épices douces, filet d'agneau et concassé de tomates, tourtière aux pruneaux et armagnac avec glace à l'armagnac. **Credit cards** Visa, Eurocard and MasterCard. **Pets** Dogs allowed (+30F). **Facilities** Parking. **Nearby** Les Baux, Saint-Rémy-de-Provence, Fontvieille – 18-hole Servanes golf course in Mouriès. **Open** All year (closed Wednesday).

The auberge is in the center of a beautifully preserved village of the Alpilles. Formerly a restaurant in an 18th-century postal relay station, it has recently become a small, seven-bedroom establishment. The three most comfortable rooms open onto a charming courtyard with trees, where meals are served in summer (our favorites are numbers 4 and 5, and 1 and 3, which have recently been renovated); the two smaller rooms look out over the Place de la Mairie. A bistro area also serves as a lounge for hotel guests. The young owner doubles as the chef. Meals are served on the terrace in good weather or in the restaurant, which has a beautiful fireplace. The excellent cuisine is based on seasonal market produce, and the menu changes often. The hospitality is generous.

How to get there (Map 33): 13km southeast of Cavaillon via A7, Cavaillon exit, then D99 and D74a.

Mas doù Pastré

Quartier Saint-Sixte, 13810 Eygalières (Bouches-du-Rhône)
Tel. (0)4★ 90.95.92.61 - Fax (0)4★ 90.90.61.75
M. and Mme Roumanille

Rooms 8 with telephone, bath or shower, WC, TV and 5 with minibar. **Price** Double 320-550F. **Meals** Breakfast 48F, served 8:00-10:30. No restaurant. **Credit cards** All major. **Pets** Dogs not allowed. **Facilities** Swimming pool, parking. **Nearby** Les Baux, Saint-Rémy-de-Provence, Fontvieille – 18-hole Servanes golf course in Mouriès. **Open** All year.

Mme Roumanille, who has just renovated this old farmhouse as she would have her own home, is a friendly and hospitable hostess. Throughout the house, the ceilings and walls are decked out in Provençal colors, and there is a wealth of antique furniture, paintings, engravings, prints, and local curios–enough to make you feel even better than you would at home. The evocatively named bedrooms are all different: their decor owes much to carefully chosen furnishings, and to the owners' boundless imagination in adding a touch of exuberance and humor. You can also sleep in an authentic, elaborately carved wooden trailer, which is very old but equipped with air-conditioning and every modern comfort. Breakfast is delicious (there are always fresh fruit juices), whether you have it outside or in the charming dining room. This is an excellent and very Provençal hotel. *L'Auberge Provençale* is the famous restaurant in Eygalières, and the fashionable spot is *Sous les Micocouliers*.

How to get there *(Map 33): 13km southeast of Cavaillon via A7, Cavaillon exit, then D99 and D74a.*

Le Relais de la Magdelaine ★★★★

Route d'Aix-en-Provence
13420 Gémenos (Bouches-du-Rhône)
Tel. (0)4★ 42.32.20.16 - Fax (0)4★ 42.32.02.26 - M. and Mme Marignane

Rooms 24 with telephone, bath or shower, WC and TV. **Price** Single 395-520F, double 545-750F, suite 1100F. **Meals** Breakfast 69F, served from 7:15; half board 565-850F, full board 785-1050F (per pers., 3 days min.). **Restaurant** Service 12:00-14:00, 20:00-21:30; menu 250F, also à la carte. Specialties: Galettes de grenouilles à la provençale, pavé de canard au miel de lavande, griottes au chocolat sauce pistache. **Credit cards** Visa, Eurocard and MasterCard. **Pets** Dogs allowed (+30F) but not in the swimming pool. **Facilities** Swimming pool, parking. **Nearby** Marseille, Aix-en-Provence, Cassis and the Calanques – 18-hole La Salette golf course in Marseille-La Valentine. **Open** Mar 15 – Nov 30.

To find this beautiful 18th-century country house covered in ivy and roses, you leave the highway, drive along an avenue of century-old plane trees and cross a formal garden designed by Le Nôtre. Here you will find M. and Mme Marignane, who have been welcoming an international clientele for thirty years. Their dedication and good taste in creating a very special holiday hotel is evident in the bedrooms. These have superb old furniture; those that look out on the terrace are the largest. Their son is the chef and turns out refined Provençal food. The garden and swimming pool are very pleasant; you will be delighted by the cordial welcome.

How to get there *(Map 33): 23km from Marseille via A50 towards Toulon, Aubagne-Est or Aubagne-Sud exit, then D2 to Gémenos.*

436

New Hôtel Bompard ★★★

2, rue des Flots-Bleus
13007 Marseille (Bouches–du–Rhône)
Tel. (0)4★ 91.52.10.93 – Fax (0)4★ 91.31.02.14 – M. Antoun

Rooms 46 with air-conditioning, telephone, bath, WC, TV and minibar. **Price** Single and double 370-400F. **Meals** Breakfast 45F, served 7:00-11:00. No restaurant. **Credit cards** All major. **Pets** Dogs allowed. **Facilities** Swimming pool, solarium, parking. **Nearby** Vieille Charité, Art museum, Cantini museum, M.A.C. in Marseille, Cassis and the Calanques: Port-Miou, Port Pin and Envau, Aix-en-Provence – 18-hole La Salette golf course in Marseille-La Valentine. **Open** All year.

The Hotel Bompard, which is located on the Corniche which runs around the Bay of Marseille, has the unusual advantage of having a large garden even though it is in the city. The bedrooms, most of which have a large balcony overlooking the acacias and palm trees or the grounds, are charming. The best rooms are those in the main building which are tastefully furnished, combining elegance, practicality and comfort. For longer stays, or for family groups, there are bungalows, some with kitchenettes. The tranquillity and the cordial welcome at the new Hôtel Bompard make it a good place to stay, but as it is ten minutes from the center of the city you will need a car or taxi to get to and fro. (You can rent a car at the hotel.) For the best *bouillabaisse* in town, try *Chez Michel, Le Chaudron Provençal, Chez Foulon* or, more reasonably priced, *Chez Etienne*. For a beautiful view, there are also *La Nautique* and *Chez Péron*.

How to get there *(Map 33): On the J. F. Kennedy Corniche, follow signs from Le Ruhl restaurant.*

L'Oustaloun ★★

Place de l'église
13520 Maussane-les-Alpilles (Bouches-du-Rhône)
Tel. (0)4★ 90.54.32.19 - Fax (0)4★ 90.54.45.57 - M. Fabrégoul

Rooms 10 with telephone, bath or shower, WC and 8 with TV. **Price** Double 260-395F. **Meals** Breakfast 34F, served 7:30-9:30. **Restaurant** Service 12:15-13:45, 19:15-21:30; menu, also à la carte. Specialties: Provençal and Italian cooking. **Credit cards** Amex, Visa, Eurocard and MasterCard. **Pets** Dogs allowed. **Facilities** Garage (20F). **Nearby** Avignon, Arles, St-Rémy-de-Provence, Les Baux and le Val d'enfer, Alphonse Daudet's windmill in Fontvieille – 9-hole golf course in les Baux, 18-hole Servanes golf course in Mouriès. **Open** All year except Jan 8 – Feb 6.

In 1792, this was the first town hall of the village, then the gendarmerie (and the prison). Today, L'Oustaloun is a typical small Provençal auberge looking out on - what else? - a square shaded with towering plane trees and a tinkling fountain. The bedrooms are lovely and comfortable; all are decorated with Provençal fabrics and antique furniture. Although some bathrooms are somewhat old-fashioned, that will soon change because the hotel has just been bought by new owners who are planning to renovate. With the first good weather, the Oustaloun spills out to the center of the square, where a bar-terrace is set up, shaded by large parasols. This is a charming spot just several minutes out of spectacular (and gastronomically acclained) town of Les Baux. The prices are reasonable and you will be welcomed with a very warm Provençal smile.

How to get there (See Map 33): 40km south of Avignon via A7, exit Cavaillon, then D99 to Saint-Rémy and D5.

Le Berger des Abeilles ★★

13670 Saint-Andiol (Bouches-du-Rhône)
Tel. (0)4★ 90.95.01.91 - Fax (0)4★ 90.95.48.26
Mme Grenier

Rooms 6 with telephone, bath or shower, WC and TV. **Price** 300-350F.
Meals Breakfast 50F, served 8:00-10:00; half board 450F (per 1 pers.), 700F (per 2
pers., 3 days min.). **Restaurant** Closed Sunday evening and Monday except for
residents. Service 12:30-13:30, 20:00-21:30; menus 120-270F, also à la carte.
Specialties: Provençale cooking, mousse au miel de lavande, vieux marc de Provence.
Credit cards Amex, Visa, Eurocard and MasterCard. **Pets** Dogs allowed (35F).
Facilities Parking. **Nearby** Les Baux, Saint-Rémy-de-Provence, Avignon. **Open** Mar
4 – Dec 31.

L e Berger des Abeilles is as welcoming as a hotel could possibly
be. There are only six bedrooms and so the owners provide a
personal style of service. All the rooms are perfectly comfortable,
but you should choose our favorites if they're available, *Alexia* or
Caroline. (The rooms are named after the women in the family.)
A few items of period furniture set the trend for the cheerful,
intimate decor. Mme Grenier does the cooking herself and her
cuisine has an excellent reputation. Dinner is served in a beautiful,
rustic dining-room or outside in the shade of a gigantic plane tree.
The noise of traffic on the main road, muffled by luxuriant
vegetation, can hardly be heard in the hotel garden, and not at all
indoors (thanks to the thick walls). This is a lovely place to stay.

How to get there *(Map 33): 13km south of Avignon via N7 (2km from
north of Saint-Andiol). On A7, Avignon-Sud exit, 5km south.*

Hostellerie de Cacharel ★★★

Route de Cacharel
13460 Les Saintes-Maries-de-la-Mer (Bouches-du-Rhône)
Tel. (0)4★ 90.97.95.44 – Fax (0)4★ 90.97.87.97 – M. Colomb de Daunant

Rooms 11 with telephone, bath or shower and WC. **Price** Single and double 530F. **Meals** Breakfast 45F, served 8:00-10:30. **Restaurant** Snacks available: 80F "assiette campagnarde". **Credit cards** Amex, Visa, Eurocard and MasterCard. **Pets** Dogs allowed. **Facilities** Swimming pool, horse trekking, parking. **Nearby** Church of Saintes-Maries-de-la-Mer, gypsy pilgrimage (May 24 and 25), sea wall (30km), Arles – 18-hole Servanes golf course in Mouriès. **Open** All year.

The Hostellerie is an old farmhouse on the borders of the Camargue, a land of nature reserves, placid lakes and white horses. The ground-floor bedrooms are furnished charmingly and look out either on a flower-filled inner courtyard or on the lakes and salt marshes. As the hotel is part of the farm, guests can walk or ride horses on the property. There is no restaurant but snacks can be provided. You will receive a good welcome at this tranquil and genuine Camargue house in its popular tourist region.

How to get there *(Map 33): 38km southwest of Arles. 4km north of Saintes-Maries-de-la-Mer by D85a, called the Route de Cacharel.*

Mas du Clarousset ★★★

Route de Cacharel
13460 Les Saintes-Maries-de-la-Mer (Bouches-du-Rhône)
Tel. (0)4★ 90.97.81.66 – Fax (0)4★ 90.97.88.59 – Mme Eyssette

Rooms 10 with telephone, bath, WC, TV and minibar. **Price** Double 750F. **Meals** Breakfast 50F, served 7:00-11:00; half board 1350F, full board 925-1300F (per pers., -10% from 3 days). **Restaurant** Closed Sunday evening and Monday. Service 12:00-14:00, 20:00-22:00; menus 250-350F, also à la carte. Specialties: Terrine de canard colvert, loup en croûte, terrines à la provençale, daube de taureau, Aïgue Saoü. **Credit cards** All major. **Pets** Dogs allowed (+50F). **Facilities** Swimming pool, gypsy evenings (on request), parking. **Nearby** Church of Saintes-Maries-de-la-Mer, gypsy pilgrimage (May 24 and 25), sea wall (30km), Arles – 18-hole La Grande Motte golf course. **Open** All year.

The very pleasant Mas du Clarousset is an ideal place to absorb the spirit of Provence. Here, Henriette gives a special welcome to lovers of the Camargue and likes to introduce them to the local way of life with gypsy evenings, walks on little-known beaches, and a midnight Christmas mass to which everyone rides on horseback. She can also reserve a horse or a boat for you. The pretty and comfortable bedrooms all have private terraces and views over the Camargue. Each room has a separate private entrance with a parking space right in front of the door. After a day's excursion in the area you can relax and cool off in the swimming pool in the garden. Afterwards, you can enjoy the very good restaurant at the Mas, where Henriette offers traditional cuisine, featuring many regional specialties.

How to get there *(Map 33): 38km southwest of Arles, then D85a (7km from Saintes-Maries).*

Lou Mas doù Juge ★★★

Quartier Pin Tourcat
13460 Saintes-Maries-de-la-Mer (Bouches-du-Rhône)
Tel. (0)4★ 66.73.51.45 – Fax (0)4★ 66.73.51.42 – M. and Mme Granier

Rooms 7 with bath or shower, WC, and TV. **Price** Single with half board 750F (1 pers.), 1200F (2 pers.). **Restaurant** Table d'hôtes with reservation. Service 12:00-13:00, 20:00-21:00. Menus 350F. Specialties: Anchoïades, terrine maison, salade frisée à l'aïl avec fromage frais de brebis, sandre et turbot grillés, gardianne pâtes fraîches. **Credit cards** Not accepted. **Pets** Dogs not allowed. **Facilities** Parking. **Nearby** Church of Saintes-Maries-de-la-Mer, gypsy pilgrimage May 24 and 25, sea wall (30km), Arles – 18-hole Servanes golf course in Mouriès. **Open** All year.

As you drive through the Camargue you will see a giant bottle at the side of the road; this tells you that you are on the right road and that the farm hotel Lou Mas doù Juge is not far off. It is known for its true Camargue spirit, its cuisine, and its parties put on by your convivial host. The large farm has several bedrooms, all of them pleasant, spacious, and prettily furnished with old furniture. Each one has a large bathroom and a good view of the Camargue countryside. There is what some might consider a slight snag, namely that the Mas is very much sought after for receptions. However, the proprietors are very good at creating a friendly atmosphere among all the guests.

How to get there (Map 33): 38km southwest of Arles, then D85, the route du Bac du Sauvage.

Château des Alpilles ★★★★
Ancienne route des Baux
13210 Saint-Rémy-de-Provence (Bouches-du-Rhône)
Tel. (0)4★ 90.92.03.33 – Fax (0)4★ 90.92.45.17 – Mmes Bon

Rooms 19 with telephone, bath, WC, TV, and minibar (some air-conditioned).
Price Single 860-1030F, double 900-1080F, suite 1290-2000F. **Meals** Breakfast
74F, served 7:30-12:00. **Restaurant** Snacks available with reservation, also à la
carte 180-220F. **Credit cards** All major. **Pets** Dogs allowed (+50F). **Facilities**
Swimming pool, tennis, sauna, parking. **Nearby** Frédéric Mistral museum in Maillane,
Eygalières, Les Baux, Avignon, Arles – 9-hole golf course in Les Baux, 18-hole
Servanes golf course in Mouriès. **Open** All year except Nov 13 – Dec 19 and Jan 9 –
Feb 17.

The château was built at the beginning of the 19th-century by
one of the oldest families of Arles and became the meeting
place of politicians and writers staying in the region. It still has the
feeling of a holiday château. The lounge, the bar, and the dining
room, richly decorated with plasterwork and mirrors, are all very
pleasant rooms and open out onto the garden. The comfortable
bedrooms have period furniture and large bathrooms. The large
park, with a swimming pool and tennis court, is planted with
hundred-year-old trees and rare plant species. The Château des
Alpilles is very well adapted to the chic clientele who are coming
more frequently to the villge.

How to get there *(Map 33): 14km west of Cavaillon via A7, exit Cavaillon,
then D99; 1km from Saint-Rémy-de-Provence.*

Château de Roussan

13210 Saint-Rémy-de-Provence (Bouches-du-Rhône)
Tel. (0)4★ 90.92.11.63 - Fax (0)4★ 90.92.50.59

Rooms 21 with telephone, bath or shower and 18 with WC - Wheelchair access. **Price** Double 360-750F. **Meals** Breakfast 60-70F in room, served 8:00-11:00; half board 365-610F (per pers., 3 days min.). **Restaurant** Service 12:00-14:00, 19:30-21:30; also à la carte. Specialties: Sole au beurre blanc, rognons à la cartagéne. **Credit cards** Amex, Visa, Eurocard and MasterCard. **Pets** Dogs allowed. **Facilities** Parking. **Nearby** Museum Frédéric-Mistral in Maillane, Eygalières, les Baux, Avignon, Arles – 9-hole golf course in Baux, 18-hole Servanes golf course in Mouriès. **Open** All year.

An avenue of superb, century-old plane trees leads up to this fanciful and splendid house which was built at the beginning of the 18th-century by the Marquis of Ganges. A hotel since l951, the château has nevertheless retained all its original character. The salons, the dining room, the library, and many bedrooms are still furnished with beautiful antiques; and the floors still have beautiful old parquet and terra-cotta tiles. If you like modern accommodations, ask for the bedrooms behind the library, or the rooms named *Laurier-Rose, Lilas,* or *Lavande*. History buffs should ask for the rooms named *Alix, Mistral,* or *Marquise*. The château is surrounded by a 15-acre park, an orange grove, a basin, and a lake with a small island. It is said that the elegant Marquis used to give sumptuous suppers here.

How to get there *(Map 33): 14km west of Cavaillon via A7, exit Cavaillon, then D99; 2km from Saint-Rémy, take road to Tarascon.*

Le Mas des Carassins ★★★

1, chemin Gaulois
13210 Saint-Rémy-de-Provence (Bouches-du-Rhône)
Tel. (0)4★ 90.92.63.47 - Fax (0)4★ 90.92.63.47 - M. and Mme Ripert

Rooms 10 with telephone, bath and WC - Wheelchair access. **Price** Single 350-500F, double 380-500F. **Meals** Breakfast 49F, served 8:00-9:30. No restaurant. **Credit cards** Visa, Eurocard and MasterCard. **Pets** Dogs not allowed. **Facilities** Parking. **Nearby** Frédéric Mistral museum in Maillane, Eygalières, Les Baux, Avignon, Arles – 9-hole golf course in Les Baux, 18-hole Servanes golf course in Mouriès. **Open** Mar 15 – Nov 15.

This 19th-century farm is now a small family hotel. It is just outside the center of Saint Rémy-de-Provence in what has become the residential quarter. In its pretty garden, however, you can imagine yourself in the middle of the country. The bedrooms are all different. In *Magnaneraie,* for example, there is a rustic ambience with stone walls, while the *Jassé* room is the only one with a terrace. There is a pretty dining room and a small, pleasant lounge with cane furniture. There is no restaurant, but if you are staying in the hotel, the helpful Mme Ripert will prepare a snack for you. The restaurants we recommend are: *Bistrot des Alpilles, Café des Arts, Jardin de Frédéric* in the village, or *L'Oustalet* in Maillane.

How to get there *(Map 33): 14km west of Cavaillon via A7, Cavaillon exit, then D99.*

Le Mas de Peint

Le Sambuc
13200 Arles (Bouches-du-Rhône)
Tel. (0)4★ 90.97.20.62 – Fax (0)4★ 90.97.22.20 – Mme and M. Bon

Rooms 8 and 2 suites with air-conditioning, telephone, bath, WC, minibar, safe, and cable TV. **Price** Double 980-1500F, suite 1700-1900F. **Meals** Breakfast 80F, served 8:00-10:00; half board 730-930F, 1090-1190F (suite) (per pers., 3 days min.). **Restaurant** Service 12:00-14:30, 20:00-22:00; menus 165F (lunch), 210F (dinner). Specialties: Produits de la ferme, taureau de notre élevage, riz du marais. **Credit cards** All major. **Pets** Dogs allowed (+75F). **Facilities** Swimming pool, mountain bikes rentals, parking. **Nearby** Saintes-Maries-de-la-Mer (gypsy pilgrimage, May 24 and 25), sea wall (30km), Arles (féria for easter) – 18-hole La Grande Motte golf course. **Open** Mar 20 – mid-Jan.

The Mas de Peint is a formidable compromise between the friendliness of a Camargue guest house and the modern accommodations of a luxurious hotel of character and charm. The owner of a famous herd of horses and bulls, Jacques Bon, is always proud to discuss (and show) his 1235 acres devoted to growing rice and breeding horses and bulls. Mme Bon has contributed her art as a talented architect and interior decorator to the Mas de Peint, which feels like a house for entertaining friends. There is a large table with a bouquet of fresh flowers in the entrance, and a comfortable sofa surrounded by bookshelves. You will find a small reading room and a larger room with a fireplace. In the kitchen, guests gather for an informal meal offering regional specialties. The bedrooms are extraordinarily large, some have bathrooms on a mezzanine, and every room has its personal charm.

How to get there *(Map 33): 20km south of Arles via D36, towards Salin de Giraud; at the exit from Sambuc, 3km to the left.*

Hôtel Le Chrystalin ★★★

83600 Les Adrets-de-l'Estérel (Var)
Tel. (0)4★ 94.40.97.56 – Fax (0)4★ 94.40.94.66
Mme Butor Blamont and M. Pandelle

Rooms 15 with telephone, bath, WC and TV - Wheelchair access. **Price** Single and double 380-430F, triple 480-530F, quadruple 580-630. **Meals** Breakfast 40F in room, 50F in bedroom, served 8:00-10:00; half board 350-385F (per pers.). **Restaurant** Service 11:30-15:00, 18:30-23:00; menus 95-170F, also à la carte. Specialties: Fish, aioli, bouillabaise, bourride. **Credit cards** Amex, Visa, Eurocard and MasterCard. **Pets** Dogs allowed. **Facilities** Swimming pool, tennis, parking. **Nearby** Lake of Saint-Cassien, Estérel Mountains between Saint-Raphaël and La Napoule, Saint-Tropez – 18-hole golf course in Valescure. **Open** Feb – Oct.

This lovely hotel is made up of three buildings in the heart of the spectacular unspoiled Esterel Mountains. In the first building, facing the church, you will find the friendly village bar and the Chrystallin's panoramic restaurant. Ask for a table near the large bay window and you will enjoy a stunning view out over one of the most beautiful regions of Provence. The bedrooms, in two other buildings away from the street, are surrounded by flowers and look out over a superb swimming pool and, in the distance, the craggy red escarpments of the Esterel. All the rooms are comfortable and bright, decorated with cheerful Provençal fabrics, and have large terraces with a magnificent view. There are also duplex suites which are beautifully decorated and perfect for a group.

How to get there *(Map 34): 14km west of Fréjus via A8, exit Les Adrets. On the Place de l'Eglise.*

Logis du Guetteur ★★★

Place du Château
83460 Les Arcs-sur-Argens (Var)
Tel. (0)4★ 94.73.30.82 - Fax (0)4★ 94.73.39.95 - M. Callegari

Rooms 10 with telephone, bath or shower, WC, TV and minibar. **Price** Double 450F.
Meals Breakfast 48F, served 8:00-10:30; half board 430F, full board 550F (per pers.,
2 days min.). **Restaurant** Service 12:00 and 19:15; menus 130-330F, also à la carte.
Specialties; Saumon fourré à l'écrevisse, Saint-Jacques au beurre de muscat, pigeon
de ferme aux truffes, ris de veau aux oranges, bourride. **Credit cards** All major.
Pets Dogs allowed (+30F). **Facilities** Swimming pool, parking. **Nearby** Sainte-
Rosaline chapel (4km from Arcs), Château d'Entrecasteaux, Thoronet abbey, Seillans,
Simon Segal museum in Aups – Saint-Andiol golf course. **Open** All year (closed Jan
15 – Feb 15).

The old 11th-century Château du Villeneuve, which houses
the Logis. However, was restored in 1970 its rough stone
medieval walls have been preserved. In your comfortable,
pleasantly furnished bedroom, you can be assured that no enemies
will scale the castle walls. On the contrary, you can relax and take
in the magnificent, panoramic views. The dining room, which is
in the old cellars, has a covered terrace that looks out over the
charming belltower and rooftops below. There is a lovely
swimming pool, delicious cuisine, and a very kind welcome.

*How to get there (Map 34): 12km south of Draguignan via N555 and
D555; in the medieval village.*

Hostellerie Bérard ★★★

Rue Gabriel-Péri
83740 La Cadière-d'Azur (Var)
Tel. (0)4★ 94.90.11.43 – Fax (0)4★ 94.90.01.94 – Mme Bérard

Rooms 40 with telephone, bath or shower, WC, TV and minibar. **Price** Single 425-640F, double 425-740F, suite 900-1200F. **Meals** Breakfast 65F, served 7:30-9:30. **Restaurant** Closed Sunday evening and Monday in low season. Service 12:30-13:30, 19:30-21:30; menus 95-410F, menu lunchtime in the garden 65-95F, also à la carte. Specialties: Mille-feuille de coquilles Saint-Jacques aux pousses d'épinards à l'aceto balsamico, Saint-Pierre rôti à la peau au jus court de lapereau à la badiane. **Credit cards** Amex, Visa, Eurocard and MasterCard. **Pets** Dogs allowed (+40F). **Facilities** Swimming pool, tennis, cooking school, parking. **Nearby** Sanary exotic garden, Bandol, village of Le Castellet, beach (3km) – 18-hole La Frégate golf course in Saint-Cyr-sur-Mer. **Open** All year except Jan 10 – Feb 20.

You will enjoy the festive atmosphere of the Thursday market and don't worry about being disturbed by it: the hotel has a quiet garden behind medieval walls. The bedrooms in this former convent are large, cool in summer, and decorated in varied tones of brown. The bathrooms beautiful are also quite. The rooms in the *bastide* are more traditional, but also more colorful with their pretty Provençal curtains and bedcovers. All are comfortable and well furnished. You can have a view of the rooftops, the garden, the ramparts, the village itself, or the countryside with the medieval village of Le Castellet in the distance. You will be charmed by Danièle Bérard's friendly welcome,. The highly reputed cuisine here is excellent.

How to get there (Map 34): 20km west of Toulon via A50, La Cadière d'Azur exit.

Hostellerie Les Gorges de Pennafort ★★★
83830 Callas (Var)
Tel. (0)4★ 94.76.66.51 - Fax (0)4★ 94.76.67.23
Mme and M. Da Silva

Rooms 16 with telephone, bath, WC, TV and minibar. **Price** Single and double 480-630F, suite 800-1000F. **Meals** Breakfast 50F, served 8:00-11:00; half board 500F (per pers., 2 days min.). **Restaurant** Closed Sunday evening and Monday in low season. Service 12:00-14:00, 19:30-22:00; menus 190-250F, also à la carte. Specialties: Fricassée de petits gris et pied de porc aux asperges, filet de rouget à la crème d'olive et marjolaine, lapereau rôti aux petits oignons et artichauts, ananas et pruneaux au gingembre glace à l'armagnac. **Credit cards** Amex, Visa, Eurocard and MasterCard. **Pets** Dogs allowed (+50F). **Facilities** Parking. **Nearby** Le Malmont, villages of Bargemon, Seillans, Salernes, Tourtour, Aups (Simon-Segal museum), Les Arcs (Sainte-Roseline chapel), château of Entrecasteaux, Thoronet Abbey. **Open** Mar 15 – Jan 15 (closed Sunday evening and Monday in low season).

This pretty, ochre-colored Provençal hotel lies in the heart of dramatic mountain gorges. At night, the trees, the craggy cliffs, and the nearby lake are beautifully illuminated by invisible projectors. Decorated with colorful fabric wall coverings, the bedrooms are prim and modern, impeccably kept, and very comfortable; all have gleaming bathrooms. The lounges, the bar, and the dining room (where you will enjoy excellent Provençal specialties) are decorated in the same charming style. There is a ravishing shady terrace, and the service is attentive.

How to get there (Map 34): 20km northeast of Draguignan via D56 and D25. On A8, exit Le Muy and then D25.

Auberge du Puits Jaubert *

Route du Lac de Fondurane
83440 Callian (Var)
Tel. (0)4* 94.76.44.48 - M. Fillatreau

Rooms 8 with bath or shower and WC. **Price** Double 225-250F. **Meals** Breakfast 35F, served 8:00-10:30; half board 300-320F, full board 400-420F (per pers., 3 days min., obligatory in summer). **Restaurant** Service 12:00-13:30, 20:00-21:30 (closed Tuesday); menus 145-260F, also à la carte. Specialties: Thon roti à la flamme, coquelet à l'estragon, rognond de veau à la provençale, magret de canard au thyn et vin rouge. **Credit cards** Visa, Eurocard and MasterCard. **Pets** Dogs allowed. **Facilities** Parking. **Nearby** Saint-Cassien lake, massif du Tanneron, chapel of Notre-Dame-de-Peygros, Auribeau-sur-Siagne – 18-hole golf course in Valescure. **Open** Dec 15 – Nov 15 (closed Tuesday).

To the west of Cannes lies the massif of Tanneron, the land of mimosa, and it is in this beautiful area, in the middle of the countryside, that you will find the Auberge du Puits Jaubert. Converted from a 15th-century farm, it lies at the end of a track winding along the banks of Lake Saint-Cassien. It is a lovely dry stone building roofed in round Genoese tiles. The same lovely stonework is found in the large dining room where a collection of old farming implements adds to the country atmosphere. The cooking is good and in summer it is a real pleasure to dine under the foliage of the veranda or in the shade of the plane trees. The bedrooms are simple but not lacking in comfort. They have just been completely renovated and prettily decorated in pastel colors.

How to get there *(Map 34): 33km from Fréjus via A8, exit Les Adrets-de-l'Estérel, then D37 towards Montauroux and D560; follow signs.*

451

Hostellerie Lou Calen ★★★

1, cours Gambetta
83850 Cotignac (Var)
Tel. (0)4★ 94.04.60.40 – Fax (0)4★ 94.04.76.64 – M. and Mme Mendes

Rooms 16 with telephone, bath or shower, WC and TV. **Price** Double 290-620F. **Meals** Breakfast 45F, served 7:30-10:30; half board 650-985F, full board 920-1256F (2 pers.). **Restaurant** Closed Wednesday in low season. Service 12:00-14:30, 19:30-21:30; menus 105-250F, also à la carte. Specialties: Foie gras maison. **Credit cards** All major. **Pets** Dogs allowed (+40F). **Facilities** Swimming pool, parking. **Nearby** Abbey of Le Thoronet, château d'Entrecasteaux, Verdon gorges, Sainte-Croix lake – 18-hole Barbaroux golf course in Brignoles. **Open** Mar 15 – Jan 2.

The hotel is at the entrance of the village, near the old wash house; it is in the center of things, but it is still surrounded by countryside and has a garden hidden behind its façade. The dining room extends into a garden terrace with the swimming pool below. The bedrooms are in various styles, sizes, and prices, but they are all charming and comfortable. Some have a loggia, while others have fireplaces. However, the soundproofing in some of the rooms is not good. All around Cotignac there are cliffs topped by Saracen towers. The village itself, with its squares shaded by plane trees, pavement cafés, and moss-covered fountain, is an ideal place for enjoying the life of a Provençal village.

How to get there (Map 34): 24km north of Brignoles via A8, Brignoles exit, then D562 towards Carcès and D13 towards Cotignac.

Château de Valmer ★★★

Route de Gigaro
83420 La Croix Valmer
Tel. (0)4★ 94.79.60.10 - Fax (0)4★ 94.54.22.68 - Mme Rocchietta

Rooms 42 (32 with air-conditioning) with telephone, bath or shower, WC, TV and minibar; elevator - Wheelchair access. **Price** Double 670-1260F, suite 1615-1800F. **Meals** Breakfast 80F, served 8:00-10:30. **Restaurant** Grill on the beach, service 12:30-15:00 – "La Pinède", service 19:30-21:00. **Credit cards** All major. **Pets** Dogs allowed (+50F). **Facilities** Swimming pool, tennis, parking. **Nearby** Saint-Tropez gulf, Les Maures, islands of Porquerolles and Port-Cros. **Open** Apr 1 – Sept 30.

A comfortable, elegant, and luxurious hotel, the Château de Valmer is surrounded by a 12-acre park with a century-old palm grove and a private beach. The interior of the Valmer has just been magnificently renovated. In the lounges, there are antiques and deep sofas which are elegantly covered with printed fabrics coordinated with those of the drapes. The decor matches the handsome paintings. The bedrooms are beautiful and impeccably kept, and they have very luxurious bathrooms. Prices vary according to the size of the room and the view. Lovely terraces with stone colonnades lend charm to the façade of the château– and there are also tables here where you can have breakfast.

How to get there *(Map 34): A8, Le Muy exit, towards La Garde-Freinet, Grassin and La Croix-Valmer.*

Moulin de la Camandoule ★★★

Chemin Notre-Dame-des-Cyprès
83440 Fayence (Var)
Tel. (0)4★ 94.76.00.84 - Fax (0)4★ 94.76.10.40 - Mme Rilla

Rooms 12 with telephone, bath, shower, WC and TV. **Price** Single 265-460F, double 460-655F, suite 690F. **Meals** Breakfast 51F, served 8:00-10:00; half board 465-570F (obligatory March 15 – Oct 31). **Restaurant** Closed Tuesday noon. Service 12:30-15:00, 20:00-22:00; menus 183-265F, also à la carte. **Credit cards** Visa, Eurocard and MasterCard. **Pets** Dogs allowed (+41F). **Facilities** Swimming pool, parking. **Nearby** Seillans, Bargenon, Sainte-Roseline chapel (4km from Arcs), château d'Entrecasteaux, abbey of Le Thoronet – 18-hole golf course in Roquebrune-sur-Argens. **Open** All year except in Feb.

This old olive oil mill has been well preserved and today belongs to an English couple who run it like an old-fashioned English guest house. You will enjoy a warm, friendly welcome and all the services and comforts of a good hotel. The interior decoration is in excellent taste. The bedrooms are furnished in an attractive Provençal style, although the attention to detail is uneven. In the unusual lounge the old machinery of the oil press has been cleverly incorporated into the decor. Around the hotel are large grounds through which the River Camandre flows. A look at the menus on the walls of the swimming pool bar will tell you much about the care given to the cooking. Mme Rilla, who has worked on many radio and TV food programs, has made La Camandoule a favorite destination for travelers with a passion for good food.

How to get there (Map 34): 31km north of Fréjus via D4, then D19.

454

La Grillade au feu de bois **

Flassans-sur-Issole
83340 Le Luc (Var)
Tel. (0)4★ 94.69.71.20 – Fax (0)4★ 94.59.66.11 – Mme Babb

Rooms 16 with telephone, bath or shower, WC and TV. **Price** Single and double 400-550F, suite 900F. **Meals** Breakfast 50F, served 8:00-10:30. **Restaurant** Service 12:00-13:45, 19:30-21:00; menu 180F, also à la carte. Specialties: Traditional Provençal cooking. **Credit cards** Amex, Visa, Eurocard and MasterCard. **Pets** Dogs allowed. **Facilities** Heated swimming pool, parking. **Nearby** Abbey of Thoronet, tour of Luc, abbey of La Celle, La Loube mountain – 18-hole Barbaroux golf course in Brignoles. **Open** All year.

This very well restored 18th-century Provençal *mas* is surrounded by lush vegetation and has a terrace shaded by beautiful trees, the oldest of which is a 100-year-old mulberry. Inside, the various living areas and the long vaulted dining room, with a fireplace at one end, are remarkably furnished. (Mme Babb, who is also an antiques dealer, has personalized the decor with numerous lovely objects, paintings, and pieces of furniture.) The bedrooms are superb, large, and comfortable, in fact immense; they are very quiet despite the proximity of the N7 highway (500m away). We can heartily recommend them. The bathrooms are also lovely. You will enjoy good Provençal cuisine and, as you would expect, there are delicious grills.

How to get there *(Map 34): 13km east of Brignoles via N7. On A8, Le Luc exit.*

Auberge du Vieux Fox ★★

Place de l'Eglise
83670 Fox-Amphoux (Var)
Tel. (0)4★ 94.80.71.69 – Fax (0)4★ 94.80.78.38 – M. Martha

Rooms 8 with telephone, bath or shower, WC and 4 with TV. **Price** Double 280-380F.
Meals Breakfast 35F, served 8:30-10:00; half board 600-750F, full board 750-850F
(per 2 pers.). **Restaurant** Service from 12:30 and 19:15; menus 115-245F, also à la
carte. Specialties: Agneau de Haute-Provence, galette du berger. **Credit cards** Amex,
Visa, Eurocard and MasterCard. **Pets** Dogs allowed (+35F). **Facilities** Parking.
Nearby Abbeys of Le Thoronet and La Celle, Verdon lake and gorges – 18-hole
Barbaroux golf course in Brignoles. **Open** All year (closed Tuesday and Wednesday
noon in low season).

The old village of Fox-Amphoux, perched on its wooded crag,
was first a Roman camp and then became a headquarters of
Knights Templars. The hotel is in the old presbytery adjoining the
church in the center of the village. The interior will instantly charm
you: there is a delightful dining room with prettily set tables
alongside lovely old furniture. In summer you can also have dinner
on the enchanting little terrace in the shade of a large fig tree. The
bedrooms and bathrooms have been recently renovated. They are
comfortable and look out on the massifs of Sainte-Victoire and
Sainte-Baume. In addition to the comfort and charm of this small
hotel (where *demi-pension* is recommended), you will enjoy very
good cuisine and reasonable prices.

How to get there *(Map 34): 32km north of Brignoles via A8, Saint-*
Maximin-la-Sainte-Baume exit, then D560 to Tavernes, D71 and D32.

La Boulangerie ★★★

Route de Collobrières
83310 Grimaud (Var)
Tel. (0)4★ 94 43.23.16 – Fax (0)4★ 94.43.38.27 – Mme Piget

Rooms 11 (4 with air-conditioning) with telephone, bath, WC, 2 with TV and 1 with minibar. **Price** Single 560F, double 660-690F, suite 780-1320F. **Meals** Breakfast 50F, served 7:45-11:00. **Restaurant** For residents only. Service 12:00-13:30; à la carte. Specialties: Aïoli de poissons, poulet fermier aux truffes. **Credit cards** Amex, Visa, Eurocard and MasterCard. **Pets** Dogs allowed (+60F). **Facilities** Swimming pool, tennis, table tennis, parking. **Nearby** La Garde-Freinet, ridgeway to the Notre-Dame-des-Anges hermitage, Collobrières, Carthusian monastery of La Verne, Saint-Tropez – 9-hole Beauvallon golf course in Sainte-Maxime. **Open** Apr 1 – Oct 10.

This place has nothing to do with bakeries as its name would suggest–it is named after a small village–and additionally, it has a very different atmosphere from a traditional hotel. Far from the crowds in a tranquil spot in the Massif des Maures, it is more like a holiday house in the interior of Provence. Everything conspires to produce this impression: both the terrace where you can have meals, and the dining room, which is part of the lounge. There is a happy informality that makes you feel instantly at ease. The bedrooms have the same homey atmosphere and are more like guest rooms in a friend's house. This is a beautiful hotel where you will be warmly received.

How to get there *(Map 34): 10km west of Saint-Tropez via D14; 1km from the village.*

Le Verger

Route de Collobrières
83310 Grimaud (Var)
Tel. (0)4★ 94.43.25.93 – Fax (0)4★ 94.43.33.92 – Mme Zachary

Rooms 9 (first floor with air-conditioning) with telephone, bath or shower, WC, TV and 3 with air-conditioning. **Price** Double 550-850F. **Meals** Breakfast 60F, served 8:30-11:30. **Restaurant** Service 12:00-14:30, 19:30-23:30; à la carte. Specialties: Salade de foie gras aux truffes, médaillon de lotte au curry, carré d'agneau au miel, sabayon chaud aux framboises, bourride. **Credit cards** Visa, Eurocard and MasterCard. **Pets** Dogs allowed. **Facilities** Swimming pool, parking. **Nearby** La Garde-Freinet, ridgeway to the Notre-Dame-des-Anges hermitage, Collobrières, Carthusian monastery of La Verne, Saint-Tropez – 9-hole Beauvallon golf course in Sainte-Maxime. **Open** Mar – Nov.

This pretty house looks like a private dwelling. The bedrooms have French windows which open onto a terrace or a lawn with fruit trees. The tasteful Provençal decor is enhanced with lovely fabrics and beautiful bathrooms. You will find your bed turned down every evening, and bouquets of flowers add a pleasant touch. Every day the restaurant is filled with loyal followers of M. Zachary who remember him when he was the excellent chef at the Bigorneaux in Saint-Tropez. His delicious cuisine is made with aromatic herbs and vegetables from the kitchen garden. Shielded by a bamboo grove on the small river in back, the Verger is very quiet. And the hospitality is charming.

How to get there *(Map 34): 9km west of Saint-Tropez. From A8, exit Le Luc, then D558 towards Saint-Tropez; before Grimaud take D14 for 1km towards Collobrières and follow signs.*

Le Manoir ***
Ile de Port-Cros
83400 Hyères (Var)
Tel. (0)4★ 94.05.90.52 – Fax (0)4★ 94.05.90.89 – M. Buffet

Rooms 23 with telephone, bath or shower and WC. **Price** Double with half board 720-980F (per pers., 3 days min.). **Meals** Breakfast 60F, served 7:45-10:00. **Restaurant** Service from 13:00 and 20:00; menus 250F, also à la carte. Specialties: Bourride provençale, baron d'agneau à la broche, fricassée de gambas au whisky. **Credit cards** Visa, Eurocard and MasterCard. **Pets** Dogs not allowed. **Nearby** Nature trails in the Port-Cros national park, Porquerolles. **Open** Mid Apr – beg. Oct.

The eucalyptus, palm trees, white walls, and graceful columns of the Manoir evoke an exotic dream, a lost island. And yet Toulon is so close. The island of Pont-Cros is a nature reserve and no vehicles are allowed. The hotel was opened just after the war in this private house and it still preserves a family atmosphere, blending conviviality with elegance. There is a large lounge and several small ones, which card players frequent towards the end of the summer season. The bedrooms are cool and charming and some have little loggias; from Room 4 you can see the sea through the trees. A beautiful, quiet 30-acre park adds to the considerable charm of this lovely hotel.

How to get there *(Map 34): Ferry connection from Le Lavandou and Cavalaire (tel. 94.71.01.02), from Hyères (tel. 94.58.21.81). Cars not allowed on the island. Airport Toulon-Hyères.*

Les Glycines ★★★

Place d'Armes - Ile de Porquerolles
83400 Hyères (Var)
Tel. (0)4★ 94.58.30.36 - Fax (0)4★ 94.58.35.22 - M. Fanara

Rooms 12 with air-conditioning, telephone, bath or shower, WC and TV. **Price** Double 500-650F. **Meals** Breakfast (buffet) 50F, served from 8:30; half board 450-900F (per pers.). **Restaurant** Service 19:30-22:30: menu 140F, also à la carte. Specialties: Loups au gros sel grillés, thon grillé, sardines rôties, souris d'agneau. **Credit cards** Amex, Visa, Eurocard and MasterCard. **Pets** Dogs not allowed. **Nearby** Bike rides along island paths, beaches, boat rental. **Open** All year.

The hotel set in a garden with a century-old fig tree, is on the main square of the village, but as there are no cars on the island it is very peaceful. The hotel, with its whitewashed walls and blue shutters has been completely refurbished and still has the peaceful atmosphere of Provençal houses of yesteryear. The bedrooms, all comfortable and air-conditioned, open onto the garden or the square, and have a pleasant atmosphere with pastel tinted walls, Provençal fabrics, and ceramic floor-tiles. The bathrooms are also elegant and have every facility. The meals include Mediterranean specialties and are served on tables with brightly patterned tablecloths in the cool shady garden.

How to get there *(Map 34): Ferry connection from Hyères or La Tour Fondue (tel. 94.58.21.81) or boat-taxi (tel. 94.58.31.19) at any time. Cars not allowed on the island. Airport Toulon-Hyères (7km).*

Hôtel Le Calalou ★★★

Moissac-Bellevue
83630 Aups (Var)
Tel. (0)4★ 94.70.17.91 – Fax (0)4★ 94.70.50.11 – Mme Vernet

Rooms 36 with telephone, bath, WC, 5 with shower, 31 with TV and minibar.
Price Single 320-380F, double 510-600F, 800F with salon. **Meals** Breakfast 65F,
served 8:00-10:00; half board 515-560F, full board 715-760F (per pers.).
Restaurant Service 12:00-14:00, 19:30-22:00/23:00 (Dec 16 – Feb 27 open just the
week-end); menus 150-250F, also à la carte. Specialties: Petit clin d'œil piémontais,
carré d'agneau à la broche avec sa mijotée de légumes, abricot rôti et son sorbet aux
pêches. **Credit cards** All major. **Pets** Dogs allowed (+40F). **Facilities** Swimming pool,
tennis, parking. **Nearby** Aups: Simon-Segal museum, villages of Salernes (pottery),
Tourtour, Cotignac Château d'Entrecasteaux, abbey of Thoronet, gorges du Verdon,
lake of Sainte-Croix – 18-hole Barbaroux golf course. **Open** Mar 27 – Oct 16, Dec 16
– Feb 27.

L e Calalou looks way out over splendid countryside and a flower
garden. Inside, antique furniture, pretty regional fabrics, old
tiles, and immense bouquets of flowers all create a warm and
cheerful atmosphere in the vast reception rooms. Out of season,
meals are served in a fine, sunny colored dining room; in summer,
it opens onto the garden, The cuisine turned out by young Olivier
is refined and savory. The bedrooms detract somewhat from the
charm of the place. However, the bedrooms (many of which are
small) and the baths are comfortable. But improvements are in the
works and you should ask for those which have already been
redone: they are very charming.

How to get there (Map 34): 35km northwest of Draguignan; via A8, Le
Muy or Saint-Maximin exit.

La Maurette

83520 Roquebrune-sur-Argens (Var)
Tel. (0)4★ 94.45.46.81 – Fax (0)4★ 94.45.46.81
M. and Mme Rapin

Rooms 9 with telephone, bath or shower and WC (5 with kitchenette). **Price** Double 350-450F. **Meals** Breakfast 45F, served 8:00-10:00. **Restaurant** Occasional meals for residents only. **Credit cards** Visa, Eurocard and MasterCard. **Pets** Dogs not allowed. **Facilities** Swimming pool, parking. **Nearby** Roquebrune, Fréjus cathedral, massif de l'Estérel – 18-hole golf course in Roquebrune. **Open** Easter – mid-Oct.

M. Rapin may well owe his vocation as a hotelier to a grandfather who owned a hotel in Cannes. But is "hotelier" the right word in his case? For La Maurette is really more like a guest house. It is the kind of place where you will almost feel you have been invited. And anyway, would a hotel really choose such a secluded location, so removed from the crowds? This could be the setting for a monastery, facing the rock of Roquebrune and the foothills of the Massif des Maures. And in the back, there are the Estérel, the Mediterranean, and the valley. The bedrooms are bright, cheerful, and very comfortable, with charming, carefully chosen furniture, curios, and paintings. The *table d'hôte* meals are delicious, with good family-style Provençal gratins, meats roasted in a woodburning oven, and desserts. Then there is the large swimming pool and your hosts' warm, friendly hospitality. Who could ask for more?

How to get there *(Map 34): 10km west of Fréjus via N7 and D7; then after the Pont de l'Argens follow signs; from A8, Le Muy or Puget-sur-Argens exit.*

Hôtel plein Soleil

83700 Saint-Aygulf (Var)
Tel. (0)4★ 94 81 09 57 – Fax (0)4★ 94 81 76 65
Mmes Jamgotchian

Rooms 12 with telephone, bath, WC and minibar. **Price** Double 650-850F. **Meals** Breakfast incl., served 8:00-12:00. **Restaurant** By reservation for residents only. Menu 120F - also à la carte. **Credit cards** All major. **Facilities** Swimming pool, parking. **Pets** Dogs allowed. **Nearby** Beach (300m); Fréjus Cathedral, massif de l'Estérel, Saint-Tropez – 18-hole golf course in Roquebrune. **Open** All year.

The Hôtel Plein Soleil still has the look of a villa. Nine comfortable bedrooms equipped with modern bathrooms have been installed in a new wing which has not altered the character of the house. The three other rooms, which are also pleasant, are in the original villa. In the garden, you will find a swimming pool and deck chairs for soaking up the sun, unless you prefer the beach next door. For breakfast on the terrace, you are served a generous buffet with fruits, cheeses, and all kinds of homemade pastries. If you simply don't want to go out, you can be served a light meal provided you have ordered it in the morning. A reassuring family atmosphere permeates the Hôtel Plein Soleil.

How to get there *(Map 34): 5km from Fréjus, towards Saint-Tropez.*

Hôtel Le Pré de la Mer ★★★

Route des Salins
83990 Saint-Tropez (Var)
Tel. (0)4★ 94.97.12.23 – Fax (0)4★ 94.97.43.91 – Mme Blum

Rooms 3 and 9 studios (with kitchenette) with telephone, bath, shower, WC, TV and minibar. **Price** Single and double 490-680F, studio 640-890F. **Meals** Breakfast 55F, served 8:30-12:00. No restaurant. **Credit cards** Visa, Eurocard and MasterCard. **Pets** Dogs allowed (+50F). **Facilities** Parking. **Nearby** L'Annonciade museum in Saint-Tropez, Ramatuelle festival in July, La Nioulargue in October, la Garde-Freinet, ridgeway to Notre-Dame-des-Anges hermitage, Collobrières, Carthusian monastery of La Verne – 9-hole Beauvallon golf course in Sainte-Maxime. **Open** Easter – Sept 30.

This is a low-roofed white house built in Saint-Tropez–Mexican style. The bedrooms are large and comfortable, cooled by large fans. Some have a kitchen (which helps you forget the prices of the restaurants in Saint-Tropez) and all have a private terrace with white wooden table and chairs, perfect for breakfast and meals. The terraces lead out into a pleasant garden where lemon and pomegranate trees and oleanders bloom. But to get into this peaceful haven just minutes from Saint-Tropez, you will have to charm Joséphine Blum, the owner, who likes to choose her clientele. Restaurant fashions come and go here, but there are always *Le Gorille* and *Le Sénequier* on the port; *Le Bistrot des Lices* and *Le Café des Arts* on the Place des Lices; *Chez Fuchs* and *La Table du Marché*; and on the beaches, *Le Club 55*, *Le Nioulargo* for his Thai cuisine. Or try *Les Jumeaux*.

How to get there *(Map 34): 3km east of Saint-Tropez on the Salins road.*

La Ferme d'Augustin ★★★

83350 Ramatuelle - Saint-Tropez (Var)
Tel. (0)4★ 94.97.23.83 - Fax (0)4★ 94.97.40.30
Mme Vallet

Rooms 46 with telephone, bath (5 with shower), WC, TV, safe and minibar, 30 with air-conditioning; elevator. **Price** Double 580-1600F, suite 1800F. **Meals** Breakfast 75F, served 6:00-14:00. No restaurant but snacks available. **Credit cards** Amex, Visa, Eurocard and MasterCard. **Pets** Dogs allowed (+70F). **Facilities** Heated swimming pool, parking. **Nearby** L'Annonciade museum in Saint-Tropez, Ramatuelle festival in July, La Nioulargue in October, la Garde-Freinet, ridgeway to the Notre-Dame-des-Anges hermitage, Collobrières, Carthusian monastery of La Verne – 9-hole Beauvallon golf course in Sainte-Maxime. **Open** Mar 25 – Oct 15.

This former family farmhouse has now been completely renovated. As soon as you arrive, you will be captivated by the pine grove and the garden full of wisteria, bougainvillea, rambling roses, and the great parasol-shaped mulberry trees. In the lounges, antique country-style furniture is tastefully combined with modern sofas. The bedrooms have pretty bathrooms with wall tiles from Salernes. They all overlook the garden and have a balcony or terrace commanding sea views. The hotel occupies a truly enviable position, just off Tahiti Beach, 200 meters from hiking paths and mountainbiking trails. If you want to stay on the beach all day, ask for a box lunches; the bar serves light meals and provides 24-hour room service. Ask your hotel for restaurant recommendations; or see ours on page 465.

How to get there *(Map 34): 5km from Saint-Tropez on the Tahiti Beach road.*

Hôtel Les Bouis ★★★
Route des Plages-Pampelonne
83350 Ramatuelle - Saint-Tropez (Var)
Tel. (0)4★ 94.79.87.61 - Fax (0)4★ 94.79.85.20

Rooms 14 plus 4 duplexes with air-conditioning, telephone, bath, WC, TV, safe and minibar. **Price** Double 750-1150F, duplex +350F. **Meals** Breakfast 70F, served 8:00-12:00. No restaurant, but grill by the swimming pool at lunchtime. **Credit cards** Amex, Visa, Eurocard and MasterCard. **Pets** Dogs allowed (+50F). **Facilities** Swimming pool, parking. **Nearby** L'Annonciade museum in Saint-Tropez, Ramatuelle festival in July, La Nioulargue in October, la Garde-Freinet, ridgeway to the Notre-Dame-des-Anges hermitage, Collobrières, Carthusian monastery of La Verne – 9-hole Beauvallon golf course in Sainte-Maxime. **Open** Mar 22 – Oct 25.

Les Bouis' special attraction in this town of many charming hotels is its exceptional location, high in the hills yet only a kilometer from the sea, commanding an impressive view out over Pampelonne and Camarat Beaches, and one of the most beautiful gulfs of the Côte d'Azur. Recently constructed, the hotel has only a few bedrooms; some open directly onto the garden and have a private terrace with a panorama of the swimming pool and the coast. All the rooms are very comfortable. Breakfast, which is special, can be served in your room or around the swimming pool until noon. Here also, a grill is set up in the summer. The atmosphere is relaxed and the service is charming. The owner will give you good restaurant recommendations; our own are given on page 465.

How to get there *(Map 34): 5km from Saint-Tropez, on the road to Pampelonne Beach.*

La Ferme d'Hermès ★★

Route de l'Escalet – Val de Pons
83350 Ramatuelle – Saint-Tropez (Var)
Tel. (0)4★ 94.79.27.80 – Fax (0)4★ 94.79.26.86 – Mme Verrier

Rooms 8 and 1 suite with telephone, bath, WC, TV, minibar and kitchenette. **Price** Double 600-850F, suite 950-1000F. **Meals** Breakfast 70F, served 9:00-12:00. No restaurant. **Credit cards** Visa, Eurocard and MasterCard. **Pets** Dogs allowed (+50F). **Facilities** Swimming pool, parking. **Nearby** L'Annonciade museum in Saint-Tropez, Ramatuelle festival in July and Aug, La Nioulargue in Oct, Grimaud. **Open** Apr 1 – Oct 31.

A dirt path through the vineyards, a fragrant garden full of rosemary bushes and olive trees, a pink house: this is the address in the Midi you have always dreamed of, a place where you want to welcome your friends. Madame Verrier, the owner, has thought of every detail. The fireplace, homemade preserves and pastries for breakfast, bouquets of flowers–all make this house thoroughly charming. The rooms are lovely, and some have a small terrace right on the vineyard. Most have a pleasant kitchenette. Madame Verrier can advise you on restaurants; otherwise, see our note on page 465.

How to get there *(Map34): 2km south of Ramatuelle on L'Escalet Road.*

La Figuière ★★★

Route de Tahiti – 83350 Ramatuelle – Saint-Tropez (Var)
Tel. (0)4★ 94.97.18.21 – Fax (0)4★ 94.97.68.48
M. Béraud and Mme Chaix

Rooms 42 with air-conditioning, telephone, bath (3 with shower) and WC (31 with TV, 42 with safe and minibar). **Price** Double 500-900F, suite 1300-1400F. **Meals** Breakfast 65F, served 8:00-11:00. **Restaurant** Service 12:00-15:00, 20:00-23:00; also à la carte. Specialties: Grills. **Credit cards** Visa, Eurocard and MasterCard. **Pets** Dogs allowed (+50F). **Facilities** Swimming pool, tennis, parking. **Nearby** L'Annonciade museum in Saint-Tropez, Ramatuelle festival in July, La Nioulargue in Oct, La Garde-Freinet, ridgeway to the Notre-Dame-des-Anges hermitage, Collobrières, Carthusian monastery of La Verne, Saint-Tropez – 18-hole Beauvallon golf course in Sainte-Maxime. **Open** Apr 4 – Oct 10.

In the morning, opening the shutters to a vista of sunny vineyards is one of the many charms of this hotel in the countryside a few kilometers from Saint-Tropez. La Figuière is composed of five small typical Provençal buildings in a garden full of fig trees. The bedrooms are spacious and quiet and open onto a small private terrace. The regional decoration is sober and the bathrooms are comfortable—some have a double washbasin, shower, and bath. Our favorites have numbers ending in 30 and 40 and enjoy pretty, private terraces surrounded by lavender and lantanas; they have a panoramic view over the vineyards and hills covered with parasol pines. Good breakfasts are served with the morning newspaper. Grills are served at lunchtime around the swimming pool bordered with pink oleander and japonica. A tennis court is hidden behind the hotel, and the staff is very friendly.

How to get there *(Map 34): 2.5km south of Saint-Tropez on the Tahiti Beach road.*

Hôtel des Deux Rocs ★★★

Place Font d'Amont
83440 Seillans (Var)
Tel. (0)4★ 94.76.87.32 – Fax (0)4★ 94.76.88.68 – Mme Hirsch

Rooms 15 with telephone, bath or shower, WC and minibar. **Price** Double 260-520F.
Meals Breakfast 43F, served 8:00-10:00; half board 310-440F, full board 410-540F
(per pers., 3 days min.). **Restaurant** Closed Tuesday and Thursday lunchtime. Service
12:00-14:00, 19:30-21:00; menus 90F (lunchtime in week)-140-220F, also à la carte.
Specialties: Crotin de chavignol en croûte, filet de loup à la crème de basilic, feuilleté
aux pommes. **Credit cards** Visa, Eurocard and MasterCard. **Pets** Dogs allowed.
Nearby Chapel of Saint-André in Comps-sur-Artuby, Fayence, les Arcs and the
Sainte-Roseline chapel (4km), château d'Entrecasteaux, abbey of Le Thoronet – 18-
hole golf course in Roquebrune-sur-Argens. **Open** Apr 1 – Oct 31.

Standing at the top of the splendid village of Seillans, close to
the city walls and the old castle, is the Hôtel des Deux Rocs, a
large Provençal house which is a modest, rustic replica of certain
Italian residences. Variety is the keynote of the decor, which is
exquisite. You will feel at home and relaxed in the small lounge
with a fireplace. The bedrooms are all individually designed: period
furniture, wall fabrics, curtains, and bathroom towels are unique to
each one of them. Breakfast can be served at tables set up in the
pleasant little square not far from Max Ernst's *Génie de la Bastille*;
homemade preserves are just one of the many delicious details
which make a stay here memorable. You will love this hotel, and
prices are very reasonable.

How to get there *(Map 34): 34km north of Fréjus via A8, Les Adrets exit,
then D562 towards Fayence and D19.*

1996

Les Bastidières ★

2371 avenue de la Résistance
83100 Toulon Cap Brun (Var)
Tel. (0)4★ 94.36.14.73 - Fax (0)4★ 94.42.49.75 - Mme Lagriffoul

Rooms 5 with telephone, bath or shower, WC, TV and minibar. **Price** Double 450-800F. **Meals** Breakfast 60-70F, served 8:00-10:00. No restaurant. **Credit cards** Not accepted. **Pets** Dogs allowed. **Facilities** Swimming pool, parking. **Nearby** Mont Faron; gorges of Ollioules and Evenos; villages of the Castellet and The Cadière d'Azur; cap Siciè; Porquerolles; Port-Cros; Saint-Tropez. **Open** Apr 1 – Oct 31.

This beautiful villa stands on the lush heights of Cape Brun in Toulon and is surrounded by a garden where exoticism and the air of Provence mingle harmoniously. Palm trees, yuccas, and ancient pine trees cast shade over large earthenware jars overflowing with impatiens and geraniums. The owners live in the main house. Just next door, there is an annex with five spacious bedrooms that are comfortably equipped with very functional bathrooms. Each room opens onto a small flowery terrace where it is pleasant to have breakfast. The food is excellent and is presented on beautiful silver service. The quietest and most intimate rooms are near the swimming pool, which is beautifully large and surrounded by trees, exotic plants, and Mediterranean flowers. It is midway between the hotel and the guest house–"guest" in the sense that you live very independently of the main house, and that all the services of a hotel are not provided (the lounge is in the owners' house). But Les Bastidières is a beautiful place to stay.

How to get there (Map 34): On A8, Toulon exit; center of town and toward Le Pradet.

Auberge Saint-Pierre ★★★

Quartier Saint-Pierre
83690 Tourtour (Var)
Tel. (0)4★ 94.70.57.17 – Fax (0)4★ 94.70.59.04 – M. and Mme Marcellin

Rooms 18 with telephone, bath or shower and WC. **Price** Double 360-510F.
Meals Breakfast 50F, served 8:00-11:00; half board 760-910F (per 2 pers., 3 days
min.). **Restaurant** Closed Wednesday. Service 12:00-13:00, 20:00-20:30; menus
170-200F. Specialties: Brouillade aux truffes, pigeonneau truffé, jambonnette
d'agneau à la broche, lapereau farci sauce sariette. **Credit cards** Visa, Eurocard
and MasterCard. **Pets** Dogs allowed (+30F). **Facilities** Swimming pool, tennis, sauna
(80F), bikes, archery, table tennis, parking. **Nearby** Caves of Villecroze, chapel of
Saint-André in Comps-sur-Artuby, abbey of Thoronet, Bargème, Simon-Segal
museum in Aups. **Open** Apr 1 – Oct 15.

The Auberge is a 16th-century *bastide* which once belonged to
the lords of Tourtour. Its secluded position in the middle of
the lush countryside makes it just the place to relax. In the lounge,
country furniture is arranged around a fireplace and there is a
collection of prehistoric objects, which were found on the
property. The dining room, decorated in Provençal style, was once
the courtyard of the *bastide*. The bedrooms are comfortable. The
Marcellin family's warm welcome and good Provençal cooking
made with natural products make the Auberge a delightful place
to stay.

How to get there *(Map 34): 19km west of Draguignan via A8, Le Muy
exit; 3km from Tourtour.*

Château de Trigance ★★★

83840 Trigance (Var)
Tel. (0)4★ 94.76.91.18 – Fax (0)4★ 94.85.68.99
M. Thomas

Rooms 10 with telephone, bath, WC and TV. **Price** Double 550-700F, suite 850-900F. **Meals** Breakfast 68F, served 7:30-10:00; half board 550-720F (per pers.). **Restaurant** Closed Wednesday lunchtime in low season. Service 12:00-14:00, 19:30-21:00; menus 195-360F, also à la carte. Specialties: Fondant de lapereau truffé jus court balsamique aux raisins noirs, croustillant d'agneau des Alpilles à la moutarde violette, tagliatelles persillées du maraîcher, gigotin de lotte en tapenade, tulipe de poivrons doux. **Credit cards** All major. **Pets** Dogs allowed. **Facilities** Parking. **Nearby** Verdon canyon, ridgeway from La-Palud-sur-Verdon, Moustiers-Sainte-Marie – 9-hole château de Toulane golf course in La Martie. **Open** Mar 20 – Nov 7.

Originally a fortress built in the 9th-century by the monks of the Abbey of Saint-Victor, the château de Trigance became a castle of the Counts of Provence two hundred years later. A massive structure perched like an eagle's nest on the top of a hill, it has been restored with local stones. The salon and the barrel-vaulted dining room have retained their medieval character, including the ancient music. The bedrooms are arranged around an enormous, magnificent terrace, making them quieter and more intimate. They are very comfortable. Excellent regional cuisine is served inside only, but you can enjoy drinks at the bar on the terrace facing this fantastic panorama. In summer plays are performed on the esplanade by the ramparts. The owners extend a warm welcome.

How to get there *(Map 34): 44km north of Draguignan via D995 to Comps-sur-Artuby; then D905 to Trigance.*

Hôtel de la Mirande ★★★★

Place de la Mirande
84000 Avignon (Vaucluse)
Tel. (0)4★ 90.85.93.93 – Fax (0)4★ 90.86.26.85 – M. Stein

Rooms 19 with air-conditioning, telephone, bath, shower, WC, TV and minibar.
Price Double 1400-2100F, suite 2800F. **Meals** Breakfast 95F, served until 11:30.
Restaurant Service 19:00-21:45; menus 190-350F, also à la carte. Specialties: Filet
rouget barbet dans son croustillant Provençal, raviolis de homard aux poireaux.
Credit cards All major. **Pets** Dogs allowed (+80F). **Facilities** Parking (+80F).
Nearby Palace of the Popes, Notre-Dame des Doms, Campana collection at the Petit-
Palais, Calvet museum, theater festival at Avignon in July, Villeneuve-Lès-Avignon,
la Provence romaine and les Alpilles, le Lubéron – 18-hole Châteaublanc golf course
in Avignon. **Open** All year.

This marvelous hotel in Avignon is charming, to say the least.
The inner courtyard has been turned into a delightful
conservatory, where the wicker armchairs in delicate caramel colors
set the tone. Off the courtyard there is a stunning sequence of
rooms richly decorated with beautiful antiques, Provençal style
fabrics, and chintzes. The bedrooms are spacious, elegant and
comfortable, and all have a lounge or anteroom. Those on the
premier étage are more spacious, while those on the mezzanine and
deuxième étage are more intimate. Some rooms on the last floor have
a lovely terrace which is very pleasant at lunchtime. The
ancient–and baroque–music evening concerts in the autumn or
the cooking workshops directed by leading chefs will perhaps give
you the opportunity to discover this hotel, which is both exquisite
and sumptuous. If you are simply passing through Avignon, the
tea room and the piano bar are also very pleasant places to spend
a lovely afternoon. Last, but not least, the people are very charming.

How to get there *(Map 33): In the town center, at the foot of the Palais des Papes.*

Hôtel d'Europe ★★★★
12, place Crillon
84000 Avignon (Vaucluse)
Tel. (0)4★ 90.82.66.92– Fax (0)4★ 90.85.43.66 – M. Daire

Rooms 47 with air-conditioning, telephone, bath, WC, TV (24 with minibar).
Price Single and double 620-1650F, suite 1990-2400F. **Meals** Breakfast 90F,
served 6:30-11:00. **Restaurant** Closed Monday noon and Sunday. Service 12:00-
14:00, 19:30-22:00; menu, also à la carte. **Credit cards** All major. **Pets** Dogs allowed
(+50F). **Facilities** Garage. **Nearby** Palace of the Popes, Notre-Dame des Doms,
Campana collection at the Petit-Palais, Calvet museum, theater festival at Avignon
in July, Villeneuve-Lès-Avignon, la Provence romaine and les Alpilles, le Lubéron –
18-hole Châteaublanc golf course in Avignon. **Open** All year.

The seigneurial 17th-century Hôtel d'Europe was once the
mansion of the Marquis de Graveson. The refinement of the
hotel has been carefully preserved: handsome antique furniture and
paintings along with brilliant Aubusson tapestries decorate the
salons and the very beautiful dining room. The bedrooms, which
are of varying size, are all furnished with antiques and have very
comfortable accommodations. Three suites have been opened and
from their private terrace in the evening, you will enjoy a unique
view the illuminated Palace of the Popes and the medieval ramparts
surrounding the town. In summer, you can dine in the pretty patio,
shaded by plane and palm trees, which are planted in huge
traditional pots made in the nearby village of Anduze. The cuisine
is excellent, and there is a very good wine cellar. Note the private
garage, which solves the thorny problem of parking in the old
town.

How to get there (Map 33): *Inside the ramparts.*

474

L'Anastasy

Ile de la Barthelasse
84000 Avignon (Vaucluse)
Tel. (0)4★ 90.85.55.94 – Fax (0)4★ 90.82.59.40 – Mme Manguin

Rooms 4 with bath or shower. **Price** Single and double 300-350F. **Meals** Breakfast incl.
Restaurant For residents only. Service from 13:00 and 20:30; menu 100F. Specialties:
Provençal and Italian cooking. **Credit cards** Not accepted. **Pets** Dogs allowed.
Facilities Swimming pool, parking. **Nearby** Palace of the Popes, Notre-Dame des Doms,
Campana collection at the Petit-Palais, Calvet museum, Villeneuve-lès-Avignon – 18-
hole Châteaublanc golf course. **Open** All year.

L'Anastasy used to be a farm typical of the area surrounding
Avignon, where animals and harvests were the sole concern.
Now the barns and stables have been converted to make a large
family house where friends and guests can be welcomed. On the
ground floor there is now a spacious lounge and kitchen–dining
room which is the very heart of the house, for the warm and friendly
hostess, Olga Manguin, enjoys nothing more than cooking for her
guests; indeed, the Provençal and Italian specialties she excels at
are delicious. The bedrooms are pretty. The attractions of the house
are many, including the terrace leading into the garden planted
with lavender and rosemary, hollyhocks and acanthus. Although
the atmosphere is convivial, you nevertheless can be left on your
own, but it would be a shame not to join in the activities here.
Olga's friends, including journalists, directors, stage designers and
actors, wouldn't dream of staying anywhere else during the
Avignon Festival.

How to get there *(Map 33): 6km north of Avignon; from Avignon head for
Villeneuve-lès-Avignon over the Daladier bridge.*

Les Géraniums **

Place de la Croix
84330 Le Barroux (Vaucluse)
Tel. (0)4★ 90.62.41.08 – Fax (0)4★ 90.62.56.48 – M. and Mme Roux

Rooms 22 with telephone, bath or shower and WC. **Price** Single and double 210-250F. **Meals** Breakfast 35F, served 8:00-10:00; half board 230-250F, full board 310-330F (per pers., 3 days min.). **Restaurant** Service 12:00-14:00, 19:00-21:00; menus 80-250F, also à la carte. Specialties: Omelette aux truffes, lapin à la sarriette, chevreau au romarin, terrine maison aux pruneaux. **Credit cards** All major. **Pets** Dogs allowed (+30F). **Facilities** Parking. **Nearby** Château de Barroux, pharmacy museum at the Hôtel-Dieu in Carpentras, Mazan Gallo-Roman cemetery, dentelles de Montmirail – 18-hole Le Grand Avignon golf course. **Open** Feb 1 – Dec 31 (closed Wednesday in low season).

Le Barroux is a village set high on a hill between the Ventoux and the jagged peaks of Montmirail, commanding stunning views of the whole Avignon area. The place has a charm of its own, and this small hotel provides pleasantly comfortable accommodation. It also serves as that typical French institution, the *café de la place*, thus offering first-hand insight into local village life. The bedrooms are simple but pleasant and have recently been improved. The nicest have a small terrace. The menu features good local dishes based on fresh products and is likely to include game in season. Meals can be served on the terrace or in the dining room.

How to get there *(Map 33): 9km from Carpentras via D938; between Carpentras and Malaucène.*

Château de Rocher–La Belle Ecluse ★★★

42, rue Emile Lachaux
84500 Bollène (Vaucluse)
Tel. (0)4★ 90.40.09.09 – Fax (0)4★ 90.40.09.30 – M. Carloni-Fassetta

Rooms 20 with telephone, bath or shower, WC and TV. **Price** Single and double 220-370F. **Meals** Breakfast 45-55F, served 7:30-10:00; half board 260-380F (per pers., 3 days min.). **Restaurant** Service from 12:00 and 19:00; menus 100F (lunchtime)-150-250F; also à la carte. Specialties: Duo de foie gras mi cuit et poëllé, filet de bœuf aux truffes, nougat glacé au miel de lavande. **Credit cards** All major. **Pets** Dogs allowed (+30F). **Facilities** Parking. **Nearby** Arc de triomphe and old theatre in Orange, Henri Fabre museum in Sérignan – 18-hole Grand Avignon golf course. **Open** All year.

A beautiful aristocratic mansion built in 1828, the château is set in the middle of a lovely 10-acre park containing both domestic and wild animals and a large garden. The bedrooms are big, comfortable and light. The most attractive is room 6, with a terrace overlooking the garden, and the most amusing is room 8, in the former chapel, which has stained glass windows. The elegant cuisine can be served outside on the terrace, in summer, or in the Richelieu dining room, which has a painted wooden ceiling, a beautiful carved stone chimney and a portrait of the famous Cardinal above the mantel.

How to get there *(Map 33): 25km from Orange via A9, Bollène exit, towards town center then towards Gap, Nyons road.*

Hostellerie du Prieuré ★★★

84480 Bonnieux (Vaucluse)
Tel. (0)4★ 90.75.80.78 – Fax (0)4★ 90.75.96.00
Mme Keller and M. Chapotin

Rooms 10 with telephone, bath, WC and TV. **Price** Single 350F, double 500-590F.
Meals Breakfast 40F, served 8:00-11:00. **Restaurant** Closed Tuesday and Wednesday
Tuesday noon. Service 12:00-13:30, 19:00-21:00; menu 145-200F. Specialties: Aïoli,
caille farcie braisée au miel, daurade au thym et au fenouil, gâteau au chocolat.
Credit cards Visa, Eurocard and MasterCard. **Pets** Dogs allowed (+suppl.).
Facilities Parking. **Nearby** Avignon, Aix-en-Provence, Lubéron villages – 18-hole
Saumane golf course. **Open** Feb 16– Nov 4.

L'Hostellerie du Prieuré is in the village, but the main reception
rooms and bedrooms face the garden and the valley. The
interior decoration is very comfortable and elegant – indeed
opulent – creating an atmosphere that is both intimate and cozy.
The bedrooms are delightful; all are different, but Number 9 has
a terrace with a view of the valley. In summer there is a bar and
restaurant service in the garden. There is no à la carte menu, but
there are two set-price menus which, although unimaginative, do
offer a good choice of specialties.

How to get there *(Map 33): 27km east of Cavaillon via D2 and N100
towards Apt, then D36.*

Hostellerie de Crillon-le-Brave ★★★★

Place de l'église
84410 Crillon-le-Brave (Vaucluse)
Tel. (0)4★ 90.65.61.61 - Fax (0)4★ 90.65.62.86 - M. Chittick

Rooms 16 and 8 suites (2 suites and 1 room with air-conditioning) with telephone, bath or shower, WC and TV on request. **Price** Single and double 750-1450F, suite 1250-2500F. **Meals** Breakfast 75F, served 7:30-11:00; half board +280F, full board +420F (per pers., 3 days min.). **Restaurant** Closed in week for lunchtime. Service 12:00-14:30 (grills on the swimming pool in summer), 19:30-21:30; menus 240-340F, also à la carte. **Credit cards** Amex, Visa, Eurocard and MasterCard. **Pets** Dogs allowed (+80F). **Facilities** Swimming pool, bike, garage. **Nearby** Bédoin, dentelles de Montmirail, chapel of Le Grozeau, château du Barroux, pharmacy museum at Hôtel-Dieu in Carpentras – 18-hole Grand Avignon golf course. **Open** Apr – Dec.

Just next to the church stands this beautiful hotel: formerly a large family house, its bedrooms are still named after the former occupants. The building still has its worn flagstone floors and is tastefully decorated with terracotta objects and Provençal antiques found at nearby Isle-sur-la-Sorgue. The bedrooms are extremely comfortable and cozy, and their yellow-ochre walls evoke the Midi sun. The two lounges contain shelves loaded with old books, comfortable sofas and windows looking over the pink rooftops of the village. A terraced garden, with pretty wrought-iron furniture in its many shady corners, leads down from a waterlily pond to the swimming-pool, where a grill has been set up.

How to get there *(Map 33): 15km north of Carpentras via D974 and D138.*

Hostellerie La Manescale

Route de Faucon
Les Essareaux – 84340 Entrechaux (Vaucluse)
Tel. (0)4★ 90.46.03.80 – Fax (0)4★ 90.46.03.89 – Mme Warland

Rooms 6 with telephone, bath or shower, WC, TV and minibar. **Price** Double 400-560F, suite 800F. **Meals** Breakfast 65F, served 8:30-10:00; half board 425-650F (per pers., 2 days min). **Restaurant** For residents only, closed Monday evening. Service at 19:45; menu 170-185F. Specialties: Cooking with fresh local produce. **Credit cards** All major. **Pets** Dogs allowed (+60F). **Facilities** Swimming pool, parking. **Nearby** Cathedral of Notre-Dame-de-Nazareth in Vaison-la-Romaine, dentelles de Montmirail, Séguret – 18-hole Grand Avignon golf course. **Open** Easter – Oct.

Formerly a shepherd's house and now carefully rebuilt and restored, this pleasant inn stands among vineyards and olive trees between the Drôme and the Vaucluse, facing Mont Ventoux. The bedrooms are luxuriously equipped and tastefully decorated, providing every thoughtful detail. Some of them are small suites (the *Provence* room, for instance). The pleasure of a hearty breakfast on the terrace is enhanced by the magical scenery: a peaceful valley, crowned by the Ventoux, displaying a subtle and ever-changing palette of colors and light. Hotel facilities also include a superb swimming pool. This is a place one would like to keep to oneself, but enthusiastic readers' letters have made sharing the secret a pleasure.

How to get there *(Map 33): 8km east of Vaison-la-Romaine via D205. From A7, take Bollène exit.*

Les Florets ★★

Route des Dentelles
84190 Gigondas (Vaucluse)
Tel. (0)4★ 90.65.85.01 – Fax (0)4★ 90.65.83.80 – Mme Bernard

Rooms 13 with telephone, bath or shower, WC and TV. **Price** Double 350-410F.
Meals Breakfast 50F, served 8:00-10:00; half board 780F (2 pers., 3 days min.).
Restaurant Service 12:00-14:00, 19:30-21:00; menus 95-210F, also à la carte.
Specialties: Dos d'agneau et son tian belle niçoise, blanquette de lotte à l'oseille,
pintadeau au melon. **Credit cards** All major. **Pets** Dogs allowed (+40F). **Facilities**
Parking. **Nearby** Chapel of Notre-Dame-d'Aubune, Séguret, dentelles de Montmirail,
cathedral and Roman bridge in Vaison-la-Romaine – 18-hole Grand Avignon golf
course. **Open** Mar – Dec. (closed Wednesday).

Les Florets occupies an enviable position in the middle of the
countryside at an altitude of 1200 feet facing the peaks of
Montmirail and overlooking the Gigondas vineyards. This is a
simple country hotel, traditional in style, with a pleasant family
atmosphere. The jagged peaks above can be viewed from the
terrace, where an arbor provides welcome shade. The bedrooms
are simple and unpretentious, but comfortable enough and have a
view of the trees. We recommend the new and very charming
bedrooms in the annex. Each opens directly onto the garden. The
furniture is tasteful and the rooms and baths have modern
conveniences. The restaurant serves regional specialties
accompanied by local Gigondas wines. The staff are very friendly
and the owner will be happy to show you his cellars and have you
taste his wines.

*How to get there (Map 33): 25km east of Orange via D975 towards Vaison-
la-Romaine, then D8 and D80; on the Route des Dentelles de Montmirail.*

Ferme de la Huppe

Route D 156
Les Pourquiers – 84220 Gordes (Vaucluse)
Tel. (0)4★ 90.72.12.25 – Fax (0)4★ 90.72.01.83 – Mme Konings

Rooms 8 with telephone, bath, shower, WC, TV and minibar. **Price** Single 400F, double 600F. **Meals** Breakfast incl., served 8:00-10:00. **Restaurant** Open the night and Saturday noon, closed Thusday. Service 12:00-13:30, 19:30-21:00; menus 145-200F, also à la carte. Specialties: Seasonal cooking. **Credit cards** Visa, Eurocard and MasterCard. **Pets** Dogs not allowed. **Facilities** Swimming pool, parking. **Nearby** Les Bories, Sénanque abbey, Roussillon, l'Isle-sur-la-Sorgue, Fontaine de Vaucluse – 18-hole Saumane golf course. **Open** Apr 1 – Nov 7.

The small road winding across the Luberon plain gradually turns into a track, leading to this beautifully restored, extremely secluded old farmhouse. Everything revolves around the fig tree, the olive trees and the well in the middle of a small inner courtyard. It gives access to the six delightful bedrooms named after the old parts of the building: *La cuisine, L'écurie, La cuve...* the kitchen, the stables, and the wine vat. Their terracotta floors, thick walls and typically small windows ensure both privacy and coolness. They are decorated with old objects and elegant fabrics, and all are very comfortable. A covered patio adjoining the dining room looks onto a beautiful swimming pool screened by flowers and lavender. Young chef Gérald Konings' inspired cuisine is fast gaining him a reputation. The Ferme offers an excellent reputation in this region of high gastronomic standards. Last but not least, the hospitality is charming and the prices are still very reasonable.

How to get there (Map 33): 25km northeast of Cavaillon to Gordes via D2; then toward Joucas for 2.5km, then right toward Goult for 500 meters.

Hôtel Les Romarins ★★★

Route de Sénanque
84220 Gordes (Vaucluse)
Tel. (0)4★ 90.72.12.13 - Fax (0)4★ 90.72.13.13 - Mme Charles

Rooms 10 with telephone, bath or shower, WC, TV (8 with minibar). **Price** Single and double 420-680F. **Meals** Breakfast 52F, served 8:00-10:00. No restaurant. **Credit cards** Amex, Visa, Eurocard and MasterCard. **Pets** Dogs not allowed. **Facilities** Swimming pool, parking. **Nearby** Les Bories, Sénanque abbey, Roussillon, l'Isle-sur-la-Sorgue, Fontaine de Vaucluse – 18-hole Saumane golf course. **Open** Feb 16 – Jan 14.

This 200-year-old house has just been fully refurbished and turned into a hotel; it is the only establishment in Gordes commanding a view of the old village more houses. That is a beautiful asset indeed if you delight, as we do, in that breathtaking assemblage of ancient walls, terraced gardens and cypresses. Most of the bedrooms have this view, but make sure when you reserve. They are neat and comfortable, and simply and elegantly decorated in either Directoire or contemporary style. The delicious breakfast – with the view of Gordes – can be served in a small, bright dining-room, or outside in the shade of an ancient mulberry tree. The atmosphere is friendly and informal (all the more so because of the a talking parrot on the staff!). The bird, however, is not in sole charge, and M. and Mme Charles extend an urbane and congenial welcome. There is no restaurant but those previously mentioned for Gordes will delight you. Don't forget *Le Mas Tourteron* on the Imberts road.

How to get there *(Map 33): 25km northeast of Cavaillon via D2.*

483

Mas de Cure Bourse ★★★

Carrefour de Velorgues
84800 Isle-sur-la-Sorgue (Vaucluse)
Tel. (0)4★ 90.38.16.58 – Fax (0)4★ 90.38.52.31 – M. and Mme Donzé

Rooms 13 with telephone, bath, WC and TV. **Price** Single 290-500F, double 320-550F. **Meals** Breakfast 45F; half board 400-470F. **Restaurant** Service 12:00-13:30, 20:00-21:30 (closed 3 weeks in Oct and 2 weeks in Jan, Monday and Tuesday), also à la carte. Specialties: Fleurs de courgettes farcies aux champignons, rascasse coulis de crabe, melon d'agneau aux haricots blancs, petits chèvres pané aux noisettes, nougat glacé. **Credit cards** Visa, Eurocard and MasterCard. **Pets** Dogs allowed (+30F). **Facilities** Swimming pool, parking. **Nearby** l'Isle-sur-la-Sorgue, flea market and Provençal market on Sunday, Fontaine de Vaucluse, Gordes, les Bories, abbey of Sénanque – 18-hole Saumane golf course. **Open** All year.

The Mas de Cure Bourse is a former postal relay station which was built in 1754 in the plain of Isle-sur-la-Sorgue. And it is in this very charming old Provençal *mas,* surrounded by orchards and a 5-acre park, that M. and Mme Donzé receive their visitors. Françoise Donzé is a renowned chef and will make outstanding meals of succulent regional specialties. You will be served in the pretty dining room in front of a large fireplace or on the shady terrace. Through the large glassed-in opening between the reception area and the kitchen, you can even watch the chef and her helpers at work. The decoration and the modern amenities in the bedrooms are impeccable. We prefer *La Chambre du Bout*, the Room at the End, with its small balcony and view over the swimming pool.

How to get there *(Map 33): On A7, exit Avignon-sud or Cavaillon. 3km from Isle-sur-la-Sorgue, on D938, road from Carpentras to Cavaillon.*

484

Le Mas des Grès ★★

Route d'Apt
84800 Lagnes (Vaucluse)
Tel. (0)4★ 90.20.32.85 – Fax (0)4★ 90.20.21.45 – M. and Mme Hermitte

Rooms 12 with telephone, bath, WC and 6 with TV. **Price** Double 400-600F, suite 1000F. **Meals** Breakfast 50F, served 8:00-11:00. **Restaurant** Residents only. Menu 140F. Specialties: Provençal cooking. **Credit cards** Visa, Eurocard and MasterCard. **Pets** Dogs not allowed. **Facilities** Swimming pool, parking. **Nearby** Isle-sur-la-Sorgue, Fontaine de Vaucluse, Gordes, les Bories, Sénanque abbey – 18-hole Saumane golf course. **Open** Mar 1 – Nov 31, Dec week-end, Christmas and New Year's day.

Set among orchards, this beautiful place is a truly marvelous hotel, a bit like your own home in the Luberon, full of joie de vivre and even a touch of eccentricity. The owner, an interior decorator from Savoy, jokes about the "rustico-Byzantine" style, but the decoration has in fact been very tastefully handled. The lounge and bedrooms are elegantly simple and as charming as the guest room you would expect to find in a friend's house. Room 8 can accommodate a whole family, and Room 6 is perfect for children. The restaurant, for guests only, serves family-style meals, which can be enjoyed under an arbor. M. Hermitte's warm and friendly hospitality makes dinner a special pleasure. Meals are available on a half-board basis.

How to get there *(Map 33): On A7, take Avignon exit toward l'Isle-sur-la-Sorgue, then toward Apt via N100 for 5km.*

Mas des Capelans

84580 Oppède (Vaucluse)
Tel. (0)4★ 90.76.99.04 - Fax (0)4★ 90.76.90.29
Poiri Family

Rooms 8 with telephone, bath, WC and TV. **Price** Double 400-800F, suite 600-900F.
Meals Breakfast 50F, served 8:30-10:30; half board 400-600F (per pers., 3 days
min.). **Restaurant** Evening meals. Service at 20:00; menu 155F. Specialties:
Lapereau au romarin, navarin aux petits légumes, pintade aux cerises.
Credit cards All major. **Pets** Dogs allowed (+70F). **Facilities** Heated swimming pool,
billiards, parking. **Nearby** The north of Luberon (Ménerbes, Lacoste, Bonnieux, Saint-
Symphorien priory, Buoux, Saignon, Apt) – 18-hole Saumane golf course. **Open** Feb
15 – Nov 15 (closed Sunday).

The Mas des Capelans once belonged to the monks of the abbey
of Sénanque, who used the building to breed silkworms. The
guest bedrooms are large and very comfortable, and have been
carefully decorated. Each one is named after the view it commands
– *Roussillon, Gordes* – or simply after the vineyard it overlooks, like
some of the ground-floor rooms (which have private entrances).
The living room, dominated by high roof beams, is decorated with
comfortable furniture. The surroundings are pleasant, and dinner
in the courtyard beneath the mulberry-trees and acacias is one of
the highlights of a stay.

How to get there *(Map 33): 10km east of Cavaillon. Via A 7, exit Avignon-*
Sud, toward Apt, N100 between Coustellet and Beaumette, then follow signs.

Hôtel Arène ★★★
Place de Langes
84100 Orange (Vaucluse)
Tel. (0)4★ 90.34.10.95 – Fax (0)4★ 90.34.91.62 – M. and Mme Coutel

Rooms 30 with air-conditioning, telephone, bath or shower, WC, minibar and TV.
Price Single and double 340-440F. **Meals** Breakfast 44F, served 7:00-12:00. No
restaurant. **Credit cards** All major. **Pets** Dogs allowed. **Facilities** Garage. **Nearby** Old
theatre and Arc de Triomphe in Orange, Mornas, Henri Fabre museum in Sérignan,
gorges of Ardèche, Vaison-la-Romaine – 18-hole Grand Avignon golf course.
Open Dec 15 – Oct 31.

Ideally located close to the Roman Theatre in a small pedestrian
square shaded by hundred-year old plane trees, the Arène is the
most sought-after hotel in town. M. and Mme Coutel devote lavish
amounts of care to their guests' well-being and are constantly
refurbishing the hotel. The bedrooms, all different, very
comfortable and cheerful, though some are a little dark. There is
no restaurant, but there is a pleasant lounge with a large fireplace
and period furniture. Guests very much enjoy the hospitality of
the hotel, where it is necessary to reserve well ahead, especially
during the Festival. *Au Goût du Jour* is a charming restaurant with
very reasonable prices.

How to get there *(Map 33): In the old town center.*

487

Auberge de L'Orangerie

4, rue de L'Ormeau
84420 Piolenc (Vaucluse)
Tel. (0)4★ 90.29.59.88 – Fax (0)4★ 90.29.67.74 – Mme De Larocque

Rooms 5 with bath or shower and WC. **Price** Single 190-300F, double 190-380F.
Meals Breakfast 45F, served from 8:30; half board 265F (obligatory in summer),
full board 355F. **Restaurant** Service 12:00-14:00, 19:30-21:30; menus 90-200F.
Specialties: Foie gras, crabe farci, ossobuco de langouste, zarzuela, magret aux
airelles. **Credit cards** Visa, Eurocard and MasterCard. **Pets** Dogs allowed (+40F).
Facilities Parking. **Nearby** Henri Fabre museum in Sérignan, old theatre and Arc
de Triomphe of Orange, Chorégies of Orange in July and August, Mornas – 18-hole
Moulin golf course. **Open** All year.

The vegetation has overrun the interior courtyard of the
Orangerie where everything is in charming disorder. Set back
in a tiny street of Piolenc, a small village only 6km from Orange,
the hotel is very quiet. The dense tangle of flowers and climbing
plants makes the house delightfully cool in summer. Once the
principal attraction of the property, the restaurant is in a beautiful
vaulted room at the back. The simple bedrooms, decorated with
several regional antiques, have an endearing provincial charm; and
one room has a small, pretty terrace. The hospitality is very friendly,
as are the prices.

How to get there *(Map 33): 6km north of Orange. Via A7, exit Orange
(or Bollène if you are coming from Lyon), N7 toward Bollène.*

Auberge de Cassagne ★★★★

450, allée de Cassagne
84130 Le Pontet - Avignon (Vaucluse)
Tel. (0)4★ 90.31.04.18 - Fax (0)4★ 90.32.25.09
MM. Gallon, Boucher, Trestour

Rooms 25 and 5 apartments with air-conditioning, telephone, bath, WC, cable TV, safe and minibar. **Price** Single 420-490F, double 490-1380F, suite 1380-1780F. **Meals** Breakfast 95F, served 7:30-10:30; half board 710-1155F, full board 900-1345F (per pers.). **Restaurant** Service 12:00-13:30, 19:30-21:30; menus 230-460F, also à la carte. Specialties: Terrine provençale au coeur de foie gras, filets de rouget au citron vert, émincé d'agneau et côtelettes de lapereau panées aux petits légumes farcis. **Credit cards** All major. **Pets** Dogs allowed (+60F). **Facilities** Tennis, parking (+20F). **Nearby** Palace of the Popes, Campana collection at the Petit Palais and Calvet museum in Avignon, Avignon festival in July, Villeneuve-les-Avignon – 18-hole Grand Avignon golf course, 18-hole Châteaublanc golf course in Avignon. **Open** All year.

Jean–Michel and Françoise Gallon will greet you in this beautiful old Provençal house only a few kilometers out of Avignon. In summer, in the magnificent flower-filled garden, you can enjoy the renowned cooking of the young chef Philippe Boucher, who trained under Georges Blanc and Paul Bocuse. The outstanding wine cellar has been entrusted to André Trestour. The bedrooms, pleasantly decorated and furnished in Provençal style, are comfortable, though rather small (the most spacious are those with a terrace facing the garden). Some are in the main building and others around the lovely swimming pool.

How to get there *(Map 33): 5km east of Avignon via A7, Avignon-Nord exit, then 5 mins. and left on small road before the lights.*

Mas de Garrigon ★★★

Route de St-Saturnin
84220 Roussillon (Vaucluse)
Tel. (0)4★ 90.05.63.22 – Fax (0)4★ 90.05.70.01 – Mme Rech-Druart

Rooms 9 with telephone, bath, shower, WC, TV and minibar. **Price** Single 700F, double 780F, suite1080F. **Meals** Breakfast 75F, served 7:30-10:30; half board 700-900F, full board 850-1050F (per pers.). **Restaurant** Closed Monday and Tuesday noon. Service 12:00-14:00, 20:00-21:30; menus 190-340F, also à la carte. Specialties: Poellée de langoustines aux fleurs de courgette, pot au feu de volaille aux truffes, soupière de fruits au vin d'épices. **Credit cards** All major. **Pets** Dogs allowed (+65F). **Facilities** Swimming pool, parking. **Nearby** Gordes, les Bories, Sénanque abbey, Isle-sur-la-Sorgue, Luberon – 18-hole Saumane golf course. **Open** All year.

This charming *mas* is typically Provençal in style. Lying at the foot of the Luberon, it is a pleasant place to stay in all seasons. The swimming pool and deckchairs are an invitation to relax in the sun, and lunch can be served there. The lounge has a magnificent fireplace and is perfect for listening to classical music or reading a book from the bookshelves. The bedrooms are tastefully furnished and all have their own terrace facing south over the Luberon. The cooking is refined and made with fresh products from the market. The Mas is ideally situated for touring Provence, as all the principal places of interest are within a 100km radius.

How to get there *(Map 33): 48km east of Avignon via N100 towards Apt, then D2 towards Gordes and D102.*

Auberge du Presbytère

Place de la Fontaine
Saignon – 84400 Apt (Vaucluse)
Tel. (0)4★ 90.74.11.50 – Fax (0)4★ 90.04.68.51 – Mme Bernardi

Rooms 10, 8 with bath and WC. **Price** Double 220-400F. **Meals** Breakfast 45F, served 8:30-10:00. **Restaurant** Service 12:30-14:00, 20:00-21:00; menu 160F. Specialties: Provençal cooking. **Credit cards** Amex, Visa, Eurocard and MasterCard. **Pets** Dogs allowed (+35F). **Nearby** Saignon church, Luberon, Buoux, Saint-Symphorien priory, Bonnieux, Lacoste, Ménerbes, Oppède, Maubec, Robion – 18-hole Saumane golf course. **Open** All year except Nov 15 – 30 and 15 days in Jan (closed Wednesday).

The Auberge du Presbytère is made up of three village houses joined together, making for an entertaining variety of floor levels. The interior decoration is that of a country house with old furniture. The bedrooms are charming, and the two which share a bathroom in the corridor will delight those on a small budget. The restaurant offers two daily menus featuring delicious traditional and local dishes. The Auberge is a charming and friendly place to stay in the heart of the Luberon where M. and Mme Bernardi will greet you like friends.

How to get there *(Map 33): 3.5km southeast of Apt; in the village.*

Hostellerie du Vieux Château

Route de Sainte-Cécile
84830 Sérignan (Vaucluse)
Tel. (0)4★ 90.70.05.58 – Fax (0)4★ 90.70.05.62 – M. and Mme Truchot

Rooms 7 with telephone, bath, WC, TV and minibar - Wheelchair access. **Price** Double 300-800F. **Meals** Breakfast 40F, served 8:00-10:00. **Restaurant** Closed Sunday evening and Monday in low season. Service 12:30-13:30, 19:30-21:00; menus 145-185F, also à la carte. Specialties: Jambon persillé, foie gras au Beaume de Venise, canard aux cassis, agneau de la Drôme, truffes au chocolat et raisins au marc. **Credit cards** Amex, Visa, Eurocard and MasterCard. **Pets** Dogs allowed (+50F). **Facilities** Swimming pool, parking. **Nearby** Arc de triomphe and old theatre in Orange, Chorégies of Orange in July and Augut, Mornas, Henri Fabre museum in Sérignan. **Open** All year except late Dec, 1 week in Nov (closed Sunday evening and Monday in low season).

This was originally a farmhouse with a mill in the back whose only remaining trace is a canal which flows by the house. Today, the hotel is a large village house flanked by a small vegetable garden and a pleasant flower garden filled with fragrant lavender around the swimming pool. The owners run a very traditional hotel, with M. Truchot in the kitchen and his wife at the reception. The atmosphere is that of a quiet, family-style provincial auberge. The bedrooms are all individually decorated, with the decor occasionally overdone. Our favorite is number 6, with the poppies. In summer, meals are served in the shade of the beautiful plane trees in the garden, making for a very Provençal setting.

How to get there (Map 33): 7km northeast of Orange. Via A7, Orange exit, (or Bollène if you are coming from Lyon), in the toward of Bollène and D976 in the toward of Sérignan.

Hostellerie Le Beffroi ★★★
Haute Ville - Rue de l'Evêché
84110 Vaison-la-Romaine (Vaucluse)
Tel. (0)4★ 90.36.04.71 - Fax (0)4★ 90.36.24.78 - M. Christiansen

Rooms 22 with telephone, bath or shower, WC, TV and minibar. **Price** Single 320-415F, double 435-630F, suite 630-725F. **Meals** Breakfast 45F, served 7:30-9:45; half board 430-525F, full board 525-685F (per pers., 3 days min.). **Restaurant** Closed weekday afternoons. Service 12:00-13:45, 19:15-21:30; menus 98F (lunchtime), 195F, also à la carte. Specialties: Aïgo boulido, tourte au vert, gigot d'aubergine, daube d'agneau à l'Avignonnaise, crème brûlée au miel et à la lavande. **Credit cards** All major. **Pets** Dogs allowed (+35F). **Facilities** Minigolf, games, table tennis, garage (40F). **Nearby** Arc de Triomphe and old theatre in Orange, Mornas, Henri Fabre museum in Sérignan. **Open** Mar 15 – Nov 15 and Dec 15 – Feb 15.

This hotel high up in the medieval part of Vaison consists of several mansions joined together. The buildings' character has been preserved with tiled floors, polished paneling, spiral staircases and beautiful antiques, paintings and curios. The bedrooms are all different; antique lovers will be especially taken by the quality of the period furniture. The lounges are also pleasantly furnished and have open fireplaces. A superb terrace garden gives lovely views over the rooftops of the town. In summer, meals are served here, along with very reasonably priced salads.

How to get there *(Map 33): 30km northeast of Orange via D975; at the top of the town.*

Hostellerie La Grangette ★

Chemin Cambuisson
84740 Velleron (Vaucluse)
Tel. (0)4★ 90.20.00.77 – Fax (0)4★ 90.20.07.06 – Mme and M. Blanc-Brude

Rooms 16 telephone, bath or shower, WC, TV on request. **Price** Double 550-950F, suite 1050F. **Meals** Breakfast 70F, served 8:00-10:00; half board +180F (per pers.). **Restaurant** Service 12:00-14:00, from 20:00; menu 165-235F, also à la carte. Specialties: Poutargue provençale aux petits légumes, le délice des calanques, dentelles aux fraises. **Credit cards** Amex, Visa, Eurocard and MasterCard. **Pets** Dogs allowed (+140F). **Facilities** Swimming pool, parking. **Nearby** Isle sur Sorgue; Fontaine de Vaucluse; Gordes; les Bories; abbey of Sénanque; Avignon; Le Lubéron– 18-hole Saumane golf course. **Open** All year.

On a farm which neighbors still remember, La Grangette has had a beautiful past. Now it is reopened in the heart of nature. Sixteen beautiful bedrooms, all different, are decorated in Provençal colors and offer you comfort and silence. There are *La Mistrale, La Mule du Pape, La Mireillo* and the lovely *L'Arlesienne* room, with a terrace and two windows facing the evening light. Brightly waxed antique furniture throughout is combined with a gaily regional decor. There is an immense swimming pool, a shady terrace for meals and a large garden with trees which can be the starting point for pleasant walks. Add the friendly hospitality and you have a very pleasant hostelry.

How to get there *(Map 33): 20km from Avignon. On A7, take Avignon exit toward L'Isle-sur-la-Sorgue; in L'Isle, take toward Pernes-les-Fontaines via D938 for 4km, then signs on right.*

Auberge de la Fontaine

Place de la Fontaine
84210 Venasque (Vaucluse)
Tel. (0)4★ 90.66.02.96 - Fax (0)4★ 90.66.13.14 - M. and Mme Soehlke

Rooms 5 suites with air-conditioning, telephone, bath, WC, TV and minibar.
Price Suite 700F. **Meals** Breakfast 50F. **Restaurant** Closed Wednesday and from
mid-Nov to mid-Dec. Service every evening 20:00-22:00 and Sunday 12:00-14:00;
menu 200F, also à la carte. Specialties: Assiette du pêcheur, choucroute au foie gras,
gibier frais en saison, pigeonneau aux airelles. "Bistro": menu 80F, also à la carte
(closed Sunday evening and Monday). **Credit cards** Visa, Eurocard and MasterCard.
Pets Dogs allowed. **Facilities** Mountain bikes, parking. **Nearby** Venasque church,
Gallo-Roman cemetery in Mazan, Pernes-les-Fontaines, Carpentras – 18-hole
Saumane golf course. **Open** All year.

The Auberge de la Fontaine is a beautiful old village house
which Ingrid and Christian Soehlke have completely
restructured inside, creating an amusing maze of mezzanines,
terraces and stairways. While conserving the structure's noble
appearance, they particularly sought to create the informal
atmosphere of a house for friends. And it would be difficult not to
feel at ease: each suite includes a bedroom and a lounge with a
fireplace, tastefully decorated and furnished in very Provençal style
and equipped with a direct-dial phone, television, and cassette, CD
players, fax and minitel. Each has a secluded terrace and a
kitchenette, but the charming dining room and the Soehlkes'
succulent cuisine should not be missed. There is a dinner concert
each month, and in the low season, the hotel proposes a 5-day
package with cooking lessons.

How to get there *(Map 33): 11km south of Carpentras via D9.*

Auberge Les Bichonnières **

Route de Savigneux
01330 Ambérieux-en-Dombes (Ain)
Tel. (0)4★ 74.00.82.07 - Fax (0)4★ 74.00.89.61 - M. Sauvage

Rooms 9 with telephone, bath or shower and WC. **Price** Single 220F, double 240-320F. **Meals** Breakfast 40F, served 8:00-10:00; half board 260F (per pers., 3 days min.). **Restaurant** Service 12:15-13:45, 19:30-20:45 (closed Monday in July and Aug); menus 98-250F, also à la carte. Specialties: Grenouilles fraîches, volaille de Bresse. **Credit cards** Amex, Visa, Eurocard and MasterCard. **Pets** Dogs allowed. **Facilities** Parking. **Nearby** Trévoux, bird reserve in Villard-les-Dombes, Montluel, Pérouges – 18-hole Le Clou golf course in Villard-les-Dombes. **Open** All year except Christmas holiday (closed Sunday evening and Monday in low season).

Not far north of Lyon, this roadside (yet quiet) inn is an old farmhouse that has been restored but still retains its rustic character – not a fake, kitsch version of rustic, as is too often the case, but the genuine article with all its charm. The flower-filled courtyard where meals can be enjoyed in the shade of large white parasols brings to mind Italian sidewalk cafés. The bedrooms are comfortable, with pleasant decor in keeping with the rural character of the building. This hotel provides a good stopping place just before Lyon and an ideal base for exploring the picturesque, lake-dotted Dombe area. Chef Marc Sauvage trained with Fernand Point and prepares regional specialities using fresh local produce.

How to get there *(Map 26): 30km north of Lyon via A6, Villefranche exit, then D904 towards Bourg-en-Bresse, then Villars-les-Dombes.*

Auberge des Chasseurs ★★★

Naz–Dessus
01170 Echenevex (Ain)
Tel. (0)4★ 50.41.54.07 – Fax (0)4★ 50.41.90.61 – M. Lamy

Rooms 15 with telephone, bath or shower, WC and TV. **Price** Single 350-500F, double 400-600F. **Meals** Breakfast 55F, served 8:00-10:00; half board 480-600F (per pers.). **Restaurant** Service 12:00-13:30, 19:00-21:30; menus 180-300F (125F lunchtime except Saturday and Sunday), also à la carte. Specialties: Salade de cocos et écrevisses petite raviolle mœlleuse, cannelloni de homard, ris de veau poêlés barigoule d'artichauts et girolles. **Credit cards** All major. **Pets** Dogs allowed (+40F). **Facilities** Swimming pool, tennis, parking. **Nearby** Le Pailly and col de la Faucille, château of Fernet-Voltaire – 27-hole Maison Blanche golf course in Echenevex. **Open** March 10 – Nov 15.

Standing on the slopes of the Jura, amidst fields and woods, and yet just 15 minutes from Geneva, the Auberge des Chasseurs is an old farmhouse which has been very well restored. The homey atmosphere inside is very charming. The beamed ceilings, chairs and bedroom doors are decorated with floral frescos recently done by a Swedish artist. In the restaurant, there is a magnificent series of photographs by Cartier-Bresson. Upstairs, you will find a very inviting lounge and bar. The bedrooms are beautifully decorated with Laura Ashley fabrics and wallpapers, English-pine furniture and their charming bathrooms are as lovely. Outside, the oak garden furniture was designed by an artist, as was the mosaic of the terrace floor. The garden is full of flowers and shady spots, and the view is splendid. The cuisine is excellent, the service attentive and Dominique Lamy is a very hospitable owner.

How to get there *(Map 20): 17km northwest of Genève via D984 towards St-Genis-Pouilly, then D978c towards Echenevex; at Chevry head for Naz-Dessus.*

Hostellerie du Vieux Pérouges ★★★★

Place du Tilleul
01800 Pérouges (Ain)
Tel. (0)4★ 74.61.00.88 – Fax (0)4★ 74.34.77.90 – M. Thibaut

Rooms 28 with telephone, bath, shower, WC and 4 with TV. **Price** Single 390-700F, double 450-900F, suite 980F. **Meals** Breakfast 60F, served 8:00-10:00. **Restaurant** Service 12:00-14:00, 19:00-21:00; menus 180-390F, also à la carte. Specialties: Filet de carpe farci à l'ancienne, volaille de Bresse, panaché pérougien, galette de l'hostellerie. **Credit cards** Visa, Eurocard and MasterCard. **Pets** Dogs allowed. **Facilities** Parking. **Nearby** Trévoux, bird reserve in Villard-les-Dombes, Montluel – 18-hole Le Clou golf course in Villard-les-Dombes. **Open** All year.

Pérouge is an exceptional small medieval town that you should be sure to visit and to plunge yourself into the atmosphere, what more appropriate than this inn which is made up of several very old houses. Stone stairways, stained glass windows, French ceilings, fireplaces... nothing is amiss. The most luxurious bedrooms are resplendent with Haute Epoque furniture and marble baths. The other, simpler rooms are also well furnished and offer excellent modern amenities. Each house borders on a small paved lane with, here and there, a small garden or open ruins overgrown with vegetation. The house opens onto the main square where the restaurant is located. Here too, the medieval atmosphere is prevalent; a wide-board floor, a baker's kneading trough, china cupboards, a large fireplace in which several large logs are often burning, all combine to whet the appetite for the Ostellerie's regional cuisine which is served by waiters in traditional dress.

How to get there (Map 26): 35km northeast of Lyon via A42, Pérouges exit.

Hôtel de la Santoline ★★★

07460 Beaulieu (Ardèche)
Tel. (0)4★ 75.39.01.91 - Fax (0)4★ 75.39.38.79
M. and Mme Espenel

Rooms 7 with telephone, bath, WC and minibar (some with air-conditioning).
Price Double 290-370F, suite 580F. **Meals** Breakfast 40F, served 8:00-10:00; half
board 310-460F (per pers., 3 days min.). **Restaurant** Service 19:30-21:30; menus
165-240F, also à la carte. Specialties: Blinis au saumon et aux épinards, assiette
d'agneau, pieds et paquets. **Credit cards** Visa, Eurocard and MasterCard. **Pets** Dogs
allowed (+30F). **Facilities** Swimming pool, parking. **Nearby** La Cocalière cave, bois
de Païolive, corniche du Vivarais, Les Vans to la Bastide-Puylaurent. **Open** March –
Nov.

Standing right in the middle of Provençal Ardèche, la Santoline is a converted stone hunting lodge. It is a haven of peace and commands views as far as the Cévennes. A beautiful vaulted cellar has been turned into a dining-room, and the simple decor of the bedrooms, all of which have pretty bathrooms, is perfectly in tune with the unadorned style of the building. Our favorites are Room 5 and especially Room 4, under the eaves; both have marvelous view of the surrounding country side and are equipped with air conditioning. The swimming pool is much appreciated in summer, as is the pleasant flowery terrace where breakfast and dinner can be served. Pierre and Marie-Danièle Espenel are friendly hosts, and prices are very reasonable.

How to get there *(Map 32): 84km north of Nîmes via N106 to Alès, then D904 and D104 to La Croisée de Jalès, then D225.*

Château d'Urbilhac ★★★

07270 Lamastre (Ardèche)
Tel. (0)4★ 75.06.42.11 – Fax (0)4★ 75.06.52.75
Mme Xompero

Rooms 13 with telephone, bath or shower and WC. **Price** Single 500F, double 550-700F. **Meals** Breakfast 65F, served 8:00-11:00; half board 550-625F (per pers.). **Restaurant** Closed lunchtime except weekends. Service at 12:30 and 19:30; menus 230-270F. **Credit cards** All major. **Pets** Dogs allowed. **Facilities** Heated swimming pool, tennis, parking. **Nearby** Tournon, Vivarais steam train between Tournon and Lamastre – 18-hole golf course in Chambon-sur-Lignon. **Open** May 1 – Oct 5.

The Château d'Urbilhac, built in the last century in Renaissance style over the cellars of a 16th-century fortified house, is set in 148-acres of parkland. In the reception rooms, 19th-century style is predominant. The bedrooms, each with its own style, are equally beautiful. Restful and comfortable, they are further enhanced with superb bathrooms and often look out on a sublime panorama. In the spring, the dining room is moved out onto a vast veranda. You will enjoy outstanding cuisine, which is intelligently original and which reflects great respect for the proper use of farm products. (The prices are expensive at first but the reasonable *demi-pension* price is applicable beginning with the first night.) Mme Xompero is especially attentive, going from table to table, ensuring that everyone is pleased and generally contributing to the excellent atmosphere here. Finally, you should not leave Urbillac without first stepping onto the immense terrace and looking out over the valley where distant Ardèche farms are scattered between pastures and chestnut groves.

How to get there *(Map 26): 36km west of Valence via D533.*

500

Domaine de Rilhac ★

07320 Saint-Agrève (Ardèche)
Tel. (0)4★ 75.30.20.20 - Fax (0)4★ 75.30.20.00
Mme and M. Sinz

Rooms 8 with telephone, bath or shower, WC and TV. **Price** Single and double 330-430F, apart. 660F. **Meals** Breakfast 50F, served 8:00-10:30; half board 390F, full board 440F (per pers., 2 days min.). **Restaurant** Service 12:30-13:30, 20:00-21:30, menus 110-270F (70F child), also à la carte. Specialties: Ecrevisses, saumon de Fontaines, bœuf salers, chataignes, myrtilles. **Credit cards** Visa, Eurocard and MasterCard. **Pets** Dogs allowed (+40F). **Facilities** Parking. **Nearby** Mont-Gerbier-des-Joncs; gorges de l'Eyrieux – 18-hole Chambon-sur-Lignon golf course. **Open** All year except Feb (closed Monday evening and Tuesday except July).

Behind Saint-Agrève, an immense plateau lies at an altitude of 1000 meters facing Mounts Gerbier de Jonc and Mézenc. The air is pure, brown cows lead a peaceful existence there and several trout streams wind through the valley hollows. Ludovic Sinz, *hôtel de charme* shows that not only is he a talented young chef but also, with his wife Florence, he knows how to restore charming places. A stairway with a beautiful wrought-iron railing crafted by a local artisan leads to the comfortable bedrooms. They are named after flowers and each has a framed alphabet. The colors of the embroideries are repeated in the coordinated bedcover fabrics, drapes and table skirts, all contributing to a fresh and tasteful decor. The view is magnificent throughout, with large bay windows affording fine panoramas. The yellow plaster in the entrance, the small lounge and the dining room creates a joyful, almost Provençal atmosphere in all seasons. You will find the same refinements in the shady garden outside, which is protected by an old wall and is very carefully tended.

How to get there (Map 26): 56km west of Valence via D533.

Grangeon

07800 Saint-Cierge-la-Serre (Ardèche)
Tel. (0)4 75.65.73.86
Mme Valette

Rooms 5 of which 4 with bath, 1 with shower and 2 with WC. **Price** Double 290-490F. **Meals** Breakfast 37F, served 8:00-9:00; half board in July and Aug. **Restaurant** Evening meals for residents only. Service 19:30; menu 160F. Specialties: Agneau au miel, papillotes de lapin à l'aneth et au pastis. **Credit cards** Not accepted. **Pets** Dogs not allowed. **Facilities** Parking. **Nearby** Valence museum, villages romanesque church and châteaux of the Ardèche – 18-hole Valence golf course in Saint-Didier-de-Charpey. **Open** By reservation Apr 10 – Nov 1.

Grangeon is the ideal place for those seeking a peaceful retreat and for nature lovers. It is an estate of 155-acres of parkland and forests, 4km away from the nearest village, and is reached by a small road winding through hills and woods. The house itself was built at the beginning of the 18th century and has seven bedrooms. The decoration combines wood and stone to create a warm country atmosphere. (Guests can play the piano.) All kinds of vegetables grow in Mme Valette's lovely terraced garden, and as she bakes her own bread and raises sheep, she is almost self-sufficient. Set in the heart of the Ardèche region and yet only 15km from the motorway, Grangeon provides an opportunity to relax in the countryside.

How to get there (Map 26): 35km south of Valence via A7, Loriol exit, then N104 towards Privas-Aubenas; at Les Fonts-du-Pouzin D265 towards Saint-Cierge (follow signs).

Hôtel Bellier ★★

Avenue de Provence
26420 La Chapelle-en-Vercors (Drôme)
Tel. (0)4★ 75.48.20.03 - Fax (0)4★ 75.48.25.31 - Mme Bellier

Rooms 12 with telephone, bath or shower, WC and TV. **Price** Single 160-200F, double 300-440F. **Meals** Breakfast 40F, served 8:00-11:30; half board 280-380F, full board 400-490F (on request, per pers., 3 days min.). **Restaurant** Service 12:30-13:30, 19:30-20:30; menus 90-210F, also à la carte. Specialties: Truite Bellier, poulet aux morilles, pintadeau au genièvre, gratin dauphinois. **Credit cards** All major. **Pets** Dogs allowed. **Facilities** Swimming pool, parking. **Nearby** Pont-en-Royans, road des Petits and Grands Goulets, La Luire cave, Col of Rousset, Lente forest, Draye Blanche cave – 9-hole golf course in La-Chapelle-en-Vercors. **Open** All year (closedTuesday evening and Wednesday).

This inn stands on a rise at the entrance to La Chapelle-en-Vercors, one of the most charming villages of the very beautiful Vercors Mountain region. From the terrace and a flower-filled garden, you will have a beautiful view over the fields, mountains, and the swimming pool. As this is a mountain hotel, the interior decoration has been designed very much in the Alpine style. The bedrooms are quiet, comfortable but all should be extensively renovated. The restaurant offers varied, refined cuisine and meals can be served in the shady garden. You will enjoy friendly hospitality at this inn, a starting point for discovering a region of steep roads, pastures and forests, cascading waterfalls, grottos and caves much prized by speologists.

How to get there *(Map 26): 63km east of Valence. 62km southwest of Grenoble via D531 to Villard-de-Lans, then D103.*

La Treille Muscate ★★★
26270 Cliousclat (Drôme)
Tel. (0)4★ 75.63.13.10 – Fax (0)4★ 75.63.10.79
Mme Delaitre

Rooms 12 with telephone, bath, WC and TV. **Price** Double 280-500F. **Meals** Breakfast 45F, served 8:00-10:00. **Restaurant** Closed Tuesday. Service 12:00-13:30, 20:00-21:30; menus 89-129F, also à la carte. Specialties:Croustillant de pigeon laqué au miel d'épices. **Credit cards** Visa, Eurocard and MasterCard. **Pets** Dogs allowed. **Facilities** Swimming pool. **Nearby** Mirmande, Poët-Laval; le quartier des Forts in Nyons – 18-hole Valdaine golf course. **Open** All year except Jan and Feb.

La Treille Muscate is exactly the kind of small hotel you hope to find in a Provençal village. Beautiful sunny yellow walls brighten the on the ground floor rooms; here you will find the dining room with its bright Provençal table linens, the corner bar and the small TV room. There are several pieces of handsome regional furniture, large watercolors, varnished jugs and splendid dinnerware crafted by a skilled potter, a neighbor and friend; all create a decor that makes you feel truly at home. Upstairs, pretty bedrooms have recently been installed and beautifully decorated. They have a lovely view out over the quiet village or the countryside.The excellent cuisine is enhanced with aromatic herbs and local products. In good weather, a few tables are set out on the village side or in a small garden, bordered with terraced walls. "The Muscat Arbor" is a hospitable, charming small hotel with extremely reasonable prices.

How to get there *(Map 26): 16km north of Montélimar via A7, Loriol exit, then 5km. On N7 Loriol-Montélimard toward*

Manoir de la Roseraie ★★★

26230 Grignan (Drôme)
Tel. (0)4★ 75.46.58.15 - Fax★ (0)4 75.46.91.55
M. and Mme Alberts

Rooms 15 with telephone, bath or shower, WC and TV - Wheelchair access.
Price Single and double 630-1050F, suite 1600F. **Meals** Breakfast 90F, served 8:00-
10:30; half board 610-820F (per pers., 3 days min.). **Restaurant** Service 12:00-
13:30, 20:00-21:15; menus 180-230F. Specialties: Croustillant de filet d'agneau au
miel de tapenade, filet de bar en croûte de pipenade, foie gras maison, belle cave
de côte du Rhône. **Credit cards** All major. **Pets** Dogs allowed (+60F).
Facilities Heated swimming pool, tennis, sauna, parking. **Nearby** Château and
museum of Mme de Sévigné in Grignan, Poët-Laval, Dieulefit – 9-hole Valaurie golf
course. **Open** All year except Jan 5 – Feb 14 and Nov 6 – 13 (closed Monday in low season).

In this beautiful private mansion built in 1850 by the mayor of
Grignan, Michèle Alberts and her husband have tastefully
refurbished and decorated the bedrooms and the suite. Those on
the ground and first floors are imposingly large with their high
ceilings, and are bright and comfortable, while the ones on the
deuxième étage are more intimate. They have colorful and sometimes
unusual bathrooms. (The *Baccara* room, for instance, has a circular
bath.) The elegant salmon-pink dining room looks out onto the
ravishingly beautiful park, which is planted with cedars,
bougainvillea and 350 rose bushes. The heated swimming pool is
prettily integrated into the design of the park. Meals and the
breakfast buffet are served on the large terrace in summer. The staff
is very friendly.

How to get there *(Map 33): 90km north of Avignon via A7, Montélimar-
Sud exit, then N7 and D133.*

Domaine du Colombier ***

Route de Donzère
Malataverne - 26780 Montélimar (Drôme)
Tel. (0)4★ 75.90.86.86 - Fax (0)4★ 75.90.79.40 - M. and Mme Barette

Rooms 20 and 5 suites with telephone, bath, WC and TV. **Price** Single 400-580F, double 450-860F, suite 860-1200F. **Meals** Breakfast 70F, served 7:30-11:00. **Restaurant** Service 12:15-14:15, 19:15-21:30; menus 150F (lunchtime), 190-360F, also à la carte. Specialties: Assiette des Mareyeurs au ravioles de Royans, panaché d'agneau aux herbes de la garrigue, chariot de desserts. **Credit cards** All major. **Pets** Dogs allowed (+50F). **Facilities** Swimming pool, bowling alley, bicycles, parking. **Nearby** Poët-Laval, Nyons, château and museum of Mme de Sévigné in Grignan, villages of the Drôme between Montélimar and Orange. **Open** Feb 10 – Nov 27, Dec 9 – Jan 27.

Formerly a 14th-Century abbey, the Domaine du Colombier maintains its tradition of hospitality to travelers to this day, as it is now a pleasant hotel conveniently located on the road south. Although only minutes off the highway, it seems to be in the middle of the countryside. When you walk through the door be prepared to find furniture and fabrics piled up in the entrance hall, for it is also a shop. The bedrooms are bright, colorful and comfortably decorated; three of them have a small mezzanine. In the garden, the swimming pool, surrounded by chaises longues, is a lovely place to relax. The lavender-blue furniture in the dining room is Provençal in style, and dinner or an evening drink can also be served on the patio.

How to get there *(Map 33): 9km south of Montélimar via N7 and D144a (2km after Malataverne).*

La Capitelle **
Rue du Rempart
26270 Mirmande (Drôme)
Tel. (0)4★ 75.63.02.72 – Fax (0)4★ 75.63.02.50 – M. and Mme Melki

Rooms 10 plus 2 apartments with telephone, bath or shower (10 with WC). **Price** Single and double 290-460F, apart.520-550F. **Meals** Breakfast 47-52F, served 8:00-11:00; half board 327-457F. **Restaurant** Service 12:00-13:30 (14:00 in hight season), 19:30-21:30; menu 95-260F, also à la carte. Specialties: Brouillade aux truffes, demi pigeon farci au foie gras, marmite de poissons safranée, tirami-sù aux fruits rouge, nougat glacé. **Credit cards** Amex, Visa, Eurocard and MasterCard. **Pets** dogs allowed (+35F). **Facilities** Garage (+50F). **Nearby** Mirmande church, Pöet-Laval, Nyons – 18-hole Valdaine golf course. **Open** Feb 20 – Jan 15 (closed Tuesday and Wednesday lunchtime).

L a Capitelle is a tall Renaissance building with mullioned windows. The lounge and dining-room have vaulted ceilings and handsome stone fireplaces. Items of period furniture combine well with more simple contemporary furnishings to create an elegant and yet warm atmosphere. A sober and sure taste is also in evidence in the bedrooms, most of which have a beautiful antique wardrobe with a bouquet of dried flowers. All the rooms are different and most enjoy a magnificent view over the plain below. Breakfast and drinks can be served on the ramparts, while meals are served in the dining room or on the shady terrace in summer: the regional cuisine is excellent. To enjoy optimum service as well as the beauty of the site, guests are kindly requested to arrive by 8:30 P.M. at the latest. The staff is hospitable and very friendly.

How to get there *(Map 26): 17km south of Valence via N7, then D204; at the entrance to Mirmande.*

Ferme Saint-Michel **
26130 Solérieux (Drôme)
Tel. (0)4★ 75.98.10.66 – Fax (0)4★ 75.98.19.09
M. Laurent

Rooms 15 (5 with air-conditioning) with telephone (13 with bath and WC, 10 with TV). **Price** Single 300-330F, double 310-350F. **Meals** Breakfast 38F, served 9:00-10:00. **Restaurant** Service 12:30-14:00, 20:00-21:15 (closed Dec 23 – Jan 24, Sunday evening and Monday); menus 130-180F, also à la carte. Specialties: Menu-truffe. **Credit cards** Visa, Eurocard and MasterCard. **Pets** Dogs not allowed. **Facilities** Swimming pool, tennis, parking. **Nearby** Château and museum of Mme de Sévigné in Grignan, Forts in Nyons, Poët-Laval, Dieulefit, villages of the Drôme – 9-hole Valaurie golf course. **Open** All year.

Partially renovated and under new ownership, the Ferme Saint-Michel is a traditional old Provençal *mas*, isolated from the road by thick vegetation, whose origins go back to the 16th century. The Ferme opens onto an inviting terrace where, in summer, a few tables are set for dinner. You will savor excellent local products such as the truffles harvested on the property, and game in season. Large trees afford lovely shade over the terrace, while a few steps away, there is the swimming pool. For the moment, we can recommend only the bedrooms which have been renovated. They are simple with modern conveniences, and they are decorated with local Souleïado fabrics, which harmonize beautifully with the Provençal furniture. On the ground floor, there is a cool dining room, a small bar and inviting lounges with fireplaces.

How to get there *(Map 33): North of Bollène. On A7, Bollène or Montélimar-Sud exit, toward Saint-Paul-Trois-Châteaux.*

Auberge de la Rochette

La Rochette
26400 Vauvaneys-la-Rochette (Drôme)
Tel. (0)4★ 75.25.79.30 – Fax (0)4★ 75.25.79.25 – A. Cordonier and P. Danis

Rooms 5 with telephone, bath or shower, WC, TV, safe and minibar. **Price** Double 400-450F, duplex 600F (4 pers.). **Meals** Breakfast-brunch 60F, served 8:00-10:00; half board 370-380F (per pers., 3 days min.). **Restaurant** Service 12:00-13:30, 19:30-21:00 (on reservation); menus 125-195F. Specialties: Foie gras de canard maison, agneau de la Drôme à la crème d'aïl doux, pavé de turbot à l'huile d'olive parfumée, crème brûlée à la lavande. **Credit cards** Visa, Eurocard and MasterCard. **Pets** Dogs allowed (+50F, on reservation). **Facilities** Swimming pool, parking. **Nearby** Shoe Museum in Romans, Facteur Cheval's Palace in Hauterives, Massif du Vercors, villages of the Drôme. **Open** All year except 15 days in Oct, 15 days in Feb and Wednesday.

Located in the stunningly beautiful setting of Provençal Drôme, the Auberge is an old barn which has been restored in the regional style. The small size allows the owners to receive guests informally, like friends. The beautiful rooms have been carefully designed down to the last detail. (A room with a mezzanine and high ceilings was designed with families or groups of friends in mind). The décor includes warm sand-colored walls, Provençal quilted bedspreads and matching drapes, terracotta-tile floor and antique furniture. An elegant small dining room opens onto a flower-filled terrace where regional specialties are served. This is a charming, very friendly inn.

How to get there *(Map 26): 20km south of Valence, on A7 exit Loriol or Valence-Sud, toward Crest; before Crest, take road for Vauvaneys, then La Rochette on D538 coming from Valence.*

Château de Passières ★★

38930 Chichilianne (Isère)
Tel. (0)4★ 76.34.45.48 – Fax (0)4★ 76.34.46.25
Mme and M. Perli

Rooms 23 with telephone, bath, shower and 20 with WC. **Price** Single 280F, double 280-450F. **Meals** Breakfast 40F, served 7:30-9:30; half board from 310F on request (per pers., 3 days min.). **Restaurant** Closed Monday in low season and Nov – Jan. Service 12:15-13:30, 19:15-21:00; menus 95-200F, also à la carte. Specialties: Fricassée de cèpes et escargots, escalope de saumon du miel de pissenlit, crêpe d'agneau, truffes. **Credit cards** Visa, Eurocard and MasterCard. **Pets** Dogs allowed (+20F). **Facilities** Swimming pool, tennis, sauna, parking. **Nearby** Mont Aiguille, Vercors plateau, Grenoble. **Open** Feb 1 – Nov 1 (closed Sunday evening and Monday in low season).

Restored by a very friendly family, this 15th-century château occupies a truly exceptional position at the foot of Mont Aiguille, a magnificent rock wall which creates a somewhat unreal atmosphere throughout the region. We particularly recommend the three bedrooms with dark-brown antique wood paneling and red carpets; they have great character and are very warm and inviting. The other rooms are more modern and impersonal. On the ground floor there is an irresistible salon, with almond-green, figured paneling, antique furniture and, above all, a superb collection of paintings. In good weather, dining tables are set out on the terrace and in winter, the good regional cuisine is served in the large dining room. On the walls, several paintings by Edith Berger remind art lovers that a small museum dedicated to her works is located on the top floor. This very hospitable château is a must in a region which is not to be missed.

How to get there (Map 26): 50km south of Grenoble via N75 towards Sisteron until Clelles, then D7 and D7b.

Domaine de Clairefontaine ★★

38121 Chonas–L'Amballan (Isère)
Tel. (0)4★ 74.58.81.52 – Fax (0)4★ 74.58.80.93
M. Girardon

Rooms 14 and 2 apartments with telephone and 13 with bath and WC (TV on request). **Price** Single and double 180-380F, suite 360-710F. **Meals** Breakfast 45F, served 7:30-9:00. **Restaurant** Closed Sunday evening except in July and Aug. Service 12:00-13:45, 19:00-21:00; menus 140-350F, also à la carte. Specialties: Homard roti à la minute, minestrone de légumes aux arômates, rosace d'agneau jus court au romarin et tatin de pommes dauphinoises, cône chocolat et liqueur de chartreuse, crème pralin. **Credit cards** All major. **Pets** Dogs allowed. **Facilities** Tennis, parking, garage. **Nearby** Saint-Pierre church and lapidary museum in Vienne, wine tasting. **Open** Feb 1 –Oct 31.

Clairefontaine is a family hotel run by M. Girardon and his two sons, who will soon replace him (brilliantly); but they are above all responsible for the excellent cuisine served here. One son makes the morning croissants, pastries and desserts, while the other prepares the main dishes, from stocks to sauces. The bright dining room is very beautiful and the lounge is inviting. The bedrooms have the style of old provincial houses with their high ceilings, creaking floors and classic furniture. Ask for those on the *premier étage*, particularly number 3; there is also a large apartment for big families and other bedrooms in an annex which has just been renovated.

How to get there *(Map 26): 12km south of Vienne via A7, Vienne exit, then N7 or N86 and D7 towards Le Péage-en-Roussillon or Chanas exit then N7 Vienne toward.*

Chalet Mounier ★★★

38860 Les Deux-Alpes (Isère)
Tel. (0)4★ 76.80.56.90 – Fax (0)4★ 76.79.56.51
M. and Mme Mounier

Rooms 48 with telephone, bath or shower, TV and 44 with WC. **Price** Single 290-510F, double 335-780F. **Meals** Breakfast incl., served 7:30-9:30; half board 305-590F, full board 385-650F (per pers., 3 days min.). **Restaurant** Service 12:30-14:00, 19:30-21:00; menus 125-290F, also à la carte. **Credit cards** Visa, Eurocard and MasterCard. **Pets** Dogs allowed. **Facilities** Heated swimming pool, covered swimming pool, sauna, hamman, health center, garage (+40F). **Nearby** Ski lifts (100m), village of Venosc, Bézardé valley, Ecrins park, massif of La Meije. **Open** Dec 15 – May 1, June 29 – Sep 1.

This chalet was originally a mountain refuge and farm but since 1933 has grown into a large and modern hotel while retaining its charm. The welcoming entrance hall immediately establishes the atmosphere of the hotel. You will be charmed by the decor of the lounge and the restaurant, whose large windows open onto the garden and the swimming pool and onto the snow-clad slopes in winter. The bedrooms are all comfortable and have balconies with unrestricted views of the mountains. Chef Robert Mounier prides himself on his hearty, succulent cuisine, which is very professionally served. There is also a newly opened small restaurant for gourmet fare. The hotel is very quiet and the people are very friendly.

How to get there *(Map 27): 74km southeast of Grenoble (detour from Grenoble via Pont-de-Claix) via N85 to Vizille; then N91 to the barrage (dam) on the Chambon via Bourg-d'Oisans, then D213 to Les Deux-Alpes.*

Château de la Commanderie ★★★

17, avenue d'Echirolles
Eybens- 38320 Grenoble (Isère)
Tel. (0)4★ 76.25.34.58 – Fax (0)4★ 76.24.07.31 – M. de Beaumont

Rooms 25 with telephone, bath or shower, WC, TV and minibar. **Price** Single 375-590F, double 415-630F. **Meals** Breakfast 55F, served 7:00-10:00. **Restaurant** Closed Saturday and Sunday lunchtime. Service 12:00-14:00, 19:30-21:45; menu 142-225F, also à la carte. **Credit cards** All major. **Pets** Dogs allowed (+50F). **Facilities** Swimming pool, parking. **Nearby** Grenoble museum, massifs of Vercors, Chartreuse and Oisans – 18-hole Bresson-Eybens golf course. **Open** All year.

Formerly a hospice of the Knights of Malta, the Château de la Commanderie is ideally located just 5km from the center of Grenoble and half an hour from the Olympic ski slopes. A large, lovely walled garden planted with centuries-old trees gives it an air of space and tranquillity rare in a town hotel. The bedrooms combine modern comforts and facilities with period furniture, old engravings and carefully chosen fabrics. Breakfast is a substantial affair served on the terrace in summer, or in vast 18th-century rooms decorated with family portraits. Next to it is a large dining room decorated with pastoral Aubusson tapestries. The superb cuisine is intelligently innovative and respectful of its ingredients. A friendly, family atmosphere prevails.

How to get there *(Map 26): 4km east of Grenoble via the bypass (south), exit Eybens (Route Napoléon); 500m from Eybens.*

Le Lièvre Amoureux ★★★

38840 Saint-Lattier (Isère)
Tel. (0)4★ 76.64.50.67 – Fax (0)4★ 76.64.31.21
M. Breda

Rooms 14 with telephone (12 with bath and 5 with TV). **Price** Double 320-460F, suite 380F. **Meals** Breakfast 60F, served 7:30-10:30. **Restaurant** Menus 179-199F, also à la carte. Specialties: Game, hare on the spit. **Credit cards** All major. **Pets** Dogs allowed (+40F). **Facilities** Swimming pool, parking. **Nearby** Saint-Bernard college in Romans, Facteur Cheval palace, Saint-Antoine abbey. **Open** Mar 1 – Oct 15 (closed Sunday evening and Monday in low season).

This comfortable and welcoming small hotel is nestled in the countryside facing the foothills of the Vercors, to the east of Valence. The bedrooms are in different buildings; those by the swimming pool are large and have a living area. Though modern, they are very charming; their large windows open onto a private terrace. (In the distance, a plantation of walnut trees reminds you of the local speciality). The other bedrooms, in a small turn-of-the-century house, are also faultless and have a lovely old-fashioned atmosphere. One slight drawback is that they are within earshot of the railway line, so visitors who like total silence should ask for the modern accommodations by the pool.

How to get there *(Map 26): 15km north of Romans via N92.*

Le Christiania ★

38250 Villars-de-Lans (Isère)
Tel. (0)4★ 76.95.12.51 – Fax (0)4★ 76.95.00.75
Mme Buisson

Rooms 24 with telephone, bath or shower, WC and TV. **Price** Single 280-400F, double 395-580F. **Meals** Breakfast 52F, served 7:30-10:00; half board 395-498F, full board 475-578F (per pers., 7 days min.). **Restaurant** Service 12:30, 19:30-21:00, menus 130-289F, also à la carte. Specialties: Ravioles de Romans, poulet fermier cuit à blanc et crème, filet de bœuf aux morilles, truite d'eau vive aux champignons des bois, croustillant aux poires, tarte au chocolat. **Credit cards** All major. **Pets** Dogs allowed (+40F). **Nearby** Massif du Vercors; skiing. **Open** Dec 15 –Apr 20, May 15 – Sept 20.

From the outside, the Christiania is architecturally classic, as are many mountain hotels, and its location on the edge of the road is not a plus. But you will be pleasantly surprised once you have gone inside and seen how charming it is. The very friendly owners have in fact decorated the hotel like their own home. Paintings, family furniture and objects lend special touches to the small lounge on the left. And a corner of the elegant dining room is bright with a collection of shining antique carafes. Mme Buisson herself is the artist behind the small floral motifs on each door. In the same spirit, the green and red tartan fabrics, the drapes and the checked eiderdowns have been tastefully selected, all creating a lovely effect (although the bedrooms are somewhat small). The owner's son is the chef, while his wife presides over the dining room. They maintain a reputation for excellent meals, which are served outdoors with the first good weather.

How to get there *(Map 26): 35km southwest of Grenoble.*

Hôtel des Artistes ★★★

8, rue Gaspard-André / Place des Célestins
69002 Lyon (Rhône)
Tel. (0)4★ 78.42.04.88 – Fax (0)4★ 78.42.93.76 – Mme Durand

Rooms 45 with telephone, bath or shower, WC, TV and 36 with minibar. **Price** Single
330-410F, double 370-450F. **Meals** Breakfast 48F, served 7:00-11:30. No restaurant.
Credit cards All major. **Pets** Dogs not allowed. **Nearby** Hôtel de Ville, art museum
in Lyon, Yzeron, Mont d'Or Lyonnais, Trévoux, Pérouges – 18-hole Lyon Verger golf
course, 9-hole Lyon Chassieux golf course. **Open** All year.

The Hôtel des Artistes (a favorite haunt of artists, as its name
and many autographs indicate) is in that old quarter of Lyon,
which lies between the embankments of the Rhône and Saône,
close to the Place Bellecour and the Célestins Theatre. The
bedrooms are decorated with very simple, modern furniture, and
differ only in their soft colors. They are all comfortably equipped,
with television and good soundproofing, and some have air
conditioning. Breakfast is very good, and there is a friendly
atmosphere. Special weekend rates are sometimes available. As
Lyons has a number of world-famous restaurants, here are several
simpler traditional bistros, which also are famous in Lyon: *Le Bistrot
de Lyon, Le Bouchon aux Vins, Le Garet,* the *Brasserie Brotteaux,* the
Café Comptoir Abel, the *Café des Fédérations,* and the *Café des
Négociants, Assiette et Marée.*

How to get there *(Map 26): In the town center near Place des Célestins.*

La Sivolière ★★★

Quartier des Chenus
73120 Courchevel (Savoie)
Tel. (0)4★ 79.08.08.33 – Fax (0)4★ 79.08.15.73 – Mme Cattelin

Rooms 30 with telephone, bath, WC and TV. **Price** Double 850-1950F. **Meals** Breakfast 75F, served at any time; half board 1010-1310F. **Restaurant** Service 12:00-14:30, 19:00-23:00; menus 180-280F. Specialties: Savoyard dishes, côte de bœuf à la cheminée, tartiflette, raclettes, gratin de potiron. **Credit cards** Amex, Visa, Eurocard and MasterCard. **Pets** Dogs not allowed. **Facilities** Sauna, jacuzzi, hamman. **Nearby** Skiing, cable car to La Saulire – 9-hole Courchevel golf course, 18-hole Méribel golf course. **Open** Dec 1 – May 1.

L ying sheltered by trees at the foot of the ski runs is Courchevel's *hôtel de charme*. Although quiet and tranquil, it is within walking distance of the village center. The hotel's friendly atmosphere reflects the personality of Mme Cattelin, who looks after her guests personally and has spent twenty years creating what some would call a little paradise. Everything in the chalet is in good taste: the decor, the food, the hospitality. Its success is due to a thousand small touches such as potpourris, fresh flowers and pretty tablecloths, the delicious *plats du jour* and homemade tarts. The same care and attention to detail is found in the ski room and living rooms. This is the kind of place that visitors tend to keep secret.

How to get there *(Map 27): 50km southeast of Albertville via N90 to Moûtiers, then D915 and D91.*

Lodge Nogentil Hôtel ★★★

73123 Courchevel 1850 (Savoie)
Tel. (0)4★ 79 08 32 32 – Fax (0)4★ 79 08 03 15
M. Manuel

Rooms 10 with telephone, bath, WC, TV and minibar. **Price** Double in half board 850-950F (per pers.); duplex (4 pers) 1050F (per pers.). **Meals** Breakfast incl., served 8:00-14:00. **Restaurant** Residents only. Service 19:30-21:30, menu. **Credit cards** Amex, Visa, Eurocard and MasterCard. **Pets** Dogs not allowed. **Facilities** Sauna, fitness center, parking. **Nearby** Skiing from hotel – 9-hole Courchevel golf course, 18-hole Méribel golf course. **Open** Nov 27 – May 1.

The new architectural policy of Courchevel is designed to encourage the construction of hotels in the traditional Savoyard style, and the Lodge Nogentil is one of the latest of its new charming chalet-hôtels. Well located at the edge of the Bellecôte ski run, the Nogentil offers only a few rooms, all very pretty indeed. They are bright with luminous wood paneling. The pleasant decor includes rustic furniture, which complements the handsome armoires from Afghanistan. There is the same exotic touch in the lounge. And you're sure of after-ski relaxation, what with the sauna and gym at your disposal.

How to get there *(Map 27): 50km southeast of Albertville via N90 to Moûtiers, then D915 and D91 to Courchevel 1850.*

La Tour de Pacoret ★★

Montailleur
73460 Grésy-sur-Isère (Savoie)
Tel. (0)4★ 79.37.91.59 – Fax (0)4★ 79.37.93.84 – M. Chardonnet

Rooms 10 with telephone, bath or shower, WC and TV. **Price** Single and double 280-450F. **Meals** Breakfast 45F, served 8:00-10:00; half board 300-400F, full board 390-490F (per pers., 3 days min.). **Restaurant** Service 12:00-13:30, 19:30-21:00; menus 90-120F, also à la carte. Specialties: Délice de Savoie, home-smoked salmon. **Credit cards** Visa, Eurocard and MasterCard. **Pets** Small dogs allowed (+30F). **Facilities** parking. **Nearby** Conflans, fort du Mont, château of Miolans – 27-hole Giez-Faverges golf course. **Open** Mid-Apr – Nov 1.

This beautiful 14th-century watchtower, standing in the middle of the countryside on a hilltop at the foot of the Alps, has been transformed into an intimate and elegant hotel. A cheerful lounge devoted to reading and music, a dining-room with chalet-style panelling, and carefully chosen watercolors and drawings make a harmonious ensemble. The bedrooms are individually decorated, with well-chosen furnishings and fully-equipped bathrooms. The terrace gardens command splendid views of the snow-capped Alps and of the Isère Valley below, and meals and drinks can be served there in the shade of the wisteria and garden umbrellas. The kitchen garden supplies fresh produce for the table. You will be warmly welcomed by the extremely friendly hosts.

How to get there (Map 27): 19km southwest of Albertville via N90 towards Montmélian until Pont-de-Grésy, then D222 and D201 towards Montailleur.

Hôtel Adray-Télébar ★★

73550 Méribel-les-Allues (Savoie)
Tel. (0)4★ 79.08.60.26 – Fax (0)4★ 79.08.53.85
M. Bonnet

Rooms 24 with telephone, bath or shower (24 with WC). **Price** Single and double 550-750F. **Meals** Breakfast 60F, served 8:00-11:00; half board 560-680F, full board 620-730F (per pers., 3 days min.). **Restaurant** Service 12:00-16:00, 20:00-22:00; menu 190F, also à la carte. Specialties: Escalope à la crème, steak au poivre, tarte aux myrtilles, fondue savoyarde, raclette. **Credit cards** Visa, Eurocard and MasterCard. **Pets** Dogs allowed. **Nearby** Skiing from hotel, Les Trois Vallées, mountain excursions – 9-hole Courchevel golf course, 18-hole Méribel golf course. **Open** Dec 20 – Apr 24.

This pretty chalet is only a few steps from the chairlift and the ski runs but it is well located above the valley, with spectacular views of pinewoods and mountains. You reach it via Méribel 1600, where you must leave your car; the hotel staff meets you and to take you to the chalet. The Adray is unrivalled at Méribel, and at lunchtime the large sunny terrace is invaded by skiers. The atmosphere is cheerful and the home cooking excellent. The bedrooms are simple but welcoming, with comfortable rustic furniture. The service is friendly and attentive. This is the place for making the most of the mountains without paying the higher prices of hotels in the village center.

How to get there (Map 27): 39km south of Albertville via N90 and D95, then D90.

Le Yéti ★★★
73553 Méribel-les-Allues (Savoie)
Tel. (0)4★ 79.00.51.15 – Fax (0)4★ 79.00.51.73
M. and Mme Saint Ghilhem

Rooms 37 with telephone, bath, WC and cable TV. **Price** Room with half board in winter 810-970F, in summer 590-750F (per pers.). **Restaurant** Service 12:00-15:00, 19:30-22:00; menus 98-210F, also à la carte. **Credit cards** All major. **Pets** Dogs not allowed. **Facilities** Swimming pool, sauna, hammam. **Nearby** Skiing from hotel, Les Trois Vallées, mountain excursions – 9-hole Courchevelle Golf Course, 18-hole Méribel Golf Course. **Open** All year except Apr 21 – June 30 and Oct 1 – Dec 16.

This chalet-hotel is located on the western slopes of Méribel, just next to the ski runs. Sophie and Frédéric Saint Ghilhem, who are both mountain guides, have decorated the hotel lovingly, and it shows. The walls are panelled in rough, hand-polished wood; the handsome furnishings include pretty objects, kilims, and comfortable armchairs in the bar and in front of the fireplace. The view is magnificent from all vantage points. The bedrooms are extremely comfortable and furnished in the loveliest mountain-chalet style. The panoramic restaurant has a terrace facing due south over a small swimming pool. Finally, when you set out for the lofty summits, Frédéric is there to advise you and to share the adventure.

How to get there *(Map 27): 39m south of Albertville via N90 and D95, then D90.*

Relais du Lac Noir *

Tioulévé 73220 Montsapey (Savoie)
Tel. (0)4★ 79.36.30.52 – Fax (0)4★ 79.36.37.80
M. Caulliez

Rooms 8 (5 with bath, WC). **Price** Single 125F, double 195F. **Meals** Breakfast 30F; half board 230F, full board 290F (per pers.). **Restaurant** Service 12:30-15:00, from 20:00; menus 90-120F. Specialties: gibier, diots (saucisses savoyardes), tartiflette, fondues, raclettes, magret, truite. **Credit cards** Visa, Eurocard and MasterCard. **Pets** Dogs not allowed. **Nearby** massif of Chartreuse, massif of the Lauzière, mountain excursions at Lac Noir (2000m) and at Grand Arc (2500m). **Open** 16 Dec – Nov 14.

The Relais du Lac Noir is located at the very end of a small, winding road which climbs up the mountainside to an altitude of 1030 meters in the heart of a natural cirque. It is surrounded by others chalets, some of which are very old. After having admired the splendid view, guests enter a large room with light-wood paneling. A corner bar, tables on a dais and a piano occupy a central foyer in front of which several comfortable chairs are arranged. M. and Mme Caulliez oversee everything, including mouthwatering mountain cuisine, and the friendly atmosphere which prevails here is due largely to them. The bedrooms, located on two floors, are small and well kept. Children will love the painted-wood closed beds upstairs, while their parents will prefer the rooms with a double bed (near the floor in some rooms); from all the rooms, you will enjoy silence, fresh mountain air and a beautiful view. The decoration is charming throughout, with old pine furniture and traditional objects contributing to an authentic and warm atmosphere. This is a special place, ideal for marvelous long walks (including, of course, a hike to Lac Noir), and there is excellent value for the money.

How to get there *(Map 27): 75km north of Grenoble, toward Aiguebelle; via A43, Aiton exit.*

Les Châtaigniers

Rue Maurice-Franck
73110 La Rochette (Savoie)
Tel. (0)4★ 79.25.50.21 - Fax (0)4★ 79.25.79.97 - Mme Rey

Rooms 3; 1 suite and 1 apartment with telephone, bath, WC (2 with TV). **Price** Single and double 350-490F, suite 600-950F. **Meals** Breakfast 65F, served 7:45-10:00; half board from 3 night min. **Restaurant** Service 12:00-13:30, 19:45-21:30; menus 125-275F, also à la carte. Specialties: Foie gras mi-cuit au torchon maison, fish, tempura de homard, andouillette de saucisson chaud maison. **Credit cards** All major. **Pets** Dogs not allowed. **Facilities** Swimming pool, parking. **Nearby** Saint-Pierre-de-Chartreuse, château of Miolans, Charmant Som, belvédère des Sangles, la Grande Chartreuse convent, Wine Route of Savoie – 18-hole Aix-les Bains golf course. **Open** Jan 21 – 2 Jan closed 8 days in Sept and Nov (closed Saturday noon, Sunday evening and Wednesday in low season).

This family home, which is now a guest house, is as charming as the surrounding valleys and mountains. From the elegant lounge with its grand piano to the beautiful dining-room and the spacious, comfortably furnished bedrooms, throughout the house, you will feel relaxed and at home. The lovely decor and ambience have been created by your two remarkable hosts, Philippe Roman and Mme Rey. Philippe, a chef and poet, has trained with several renowned chefs. Ask about his "poetic dinner." Mme Rey is a charming hostess with impeccable taste, and speaks several languages. The atmosphere is lively and light-hearted, and you will certainly want to stay for a while.

How to get there *(Map 27): 30km north of Grenoble via A41, Pontcharra exit, then D925; at La Rochette (opposite Hôtel de Ville) towards Arvillard.*

Hôtel Le Calgary ★★★

73620 Les Saisies (Savoie)
Tel. (0)4 79 38 98 38 – Fax (0)4 79 38 98 00
M. Berthod

Rooms 38 with telephone, bath, TV and minibar - 2 for disabled persons. **Price** Double and triple in half board 275-560F, full board 345-630F (per pers.). **Restaurant** Service 12:15-13:30, 19:15-21:00; menu 115-200F, also à la carte. Specialties: Saucisson de canard au foie gras, assiette "Belle de mer au homard", ragout de chevreuil luté aux essences de truffes noires, aumônière de pommes reinettes jus au calvados. **Credit cards** All major. **Pets** Dogs allowed (+40F). **Facilities** Swimming pool, hammam, sauna, garage (40F per day). **Nearby** Skiing from hotel, Olympic cross-country stadium at 200m – 18-hole Mont d'Arbois golf course in Megève (15 km). **Open** All year except May, Oct and Nov.

Le Calgary was built in Tyrolean style by the French ski champion Frank Piccard, who returned from Austria in love with the hotels there. Thus the reason for the flower-covered balconies which run along the façades and the two traditional oriel windows. Inside, the lounge recalls an Austrian pub and the dining room, with its colorful tablecloths, is very cheerful. Although the bedroom decor is somewhat standard, the rooms are spacious, and some can accommodate three people. All have a balcony with a lovely view over Beaufort and the ski trails of Les Saisies. In summer, the hotel offers a large choice of study sessions, including some for children. Le Calgary, by the way, is named after the town where Frank Piccard won an Olympic medal.

How to get there *(Map 27): 31km northeast of Albertville via D925, toward Beaufort, and D218, toward Col des Saisies.*

Le Blizzard ★★★★

73150 Val-d'Isère (Savoie)
Tel. (0)4★ 79 06 02 07 - Fax (0)4★ 79 06 04 94
M. Cerboneschi

Rooms 74 including 14 suites with telephone, bath or shower, WC and TV, minibar in suite; elevator. **Price** Single and double 515-1260F (530-660F in summer). **Meals** Breakfast incl.; half board 395-770F per pers. (400-470F in summer). **Restaurant** Service 12:30-15:00, 19:30-22:00; menu from 150F, also à la carte. Specialties: Regional cooking. **Credit cards** All major. **Pets** Dogs allowed (+50F). **Facilities** Swimming pool, sauna, hammam, jacuzzi, parking. **Nearby** Ski lift (100m), Parc de la Vanoise. **Open** All year except May – June and Sept – Nov.

This has long been "the" hotel of Val d'Isère. Frequented by a chic clientele of habitués and famous people, there is nevertheless a sporty atmosphere marked by everyone's passion for skiing; if guests stay late at the bar, they are ready to go the next morning when the cable cars start up. Le Blizzard has just had a face lift. All the bedrooms have been redone in a style which is both modern and warm. Those on the south side are quieter and have a large balcony with a beautiful view. A large swimming pool has been built and is be open in both winter and summer. The restaurant serves excellent cuisine – on the terrace in summer and winter. Note also *Le Knack*, the hotel's nightclub; and *La Luge*, the restaurant which is open until 2 AM.

How to get there *(Map 27): 85km southeast of Albertville, voie express toward Moûtiers, then N90 to Bourg-Saint-Maurice, then D902 to Val-d'Isère. Airport: Genève, Lyon Satolas, Chambéry. SNCF: TGV every Fridays Paris-Bourg-Saint-Maurice.*

La Savoyarde ★★★

73150 Val-d'Isère (Savoie)
Tel. (0)4★ 79.06.01.55 – Fax (0)4★ 79.41.11.29
Mme Carrier

Rooms 44 and 2 suites with telephone, bath, WC, cable TV and 3 with minibar.
Price Double 400-580F (per pers.). **Meals** Breakfast 46F, served from 7:00.
Restaurant Service 12:00-14:00, 19:30-21:30; menu 195F (lunchtime 100F), also
à la carte. Specialties: Raclette, tartiflette, fondue. **Credit cards** Visa, Eurocard and
Master. **Pets** Dogs allowed. **Facilities** Sauna, jacuzzi, solarium, fitness center,
massage, parking. **Nearby** Skiing from hotel, Col de l'Iseran. **Open** All year except
May 9 – 23 and Dec 2 – 19.

The Savoyarde is in the heart of the Espace Killy in the old
village: it is the "classic" hotel of Val d'Isère and has been
owned by the same family for four generations. Each has added its
personal touch, but with the constant aim of putting comfortable
furnishings first. The bedrooms have been recently refurbished, in
simple good taste. Some have exposed beams, which fit in well
with the pine furniture and patchwork bedcovers; others have
pleasant balconies with unrestricted views of the ski runs and the
Manchet Valley. All have pleasant bathrooms. The dining room is
also very pleasant and lively at dinner, and the cooking is refined.
This hotel is a favorite with the loyal clientele of Val-d'Isère.

*How to get there (Map 27): 85km southeast of Albertville via N90 to Bourg-
Saint-Maurice, then D902 to Val-d'Isère.*

Hôtel Fitz Roy ★★★★

73440 Val Thorens (Savoie)
Tel. (0)4★ 79 00 04 78 – Fax (0)4★ 79 00 06 11
Mme Loubet

Rooms 36 with telephone, bath, TV and minibar; elevator. **Price** Double in half board 800-1700F, full board 1000-1900F (per pers.). **Meals** Breakfast 90F, served 8:00-11:00. **Restaurant** Service 12:00-15:00, 19:00-22:00; menu 220-500F, also à la carte. Specialties: Regional cooking. **Credit cards** Amex, Visa, Eurocard and Mastercard. **Pets** Dogs allowed (+90F in rooms only). **Facilities** Covered swimming pool, sauna, health center, beauty salon, parking. **Nearby** Skiing from hotel. **Open** Dec 1 – May 6.

In the heart of Val Thorens, the Fitz Roy is a luxurious modern chalet. The interior is decorated very elegantly, with blond woodwork, predominantly white and pastel fabrics, and tasteful furniture. The large lounge, where vast sofas surround the fireplace, looks out due south over the ski runs. The bedrooms, which are all different, are spacious, with very refined decor and accommodations. Each has a balcony and a bathtub with whirlpool. In the evening, enjoy traditional Savoyard country cooking and professional service by candlelight. From the large terrace-solarium, you will also enjoy the superb sunsets over the resort. For *l'après-ski*, there is a swimming pool and excellent exercise equipment. In a resort which can be criticized for being artificial, the Fitz Roy has successfully combined luxury, modernity and the finest hotel tradition.

How to get there *(Map 27): 62km southeast of Albertville via N90 to Moûtiers, then D915 and D117.*

Chalet Rémy ★

74170 Saint-Gervais (Haute-Savoie)
Tel. (0)4★ 50.93.11.85
Mme Didier

Rooms 19 with basin. **Price** Double 220F. **Meals** Breakfast 30F, served 8:00-10:00; half board (obligatory in winter) and full board 280-350F (per pers., 3 days min.). **Restaurant** Service 12:00-14:00, 19:00-21:00; menu 90F, also à la carte. Specialties: Family cooking. **Credit cards** Visa, Eurocard and MasterCard. **Pets** Dogs allowed. **Nearby** Ski lift (300m), Chamonix, Megève – Mont-d'Arbois golf course in Megève (15km). **Open** All year.

This exceptional hotel is housed in an 18th-century farmhouse which through the centuries has preserved all its old woodwork. Panels, ceilings, moldings and the staircase leading to the superb gallery serving the bedrooms, all create a lovely harmony of dark red tones. The dining room is set with small tables lit by candles, and the family cuisine is excellent. Mme Didier loves classical music, which accompanies meals. It is the simplicity of the bedrooms that makes them charming; and though the bathroom facilities are merely basic, the bedrooms are absolute jewels with their lovely wood walls, floors and ceilings. The location of the Chalet Remy is another major asset. It is on the outskirts of Saint-Gervais and is reached by a winding road surrounded by pine woods and meadows facing the impressive snowy peaks of Mont Blanc.

How to get there *(Map 27): 50km northeast of Albertville via N212 and D909 to Robinson and Le Bettex. By A40, Le Fayet exit.*

Hôtel La Savoyarde ★★★

28, route des Moussoux
74400 Chamonix (Haute-Savoie)
Tel. (0)4★ 50.53.00.77 – Fax (0)4★ 50.55.86.82 – Mme Janin

Rooms 14 with telephone, bath, WC and TV. **Price** Double 400-580F. **Meals** Breakfast 46F, served from 7:00. **Restaurant** Service 12:00-14:00, 19:30-21:30, menu 88F (38F child), also à la carte. Specialties: Raclette, tartiflette, fondue. **Credit cards** Visa, Eurocard and MasterCard. **Pets** Dogs allowed. **Facilities** Garage (+48F), parking. **Nearby** Skiing, mountain excursions – 18-hole Praz golf course. **Open** All year except May 9 – 23 and Dec 2 – 19.

This hotel at the foot of Mount Brévent is surely one of the best located hotels in Chamonix. It overlooks the village and has a superb view of the Aiguille du Midi. Refurbished in the last two years, its style evokes both an English country cottage and an Alpine chalet. There are two adjoining buildings, both well cared for and, in summer, surrounded by flowers. The attractive entrance hall sets the tone of the house: painted ceilings, white walls and a cozy atmosphere. The owners have resisted the temptation to go in for a pseudo-rustic decor. The bedrooms are light and airy and have specially designed furniture. All have balconies or terraces and only two are at the back of the hotel. Among our favorites are Room 5, which has a large balcony, and Room 14, with its exposed beams. One drawback: in the bedrooms near the stairs, early-morning skiers can sometimes wake guests who are less enthusiastic early risers. This is a marvelous place to stay in Chamonix.

How to get there *(Map 27): 67km northeast of Albertville via N212 to Saint-Gervais, then N205. By A40, Le Fayet exit.*

Hôtel du Jeu de Paume ★★★★

705, route du Château – Le Lavancher
74400 Chamonix (Haute-Savoie)
Tel. (0)4★ 50.54.03.76 – Fax (0)4★ 50.54.10.75 – Mmes Prache and Blanc

Rooms 24 with telephone, bath, shower, WC, TV, hairdryer and minibar. **Price** Single and double 790-990F, suite 1290F. **Meals** Breakfast 65F, served 7:30-10:30; half board 625-875F (per pers.). **Restaurant** Service 12:00-14:30, 19:30-21:30; menu 170F, also à la carte. **Credit cards** All major. **Pets** Dogs allowed (+50F). **Facilities** Swimming pool, tennis, sauna, car rental, parking. **Nearby** Skiing in Argentières (Les Grands Montets, 3km), and in Chamonix – 18-hole Praz golf course. **Open** Dec 15 – Nov 10.

Elyane and Guy Prache, who own the elegant Hôtel du Jeu de Paume in the heart of the Ile Saint-Louis in Paris, have just opened this delightful chalet-hôtel at Lavancher, 7km from Chamonix, on the edge of a pine wood overlooking the Argentière Valley. The hotel is luxurious, refined and very comfortable; it is the chalet "re-invented", with wood playing a major role in the decor. The bedrooms are all very functional and furnished with warmth and good taste; nearly all have balconies. There is the same comfortable coziness in the bar and lounges. Throughout the hotel there are lovely pieces of antique furniture, mirrors and paintings. The traditional cooking is excellent and is served in a convivial atmosphere. The staff is very welcoming and in winter the hotel car will take you to the departure points for the ski runs.

How to get there (Map 27): 67km northeast of Albertville via N212. By A40, Le Fayet exit.

Chalet-Hôtel Beausoleil ★★

74400 Chamonix - Le Lavancher (Haute-Savoie)
Tel. (0)4★ 50.54.00.78 – Fax (0)4★ 50.54.17.34
M. Bossonney

Rooms 15 with telephone, bath or shower, WC and TV. **Price** Single 295F, double 350-565F. **Meals** Breakfast 42F, served 7:30-11:00; half board 290-400F, full board 350-460F (per pers., 3 days min.). **Restaurant** Service 12:30-13:30, 19:30-20:30; menu 90-150F, also à la carte. Specialties: Entrecôte sauce morilles, escalope de veau savoyarde, filet de truite au Crepy, fondue, raclette. **Credit cards** Visa, Eurocard and MasterCard. **Pets** Dogs allowed in rooms. **Facilities** Tennis. **Nearby** Ski lift (3 km), overland skiing from hotel – 18-hole Praz golf course. **Open** Dec 20 – Sept 20.

This peaceful hotel has been run by the Bossonney family for fifty years. Lying at the foot of the Aiguille du Midi and Mont Blanc, it is surrounded by gentle fields and peaceful tranquility. The recently renovated bedrooms are small but all offer modern accommodations and pleasant bathrooms; the rooms upstairs have balconies. The dining room opens onto a terrace which in turn gives onto a lovely flower garden bordered with evergreens. You will enjoy good family cooking at the Beausoleil, along with a friendly welcome.

How to get there *(Map 27): 67km northeast of Albertville via N212. Via A40, Le Fayet exit. (4km north of Chamonix via N506, toward Argentière).*

Hôtel Le Labrador ★★★

Route du Golf, 101
74400 Chamonix - Les Praz (Haute-Savoie)
Tel. (0)4★ 50.55.90.09 - Fax (0)4★ 50.53.15.85 - M. Bartoli

Rooms 32 with telephone, bath, WC, TV and minibar. **Price** Double 530-850F. **Meals** Breakfast incl., served until 10:30; half board 390-630F, full board 495-755F (per pers., 3 days min.). **Restaurant** Service 12:00-22:30; menu from 85F, also à la carte. Specialties: Saumon fumé maison, côte de bœuf gros sel. **Credit cards** All major. **Pets** Dogs allowed. **Facilities** Sauna, fitness center, whilpool, parking. **Nearby** Skiing from hotel, Alpine skiing: La Flégère (250 m), Chamonix (3 km) – 18-hole Praz golf course. **Open** Dec 15 – Oct 15.

Built on the Chamonix Golf Course facing Mont Blanc, the Labrador enjoys an outstanding location. A combination of Scandinavian and Savoyard architecture, the various buildings of the hotel fit harmoniously into the natural setting. The bedrooms are not very large but they are comfortable, and those on the front have balconies. The restaurant, *La Cabane*, is more typically Finnish, with a traditional *kelo* roof which is made of actual turf. (It is mowed every week!) The *Cabane* offers simple, hearty cuisine with specialties which vary with the seasons. (Try the roast beef ribs with coarse salt). The only drawback is its large size, which makes it somewhat lacking in intimacy. The service is attentive. And the hotel will also suggest ski, golf or mountain package trips if you wish.

How to get there *(Map 27): 67km northeast of Albertville, via N212. Via A40, exit Le Fayet. (3km north of Chamonix via N506, toward Argentière; on the golf course).*

Au Cœur des Prés ★★★

74920 Combloux (Haute-Savoie)
Tel. (0)4★ 50.93.36.55 – Fax (0)4★ 50.58.69.14
M. Paget

Rooms 34 with telephone, bath, WC and TV. **Price** Single and double 330-500F.
Meals Breakfast 44F, served from 7:30; half board and full board 390-430F (per
pers.). **Restaurant** Service 12:30-14:00, 19:30-20:30; menu 145-190F, also à la
carte. **Credit cards** Visa, Eurocard and MasterCard. **Pets** Dogs allowed.
Facilities Tennis, sauna, whirlpool, garage (30F), parking. **Nearby** Ski lifts (1km),
Megève, Chamonix – 18-hole Mont d'Arbois golf course in Megève. **Open** May 20 –
Sept 25 and Dec 19 – Apr 15.

This hotel has the advantage not only of a superb view of Mont
Blanc and the Aravis Mountains, but it is also surrounded by
a large, quiet meadow. Most of the bedrooms overlooking Mont
Blanc have a balcony; they are comfortable and all have now been
renovated. Those on the *troisième étage*, which have mansard
ceilings, are the most charming. The lounge has comfortable
armchairs and a big fireplace, and the dining room is charming
with its tiled floor, exposed beams, pink tablecloths and panoramic
view. Guests very much enjoy chef Nicolas' cuisine. The hotel has
been awarded prizes by the community for its summer flower
display and is ideal for those who like peace and tranquillity amid
impressive scenery. During the winter-sports season, the hotel has
a shuttle to take clients to the various ski areas.

How to get there *(Map 27): 36km northeast of Albertville via N212 to
Combloux through Megève. Via A40, Le Fayet exit.*

Les Roches Fleuries ★★★

74700 Cordon (Haute-Savoie)
Tel. (0)4★ 50.58.06.71 - Fax (0)4★ 50.47.82.30
J. and G. Picot

Rooms 28 with telephone, bath, WC and cable TV. **Price** Double 460-650F, suite 750-950F. **Meals** Breakfast 58F, served 7:30-10:00; half board 390-560F (per pers., 3 days min.). **Restaurant** Service 12:30-14:00, 19:30-21:30; menus 140-295F also à la carte. Specialties: Tartiffle de lapin au Beaufort, pigeon fermier mi-cuit aux pousses d'épinard, "la boite à fromages". Regional restaurant 155F. **Credit cards** All major. **Pets** Dogs allowed (+35F). **Facilities** Heated swimming pool, health center, ranning salon, whirlpool, hamman, Mountain bikes rental, mountain guides, parking, garage (30F). **Nearby** Ski lifts (700m), Megève, Chamonix – 18-hole Mont d'Arbois golf course in Megève. **Open** Mai 8 – Oct 1, Dec 17 – Apr 8.

Cordon lies between Combloux and Sallanches on the threshold of Mont Blanc and is a delightful village all year round. In summer the chalets nestle among cherry and walnut trees, and in winter there are sensational views of the Aiguilles de Chamonix and the Aravis Mountains. The bedrooms are prettily furnished and most have terraces on which you can enjoy the magnificent view, the peace and the sun. Like the bedrooms, the lounge and dining room are furnished in a comfortable rustic style. In winter the blaze in the fireplace creates a warm and cozy ambience. The cooking is good and the service attentive and friendly.

How to get there (Map 27): 43km northeast of Albertville via N212 to Sallanches, then D113. Via A40, Le Fayet exit.

Marceau Hôtel ★★★

115, chemin de la Chappelière
74210 Doussard (Haute-Savoie)
Tel. (0)4★ 50.44.30.11 – Fax (0)4★ 50.44.39.44 – M. and Mme Sallaz

Rooms 16 with telephone, bath or shower, WC (14 with TV). **Price** Double 470F, suite 680F. **Meals** Breakfast 50F, served 7:30-10:00; half board 470-750F, full board 490-820F (per pers., 3 days min.). **Restaurant** Service 12:30-14:00, 19:30-21:00; menus 130-330F, also à la carte. Specialties: Longe de veau Marceau, féra du lac au chignin, blanquette de homard. **Credit cards** All major. **Pets** Dogs allowed (+50F). **Facilities** Tennis, parking. **Nearby** Lake of Annecy, le Semnoz by the ridgeway, gorges of Le Fier – 18-hole Annecy golf course in Talloires. **Open** Feb 1 – Oct 10.

In one of the most touristic areas of France, how lovely it is to find a peaceful haven well off the beaten track! Set in the middle of the countryside with a beautiful view of the lake and valley, this elegantly comfortable hotel is precisely that and much more. In the dining-room, subtle shades of pink blend perfectly with the colors of the wood, and large windows open onto beautiful surroundings. There is an attractive lounge for watching television or reading by the fireside. In summer, both view and sunshine can be enjoyed on a delightful terrace next to the kitchen garden. The bedrooms are tastefully decorated, with carefully chosen furniture. There are fresh flowers everywhere and the welcome is warm.

How to get there (Map 27): 20km south of Annecy via N508 towards Albertville.

Chalet-Hôtel Crychar ★★★

74260 Les Gets (Haute-Savoie)
Tel. (0)4★ 50.75.80.50 – Fax (0)4★ 50.79.83.12
Mme Bouchet

Rooms 12 with telephone, bath, WC and TV. **Price** Double 350-595F, suite 630-820F. **Meals** Breakfast 47,50F. No restaurant. **Credit cards** All major. **Pets** Dogs not allowed. **Facilities** Sauna (60F), solarium, garage (+40F), parking. **Nearby** Skiing from hotel, Morzine, Avoriaz, Chamonix, Evian. **Open** Dec 15 – Apr 15, June 30 – Sept 15.

In the middle of the ski slopes in winter (yet only 100 metres from the center of the village) and surrounded by green Alpine meadows in summer, this modern hotel feels like a traditional mountain chalet because it has a limited number of rooms. The bedrooms are light, airy, well decorated and comfortable, with balconies and bathrooms. The hotel is well- equipped with leisure facilities including table tennis, a swimming pool, an authentic Finnish sauna and various kinds of exercise equipment. The lack of a restaurant makes for peace and quiet in the hotel but there are many restaurants close by.

How to get there *(Map 27): 86km northeast of Annecy via A41, then A40 Cluses exit, then D902 to Les Gets via Taninges.*

Chalet-Hôtel Peter Pan

74310 Les Houches (Haute-Savoie)
Tel. (0)4★ 50.54.40.63
M. and Mme Bochatay

Rooms 13 (2 with bath, 4 shower and 2 with WC). **Price** Double 195-270F.
Meals Breakfast 38F, served 8:00-10:00; half board 235-255F, full board 270-290F
(per pers., 3 days min.). **Restaurant** Service at 12:30 and 19:30; menus 95-145F,
also à la carte. Specialties: Saumon frais à l'oseille, braserades, tarte tatin, nougat
glacé, filet de ferra au genepy, curry de ris de veau, tournedos aux morilles. **Credit
cards** Not accepted. **Pets** Dogs allowed. **Facilities** Parking. **Nearby** Ski lifts (1km)
– 18-hole Praz golf course in Chamonix (7km). **Open** All year except in May and Nov
1 – Dec 14.

Michel Bochatay and his wife have been in this beautiful
converted 18th-century farm for seventeen years. It is on a
hilltop near Les Houches and has a superb view of the valley of
Chamonix. In this delightful place the owners have created an
original and welcoming ambience, with excellent food at
reasonable prices. The two chalets are constructed entirely of wood
and are veritable small museums. Meals are served by candlelight
on prettily set little wooden tables bright with bouquets of flowers.
The bedrooms vary in size and style. Rooms 1 and 2 are spacious
(2 has a bathroom) and Room 6 on the top floor is more intimate;
the three look out on the valley. The rooms in the annex are smaller
and four of them have only a washbasin. Nevertheless, thanks to
the tranquillity, the charming ambience and the warm welcome,
the Peter Pan is a great place to stay.

How to get there *(Map 27): 59km northeast of Albertville via N212, then*

537

Hôtel de La Croix Fry ★★★

Manigod – 74230 Thônes (Haute-Savoie)
Tel. (0)4★ 50.44.90.16 – Fax (0)4★ 50.44.94.87
Mme Guelpa-Veyrat

Rooms 12 with telephone, bath (3 with balneo), WC and cable TV. **Price** Double 500-1500F(suite). **Meals** Breakfast 80F, served 8:00-10:00; half board 550-850F (per pers., 3 days min.). **Restaurant** Service 12:30-13:30, 19:30-20:30; menus 140-360F, also à la carte. Specialties: Tartifflette maison, viande et omelette avec bolets et chanterelles, foie gras cuit maison, desserts aux fruits sauvages. **Credit cards** Amex, Visa, Eurocard and MasterCard. **Pets** Dogs allowed (+25F). **Facilities** Heated swimming pool, tennis, parking. **Nearby** Skiing in La Croix-Fly/l'Etoile (1km), La Clusaz, Manigod valley, village of Chinaillon, gorges of Le Fier, Annecy lake – 18-hole Annecy golf course in Talloires. **Open** June 15 – Sept 15, Dec 15 – Apr 15.

This is the kind of hotel we would like to find more often in the French Alps without having to go to the five-star establishments. It is comfortable and cozy and its bedrooms – all named after mountain flowers – have had great care lavished on them over the years: beamed ceilings and old furniture create a snug chalet atmosphere. The ones facing the valley have breathtaking views and are very sunny. All have either a balcony, a terrace or a mezzanine to make up for the tiny bathrooms. (Some have balneotherapy bathtubs.) The former stables, converted into a bar with seats covered in sheepskin, lead into the dining-room, which faces the Tournette Mountains. This is a great spot in summer or winter, and you are strongly advised to reserve well in advance, for the hotel has a large and faithful following.

How to get there (Map 27): 27km east of Annecy via D909 to Thônes, then D12 and D16 to Manigod, then La Croix Fry.

Le Mont Blanc

Place de l'église, rue Ambroise Martin
74120 Megève (Haute-Savoie)
Tel. (0)4★ 50.21.20.02 – Fax (0)4★ 50.21.45.28 – M. Sibuet

Rooms 39 with telephone, bath, WC, TV, minibar and safe. **Price** Single and double 600-1030F (per pers.). **Meals** Breakfast incl. **Restaurant** Service 12:00-14:00, 19:30-22:30; carte 250 F. Specialties: Regional cooking, fish. Cheeses restaurant: menu 220F. **Credit cards** All major. **Pets** dogs allowed (+suppl.). **Facilities** Steam bath, sauna, jacuzzi, health center - Piano-bar. **Nearby** ski lifts (50m), Chamonix valley – 18-hole Mont d'Arbois golf course. **Open** June 15 – May 1.

Successful, talented Jocelyne and Jean-Louis Sibuet are in charge of the Mont Blanc's «new life». The Mont Blanc! This was one of the symbolic places of the prosperity and carefree spirit of the 1960s when anybody who was a celebrity emigrated from Saint Tropez to Megève for the winter. Guests came down to enjoy the hotel's cozy comfort late in the day because most had spent the wee hours in Les Enfants Terribles, the hotel's famous, sophisticated bar which was decorated by Jean Cocteau. Reviving this spirit was a difficult challenge. Today, the Mont Blanc has a very beautiful decor, which nevertheless lacks a touch of fantasy. And yet everything is there: the woodwork, the polished furniture, the reds and greens of the new fashion in decoration, very modern amenities, excellent service... The only thing lacking is the «spirit» that will give Le Mont Blanc a new soul.

How to get there (Map 27): 34km northeast of Albertville via N212. Take A40, exit Sallanches. (Toward Rochebrune, on left at the corner of the Maison de la Montagne, in the pedestrian zone.)

Les Fermes Marie ★★★

Chemin de Riante Colline
74120 Megève (Haute-Savoie)
Tel. (0)4★ 50.93.03.10 – Fax (0)4★ 50.93.09.84 – M. Sibuet

Rooms 52 with telephone, bath, WC and TV. **Price** Single and double in half board 770-1030F (per pers.). **Restaurant** Service 12:00-14:00, 19:30-22:30; carte 250 F. Specialties: Regional cooking, fish. Cheeses restaurant: menu 220F. **Credit cards** Amex, Visa, Eurocard and MasterCard. **Pets** dogs allowed (+suppl.). **Facilities** Steam bath, fitness center, hammam, sauna, jacuzzi, health center, swimming pool. **Nearby** ski lifts (500m), Chamonix valley – 18-hole Mont d'Arbois golf course. **Open** Dec 17 – Apr 15 and June 23 – Sept 15.

After opening their delightful hotel in Rochebrune, Le Coin du Feu, and the chaming restaurant Le Saint-Nicolas, Jocelyne and Jean-Louis Sibuet recently opened Les Fermes de Marie, another charming hotel in Megève. This is in fact a small hamlet composed of several chalets which have been reconstructed from old mazots - tiny traditional Savoyard mountain chalets - and built entirely with old wood. The reception area, the two restaurants, the library, and the bar occupy the main building. All the bedrooms face due south and are delightfully decorated in the most attractive mountain style; they are very comfortable and have a balcony-terrace along with a corner lounge. Scouring the region for antiques, Jocelyne found more than 450 pieces of traditional furniture to decorate the hotel. Similar care has been paid even to the breakfasts, which include delicious homemade preserves, country bread and crusty baguettes. The evening meal is simple but nutritious and succulent.

How to get there *(Map 27): 34km northeast of Albertville via N212. Take A40, exit Le Fayet. (The hotel is on the road to Rochebrune).*

Le Coin du Feu ★★★

Route de Rochebrune
74120 Megève (Haute-Savoie)
Tel. (0)4★ 50.21.04.94 – Fax (0)4★ 50.21.20.15 – M. and Mme Sibuet

Rooms 23 with telephone, bath, WC and TV. **Price** Single and double 500-1000F.
Meals Breakfast 35F; half board 620-770F (per pers.). **Restaurant** Service 19:30-
22:30; menu 250F, also à la carte. Specialties: Regional cooking and fish from the
lake. **Credit cards** Amex, Visa, Eurocard and MasterCard. **Pets** Dogs allowed.
Nearby Ski lifts (200m), Chamonix valley – 18-hole Mont d'Arbois golf course.
Open Dec 20 – Apr 5 and July 20 – Aug 31.

This hotel has long been known to those who like tradition as
the most appealing place to stay in Megève. Its success lies in
its handsome pine furniture, oak panelling, the flowered fabrics
and above all its welcoming fireplace. The hotel's restaurant, the
Saint-Nicholas, attracts Megève regulars who come here for its
simple but delicious cuisine or the traditional *raclettes* and fondues.
The bedrooms are cheerful and pretty and you will receive a very
friendly welcome.

How to get there *(Map 27): 34km northeast of Albertville via N212. By
A40, Le Fayet exit. (The hotel is on the road to Rochebrune).*

Le Fer à Cheval ★★★

36, route du Crêt-d'Arbois
74120 Megève (Haute-Savoie)
Tel. (0)4★ 50.21.30.39 – Fax (0)4★ 50.93.07.60 – M. Sibuet

Rooms 41 with telephone, bath, WC, TV and 41 with minibar. **Price** Double with half board 565-860F (per pers.). **Meals** Breakfast 50F, served 7:45-11:30. **Restaurant** Service 19:30-21:30; menu savoyard, also à la carte. **Credit cards** Amex, Visa, Eurocar and MasterCard. **Pets** Dogs allowed (+45F). **Facilities** Swimming pool, sauna, whilpool, hammam, health center, parking, garage. **Nearby** Ski lifts (450m), Chamonix valley – 18-hole Mont d'Arbois golf course. **Open** Dec 14 – Easter and July 1 – Sept 11.

This is one of the most charming hotels in Megève, from every point of view. The chalet has been very well refurbished; exposed beams and lovely wood panelling create a warm and comfortable decor, as do the patinated and polished antique furniture and the variety of fabrics and *objets d'art*. We can't recommend any particular bedroom – they are all delightful and any variation in price is only due to size. In winter, meals are served by the fireplace in the dining room, and in summer by the swimming pool. If there isn't enough snow, a hotel shuttle will take you to the nearby resorts, Les Contamines or Chamonix. You can also make an excursion into the mountains (La Vallée Blanche, for example) with a guide. Guests receive a warm welcome.

How to get there *(Map 27): 34km northeast of Albertville via N212. By A40, Le Fayet exit.*

Ferme Hôtel Duvillard ★★★

Le Mont d'Arbois
74120 Megève (Haute-Savoie)
Tel. (0)4★ 50.21.14.62 – Fax (0)4★ 50.21.42.82 – Mme Mouroux

Rooms 19 with telephone, bath or shower, WC and cable TV. **Price** Single 677-804F, double 811-1054F, triple 895F, duplex (4 pers.) 991-1299F. **Meals** Breakfast 60F, served 7:30-9:30; half-board 588-724F (per pers. in double room). **Restaurant** Service 12:00-14:00, 19:30-21:00; menu 150F, also à la carte. Specialties: Pierrade, fondue, raclette, pela, farcement. **Credit cards** All major. **Pets** Dogs allowed (+60F). **Facilities** Heated swimming pool, sauna, parking. **Nearby** Skiing from hotel with Mont-D'Arbois chairlift – 18-hole Arbois golf course. **Open** Dec 20 – Apr 15 and July 1– Sept 15.

This is an old family farm which has been converted into a lovely mountain hotel. It is very conveniently located at the foot of the ski trails, the cable car, ski lift and the Mont d'Arbois Golf Course. The interior is warm and inviting. The bedrooms are not very large but they have full modern accommodations, which are welcome in the mountains: television, hair dryer, and there is a sauna upstairs. In the restaurant, the cuisine is simple, with the emphasis on hearty Savoyard specialties, which are served in a half-Savoyard, half-Tyrolean decor. And the owners know something about skiing and running a hotel: Adrien Duvillard is a native son of Megève and a member of the French Ski Team, and his wife, Eva, is a graduate of the Innsbrück Hotel School. The service is somewhat distant at first but quickly becomes friendly.

How to get there *(Map 27): 34km northeast of Albertville viaN212. Take A40, exit Le Fayet. (The hotel is at the foot of the Mont d'Arbois cable car).*

Hôtel Le Mégevan

Route de Rochebrune
74120 Megève (Haute-Savoie)
Tel. (0)4★ 50.21.08.98 – Fax (0)4★ 50.21.79.20 – M. Demarta

Rooms 11 with telephone, bath, WC, minibar and TV. **Price** Double. **Meals** Breakfast incl., served from 7:00; half-board 588-724F (per pers. in double room). No restaurant. **Credit cards** Amex, Visa, Eurocard and MasterCard. **Pets** Dogs allowed. **Facilities** Heated swimming pool, sauna, parking. **Nearby** Skiing from hotel with Rochebrune chairlift, valley of Chamonix – 18-hole.Arbois golf course. **Open** Dec 17 – Sept 16.

Frequented largely by faithful clients, the Mégevan is a small, unpretentious hotel, very refined, but a true hotel of character and charm. There are no rigid hotel rules here, refusing you breakfast service at 10:03: hours are flexible and the staff is pleasant. Down from the Rochebrune road, the Demartas' old family house has eleven very beautiful bedrooms. All have a small balcony in the larches; the bedrooms are spacious and discreetly decorated in a 1930s style with pretty engravings, wood, soft carpets and charming bathrooms. The salon-bar with its deep sofas is an invitation to after-ski relaxation around the fireplace. The Rochebrune chairlift is only 100 meters away. The hotel has no restaurant but the choice is vast in Megève. Nearby, try the fondue at *Le Chamois* in the village or *Le Saint-Nicolas*, which is more «in»; for lunch, there is the beautiful terrace of *L'Alpette* in Rochebrune.

How to get there *(Map 27): 34km northeast of Albertville via N212. Via A40, exit Le Fayet. The hotel is on the road to Rochebrune.*

La Bergerie ★★★
Rue de Téléphérique
74110 Morzine (Haute-Savoie)
Tel. (0)4★ 50.79.13.69 - Fax (0)4★ 50.75.95.71 - Mme Marullaz

Rooms 27 rooms, studios or apartments with telephone, bath, WC, TV (21 with minibar). **Price** Room 350-500F, studio 450-700F, apart. (2-4 pers.) 600-900F. **Meals** Breakfast 60F, served 7:00-11:00. **Restaurant** Table d'hôtes 1 day by week. **Credit cards** Visa, Eurocard and MasterCard. **Pets** Dogs allowed. **Facilities** Swimming pool, sauna, solarium, health center, games room, parking, garage. **Nearby** Ski lifts (50m), Avoriaz, Evian – 9-hole Morzine golf course, 18-hole Royal Hôtel golf course, Evian. **Open** Dec 19 – Apr 20 and July 1 – mid. Sept.

This is the favorite hotel of Morzine residents, although it has changed somewhat. There are now studios and apartments as well as individual bedrooms, all sharing the hotel's services. The Mourgues armchairs and the orange-and-yellow check fabrics on the Knoll-style chairs in the lounge make for a delightful 1970s style. The best bedrooms are those facing south which look out over the garden and swimming pool. There is no restaurant but light snacks are served. The most popular restaurants with the resort's regulars are *Le Cherche Midi* on the road to Les Gets, or *La Crémaillère* in Les Lindarets-Montrionds, which you can also get to in winter via the ski trails. *La Taverne des Dromonts* in Avoriaz is also very charming.

How to get there *(Map 27): 93km northeast of Annecy via A41 and A40, Cluses exit, then D902. The hotel is near the E.S.F (ski school).*

Hôtel Beau Site ★★★

74290 Talloires (Haute-Savoie)
Tel. (0)4★ 50.60.71.04 – Fax (0)4★ 50.60.79.22
M. Conan

Rooms 29 with telephone, bath or shower, WC and TV (10 with minibar). **Price** Single and double 410-795F, suite 900-950F. **Meals** Breakfast 52F, served 7:30-10:30; half board 430-630F, full board 450-670F (per pers., 2 days min.). **Restaurant** Service 12:30-14:00, 19:30-21:15; menus 170-280F, also à la carte. Specialties: Fish from the lake. **Credit cards** All major. **Pets** Dogs allowed. **Facilities** Tennis (+60F), private beach, parking. **Nearby** Ermitage Saint-Germain, château de Menthon-Saint-Bernard, Thorens and Montrottier, château, lake, museum and olg city in Annecy – 18-hole Annecy golf course in Talloires. **Open** May 10 – Oct 10.

With grounds reaching right down to the banks of Lake Annecy, the Hôtel Beau Site is reminiscent of a hotel on the Italian lakes. A family estate converted into a hotel at the end of the 19th century, it has retained many gracious features: a vast, sunny dining-room-cum-verandah decorated with old plates; a delightful lounge with period furniture; and lawns well provided with deck chairs. The charming bedrooms have been completely refurbished; they have a terrace and many look out on the lake. Some are decorated with antiques, others are more modern, and some have a mezzanine. The food is excellent. The hotel is specially noted for its warm and friendly welcome.

How to get there *(Map 27): 13km from Annecy via A41, Annecy exit. At Annecy, take east bank of lake towards Thônes until Veyrier, then Talloires.*

INDEX

INDEX

A

Abbaye (Auberge de l') *Le Bec-Hellouin* 348
Abbaye (Hôtel de l') *Beaugency* 215
Abbaye (Hôtel de l') *Longpont* 219
Abbaye (Hôtel L') *Saint-Cyprien-en-Périgord* 76
Abbaye de Villeneuve *Les Sorinières* 373
Adray Télébar (Hôtel) *Méribel* 520
Aiglon (Hôtel L') *Serriera* 235
Aïtone (L') *Evisa* 232
A l'Orée du Bois *Futeau* 226
Ajoncs d'Or (Hostellerie Les) *Plouharnel* 189
Alisiers (Auberge Les) *Lapoutroie* 46
Anastasy (L') *Avignon* 475
Anne d'Anjou (Hôtel) *Saumur* 375
Anthon (Hôtel) *Obersteinbach* 36
Antiquité (Hôtel de l') *Challans* 383
Arcades (Hôtel Les) *Aigues-Mortes* 264
Arcé (Hôtel) *Saint-Etienne-de-Baïgorry* 103
Arène (Hôtel) *Orange* 487
Argouges (Hôtel d') *Bayeux* 338
Arlatan (Hôtel d') *Arles* 427
Arnold (Hôtel) *Itterswiller* 32
Arraya (Hôtel) *Sare* 105
Artistes (Hôtel des) *Lyon* 516
Artzaïn Etchea *Esterençuby* 102
Atalaya (Auberge L') *Llo* 288
Ascott (Hôtel L') *Saint-Malo* 177
Atelier (Hôtel de l') *Villeneuve-lès-Avignon* 279
Avaugour (Hôtel d') *Dinan* 148

B

Bains (Hôtel des) *Granville* 360
Balanea (Hôtel) *Calvi* 236
Barbacane (Hôtel La) *Tiffauges* 389
Bas-Rupts (Hostellerie des) *Gérardmer* 57
Bastard (Hôtel de) *Lectoure* 303
Bastide de Moustiers *Moustiers-Sainte-Marie* 403
Bastidières (Les) *Toulon* 470
Beau Site (Hôtel) *Talloires* 546
Beffroi (Hostellerie Le) *Vaison-la-Romaine* 493

Belle Gasconne (A la) *Poudenas* 94
Bellier (Hôtel) *La Chapelle-en-Vercors*.................................503
Bégude Saint Pierre (La) *Les Coudoulières*.......................267
Benvengudo (Hôtel La) *Les Baux-de-Provence* 430
Bérard (Hostellerie) *La Cadière d'Azur*..............................449
Berger des Abeilles (Le) *Saint-Andiol*................................439
Bergerayre (Auberge du) *Saint-Martin-d'Armagnac* 306
Bergerie (La) *Ile-Rousse*...240
Bergerie (La) *Rugy*...54
Bergerie (La) *Morzine* 545
Bichonnières (Auberge Les) *Ambérieux-en-Dombes*......496
Blizzard (Le) *Val d'Isère* 525
Bon Accueil (Au) *Limeuil*...70
Bon Fermier (Auberge du) *Valenciennes*.............................333
Bon Laboureur et du Château (Hôtel du) *Chenonceaux* 201
Bonne Idée (A la) *Saint-Jean-aux-Bois* 225
Bordeaux (Hôtel de) *Pons*...395
Bouis (Hôtel Les) *Saint-Tropez* 466
Boulangerie (La) *Grimaud*..457
Boule de Neige (La) *Serre-Chevalier*....................................409
Boule d'Or (Auberge de la) *Beuvron-en-Auge*..................339
Bourgogne (Hôtel de) *Cluny* 138
Brise Marine (Hôtel) *Saint-Jean-Cap-Ferrat*......................420
Brittany (Le) *Roscoff*..168
Buisonnière (La) *Aigaliers*...263

C

Cacharel (Hostellerie de) *Saintes-Maries-de-la-Mer* 440
Cala Rossa (Grand Hôtel) *Cala Rossa - Porto-Vecchio* 231
Calalou (Hôtel Le) *Moissac-Bellevue*...................................461
Calgary (Hôtel Le) *Les Saisies* 524
Capitelle (La) *Mirmande* 507
Casa Païral (Hôtel) *Collioure*...287
Castel Brando (Hôtel) *Erbalunga*...242
Cassagne (Auberge de) *Le Pontet*...489
Castel (Le) *Mailly-le-Château*..144
Castel Mouisson (Hôtel) *Barbentane* 429
Castel-Hôtel 1904 *Saint-Gervais-d'Auvergne*....................128
Castellas (Hostellerie le) *Colias* 266
Chaîne d'Or (La) *Les Andelys*...345
Chalet (Le) *Coulandon* 108
Chalet Mounier *Les Deux-Alpes*...512
Chalet Rémy *Le Bettex - Saint-Gervais* 528
Chalet Hôtel Beausoleil *Chamonix-Le Lavancher*............531
Chalet Hôtel Crychar *Les Gets* 536
Chalet Hôtel Peter Pan *Les Houches* 537
Chalets des Ayes *Le Thillot* 60
Chantoiseau (Hôtel) *Le Pont-de-Montvert*..........................284
Charembeau (Auberge) *Forcalquier*.....................................401
Charmilles (Hôtel Les) *Nouan-le-Fuzelier* 210
Chartreuse du Val Saint-Esprit *Gosnay* 334
Chasseurs (Auberge des) *Echenevex* 497
Chat Botté (Hôtel Le) *Ile-de-Ré*..394
Châtaigniers (Les) *La Rochette*...523

Château (Auberge du) *Val de Mercy*..................................145
Château (Hostellerie Le) *Neuville-Saint-Amand* 220
Château Haut-Gléon *Durban*..................................260
Château Lardier *Ruch* 85
Château Saint Saturnin *Saint-Saturnin-de-Lenne* 300
Château d'Adoménil *Rehainviller*..................................53
Château d'Agneaux (Hôtel du) *Agneaux - Saint-Lô* 356
Château d'Ayres *Meyrueis*..................................283
Château d'Etoges *Etoges*..................................223
Château d'Urbilhac *Lamastre* 500
Château de Barive *Sainte-Preuve*..................................221
Château de Bellecroix (Hostellerie du) *Chagny* 137
Château de Bouesse *Bouesse* 199
Château de Boussac *Target*..................................109
Château de Brécourt *Douains* 351
Château de Brélidy *Brélidy*..................................147
Château de Camon *Camon*..................................290
Château de Castelpers *Castelpers* 294
Château de Challanges *Challanges* 133
Château de Chissay *Chissay-en-Touraine*..................................209
Château de Cocove *Recques-sur-Hem*..................................335
Château de Goville (Hostellerie du) *Le Breuil-en-Bessin* 340
Château de Kernuz *Pont-L'Abbé* 166
Château de Landel *Bézancourt*..................................366
Château de Lavendès *Champagnac*..................................112
Château de L'Hoste *Saint-Beauzeuil* 331
Château de L'Isle (Hostellerie du) *Civray-en-Touraine*..................202
Château de Madières *Madières*..................................280
Château de Mavaleix *Mavaleix*..................................72
Château de Montlédier *Pont-de-L'Arn*..................................329
Château de Nieuil *Nieuil*..................................392
Château de Passières *Chichilianne* 510
Château de Projan *Projan* 305
Château de Prunoy *Charny-Prunoy* 143
Château de Rocher-La Belle Ecluse *Bollène* 477
Château de Roussan *Saint-Rémy-de-Provence* 444
Château de Saint-Paterne *Saint-Paterne* 380
Château de Sassetot-le-Mauconduit *Sassetot-le-Mauconduit* 369
Château de Seignan *Saint-Girons*..................................293
Château de Trigance *Trigance*..................................472
Château de Valmer *La-Croix-Valmer*..................................453
Château de Vieux-Mareuil *Vieux-Mareuil*..................................80
Château de la Beuvrière *Saint-Hilaire-de-Court*..................................194
Château de la Bourdaisière *Montlouis-sur-Loire* 206
Château de la Commanderie *Grenoble-Eybens*..................................513
Château de la Motte Beaumanoir *Pleugueneuc*..................................174
Château de la Rapée *Bazincourt-sur-Epte* 347
Château de la Treyne *Lacave* 314
Château de la Roque *Hébécrevonne*..................................361
Château de la Vallée Bleue *Saint-Chartier* 200
Château de la Vérie *Challans* 382
Château de la Voûte *Troo*..................................213
Château des Alpilles *Saint-Rémy-de-Provence* 443
Château des Bondons *La Ferté-sous-Jouarre* 253

Château des Briottières *Champigné*..................................374
Château des Tertres (Hôtel) *Onzain*..................................211
Château du Clair de Lune (Le) *Biarritz* 98
Château du Foulon *Castelnau-de-Médoc* 83
Château du Vivier *Le Vivier - Argenton-sur-Creuse*.............196
Chatenet (Le) *Brantôme*..62
Chaufourg en Périgord (Le)*Sourzac*................................78
Chaumières de Kernavien (Les) *Hennebont* 181
Chenevière (La) *Escures-Commes*.................................342
Chez Camille *Arnay-le-Duc*..130
Chez Chilo *Barcus*..96
Chez Marcel *Cardaillac*..312
Cholotte (Auberge de la) *Les Rouges-Eaux* 59
Christiania (Le) *Villars-de-Lans*....................................515
Chrystalin (Hôtel Le) *Les-Adrets-de-L'Estérel* 447
Clairière (Hôtel La) *Illhaeusern* 44
Clarion (Hôtel) *Aloxe-Corton*.......................................129
Claude Marco *Lamagdelaine-Cahors* 319
Clé d'Or (Hostellerie de la) *Barbizon* 251
Cléry (Hôtel) *Hesdin-l'Abbé*...336
Clos de Chantemerle (Le) *Serre-Chevalier - Saint-Chaffrey*..........408
Clos des Arômes (Le) *Cassis* 433
Clos Normand (Auberge du) *Martin-Eglise* 368
Clos Saint-Vincent (Hôtel Le) *Ribeauvillé*.......................47
Clos Sorel (Auberge du) *Les Molanes-Praloup*................405
Closerie des Vignes (La) *Saint-Ciers-de-Canesse*.............86
Cœur des Prés (Au) *Combloux* 533
Coin du Feu (Le) *Megève*..541
Colombier (Auberge du) *Roquefort-les-Pins* 419
Combreux (L'Auberge de) *Combreux*...............................217
Concasty (Auberge de) *Boisset* 111
Conquérant *Barfleur* 357
Corniche (Hôtel de la) *San-Martino-di-Lota* 243
Cour d'Alsace (La) *Obernai*..34
Courpain (Auberge de) *Fontaine-la-Rivière* 249
Couvent aux Herbes (Le) *Eugénie-les-Bains* 87
Crillon le Brave (Hostellerie de) *Crillon-le-Brave* 479
Cro-Magnon (Hôtel) *Les Eyzies-de-Tayac*......................67
Croix Blanche (Hôtel de la) *Chaumont-sur-Tharonne*...................208
Croix Fry (Hôtel de La) *Manigod*...................................538
Cuq-en-Terrasse *Cuq-Toulza* 327

D

Dame Carcas *Carcassonne*..259
Demeure de Flore *Lacabarède* 328
Demeure d'en Jourdou (La) *Cadours* 309
Demeures du Ranquet *Tornac-Anduze*............................276
Demeure Océane (La) *Portsall*......................................167
Désirade (Hôtel Village La) *Belle-Ile-en-Mer* 178
Deux Frères (Hôtel Les) *Roquebrune Village*....................418
Deux Rocs (Hôtel des) *Seillans*....................................469
Devinière (La) *Saint-Jean-de-Luz*..................................104
Diderot (Hôtel) *Chinon* 203
Dolce Vita (Hôtel) *Ajaccio*...228

Domaine de Bassibé *Segos*...307
Domaine de Bodeuc *La Roche-Bernard - Nivillac*............190
Domaine de Chicamour *Sury-aux-Bois* 218
Domaine de Clairefontaine *Chonas-l'Amballan* 511
Domaine de Kéréven *Bénodet* 161
Domaine de l'Etape *Le Blanc* 198
Domaine de la Roseraie *Brantôme* 63
Domaine de la Tortinière *Montbazon-en-Touraine*........205
Domaine de la Rhue *Rocamadour - La Rhue* 321
Domaine de Rieumégé *Olargues*.................................282
Domaine de Rilhac *Saint-Agrève*.................................501
Domaine de Rochevilaine *Billiers-Musillac* 180
Domaine des Mouillères *Saint-Georges-la-Pouge* 126
Domaine du Colombier *Malataverne* 506
Domaine du Val *Planguenoual*....................................152
Dragon (Hôtel du) *Strasbourg*....................................39

E

Ecailler (Hôtel l') Ile d'Oléron 393
Echo et de l'Abbaye (Hôtel de) *La Chaise-Dieu* 118
Ecrin (Hôtel l') *Honfleur* 343
Enrose (Auberge d') *Solomiac* 308
Entraigues (Hôtel d') *Uzès*..278
Ermitage (Hôtel L') *Saulges* 376
Europe (Hôtel d') *Avignon* 474
Eychenne (Hôtel) *Saint-Girons*..................................292

F

Falaises (Hôtel Les) *Gluges* 313
Fanal (Le) *Plévenon* 154
Fare (La) *Pierrerue-Forcalquier* 402
Fer à Cheval (Le) *Megève* 542
Ferme aux Grives (Auberge de) *Eugénie-les-Bains* 89
Ferme Rose (La) *Moustiers-Sainte-Marie* 404
Ferme d'Augustin (La) *Saint-Tropez* 465
Ferme d'Hermès (La) *Saint-Tropez* 467
Ferme de Cocherel (La) *Cocherel*...............................349
Fermes de Marie (Les) *Megève* 540
Ferme de la Huppe *Gordes*..482
Fermes Hôtel Duvillard *Megève*.................................543
Ferme Hôtel La Rançonnière *Crépon*..........................341
Ferme Saint-Michel *Solérieux* 508
Fiacre (Auberge Le) *Fontaine-la-Rivière*......................227
Figuière (La) *Saint-Tropez*..468
Fitz Roy (Hôtel) *Val-Thorens* 527
Florets (Les) *Gigondas* 481
Fleur de Sel *Noirmoutier-en-l'Ile* 386
Flux (Hôtel) *Ile d'Yeu* 384
Fontaine aux Muses (La) *La Celle-Saint-Cyr*................142
Fontaine Stanislas (Hôtel de la) *Plombières-les-Bains* 58
Fontaine (Auberge de la) *Venasque* 495
France (Hôtel de) *Les Rousses* 248
France et des Fuchsias (Hôtel de) *Saint-Vaast-la-Hougue*..........362
France et d'Angleterre et Champlain (Hôtel) *La Rochelle* 396

G

Général d'Elbée (Hôtel du) *Noirmoutier-en-l'Ile*.........................385
Genovese (Hôtel) *Bonifacio*.........................229
George Sand (Hôtel) *Loches* 204
Géraniums (Les) *Le Barroux*.........................476
Gilg (Hôtel) *Mittelbergheim* 33
Glycines (Hôtel Les) *Les Eyzies-de-Tayac* 68
Glycines (Les) *Ile de Porquerolles* 460
Golf (Hôtel du) *Le Vaudreuil*.........................355
Gonfalon (Hôtel Le) *Germigny-L'Evêque*.........................258
Gorges de Pennafort (Hostellerie Les) *Callas*.........................450
Grand Duc (Hostellerie du) *Gincla* 261
Grande Marque *(La) Marnac*.........................71
Grandes Roches (Les) *Trégunc*.........................170
Grangeon *Saint-Cierge-la-Serre*.........................502
Grangette (Hostellerie La) *Velleron*.........................494
Grillade au feu de bois (La) *Flassans-sur-Issole* 455

H

Hacienda (L') *Marguerittes* 269
Hameau (Hôtel Le) *Saint-Paul-de-Vence*.........................421
Haras de la Potardière La Potardière – *Crosmières* 379
Hauterive Hôtel Saint-James *Bouliac* 82
Hirondelles (Les) *Illhaeusern* 45
Home (Hôtel Le) *Beaune* 131
Horizon (L') *Thionville*.........................55

I

Imperator Hôtel *Nîmes*.........................271
Imsthal (Auberge d') *La Petite-Pierre* 37
Iroise (Hôtel de L') *Pointe-du-Raz* 164
Ile du Saussay (Auberge de l') *Itteville* 250

J

Jardin Fleuri (Le) *Sebourg* 332
Jeu de Paume (Hôtel du)*Chamonix-Le Lavancher* 530

K

Kastell Dinec'h *Tréguier*.........................159
Kerhinet (Auberge de) *Saint-Lyphard* 372
Kerlon (Hôtel de) *Plouhinec* 188
Kiboki (Auberge du) *Turquestein*.........................56
Korrigane (La) *Saint-Malo*.........................176

L

Labrador (Hôtel Le) *Chamonix-Les Praz*.........................532
Laminak (Hôtel) *Arbonne-Biarritz*.........................97
Lehen Tokia *Ciboure* 101
Lièvre Amoureux (Le) *Saint-Lattier*.........................514
Lodge Nogentil (Le) *Courchevel* 518
Loges de l'Aubergade (Les) *Puymirol*.........................95
Logis de La Couperie *La Roche-sur-Yon*.........................388
Logis du Guetteur *Les Arcs-sur-Argens* 448
Logis Parc er Gréo *Le Gréo* 182

Logis Saint-Martin (Le) *S399t-Maixent-l'Ecole*...............399
Longcol (Hôtel) *La Fouilla295Najac*...............295
Lou Calen (Hostellerie) *Cot452ac*...............452
Lou Rouballou *Mont-Lo289*...............289
Louvèterie (La) *Saint-Augustin*...............256
Lucarne aux Chouettes (La) *Villeneuve-sur-Yonne*...............146

M

Madone (Auberge de la) *Peillon*...............417
Magnolias (Hostellerie Les) *Plaisance*...............298
Maison Anglaise (La) *Saint-Robert*...............123
Maison des Chanoines *Turenne*...............125
Maison des Consuls (La) *Mirepoix*...............291
Maison Rose (La) *Eugénie-les-Bains*...............88
Manassès (Le) *Curtil-Vergy*...............134
Manescale (Hostellerie La) *Entrechaux*...............480
Manoir (Le) *Ile de Port-Cros*...............459
Manoir d'Hautegente *Coly*...............66
Manoir de Bellerive (Hôtel du) *Le Buisson-de -Cadoin*...............64
Manoir de Boisvillers *Argenton-sur-Creuse*...............197
Manoir de Crec'h-Goulifen *Beg-Leguer Lagnon*...............158
Manoir de l'Etang (Le) *Mougins*...............414
Manoir de Moëllien *Plonévez-Porzay*...............163
Manoir de Rigourdaine *Plouers-sur-Rance*...............156
Manoir de Roche Torin *Courtils*...............358
Manoir de Sornat *Bourbon Lancy*...............136
Manoir de Vaumadeuc *Pleven*...............153
Manoir de la Forêt *La Ville-aux-Clercs*...............214
Manoir de la Rance *Pleurtuit*...............175
Manoir de la Roseraie *Grignan*...............505
Manoir des Saules (Le) *La Saussaye*...............354
Manoir du Cleuziou *Louargat*...............149
Manoir du Lys *Bagnoles-de-l'Orne*...............365
Maquis (Le) *Porticcio*...............234
Marais (Au) *Coulon*...............398
Marceau (Hôtel) *Doussard*...............535
Mare e Monti (Hôtel) *Feliceto*...............239
Maréchal Hostellerie (Le) *Colmar*...............43
Marie d'Agoult (Hôtel) *Uzès - Arpaillargues -*...............277
Marine (Hôtel de la) *Ile de Groix*...............183
Marina d'Argentella *L'Argentella-Calvi*...............238
Maronne (Hostellerie de la) *Le Theil*...............115
Martinet (Hôtel du) *Bouin*...............381
Mas d'Aigret (Le) *Les Baux-de-Provence*...............431
Mas d'Oléandre (Le) *Saint-Médiers*...............273
Mas de Cure Bourse *Isle-sur-la-Sorgue*...............484
Mas de Garrigon *Roussillon*...............490
Mas de Peint *Le Sambuc*...............446
Mas de la Pagane *Antibes*...............410
Mas des Capelans *Oppède-le-Vieux*...............486
Mas des Carassins *Saint-Rémy-de-Provence*...............441
Mas des Grès *Lagnes*...............485
Mas des Trilles *Céret*...............286
Mas doù Juge *Saintes-Maries-de-la-Mer*...............442

Mas doù Pastré *Eygalières* 435
Mas du Clarousset *Saintes-Maries-de-la-Mer* 441
Maurette (La) *Roquebrune-sur-Argens* 462
Meaulnes (Auberge des) *Nançay* 193
Mégevan (Le) *Megève* 544
Ménez (Hôtel) *Saint-Antoine* 171
Métairie (La) *Millac* 73
Métairie Neuve (La) *Pont-de-L'Arn* 330
Meunière (Auberge La) *Thannenkirsch* 51
Midi-Papillon (Hôtel du) *Saint-Jean-du-Bruel* 299
Minaret (Le) *Bénodet* 160
Mirande (Hôtel de la) *Avignon* 473
Mont Blanc (Le) *Megève* 539
Montagnes (Auberge des) *Pailherols* 116
Montagne de Brancion (La) *Tournus* 141
Montespant-Talleyrand (Grand Hôtel) *Bourbon-L'Archambault* 107
Moulin (Au) *Flagy* 254
Moulin (Hôtel Au) *Sainte-Croix-en-Plaine* 50
Moulin d'Hauterive *Saint-Gervais-en-Vallière* 140
Moulin de Bourgchâteau *Louhans* 139
Moulin de Chaméron (Auberge du) *Bannegon* 191
Moulin de Connelles *Connelles* 350
Moulin de Lesnuhé *Saint-Avé* 186
Moulin de Rosmadec *Pont-Aven* 165
Moulin de Villeray *Condeau* 364
Moulin de la Beune *Les Eyzies-de-Tayac* 69
Moulin de la Camandoule *Fayence* 454
Moulin de la Gorce *La Roche l'Abeille* 127
Moulin de la Mère Michelle (Le) *Les Planches-près-Arbois* 247
Moulin de La Wantzenau (Le) *La Wantzenau* 41
Moulin du Plain (Auberge Le) *Goumois* 244
Moulin du Pré (Hostellerie du) *Bavent* 337
Moulin Fouret (Hostellerie du) *Saint-Aubin-le-Vertueux* 353
Muse et des Rosiers (Grand Hôtel de la) *Peyrereau-le-Rozier* 297

N
Neuhauser (Hôtel) *Les Quelles* 38
New Hôtel Bompard *Marseille* 437
Nord-Pinus (Grand Hôtel) *Arles* 428
Noyer (Auberge du) *Le Reclaud-de-Bouny-Bas* 74

O
Orangerie (L') *Piolenc* 488
Oustal del Barry *La Fouillade-Najac* 296
Oustaloun (L') *Mausanne-les-Alpilles* 438

P
Paillère (Auberge de la) *Mus* 270
Pain, Adour et Fantaisie *Grenade-sur-Adour* 90
Parc Hôtel (Le) *Levernois* 132
Parc Hôtel *Wangenbourg* 40
Paris (Hôtel de) *Cannes* 411
Patoula (Hôtel La) *Ustaritz* 106
Pelissaria (Hôtel de la) *Saint-Cirq-Lapopie* 323

Perce-Neige (Hostellerie Les) *Vernou-sur-Brenne*.........................207
Pérouse (Hôtel La) *Nice*..415
Petite Auberge (La) *Lascabanes* 316
Pigeons Blancs (Les) *Cognac* 391
Pins (Auberge des) *Sabres*..92
Plage (La) *Sainte-Anne-la-Palud* 169
Pléiades (Les) *Barbizon*...252
Plein Soleil (Hôtel) *Saint-Aygulf*..463
Plume d'Oie (La) La Roque-Gageac 75
Poids Public (Auberge du) *Saint-Félix-Lauragais*.......................310
Pont de l'Ouysse (Le) *Lacave*...315
Pont de Lanau (Auberge de) *Lanau-Chaudes-Aigues*...................114
Pont Romain (Auberge du) *Sommières* 274
Port des Roches (Auberge du) *Luché-Pringé* 378
Pougnots (Petit Hôtel des) *Belle-Ile* 179
Prateaux (Hôtel les) Noirmoutier-en-l'Île....................................387
Pré Bossu (Le) *Moudeyres*...119
Pré de la Mer (Hôtel Le) *Saint-Tropez*.....................................464
Prés de la Vézère (Auberge des) *Saint-Viance*...........................124
Presbytère (Auberge du) *Saignon*..491
Prieuré (Hostellerie du) *Bonnieux* 478
Prieuré (Hôtel Le) *Ermenonville* 224
Provençale (Auberge) *Eygalières*...434
Puits Jaubert (Auberge du) *Callian*..451
Pyjama(Le) *Super-Sauze* 407

Q
Quatre Dauphins (Hôtel des) *Aix-en-Provence*...........................426

R
Reillanne (Auberge de) *Reillanne*...406
Relais Chantovent *Minerve* 281
Relais Cicéro *La Flèche*...377
Relais de Fréhel *Le Fréhel* 155
Relais de Saint-Jacques-de-Compostelle *Collonges-la-Rouge*........121
Relais de la Magdelaine *Gémenos* 436
Relais des Landes *Ouchamps*..212
Relais des Marches de l'est) *Oberhaslach* 35
Relais du Lac Noir (Le) *Montpasey-Aiguebelle* 522
Relais du Touron (Le) *Le Touron - Carsac-Aillac* 65
Relais du Val d'Orbieu *Ornaisons*..262
Relais Moulin de Balisne *Balines*...346
Relais Sainte-Anne *Martel* 318
Rendez-Vous des Pêcheurs (Au) *Pont du Chambon*....................122
Repaire de Kerroc'h (Le) *Paimpol* 150
Résidence de Rohan *Vaux-sur-Mer*...397
Résidence du Centre Nautique *Bonifacio*...................................230
Ric (Hôtel) *Saint-Céré*..322
Richeux (Hôtel) *Cancale*..172
Rimains (Les) *Cancale*...173
Ripa Alta (Le) *Plaisance-du-Gers*..304
Rivière (Auberge de la) *Velluire* 390
Roches Blanches (Les) *Cassis*...432
Roches Fleuries (Les) *Cordon*...534

Roches Rouges (Les) *Piana* 233
Rochette (Hôtel de la) *La Rochette* 49
Rochette (Auberge de la) *Vauvaney-la-Rochette* 509
Roseraie (La) *Vence* 423
Romarins (Les) *Gordes* 483
Roumanin (Le) *Esparron-de-Verdon* 400
Royal Hôtel *Nîmes* 272

S

Saint-Antoine (Hostellerie) *Albi* 326
Saint-Barnabé (Hostellerie) *Buhl - Murbach* 42
Saint-Charles (Le) Biarritz 99
Saint-Christophe (Auberge) *Pont-d'Ouilly* 344
Saint-Jacques (Hostellerie) *Saint-Saud-en-Périgord* 77
Saint-Jacques (Hostellerie) *Cloyes-sur-le-Loir* 195
Saint-Pierre (Auberge) *Tourtour* 471
San Francisco (Le) *Ile aux Moines* 184
Sant' Agnellu (U) *Rogliano* 241
Santoline (Hôtel de la) *Beaulieu* 499
Savoyarde (Hôtel La) *Chamonix* 529
Savoyarde (La) *Val d'Isère* 526
Scierie (Auberge de la) *La Vove* 222
Seigneur (Auberge du) *Tavel* 275
Seigneurs de Ribeaupierre (Hostellerie des) *Ribeauvillé* 48
Seigneurs et du Lion d'Or (Auberge des) *Vence* 422
Sélune (Auberge de la) *Ducey* 359
Sénéchal (Le) *Sauveterre-de-Rouergue* 301
7 Molles (Hostellerie des) *Sauveterre-de-Comminges* 311
Signoria (Auberge de la) *Calvi* 237
Sivolière (La) *Courchevel* 517
Soleil (Auberge du) *Coaraze* 412
Sologne (Hôtel de la) *Beaugency* 216
Solognote (La) *Brinon-sur-Sauldre* 192
Sombral (Auberge du) *Saint-Cirq-Lapopie* 324
Source Bleue (La) *Touzac* 325
Sphinx (Hôtel Le) *Perros-Guirec* 151
Square (Le) *Astaffort* 93
Sud Bretagne (Hôtel) *Pornichet* 371

T

Taillard (Hôtel) *Goumois* 245
Templiers (Hôtel Les) *Aigues-Mortes* 265
Terrasse (Hôtel de la) *Varengeville* 370
Terrasse au Soleil (La) *Céret* 285
Ti Al-Lannec *Trébeurden* 157
Tomette (Auberge de la) *Vitrac* 117
Tour de L'Esquillon (La) *Miramar Théoule* 413
Tour de Pacoret (La) *Grésy-sur-Isère* 519
Treille Muscate (La) *Cliousclat* 504
Trois Fontaines (Hôtel des) *Locmariaquer* 187
Trois Lys (Hôtel des) *Condom* 302
Tronçais (Le) *Tronçais* 110
Turenne (Hôtel le) *Beaulieu-sur-Dordogne* 120
Ty-Mad (Hôtel) Douarnenez 162

V

Val au Cesne (Auberge du) *Croix-Mare* 367
Val Joli (Auberge du) *Le Valtin* 61
Val-Suzon (Hostellerie du) *Val-Suzon* 135
Verger (Le) *Grimaud* 458
Vert (Hostellerie Le) *Mauroux* 317
Verte Campagne *Trelly* 363
Vieille Auberge (La) *Port-de-Lanne* 91
Vieille Fontaine (La) *Cornillon* 268
Vieilles Tours (Hôtel Les) *Rocamadour - Lafage* 320
Vieux Château (Hostellerie du) *Sérignan* 492
Vieux Chêne (Au) *Landevant* 185
Vieux Chêne (Auberge du) *Champs-sur-Tarentaine* 113
Vieux Fox (Auberge du) *Fox-Amphoux* 456
Vieux Logis (Le) *Trémolat* 79
Vieux Logis (Hostellerie Le) *Thomery* 257
Vieux Pérouges (Ostellerie du) *Pérouges* 498
Vieux Puits (Auberge du) *Pont-Audemer* 352
Vieux Raquine (Hostellerie du) *Lugon* 84
Vieux Remparts (Hostellerie aux) *Provins* 255
Villa Gallici *Aix-en-Provence* 425
Villa L'Arche *Bidart-Biarritz* 100
Villa Thérésa-Hôtel Sémiramis *Arcachon* 81
Violettes (Hôtel Les) *Thierenbach* 52
Vouivre (Hôtel de la) *Champagnole* 246

W

Welcome (Hôtel) *Villefranche-sur-Mer* 424
Windsor (Hôtel) *Nice* 416

Y

Yéti (Le) *Méribel-les-Allues* 521

ILE DE FRANCE - CHAMPAGNE-PICARDIE

VALLEES DE LA BEAUCE, VALLEE DE LA JUINE ET DE LA CHALOUETTE

Fontaine-la-Rivière (47km from Paris)
– Auberge de Courpain (350F) 249

Itteville (44km from Paris)
– Auberge de l'Ile du Saussay (350F)..................................250

FORET DE FONTAINEBLEAU

Barbizon (57km from Paris)
– Hostellerie de la Clé d'Or (420-480F)........................251
– Hostellerie Les Pléiades (420-550F)...........................252

Flagy (98km from Paris)
– Au Moulin (310-500F) 254

Thomery - Fontainebleau (74km from Paris)
– Hostellerie Le Vieux Logis (400F)...............................257

VALLEE DE LA MARNE, VALLEE DU PETIT MORIN ET DU GRAND MORIN

La Ferté-sous-Jouarre (66km from Paris)
– Château des Bondons (400-550F).................................253

Saint-Augustin (65km from Paris)
– La Louveterie (500F) 256

Germigny-L'Evêque (66km from Paris)
– Hôtel Le Gonfalon (280-360F).......................................258

PROVINS *(86km from Paris)*
– Hostellerie Aux Vieux Remparts (395-650F) 255

PARC D'ERMENONVILLE

Ermenonville (47km from Paris)
– Hôtel Le Prieuré (450-500F) 224

FORET DE COMPIEGNE

Saint-Jean-aux-Bois - Compiègne (80km from Paris)
– A la Bonne Idée (385-430F) 225

ARTOIS PICARDIE

Longpont (85km from Paris)
– Hôtel de l'Abbaye (175-320F)...219

Neuville-Saint-Amand (145km from Paris)
– Hostellerie Le Château (330-390F).................................220

Sainte-Preuve (140km from Paris)

– Château de Barive (480–580F)..221

VIGNOBLE CHAMPENOIS
Etoges (150km from Paris)
– Château d'Etoges (550–700F)...223

CENTRE - LOIRE VALLEY

SOLOGNE
Chaumont-sur-Tharonne (167km from Paris)
– La Croix Blanche (300–500F)..208
Beaugency (151km from Paris)
– Hôtel de l'Abbaye (510–560F)..215
– Hôtel de la Sologne (250–410F)..216
Brinon-sur-Sauldre (190km from Paris)
– La Solognote (310–420F)...192
Nançay - carte 17 :
– Auberge des Meaulnes (450F)...193
Saint-Hilaire-de-Court (205km from Paris)
– Château de la Beuvrière (350–480F).....................................194

CHATEAUX DE LA LOIRE
Chissay-en-Touraine (219km from Paris)
– Château de Chissay (550–910F)...209
Nouan-le-Fuzelier (177km from Paris)
– Hôtel Les Charmilles (340–380F)...210
Onzain (198km from Paris)
– Hôtel Château des Tertres (390–500F)..................................211
Ouchamps (198km from Paris)
– Relais des Landes (495–745F)..212

CHATEAUX DE LA LOIRE, VAL DU LOIR
Troo (197km from Paris)
– Château de la Voûte (370–550F)..213
La Ville-aux-Clercs (157km from Paris)
– Manoir de la Forêt (290–340F)..214
Cloyes-sur-le-Loir (142km from Paris)
– Hostellerie Saint-Jacques (320–480F) 195

CHATEAUX DE LA LOIRE, FORET DOMANIALE D'ORLEANS
Combreux (110km from Paris)
– L'Auberge de Combreux (315–495F).....................................217
Sury-aux-Bois (119km from Paris)
– Domaine de Chicamour (365F)..218

BOURGOGNE

L'AUXERROIS
La Celle-Saint-Cyr (155km from Paris)
– La Fontaine aux Muses (390F) 142
Villeneuve-sur-Yonne (135km from Paris)
– La Lucarne aux Chouettes(490–650F)...................................146

L'AUXERROIS ET LA VALLEE DE LA CURE

Mailly-le-Château (197km from Paris)
  – Le Castel (230-340F) 144

LA PUISAYE ET SAINT-FARGEAU

Prunoy (140km from Paris)
  – Château de Prunoy (500-700F)...143

NORMANDIE

NORMANDIE, VALLEE DE LA SEINE

Les Andelys (93km from Paris)
  – La Chaîne d'Or (395-740F) 345

Bazincourt-sur-Epte (75km from Paris)
  – Château de la Rapée (410-510F)..347

Douains (90km from Paris)
  – Château de Brécourt (670-1040F) 351

Cocherel (90km from Paris)
  – La Ferme de Cocherel (350-400F)...349

Connelles (100km from Paris)
  – Le Moulin de Connelles (600-800F)..350

Balisnes (120km from Paris)
  – Relais Moulin de Balisne (350-450F)......................................346

Saint-Aubin-le-Vertueux (155km from Paris)
  – Hostellerie du Moulin Fouret (235F).......................................353

La Saussaye (125km from Paris)
  – Le Manoir des Saules (450-1150F)..354

Le Vaudreuil (140km from Paris)
  – Hôtel du Golf (225-350F)...355

PAYS D'AUGE

Beuvron-sur-Auge (224km from Paris)
  – Auberge de la Boule d'Or (230F) 339

COTE FLEURIE ET ARRIERE PAYS

Honfleur (192km from Paris)
  – Hôtel l'Ecrin (370-900F)...343

Le Bec-Hellouin (157km from Paris)
  – Auberge de l'Abbaye (380-420F) 348

Pont-Audemer (168km from Paris)
  – Auberge du Vieux Puits (270-420F) 352

COTE DE SEINE-MARITIME ET PAYS DE CAUX

Sassetot-le-Mauconduit (215km from Paris)
  – Château de Sassetot-le-Mauconduit (470-730F) 369

Croix-Mare (177km from Paris)
  – Auberge du Val au Cesne (350F) 367

COTE DE DIEPPE, FORET D'ARQUES

Varengeville (180km from Paris)
  – Hôtel de la Terrasse (240-310F)..370

Martin-Eglise (175km from Paris)
– **Auberge du Clos Normand** (270-370F) 368

ANJOU

Champigné (202km from Paris)
– **Château des Briottières** (550-750F) 374

Bézancourt
– **Château de Landel** (470-750F) 366

* We have limited our selection to hotels located in an area distant of about 200km from Paris but this should not keep you from exploring further... For more details please refer to the relevant page.

Notes

Notes

Notes